RICHARD J. MORSE

THE SUBSTANCE OF SOCIOLOGY

SOCIOLOGY SERIES

John F. Cuber, *Editor*

Alfred C. Clarke, *Associate Editor*

THE SUBSTANCE

OF

SOCIOLOGY

Codes, Conduct and Consequences

*Edited with Introduction
and Notes by*

EPHRAIM H. MIZRUCHI

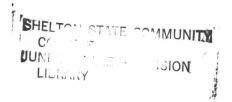

New York

APPLETON-CENTURY-CROFTS

DIVISION OF MEREDITH PUBLISHING COMPANY

TO MY PARENTS

PREFACE

THE DISCIPLINE OF SOCIOLOGY has undergone many changes since its founding by Henri St. Simon and August Comte early in the nineteenth century. The transformation from a concern with "stages" of societal development to a focus on social interaction and from a view of total societies as units of analysis to units as small as two-person groups has had profound influences on the several generations of students of society.

Sociology may be characterized as a field which has two basic methodological approaches and still only one fundamental objective. While the approaches to the study of sociology may be described as the *Verstehen*, or *intuitive understanding* method, on the one hand, and the *formal scientific*, on the other, all sociologists are primarily concerned with *understanding* societal processes and discovering the order which makes life in society possible.

Our objective in this collection of essays is two-fold: (1) to provide the beginning student of society with the kinds of materials which will markedly increase his *awareness* of the processes in which he participates; and (2) to stimulate greater *understanding* of these processes on an elementary level.

Avoiding Pitfalls. There are numerous problems associated with the learning of basic ideas in the social sciences yet few solutions to these problems. What is required of the student is the development of capacities of abstraction, precision, objectivity and generalization, in relation to a body of data which are really the stuff of ordinary life in society. Skepticism in relation to the kinds of observations made by social scientists is not uncommon and generalizations are often described by the layman as "common sense." Demonstration of the meaningfulness of sociological concepts is particularly difficult for the person who has only limited background in the literature produced by social science. Concepts which have meaning for a relatively limited group of knowledgeable students of society and its processes typically sift down to lower levels of shared understanding, i.e., lower common denominators in the process of communication (cf. Simmel, below). In time rough approximations of these concepts make their way into the everyday language of the lay public. Since the process reflects timely issues it is especially important that at least the educated in our society have clear conceptions of what is being communicated by the social scientist. There is, consequently, no substitute for careful, extensive reading and precise understanding of concepts.

At least three possible sources of misunderstanding may be anticipated in reading these essays: (1) taking a *concept* to mean what a similar term means to the layman; (2) confusing statements of probability with "either-or" generalizations; and (3) accepting *ideal type* constructs as descriptions of reality.

On the most elementary level of interpretation, the problem of imprecise meaning in the usage of descriptive terms as synonyms for concepts typically revolves about words like: "culture," which does *not* simply refer to the aesthetic aspects of learning; "group," which may be defined in various ways depending upon the sociological context in which it is used; "institution," which is only rarely used by sociologists to refer to hospitals, prisons or sanatoria (cf. Hamilton, below); and "individual," which may refer to a variety of meanings. Careful reading of the essays included here will aid the student in his efforts to attain a more meaningful interpretation of sociological materials as well as a deeper understanding of the processes in which he is a participant.

On another plane is a problem which sociologists themselves often forget to make explicit. This refers to what Robert K. Merton has called "single term, diverse concepts," and "single concept, diverse terms" (c.f., *Social Theory and Social Structure*, New York: The Free Press of Glencoe, 1957, pp. 20-25). The term "alienation," for example, is often used to describe such diverse processes as social isolation (which has similarly been used to describe diverse concepts); personal feelings of apartness from others, things and processes; and mental disorders, e.g., psychiatrists were once called "alienists." Similarly the person who is described as being confused in complex, contemporary societies has simultaneously been characterized as suffering from "alienation," "meaninglessness," "anomie," and "loss of identity." Thus, for clarity of thought it is well to be alert to the problems of meaning which are necessary for adequate communication of idea and description.

Another possible pitfall to avoid is the tendency to confuse the limited generalizations of probability with the unlimited generalizations of absoluteness. We are not in this context suggesting a lack of confidence in the results of social scientific observation. What we are saying instead is that we very rarely make "either-or" generalizations in sociology. A statement, for example, that there is a direct relationship between level of education and membership in formal associations (lodges, P.T.A., and similar organizations) tells us not that all people with limited formal education will have no associational ties. To the sociologist such a statement means that if we systematically selected a cross-section of a population we would find that those with more formal education would be significantly, by mathematical standards, more likely to belong to associations than those with less formal education. The statement does not mean that a *particular person* with a great deal of formal education will necessarily belong to a great number of associations. Our generalizations in sociology refer not to what *particular* people will do but what people *in general* will do when acting in relation to one another. Because of the complexities of sociological generalizations and probability statements it is important to have a clear idea as to the units of analysis and the limits of generalizations.

Still another possible pitfall is confusing *ideal types* with descriptions of reality. Ideal types are mental constructs, conceptual tools, which provide baselines in relation to which realities may be described and intuitively measured. Thus, for example, if we characterize social relationships in contemporary urban areas as instrumental, i.e., people use their associations with others as *means* for achieving other ends (being friendly with people in order to sell them something, use them, etc.) as contrasted with relationships in nonurban areas in which associations are supposedly ends in themselves (being friendly for the sake of friendship), we would be using ideal type constructs in relation to types of social interaction. In reality we probably could not find an urban area in which we would find *instrumental* relations in a pure form as a dominant mode of interaction. Nor could we find nonurban areas in which relationships as ends were the dominant mode. We would find *approximations in reality* and we could place descriptions of dominant modes on a continuum from those which most closely approximate the ideal type to those which are most divergent. In this way we may discuss and understand ongoing processes in one setting as compared with another. (e.g., see Mizruchi and Perrucci, below).

In concluding this Preface we repeat that there is no substitute for careful, thoughtful reading. Reading from "the substance of sociology" can be a richly rewarding experience and it is the accomplishment of that experience which has guided us in our selection of materials.

ACKNOWLEDGMENTS

The organization and preparation of this volume represents the efforts of a number of persons. While many have made direct and indirect contributions and will remain unmentioned here several are conspicuous as contributors. Professors Paul Meadows and Byron Fox made suggestions and assessments which were crucial to the final outcome of my efforts. Robert Morrison, Keith Johnson, George Christie, Katherine Rohrer and Marguerite Hurley located materials, saw them through the process of reproduction and typing and have contributed much in the form of research assistance. I thank also Mary Belle-Isle and Joy Meadows who typed some of the essays and correspondence relevant to this project. Without the generous response of my colleagues and their publishers, all of whom gave us permission to reprint the materials which follow, this book would not have been possible. The students at Syracuse University who used earlier versions of this collection, some of whom explicitly commented on the pedagogic value of the selections, are also to be thanked. Finally, although my contributions to this work are dedicated to my parents, my wife Ruth and our children, Mark, David and Susan have aided my effort by their willingness to tolerate a sometimes absent and occasionally preoccupied husband and father.

Syracuse, New York

E. H. M.

A NOTE TO THE INSTRUCTOR

THIS BOOK has been used, in earlier forms, both as a text and as collateral reading with a standard text. We have attempted to provide the kind of organization which would assure coverage of major theoretical areas of sociological concern while at the same time including materials in a wide variety of substantive areas. Thus our selections have been made according to whether or not they represent a combination of sociological interests which we feel are of pedagogic value. A typical essay will provide coverage of a substantive problem and a methodological or theoretical approach. In Part I, for example, 4 types of methodologies are represented in the Johnson, Snyder, Stoodley and Lazarsfeld papers while at the same time providing interesting substantive contexts which illustrate the variety of problems which attract sociologists.

Throughout we have tried to cover as many approaches to the field as are pedagogically meaningful to the beginning reader. Conspicuously absent are advanced types of interests which revolve about mathematical and statistical models, scaling and the more esoteric aspects of substantive theory. A carefully selected bibliography provides direction for the student who desires to go beyond these materials to more specialized areas.

Finally, this is an intentionally eclectic book. There are several themes which make their way into the selection and organization process but these do not represent an attempt at a truly systematic work. The general course in sociology should, we believe, provide an introduction to the various viewpoints in the field, their vocabularies and sufficient guidance and stimulation for interest in reading and advanced study. It must contribute first to making of the student an educated and intelligent member of a cosmopolitan society. Second, it must convince the student that systematic scientifically derived knowledge about societal processes is more reliable and thus preferable to unsystematically gathered and assessed information. And, third, it must play a role in attracting outstanding students to the field as a major vocational area. Thus, this collection is directed to the preprofessional or premajor student. As in the case of all such books its primary value will ultimately be determined by its use in the hands of a critical and perceptive teacher.

E. H. M.

Selected Bibliography: Texts in Introductory Sociology

Bensman, Joseph and Rosenberg, Bernard. *Mass, Class and Bureaucracy,* Englewood Cliffs, New Jersey: Prentice-Hall, Inc., 1963.

Bertrand, Alvin L. *Basic Sociology: An Introduction to Theory and Method,* New York, Appleton-Century-Crofts, 1967.

Bottomore, Thomas B. *Sociology,* Englewood Cliffs, New Jersey: Prentice-Hall, Inc. London: George Allen and Unwin, Ltd., 1963.

Bredemeier, Harry C., and Richard M. Stephenson. *The Analysis of Social Systems,* New York: Holt, Rinehart and Winston, Inc., 1962.

Broom, Leonard, and Philip Selznick. *Sociology,* 3d ed. New York: Harper & Row, Publishers, 1963.

Chinoy, Ely. *Society,* New York: Random House, 1961.

Cuber, John F. *Sociology,* 5th ed. New York: Appleton-Century-Crofts, 1963.

Gouldner, Alvin and Gouldner, Helen. *Modern Sociology,* New York: Harcourt, Brace & World, Inc., 1963.

Green, Arnold W. *Sociology,* 4th ed. New York: McGraw-Hill Book Company, Inc., 1964.

Horton, Paul B., and Chester L. Hunt. *Sociology,* New York: McGraw-Hill Book Company, Inc., 1964.

Inkeles, Alex. *What Is Sociology?,* Englewood Cliffs, New Jersey: Prentice-Hall, Inc., 1964.

Johnson, Harry M. *Sociology,* New York: Harcourt, Brace & World, Inc., 1960.

Lundberg, George A., Clarence C. Schrag, and Otto N. Larsen. *Sociology,* 3d ed. New York: Harper & Row, Publishers, 1963.

MacIver, Robert M. and Page, Charles H. *Society,* New York: Holt, Rinehart and Winston, Inc., 1949.

Mott, Paul B. *The Organization of Society,* Englewood Cliffs, New Jersey: Prentice-Hall, Inc., 1965.

Ogburn, William F., and Meyer F. Nimkoff. *Sociology,* 5th ed. Boston: Houghton Mifflin Company, 1964.

Rose, Arnold M. *Sociology,* 2nd ed., New York: Alfred A. Knopf, Inc., 1965.

Wilson, Everett K., *Sociology,* Homewood, Ill.: Dorsey Press, 1966.

Young, Kimball, and Raymond W. Mack. *Sociology and Social Life,* 2d ed. New York: American Book Company, 1962.

CONTENTS

4. GROUPS AND INTERACTION

5. THE SELF AND INTERACTION

6. MEANING AND ITS CONSEQUENCES

9. URBANIZATION AND SOCIAL CHANGE

10. BUREAUCRATIZATION AND SOCIAL CHANGE

11. INDUSTRIALIZATION AND SOCIAL CHANGE

12. MASS SOCIETY AND MASS CULTURE

Our deeds determine us, as much as we
determine our deeds; and until we know
what has been or will be the peculiar
combination of outward with inward facts,
which constitute a man's critical
actions, it will be better not to think
ourselves wise about his character.

GEORGE ELIOT, *Adam Bede*

INTRODUCTION

THAT WHICH CHARACTERIZES the sociological dimension as contrasted with others in the analysis of human behavior is the coercive factor in patterned social relationships. This idea is directly derived from the French sociologist, Émile Durkheim, who focused on "social facts."

> Here then is a category of facts with very distinctive characteristics: it consists of ways of acting, thinking, and feeling, external to the individual, and endowed with a power of coercion, by reason of which they control him. These ways of thinking could not be confused with biological phenomena, since they consist of representations and of actions; nor with psychological phenomena, which exist only in the individual consciousness and through it. They constitute, thus, a new variety of phenomena; and it is to them exclusively that the term "social" ought to be applied. . . . These ways of thinking and acting therefore constitute the proper domain of sociology. It is true that, when we define them with the word "constraint," we risk shocking the zealous partisans of absolute individualism. For those who profess the complete autonomy of the individual, man's dignity is diminished whenever he is made to feel he is not completely self-determinant. It is generally accepted today, however, that most of our ideas and our tendencies are not developed by ourselves but come to us from without. How can they become a part of us except by imposing themselves upon us? This is the whole meaning of our definition.*

By this we mean that the person acting in a situation in relation to others is directly and indirectly compelled to behave as others expect. In other words the presence of others exerts more or less pressure to act in accordance with what they feel is appropriate and desirable conduct. Since we too are present as actors in a situation there is greater or lesser probability that what our associates in a given situation expect of us is essentially what we would expect of them and of ourselves as well. Thus the idea embodied in what we have designated the coercive factor is that groups arise and persist both because: (1) actors adhere to what others expect of them; and (2) they want and expect to do more or less the same. It will be noted that sociologists are often less than explicit in the generalizations they make. So, for example, we have said that people "more or less" expect to do what others want them to do. We do this to anticipate the fact that there is a great deal of variation in personal behavior even though there is

---

* *The Rules of Sociological Method*, ed. by G. Catlin, translated by Sarah Solovay and John Mueller, New York: The Free Press, 1950, pp. 3-4. Originally published in 1895.

1

much uniformity in group action. In a given setting there may be some who are enthusiastic adherents to a code of conduct because they personally desire to act in the expected way while others may conform in anticipation of group pressures to "toe the line." Still others may decide not to adhere regardless of the anticipated consequences. Every situation requires *some* degree of organization of activity. It is doubtful that most group behavior requires total conformity of all those engaged in a given task. Thus one assumption which we make is that in a given setting *most* people will behave in a predictable manner regardless of their personal motives for so doing and that this process of predictability, which we call a *pattern* is a direct outgrowth of the coercive factor. The major concern of sociology, from this point of view, then, is to understand the processes by which group activities become organized and changed. Central to the process of organization is the coercive factor, broadly defined.

What then is coercion? The use of so strong a word is surely objectionable to some social scientists and many laymen. Perhaps it is more desirable than similar words like *compulsion, constraint, restraint, restriction, prohibition.* What we have in mind is a process by which the group rather than the person directly or indirectly influences one's decision to think, believe, or act in a prescribed or proscribed way. Although most of the essays selected here deal with at least some aspect of conformity and deviance the issues we have in mind are most succinctly presented in intentionally exaggerated form in the essay by Dennis Wrong, "The Oversocialized Conception of Man in Modern Sociology" (Chapter 5).

For purposes of orientation we assume that any pattern of group behavior is coercive. Directives to act in a given way emerge from two sources which are focal points of sociological study: the normative order and the factual order. While the former refers to the way people *should* think, believe or act the latter refers to the way people *do* think, believe or act. Thus, for example, one proposition which will inform our approach to both the study of the normative order and deviance is, *adherence to group expectations is not the same as conformity to norms.* In our second selection, "Negro Reactions to Minority Status," we observe a well-organized pattern of behavior in which many persons are engaged. The participants—Negroes and whites—behave in a predictable manner which conforms to the expectations of the Negro. Here we have a clearly discernible pattern of expectations which is non-normative. Instead of patterns based on what one *should* or *ought* to do we have patterns based on "the realities of the situation."

In organized criminal activities, for example, patterned expectations make it possible for the attainment of desired goals. Thus, in a "price-fixing scandal" several years ago an elaborate scheme was worked out and adhered to by executives of large electrical manufacturing firms which made possible the "rigging" of bids for government contracts.

Contrast these descriptions of reality with Snyder's description of the normative aspects of Orthodox Jewish drinking behavior which does not describe what people *do* but what they *should* do. In Chapter 8, where we present essays dealing with these phenomena we see the contrast reflected in the divergence of viewpoint between Sumner and Malinowski.

One problem then, in describing and coming to understand how groups are organized in given situations, is to understand the primary sources of the coercive process. Is it primarily in the normative order, that is the value system of the group, or is it primarily in the factual order, that is the pattern by which people influence one another regardless of what they believe they should do? In a concrete sense the organization of behavior may be described as an outcome of the interplay between both values and direct interaction since regardless of how people go about attaining given group goals there is a tendency for their overt behavior to approximate normative patterns.

Behavior then is organized not only by norms—or what all participants are supposed to do in a specific setting—but by *role expectations* as well. Whereas the norms are prescriptions and proscriptions for everyone in a social situation, role expectations apply only to the occupants of given *status* positions. In a college classroom, for example, aggressive behavior is pro-scribed for all. The professor has no more right to physically abuse a student than do students to abuse professors. Nevertheless the professor has the sole right to formally assess the quality of the student's academic perform-ance. The performance of rights and obligations by group members as part of their *roles* represents, then, a crucial dimension of group organization. Since the parts played by actors assigned to specific social positions, i.e., roles, involve rights and obligations they too may be thought of as aspects of group coercion. It should be clear at this point that coerciveness is a crucial dimension in the analysis of group behavior and that organized social life implies coercion.

Our selections revolve about the general problem of social organization and change. First of all, what do sociologists do (Chapter 1)? Secondly, what issues surround their efforts to pursue their interests (Chapter 2)? Thirdly, what factors play a role in the process of organized life in society and how they are interrelated (Chapters 3 through 7)? Fourthly, what are the processes which contribute to stability and change and their interre-lationship (Chapter 8)? Finally, what are the major focal processes giving rise to new and emergent forms of social organization and what are some of the problems associated with these processes (Chapters 9 through 13)?

Our efforts are directed to an understanding of these processes within a dynamic framework, for social organization is a dynamic process, con-stantly emerging, constantly taxing man's capacity for innovation and adaptation, sometimes progressing and—at other times—regressing, but al-ways on the move. Awareness of the processes which enhance and inhibit our efforts to bring about the kind of world in which we would want to persist both as creatures and creators requires a dynamic orientation. These essays contribute to such a perspective.

1

VARIETIES OF
SOCIOLOGICAL STUDY

Introduction

THE SOCIOLOGISTS' LABORATORY is the universe of man's experience. From the libraries to the streets of cities, from the home to the small-group laboratory, sociologists read, interview, watch and count in a constant proliferation of techniques for the observation of group behavior.

We have selected four types of studies for inclusion in this chapter which provide not only methodological variety but data which are substantively interesting. The Snyder essay provides an example of the use of classical sources in understanding the way group behavior is supposed to be. It deals with a fascinating substantive problem, alcohol beverage consumption, which contributes to an understanding of the dynamics of pathological and nonpathological drinking behavior. It may be reread with profit in the context of the materials in both Chapter 3, The Normative Order, and Chapter 7, Deviance.

Stoodley's paper provides both an example of insightful social psychological analysis and a challenging description of interaction in the college setting. A review of this essay along with the materials in Chapter 4, Groups and Interaction, and Chapter 5, The Self, will add to its usefulness in understanding its substantive contribution. The paper by Johnson is a veritable storehouse of sociological treasures. Not only does it deal with an immediate and interesting problem, which applies to the processes of reaction by all groups playing subordinate roles in relation to others, but it displays a number of methodological and analytical approaches. The interview and the participant observation are closely bound up with imaginative organization of research findings into substantive typologies which provide sensitive understanding of this phenomenon. In addition to its values in rounding out the materials in Chapter 7, Deviance, it provides data on a social problem which adds to our essay in Chapter 13, Alienation and Anomie. The excerpt from Lazarsfeld's article provides an example of quality survey research, reflected in several studies included in this volume, and the need for scientifically gathered and analyzed data in interpreting group processes. In the latter case it is applicable to some of the issues in Chapter 2.

Orthodox Jewish Drinking Patterns

CHARLES R. SNYDER

A NATURAL STARTING POINT in studying Jewish drinking patterns is a description of the traditional religious rituals and ceremonies in which alcoholic beverages are used. There are at least two reasons for beginning in this way before turning to the findings from field research. The first has to do with the fact that the vast majority of American Jews are of Eastern European origin, having been in this country for only one or two generations. Most of the Jewish men interviewed in New Haven were of Eastern European background, as were a majority of the Jewish student respondents in the College Drinking Survey. The countries, such as Poland and Russia, from which these Jews or their recent forebears emigrated were distinguished from the countries of the "emancipated" West (e.g., Germany) as strongholds of Jewish traditionalism and religious orthodoxy. The drinking patterns embodied in the Orthodox religious culture therefore provide an appropriate base line against which to view variations in patterns among American Jews in different degrees and phases of acculturation. The second reason is that the extensive integration of drinking in the rituals of Orthodox Judaism has been seen as the source of normative attitudes thwarting the development of drinking pathologies among Jews.

The most fruitful way of describing and suggesting the behavioral effects of traditional Jewish drinking patterns is to consider the ways in which culturally defined drinking situations impinge on the Orthodox Jew in the course of life, from the time of birth until death. A threefold classification of drinking occasions into (a) *rites de passage*, (b) weekly Sabbath observances, and (c) annual holy days and festivals will aid the organization of the materials, although departure from this scheme will sometimes be necessary in following the course of the life cycle. Since the labor of piecing together the occasions for drinking and the norms, ideas and sentiments associated with drinking among recent generations of Orthodox

From *Quarterly Journal of Studies on Alcohol,* 16, 1955, pp. 106-123. Reprinted by permission of the publisher and author.

Jews was begun by Bales, his work is used as our major reference. There are, however, some noteworthy gaps and misplacements of emphasis in Bales' description. Of special importance is his stress on the use of wine for religious and ceremonial purposes to the virtual exclusion of other alcoholic beverages, although Jewish tradition and practice incorporates their use in many instances. Hence, in summarizing traditional Jewish drinking Bales' work is supplemented at a number of points, particularly by reference to the *Shulchan Aruch*. This is the last great codification of Jewish law and custom and is authoritative among Orthodox Jews today.

1. EARLY RITES DE PASSAGE

The first rite de passage and the first drinking occasion in the life of the Jewish boy is his circumcision, which takes place on the eighth day after birth. The day of the circumcision is marked as a semifestival. The guests at the ceremony wear their best clothes, and the room where the operation is performed is decorated for the occasion. Tradition requires the presence of at least 10 adult males, including the operator (*mohel*) and the child's godfather. The minimum of 10 (*a minyan*) represents the quorum required for acts of public worship among Orthodox Jews. During the circumcision ceremony the child is placed on a special chair, called the "Seat of Elijah." The godfather holds the child on his lap for the operation proper. The mohel recites a benediction over a cup of wine, at the same time giving the child its name. The godfather drinks of the wine and a few drops are customarily given to the child. A lunch or banquet follows the ceremony.

The rite of circumcision marks the entry of the child into the moral community of Orthodox Judaism, making the child a party to the covenant with Jehovah and binding him to Jehovah's Commandments. The ceremony concretely dramatizes the child's entrance into and membership in the traditional moral community. Commenting on the significance of the wine on this occasion, Bales observes:

> The cup of wine [at circumcision] may be considered a visible symbol and seal of the completed act of union, and in its significance as "The Word of God," "the commandment of the Lord," may be conceived as representing His part in the covenant. On this symbolic level there appears to be at least a partial identification of the moral community and its norms with Jehovah and His Commandments, with the wine serving as the concrete symbol of both . . .

If the Jewish child is the first son, the second important rite in his life is the redemption of the first-born son, which ordinarily takes place 30 days after birth. In this ceremony the father presents the child before the *cohen* who pronounces a benediction and then formally inquires whether the father prefers to give the child up or redeem him for value. The father pays redemption money and the child is declared redeemed, in accord with ritualized procedure. This part of the rite is followed by a banquet at the father's house, but first a blessing is recited by the cohen over a cup of wine, as Bales describes the ritual following Glover. However, the *Shulchan Aruch* specifies, in addition, that after blessing the child, the cohen "says the benediction over a goblet of wine; and if there be no wine obtainable he says the blessing over some other beverage which is used there [in the locale]."

At the rites of his own circumcision and redemption, the child is unable to understand and appreciate the ideas and sentiments involved. Nonetheless, as he grows older, he will see these ceremonies performed for other children and know that he was once the central participant. In later life, he will probably participate in these ceremonies as a member of the minyan and insure their reenactment for his own sons.

2. SABBATH DRINKING: KIDDUSH AND HABDALAH, AND THE CUP OF BENEDICTION

It is otherwise with the drinking rituals of the Sabbath, of which the principal ones are *Kiddush* and *Habdalah*. The *Shulchan Aruch* prescribes that the father instruct his son in these rituals as soon as he is old enough to understand what Sabbath means: "The time for training a child for the performance of the positive commandments depends upon the ability and understanding of each child. Thus, if he knows what Sabbath signifies, it becomes his duty to hear Kiddush and Habdalah, and the like." The Sabbath being a weekly occurrence, the ideas and sentiments associated with it have an inescapable recurrent impact on the Jewish child brought up in a religious home.

Among Orthodox Jews, Sabbath observance includes three essential rituals in which drinking is of central significance. The first of these is the Kiddush (literally "sanctification") which marks the transition from the secular part of the week to the day set apart as sacred. The Kiddush ritual may be thought of as an instance of the broader principle of sanctification and the embracing idea of holiness which Kohler brings out as basic to Orthodox Judaism in this passage:

> The Jewish religion, having for its fundamental ethical principle the law of holiness: "Ye shall be holy: for I the Lord your God am holy" (Lev. XIX, 2) accentuates the perfectibility of the whole man, while demanding the sanctification of all that pertains to human existence. "The Lord did not create the world for desolation; he formed it for human habitation" (Isa. XLV, 18) is the principle emphasized by the rabbis (Pesachim, 88b). In the ideal state of things nothing should be profane. "In that day there shall be (inscribed) upon the bells of the horses: Holiness unto the Lord! And the pots in the Lord's house shall be like bowls before the altar."

The Kiddush immediately precedes the Friday evening Sabbath meal, after services at the synagogue. During the ritual the men and boys keep their heads covered, as in the synagogue. There is ordinarily some recitation and singing of hymns, followed by a brief recitation from Genesis (ch. 2, verses 1, 2 and 3) which marks the beginning of the Kiddush text proper. After this introductory the blessing over the cup of wine is uttered: "Blessed art Thou, O Lord our God, King of the universe, Who hast created the fruit of the vine." The sanctification is then completed, ending with the words, "Blessed art Thou, O Lord, who sanctifiest the Sabbath," and the wine is drunk. Of the wine to be used and the procedure on this occasion, the *Shulchan Aruch* declares:

> It is mandatory to say kiddush upon old wine; it is also mandatory to select good wine, and if possible an effort to obtain red wine should be made. Where suitable grape wine cannot be obtained, kiddush may be said upon raisin wine. While saying "and the heavens and earth were finished," one should stand and gaze at the candles, thereafter he may sit down, gaze at the goblet and say the benediction "who createst the fruit of the vine" and "who hallowest us." If one has no wine, he should say kiddush upon bread but not on any other beverage.

In drinking the wine, the head of the household drinks first and then passes the cup around to the various members of the household in the order of their status. The drinking is followed by the ritual washing of hands and the "breaking of the bread." There are two special Sabbath loaves which commemorate the double portion of manna that fell in the wilderness on the day before Sabbath. Everyone present partakes of the special loaves and the meal itself begins.

The second drinking ritual of the Sabbath is often called the Great Kiddush. In spite of its name, Great Kiddush is a small one. Nonetheless, its performance is essential to proper Sabbath observance. This drinking ritual takes place on the morning of the Sabbath or other festival days after the recital of prayers. It is immediately followed by the benediction over bread before breakfast. According to Bales, Great Kiddush is ritually identical with the Sabbath evening Kiddush, but the tradition of the *Shulchan Aruch* specifically permits the use of beverages other than wine on this occasion:

> In the day time [on the Sabbath] at the morning meal, one should also say the kiddush upon a glass [of wine]. This kiddush consists in simply pronouncing the benediction "The fruit of the vine." This kiddush is obligatory also upon women. Before this kiddush is said it is also forbidden to partake of anything, even water, as was laid down concerning the kiddush at night, and it is fulfilling the precept in the best manner to say that kiddush also over wine. If one, however, is fond of brandy and he says kiddush thereon, he has fulfilled his obligation. He should be careful to observe that the glass contains a capacity of one and a half egg-shells and he should drink a mouthful without interruption.

In the careful specifications for drinking brandy on this occasion—a mouthful without interruption—is found the prototype for the "shot" of spirits before a meal which will later be shown to be typical of many Jews today.

The third essential drinking ritual of the Sabbath is Habdalah (literally "separation"). Like the inaugural Kiddush, Habdalah marks a transition, this time from the holy Sabbath to the secular week. The *Shulchan Aruch* emphasizes the importance of the Habdalah in these terms:

> Just as it is mandatory to sanctify the Sabbath on its inception, so it is mandatory to sanctify the Sabbath on its conclusion upon a cup of wine that is the habdalah. Benedictions should also be pronounced upon spices and upon the light. Women are also duty bound to hear the habdalah, they should therefore listen well to the benediction.

In contradistinction to the requirement of wine for the Friday evening Kiddush, the *Shulchan Aruch* allows the substitution of other beverages at the Habdalah: "When wine cannot be procured, the habdalah should be pronounced upon another beverage which is the national drink, water excepted."

The ritual of Habdalah ordinarily takes place after dark, after the stars are out, and after evening prayers at the synagogue. During its performance the family stands at the table, the males again with their heads covered, while the father recites a prayer of separation. The usual blessing is given over a cup of wine (a special Habdalah cup may be used) and this is followed by blessings over a box of spices and over a lighted candle. The spice box is passed around the table; then all look at their fingernails by the candlelight, which symbolizes the resumption of work during the secular week. The father alone drinks, then moistens his eyes with wine and recites, "The commandment of the Lord is pure, enlightening the eyes." The *Shulchan Aruch* directs, "One should fill up the goblet of habdalah to its very brim, letting it slightly overflow as a token of blessing. . . ." After the father drinks, the remaining wine is poured on a tray and the candle is extinguished in it, thereby ending the ritual of separation. It is also quite proper for the father to repeat the Habdalah for the purpose of instructing the children: "One who had already said the habdalah may repeat it for the sake of his sons who have reached the age of religious training, in order that they may thus fulfill their obligations. . . ."

Bales has suggested that the order of precedence in drinking and abstaining during the Kiddush and Habdalah ceremonies implicitly dramatizes the ideal organization of authority in the Jewish family:

> It is interesting and important to note that the order in which the family members partake of the wine, first the father, then the lesser males, then the females, and then the domestics, emphasizes their relative status, also their relative closeness to the sacred. The same order in reverse is observed in the Habdalah, where first the females abstain, and then the lesser males, so that finally only the father drinks. The various members are separated from the sacred in the order of the lesser first and finally the most important.

How far this interpretation can be pressed for the Habdalah is questionable, for variations have been reported, such that others may partake of the wine after the father has completed his part of the ritual. But it is certainly important to note how alcoholic beverages and drinking are woven into these recurrent ceremonies which, in a general way, symbolize and reinforce solidarity and the organization of authority in the family, and at the same time affirm, through symbolism and ritual, the community of the entire family with the broader network of religious values.

Although Kiddush and Habdalah are properly performed in the home, they have also been performed in the synagogue since Talmudic times at the conclusion of the Friday and Saturday and Festival evening services. Except on the first two nights of Passover, the leader in prayer blesses over a cup of wine, but does not himself partake. Rather, he lets some of the children drink a little from the cup. While its origins are obscure, this custom probably represents a response to conditions in which it was not assured that all could observe the Kiddush and Habdalah rituals at home, necessitating their public enactment. This custom is apparently looked upon somewhat askance by the very Orthodox, since it is axiomatic among them that everyone will participate in Kiddush and Habdalah at home after the synagogue services. It is evidently on the assumption that he will later make Kiddush or Habdalah in his own home that the leader in prayer abstains from drinking in the synagogue and gives the wine to the children.

At the conclusion of Sabbath (and other formal) meals, it is also customary to say Grace, bless and partake of the Cup of Benediction. Although this custom lacks the essential character of Kiddush and Habdalah, where it is regularly observed there will be three additional drinking rituals corresponding to the three feasts required on the Sabbath. Often the third Sabbath meal is taken by the men at the synagogue, at dusk, between the late afternoon and evening prayer services—a token communal meal in which wine, beer or other beverages may be served, and this meal will be concluded by the Cup of Benediction ritual. In brief allusion to this ritual, Bales says that wine drinking for the Cup of Benediction used to be part of every Jewish meal, but is generally taken only on the Sabbath or on festivals or other joyous occasions in modern times. However, in referring to Grace and the Cup of Benediction as a part of every meal, the *Shulchan Aruch* makes it clear that wine was not the only beverage used:

> If three men ate together it is their duty to unite in saying the grace after meals, and they must say it over a glass of liquor. If possible, a glass of wine should be used; if it be impossible then beer, mead or brandy may be used, when such liquid is the common beverage of the locality, i.e., where vine culture does not obtain and one has to walk a whole day to obtain it, consequently wine is expensive and these beverages are substituted in the place of wine. Some authorities are of the opinion that even a single person is required to say Grace over a glass. Stringent people are accustomed, when saying Grace alone, not to hold the glass in their hands, but place it on the table in front of them.

It is also important to note that during Sabbath and other festival meals the drinking of wine, beer or spirits may often accompany the meal.

3. THE ANNUAL CYCLE OF HOLY DAYS AND FESTIVALS

The Orthodox Jew is commanded to honor the annual festivals as he honors the Sabbath. He must recite the Kiddush over wine before a festival meal and divide the portions of bread just as for the Sabbath meal. When a festival is followed by an ordinary week-day or by a day designated as "intermediate," i.e., between the first and last days of a week-long festival, he is also required to perform the Habdalah over a cup of wine, but omitting the benedictions of the spices and the light.

Bales has called attention to the "swing of the pendulum" in the annual religious cycle from the most serious holy days of New Year's (Rosh Hashanah) and the Day of Atonement (Yom Kippur) to the gay festival of Purim at the other extreme. While it is required that one rejoice appropriately on a joyous festival in the Jewish year, as indeed it is requisite to rejoice on the Sabbath, hedonistic indulgence is inappropriate for even the most festive occasion. The *Shulchan Aruch* is quite explicit on this:

> When one rejoices on a Festival one should not prolong in wine drinking, jesting and levity and say that whoever increase to do this thereby adds to the rejoicing of the festival; for drunkenness, jesting and levity is not rejoicing but mere foolishness, which is not according to the command. The rejoicing should be consistent with the worship of the Creator of the universe, for it is said, "Because thou hast not served the Lord thy God with joy and kindness of heart," from this may be inferred that worship is joy and one cannot serve God out of jesting, levity or drunkenness.

The conception of festive rejoicing in traditional Judaism is hardly to be equated with the individual pleasure seeking or spontaneous recreation which many Americans consider as the essence of "a good time" or "having fun." Even the most general ideas regarding what constitutes festivity and enjoyment, and the norms of how one ought to rejoice and be festive, are clearly defined by the religious code. True rejoicing and festivity are conceived of as integral with worship and contingent upon conformity with religious customs and fulfillment of ritual obligations. Nonetheless, there are differing emphases upon festivity and solemnity in the course of the annual cycle of holy days and festivals.

The Jewish year starts in the fall with the Ten Days of Penitence, which begin with the 2-day festival of Rosh Hashanah, the New Year proper. Rosh Hashanah is a time of judgment which anticipates the most solemn occasion of the year, the Day of Atonement. Since Rosh Hashanah is a festival, however, fasting is prohibited. After the evening services of worship on the first day of the festival (Jewish days begin at sundown) a feast is held which is preceded by the Kiddush drinking ritual. On the following noon Kiddush will also be performed. The second day of the festival repeats the pattern of the first, with variation in the reading from Scripture in the synagogue, and the festival is concluded with the ritual of Habdalah.

During the interim between Rosh Hashanah and the Day of Atonement time and energy are ordinarily devoted to settling quarrels and arguments, and, in general, to acts of penitence, restitution and reconciliation. On the third day of this first month (Tishri) of the religious calendar falls the Fast of Gedaliah, commemorating the slaying of the last governor of Judah in the time of Nebuchadnezzar. Abstention from food and drink is required during the day.

The Day of Atonement (Yom Kippur) climaxes the Ten Days of Penitence. It is a day of repentance and expiation in the fullest sense, and the most solemn occasion in the annual religious cycle. Although Yom Kippur is not a day of mourning, as is Tish'ah b'Ab, a rigorous fast of some 24 hours is mandatory. The seriousness of the occasion is suggested by the fact that the Day of Atonement is the one instance in the Jewish calendar when fasting is mandatory even if the day falls on the Sabbath. During Yom Kippur all labor, eating, drinking, bathing, and even the wearing of leather shoes (in ancient times a luxury) is forbidden.

Five days after Yom Kippur comes Succot, the Festival of Booths, a 9-day period of thanksgiving and joy. Succot commemorates the days of the wandering in the Desert of Sinai. As a symbol of this period, the pious Jew constructs a kind of leafy bower (a *succah*) in which to live for a week's time during the festival. At the minimum, Jews who observe the festival will eat a token of food and recite the Kiddush over wine in the succah on the first evening. In the Orthodox tradition Kiddush will be performed on the first two days and again on the last two days. The eighth and ninth days of this period are festivals in their own right: Sh'mini Azeret and Simchat Torah, respectively. Sh'mini Azeret climaxes the thanksgiving season, which began with Succot, and is marked by the prayer for rain at the additional service in the synagogue. On Simchat Torah, the Day of Rejoicing in the Law, the annual reading cycle of the Pentateuch is completed and begun again. As its name suggests, this latter day is a particularly festive occasion. Kiddush is performed before meals during both these festivals, as on the Sabbath.

Hannukkah begins two months after Simchat Torah, and roughly coincides with the Christmas season. This 8-day festival commemorates the purification and rededication of the Temple by the Maccabees. Lights are kindled each Hannukkah evening in remembrance of the light which miraculously burned for 8 days in the Temple with oil enough to last only a day. Half of every feast is supposed to be devoted to study, the other half to eating and drinking.

Approximately 10 weeks after Hannukkah comes Purim, the most frivolous festival in the annual cycle. It is also the most secular of all the festivals, and may be thought of as the "liberal extreme" in the Jewish calendar. Purim is an occasion for especial merrymaking which commemorates the triumph of the Jewish people over Haman, as narrated in the Book of Esther. Haman is the archetype of persecutors in Jewish history and the traditional symbolic focus for pent-up feelings of aggression toward politically dominant groups. Except for Hannukkah and the intermediate days of festivals, Purim is the only festival during which business and work are permitted. It is customary for gifts to be exchanged among friends and for alms to be given to the poor. In regard to drinking, Purim is a time of relative license. The *Shulchan Aruch* declares that "it is obligatory to eat, drink and be merry on Purim" and elaborates on the importance of drinking thusly:

> As the whole miracle was occasioned through wine: Vashti was troubled in the wine feast and Esther was put in her stead; also the downfall of Haman was due to wine, therefore the sages made it obligatory on one to become drunk, until he should not be able to differentiate between "Cursed be Haman" and "Blessed be Mordecai." At least one should drink more than he is accustomed to of wine or of another intoxicating beverage; one, however, who is of a weak disposition, likewise one who knows that it will cause him to despise some precept, a benediction or a prayer, or that it will lead him to levity, it is best not to become intoxicated; and all his deeds shall be done for the sake of Heaven.

In view of the ritual requirements of traditional Judaism, one could certainly not become drunk without running the risk of disrespect to some precept, benediction, or prayer, or of falling into levity. Nonetheless, the idea of relative license remains in the tradition of Purim and the appearance of mild intoxication is not inappropriate. Bales suggests that the dramatization of drunkenness and the sanctioned, directed variation from the ritual and sacred uses of wine on Purim has its own "subtle educational purpose." This is because it sharpens the contrast between the ordinarily sober and dignified Jew, and the ridiculous, tipsy merrymaker in the context of the particular festival which emphasizes the hatred and dangers of the persecutor (whose downfall was due to wine). We may add that the tradition of Purim probably helps structure and reinforce the stereotypes of sober Jews and drunken Gentiles, to be discussed in Chapter 4.

Passover follows Purim by a month and at this time the pendulum swings back to more serious religious observances. Passover commemorates the deliverance of the Jews from Egyptian bondage, and during its course leaven is banned from the home in accord with Biblical injunction. Although this prohibition does not extend to wine, great care must be taken to see that it is ritually pure. Of the wine to be used on Passover, the *Shulchan Aruch* declares:

> It is mandatory to acquire choice wine wherewith to perform the precept of drinking four goblets. If one can obtain red wine which is of the same quality as the white, and is also as valid for the use on Passover as the white, the

former is to be preferred to the latter, for it is written: "Do not observe wine
when it becomes red," from which it may be inferred that the value of wine
lies in its being red.

However, some latitude is given in regard to alcoholic beverages for ritual
use even on Passover. In the case of "one who abstains from wine during
the year because it is injurious to him" the *Shulchan Aruch* rules that on
Passover, "he may dilute it with water or he may drink raisin wine or mead,
if this is a local beverage."

The first two evenings of Passover are *Seder* (literally, "order") nights.
On the first evening certain symbolic foods are placed on the table before
the regular meal. These include the *matzoth,* or unleavened bread, the
"bread of affliction"; the roasted shankbone of a lamb, or a substitute, representing the Passover lamb which was annually offered up at the Temple
in Jerusalem; the bitter herbs and a cup of salt water into which the herbs
are dipped as a symbol of the bitterness of Egyptian slavery; the *charoseth,*
a paste made of apples, almonds, spices, wine and other ingredients, representing the mortar which the Jews made for the Egyptians; and an egg,
symbolizing another sacrifice made in Temple days.

The Passover ritual begins with the blessing of the children, first by the
father, and then by the mother. The Kiddush is recited and all partake of
the wine. The wine cups are refilled and the youngest child then asks the
meaning of the festival and the special foods. A historical account of Passover is recited. Some of the special foods are passed around and all partake.
Hymns are recited or sung, after which the benediction over wine is repeated and all drink the second cup. The festival meal is served, the wine
cups are filled again, following which the Grace is said, ending with the
drinking of the third cup. Immediately thereafter the wine cups are filled
again. An extra cup, called the Cup of Elijah, is poured in expectation of
the visit of the prophet Elijah. One of the children is sent to open the door
for Elijah. Then psalms and other traditional songs are sung, after which
the wine blessing is repeated and the final cup is finished. After this fourth
cup, no more wine may be drunk that night. To the master of the house the
Shulchan Aruch recommends that "He should urge his household to drink
at least the greater part of each cup at one time, and of the fourth cup they
should drink a quarter of a cup at one time." Traditionally, then, on the
first and second nights of Passover, the usual Kiddush ceremony is woven
into the Seder, at which the wine is blessed and drunk four successive
times. In addition there is a Kiddush in the middle of the day and a
Habdalah at the close of the second day, i.e., before the intermediate days
of the festival. The final two days of Passover are once again Kiddush days.

Seven weeks after the beginning of Passover comes Shavuot, the 2-day
Festival of Weeks, or Pentecost, and the last festival of the year. This holiday celebrates the giving of the Torah. It is a joyous occasion and wine is
used as on other feast days, the pattern of Kiddush and Habdalah being the
same as on Rosh Hashanah.

The Fast of the Seventeenth of Tammuz, which occurs during the summer, commemorates the breach in the wall of Jerusalem and on this day abstention from food and drink is required. From the Fast of the Seventeenth of Tammuz to the Fast of the Ninth of Ab (a period of 3 weeks) it is customary for the pious to observe some degree of mourning. It is forbidden to eat meat or to drink wine during the 9 days preceding the Fast of the Ninth of Ab, or Tish'ah b'Ab, which commemorates both the first and the second destruction of the Temple. All the regulations concerning this 9-day period have to do with mourning; one should not do anything for pleasure during this time. On the Ninth of Ab one is forbidden to eat or drink, to bathe, to wear leather shoes, and so forth, from the preceding day at nightfall. The abstention from meat and drink ideally is to last until noon on the tenth of Ab. Tish'ah b'Ab is the most rigorous fast day of the Jewish year except the Day of Atonement and concludes the important occasions in the cycle of the Jewish year.

4. LATER RITES DE PASSAGE

By the time the Jewish boy brought up in a traditionally religious home approaches his teens, he has experienced the rite of circumcision and actively participated in the Sabbath observances and festivals of which ritualized uses of alcoholic beverages are a part. It is also likely that he has been a spectator at a *Bar Mitzvah*, wedding or funeral, although he has yet to play an active or central role in these ceremonies.

The ceremony of the Bar Mitzvah marks a stage in the Jewish boy's religious education and his formal transition to adult status. The Bar Mitzvah takes place around the thirteenth birthday and makes the boy a full member of the religious community, eligible to be reckoned among the 10 men making up a minyan. There is first a religious ceremony at the synagogue, where the boy usually reads part of the Scriptures in Hebrew. This is customarily followed by a family reunion and celebration. Speeches may be given, the boy is blessed by the rabbi and receives gifts from family and friends. There is no special use of wine or alcoholic beverages on this occasion as at the circumcision, but these beverages will be sanctified and used as a part of the meal of celebration.

Ordinarily, the next important status transition after the Bar Mitzvah occurs with marriage. Marriage is held in great reverence among Jews, for the founding of a family is accounted a religious duty as well as a social ideal. The traditions and rules for the preparation and conduct of an Orthodox wedding are much too elaborate to be outlined here. However, the central significance of wine and drinking in the wedding ceremony itself must be noted. During the ceremony the rabbi utters the benediction over a cup of wine and hands it to the bridal couple who partake of it. They may then pass it on to their nearest relatives who also drink. The procedure thereafter is this:

. . . The person performing the ceremony continues as follows: "Blessed art thou, O Lord, our God, King of the universe, who has sanctified us with Thy commandments concerning forbidden connections, and hast forbidden unto us those who are merely betrothed and hast permitted unto us those lawfully married to us through 'canopy' (*huppah*) and 'betrothal' (*kiddushin*). Blessed art Thou, O Lord, who sanctifiest Thy people Israel through huppah and kiddushin," after which the groom hands to the bride a ring or some object of value (not less than a perutah, the smallest current coin), saying, "Be thou betrothed (or consecrated) unto me with this ring (or object) in accordance with the laws of Moses and Israel." . . . This act of betrothal is at present combined with the rite of hometaking; and after the placing of the ring upon the finger of the bride, the marriage contract (*ketubah*) is read, to form an interval between the two acts. The recitation of another benediction over wine and of the customary seven wedding benedictions forms the completion of the wedding ceremony.

It is also customary for the groom to break a wine glass on the floor or crush it beneath his feet. Although a number of interpretations have been offered for this custom, the original meaning is obscure.

The last of the rites in the life cycle is, of course, the funeral. Jewish tradition prescribes that full mourning be limited to the death of a father, mother, son, daughter, brother, sister, wife or husband. It is also appropriate for a student to mourn for his teacher. As might be expected, during the initial period of grief, that is, until the time of burial, abstention from eating in company, from meat and from wine is enjoined (Sabbath and holy days excepted). As to the positive uses of alcoholic beverages at this time, the *Shulchan Aruch* prescribes that wine be used to wash the head of the corpse:

Then they beat an egg with some wine, and the egg should be beaten in its shell, indicating thereby the wheel of fortune that makes revolutions in this world (and where wine is unobtainable water may be substituted), and wash the head of the dead therewith. And the custom prevailing in some places that each one takes a little from this mixture and sprinkles it upon the dead, is improper; such custom should be abolished because it resembles the customs of other peoples; his head only should be washed therewith.

From the point of view of structuring cultural definitions of drinking in the personality, rites de passage cannot, in their nature, have the repetitive impact of the Sabbath ceremonies on the personality of the Jew. Perhaps, also, rites like the wedding, which are adult experiences, thereby lose some effectiveness as occasions for socialization. Nevertheless, the rites de passage are events of great significance to the individual which redefine his social status and relationships. Moreover, from the vantage point of membership in the community these rites have a recurrent character. The individual may participate in them variously as candidate, groom, father, relative, member of the congregation, fellow Jew, and so forth. More broadly, the rites de passage are tangible expressions and reinforcements of the ideal structure and solidarity of the extended family and social community. And they are occasions for expressing and reinforcing the overriding symbolism and sentiments of the religious community in the broadest sense. The fact that alcoholic beverages and drinking have either a prominent or ancillary role in all these ceremonies implies (1) the further impact of cultural definitions of drinking upon the individual, and (2) a strengthening of the links between drinking and the most powerful norms, ideas and sentiments of the group in "outer" social expression and "inner" structure of the personality. It also testifies to the consistency with which traditional Judaism incorporates these beverages and drinking in its core symbolism, sentiments and activities.

5. OTHER USES AND BASIC MEANINGS OF ALCOHOLIC BEVERAGES AND DRINKING IN ORTHODOX CULTURE

In brief conclusion to his documentary study of drinking among Orthodox Jews, Bales notes that early rabbinical writings contain references to drinking for other than religious ritual purposes. These usages, he says, seem largely to have disappeared with the exception of the drinking of *schnapps*, originally a strongly alcoholic drink made by pouring *aqua vitae* over fruit and allowing the whole to stand, now any spirits. Schnapps, according to Bales, is sometimes taken by the master of the house before a meal or is occasionally taken as medicine. The rationale for the custom is "medicinal," although for schnapps, as indeed for any drinking, a short blessing is required. In regard to specifically medicinal usages, whether at mealtime or any other time, the *Shulchan Aruch* specifies that "One who partakes of food or drink as medicine, if it be something savoury which he relishes, even if it is forbidden food, he should say the preceding and concluding benedictions appropriate thereto . . ." The clear implication of the Orthodox tradition is that even in otherwise secular situations the drinking is drawn into the realm of religious ideas and sentiments by the extension of religious symbolism. As we shall see, however, the use of schnapps in religious contexts—quite clearly provided for by the *Shulchan Aruch*—and in other situations is far more widespread among Jews than Bales' comments would suggest.

It is nonetheless pertinent to reiterate the basic meanings of alcoholic beverages and drinking in Orthodox Jewish culture as these have been summarized by Bales:

> . . . the essential uses of wine and other alcoholic beverages as they have existed to the present time are quite uniform: wine is symbolic of the *sacred source of moral authority*, God and the commandments of God, the law, the moral community and those who stand for it, such as the father; the act of drinking has the ritual significance of *creating, manifesting, or renewing a union* between the individual and the source of moral authority; and conversely, a

degree of separation of the individual from the sacred things represented by the wine is symbolically initiated, manifested, or perpetuated by an *abstention* from, or prevention of the act of drinking in certain ways . . . Virtually all of the drinking which takes place in the Orthodox Jewish culture has these socially defined meanings, and furthermore, it can be assumed that practically every Orthodox Jew associates the act of drinking (consciously or not) with these profoundly moving ideas and sentiments regarding the sacred and his relationship to it, because of the intimate integration of the meaningful act with the earliest processes of socialization, the rites de passage, the weekly and yearly cycle of religious events, and the relationships of individuals within the family.

The concept of a "ritual attitude" toward drinking, which Bales believes is at the root of the low rates of drinking pathologies among Jews was referred to in PART II. But, against the background of rituals and ceremonies which we have described, the above summary statement articulates the content of Orthodox Jewish attitudes toward drinking and the ways in which these are structured and sustained in the individual personality.* Elaboration of these ideas and their possible significance for the low rates of drinking pathologies among Jews must be postponed, however, until the actual drinking behaviors and attitudes of contemporary Jews are given fairly extensive consideration.

* It is also pertinent to spell out here more fully than in PART II the formal characteristics of ritual drinking as defined by Bales and as found, empirically, in Orthodox Jewish culture. In its ideal-type form, ritual drinking embodies these characteristics: "*1*. The ends of the act are non-empirical, that is, it is not possible to determine scientifically whether or not they are achieved, because they refer to entities and states of the 'other world'—the world which is articulated in terms of religious ideas and sentiments. The purposes, although entertained by an individual, are also the joint purposes of a 'moral community' in Durkheim's sense, not simply of the individual as an individual. The purposes are supposedly achieved in the act itself, not in further empirical effects which the act brings about. The purposes are expressive and communicative rather than procurative. *2*. Employment of the act of drinking as a means to the end is successful, not by reason of its empirical, physical character or effects, but by reason of its symbolic socially arbitrary definition. The empirical function of the act lies in the control and manipulation of the cognitive and moral modes of orientation of the participants, not of the affectional, hedonic or goal directive modes. *3*. The conditions of success lie in the proper symbolic performance of the act itself, as socially defined by the tradition of the group, rather than in conforming to any physical conditions of cause and effect. The act must be performed in the presence (real or imagined) of others who understand and concur in the meaning and purpose of the act." Bales defines the characteristics of ritual drinking as point for point opposed to utilitarian (or hedonistic) drinking, the prevalence of which in Irish culture he sees as a factor predisposing toward high rates of drinking pathologies.

The Experiential Aspects of Social Structure

BARTLETT H. STOODLEY

"Sociology," says Edward Shils, "is a continuation and elaboration of the permanent and necessary effort of man to understand himself and his species." Shils seems to feel that the sociologist makes some contribution to this effort when he can make his theory inclusive enough to cover a wide spectrum of human experience. He says that ". . . sociologists are now more able and more apt to include, in their observations, the experience of situations as they appear to those who live in them, and to heed the actual experience and the sentiments it evokes."

Admitting that progress of this sort is being made, there is little doubt that teachers of sociology have encountered difficulty in conveying the substance of sociology to beginning students. This is due in large part to the difference between the perspective the individual normally has on life and the more abstract, conceptualized view of the sociologist. But, since sociology is based on behavior and abstracts from it, the individual is entitled to ask, "What aspects of my experience form the basis of sociology?"

When we, as sociologists, answer this question we normally deal with such items as goal seeking, norm internalization, self conceptions, and so on. These are important aspects of the individual's perspective. But they fail to indicate what is probably the most important single element in the sociological point of view, the element of constraint. When the sociologist turns to the question of constraint he performs a peculiar reversal and, instead of talking about the constraint exercised by the goal-seeking, norm-oriented *actor*, he mentions the constraint exercised over this actor by an external *alter*. No student is going to identify with this villainous alter, and in fact sociologists don't often paint alter in very human terms. The sociologist thus caters to the very bias that he struggles against in his students. The student identifies with ego who, like St. George, is struggling against the evil of a host of nameless, Argos-eyed alters.

The student of sociology must be given no opportunity to separate himself from the constraint which is part of the human condition. He should see himself as an agent of constraint, although often an unconscious one, as well as the object of constraint on the part of others. I would argue that when we see the actor as a striving *and* constraining agent in a one-package deal we are establishing the experiential basis of sociology. I think also that when we combine ego and alter in the same frame of reference, a concrete

From *Social Education,* May, 1965. Reprinted by permission of the publisher and author.

individual, we can more easily detect the interrelations between ego and alter modes of activity. When I use the term ego in this paper I am referring to the motivations and orientations associated with the personality (if we may use the term loosely) of the individual. When I employ the term alter I have in mind those aspects of behavior that reflect recognition (conscious or unconscious) of an external or public set of proprieties. The locus of alter behavior is in these external, public proprieties, while the locus of ego behavior is in the dynamic of the personality, itself. These are, of course, analytic distinctions, but they are the basic analytic distinctions that serve to demonstrate the experiential basis for sociological analysis. In what follows we shall try to give a demonstration of typical behavior that involves both ego-type and alter-type behaviors and we shall improve the occasion by developing the general points made above.

If I am on my way to class, I am aware of myself as a person, of the notes I have available, of my inability to organize them satisfactorily before class, and of my hope that in front of the class they will somehow make sense. There is a vibrant external and internal world as I proceed to the classroom. There is a world of physiological vividness, too. I have the tingling of apprehension, the liberating glow of hope, the messianic fervor of imparting the "word." If I am relaxed, I may hum a tune—perhaps a line of poetry will come from nowhere. All this is a continuous record—my *ego* record, perhaps. And now I have come to the classroom.

But what have I left out? In my concentration on the last mile, I failed to see the janitor who has put himself in my way to say good morning and make a pronouncement on the day's weather. I have noted that he respects teachers. He is new and before long this attitude will change. I have now started him on his way toward a more enlightened view. I shall not again be flattered with deference. For as I pass unseeing the janitor feels the uncomfortable emotion of rejection. This is going to lead to doubts and re-examination. I have started a discontinuous record—my *alter* record. To start my alter record going it was not necessary for me to intend anything or even perceive anything. I was *there,* that is all.

But this is not all. I pass the bulletin board. An uncommonly pretty student is looking at it and turns toward me as I pass. Anyone who is looking at the sociology bulletin board is on the right track and if she is pretty, so much the better. I give this girl my warmest smile. Now I really do remember this. It is in my ego record, but I might have repressed it a little.

As I come to the classroom the bell rings. It hardly causes a ripple on the surface of my preconscious I am so used to it. But I sense that it is now late for all but teachers to get to class. A student brushes past me seeking to get into the classroom at the last moment. She is late. My placid but not fully mobile face, my retarded response, means nothing at all to me, but to her it is the expected price for tardiness, one of those things it is as well to avoid if you can.

My walk from the office to the classroom has resulted in three different types of behavior. In the first place I have failed to satisfy the expectations of someone else and this is a fact with predictable consequences. My ego is entirely innocent of sin. When I see the janitor next, I shall be disappointed by a suggestion of coldness and I will conclude he really isn't the pleasant person I thought he was, and his deference was put on. He was pulling my leg.

The student at the bulletin board occupied my attention only for the merest second. Yet, let's face it, my smile had an element of wistfulness. My unconscious stirred on certain Caliban-like promptings of the id. I moved on. But behind me the smile prompted a pretty student to think again, a little differently—perhaps she gave a fleeting thought to electing a course in sociology. No one will say I was not acting as a teacher should in rewarding her intellectual interests (if she was not looking at the cartoons on the bulletin board) and this was not apart from my intention. The realest thing to me was that vision of forbidden youth, but the realest thing to her, out of that brief encounter, was the possible uses of sociology.

It cannot be said that I was angry in the slightest as the next student brushed past me to get into the classroom. But the bell had rung. My pre-conscious could not but know that she was late. If I would not penalize her—and that amount of involvement was completely foreign to me—yet I could not be actively interested in her. My ego lived on without a stir. But to the late student this disinterest was measured from what it might have been. Personal indifference on my part became active sanction in her eyes, a thing as well to avoid.

It should be noticed that the things that were realest to me and destined for my diary were actually of little lasting significance. My report of my journey from my desk to the classroom would indicate nothing of any moment. Except for a vague stirring of youth nothing happened. Yet, from another point of view, everything happened. My walk brought about three different sets of stimulation that could have important influence on the behavior of others.

How did this situation come about? In none of the three situations mentioned above was I really involved. What, in the first place, was the view of the janitor? He was not thinking of me as I like to think of myself, as a total, dynamic process too deep even for me. I took my meaning for the janitor from my membership in a larger complex. I was a part of American society, I was at a college, I was a teacher. In other words, I belonged to a set of intersecting classifications. As a member of American society I *could be expected* to accept sociability and friendliness as a value; as a member of the college community I shared a basic orientation with the janitor; as a teacher I held a certain position in the hierarchy of persons in the college community. While I might be the object of respect (highly problematical), I was the more bound to a demonstration of equalitarianism. The weather would serve very well. But the friendly tongue, the eager, the nascent smile of the janitor—all were lost on the stiff, unbending figure that walked vacantly down the hall. The janitor's good opinion of me will be hard to reclaim. Especially hard since I do not even know that I have lost it. Before it has been reclaimed by good works the janitor's point of view may have been communicated to others and so have taken its place in those systems of concentric circles that we call interpersonal communication. Those spreading circles, started before I have returned to the good graces of the janitor— if I *do* return—cannot be reclaimed. And they cannot be really traced beyond their earlier stages.

All this is a pity when you think that I simply did not see the janitor. I was too busy wrestling with my thought, with my encounter with the class. This may be the whole explanation, and it certainly is often the explanation of waves of communication which emanate from us with which we feel in no way identified and of which we may not even be conscious. Yet these waves of communication win friends and influence people. Our intentions or our consciousness does not impede their spread, nor can our regrets call them back. They are "objective results" of our "being in this world." Individuals, in their encounters with others, can only rarely measure behavior from the roots of the secret self (I just admitted above that I was unfathomable to myself!). They must use some kind of external measure as a referent. With new acquaintances the small talk of "Where do you come from?" "Whom do you know?" "What part of town do you live in?" serve as referent points to define the meaning of a person's behavior. In other circumstances the fact that a person is a teacher, a judge, a doctor, gives clues to the behavior to be expected and to the explanation of the behavior after it has taken place.

But the classification serves a further purpose. When the behavior does not conform in all respects to the classification, and we search for further clues, we measure the meaning of the behavior from the manner and distance it deviates from the expected behavior. The janitor measured me according to an image in his mind. My innocence did not keep the moving finger from writing, and it is doubtful if I shall be able to repeal a word. This is not my ego record, my real self in action; it is my alter record, my record of meaning to others. In this case the two records did not touch at any point. The external observer, however, the sociologist, would have to observe the consequences of this encounter in terms of the change in the janitor's attitudes and his communication of this change to others. In rather more serious circumstances than we would expect here, the sociologist might observe a severe dip in the morale of the janitors at this institution. When he traced the cause to me I would certainly feel unjustly accused and would probably respond aggressively against the sociologist and thus start a new wave of social change.

In this instance, when I passed the janitor by, I was both an alter and an ego. As an alter I had meaning for the janitor which in this instance resulted merely from my physical presence and appearance; as an ego I was palpitating with moods of the morning and wondering how things would go in the classroom. At the time of the encounter with the janitor both the ego record and the alter record were being written. I was ego and alter at once. I was, however, only conscious of being ego and only interested in being ego. But the major event, as it happens, was written in the alter record.

Let us take another look at the pretty girl at the bulletin board. Here, there was also an ego record and an alter record. And I cannot say that I did not perceive the student there. It will be written in my diary that I saw the student there with my ego, my whole self, for one fleeting instant. But, and this is the glory of social systems, she did not perceive me with her whole self. She perceived me as a classification, much as the janitor did. Her smile was a response to a classification, and I was saved from temptation. I was isolated in my fantasy. The student thought only of sociology.

Yet, if the student thought of me only as a congeries of classifications, perhaps I masked my real self after all and acted as a teacher should. I know how to act as a teacher, just as the student knows how to act as a student, because this is a kind of public position that one can learn about. Since the student responded to my smile in terms of my public self (my alter record), it is possible that my smile was modeled correctly on my public self. So here two public selves had an encounter, two alters wrote their stories.

Was there a whisper of ego in this encounter? Was I able to keep my personal interest out of my smile: Perhaps not. And the student, did she see the smile as only an emanation from the alter? If we assume that I transgressed here (and who does not?), then the student may not only have felt the approval of a teacher for a student but also the approval of a man for a pretty girl; and her response may not have been entirely that of a student.

In most encounters ego and alter stimulations and responses are part of the strategy of communication and they are empirically inseparable. In encounters like the one above the public self is dominant, and I feel obligations to it, as does the student. In fact, it is the mutual awareness of the legitimate dominance of the public self in each case that encourages a little dalliance behind the alter scene. The ego is saying, "I can dream, can't I?" And, in fact, this fantasy is dependent on the stability and continuity of the public facade. It is the public facade, the exchange between alters, that defines the real relation and thus insures that fantasy will not take the wheel.

If either party fails to carry out the expectations of the public self (i.e., the alter dimension of action), it would constitute an invitation to a relation different from the teacher-student relation. This, of course, introduces instability and ambiguity into the relation, and if other alters detect it, there is likely to be gossip. If the invitation is accepted by the other party, then a new relationship is established. It then may be necessary to make believe that the former student-teacher relation still is in effect, for other alters (other students, teachers, and members of the administration) are likely to feel that the maintenance of the alter relation is necessary to achieve the aims of education.

This episode tells us a number of things. In the first place it tells us that it is quite possible for us to carry on alter activity and ego activity at the same time. It also tells us that our alter activity is very different from our ego activity even when we are conscious of both of them. Perhaps the most important thing it calls to mind is that alter activity involves, as we said, a public self. This public self is considerably different from a private self. It is not a self that the individual thought up. It is something that was already in existence outside of him which he picked up in his voyage through life. What he observed, external to himself, was a series of intersecting opinions, attitudes, and expressions, having as their focus a certain social situation like, for instance, that of the teacher. We know now that these are largely alter emanations of other individuals, but in any event they serve to define conduct for the individual in that situation. When the individual enters the situation of teacher he finds that the opinions, attitudes, and verbalizations focusing on this position serve as the basis of evaluation by others of his behavior. He finds that his students rely on his observance of these behaviors. And, truth to tell, he also finds that he relies on his students' observances of the opinions and attitudes focusing on *their* position.

A society consists of innumerable social positions that serve as the focus for opinions that define the proprieties of conduct. These opinions are aimed at the position and not the person. They require the individual to observe them so long as he is in the position. Thus, they are external to the individual. But he is beholden to these definitions in order to communicate to others and in order to understand communication from them. When the individual is in such a position he is the target of these public opinions, expectations, and evaluations whether he wishes it or not. Notice my unfortunate encounter with the janitor. Much of my influence in the world is brought about from the behavior of my public self, my alter, regardless of my heart's desire.

But it is time we went back to my walk to class. We can hope to show yet another aspect of the alter-ego relation. You will remember that when I had greeted the girl at the bulletin board I proceeded toward the classroom. In my unconscious there was a hum resembling the tune, "A pretty girl is like a melody." This faded away. I came to the door as the bell rang announcing the beginning of the next period. A student brushed past ahead of me as I opened the door to the classroom. Her furtive glance at me received no encouraging smile. She was late for class, and in general there was nothing special to enthuse over. She, too, was good-looking, but she was also late. It would be hard to say that I consciously or unconsciously expressed my displeasure and thus sanctioned the girl for being late. I really scarcely heard the bell, and it is not my practice to single out late students for criticism. The fact remains that, under the circumstances, I showed no concrete awareness of the student, no fleeting admission of a social relationship. In fact, since my mind was on the class presentation the bell was a welcome event. It gave me an excuse, perhaps, to avoid recognition of the student that passed by me and to continue my line of thought about my lecture. It is even conceivable that I was just a little grateful to the student for this excuse for ignoring her.

As you can see, it is not entirely certain why I did preserve a kind of social distance between myself and the student.

But now let us look at it from the view of the student. She had no access to the private world I lived in. She could not sort out my motivations. And it is easy to see that even if she did have access to my private world, she would have found it all but impossible to sort out the effective motivation for my act. It was really a blend of motivations. Fortunately, the student did not embark on such a wild goose chase. She worked with the public meaning of my behavior and the public significance of her behavior. She may have had many excuses for being late, but she was late. And while I did not have the reputation of being hard on late students, I was still a teacher. So the student expected to be sanctioned in view of her behavior as a student and my position as a teacher. She was committed to seeing a sanction where it was justified. My social reticence was enough. She moved quickly through the door to her seat with a brief feeling of discomfort and even a stirring of self-disapproval.

In this situation the alter aspects of two selves were in collision. One alter was subject to sanction in terms of the public proprieties of her position and thus she expected not reward but punishment from the reciprocal alter of another individual who had the public right to dispense both reward and punishment. And, being subject to sanction, she was inclined to perceive sanction; that is to interpret the behavior of the relevant alter as conveying sanction whether it was in any sense intended or not.

There is something else to be learned from this episode. It is quite likely that I took advantage of my rights as alter to carry on an ego interest of my own. I was preparing my lecture in that language that George H. Mead calls the "conversation of gestures." The girl's tardiness gave me an excuse to avoid the ritual of a social encounter and to continue, undisturbed, the pursuit of my lecture. Here my self took advantage of my rights as alter. Thus my public self performed a definite function for my inner self.

CONCLUSION

I have shown that I was dichotomized on the morning I took that walk to the classroom. I was an ego system and in that system I was aware of myself, my feelings, my plans. But I was at the same time an alter system; I was subject to a host of expectations and evaluations which clustered around the classifications or positions that applied to me. I was an American, a member of an educational community, a teacher. We have dealt mainly with the position of teacher. My alter record and my ego record do not run concurrently nor synchronously. With the janitor my alter record consisted only in my existence and presence at the fateful conjunction between the janitor and myself. In the case of the girl at the bulletin board I was aware of some disparity between my alter record and my ego record. But I was willing to recognize the legitimacy of the alter record and the illegitimacy of the ego record. This, in fact, freed my ego for a little wishful thinking. It was not in the business of making reality decisions, for this job was being done by my public self, the alter. When I came to the door of the classroom my ego made yet another use of the alter. It took advantage of an alter right to maintain its own privacy. Thus my behavior had two important consequences: it served to remind the student of her obligations to her public performance as a student, and it made it possible for me to continue the inward preparation of my lecture.

Let us reverse the coin. The janitor applied to me expectations that applied to my position as citizen, member of the community, and teacher. He chose to take my default seriously, that is, he took it to his ego. He might have merely disapproved of me as a teacher, but instead he chose to interpret my disregard as a personal slight. In this situation my alter did me a lot of personal harm. The student at the bulletin board received a public and a personal reward. She was approved as a person, but she was also approved as a student. She had a stake, not only in her ego, but in her alter performance, for she hoped to go to graduate school. She was, therefore, involved in her public performance. It held the promise of personal rewards in education and career rewards in graduate school. The student in the classroom interpreted a public act as a public sanction for her own deficient alter performance. She had accepted to some extent the legitimacy of the public expectations of her position, for she was somewhat disappointed in herself as she went to her seat.

Thus I am dichotomized, and they are dichotomized, and so are we all. Our selves as egos are aware of our own life space; but as alters we are aware of the public intersection of proprieties and expectations converging on the positions that we occupy. We all perform alter functions as well as ego functions, although we are much more conscious of our ego functions. Sometimes we are unaware of our alter significance, sometimes we use it to our advantage, sometimes we use it to exert our alter rights, but in any event we act as alters continuously.

It seems to the writer that advantages accrue from combining the ego and alter aspects of behavior into a package that relates to the action of the individual rather than separating off alter behavior and looking upon it as a constraint to which the actor responds. First, it helps the sociologist, in Shils' words, ". . . to include . . . the experience of situations as they appear to those who live in them. . . ." Second, the opening gambit for which I argue establishes the experiential basis of sociology. When the sociologist moves to the "situation of action" where alter behavior is separated from ego behavior it can be readily seen that this is a methodological convenience. When the individual is concentrated on an ego goal the external impediments in the form of alter behavior of others is more germane to the goal striving than the alter behavior of the goal seeker. Third, the analysis of alter behavior in its association with ego behavior in the same individual opens up a field of research in the dynamics of the self and particularly invites attention to the variety of functions and dysfunctions of alter behavior in the individual. It also favors the treatment of trends in ego behavior, "ego press," that may bring massive pressure to bear on social organization.

Negro Reactions to Minority Group Status

ROBERT JOHNSON

I. INTRODUCTION

IN THE CURRENT INTERNATIONAL CRISIS of conflicting group attitudes, sentiments and loyalties, men are fortunate in having available to them a vast amount of academic and empirical literature on the subject of minority group relations in world society. Most of these studies of minority group problems have dealt with (a) the position of minorities in the stratification of social structures; (b) the clarification of thinking on the subject of race, and on the relation of race and culture; (c) the psychological, sociological and economic analyses of the nature of race prejudice and discrimination; and (d) the discussion of techniques for the reduction of intergroup tension and the improvement of minority group status.

The present article is an attempt to contribute to a fifth area of interest: the differential reaction of minority group members to their minority group status. This subject has received intensive study by Myrdal, Frazier, Johnson, Strong, Rose, Cox, and numerous other social scientists. However, this study is the outgrowth of an intensive two-year investigation in a single community, using as a setting the general community as well as the rest of the American Negro world. In this study, the research techniques of participant-observation and of the cross-sectional survey method have been combined to determine how the American Negro in this community feels and reacts toward his minority status.

We are generally familiar with the current credo of the American Negro as expressed by Negro leaders, organizations and publications on the national level. This credo implies the desirability of concerted movement toward two goals: (a) the promotion of a general American drive toward the 'More Perfect Union,' and (b) the improvement of the Negro's status within the framework of the democratic creed. Militancy is urged, self-hatred is decried,

From *American Minorities*, edited by Milton Barron, New York: Alfred A. Knopf, 1957, pp. 192-212. Reprinted by permission of Professor Barron.

interest in international events is encouraged, friendliness and goodwill toward whites are advocated (with notable exceptions). In addition, a seemingly contradictory but actually realistic dual value is implied: (a) the desirability of strengthening Negro group identification and race pride, and (b) the desirability of struggling for full integration into American society.

On a local community level, it is evident that adherence to this National Negro Credo will be strongly affected by the socio-economic position of the individual Negro, by the background of racial experience that colors his current attitudes, by the nature and frequency of his interracial contacts, and by the attitudes of his reference groups and 'significant others.' This intensive community-wide examination of intergroup contacts, attitudes and social relations has selected, as part of its scope, the relevance of the national Negro credo to Negro attitudes in a specific locus.

II. THE GENERAL COMMUNITY SETTING

The study was made in a middle-sized, upstate New York community of 60,000 persons which we shall call 'Hometown.' It is a predominantly industrial community boasting twelve locally-owned and twelve absentee-owned relatively small industries, and one large industrial plant with 7000 employees. The city was selected on the basis of these criteria: (a) its economic and industrial organization was relatively representative of most middle-sized American cities, (b) it was not a 'boom town' nor was it 'dominated' by large nearby cities, large industries or educational institutions, (c) it had a fair distribution of ethnic groups. The Negro and Jewish communities were of approximately equal size, each comprising close to three per cent of the city's population. Roughly, 6% of the community members were of Italian-American descent. In addition, the community contained several Irish, Russian-Ukrainian and Polish families.

After compiling relevant data on the history, demography and ecology, economic organization and social structure of the community, and after making 'quickie' surveys in six similar cities, the research group devised a questionnaire which was administered to 529 adult 'NaM's (native American white gentiles), 150 Jews, 150 Negroes and 150 persons of Italian ancestry. The questionnaire contained an exhaustive inventory of contacts between majority and minority group members, an inventory of personality traits (authoritarianism, 'Jungle' outlook, frustration, and indices of psychoneurosis) and an intensive inventory of the elements of prejudice—hostility, antipathy, scapegoating, social distance, and stereotyped thinking.

When the majority group was asked about the Negro community, it soon became evident that most majority group members had (a) very little contact with Negroes, and (b) a great deal of prejudice against them. Half of the majority group members in the community had *no* contact with *any* minority group member (Negro, Jew or Italian) in any of the four areas investigated—job, neighborhood, organization or informal social group.

Respondents were asked about actual and hypothetical contacts with Negroes in these four areas. Fourteen per cent stated that there were Negroes living within a block or two of their home, 13% reported contact with a Negro fellow-worker or employee on their job, 10% belonged to organizations with Negro members (half of these were unions or veteran's organizations) and none of the respondents interviewed reported any Negroes in their informal social group. Attitudes toward Negroes in these four areas took this form:

Those who had Negroes	Respondent 'feels different'	Others 'feel different'
In their club (52)	10%	23%
On their job (67)	17%	33%
In their neighborhood (74)	27%	46%
In their social group (0)	—	—

Those who contacted no Negroes in these areas were asked:

Suppose a Negro wanted to come into:	Respondent would object:	Others would object:
Your club (205)	43%	68%
Your work group (226)	33%	47%
Your neighborhood (448)	60%	86%
Your social group (293)	77%	93%

It may be consistently shown that respondents reacted more favorably to the presence of Negroes in these four areas than they responded to the *hypothetical* possibility of Negroes in these areas, and also that in every single case, the respondent was more likely to say that *others* would object than to admit that he himself would object.

The researcher began the study with the assumption that most prejudices arise not from contact with minorities but from contact with other prejudiced people. This was confirmed by the fact that despite the lack of contact with Negroes, most whites expressed some type of prejudice against them. When presented with a social-distance scale (known as the 'distastefuls') Hometown whites answered as follows:

I would find it distasteful:

1. To eat with a Negro	49%
2. To dance with a Negro	82%
3. To go to a party and find that most of the people there are Negro	80%
4. To have a Negro marry somebody in my family	99%

When asked a modified version of the 'Chicago Tension Barometer,' 20%
of Hometown residents said that they disliked Negroes, 22% thought that
Negroes are demanding more than they have a right to (and 26% of these
said that this made them feel 'pretty angry'); 41% felt that Negroes were
pushing in where they were not wanted (of these, 23% averred that it
bothered them a good deal). In addition, 42% agreed with the stereotyped
statement that "generally speaking, Negroes are lazy and ignorant."

Allied to this statistical picture of anti-Negro prejudice in Hometown
(though not always directly related to it) is the pattern of racial discrimination in the community and the configuration of operating policies and procedures by which Negroes are admitted to or barred from various institutional and organizational structures, depending on the will of 'gatekeepers'
in power roles. In a state that has reasonably strong civil rights laws for the
protection of minorities, outright discrimination against Negroes in jobs and
housing, public facilities, or social groups is difficult to enact in a direct
manner, and is, in some cases, impossible. However, more subtle ways of
practicing racial discrimination often take their place. For example, although
a direct refusal to serve a Negro in a restaurant might bring about a legal
suit, the Negro may be otherwise discouraged by such devices as slow or
careless service, overcharging, caustic glances and remarks, or the breaking
of the Negro's dishes after the meal. In the face of this partial discrimination
and fuzzy uncertainty about the possibility of 'runarounds,' the Negro frequently finds it easier to completely avoid the situation.

III. BARRIERS TO COMMUNICATION:
ON THE WHITE MAN'S SIDE

In addition to the factors of prejudice and discrimination against the
Negro, a third factor contributes to his isolation from the general life of the
community. Woven into the speech of many Americans are elements of 'the
language of prejudice,' derogatory remarks, slurs, and epithets that are insulting to the Negro. The content of interracial contacts is frequently (and
negatively) loaded and charged with affect by the white person's careless
or non-insightful employment of these elements.

The following are some of the elements of the language of prejudice,
ranging from little minded careless expressions to the words that make any
Negro "spit fire."

1. Phrases pertaining to color; equating whiteness with desirability and black-
   ness with evil: 'that's darn white of you,' 'free, white, and twenty-one,'
   'your face may be black but your heart is as white as mine,' 'he treated
   me white.'
2. Racial 'testimonials'—Statements from whites explaining that 'you're as

good as I am,' 'I like you people,' 'I've loved the colored every since I was rocked to sleep in the arms of my black mammy' (a popular southern eulogy and indirect status attribute).

3. Jokes about other minorities, or disparagement of other minorities: 'You people are all right with me, but it's those Jews. . . .'

4. Imitating Negro dialect, staging minstrel shows or parodying the stereotype of the Negro, referring to Negroes as 'boy' or as 'Sambo,' 'Nicodemus,' 'Rastus,' etc.

5. Prejudgements and stereotypes—expecting the Negro to be able to dance, sing and clown merely because he is Negro, assuming that every Negro knows all there is to know about Negro history, traditions, attitudes on every subject, assuming that each Negro in America knows the other fifteen million.

6. 'Darky jokes,' comic stories about Negroes using dialect, or songs with racially derogatory content such as 'you can hear those darkies singing.'

7. 'Slips'—accidental use of racial epithets as: 'I worked like a nigger,' 'I Jewed him down,' 'there's a nigger in the woodpile.'

8. Intentional use of racial epithets such as "coons," "shines," "jigaboo," "smoke."

The varied interrelationships of these three factors: the patterns of prejudice, the patterns of discrimination, and the elements of the 'language of prejudice' constitute the 'Gestalt' that confronts the Hometown Negro. The expectation of prejudice in most whites, the fear of a rebuff or ambiguously embarrassing discrimination, the tense wait for the almost inevitable 'language of prejudice' (including what one Negro called the possibility of being 'stabbed with the word nigger') produces in the Hometown Negro a pattern of avoidance and defensive insulation, prompting the frequent white statement that 'the Negroes prefer to be by themselves.'

IV. BARRIERS TO COMMUNICATION: ON THE NEGRO'S SIDE

While observing a variety of superficial, uncomfortable and sometimes frictional interracial contacts, the participant-observer developed a series of hunches on Negro reaction to these contacts. By interviewing a cross-section of 150 Negro adults, the researchers were able to verify some of these hunches in three areas: the interracial situations that make Negroes uncomfortable, the barriers to interracial contact, and the Negro's reaction to the language of prejudice. The results were these:

A. SITUATIONS THAT MAKE THE NEGRO FEEL UNCOMFORTABLE

When a group of Negroes gets noisy and boisterous around white people	88%
When a white person tells you "you're as good as I am"	44%

When you are with Negroes that are trying hard to impress the white people	37%
When a white person starts talking to you about Paul Robeson	31%
When a white person asks you how it feels to be a Negro	29%
When you are discussing race relations with white people	23%
When you are the only Negro in a group of people	21%
When you see white people in the Negro business establishments	9%
When a white person talks to you about Jackie Robinson, Ralph Bunche and other 'credits to your race'	0

(Only 8 Negroes [5%] stated that none of these situations made them feel uncomfortable.)

B. Factors That Deter Contact

Since avoidance patterns are developed in the American Negro as part of the socialization process, at an extremely early age, it is often difficult for him to articulate his reasons for avoiding contacts with whites as an adult. Many respondents were not sufficiently in touch with their own feelings to give a definite answer on the question of self-limiting contact. Thirty-two percent of the Negroes were unable to select any answer to this card question although the pattern of their group memberships and informal associations showed that they clearly *did* avoid interracial contacts. However, the 102 respondents who gave an answer other than 'nothing' replied, in answer to the question:

"Which of these things keeps you from contacting more white people than you do now?"

"I expect the white person to make a 'slip' and say something wrong about Negroes"	50%
"I have to keep up appearances so I won't reflect badly on the Negro Race"	30%
"I expect most white people to be prejudiced"	27%
"I have to avoid touchy subjects like intermarriage"	21%
"I don't understand white people"	21%
"I'm afraid my family and friends wouldn't like it"	11%
"I suspect that most white people are 'after something' "	9%
"I don't like white people"	3%
Other answers	13%

C. Reactions to the 'Language of Prejudice'

The four paramount elements of the 'language of prejudice' were considered to be the 'testimonial,' the faulty rapport device, the 'slip' and the epithet. The 150 Negro respondents were asked: "Which of these things make you angry, which just annoy you, and which don't bother you at all." The response was as follows:

	Makes Me Angry	Annoys Me	Doesn't Bother Me
When a white person tells you how much he like Negroes ('testimonial')	9%	32%	59%
When a white person tells you how much he dislikes some other minority such as Jews or Catholics (faulty rapport device)	26%	36%	38%
When a white person forgets or "slips" and uses the word 'darky' (the 'slip')	57%	26%	17%
When a white person uses the word 'nigger' (the epithet)	74%	15%	11%

Violent negative reaction to the epithet was further documented by the Negro youths. At the end of a battery of questions about their white best friend, they were asked: "If your white *best* friend 'slipped' and called you a nigger, what would you do?" The response was explosive. Only six youths said they would assume the white friend didn't mean it. 13% said they would ignore it, or do nothing, 2% said they would sympathize, 23% said they would make a vigorous verbal protest ('wise him up,' 'tell him to watch his tongue,' 'I'd resent it and tell him so in strong words.'). Twenty-four per cent mentioned physical violence ('Slap her face, but good,' 'I think I would find myself fighting,' 'I would dip my fist into his mouth,' 'give him a black eye,' 'Sock him in the teeth.'). Only one charitable-hearted thirteen year old girl said:

"I would forgive."

V. THE NEGRO COMMUNITY

The Negro's expectation of white prejudice, discrimination, and careless 'language of prejudice,' coupled with the linkages caused by family and kinship ties, membership in the segregated Negro lodges and churches, physical proximity and mutual use of the community's contact centers produces a heterogeneous but isolated ghetto of individuals, who are generally lumped together in the minds of whites under the heading 'Negro community.' The researchers went into the field employing this unreflective term, and regarding all community members as one. Soon, an obvious division emerged: that between old settlers and newcomers, or floaters, transients, 'beanpickers' and 'gandies' (transient railroad workers). This evolved into a fourfold division based on length of residence; it became apparent that the lifetime residents were almost as inactive in their social participation as were the newcomers (5 years or less), while the people who had lived in the Negro community over twenty years (but not life) were by far the most active participants. Later, the community was divided into five discrete strata on the basis of socio-economic status: (a) the isolated 'elites,' (b) the 'stable pillars,' (c) the 'steady industrious' migrants, (d) the working 'floaters,' and (e) the indigents, seniles and 'winoes.'

Still later, using criteria of sex, age, status and social participation, it was possible impressionistically to place sub-groupings at various points until approximately *fifty* clearly discernible sub-worlds were plotted, each with its own style of behavior, physical locus, pattern of belief, and reference group. When these divisions are viewed, one after another, it becomes evident that it is difficult to generalize about a 'Negro community.' It becomes a unit only because the general community (with a few exceptions based on social status or personal intimacy) defines nearly all Negroes in a similar, and usually negative, manner.

The 'Negro community' is an isolated one and there are several evidences of it. Questionnaire evidence shows not only that contacts with whites are quite limited in quantity and in depth, but also that Negroes viewed many issues more as part of a psychological community of 1200 members than as part of a Hometown community of 60,000. For example, when asked the question: "If you were asked to put yourself and your family into one of these classes, which would you say you are in: the upper class, the middle class, the working class or the lower class?" 20% of the 150 Negro adults said *upper* class, because their reference group was the working-class Negro community rather than the predominantly middle-class general community.

Casual statements of community members also reflected the isolated social world. The statement 'It's all over town' generally meant 'all over the Negro community' and even this takes in only the solid core of the Negro community, and not its indefinite periphery. 'The prettiest girl in town,' or 'the meanest man in town' referred not to Hometown but to its Negro community. The term 'we' usually turned out, under probe, to refer to Hometown Negroes or to Negroes throughout the country, rather than to Hometown in general. At one time, the observer was reassured by a lifetime resident that he could feel free to discuss confidential subjects over the telephone, since the only people who would possibly be listening on the party line were white people who were so removed from the Negro's life that it didn't matter what *they* heard.

VI. THE NEGRO'S RACE ATTITUDE COMPONENTS

A general survey of the Negro's reaction to his minority status indicates these facts: The historical position and past southern experience of the Hometown Negro strongly affect his present relations with whites; the Hometown Negro community is socially almost completely isolated from the general community; the Hometown Negro feels strongly identified with the national Negro community and much less identified with the Hometown community; the Hometown Negro maintains a high level of consciousness on intergroup relations; a good deal of confusion, status dilemma and bitterness is produced by the Hometown Negro's uncertainty of his position in inter-racial situations; a number of the face-gaining and face-losing attributes in the Negro community are connected with ingroup-outgroup relations; the undefined nature of many interracial contacts, and the fear of insult or rebuff from outsiders erect strong barriers to interracial communication; the attitude of the Hometown Negro toward other minorities and toward himself are strongly conditioned by the majority definition of minority groups; the inte-gration of the Negro into general community life is most likely when a new in-group definition is created, transcending racial lines.

Yet, complete unanimity in the Negro community seems to hang only around realization of minority status, expectation of white prejudice, and reactions to racial epithets. Even within the realm of racial attitudes, there is a vast difference of opinion within the community depending on (a) per-sonality factors, (b) regional origin and length of residence, (c) current contacts and experiences with whites, (d) exposure to the media of Negro life and Negro protest, (e) exposure to "significant others" who mold opinion on race as well as other issues, (f) social position and social mobility, (g) conforming to the role that the community has created for the indi-vidual, and (h) success or failure in the enactment of that role. The Negro's reaction to his minority status may be described (in addition to differential reactions to the "language of prejudice") in terms of five main continuums:

1. Hostility	Friendliness
2. Insulation	Integration
3. Lassitude	Militance
4. Avoidance	Whiteward mobility
5. Self-hatred	Race pride

These five continuums cannot be separated within the individual personality, but rather, hang together in a configuration of "creeds" as we shall show. However, they may be discussed separately.

1. Hostility and Friendliness

It is certain that every Hometown Negro has encountered at one time or another, evidences of white prejudice or differential treatment from whites. In addition to his own experiences, he may feel *vicariously* the ex-periences of other Negroes, transmitted through the endless racial conversa-tions, and through the militant Negro press which seldom hesitates to present in graphic detail the inequities, discriminations and atrocities perpetrated on Negroes throughout the country. Consequently, every Negro has experienced the emotion of hostility toward whites at one time or another. This hostility is usually only sporadic and occasional, rising under stress, and receding under pressure of a favorable interracial contact or under the necessity of turning attention to other things. However, in several cases, this hostility is generally resting near the surface, and is tapped in our questionnaire through reactions to the following questions, based on the responses of 150 adult Negroes:

"I would like to get even with the white man for some of the things he has done to Negroes." (25% agree.)

"No matter how nicely he treats a Negro, a white man doesn't really mean it." (26% agree.)

"Sometimes I hate white people." (33% agree.)

In general, Negro hostility is more prevalent among the less educated, among the southern-born, the youths and adults under 45, the female, the isolated, and the Negroes whose interracial contact was minimal. Often, this hostility is deflected at specific groups, particularly the foreign born, who are resented as having greater privilege on their first day in America than the Negro.

Hostility in the Hometown Negro community was most closely related to place of birth. Lifetime residents were least hostile, and the southern born were most hostile. As C. S. Johnson states:

There is a considerable amount of racial discrimination in the north but it is a common observation that the Negroes who discuss these discriminatory practices most frankly are those who originally came from the south. The Negro pattern of behavior outside the Negro residence areas is carefully molded to permit maximum freedom within the vague margins of acceptability. Within the Negro areas, there is more realization and sense of both security and possession. Buried racial antagonisms can easily be called to the surface, however, in a variety of overt expressions with or without strong provocation. Migrants from the South in particular who have stored away memories of deep-cutting offenses discreetly tolerated in the South, may reveal undue aggressiveness in the areas of open competition.

The greater hostility of southern Negroes is shown by this table:

	Born in Hometown	Born in other Northern city	Born in South, came here from other North	Came from South
Per cent who agree that:				
I would like to get even with the white man for some of the things he has done to Negroes.	18%	13%	32%	37%
No matter how nicely he treats a Negro, a white man doesn't really mean it.	4%	24%	27%	42%
Sometimes I hate white people	12%	41%	33%	42%

2. *Insulation and Integration*

Minority group reactions have often been described in terms of a cycle; first, an absorption of majority group attitudes toward the subject's minority group and a consequent development of self-hate feelings toward his group; second, an attempt to integrate into the majority group; third, a rebuff from the majority group and a subsequent development of feelings of hostility, avoidance, and defensive insulation. According to Everett Stonequist's description of the "Marginal Man," a fourth process is possible; the development of in-group identification, pride and militancy.

There is evidence that Hometown's Negro youths may follow a cycle similar to this description. At any rate, the life history of almost every Negro's reaction to minority status will include a variety of rebuffs ending in a general withdrawal and isolation from the stresses of interracial contacts. This withdrawal results in a syndrome of attitudes that characterize what we call the "insulated personality." The insulate is characterized by his endorsement of the following statements:

"Negroes should live around their own people." (27% agree.)

"If I had a choice between an all-Negro club and a mixed club, I would join the all-Negro club." (50% agree.)

"I would find it a little distasteful to:

Eat with a white person 9%

Dance with a white person 17%

Go to a party and find that most of the people there were white 21%

Have a white person marry somebody in my family." 42%

Like the hostile personality, the "insulate" is likely to be southern-born, less educated, relatively non-participant, and predominantly female. The insulate is also likely to be older than the non-insulate. In addition, the insulation responses tend to cluster together, or "scale"; that is, any person who would find it distasteful to go to a party and find that most of the people are white will also agree that Negroes should live around their own people, and prefer an all-Negro to a mixed club.

In reference to background characteristics, the most significant variables that will condition the Negro's attitude toward insulation are his education and his regional origin. Educational level was divided between those who had some high school education or better (only two of the 150 had college training) and those who had a grammar school education or less. Regional origin was defined by whether the respondent was northern-born or southern-born. Results are as follows:

	Better educated northern born (33%)	Better educated southern born (19%)	Less educated northern born (15%)	Less educated southern born (33%)
Per cent who agree that:				
Negroes should live around their own people	12%	21%	23%	47%
I would prefer an all-Negro club to a mixed club	31%	43%	59%	69%
I do not think it is all right for a Negro to marry a white person	29%	21%	50%	49%
I would find it distasteful to: Go to a party and find that most of the people are white.	12%	11%	14%	37%

3. Lassitude and Militancy

The Negro community is also divided on the necessity and possibility of militant action to improve the status of Negroes. The existence of militant feeling on the part of some Negroes is an argument against the allegation that the northern Negro is a caste member, since one of the characteristics of caste is the member's complete acceptance of his caste position. Myrdal has stated:

> [The Protest] attitude is not so uncommon as one would think, even among Negroes of humble status. But with the individual Negro there is always a tendency for the protest to become bent into defeatism. Negroes on all class levels give vent to this feeling of defeatism in expressions such as "niggers ain't got a thing," "We're the underdogs," "Negroes can't win," "there is just no hope for Negroes," "why bother?"
>
> This cannot be said publicly though. The protest motive does not allow it. No Negro leader could preach it. No Negro newspaper could print it. It must be denied eagerly and persistently. But privately it can be said and it is said.

This ambivalence about lassitude and militancy is frequently present in the Hometown Negro. On the one hand, it is status-losing for him to articulate publicly statements of defeatism about the Negro's position, except in an intimate circle of friends. On the other hand, disparagement of the Negro and joking references to the Negro's incapacity is sometimes acceptable and is often the subject of much banter and levity. Even the Race Leader sometimes pauses from his denouncement of prejudiced whites and directs amused or angry criticism at the Negro community, provided no whites are present. At an NAACP meeting, the chairman of its membership campaign shouted:

I get sick of working for people with no thanks and no help. I asked one man to join the NAACP and he told me: "You know what—that thing ain't legal."

Thirty-five per cent of Hometown Negroes, and 51% of the even less potent Negro youths agreed with the statement: "I don't worry about the race problem since I can't do anything about it." When asked what they would do if refused service in a Hometown restaurant, 60% of the adults said they would leave without saying anything, 12% said they would protest to the manager, 13% said they would try to sue, 8% would report it to the NAACP, and 7% gave other answers. Like the hostiles and insulates, the lassitudinous Negroes tended to be older, less educated, southern-born, less participant, and female.

4. Avoidance and 'Whiteward Mobility'

Most Negroes tend to avoid the ambiguous interracial contacts that abound in northern cities. Sixty-four per cent of Negro adults agreed that "Negroes shouldn't go into business establishments where they think they are not wanted." The 100 Negro youths were also asked a battery of avoidance questions, and showed a similar tendency. Ten per cent of the youths agreed that "I keep away from white people as much as I can," 29% agreed that "it is best to stay away from white people; then you will avoid all embarrassing situations," 57% agreed that "Negroes shouldn't go into business establishments where they think they're not wanted," and 77% agreed that "If a business place refuses to serve me, I think I should leave without causing any trouble."

On the other hand, 38% of Negro adults and 39% of youths agreed that "I would prefer to live in a neighborhood where there are not many Negroes"; 46% of adults and 62% of youths said they would prefer a mixed social club to an all-Negro club. Statements like "I would like to know more white people than I know now," "Colored and white people should try to mix together more often," and "I wouldn't mind having white people in my social group" were dropped from the youth questionnaire after the first 25 interviews because everybody agreed with them.

5. Self-Hate and Race Pride

The nature of self-hatred has been clearly expressed by the late social psychologist, Kurt Lewin:

> There . . . seems to exist in every underprivileged group a tendency to accept the values of the more privileged group in a given society. The member of the underprivileged group therefore becomes excessively sensitive to everything within his own group that does not conform to these values, because it makes him feel that he belongs to a group whose standards are lower. Such feelings against one's own group conflict with the natural tendency of the individual in favor of it. The result is a typically ambivalent attitude on the part of members of an underprivileged group toward their own group.

The Negroes of Hometown are caught in this cross-pressure between the high value placed on race pride and group identification of the National Negro creed, and the disparaging view of the Negro which they have absorbed from the general community. The tendency to disparage the in-group was strongly shown by Negro youths in response to these questions:

	Per cent who agree
If Negroes would prepare themselves, the white man would give them good jobs	59%
Negroes blame whites for their position, but it is really their own fault	50%
Negroes in this country need a lot more education before the white man gives them equal rights	47%
Negroes will never get ahead, because when one is succeeding, the others pull him down	41%
The white man is always trying to help the Negro but the Negroes won't try to help themselves	31%
Negroes are always shouting about their rights, and have nothing to offer	28%
Negroes would be better off if they acted more like white people	20%

On the other hand, it is status-losing to admit to others or even to one's self that one has no race pride or strong group identification. Most respondents said they were proud to be Negro and hopefully pointed to the Negro's past, his progress, and to current Negro heroes like Ralph Bunche, Jackie Robinson and Marian Anderson, as the basis of their pride. Only 28% of Negro youths said they would rather work for a white person than a Negro; 23% agreed that "Sometimes I wish I were anything but a Negro," 9% agreed that they would rather play with white kids than with Negro kids, and only 5% agreed that "If I could be born again, I would like to be born white." Eight per cent indicated 'white American' as the group they would like most to be born into, while 46% mentioned it as the group they would like *least* to be born into. Eighty-two per cent maintained that they would like most to be born Negro, 26% mentioned 'Spanish,' 17% mentioned 'Mexican,' and 17% said 'French.'

Efforts to work up a spirit of pride often conflicted with the obvious disadvantages of minority group status, as shown in these ambivalent statements:

"I'm proud to be a Negro, but it's an ordeal and a struggle. You have a hard time to get anywhere. In view of the treatment, I wouldn't 'pick to scuffle.' "

"Lots of people are worse off than we are. Negroes are advancing faster than any other race."

"I'm proud of being a Negro—no use wishing—I've got to bear with it and make the best of what comes."

One 78-year-old Negro woman summed it up by saying: "Being a Negro is no disgrace, but it sure is an inconvenience."

VII. A SOCIAL TYPOLOGY

In a study of Negroes in Chicago, Samuel Strong adopted the method of empirical typology to reflect the nature of race relations in a large metropolis. Strong says:

> The assumption is that socially isolated minority groups, resenting their exclusion from the larger society, develop their own universe of discourse which is likely to express many reactions usually withheld in conventional communication with the outgroup. Under such conditions indigenous social types arise and are referred to in the everyday language of the group in a distinctive way that reveals their connotation. By isolating empirically the significant social types recognized by a minority group and studying the various characterizations attributed to them, it is possible to ascertain the meaning they have in the life of the community.

Since the main focus of the Hometown research was intergroup relations, certain individuals in the Negro community attained special significance because of the role they played in Negro-white relations. It soon became apparent that as far as race relations were concerned, there were discrete 'types' in the Negro community who were expected by the community to play certain roles in interracial elements of community life. Some of the more articulate community members were asked to formulate the racial types in Hometown and other communities. One picturesquely expressive respondent explained:

> (a) The type that accepts first-hand impressions—they don't think. (b) The "overbearing" type—he craves white people. (c) Always looking for "Uncle Charlie" to give them something—the freebe (gift-hunting) type. Can change conditions, but won't. (d) The type that thinks white folks owe us something. (e) The cautious type Negro—so scared he's gonna hurt the white man's feelings. (f) Untrained Negroes—don't know how to act around white people. (g) Uncle Tom type—the "white man's nigger"—always hanging on to some white peck.

Combining this community articulation with the observer's impressions, it was possible to designate five social types in the Negro community which we have designated as (a) the "Race Men," (b) the "Interracial Duty Squad," (c) the "Whitewardly Mobiles," (d) the "Uncle Toms" and (e) the "Hostiles."

1. *The Race Man* is generally the spearhead of militant race leadership in these smaller communities. He has achieved a measure of person-

ality adjustment on racial matters, but sees the world through race-colored glasses and interprets most events in their racial context—how they will affect the Negro. He strongly distrusts whites, has a life history of frictional interracial experiences about which he is very bitter, and is uncompromisingly militant and hostile toward whites in general. However, he is able to completely waive this hostility when he encounters whites of whatever motivation, who are interested in helping the Negro through militant action. The Race Man is bitter not only at whites but also at more accommodating Negro leadership, at the indifferent Negro masses who won't support him, at the more disorganized areas of Negro life, and at all persons who are able or qualified to help in the struggle for Negro rights, but refuse to do so.

On the other hand, Race Men are favorably disposed toward all liberal elements in the community who are willing to help them—unions, the Democratic party, Jews, and many organizations that the general community regards as left wing. The credo of the Race Man may be summed up thusly:

> The white man has been depriving us for years; profiting off our labor and taking our women. He can't be trusted; he will smile in your face and then stab you in the back. I will fight him at every opportunity and make him accord our people their rights. If I encounter discrimination through the courts, through picketing, through boycott, I will fight back by any legal means available. "Our people" take too much of this discrimination lying down. We should stick together, give each other a boost, and fight the white man until he gives us our rights.

2. *The Interracial Duty Squad* (researcher's term) are middle-class Negroes, generally in the highest socio-economic strata of the Negro community. They are actively participant in community life, particularly in interracial activities. They feel it their duty to represent the Negro at interracial gatherings, at banquets where a brown face is wanted at the "Democracy in Action" table, in organizations that encourage a *few* Negro members or in programs where the four "faiths" (Catholic, Protestant, Jew and Negro) are represented. They generally feel that Negroes should take advantage of these invitations to interracial activities; however they feel that they should delegate *themselves* rather than some other less middle-class Negro who might reflect badly on the race as a whole. One prominent middle-class Negro woman explained:

> The colored people don't like it because my husband and I are active in the Little Theater. They say "Humph, she thinks she's white folks." But the white people have invited Negroes to participate and *somebody* ought to go. And my husband and I get along with whites better than most people do.

This group is frequently placed in a "representative leadership" role by the Negro community. However, they are less militant than the Race Men, more inclined to disparage the working-class Negro, and more likely to participate in conciliatory negotiation with whites than in contention.

3. *The "Whitewardly Mobiles"* (researcher's term) are also usually of higher socio-economic status, but have an almost minimal identification with the Negro community and a low degree of group identification. They idealize all things white and disparage all things Negro. They have somewhat concealed but strong self-hate feelings and resent being classified with the Negro community in general. They are upwardly mobile but must strain toward integration into white middle-class life since they are already near the top of the Negro status hierarchy. Because of their obsequious and ingratiating behavior toward whites, they are often despised and disparaged by Negroes with stronger in-group ties and loyalties. On the surface, their hostilities are turned back toward the Negro group, and whatever hostility they bear toward whites is deeply buried, except under stress. They are in the extremely small proportion of the Negro community (5% to 10%) who admit that they would rather be white than Negro and would rather associate with whites than with other Negroes. Such admissions are so face-losing that they must be uttered in secret, if at all.

4. *The "Uncle Toms"* are such a familiar part of Negro community life in America that the term is now being employed in the general community to describe an ingratiator and a "sellout." This is the term most frequently recognized and used by Negroes, and is probably the worst epithet that one Negro can hurl at another. Myrdal has stated:

> Especially since the time of the Washington-Dubois controversy, Negroes have been somewhat divided in their ideas as to what they should do about different aspects of the Negro problem. The major division today is between those who would be aggressive in the Negro protest and those who would compromise. The former call the latter "Uncle Toms" and "handkerchief-heads," while the latter call the former "radicals" and "hotheads." It is a serious charge in the Negro community today to call a person an "Uncle Tom."

On the local community level, whether it be deep south or extreme north, the "Uncle Tom" is characterized as a person who "sells out" the Negro race, grins, clowns and ingratiates in the presence of whites (while other Negroes grit their teeth), tells the gossip and secrets of the Negro community to whites, and places self-advancement and white favors ahead of allegiance and loyalty to the Negro community.

The person designated by the community as an "Uncle Tom" usually tries to rationalize his behavior by explaining that the whites are fine and generous and that the Negroes themselves are responsible for the prejudice and discrimination that exists. However, the social pressures in the Negro community are so strong in the current era of growing group identification that it is now difficult for any person to practice "Uncle Tom" behavior and still be accorded respect from the Negro community.

5. *The "Hostiles"* are not frequently found in these smaller northern

communities although they abound and are well recognized in the south. Recall Richard Wright's statement in "Black Boy":

> Having grown older and taller, I now associated with older boys, and I had to pay for my admittance into their company by subscribing to certain racial sentiments. The touchstone of fraternity was my feeling toward white people, how much hostility I had toward them, what degree of value and honor I assigned to race. None of this was premeditated but sprang spontaneously out of the talk of black boys who met at the crossroads.

In the Hometown community, a Negro who was articulately and violently hostile would not be supported by the community in quite the same manner; he would more likely be thought "queer" or "soreheaded." However, a few are known. One 25-year-old Negro male referred the researcher to one of his friends, saying:

> He hates a white man's guts. If he hears a man was killed somewhere, he'll ask, "White or colored?" If twenty white men get killed somewhere, he'll say, "Good. Should have been two hundred." He loves to read in the papers about some white man getting killed. He is the only guy in this town who *really* don't like a "paddy" (white man). My father don't like 'em either. But what you gonna do? You got to like 'em. They got all the money—they control the wealth. We'd look mighty funny not liking "paddies." We'd starve to death.

Interviews with "hostile" Negroes show that they usually have a basis for their hostility, rooted in a bitter past experience. However, the fact that many less hostile Negroes (even "Uncle Toms" and "Whitewardly Mobiles") have had equally bitter experiences suggests that the violent hostility toward whites may be the outgrowth of a larger personality problem.

In terms of approval or disapproval on these five social types, the Negro community was asked: "How do people in this town feel about this kind of person: would you say they strongly approve, mildly approve, mildly disapprove, or strongly disapprove?" They answered as follows:

	Race Man	Interracial Duty Squad	White-wardly Mobile	Uncle Tom	Hostile
Strongly approve	45%	50%	12%	9%	7%
Mildly approve	39%	30%	23%	5%	7%
Don't care either way	2%	5%	12%	12%	23%
Mildly disapprove	3%	2%	17%	15%	25%
Strongly disapprove	2%	2%	22%	45%	24%
I don't know	9%	11%	17%	14%	14%

The results of this cross-sectional inventory of social types clearly indicate that the Negro community is aware of these types, is willing to identify them, and has a clear-cut perception of Negro community approval or disapproval, depending on the service that each social type performs for the Negro race.

VIII. SUMMARY

From observation of hostile "Race Men" and ingratiating "whitewardly mobiles" in action, it was assumed that hostility in the Negro community would correlate with militance and that friendliness would correlate with lassitude. Analysis of the questionnaire results did not bear out this assumption, mainly because the social types are deviant cases, and are noticeable and outstanding in the community because of their atypicality. Actually, the community is divided into two opposed configurations of attitude which we may call the "Old Negro Creed" and the "New Negro Creed," with the social types falling somewhere between them. Omitting the Interracial Duty Squad (which represents more of a high-status pressure for participation than a configuration of attitudes), we could diagram the social types and the "creeds" in a six cell table, as follows:

	Lassitude-Hostility-Insulation	Lassitude-Friendliness-Insulation	Non-lassitude-Hostility-Insulation
"Old Negro Creed"	The "Uncle Toms"	The "Hostiles"	
	Lassitude-Friendliness-Integration	Militancy-Hostility-Integration	Non-Lassitude-Friendliness-Integration
	The "Whitewardly Mobiles"	The "Race Men"	The "New Negro Creed"

The characteristic racial attitude of the "Race Man" is directly opposed to that of the "Uncle Tom," the "Hostile" is the opposite of the "Whitewardly Mobile," and the old and new Negro creeds are diametrically opposed to each other. Since the vast majority of community members in the cross-sectional survey fall into either the old or the new Negro creed, we may summarize by describing the two creeds as follows:

1. The Old Negro Creed

The people who endorse this creed are generally likely to be older, less educated, of lower socio-economic status, southern-born, less participant in either all-Negro or interracial activities. They are likely to endorse all the items of lassitude, hostility, insulation, self-hatred, avoidance, and "angry" reactions to the "language of prejudice." They are likely to have fewer interracial contacts than the rest of the community, likely to avoid or withdraw from interracial contacts, likely to feel "uncomfortable" in most interracial situations, and likely to have a high number of "distastefuls." They are strongly opposed to racial intermarriage. Their hostility is also directed towards the foreign-born, though not toward Jews. They are likely to admire any Negro who fights vigorously for the rights of Negroes in preference to the Negro leader who concentrates on general community improvements, but express inability, disinterest, or lack of qualification to fight the Race's battle themselves.

2. The New Negro Creed

Community members who endorse this creed are the younger, better educated, of higher socio-economic status and likely to be northern-born. (Exception—the educated southern-born.) They have almost no "distasteful" reactions, express a belief in militancy, and maintain an attitude of friendliness toward whites in general. They have a large number of favorable interracial contacts and are interested in joining interracial clubs and promoting more tranquil contacts between the races. They have few discomforts in interracial situations and have a more temperate reaction to the language of prejudice, i.e., they are more likely to be annoyed than angry.

They are likely to deplore the incendiary aspects of the Negro press or the all-out, violent crusades of the "Race Man," but on the other hand, they have a high degree of racial optimism and are committed to an unwavering race pride and support of militant endeavor. They strongly believe in the possibility and desirability of an integrated society in which the Negro is accorded equal rights which are reinforced by law. They hold complete integration as their goal, have a somewhat more permissive attitude toward intermarriage, and regard the struggles of the Negro as part of a general drive toward "The More Perfect Union."

Thus, the National Negro Creed which is continually reiterated by Negro leaders, organizations and publications, finds its almost exact counterpart in the Hometown community, and, to varying degrees in all Negro communities throughout the American land.

The Nature of Attitude Surveys

PAUL LAZARSFELD

THE LIMITATIONS OF SURVEY METHODS are obvious. They do not use experimental techniques; they rely primarily on what people say, and rarely include objective observations; they deal with aggregates of individuals rather

"The American Soldier—An Expository Review," from *Public Opinion Quarterly*, 13, 1949, pp. 378-380. Reprinted by permission of the publisher.

than with integrated communities; they are restricted to contemporary problems—history can be studied only by the use of documents remaining from
earlier periods.

In spite of these limitations survey methods provide one of the foundations upon which social science is being built. The finding of regularities
is the beginning of any science, and surveys can make an important contribution in this respect. For it is necessary that we know what people
usually do under many and different circumstances if we are to develop
theories explaining their behavior. Furthermore, before we can devise an
experiment we must know what problems are worthwhile; which should be
investigated in greater detail. Here again surveys can be of service.

Finding regularities and determining criteria of significance are concerns the social sciences have in common with the natural sciences. But
there are crucial differences between the two fields of inquiry. The world
of social events is much less "visible" than the realm of nature. That bodies
fall to the ground, that things are hot or cold, that iron becomes rusty, are
all immediately obvious. It is much more difficult to realize that ideas of
right and wrong vary in different cultures; that customs may serve a different function from the one which the people practising them believe they
are serving; that the same person may show marked contrasts in his behavior as a member of a family and as a member of an occupational group.
The mere description of human behavior, of its variation from group to
group and of its changes in different situations, is a vast and difficult undertaking. It is this task of describing, sifting and ferreting out interrelationships which surveys perform for us. And yet this very function often leads
to serious misunderstandings. For it is hard to find a form of human behavior that has not already been observed somewhere. Consequently, if a
study reports a prevailing regularity, many readers respond to it by thinking
"of course that is the way things are." Thus, from time to time, the argument is advanced that surveys only put into complicated form observations
which are already obvious to everyone.

Understanding the origin of this point of view is of importance far
beyond the limits of the present discussion. The reader may be helped
in recognizing this attitude if he looks over a few statements which are
typical of many survey findings and carefully observes his own reaction.
A short list of these, with brief interpretive comments, will be given here
in order to bring into sharper focus probable reactions of many readers.

1. Better educated men showed more psycho-neurotic symptoms than those
   with less education. (The mental instability of the intellectual as compared
   to the more impassive psychology of the-man-in-the-street has often been
   commented on.) B, 439.
2. Men from rural backgrounds were usually in better spirits during their
   Army life than soldiers from city backgrounds. (After all, they are more
   accustomed to hardships.) A, 94.
3. Southern soldiers were better able to stand the climate in the hot South

Sea Islands than Northern soldiers (of course, Southerners are more accustomed to hot weather). A, 175.

4. White privates were more eager to become non-coms than Negroes. (The lack of ambition among Negroes is almost proverbial.) A, 583.

5. Southern Negroes preferred Southern to Northern white officers. (Isn't it well known that Southern whites have a more fatherly attitude toward their "darkies"?) A, 581.

6. As long as the fighting continued, men were more eager to be returned to the States than they were after the German surrender. (You cannot blame people for not wanting to be killed.) B, 561.

We have in these examples a sample list of the simplest type of inter-relationships which provide the "bricks" from which our empirical social science is being built. But why, since they are so obvious, is so much money and energy given to establish such findings? Would it not be wiser to take them for granted and proceed directly to a more sophisticated type of analysis? This might be so except for one interesting point about the list. *Every one of these statements is the direct opposite of what actually was found.* Poorly educated soldiers were more neurotic than those with high education; Southerners showed no greater ability than Northerners to adjust to a tropical climate; Negroes were more eager for promotion than whites; and so on. (The references following the above statements indicate where the evidence for the true findings can be located.)

If we had mentioned the actual results of the investigation first, the reader would have labelled these "obvious" also. Obviously something is wrong with the entire argument of "obviousness." It should really be turned on its head. Since every kind of human reaction is conceivable, it is of great importance to know which reactions actually occur most frequently and under what conditions; only then will a more advanced social science develop.

FURTHER READINGS

Coser, Lewis A. *Men of Ideas.* New York: The Free Press, 1965.

Faris, Robert E. L., ed., *Handbook of Modern Sociology.* Chicago: Rand McNally and Co., 1964.

Madge, John. *The Origins of Scientific Sociology.* New York: The Free Press, 1962.

Merton, Robert K., Broom, Leonard and Cottrell, Leonard. *Sociology Today.* New York: Basic Books, Inc., 1959, Harper Torchbooks, 1965.

2

ISSUES IN SOCIOLOGY

Introduction

W HILE IT IS TRUE that the social sciences, and particularly, sociology have come to be accepted as scientific disciplines after many decades of resistance on the part of both layman and professionals, numerous issues remain. The boundaries between sociology and other academic areas remain somewhat in doubt, as suggested by Berger in the essay reprinted here. He thoughtfully describes the issues and attempts to explain what is at the core of the remaining resistance to sociological research by a selected group of intellectuals. In addition to relations with nonsociologists, some problems persist within the field itself. Some sociologists, like the late C. Wright Mills, see sociology as a humanistic science, fusing older intellectual traditions with scientific techniques. Others like George Lundberg stress pure science fashioned after the approach of the physical sciences. Still another issue revolves about the conception of sociology as a behavioral science. Charles Bolton reviews the issues and comes to a conclusion shared by a great many sociologists.

It should be kept in mind that although these essays do describe differences within the field, they reflect much less variation in viewpoint among sociologists than that which characterizes the contrast between sociological and psychological or historical viewpoints. Sociology is oriented to empirical research which is closely bound up with theoretical generalizations. Few, if any, who call themselves sociologists would deny that this represents the core of sociological study.

Sociology and the Intellectuals:
An Analysis of a Stereotype

BENNETT M. BERGER

I

FOR SOME YEARS, humanist intellectuals have been cultivating a hostile stereotype of sociology and sociologists. Like other stereotypes, this one has its foundation in fact; like other stereotypes too, its exaggerations, whether expressed in the language of annihilating wit or of earnest bludgeoning, call for some serious comment. It is surprising therefore, that the responses of sociologists have been anything but dispassionate. These responses range all the way from (1) Daniel Lerner's polemical defense of sociology in his article analyzing the book reviews of *The American Soldier*, to (2) the posture of tolerant disdain toward the "misguided" stereotype, to (3) a sort of nervous embrace of the stereotype by sociologists themselves (which attempts—usually unsuccessfully—to demonstrate that they do *too* have a sense of humor), often involving a self-parody whose furtive masochism is almost startling.

There is no real need to document the stereotype with exhaustive quotations since it is rife enough in intellectual circles for everyone to have had his own personal experience of it. The overt expression of the stereotype in print is the exception, and whole articles devoted to it are rare. The most common vehicle for its expression is the derisive "remark" and the parenthetical aside. Occasionally, one finds a curiously ambiguous statement like the following:

> Popular images are rarely entirely wrong; and if the mass media and the popular mind today see the social scientist as a man with pencil and pad in hand, buttonholing hapless citizens on the street, the error is not in the observation—it is only in seeing the social scientist as the interviewer. . . . Today, no matter what the question put to the social scientist, he begins his answer by composing a questionnaire, which he then gets filled out by having an appropriate number of respondents interviewed. (In an introductory note by Nathan Glazer to I. L. Peretz' "The Interviewer at Work," *Commentary*, February, 1953, p. 195.)

One of the interesting things in this statement is the apparent convergence of images held by the "popular mind" with those held by intellectuals like Glazer. I say "apparent" because intellectuals do not often share the stereo-

From *The Antioch Review*, Vol. XVII, Number 3. Reprinted by permission of the publisher and author.

types of the popular mind, and the quoted instance is not one of the exceptions. Glazer does not describe a *popular* image in his remarks, but a stereotype held by intellectuals. Anyone who has done extensive interviewing of the "popular mind" knows that ordinary people are generally naïvely interested as well as pleased and flattered to be interviewed by a social scientist; it takes considerable sophistication to feel disdainful of and superior to the poised pencil of the interviewer. But in a curiously inverted "proof by authority" Glazer attributes an image to the popular mind in order to validate his own.

Using evidence like this demands some reading between the lines. For example, nowhere in the above quotation does Glazer explicitly state that the image supposedly held by the popular mind is an invidious one; it is largely a matter of tone, created by key connotative words like "buttonholing," and "hapless," and "appropriate." Many expressions of the stereotype are of this hit-and-run kind, and depend for their meaning and effect upon one's being "in" on the current scapegoatology. For example, the poet and critic Randall Jarrell explicates a few lines from a Robert Frost poem, then says, "if you can't feel any of this, you *are* a Convention of Sociologists." A remark like this would be meaningless to someone not "in" on the current stereotype; to those who *are* "in," and presumably a good number of readers are, it is very funny indeed. There are, of course, more elaborate and heavy handed assaults, J. P. Marquand's portrait of W. Lloyd Warner in *Point of No Return* not being the only one. Still, it is the light touch of people like Auden and Jarrell which is most effective in spreading the stereotype.

Stereotypes, and hostile stereotypes especially, do injury to the group stereotyped, and it is or ought to be our responsibility to correct them. But stereotypes are not generally exorcised by pretending they do not exist; nor are they dispelled by polemic or a demonstration of innocence. Although founded in fact, stereotypes are nonrational, and flourish in spite of the preponderance of evidence against them. Thus arguing from facts to correct an emotional excrescence is vain. What we want to know are the conditions that have generated the stereotype and permitted it to grow. Knowing these, we can transcend polemic and use our understanding in more effective ways.

II

The stereotype of the sociologist has two dimensions, founded in contradictory beliefs which, in turn, have their source in the structure of the intellectual professions. The image of the sociologist as a pathetically ignorant and pompous bumbler (jargon-ridden, pretentious, and without insight) is based on the conviction that sociology has no special subject matter, and is therefore no science; its technical apparatus and methodological strictures are hence not only presumptuous but futile, and result only in pretentiousness and banality. The image of the sociologist as a Machiavellian manipulator, however, clearly rests on a recognition of the efficacy of scientific, especially statistical, techniques in dealing with a human subject matter. But both of these—the perceived failure as well as the perceived success of sociology—have elicited from the intellectuals a hostile response.

A. THE PROBLEM OF SUBJECT MATTER: THE SOCIOLOGIST AS BUMBLER

The tendency to specialization in the intellectual professions submits them to pressure to define specifically a subject matter uniquely their own, in order to justify their existence in a profession- and specialty-conscious culture, to establish and preserve their identities with foundations and university administrations, and to demonstrate their utility and their consequent right to public support. As new specializations develop, and claim professional status, entirely reasonable questions of justification can be raised. What can you do that others not trained in your profession cannot do? What competence has your training conferred on you that is denied to others because of their lack of such training? I take it that the flourishing health of the image of the sociologist as bumbler can in part be attributed to the failure of sociologists to answer these questions satisfactorily. Any discipline which claims as its special subject matter the domain of "social relations" or "social systems" or "society" or any of the other textbook-preface definitions claims not a special subject matter but the whole gamut of human experience, a claim which thousands of scholars and intellectuals are with good reason likely to dispute. Louis Wirth's definition of sociology as the study of that which is true of men by virtue of the fact that they have everywhere and at all times lived a group life, strikes the eye as somewhat better, but runs into the difficulty of generally assuming that pretty nearly everything that is true of men is true by virtue of this fact.

It is in part due to this failure to meet the responsibility of defining one's professional competence simply and clearly to interested laymen that sociological "jargon," for example, is met with such resistance and resentment. Laymen react with no such rancor to the technical vocabularies of mathematics, the physical and natural sciences, and engineering because by an act of faith (based, to be sure, on a common-sense understanding of what these disciplines do) they decide that behind the jargon, which they do not understand (because it is a descriptive shorthand, familiarity with which requires special training), lies a *special subject matter amenable to technical treatment* which they *could* understand *if* they took the trouble. Thus the intelligent layman feels no shame or outrage at not being able to understand a technical article in a chemistry journal—or, for that matter, in not understanding the job specifications in a newspaper want ad for engineers. No such toleration is likely toward the technical vocabulary of sociology until it is accepted as a legitimate scientific profession.

That this acceptance is not forthcoming is due partly to the belief of many intellectuals that the technical vocabulary is not a natural concomitant of scientific enterprise, but rather an attempt to disguise the banality of the results of sociological studies: sociologists "belabor the obvious"; they lack insight, and substitute in its place a barrage of carefully "proven" platitudes. Doubtless, some sociologists do, but every intellectual discipline has its share of brilliant people, as well as hacks, and there is no reason to suppose that sociology has more than a normal complement of either. That the hacks are identified as *representative* of sociology is probably due more to judgments regarding the quality of sociological prose rather than to any analysis of the significance of its contents. Certainly, the prose of sociologists may seem clumsy when compared to the efforts of those whose business it is to write well. But whereas the results of scientific endeavor can legitimately be expected to be true and important, one cannot legitimately expect either that science be beautiful or that scientists be literary stylists.

In short, then, the hue and cry about the jargon and turgidity of sociological prose, about the pretentiousness of its methodology and the banality of its preoccupations, is meaningful as criticism only if one assumes that sociology has no special subject matter amenable to technical treatment; if it has not, then it must be judged by the same criteria as general essays on social and cultural topics. But as long as sociologists commit themselves to the traditions of science, and address their work not to a general literate audience, but to a community of their colleagues, these criticisms cannot seem other than beside the point. For the continuing application of aesthetic criteria of judgment to a nonaesthetic pursuit reveals only a refusal to grant to sociology the status of a science.

B. The Threat of Technique: The Sociologist as Diabolist

Stereotypes generally contain contradictory elements, and the stereotype of the sociologist is no exception. For along with his alleged gifts for the labored cliché and the clumsy, inept sentence, the sociologist is also credited with the diabolical potential of making puppets out of men, of destroying their individuality with IBM machines, of robbing them of their "individual human dignity," and presiding, finally, over their total mechanization. This image of the sociologist as diabolist rests not on a conviction regarding the failure to define a specific subject matter, but on a fear regarding the success of sociological techniques, particularly statistics, which is seen by some intellectuals as *threatening* in two ways. First, the possibility of a science of society apparently implies the possibility of human behavior being controlled or manipulated by those who know its "causes" or by those with access to this knowledge. This vision, fostered by stimulus-response psychology, nourished by the "sociological perspective," which finds the source of individual behavior in group influences (and thus runs head on into the myth of the autonomous individual), and made fearful by reports of brain washing and by novels like *1984* and *Brave New World*, is perhaps responsible for the peculiar ambivalence felt by some intellectuals toward

the very *desirability* of a science of society. Sociology is thus seen as a potential threat to democratic society. Second, and more relevant in the present context, is the fact that the application of the techniques of science to
human behavior is perceived as a threat to the viability of the most basic
function of intellectuals in the Western tradition: to comment on and to
interpret the meaning of contemporary experience.

III

The noun "intellectual" is one of those words which, in spite of lack of
consensus regarding their meaning, continue to flourish in common usage.
Attempts to define the term, to ask who the intellectuals are or what the
intellectuals do, while useful, have seemed to me inconclusive. Certainly
some intellectuals are "detached" or "free-floating"; surely a great number
are "alienated"; doubtless "neurosis" is widespread among them; "irrespon-
sibility," although currently out of fashion, is nevertheless affirmed by some
of them. There is great magic in some of their bows; but, like Philoctetes,
they often carry a corresponding wound whose stench forces them to live
somewhat marginally. Finally, it is true that they create and transmit cultural values—sometimes. There are, however, two difficulties with these and
similar attempts at definition. First, the relation between the key criteria
of the definitions and the perspectives of the definers is generally only too
transparent. Second, and for my purposes more interesting, is that although
the word is part of common usage, the attempts to define it have generally
ignored this fact. I propose here first to ask not who the intellectuals are
or what they do, but rather who they are *thought* to be—whom do people
have in mind when they use the term?—and only then to go on to the other
questions.

In this connection, I was present a few years ago at a forum on "The
Role of the Intellectual in Modern Society" held at the Museum of Modern
Art in New York. The panel members were Granville Hicks, Clement Greenberg, W. H. Auden, and Robert Gorham Davis. Auden spoke last, and at
one point in his remarks he looked around at his colleagues on the platform
as if to take note of the experts chosen to talk on this topic. Hicks, he said,
was a novelist and literary critic; Davis was a literary critic and English
professor; Greenberg was an art critic and an editor of *Commentary;* and
Auden identified himself as a poet and critic. Had this forum been held in
the Middle Ages, he pointed out, we panel members would have been
mostly members of the clergy; in the sixteenth and seventeenth centuries,
we would have been mostly natural scientists; in the twentieth century,
we are mostly literary men. Auden did not attempt to answer the question
that he had left implicit, but the question is a very leading one because
the contemporary image of the intellectual *is*, I believe, essentially a literary
one—and in two senses: he is conceived *as* a literary man, and this concep-

tion has been reinforced by the fact that it is literary men who have been most interested in, and who have written most on, the problem of the intellectual.

But it would be a mistake to assume that, because the intellectual is conceived in the image of the literary man, his essential property is that he is an artist or a student of literature. His identification as an intellectual rests not on the aesthetic value of his novels, plays, poems, essays, or literary criticism, but on his assumption, through them, of the role of *commentator on contemporary culture and interpreter of contemporary experience*. But if the intellectuals are those who assume this role, Auden's implicit question still remains: Why, in our time, has it been typically literary men who have assumed the role of the intellectual? It is in attempting to answer this question that the relation between "the intellectuals" and the stereotyping of sociologists will become clear.

In our time literary men have pre-empted the intellectual's role because of (A) their maximal freedom from the parochial demands of technical specialization, (B) their freedom (within their status as literary men) to make large and uncompromising judgments about values, and (C) their maximal freedom from institutional restraints.

A. SPECIALIZATION

Intellectuals, I have said, are commentators on contemporary culture and interpreters of contemporary experience; they are critics, liberal or conservative, radical or reactionary, of contemporary life. The range of their competence is not circumscribed; it includes nothing less than the entire cultural life of a people. If they are academic men, they may be specialists in various subjects; but their professional specialties do not generally interfere with their being intellectuals. In the humanities, and particularly in literature, a specialty usually consists of *expertise* regarding a given historical period and the figures important to one's discipline who are associated with it: Dr. Johnson and the English literature of the eighteenth century; the significance of Gide in the French literature of the twentieth century; Prince Metternich and the history of Europe after 1815; Kant, Hegel, and German Idealism 1750-1820. Specialties like these do not militate against one's assuming the role of the intellectual, because the traditions of humanistic study encourage the apprehension of cultural wholes; they encourage commentary and interpretation regarding the "backgrounds"—social, cultural, intellectual, spiritual—of the subject matter one is expert about. The humanities—and particularly literature—offer to intellectuals a professional status which impedes little if at all the fulfillment of their function as intellectuals. On the other hand, the commitment of empirical sociology to "scientific method" frequently renders it incompetent to deal with the "big problems," and often instills in sociologists a trained incapacity to say anything they cannot prove.

B. Values

In commenting on contemporary culture and in interpreting contemporary experience, intellectuals are under no seriously sanctioned injunction to be "detached" or "objective." Unlike the sociologist, who functions under the rule of strict separation between facts and values, the intellectual is expected to judge and evaluate, to praise and blame, to win adherents to his point of view and to defend his position against his intellectual enemies. In the context of free debate among intellectuals, the exercise of this function takes the form of polemics; in an academic context, it develops into the phenomenon of "schools of thought." The point is that, whereas in sociology the existence of schools of thought is an embarrassment to everyone (since it is a constant reminder that not enough is *known*—in science, opinion is tolerated only where facts are not available), in the humanities the existence of schools of thought is accepted as normal and proper, because the humanities actively encourage evaluation, the development of point of view, and heterogeneity of interpretation.

C. Freedom from Institutional Restraints

Literary men have been able, more than members of other intellectual professions, to resist the tendencies toward the bureaucratization of intellectual life. This has been possible because of the large market for fiction in the United States, and because of the opportunities of selling critical and interpretive articles to the high- and middle-brow magazines, which, in spite of repeated protestations to the contrary, continue to flourish in this country. The ability of free lance writers to support themselves without depending upon a salary from a university or other large organization maximizes their freedom to be critics of contemporary life. Such opportunities are not typically available to sociologists. In addition, major sociological research is increasingly "team" research, while literary and humanistic research in universities is still largely a matter of individual scholarship. Obviously, collective responsibility for a work restrains the commentaries and interpretations of its authors; the individual humanistic scholar, usually responsible only to himself, is free from the restraints imposed by the conditions of collective research.

The purpose of this discussion of the intellectuals has been to highlight the fact that although sociology has arrogated to itself the right to *expertise* regarding society and culture, its commitment to the traditions of science (narrow specialization, objectivity, and team research) militates against sociologists assuming the role of the intellectual. The business of intellectuals has always been the critical discussion and evaluation of the affairs of contemporary men, or, if I may repeat it once more, to comment on contemporary culture and interpret contemporary experience. When the sociologist arrogates *expertise* regarding the affairs of contemporary men, he is perceived as saying, in effect, that he *knows* more about the affairs of contemporary men than the intellectual does; and once this implication is received into the community of intellectuals, the issue is joined. The fact of this implication becomes one more fact of contemporary experience to which the intellectuals can devote their critical faculties—and with considerable relish, because the implication seems to threaten the basis of their right to the position which, as intellectuals, they hold.

Even those intellectuals with sympathies for the goals of sociology often exhibit a fundamental underestimation of the consequences of its commitment to science. The characteristic plea of these people is an exhortation to "grapple with the *big* problems." Although this advice is without doubt well intentioned, it characteristically underestimates the degree to which the mores of science and the responsibility of foundations and university research institutes can command the type of work sociologists do. I mean by this simply that the sociologist is responsible to the community of social scientists for the *scientific* value of his work, and that university research institutes are sensitive to charges of financing "biased" or "controversial" research (a possibility that is maximized when one deals with the "big problems"). And when the "big problems" *are* grappled with, for example, in books like *The American Soldier* and *The Authoritarian Personality*, or in other types of work like *The Lonely Crowd, White Collar,* and *The Power Elite,* controversy and polemic follow. For the sympathetic intellectual's exhortation to the sociologist to "grapple with the big problems" says, in effect, "don't be a scientist, be a humanist; be an intellectual." This implication is supported by the respectful (if not totally favorable) reception given by intellectuals to the works of Riesman and Mills (least encumbered with the trappings of science), and their utter hostility to works like *The American Soldier,* which fairly bristles with the method of science.

There is one more source of the intellectual's hostility to sociology that I would like to examine, a source that was anticipated by Weber in his lecture on science as a vocation. For if it is true that intellectualization and rationalization, to which science commits itself and of which it is a part, means "that principally there are no mysterious incalculable forces that come into play, but rather that one can, in principle, master all things by calculation," then it is not only true, as Weber said, that "the world is disenchanted," but also true that the social scientist is perceived as challenging that tradition of humanism and art which has subsisted on the view that the world *is* enchanted, and that man is the mystery of mysteries. To the carriers of this tradition, every work of art and every poetic insight constitutes further proof that the world is enchanted, and that the source of man's gift to make art and to have poetic insight is a mystery made more mysterious by each illumination. The power of this tradition should not be underestimated; it is well rooted in the thinking of modern literature, with its antiscientific temper and its faith in the recalcitrance of men to yield up their deepest secrets to the generalizations of science. From Wordsworth's "to dissect is to kill," to Mallarmé's "whatever is sacred, whatever is to remain sacred, must be clothed in mystery," to Cummings' "mysteries alone are significant," the tradition has remained strong. And surely, it must have reached its apotheosis when, before a Harvard audience, Cummings made the following pronouncement:

> I am someone who proudly and humbly affirms that love is the mystery of mysteries, and that nothing measurable matters "a very good God damn": that "an artist, a man, a failure," is no mere whenfully accreting mechanism, but a givingly eternal complexity—neither some soulless and heartless ultra-predatory infra-animal nor any un-understandingly knowing and believing and thinking automaton, but a naturally and miraculously whole human being—a feelingly illimitable individual; whose only happiness is to transcend himself, whose every agony is to grow. (E. E. Cummings, *six nonlectures*, Cambridge: Harvard University Press, 1955, pp. 110-111.)

Intellectuals in this tradition seem to believe that the fulfillment of the goals of social science necessarily means that the creative powers of man will be "explained away," that his freedom will be denied, his "naturalness" mechanized, and his "miraculousness" made formula; that Cummings' "feelingly illimitable individual" will be shown up as a quite limited and determined "social product," whose every mystery and transcendence can be formulated, if not on a pin, then within the framework of some sociological theory. It is no wonder, then, that a vision as fearsome as this can provoke the simultaneous convictions that a science of society is both impossible and evil.

IV

It is no great step from the stereotypes consequent to ethnic and racial diversity to the stereotypes consequent to the diversity of occupational specialization. In those occupations which claim technical, professional status, occupations in which advanced, specialized training is necessary, it is likely that occupational stereotypes should find fertile ground because those on the "outside" have only secondary, derivative "knowledge" of the occupation. It is likely to be even more true of those professions which, like sociology, are so new that the nature of their subject matter is still being discussed by their members, and *still* more true if the new profession, by arrogating to itself a field of study formerly "belonging" to someone else (or to everyone else), raises, either intentionally or unintentionally by implication, invidious questions of relative competence.

Noteworthy in this regard is the fact that the social sciences which have been most active in the "interdisciplinary" tendencies of recent years are sociology, cultural anthropology, and psychology—precisely those disciplines with the most broadly defined subject matter. Each of these claims nothing less, in effect, than the totality of man's nonphysiological behavior as the field of its special competence; and it is no wonder that economics and political science, whose claims are considerably more modest (i.e., whose subject matter is relatively clearly and narrowly defined), have not found it strikingly to their interests to participate much in this convergence. For it is no doubt partly a matter of common professional interest as well as a matter of theoretical clarification that is behind this pooling of their intellectual resources by sociologists, anthropologists, and psychologists. The satire (which invokes the extant stereotype) to which social scientists are submitted is of common concern to them, for the public image of the social sciences, largely created by the commentaries of intellectuals on them, is related to the amount of public support that the social sciences receive.

The stereotype of sociology and sociologists is part of a larger configuration which stereotypes social science in general; sociology, however, is the most successfully maligned of the social sciences. This special vulnerability is due largely to its relative lack of the sources of prestige available to the other social sciences. Economics commands a respect consequent to its age, to the generally accepted legitimacy of its subject matter, to its demonstrated usefulness, and to the wide variety of jobs available to people trained in it. Cultural anthropology borrows scientific prestige from physical anthropology and archeology, and gets some of its own as a result of its concern with the esoteric subject matter of primitive peoples. Political science has the prestigious correlates of law, diplomacy, and international relations. Clinical psychology has the towering figure of Freud, an affinity to medicine, and the presence of the almost mythic dimensions of The Psychiatrist. Unlike economics, sociology has no hoary past, and no long line of employers clamoring for access to its skills. Unlike clinical psychology, it has no founding figure generally recognized as seminal in the history of western science; and the tenuousness of the concept of a "sick society" denies to sociology the status of a clinical discipline, and hence the prestige that accrues to The Healer. Unlike political science, it has neither an empirical nor an historical relation to the high concerns of nations, governments, or law; and unlike cultural anthropology, it has neither empirical roots nor an esoteric subject matter. Not only is sociology's subject matter not esoteric, but its traditional concern with such peripheral problems of social life as crime, delinquency, and divorce, and others conventionally classified under the rubric "social disorganization," quite likely tends, as Merton has suggested, to diminish its prestige.

Sociology, then, is *vulnerable* to stereotyping; its position in the contemporary structure of the intellectual professions exposes it to criticism from all sides. In numbers the weakest of the social sciences, it is the bastard son of the humanities, from which it gets its subject matter, and the sciences, from which it gets its methods. Fully acknowledged by neither parent, it finds itself in the role of *upstart*, now utilizing the existing methods of science, now improvising new scientific methods, in an attempt to make the enchanted data of the humanities yield up their mysteries.

Like ethnic stereotypes, which are fostered by segregation and reinforced by the consequent cultural isolation, intellectual stereotypes are fostered by professional specialization and reinforced by the diverse (and sometimes conflicting) perspectives developed in each. The lack of an intellectual perspective that transcends the provincialism generated by the limitations of a specialized perspective makes one susceptible to clichés and stereotypic thinking about related fields of study. In race and interethnic relations, the marginal man has, with his proverbial "one foot in each culture," provided this transcendent perspective. Humanist intellectuals can fulfill this function in intellectual life by addressing their criticisms of sociology *to sociologists*, rather than to their own colleagues; for it is the ironic fact that in writing to his own colleagues about sociology, the humanist intellectual himself tends to use obvious clichés to which his immersion in his own perspective blinds him. The kind of cross-fertilization that might be achieved by having humanist intellectual perspectives critically directed at an *audience of sociologists*, perhaps *in* a sociological journal, might go a long way toward providing this transcendent perspective.

IBM Plus Reality Plus Humanism = Sociology

C. WRIGHT MILLS

SOCIOLOGY, judging by the books of its practitioners, is a strange field of learning. In the libraries of its professors you will find books containing announcements like this: p^1 ($=p^2ij$). As well as books, also called sociology, full of mumblings like this: "Sociological theory, then, is for us that aspect of the theory of social systems which is concerned with the phenomena of the institutionalization of patterns of value-orientation in the social system, with the conditions of that institutionalization, and of changes in the patterns, with conditions of conformity with and deviance from a set of such patterns and with motivational processes in so far as they are involved in all of these." As well as (and this is the last sample) assertions of this kind: ("Militarily, economically, and politically, there is going on a struggle for the world . . . this struggle has a portentous psychological meaning: we witness and we participate in an historic contest which will decide what types of men and women will flourish on the earth."

It is possible, I suppose, that the same mind might compose all three

From *The Saturday Review*, May 1, 1954. Reprinted by permission of the publisher and Professor I. L. Horowitz, executor of the Mills estate.

statements, but it is not very likely. And, in fact, the same mind did not do so; not even the same type of mind. All of which means that American sociology, as it is revealed in books, is now divided into three main camps. Some sociologists, after having drafted a dozen articles and a hundred memoranda to the foundations, believe themselves to be statesmen of social science, and claim to see just how each of the three fit into the orderly progress of a unified field of learning. But I am not one of them.

I hold that only one of the three camps is worthy of the name sociology, and accordingly, I am not even going to mention the names of the leading members of the other two. Some of my best friends are in those camps, but they will have to blow their own horns. This decision allows me to do all that I can honestly do: give growling summaries of the other two camps (exaggerating them slightly, in order the more clearly to reveal their tendencies); pleasantly elaborate the third, to which I belong; and then mention some key books from which one working sociologist has learned something.

The first camp is that of The Scientists, who are very much concerned to be known as such. Among them, I am sure, are those who would love to wear white coats with an I.B.M. symbol of some sort on the breast pocket. They are out to do with society and history what they believe physicists have done with nature. Such a view often seems to rest upon the hope that if only someone could invent for "the social sciences" some gadget like the atom bomb, all our human problems would suddenly come to an end. This rational and empty optimism reveals, it seems to me, a profound ignorance of (1) the role of ideas in human history, of (2) the nature of power and its relations to knowledge, and of (3) the meaning of moral action and the place of knowledge within it.

Among The Scientists, the most frequent type is The Higher Statistician, who breaks down truth and falsity into such fine particles that we cannot tell the difference between them. By the costly rigor of their methods, they succeed in trivializing men and society, and in the process, their own minds as well.

In fact, several men in the social studies now enjoy enormous reputations, but have not produced any enormous books, intellectually speaking, or in fact any contributions of note to the substantive knowledge of our time. Their academic reputations rest, quite largely, upon their academic power: they are the members of the committee; they are on the directing board; they can get you the job, the trip, the research grant. They are a strange new kind of bureaucrat. They are executives of the mind, public relations men among foundations and universities for their fields. For them, the memorandum is replacing the book. They could set up a research project or even a school, but I would be surprised if, now after twenty years of research and teaching and observing and thinking, they could produce a book that told you what they thought was going on in the world, what they thought were the major problems for men of this historical epoch; and I feel sure that they would be embarrassed if you earnestly asked them to suggest what ought to be done about it and by whom. For the span of time in which The Scientists say they think of their work is a billion man-hours of labor. And in the meantime we should not expect much substantive knowledge; first there must be methodological inquiries into methods and inquiry.

Many foundation administrators like to give money for projects that are thought to be safe from political or public attack, that are large-scale, hence easier "to administer" than more numerous handicraft projects, and that are scientific with a capital S, which often only means made "safe" by trivialization. Accordingly, the big money tends to encourage the large-scale bureaucratic style of research into small-scale problems as carried on by The Scientists.

In their practice, as in that of the Grand Theorists which I will now describe, the social studies become an elaborate method of insuring that no one learns too much about man and society, the first by formal but empty ingenuity; the second, by formal and cloudy obscurantism.

The Grand Theorists represent a partially organized attempt to withdraw from the effort plainly to describe, explain, and understand human conduct and society: in turgid prose they set forth the disordered contents of their reading of eminent nineteenth-century sociologists, and in the process mistake their own beginnings for a finished result.

To at least some of those who claim to understand their work and who like it, Grand Theory is the greatest single advance in the entire history of sociology.

To many of those who claim to understand it but who do not like it, it is a clumsy piece of irrelevant ponderosity.

To those who do not claim to understand it but who like it very much— and there are many of these—it is a wondrous maze, fascinating precisely because of its often splendid lack of intelligibility.

Those who do not claim to understand it and who do not like it—if they retain the courage of their convictions—will feel that indeed the emperor has no clothes.

And of course there are many who qualify their views, and many more who remain patiently neutral, waiting to see the professional outcome.

Serious differences among sociologists are not between those who would observe without thinking and those who would think without observing. The differences have rather to do with what kind of thinking, what kind of observing, and what kind of link, if any, there is between the two. The nerve of the Grand Theorists' difficulties lies in their initial choice of so general a level of thinking that one cannot logically get down to observation; and secondly, in the seemingly arbitrary elaboration of distinctions which do not enlarge one's understanding of recognizably human problems or experience. Moreover, almost any 500 laborious pages of theirs could be translated into seventy-five straightforward pages of English containing everything said in the 500. Too much of it is a getting ready to get ready, too much more a getting ready, and through it all, there are too many promises and not enough payoffs.

The line between profundity and verbal confusion is often delicate, and no one should deny the curious charm of those who, like Whitman, beginning their studies, are so pleased and awed by the first step that they hardly wish to go any further. Of itself, language does form a wonderful world.

Yet, isn't it time for sociologists, especially eminent ones, to stop thinking about thinking and begin directly to study *something?*

The third camp is composed of sociologists who are trying to perform three major tasks, which may be stated in this way:

Whatever else sociology may be, it is a result of consistently asking: (1) What is the meaning of this—whatever we are examining—for our society as a whole, and what is this social world like? (2) What is the meaning of this for the types of men and women that prevail in this society? And (3) how does this fit into the historical trend of our times, and in what direction does this main drift seem to be carrying us? No matter how small-scale what he is examining, the sociologist must ask such questions about it, or he has abdicated the classic sociological endeavor.

I know of no better way to become acquainted with this endeavor in a high form of modern expression than to read the periodical, *Studies in Philosophy and Social Sciences*, published by The Institute of Social Research. Unfortunately, it is available only in the morgues of university libraries, and to the great loss of American social studies, several of the Institute's leading members, among them Max Horkheimer and Theodore Adorno, have returned to Germany. That there is now *no* periodical that bears comparison with this one testifies to the ascendency of the Higher Statisticians and the Grand Theorists over the Sociologists. It is difficult to understand why some publisher does not get out a volume or two of selections from this great periodical.

What the endeavor of sociology looks like may also be seen in the many classics of sociology that have become available in English duriing the last decade. The most important, I believe, are the several works of Max Weber. Do you remember the big literary rush to Vilfredo Pareto during the thirties? Well, as the general inattention to him nowadays reveals, he wasn't worth it. Max Weber would be: his voice is that of the classic liberal in a world that seemed to him, back in the first quarter of the century, all set against liberalism, and at the same time he is the most sophisticated revisionist of classic Marxism.

Other important classics now available include: Georg Simmel's *Conflict* and *The Sociology of Georg Simmel*, Emile Durkheim's *Suicide: A Study in Sociology* and *The Division of Labor in Society*. Gaetano Mosca's *The Ruling Class,*'and Robert Michels' *Political Parties*.

The later volumes of Karl Mannheim do not have the general relevance of his first two—*Ideology and Utopia* and *Man and Society in an Age of Re-*

construction. There is now a paper-backed edition of Thorstein Veblen's *Theory of the Leisure Class.* (Someone ought to do his other books, especially *Absentee Ownership.*) H. Stuart Hughes has recently written an excellent critical estimate of *Oswald Spengler.* Francis Cornford, by his magnificent translation and editing, has given us a virtually new *Republic of Plato.*

The best attempt, since Weber, to organize key concepts and formulate hunches in a one-two-three manner is Harold D. Lasswell's and Abraham Kaplan's *Power and Society,* which draws upon Weber, Michels, and Mosca in a most intelligent way. Robert A. Dahl and Charles E. Lindblom, in their *Politics, Economics, and Welfare,* have recently produced an excellent statement of the integration of total societies.

Books on social structure or on the various institutional domains that compose it include Gunnar Myrdal's two-volume *An American Dilemma,* which deals primarily with the Negro, but is also valuable for much else. Franz Neumann's *Behemoth* and E. Herbert Norman's *Japan's Emergence as a Modern State* are models of excellence for any sociological studies of social structure.

Military institutions and their meaning for modern life have been explored by Hans Speier in several important essays, contained in *Social Order and the Risks of War,* which also contains excellent pieces on politics. The classic sociological account in English is Alfred Vagts' *A History of Militarism.* And there are good materials also in *Makers of Modern Strategy,* edited by E. M. Earle.

On the social and political meaning of the economic structure, Schumpeter and Galbraith are perhaps most significant, although Schumpeter—whose work is as much used as ideological material by the Eisenhower Administration as is any economist's—is the more solid and wide ranging. Henry Durant's *The Problem of Leisure* and J. Huizinga's *Homo Ludens* are fine statements about work and play in modern life. The best single volume on religious trends in America of which I know is Herbert W. Schneider's *Religion in Twentieth Century America,* and of educational practices, A. E. Bestor's *Educational Wastelands.* The best sociological statement of international relations is E. H. Carr's *The Twenty Years Crisis.*

William H. Whyte Jr., in *Is Anybody Listening?* does not seem to be aware of—or at any rate doesn't state—the full meaning of what he so penetratingly describes, but he represents the old-fashioned Man Who Goes Into The Field, rather than sending four dozen researchers there, and his work shows it. So does Floyd Hunter's *Community Power Structure,* which is the best book on an American community since the Lynds' studies of *Middletown.*

It is shameful that sociologists have not celebrated properly the two wonderful volumes of Arnold Hauser, *The Social History of Art.* And equally shameful that no American publisher has brought out George Lukács' *Studies in European Realism.*

Most recent books of sociological relevance dealing with the individual have been influenced by the psychoanalytic tradition. Harry Stack Sullivan and Karen Horney, with great sensibility, take into account the small group and the general cultural pattern, but neither has an adequate view of social structure. That is not true of Erich Fromm, who in his *Escape From Freedom* skillfully relates economic and religious institutions to the types of personality they select and form. One of the few books I know that really locates Freud's work in a more ample philosophical framework is the wonderful little volume by Paul Tillich, *The Courage To Be.*

Perhaps the most influential book of the last decade on types of individuals is *The Authoritarian Personality,* by T. W. Adorno, Else Frenkel-Brunswik, D. J. Levinson, and R. N. Sanford, which, although not well organized and subject to quite damaging criticisms of method, still remains of outstanding importance. In the same tradition is the neat monograph by Leo Lowenthal and N. Guterman, *Prophets of Deceit,* which ought to be read widely just now to understand something of what is involved in the Republican Party split. Many of the sociologically most interesting trends in psychiatric circles may conveniently be found in *A Study of Interpersonal Relations,* edited by Patrick Mullahy.

The main drift, the historic character of our time, has not been faced up to by many sociologists. Over-shadowing all such attempts in scope and in excellence of detail is Arnold J. Toynbee's six-volume *A Study of History,* which sociologists of the third camp will be studying for many years to come. It should be read along with Gilbert Murray's lovely little essay, *Hellenism and the Modern World,* Herbert J. Muller's criticism, *The Uses of the Past,* and Pitirim Sorokin's comparisons, *Social Philosophies of an Age of Crisis.* Karl Löwith's *Meaning in History* and Paul Tillich's *The Protestant Era* are also key items for the historically grounded sociologist.

E. H. Carr, in his *The New Society*—his BBC Third Programme lectures—has produced an indispensable and commendably brief statement of major trends in modern society. David Riesman writes better essays than books, but his *Lonely Crowd* is within the third camp. A book selling in Germany much better than in America—to the loss of American readers—is Fritz Sternberg's *Capitalism and Socialism on Trial.*

All of these, of course, are samples of the kind of books from which one sociologist has learned something, and which sustain him against The Scientists—who during the decade have moved from marketing research to the foundations, and so from toothpaste and soap to higher mathematics—and against The Grand Theorists—who have moved from textual interpretation of sociological classics to careful thinking about their own possible thought.

In every intellectual age, some one field of study tends to become a sort of common denominator of many other fields. In American intellectual life today sociology could become such a common denominator, and in fact, despite everything, it is slowly becoming that. But for such a salutary development to get fully under way, theorists are going to have to do their work with a sense of reality as well as with scope and insight. Research technicians are going to have to go about their work with more imaginative concern for its larger meanings, as well as with mathematical ingenuity. Both are going to have to drop their trivialization of subject matter and their pretensions about method. Both are going to have to face up to the realities of our time. And both are going to have to acquire the humanist concern—which some American historians have retained—for excellence of clear and meaningful expression.

On the Value of Science in Human Relations

GEORGE A. LUNDBERG

I

I HAVE EXPRESSED the view that the best hope for man in his present social predicament lies in a type of social science strictly comparable to the other natural sciences. We have reviewed some of the objections that have been urged both by physical and social scientists to this proposal. I am not under the illusion that my argument can be established conclusively in so brief a compass. Actually, of course, only time and future scientific development can finally demonstrate the validity of the position which I have outlined.

In the meantime, we are confronted with the necessity of proceeding on some hypothesis as to the way out of our difficulties. It is generally agreed, even by those who differ most radically as to the proper approach, that our first need is a unified, coherent theory on which to proceed. A society cannot achieve its adjustments by mutually incompatible or contradictory behavior, any more than can an individual organism. However we may differ on details and on ends, we must agree on certain broad means, certain principles of action toward whatever ends we do agreed upon.

In short, we all apparently agree with Comte's appraisal of the situation as he saw it almost a hundred years ago. Speaking of the theological, the metaphysical, and the positive scientific approaches, he said: "Any one of these might alone secure some sort of social order: but, while the three co-exist, it is impossible for us to understand one another upon any essential point whatever."

Of course there are some who find in our present predicament merely

From *Can Science Save Us?* by George A. Lundberg, 2nd Edition, 1960. Used by permission of the publishers, David McKay Company, Inc.

This will acknowledge the receipt of

Mizruchi: THE SUBSTANCE OF SOCIOLOGY

My comment is:

Name: ....

Institution: ....

City and State: ....

- -

We take pleasure in sending to you for your consideration a copy of

Mizruchi: THE SUBSTANCE OF SOCIOLOGY
$3.95

which we have just published. We hope you will examine it soon and will send us your comments on the attached card.

List prices are given for your convenience.

APPLETON-CENTURY-CROFTS,
Division of Meredith Publishing Company

further evidence of the futility of the scientific approach in human affairs. They overlook the fact that, actually, science has as yet not been tried on social problems. Consequently, they advocate a return to theology, or "the" classics, either in their historic forms or in new versions in which the advocates of these approaches personally can play the role of major prophets. If I could see any chance of bringing about a return to theology or "the" classics, I might give it serious consideration, because any one unified approach might be better than two or more contradictory ones. But I see no such possibility in the long run. The commitments we have already made to science, chiefly in our technological culture, are of such character that we can neither go back nor stand still.

Our technological developments and our methods of communication have resulted in a fundamental interdependence which dominates our lives. This state of affairs requires, as we shall see, that we bring our social arrangements into line with this basic technological pattern, rather than vice versa. This basic technological pattern unquestionably rests upon natural science. On this ground, rather than on any assumption of absolute or intrinsic superiority of science as such, I think the following conclusion is inescapable: *In our time and for some centuries to come, for better or for worse, the sciences, physical and social, will be to an increasing degree the accepted point of reference with respect to which the validity (Truth) of all knowledge is gauged.*

If we accept this conclusion, then a number of questions arise. What are some examples of what the social sciences have done or might do in furthering sound and orderly adjustments in human relations? What, if anything, has been achieved in the social sciences to date? . . .

II

What are some examples of types of work by social scientists that are of vast importance in managing human relations?

The work of such agencies as the Census Bureau is known to all and is taken more or less for granted. Without the data and the analyses which it provides, the administration of public affairs would certainly dissolve in chaos and perhaps civil war. It is equally certain that no international organization can function without an elaborate organization of this kind to provide the essential facts regarding people and their characteristics and activities. Perhaps the most permanent contribution of the ill-fated League of Nations was the establishment of an international statistical bureau which still continues to function at Princeton University. The Office of Population Research of the same university is engaged in detailed studies of local population trends in Europe and elsewhere, including predictions of future areas of population pressure. This work would be of the utmost practical importance to the administration of any world organization. The Scripps

Foundation, the Milbank Memorial Fund, and many others are engaged in similar or related work of a character that measures up very well to the standards of the physical sciences.

In the meantime anthropologists and sociologists have greatly extended our scientific knowledge of other peoples and cultures. This knowledge has in turn thrown a flood of light on our own civilization and permits the formulation at least of hypotheses regarding human behavior in general. The importance of this kind of knowledge in facilitating our contacts with other cultures during the recent war is too well known to require review. Is it not generally agreed that increasing contacts make the accumulation of such knowledge imperative in peace as well as in war?

We mentioned in the preceding chapter the importance of instruments and methods of observation and measurements in the social as well as in the physical sciences. Hundreds of such instruments have already been invented by means of which vocational aptitudes, success in college and other undertakings, and social behavior of great variety can be accurately measured and predicted. Perhaps the best known, but by no means the only one, of these devices is the public opinion poll. We have in this technique an illustration of how the development of the social sciences may be as significant for the future of social organization as many physical inventions have been in our individual development.

The degree to which the public will can make itself reliably felt in government and in community action has always been in the foreground of political discussion. With the expansion of the areas within which public opinion must operate, many students of the problem have despaired of the capacity of the town meeting technique adequately to make operative the public will. In the face of this situation, social scientists have developed in recent years an instrument which cheaply and accurately permits us to learn the beliefs, the attitudes, and the wishes of the rank and file of the population. To be sure, the public opinion polls are at present thought of as interesting devices mainly for predicting the outcome of elections. But this is a very minor aspect of their full possible importance. These techniques also have been extensively used in the army and as a guide to the administration of liberated areas in Europe and elsewhere. Under the auspices of Allied Force Headquarters, Stuart C. Dodd developed a polling organization for determining in the invaded areas facts regarding the behavior and conditions of life as well as opinion regarding such subjects as public security, crime and the mores governing its control, the people's satisfaction with governing officials, attitudes toward co-belligerency, status of shelter and clothing, food supply and distribution, etc.

For example, complaints reached Allied authorities in Sicily regarding the malfunctioning of the rationing system. The local officials denied it and pointed to long lines of people ostensibly being served. A survey indicated that very few people had received their sugar ration for five months. Thereupon the local officials were confronted with these facts and were told to get busy. A follow-up survey in a week showed the situation greatly improved, and in two weeks practically corrected. Here we have a public which for the first time in years finds itself consulted on such matters and then observes that its complaints actually bring results. Experience of this kind probably goes farther than any propaganda for democracy that could be invented.

It may well be that in the perspective of history we have here a social invention—a technological device based on social science and on social research—which may rank in importance with gunpowder, telephone, or radio. It may be a device through which can be resolved the principal impasse of our age, namely, the apparent irreconcilability of authoritarian control on one hand and the public will on the other. It may be that through properly administered public opinion polls professionalized public officials can give us all the efficiency now claimed for authoritarian, centralized administration, and yet have that administration at all times subject to the dictates of a more delicate barometer of the people's will than is provided by all the technologically obsolete paraphernalia of traditional democratic processes. In short, it is not impossible that as advancing technology in one department of our lives leads to a threatened breakdown of democracy, so an improved social technology may restore and even increase the dominance of the people's voice in the control of human society.

I envision a time when the science of public opinion will be a science comparable to meteorology; when charts of all kinds of social weather, its movements and trends, whether it be anti-Semitism, anti-Negro sentiment, or mob-mindedness, will be at the disposal of the administrators of the people's will in every land. Dodd formulated and proposed to the United Nations plans for the establishment of a Barometer of International Security designed to detect authoritatively and early the tensions that lead to war. It is true that mere knowledge of these tensions does not automatically operate to alleviate them. But it is also true that a reliable diagnosis of the tension and an understanding of the sentiments that underlie it is essential for an intelligent approach to the problem. Right now it would be helpful to know exactly where are the pressure areas against Negroes and American-born Japanese. Is it not vitally important in postwar Europe to know where high and low pressure areas are in respect to the scores of minorities that must find their places in European society? We shall probably not hear anything more about the Barometer of International Security for the time being. The powers that be are obviously not interested in the wishes of the people who are being mercilessly bartered and moved about like so many pawns. But that does not affect the importance of the instrument as a technological achievement.

It would be easy to continue this recital of how developments in the social sciences already have ameliorated many social problems and have greatly facilitated public administration and policy. But the achievements are not merely in such obvious and practical fields as I have mentioned. The underlying theoretical and scientific knowledge upon which such practical devices rest must also be developed. As only one example of scientific work aiming directly at the construction and verification of scientific theory, I might call attention to Stouffer's study of the mobility habits of an urban population. Stouffer observed the apparently chaotic movements of the people of Cleveland in their frequent change of apartments. But isn't this much too complex for scientific study? Well, he considered various hypotheses which might constitute a generalized description of this behavior. He finally arrived at one hypothesis, which he states in rigorous mathematical terms. He then shows that a comprehensive study of the actual behavior of the people corresponds with remarkable accuracy to this hypothesis. The resulting generalization may be stated as follows: "The number of persons going a given distance is directly proportional to the number of opportunities at that distance and inversely proportional to the number of intervening opportunities." This law has subsequently been tested for other cities and larger areas, and for at least one foreign country. It has already been found to hold with certain modifications and under stated conditions for the movements of the people of the United States as a whole, and for Sweden.

We are not here interested primarily in the possible practical uses of these findings. I cite the case rather as an illustration of the possibility of arriving at scientific generalizations of social behavior essentially of the same sort as those that, in their full development, have proved so valuable in the physical sciences.

To those who constantly have their minds on quick and dramatic solutions to the world's troubles this type of research is likely to seem offensively trivial—a kind of fiddling while Rome burns. "Writers" are fond of referring contemptuously to basic scientific work as an "ivory tower" and as "lecturing on navigation while the ship sinks." Navigation today is what it is because some people were willing to study the *principles* of their subject while their individual ships went down, instead of rushing about with half-baked advice as to how to save ships that could not be saved, or were not worth saving anyway. As A. J. Carlson has recently said: "The failure of bacteria to survive in close proximity to certain moulds looked trivial at first, but few informed people would label the discovery of that initial fact *trivial* today."

So much, then, for a few illustrations, rather than a summary, of the type of work that is being done and that needs to be done in the social sciences. Is there enough of it being done? Clearly not, or we would not need to flounder as we are in national and international affairs, pursuing diametrically opposite courses within the same decade. Can the social sciences ever hope to catch up with the other sciences, the increasingly rapid advance of which constantly creates new social problems? Certainly we can, if we devote ourselves to the business with something like the seriousness, the money, and the equipment that we have devoted to physical research. Consider how the physical scientists are today given vast resources to concentrate on the invention of a new submarine detector or a new bomb, not to mention the peacetime occupations of these scientists with penicillin and sulpha drugs. Obviously, I am not criticizing this action. On the contrary, it is the way to proceed if you want results. Is there anything like that going on regarding the world organization and its numerous subsidiary problems, all of them important to peace and prosperity?

Comparatively speaking, there is almost nothing that could be called fundamental research into the basic nature of human relations. To be sure, there are endless petty projects, surveys, conferences, oratory, and arguments by representatives of pressure groups, as if argument ever settled any scientific questions. Of basic social research there is hardly anything. Why? . . . It is not yet realized that scientific knowledge is relevant to a successful world organization. We still think that common sense, good will, eloquent leaders, and pious hopes are sufficient when it comes to management of social relations.

Is Sociology a Behavioral Science?

CHARLES D. BOLTON

OVER THE LAST TEN YEARS sociology, virtually without debate, has taken on the identity of a "Behavioral Science." Like the other social sciences, sociology has been subject to periodic seizures of intellectual fashion movements, and there seems little reason to view the behavioral science nomenclature as having a significantly different origin. However, there are certain characteristics of the behavioral science identity which make it of more serious concern than most of the intellectual costumes sociologists have tried on in the past. No doubt there comes a time in the maturation of a science when it must settle on some identity. But serious examination should be made of the uncritically accepted assumptions implicit in the Behavioral Science identity.

The Behavioral Science identity is not merely a name but also an ideology. The Behavioral Science ideology involves the substitution of a methodological rationale for a theoretical one in identifying sociology. From the viewpoint of Behavioral Science, the unity of the various behavioral sciences lies in their common method; the differentiation among them becomes one of a division of labor, not a difference in point of view. A sociologist is defined as a person who has been trained in applying the scientific

From *Pacific Sociological Review*, Vol. 6, No. 1, Spring, 1963. Reprinted by permission of the publisher and the author.

method to a particular kind of behaving system: social systems. For some years, of course, hardly any one in sociology has questioned the desirability of the field's becoming methodologically more scientific. But certain implications of the logic of the Behavioral Science ideology may prove enervating to the long run development of sociology. Let us examine the logic of this ideology.

We are told by the founders of the Unified Science group that the term "behavioral science" was chosen "primarily because its neutral character made it acceptable to both social and biological scientists." Whatever the motives of its originators, the implications of "behavioral science" are by no means neutral. The clear implication to most people is that Behavioral scientists study behavior. Because of the very great importance of Behavioristic psychology in the American tradition, the study of behavior implies the study of more or less directly observable behavior of *organisms*. This constitutes a selection of data based upon methodological considerations rather than upon the point of view of the scientist or the characteristics of the subject matter.

It would not be accurate to say that the conception of behavior has been limited in Behavioral Science to the imagery of psychological Behaviorism. Rather, the emphasis has been upon the behavior of systems. The entree of sociology into the Behavioral Science fold has come through the identification of sociology as the science which studies the "behavior" of social systems. Insofar, then, as Behavioral Science is concerned with social behavior, this behavior is seen at two levels: (1) the behavior of organisms with reference to interhuman stimuli, and (2) the behavior of social systems. However, an examination of colloquies of behavioral scientists, such as that reported in Grinker, *Toward A Unified Theory of Human Behavior,* makes clear that non-sociologists conceive of living organisms as "real" systems but think of social systems as abstract or constructed systems consisting of conceptual relations between "real" systems or the behaviors of "real" systems. There is plainly implicit the reduction of social systems to forms of explanation such as the psychological and biological, which are thought to deal with "real" systems. One major devotee of the sociology-as-behavioral-science viewpoint, George Homans, has already publicly announced himself as a psychological reductionist.

Does it any longer make any difference whether or not we believe that social phenomena can be reduced to psychological or biological phenomena? Should we not all sigh with relief at the passing of the acrimonious Durkheimian debates about *sui generis*? Perhaps, but the acceptance of behavior as the subject matter of sociology involves a critical change in the sociological identity. In the past, sociology has been the study of social *interaction* and social *relationships.* The sociological mode of explanation has been to take the *forms of relationship and interaction* as having *determinant* power in explaining the behavior of the individual. In the Behavioral Science ideology this approach must be abandoned in favor of an essentially descriptive approach to social systems.

In spite of some Behavioral sociologists' valiant efforts to defend the autonomy and non-reducibility of the sociological analysis of social systems, three rising trends in sociological theory are indicative of the implications of adopting the Behavioral Science ideology.

The first is the increasing permeation of sociological thinking by terms connotative of the psychological mode of conceptualizing personality. Terms such as drive, needs, homeostasis, and tension-reduction, as well as the rich Freudian vocabulary, exemplify a mode of thinking which explains behavior in terms of predispositions brought into situations by human organisms rather than in terms of social relations and interactions specific to the episode of action.

The second trend is the increasing dependence upon the concept of the internalization of roles and norms during the socialization of the child as the explanatory mode for the functioning of the social system. That is, the orderly processes which occur in a social system are not attributed primarily to the contemporary sociological structure of the system but to the fact that the actors in the system have at some time in the *past*, usually in childhood, internalized the roles and norms of the system. For institutionalized aspects of society such a form of explanation may have a certain plausibility—though even here, Durkheim's conception of the externality and coerciveness of the collective representations is phenomenologically more acute. But for problematic and changing aspects of society, socialization cannot serve as more than a very partial explanation of the coordination of social behavior.

The third trend in contemporary theory is a drift toward an energy model of conceptualization—as illustrated not only by the equilibrium concept but also by the recent input-output mode of conceptualization. The energy form of conceptualization is inevitably reductionist. Conceiving of social relationships in terms of energy is clearly a construction of the sociologist; there is no social energy. The location of energy must finally be within the organism or its technological extensions. More importantly, the energy model involves a radical abandonment of the traditional sociological form of conceptualization. Whether followers of Mead, Cooley, Simmel, Durkheim, or Weber, sociologists have emphasized the *communicational and definitional* character of social acts and social relations. This sociological form of conceptualization is a fundamentally different one from the hydraulic model employed in most psychological and biological thinking—that is, thinking centering around such concepts as homeostasis, libidinal economics, need-reduction, tension-reduction, frustration-aggression, etc. From the traditional sociological viewpoint the actor's marshalling of energy is contingent upon his definition of the situation. From the viewpoint of energetics the definition of the situation is essentially epiphenomenal to the balance of forces which are thought "really" to determine action. Even when input-output equations are thought of in terms of information theory, the energy model is implicit; for the function of symbols is thought of simply as that of *representing* or standing for events rather than that of *transforming* events into social objects, as is involved in Mead's conception of the function of significant symbols.* That is, in information theory a universally objective character is bestowed upon stimulus events, and language symbols become merely equivalent stimuli—a view entirely contrary to the evidence of cultural relativism.

To demonstrate that the Behavioral Science identity results in reductionism and the abandonment of traditional orientations does not, of course, prove that these developments are bad. There is no point here in warming over the theoretical arguments against reductionism. But some discussion of pragmatic consequences is in order. The achievement of a unified point of view for the Behavioral Sciences may be not only historically premature but plainly detrimental to the civilizing and enriching of human understanding of the social process. The sophistication and emancipation of thought from provincial bias in recent times has derived in large measure from the existence of multiple perspectives from which to analyze the social process. Mannheim has stressed the importance of relationalism in all social knowledge. Behavioral Science ideology leads away from this development, paradoxically, in two directions. One is the imposing of a single perspective or frame of reference on all the Behavioral Sciences; the other is the abandonment altogether of intellectual perspective in favor of a methodological orientation. The former stultifies the very trend which historically has produced the possibility of objective orientations toward the social process—are we yet so sure of our way that we can commit ourselves to a single orientation? The methodological perspective almost certainly produces a gross oversimplification of the enormously complex character of the social process. Commitment to only a methodological orientation places the scientist in a situation analogous to the tourist who is satisfied that he has "seen" Yosemite by driving only to the floor of the valley because that is technologically the easiest point to reach.

More specific pragmatic consequences for sociology can be noted. Most

---

That is, Mead's conception of symbols focuses upon their function in creating objects —in the proper sense—in the field of experience during the on-going act. Words do not merely *stand* for self-constituted objects but constitute an important part of the existential character of objects. The meaning of a word is not constituted by a class of phenomenal events but by its indication of potential interactions with a class of events as experienced from a particular perspective. Perspectives may be either the goal-directedness of the on-going act or symbol structures, such as a frame of reference. Comparison of cultures makes it clear that the same class of phenomenal events may be interacted with quite differently from varying perspectives. Hence *objects* are relative to perspectives, and it cannot be said that symbols simply represent or stand for objects divorced from particular perspectives. See George Herbert Mead, *Mind, Self, and Society*, edited by Charles W. Morris, Chicago: University of Chicago Press, 1934. Sociological adherents of Behavioral Science often pay lip service to Mead's position on objects but ignore it when embracing reductionist methodologies.

crucial is the gradual abandonment by sociologists of the field of social psychology as a specific sub-field of sociology. The progression has been subtle. While much is made of the conflict-filled nature of social psychology, historical analysis reveals that psychologically-oriented and sociologically-oriented social psychologists until recently had rather distinct focuses within the general field. Psychologically-oriented students focused upon the relation of the individual to the group, and hence have been concerned with personality and with cultural influences on traditional psychological variables such as motivation, perception, and emotion. The sociologically-oriented focused on social interaction as such—thus the concern of sociological social psychologists with such things as collective behavior, interpersonal interaction, primary groups, and consensus. In recent years, however, the sociological focus has gradually shifted to socialization, especially during infancy and childhood. The result is that the interaction process, as a generic problem, is nowhere in focus. Little attention is given to consensus as a process; consensus has become a majority of votes of individuals, or, at a more sophisticated level, another term for the state of social solidarity. Small group study has become a more or less autonomous activity, unintegrated with broader social psychological theory. The primary group becomes, not a distinctive process of interaction, but another variable to be "rediscovered" in the study of large-scale formal organization. Most unfortunately, the study of collective behavior, never hardy, receives only the most minimal attention from those sociologists wearing the Behavioral Science hat. Considering the concentration of sociology in the world's most extreme mass society, the pitifully small amount of attention being given to such mechanisms as fashion, fad, social movements, mass behavior, popular culture, and collective atmospheres is a most shocking failure of sociology. In the meagerness of attention given—even in theory—to collective behavior we can see most vividly the consequences of a Behavioral Science ideology which takes some organized system, organic or social, as its unit of analysis. For such an ideology, interaction is a product of the character of the system as such. There is no place for awareness that interaction is also a *constructional* process, the fulcrum of social creativity in which new convergences of human action are constantly shaped and new social forms crystallized.

The commitment to the methodological orientation in the Behavioral Science identity is probably associated with the decline of discussion about the nature of human nature. This old philosophical problem takes on new significance for a society in the process of transition from an economy of scarcity organized around a competitive work world to an economy of abundance where life must be centered around non-work activities. Does human nature condemn us to the fate that the personal concomitant of this societal transition shall be a shift from the false-fronting promoter personality of the marketplace to a dissolute TV addict, dissolving his anxieties in drugs and achieving social apathy through privatization? Or does human nature contain the potentiality that the Leisure Time Revolution can mold the bulk of men into creative, cooperative beings searching after goodness, beauty, and truth with the same intensity with which, in the past, they have pursued money, prestige, and power? Communist dogma has an answer, but Western social science has almost nothing to say on the subject. Similarly, our social science has little to tell us about what to expect of men or nations if disarmament can be achieved.

Another set of problems for sociology arises from the foundation sponsorship of the Behavioral Science ideology. In the Behavioral Science mode of thinking there is a distinct tendency to think of knowledge as having value for the control and manipulation of human behavior. I am not concerned here with the possible malevolence in the selective support of research by foundations concerned with manipulation. There is a more subtle theoretical problem. Theoretically, control is thought of as a corollary of prediction in science. But the assumption that control is simply a corollary of prediction involves a peculiar difficulty in the social sciences. If there is anything that is clear about the nature of human nature, it is the enormous flexibility and plasticity of human development. The career of any human development, individual or collective, apparently involves many turning points at which the outcome is problematic and more than one direction of movement is possible. It is also apparent that the same end may be reached by a variety of means with human beings. A major reason for this plasticity of humans is that the determinants of action may operate at any of a number of levels: chemical, physiological, unconscious, self-conscious, cultural, societal. It is crucial to recognize that at some of these levels humans are able to convert potential determinants into alternatives—that is, into cognitive, named objects which may be mentally, and often physically, manipulated: projected into the future, reflected upon, rejected, cast in new contexts, etc. However, other determinants are partially or wholly outside the linguistic-self process by which this manipulation of objects is carried on—for example, the influence of drugs and of unconscious or dissociated processes.

The aim of control in science implies, almost by definition, an effort to restrict and, ideally, to eliminate alternatives of the subjects. A social science which takes control as a major criterion for scientific success thereby has a built-in bias to focus attention upon those so-called independent variables which human subjects are least likely to be able to convert into alternatives. If evidence to date means anything, we can say that this focus leads to a concentration upon biochemical, unconscious, presocial, and nonrational influences and a studied ignoring of the processes which mark human beings as cognitive, self-conscious, creative, act-constructing creatures. Let me give a few illustrations of what I mean.

In recent years there have been a number of discoveries about the effects of various drugs upon human behavior and mentality. I am by no means questioning the desirability of studying the effects of these drugs; their value in handling certain cases of mental disorder seems established. But a science of controlling human behavior seems to be springing up around these drugs, with a concomitant ignoring on the part of their students of alternative processes by which human action may be regulated. The success of this mode of control tends to focus attention and research funds upon this physico-chemical approach to human behavior at the expense of alternative psychological and social approaches.

Within social psychology comparable trends are observable. Social psychologists concentrating upon socialization and personality have shown an extreme predilection for attention to presocial determinants—birth traumas, mothering in infancy, toilet training, etc.—with little or no attention to linguistic and cognitive factors. Doubtless the psychoanalytic influence is important here, but fascination with presocial determinants seems to go beyond the psychoanalytic influence. For example, the lengthy chapter on socialization in *The Handbook of Social Psychology* analyzes a number of variables in addition to those suggested by Freudians, but includes no mention at all of the significance of language development, of Piaget's studies of the development of the representational function, of Mead's theory of the self, nor, indeed, of a single cognitive variable. The almost universal locating of the basic determinants of personality differentiation in infancy and early childhood betrays the same bias of avoiding the alternative-producing conditions of human conduct. Foote is almost a lone voice in pointing out that it is an illusion that personality development, in the sense of differentiation, slows down after childhood is passed. Yet one has only to reflect upon the shock felt at reunions with once bosom college friends to recognize the truth of Foote's statement that "ten close friends fan out far more in the individualization of their identities between, let us say, ages 30 and 40 than between 10 and 20." We are constantly assured that personality is stabilized by the end of childhood and merely unravels in adulthood. But where is the evidence for these assertions? For the most part, the point is merely assumed, and even the few studies that provide some scanty evidence for personality stability in adulthood fail to consider the fact that regularity of personal behavior may be as readily explained by regularities in the social scheduling of behavioral performances as by persistence in personality structure.

Sociologists too have distinctly favored formulations which omit consideration of the alternative-producing characteristics of the social process—stressing, for example, equilibrium maintaining systems, the determination of behavior by internalized norms and role expectations, prediction scales based upon presumed structural personality factors, and, at the extreme, motivational research emphasizing unconscious manipulation. The preference for the analysis of social interaction in terms of role interaction rather than as transactions between persons-as-selves similarly shuns the alternative-producing aspects of social action. Yet the few detailed studies of specific roles shatter the image of simple, mechanical role performance and make clear the interactional pressures toward proliferation for alternatives.

I am certainly not arguing that any of the above mentioned kinds of studies should not be made. They may produce quite valid knowledge. I am only suggesting that, when not balanced by studies of the creative and alternative-producing levels of human action, such studies present a one-sided image of human nature. A more comprehensively valid scientific imagery would produce equal attention to the means of maximizing the alternative-producing conditions of human action. Consider the proportion of effort going into such areas as altruistic behavior, group factors in motivation for education, psycholinguistics, sociological factors in cognition, social contingencies of creativity, turning points in adult careers, the conditions of optimum freedom in human conduct, and human judgment. Obviously the Behavioral Science vogue is not wholly responsible for deficiencies in studying these areas. But insofar as the Behavioral Science ideology is successful in promoting the notion that success in control is the measure of scientific adequacy, it is not reasonable to expect a redress of the balance. In the social sciences there is no simple relation between prediction and control. I do not mean that we should select a particular image of the human process because it is appropriate to "good" values. Quite the contrary, I am suggesting that the present partial image has come to the fore in the Behavioral Sciences because of its appropriateness for certain values which have been accepted by scientists for essentially nonrational and nonevidential reasons—fashion, methodological convenience, foundation support, etc. What is needed is an imagery that at once points to all of the socially relevant levels of human phenomena and is appropriate to the particular set of problems to which the sociologist is expected to provide answers.

THE BEHAVIORAL IMAGE

The Behavioral Science usage of the word "behavior" itself creates a fundamental problem for sociology. The image involved is that behavior is a mechanical response to or expression of some other activating force—that is, a reaction to stimuli, to organic tensions, to internalized norms, to social sanctions, to dysfunctional changes, etc. In this imagery the social system becomes one of two things. For some writers the social system is a pattern of stimuli which schedule or trigger off the responses of organisms which have been socialized to react in certain ways to given stimuli. This conception is illustrated by the following quotation from two leading social scientists:

> We will look at our American system, which largely controls our behavior, much as we would a complex maze in which animals learn to behave. In such a system we must be taught to learn our way around as we grow up if we are to live normal lives and to behave normally as adults. . . . Growing up consists in learning how to behave, and learning how to behave means acquiring the proper responses to the batteries of social stimuli which compose our social order.

For other writers, the social system is a supraindividual system operating in terms that can be formulated independently of the transactions between the human subjects in the system. The well-known equilibrium model used in structure-functional theory exemplifies the supraindividual system conception.

These two types of conceptualization involve three common assumptions. First, it is assumed that the basic problem of sociology, like the other Behavioral Sciences, is to explain or predict behavior. Second, it is assumed that human conduct *is* behavior, that is, responses to environmental or internalized stimuli. Third, it is assumed that social behavior is to be understood as learned behavior. I believe we must reject all three of these assumptions in sociology.

In the first place, sociology is just not concerned with "behavior," in the strict sense. In the sense appropriate to the methodological presuppositions of Behavioral Science, "behavior" is a physical movement or change of internal state of an organism—such as the movement of an arm through space, the physiological changes we call blushing, the movement of an organism closer to or away from a stimulus. Sociology is not concerned with these things, per se. Sociology is concerned with social acts or interactions, which always involve the meaningful aspect of human phenomena that is relative to a particular symbolic context.

Furthermore, social acts are not responses to stimuli; they are interactions with objects and subjects. Stimuli are electrical or chemical or mechanical events that impinge upon a perceptor organ. Objects and subjects are products of the process of identifying the potentialities for interaction of events in the situation—identifications made not only from the viewpoint of the actor but from the roles or points of view of others involved in the episode of interaction. Interaction is more properly called inter-indication: indications of the significance of present parts of the act for future parts and indications of the significance of one person's act for the forthcoming or preceding conduct of another actor. Nor does one even, properly speaking, "respond" to social subjects and objects. One engages in interactions or transactions with them—ordinarily it is the modifying or building up of a relationship between actors which is crucial.

Most astonishing of all, social action cannot accurately be called "learned behavior." The constant and unqualified reiteration that human behavior is "learned" is a subtle evidence of the shift in sociological thinking in recent years. To be sure, the elements of organic behavior that are employed in social acts are, for the most part, learned. But this is by no means the whole story. For human beings "conduct" their actions. Social action is an organizing—in the give and take of social transactions—of the learned elements of behavior to build up a complex act that has its meaning in reference to the acts of others and to future stages of action. Social acts are constructional in character; they are *built up* rather than being simply learned responses. George Herbert Mead's conceptions of the self process and the social act are approvingly described in an early chapter of almost all major sociological works today, yet are thereafter ignored in the effort to treat the human process as reactive, learned behavior.

I wonder if any psychologist or sociologist takes seriously the "scientific" description of behavior when applied to his own conduct. Is the preparation of a lecture or a paper to be understood as "learned" behavior? The phonetics and written symbols and certain aspects of meaning, yes; the organization, the composition, basically no. The individual words and grammar and certain elements of style have been used innumerable times, but the particular ordering of words and ideas that constitutes this particular lecture or paper has never occurred before—but this is surely the aspect of the performance with which we are most concerned.

I have chosen the lecture as the example of building up of acts by interaction because in fact this apparently individual act is built up in a series of intrapersonal transactions in which the composer takes into account various audiences, possible criticisms, and a large array of behavioral elements which never appear in the finished form. In the case of the lecture one may also— and typically does—further reorganize the behavioral elements in process of delivery as a result of transactions with the actual audience. The manner in which a lecture must be understood as being built up in social transactions is often painfully brought home when one tries to use last year's lecture and cannot figure out what in the world one was trying to say. If something so individual as preparing a lecture must be understood as a constructional process, how much more so are the more typical interpersonal performances in which we are directly required to take into account the communications and acts of others. And let us be clear that this constructional process cannot profitably be broken down into a series of minute stimulus-response events. For the objective contingencies that emerge in the pattern of transactions are "real" determinants of the course of action. For example, if individuals of heterogeneous backgrounds come into interaction, the noncongruence of their definitions of the same events will produce inaccurate predictions and anticipations of one another's behavior, with varying consequences. Neither the heterogeneity nor the noncongruence of definitions are stimuli or responses; they can be dealt with only when the *process* of interaction is taken as the unit of analysis.

But if the image of man as a "behaver" fails to do justice to reality, what image can the sociologist or social psychologist use? A favorite philosophical image is that of man as an "actor." Thus Arendt, in analyzing the transition of Western Civilization from a political to a societal basis, suggests a distinction between man as behaver and actor:

> It is decisive that society, on all its levels, excludes the possibility of action, which formerly was excluded from the household. Instead, society expects from each of its members a certain kind of behavior, imposing innumerable and various rules, all of which tend to normalize its members to make them behave, to exclude spontaneous action or outstanding achievement.

By "action" Arendt seems to mean some spontaneous, creative self-govern-ance operating outside of social determinants. Clearly this is not an imagery with which a science can deal, even though it points to aspects of the human drama which we must take into account, though in different ways than the philosopher. But this image of the spontaneous actor is not the only alterna-tive to the image of the social process as a sequence of behavioral reactions. An appropriate sociological image of the individual in the social process is neither that of 'behavior' nor 'actor' but that of 'interactor.' By viewing the basic individual unit as 'interactor' a connection is immediately made with two crucial sociological factors, situation and transaction.

Most of the theoretical problems of sociopsychological science revolve around the intricate relationships of societal organization, personality, and situated social interaction. In most theory and research the process of situ-ated social interaction is treated as the meeting ground of the other two. But almost invariably "meeting ground" becames transmuted into "product of." Those of psychological bent would explain social interactions as the prod-ucts of the personalities of the participants—of drives and instincts, habits and attitudes, needs and defenses. Those of sociological persuasion would explain social interaction as a product of societal organization—of roles and norms, status systems and institutional structures, ecological patterns and technological apparatus. Thus social interaction tends to be seen, not as a determining aspect of the social process, but as an end product, as a sum of the reciprocal behaviors of traited individuals in a societally structured situation.

I am suggesting that social interaction processes should be given an equalitarian position with personality and societal organization. What emerges from any episode of interaction—except the most ritualized—bears the stamp of what goes on *between* the interactors. Indeed, we may argue that the problem of sociology is to explain the manner in which human acts are fitted together in social interaction. Meaning arises in human conduct precisely because human acts are *not* behavioral reactions, but rather are constructional processes in which each individual organizes his act by taking into account—ordinarily through linguistic processes—the acts of other per-sons and past and future parts of the developing episode of interaction. Thus, if the sociological unit of observation and analysis is to be a unit of meaning, it cannot be a behavioral unit but must be an interactional unit.

The significance of considering the interaction process as a determinant of social action can be seen in analyzing episodes that are ordinarily de-scribed in terms of role structure. One of the fundamental errors of most role analysis is to treat each actor as occupying the same role throughout an episode, when in fact each actor ordinarily shuttles through a number of roles during an episode, some overtly expressed, some covertly. For in-stance, a teacher conferring with his principal about a matter of academic freedom may move through the roles of teacher, colleague, scientist, liberal, ACLU member, Jew, male, family provider, etc., not to mention the interspersing of overt and covert social type perspectives such as eager beaver, individualist, cynic, martyr, and scapegoat. Which role and social type perspectives will be occupied during an episode will depend partly on the structure of the situation and partly on which perspectives are available in the actor's personal repertoire, but also partly on the transactions that occur between the participants in the episode. The give-and-take of interaction will lead and force the individual from one position to another.

The reason that George Herbert Mead's conception of the self is central to sociological theory is that it permits us to deal with personality as an interactional unit. Many writers seem to see the importance of Mead's formulation only in his notion that the self-as-object derives its identity from the conceptions other people have of the individual. But actually more critical is Mead's conception of the self as a process of interaction, with the "me" being a role-taking activity through which the individual constantly introduces into his on-going act, in addition to the perspective of the "I," the perspective of the other or the "generalized other." As Mead shows, the self process is really internalized social communication involving two or more social perspectives, just as is the case in overt interpersonal transactions. From this viewpoint, such things as motivation, attitudes, and cultural norms are seen as entering into social acts by a process of identification; that is, as being some of the steps in the defining activity by which an act is built up in an episode of interaction. It is important to note that identifying in an episode what are one's own appropriate motives, attitudes, and norms is accomplished by the same kind of activity, the role-taking process of the self, by which one imputes (through taking the role of the other) the motives, attitudes, and norms of the other by which one anticipates and tries to make sense of the actions of others in the episode.

It is not my intention here to trace the process by which social interaction has lost the place of centrality it had on the sociological stage up to the 1930's. Suffice it to say that the interactionist frame of reference came to be associated with social psychology by the 1930's, and, as the broader evolution of social psychology led to the emphasis upon the relation of the individual to his groups, the concept of "socialization" gradually came to supplant "interaction" as the focus of sociological social psychologists. In time, however, thinking about the individual actor has become so infused with the imagery of psychological dynamics that the effort to connect the individual actor and the social system by the mechanism of socialization has become tenuous. With the entry of sociology into the society of Behavioral Sciences, the split threatens to become complete and sociology in turn to become essentially a descriptive science.

Neither functional analysis nor viewing the social system as a maze of stimuli affords the basis for making sociology a nomothetic science. Sociology cannot be a well-rounded explanatory science without the inclusion of social psychology. But it must be a social psychology which takes interaction rather than the individual as its unit of analysis. Only when interaction is at the center of the sociological stage can the acting personality and social structure be adequately integrated in the contemporaneous situation. Similarly, only when social organization is given an interactional dimension can there be the needed recognition that collective behavior processes—social unrest, fashion, emotional contagions, social movements, ideological drifts—are not only processes out of which new social orders arise in periods of transition but are processes interwoven with institutional activities in all social organization. It is the dynamic of social interaction which ties together the other building blocks of sociological theory: sociocultural organization, the minded individual, collective behavior, and the contingencies which emerge from their interpenetration.

FURTHER READINGS

Horowitz, Irving Louis, ed. *The New Sociology: Essays in Honor of C. Wright Mills.* New York: Oxford University Press, 1964. Galaxy Edition, 1965.

Lundberg, George A. *The Foundations of Sociology.* New York: Macmillan, 1939.

Lynd, Robert S. *Knowledge for What?* Princeton, New Jersey: Princeton University Press, 1939.

Mills, C. Wright. *Images of Man: The Classic Tradition in Sociological Thinking.* New York: George Braziller, 1960.

3

THE NORMATIVE ORDER
AND THE FACTUAL ORDER

Introduction

IN THE INTRODUCTION to this volume we suggested
that two major dimensions of sociological analysis were the normative
order and the factual order. It is to these that we now turn.

The normative order refers to the realm of beliefs and sentiments
which are thought of as right and mandatory for participants in group
activities. The two concepts which are most often used in this context
are norms and values. Cultural norms are the ideas prescribing the direction that action *should* take. Both *ends* and *means* may be prescribed or proscribed. Sumner's *mores* and *folkways* represent a more
traditional approach to norms which is directed to the relative strength
of sentiment associated with particular acts. It is important to keep in
mind that ways of thinking and believing about things may also be
mandatory and, thus, normative. The statement, "How could you even
think of doing anything so bad!" reflects our concern with how people
think and feel.

One of the conventions in writing texts for sociology courses has
been a chapter entitled "Culture." Indeed, this concept is without doubt
one of the most important in the social sciences. As described in the
essay by Miner culture includes varieties of behavior patterns and products of man's social relationships which pervade all societies. We include this essay not only because it is interesting but because it provides
both general and detailed description of this important aspect of group
behavior.

The use of the term "normative order" rather than "cultural order"
is in keeping not only with the framework of functionalism in sociology
but it is closely related to one of the principal ideas which informs our
approach. The idea of a *normative* order implies some degree of
coercion with respect to rules or goals, ways of thinking and acting.
Indeed, one of the problems in a democratic society is to assure the
person that he has a right to think and believe any way he pleases regardless of group pressures to make him conform to prescribed ways.

The excerpts from Sumner's classic work stress the role by which group members are coerced to conform to societal *norms*. Although grossly exaggerated, as is Durkheim's account in our Introduction, it makes the point that the person does not simply make his own choices in regard to social action. The essay by Mizruchi defines values and provides examples of how certain kinds of values held by people in a small city affect their chances of attaining some measure of success as they define it. Thus it analyzes the normative in relation to the factual.

Values represent basic group ideas about what is or is not worthwhile. In contrast to the specific prescription or proscription of ends and means values are more *general* conceptions of the desirable. Thus as our analysis of "success" values in America suggests, we all share some belief that success is desirable even though our conceptions of success vary. Does this mean then that the success pattern is of little significance to organized group behavior? Hardly. What a value conception does is to circumscribe the range of alternative goals and means which will be selected in a course of action.

In our last selection, Malinowski shows us that the conception of man as a slave of custom is grossly oversimplified and exaggerated.

These essays, then, suggest that man's behavior is strongly influenced by both normative and rational processes. That man is rational and calculating with respect to his social condition is something that laymen are more likely to take for granted than the view that we often act as we do out of "rightness" and propriety. This very important theme is picked up again by Wrong in Chapter 5, The Self.

Body Ritual Among the Nacirema

HORACE MINER

THE ANTHROPOLOGIST HAS BECOME so familiar with the diversity of ways in which different peoples behave in similar situations that he is not apt to be surprised by even the most exotic customs. In fact, if all of the logically possible combinations of behavior have not been found somewhere in the world, he is apt to suspect that they must be present in some yet undescribed tribe. This point has, in fact, been expressed with respect to clan organiza-

From *American Anthropologist*, Vol. 58 (1956), pp. 503-507. Reprinted by permission of the publisher and the author.

tion by Murdock. In this light, the magical beliefs and practices of the Nacirema present such unusual aspects that it seems desirable to describe them as an example of the extremes to which human behavior can go.

Professor Linton first brought the ritual of the Nacirema to the attention of anthropologists twenty years ago, but the culture of this people is still very poorly understood. They are a North American group living in the territory between the Canadian Cree, the Yaqui and Tarahumare of Mexico, and the Carib and Arawak of the Antilles. Little is known of their origin, although tradition states that they came from the east. According to Nacirema mythology, their nation was originated by a culture hero, Notgnihsaw, who is otherwise known for two great feats of strength—the throwing of a piece of wampum across the river Pa-To-Mac and the chopping down of a cherry tree in which the Spirit of Truth resided.

Nacirema culture is characterized by a highly developed market economy which has evolved in a rich natural habitat. While much of the people's time is devoted to economic pursuits, a large part of the fruits of these labors and a considerable portion of the day are spent in ritual activity. The focus of this activity is the human body, the appearance and health of which loom as a dominant concern in the ethos of the people. While such a concern is certainly not unusual, its ceremonial aspects and associated philosophy are unique.

The fundamental belief underlying the whole system appears to be that the human body is ugly and that its natural tendency is to debility and disease. Incarcerated in such a body, man's only hope is to avert these characteristics through the use of the powerful influences of ritual and ceremony. Every household has one or more shrines devoted to this purpose. The more powerful individuals in the society have several shrines in their houses and, in fact, the opulence of a house is often referred to in terms of the number of such ritual centers it possesses. Most houses are of wattle and daub construction, but the shrine rooms of the more wealthy are walled with stone. Poorer families imitate the rich by applying pottery plaques to their shrine walls.

While each family has at least one such shrine, the rituals associated with it are not family ceremonies but are private and secret. The rites are normally only discussed with children, and then only during the period when they are being initiated into these mysteries. I was able, however, to establish sufficient rapport with the natives to examine these shrines and to have the rituals described to me.

The focal point of the shrine is a box or chest which is built into the wall. In this chest are kept the many charms and magical potions without which no native believes he could live. These preparations are secured from a variety of specialized practitioners. The most powerful of these are the medicine men, whose assistance must be rewarded with substantial gifts. However, the medicine men do not provide the curative potions for their clients, but decide what the ingredients should be and then write them down in an ancient and secret language. This writing is understood only by the medicine men and by the herbalists who, for another gift, provide the required charm.

The charm is not disposed of after it has served its purpose, but is placed in the charm-box of the household shrine. As these magical materials are specific for certain ills, and the real or imagined maladies of the people are many, the charm-box is usually full to overflowing. The magical packets are so numerous that people forget what their purposes were and fear to use them again. While the natives are very vague on this point, we can only assume that the idea in retaining all the old magical materials is that their presence in the charm-box, before which the body rituals are conducted, will in some way protect the worshipper.

Beneath the charm-box is a small font. Each day every member of the family, in succession, enters the shrine room, bows his head before the charm-box, mingles different sorts of holy water in the font, and proceeds with a brief rite of ablution. The holy waters are secured from the Water Temple of the community, where the priests conduct elaborate ceremonies to make the liquid ritually pure.

In the hierarchy of magical practitioners, and below the medicine men in prestige, are specialists whose designation is best translated "holy-mouth-men." The Nacirema have an almost pathological horror of and fascination with the mouth, the condition of which is believed to have a supernatural influence on all social relationships. Were it not for the rituals of the mouth, they believe that their teeth would fall out, their gums bleed, their jaws shrink, their friends desert them, and their lovers reject them. They also believe that a strong relationship exists between oral and moral character-istics. For example, there is a ritual ablution of the mouth for children which is supposed to improve their moral fiber.

The daily body ritual performed by everyone includes a mouth-rite. Despite the fact that these people are so punctilious about care of the mouth, this rite involves a practice which strikes the uninitiated stranger as revolt-ing. It was reported to me that the ritual consists of inserting a small bundle of hog hairs into the mouth, along with certain magical powders, and then moving the bundle in a highly formalized series of gestures.

In addition to the private mouth-rite, the people seek out a holy-mouth-man once or twice a year. These practitioners have an impressive set of paraphernalia, consisting of a variety of augers, awls, probes, and prods. The use of these objects in the exorcism of the evils of the mouth involves almost unbelievable ritual torture of the client. The holy-mouth-man opens the client's mouth and, using the above mentioned tools, enlarges any holes which decay may have created in the teeth. Magical materials are put into these holes. If there are no naturally occurring holes in the teeth, large sec-tions of one or more teeth are gouged out so that the supernatural substance can be applied. In the client's view, the purpose of these ministrations is to arrest decay and to draw friends. The extremely sacred and traditional character of the rite is evident in the fact that the natives return to the holy-mouth-men year after year, despite the fact that their teeth continue to decay.

It is to be hoped that, when a thorough study of the Nacirema is made, there will be careful inquiry into the personality structure of these people. One has but to watch the gleam in the eye of a holy-mouth-man, as he jabs an awl into an exposed nerve, to suspect that a certain amount of sadism is involved. If this can be established, a very interesting pattern emerges, for most of the population shows definite masochistic tendencies. It was to these that Professor Linton referred in discussing a distinctive part of the daily body ritual which is performed only by men. This part of the rite involves scraping and lacerating the surface of the face with a sharp instrument. Special women's rites are performed only four times during each lunar month, but what they lack in frequency is made up in barbarity. As part of this ceremony, women bake their heads in small ovens for about an hour. The theoretically interesting point is that what seems to be a preponderantly masochistic people have developed sadistic specialists.

The medicine men have an imposing temple, or *latipso,* in every community of any size. The more elaborate ceremonies required to treat very sick patients can only be performed at this temple. These ceremonies involve not only the thaumaturge but a permanent group of vestal maidens who move sedately about the temple chambers in distinctive costume and headdress.

The *latipso* ceremonies are so harsh that it is phenomenal that a fair proportion of the really sick natives who enter the temple ever recover. Small children whose indoctrination is still incomplete have been known to resist attempts to take them to the temple because "that is where you go to die." Despite this fact, sick adults are not only willing but eager to undergo the protracted ritual purification, if they can afford to do so. No matter how ill the supplicant or how grave the emergency, the guardians of many temples will not admit a client if he cannot give a rich gift to the custodian. Even after one has gained admission and survived the ceremonies, the guardians will not permit the neophyte to leave until he makes still another gift.

The supplicant entering the temple is first stripped of all his or her clothes. In every-day life the Nacirema avoids exposure of his body and its natural functions. Bathing and excretory acts are performed only in the secrecy of the household shrine, where they are ritualized as part of the body-rites. Psychological shock results from the fact that body secrecy is suddenly lost upon entry into the *latipso.* A man, whose own wife has never seen him in an excretory act, suddenly finds himself naked and assisted by a vestal maiden while he performs his natural functions into a sacred vessel. This sort of ceremonial treatment is necessitated by the fact that the excreta are used by a diviner to ascertain the course and nature of the client's sickness. Female clients, on the other hand, find their naked bodies are subjected to the scrutiny, manipulation and prodding of the medicine men.

Few supplicants in the temple are well enough to do anything but lie on their hard beds. The daily ceremonies, like the rites of the holy-mouth-men, involve discomfort and torture. With ritual precision, the vestals awaken their miserable charges each dawn and roll them about on their beds of pain while performing ablutions, in the formal movements of which the maidens are highly trained. At other times they insert magic wands in the supplicant's mouth or force him to eat substances which are supposed to be healing. From time to time the medicine men come to their clients and jab magically treated needles into their flesh. The fact that these temple ceremonies may not cure, and may even kill the neophyte, in no way decreases the people's faith in the medicine men.

There remains one other kind of practitioner, known as a "listener." This witch-doctor has the power to exorcise the devils that lodge in the heads of people who have been bewitched. The Nacirema believe that parents bewitch their own children. Mothers are particularly suspected of putting a curse on children while teaching them the secret body rituals. The counter-magic of the witch-doctor is unusual in its lack of ritual. The patient simply tells the "listener" all his troubles and fears, beginning with the earliest difficulties he can remember. The memory displayed by the Nacirema in these exorcism sessions is truly remarkable. It is not uncommon for the patient to bemoan the rejection he felt upon being weaned as a babe, and a few individuals even see their troubles going back to the traumatic effects of their own birth.

In conclusion, mention must be made of certain practices which have their base in native esthetics but which depend upon the pervasive aversion to the natural body and its functions. There are ritual fasts to make fat people thin and ceremonial feasts to make thin people fat. Still other rites are used to make women's breasts larger if they are small, and smaller if they are large. General dissatisfaction with breast shape is symbolized in the fact that the ideal form is virtually outside the range of human variation. A few women afflicted with almost inhuman hypermammary development are so idolized that they make a handsome living by simply going from village to village and permitting the natives to stare at them for a fee.

Reference has already been made to the fact that excretory functions are ritualized, routinized, and relegated to secrecy. Natural reproductive functions are similarly distorted. Intercourse is taboo as a topic and scheduled as an act. Efforts are made to avoid pregnancy by the use of magical materials or by limiting intercourse to certain phases of the moon. Conception is actually very infrequent. When pregnant, women dress so as to hide their condition. Parturition takes place in secret, without friends or relatives to assist, and the majority of women do not nurse their infants.

Our review of the ritual life of the Nacirema has certainly shown them to be a magic-ridden people. It is hard to understand how they have managed to exist so long under the burdens which they have imposed upon themselves. But even such exotic customs as these take on real meaning when they are viewed with the insight provided by Malinowski when he wrote:

> Looking from far and above, from our high places of safety in the developed civilization, it is easy to see all the crudity and irrelevance of magic. But without its power and guidance early man could not have mastered his practical difficulties as he has done, nor could man have advanced to the higher stages of civilization.

Folkways and Mores

WILLIAM GRAHAM SUMNER

DEFINITION AND MODE OF ORIGIN OF THE FOLKWAYS

IF WE PUT TOGETHER all that we have learned from anthropology and ethnography about primitive men and primitive society, we perceive that the first task of life is to live. Men begin with acts, not with thoughts. Every moment brings necessities which must be satisfied at once. Need was the first experience, and it was followed at once by a blundering effort to satisfy it. It is generally taken for granted that men inherited some guiding instincts from their beast ancestry, and it may be true, although it has never been proved. If there were such inheritances, they controlled and aided the first efforts to satisfy needs. Analogy makes it easy to assume that the ways of beasts had produced channels of habit and predisposition along which dexterities and other psychophysical activities would run easily. Experiments with newborn animals show that in the absence of any experience of the relation of means to ends, efforts to satisfy needs are clumsy and blundering. The method is that of trial and failure, which produces repeated pain, loss, and disappointments. Nevertheless, it is a method of rude experiment and selection. The earliest efforts of men were of this kind. Need was the impelling force. Pleasure and pain, on the one side and the other, were the rude constraints which defined the line on which efforts must proceed. The ability to distinguish between pleasure and pain is the only psychical power which

From *Folkways*, 1906. Reprinted through the courtesy of Blaisdell Publishing Company, a division of Ginn and Company.

is to be assumed. Thus ways of doing things were selected, which were expedient. They answered the purpose better than other ways, or with less toil and pain. Along the course on which efforts were compelled to go, habit, routine, and skill were developed. The struggle to maintain existence was carried on, not individually, but in groups. Each profited by the other's experience; hence there was concurrence towards that which proved to be most expedient. All at last adopted the same way for the same purpose; hence the ways turned into customs and became mass phenomena. Instincts were developed in connection with them. In this way folkways arise. The young learn them by tradition, imitation and authority. The folkways, at a time, provide for all the needs of life then and there. They are uniform, universal in the group, imperative, and invariable. As times goes on, the folkways become more and more arbitrary, positive, and imperative. If asked why they act in a certain way in certain cases, primitive people always answer that it is because they and their ancestors always have done so. A sanction also arises from ghost fear. The ghosts of ancestors would be angry if the living should change the ancient folkways.

FOLKWAYS ARE MADE UNCONSCIOUSLY

It is of the first importance to notice that, from the first acts by which men try to satisfy needs, each act stands by itself, and looks no further than the immediate satisfaction. From recurrent needs arise habits for the individual and customs for the group, but these results are consequences which were never conscious, and never foreseen or intended. They are not noticed until they have long existed, and it is still longer before they are appreciated. Another long time must pass, and a higher stage of mental development must be reached, before they can be used as a basis from which to deduce rules for meeting, in the future, problems whose pressure can be foreseen. The folkways, therefore, are not creations of human purpose and wit. They are like products of natural forces which men unconsciously set in operation, or they are like the instinctive ways of animals, which are developed out of experience, which reach a final form of maximum adaptation to an interest, which are handed down by tradition and admit of no exception or variation, yet change to meet new conditions, still within the same limited methods, and without rational reflection or purpose. From this it results that all the life of human beings, in all ages and stages of culture, is primarily controlled by a vast mass of folkways handed down from the earliest existence of the race, having the nature of the ways of other animals, only the topmost layers of which are subject to change and control, and have been somewhat modified by human philosophy, ethics, and religion, or by other acts of intelligent reflection. We are told of savages that "It is difficult to exhaust the customs and small ceremonial usages of a savage people. Custom regulates the whole of a man's actions—his bathing, washing, cutting his hair, eating, drinking, and fasting. From his cradle to his grave he is the slave of ancient usage. In his life there is nothing free, nothing original, nothing spontaneous, no progress towards a higher and better life, and no attempt to improve his condition, mentally, morally, or spiritually." All men act in this way with only a little wider margin of voluntary variation.

THE STRAIN OF IMPROVEMENT AND CONSISTENCY

The folkways, being ways of satisfying needs, have succeeded more or less well, and therefore have produced more or less pleasure or pain. Their quality always consisted in their adaptation to the purpose. If they were imperfectly adapted and unsuccessful, they produced pain, which drove men on to learn better. The folkways are, therefore, (1) subject to a strain of improvement towards better adaptation of means to ends, as long as the adaptation is so imperfect that pain is produced. They are also (2) subject to a strain of consistency with each other, because they all answer their several purposes with less friction and antagonism when they cooperate and support each other. The forms of industry, the forms of the family, the notions of property, the constructions of rights, and the types of religion show the strain of consistency with each other through the whole history of civilization. The two great cultural divisions of the human race are the oriental and the occidental. Each is consistent throughout; each has its own philosophy and spirit; they are separated from top to bottom by different mores, different standpoints, different ways, and different notions of what societal arrangements are advantageous. In their contrast they keep before our minds the possible range of divergence in the solution of the great problems of human life, and in the views of earthly existence by which life policy may be controlled. If two planets were joined in one, their inhabitants could not differ more widely as to what things are best worth seeking, or what ways are most expedient for well being.

THE CONCEPT OF "PRIMITIVE SOCIETY";
   WE-GROUP AND OTHERS-GROUP

The conception of "primitive society" which we ought to form is that of small groups scattered over a territory. The size of the groups is determined by the conditions of the struggle for existence. The internal organization of each group corresponds to its size. A group of groups may have some relation to each other (kin, neighborhood, alliance, connubium and commercium) which draws them together and differentiates them from others. Thus a differentiation arises between ourselves, that we-group, or in-group, and everybody else, or the others-groups, out-groups. The insiders in a we-group are in a relation of peace, order, law, government, and industry, to each other. Their relation to all outsiders, or others-groups, is one of war and plunder, except so far as agreements have modified it. If a group is exogamic, the women in it were born abroad somewhere. Other foreigners who might be found in it are adopted persons, guest friends, and slaves.

SENTIMENTS IN THE IN-GROUP AND
TOWARDS THE OUT-GROUP

The relation of comradeship and peace in the we-group and that of hostility and war towards others-groups are correlative to each other. The exigencies of war with outsiders are what make peace inside, lest internal discord should weaken the we-group for war. These exigencies also make government and law in the in-group, in order to prevent quarrels and enforce discipline. Thus war and peace have reacted on each other and developed each other, one within the group, the other in the intergroup relation. The closer the neighbors, and the stronger they are, the intenser is the warfare, and then the intenser is the internal organization and discipline of each. Sentiments are produced to correspond. Loyalty to the group, sacrifice for it, hatred and contempt for outsiders, brotherhood within, warlikeness without—all grow together, common products of the same situation. These relations and sentiments constitute a social philosophy. It is sanctified by connection with religion. Men of an others-group are outsiders with whose ancestors the ancestors of the we-group waged war. The ghosts of the latter will see with pleasure their descendants keep up the fight, and will help them. Virtue consists in killing, plundering, and enslaving outsiders.

ETHNOCENTRISM

Ethnocentrism is the technical name for this view of things in which one's own group is the center of everything, and all others are scaled and rated with reference to it. Folkways correspond to it to cover both the inner and the outer relation. Each group nourishes its own pride and vanity, boasts itself superior, exalts its own divinities, and looks with contempt on outsiders. Each group thinks its own folkways the only right ones, and if it observes that other groups have other folkways, these excite its scorn. Opprobrious epithets are derived from these differences. "Pig-eater," "coweater," "uncircumcised," "jabberers," are epithets of contempt and abomination. The Tupis called the Portuguese by a derisive epithet descriptive of birds which have feathers around their feet, on account of trousers. For our present purpose the most important fact is that ethnocentrism leads a people to exaggerate and intensify everything in their own folkways which is peculiar and which differentiates them from others. It therefore strengthens the folkways.

ILLUSTRATIONS OF ETHNOCENTRISM

The Papuans on New Guinea are broken up into village units which are kept separate by hostility, cannibalism, head hunting, and divergences of language and religion. Each village is integrated by its own language, religion, and interests. A group of villages is sometimes united into a limited unity by connubium. A wife taken inside of this group unit has full status; one taken outside of it has not. The petty group units are peace groups within and are hostile to all outsiders. The Mbayas of South America believed that their deity had bidden them live by making war on others, taking their wives and property, and killing their men.

When Caribs were asked whence they came, they answered, "We alone are people." The meaning of the name Kiowa is "real or principal people." The Lapps call themselves "men," or "human beings." The Greenland Eskimo think that Europeans have been sent to Greenland to learn virtue and good manners from the Greenlanders. Their highest form of praise for a European is that he is, or soon will be, as good as a Greenlander. The Tunguses call themselves "men." As a rule it is found that nature peoples call themselves "men." Others are something else—perhaps not defined—but not real men. In myths the origin of their own tribe is that of the real human race. They do not account for the others. The Ainos derive their name from that of the first man, whom they worship as a god. Evidently the name of the god is derived from the tribe name. When the tribal name has another sense, it is always boastful or proud. The Ovambo name is a corruption of the name of the tribe for themselves, which means "the wealthy." Amongst the most remarkable people in the world for ethnocentrism are the Seri of Lower California. They observe an attitude of suspicion and hostility to all outsiders, and strictly forbid marriage with outsiders.

CHAUVINISM

That patriotism may degenerate into a vice is shown by the invention of a name for the vice: chauvinism. It is a name for boastful and truculent group self-assertion. It overrules personal judgment and character, and puts the whole group at the mercy of the clique which is ruling at the moment. It produces the dominance of watchwords and phrases which take the place of reason and conscience in determining conduct. The patriotic bias is a recognized perversion of thought and judgment against which our education should guard us.

FOLKWAYS DUE TO FALSE INFERENCE

Furthermore, folkways have been formed by accident, that is, by irrational and incongruous action, based on pseudo-knowledge. In Molembo a pestilence broke out soon after a Portuguese had died there. After that the natives took all possible measures not to allow any white man to die in their country. On the Nicobar islands some natives who had just begun to make pottery died. The art was given up and never again attempted. White men gave to one Bushman in a kraal a stick ornamented with buttons as a symbol of authority. The recipient died leaving the stick to his son. The son soon died. Then the Bushmen brought back the stick lest all should die. Until recently no building of incombustible materials could be built in any big town of the central province of Madagascar, on account of some ancient prejudice. A party of Eskimos met with no game. One of them returned to their sledges and got the ham of a dog to eat. As he returned with the ham bone in his hand he met and killed a seal. Ever afterwards he carried a ham bone in his hand when hunting. The Belenda women (peninsula of Malacca) stay as near to the house as possible during the period. Many keep the door closed. They know no reason for this custom. "It must be due to some now forgotten superstition." Soon after the Yakuts saw a camel for the first time smallpox broke out amongst them. They thought the camel to be the agent of the disease. A woman amongst the same people contracted an endogamous marriage. She soon afterwards became blind. This was thought to be on account of the violation of ancient customs. A very great number of such cases could be collected. In fact they represent the current mode of reasoning of nature people. It is their custom to reason that, if one thing follows another, it is due to it. A great number of customs are traceable to the notion of the evil eye, many more to ritual notions of uncleanness. No scientific investigation could discover the origin of the folkways mentioned, if the origin had not chanced to become known to civilized men. We must believe that the known cases illustrate the irrational and incongruous origin of many folkways. In civilized history also we know that customs have owed their origin to "historical accident,"—the vanity of a princess, the deformity of a king, the whim of a democracy, the love intrigue of a statesman or prelate. By the institutions of another age it may be provided that no one of these things can affect decisions, acts, or interests, but then the power to decide the ways may have passed to clubs, trade unions, trusts, commercial rivals, wire-pullers, politicians, and political fanatics. In these cases also the causes and origins may escape investigation.

HARMFUL FOLKWAYS

There are folkways which are positively harmful. Very often these are just the ones for which a definite reason can be given. The destruction of a man's goods at his death is a direct deduction from other-worldliness; the dead man is supposed to want in the other world just what he wanted here. The destruction of a man's goods at his death was a great waste of capital, and it must have had a disastrous effect on the interests of the living, and must have very seriously hindered the development of civilization. With this custom we must class all the expenditure of labor and capital on graves, temples, pyramids, rites, sacrifices, and support of priests, so far as these were supposed to benefit the dead. The faith in goblinism produced other-worldly interests which overruled ordinary worldly interests. Foods have often been forbidden which were plentiful, the prohibition of which injuriously lessened the food supply. There is a tribe of Bushmen who will eat no goat's flesh, although goats are the most numerous domestic animals in the district. Where totemism exists it is regularly accompanied by a taboo on eating the totem animal. Whatever may be the real principle in totemism, it overrules the interest in an abundant food supply. "The origin of the sacred regard paid to the cow must be sought in the primitive nomadic life of the Indo-European race," because it is common to Iranians and Indians of Hindustan. The Libyans ate oxen but not cows. The same was true of the Phoenicians and Egyptians. In some cases the sense of a food taboo is not to be learned. It may have been entirely capricious. Mohammed would not eat lizards, because he thought them the offspring of a metamorphosed clan of Israelites. On the other hand, the protective taboo which forbade killing crocodiles, pythons, cobras, and other animals enemies of man was harmful to his interests, whatever the motive. "It seems to be a fixed article of belief throughout southern India, that all who have willfully or accidentally killed a snake, especially a cobra, will certainly be punished, either in this life or the next, in one of three ways: either by childlessness, or by leprosy, or by ophthalmia." Where this faith exists man has a greater interest to spare a cobra than to kill it. India furnishes a great number of cases of harmful mores. "In India every tendency of humanity seems intensified and exaggerated. No country in the world is so conservative in its traditions, yet no country has undergone so many religious changes and vicissitudes." "Every year thousands perish of disease that might recover if they would take proper nourishment, and drink the medicine that science prescribes, but which they imagine that their religion forbids them to touch." "Men who can scarcely count beyond twenty, and know not the letters of the alphabet, would rather die than eat food which had been prepared by men of lower caste, unless it had been sanctified by being offered to an idol; and would kill their daughters rather than endure the disgrace of having unmarried girls at home beyond twelve or thirteen years of age." In the last case the rule of obligation and duty is set by the mores. The interest comes under vanity. The sanction of the caste rules is in a boycott by all members of the caste. The rules are often very harmful. "The authority of caste rests partly on written laws, partly on legendary fables or narratives, partly on the injunctions of instructors and priests, partly on custom and usage, and partly on the caprice and convenience of its votaries." The harm of caste rules is so great that of late they have been broken in some cases, especially in regard to travel over sea, which is a great advantage to Hindoos. The Hindoo folkways in regard to widows and child marriages must also be recognized as socially harmful.

THE FOLKWAYS ARE "RIGHT": RIGHTS, MORALS

The folkways are the "right" ways to satisfy all interests, because they are traditional, and exist in fact. They extend over the whole of life. There is a right way to catch game, to win a wife, to make one's self appear, to cure disease, to honor ghosts, to treat comrades or strangers, to behave when a child is born, on the warpath, in council, and so on in all cases which can arise. The ways are defined on the negative side, that is, by taboos. The "right" way is the way which the ancestors used and which has been handed down. The tradition is its own warrant. It is not held subject to verification by experience. The notion of right is in the folkways. It is not outside of them, of independent origin, and brought to them to test them. In the folkways, whatever is, is right. This is because they are traditional, and therefore contain in themselves the authority of the ancestral ghosts. When we come to the folkways we are at the end of our analysis. The notion of right and ought is the same in regard to all the folkways, but the degree of it varies with the importance of the interest at stake. The obligation of conformable and cooperative action is far greater under ghost fear and war than in other matters, and the social sanctions are severer, because group interests are supposed to be at stake. Some usages contain only a slight element of right and ought. It may well be believed that notions of right and duty, and of social welfare, were first developed in connection with ghost fear and other-worldliness, and therefore that, in that field also, folkways were first raised to mores. "Rights" are the rules of mutual give and take in the competition of life which are imposed on comrades in the in-group, in order that the peace may prevail there which is essential to the group strength. Therefore rights can never be "natural" or "God-given," or absolute in any sense. The morality of a group at a time is the sum of the taboos and prescriptions in the folkways by which right conduct is defined. Therefore morals can never be intuitive. They are historical, institutional, and empirical.

DEFINITION OF THE MORES

When the elements of truth and right are developed into doctrines of welfare, the folkways are raised to another plane. They then become capable of producing inferences, developing into new forms, and extending their constructive influence over men and society. Then we call them the mores. The mores are the folkways, including the philosophical and ethical generalizations as to societal welfare which are suggested by them, and inherent in them, as they grow.

TABOOS

The mores necessarily consist, in a large part, of taboos, which indicate the things which must not be done. In part these are dictated by mystic dread of ghosts who might be offended by certain acts, but they also include such acts as have been found by experience to produce unwelcome results, especially in the food quest, in war, in health, or in increase or decrease of population. These taboos always contain a greater element of philosophy than the positive rules, because the taboos contain reference to a reason, as, for instance, that the act would displease the ghosts. The primitive taboos correspond to the fact that the life of man is environed by perils. His food quest must be limited by shunning poisonous plants. His appetite must be restrained from excess. His physical strength and health must be guarded from dangers. The taboos carry on the accumulated wisdom of generations, which has almost always been purchased by pain, loss, disease, and death. Other taboos contain inhibitions of what will be injurious to the group. The laws about the sexes, about property, about war, and about ghosts, have this character. They always include some social philosophy. They are both mystic and utilitarian, or compounded of the two.

Taboos may be divided into two classes, (1) protective and (2) destructive. Some of them aim to protect and secure, while others aim to repress or exterminate. Women are subject to some taboos which are directed against them as sources of possible harm or danger to men, and they are subject to other taboos which put them outside of the duties or risks of men. On account of this difference in taboos, taboos act selectively, and thus affect the course of civilization. They contain judgments as to societal welfare.

RECAPITULATION

We may sum up this preliminary analysis as follows: men in groups are under life conditions; they have needs which are similar under the state of life conditions; the relations of the needs to the conditions are interests under the heads of hunger, love, vanity, and fear; efforts of numbers at the same time to satisfy interests produce mass phenomena which are folkways by virtue of uniformity, repetition, and wide concurrence. The folkways are attended by pleasure or pain according as they are well fitted for the purpose. Pain forces reflection and observation of some relation between acts and welfare. At this point the prevailing world philosophy (beginning with goblinism) suggests explanations and inferences, which become entangled with judgments of expediency. However, the folkways take on a philosophy of right living and a life policy for welfare. Then they become mores, and they may be developed by inferences from the philosophy or the rules in the endeavor to satisfy needs without pain. Hence they undergo improvement and are made consistent with each other.

THE SCOPE AND METHOD OF THE MORES

In the present work the proposition to be maintained is that the folkways are the widest, most fundamental, and most important operation by which the interests of men in groups are served, and that the process by which folkways are made is the chief one to which elementary societal or group phenomena are due. The life of society consists in making folkways and applying them. The science of society might be construed as the study of them. The relations of men to each other, when they are carrying on the struggle for existence near each other, consists in mutual reactions (antagonisms, rivalries, alliances, coercions, and cooperations), from which result societal concretions, that is, more or less fixed positions of individuals and subgroups towards each other, and more or less established sequences and methods of interaction between them, by which the interests of all members of the group are served. The same might be said of all animals. The social insects especially show us highly developed results of the adjustment of adjacent interests and life acts into concatenations and concretions. The societal concretions are due to the folkways in this way,—that the men, each struggling to carry on existence, unconsciously cooperate to build up associations, organization, customs, and institutions which, after a time, appear full grown and actual, although no one intended, or planned, or understood them in advance. They stand there as produced by "ancestors." These concretions of relation and act in war, labor, religion, amusement, family life, and civil institutions are attended by faiths, doctrines of philosophy (myths, folklore), and by precepts of right conduct and duty (taboos). The making of folkways is not trivial, although the acts are minute. Every act of each man fixes an atom in a structure, both fulfilling a duty derived from what preceded and conditioning what is to come afterwards by the authority of traditional custom. The structure thus built up is not physical, but societal and institutional, that is to say, it belongs to a category which must be defined and studied by itself. It is a category in which custom produces continuity, coherence, and consistency, so that the word "structure" may properly be applied to the fabric of relations and prescribed positions with which societal functions are permanently connected. The process of making folkways is never superseded or changed. It goes on now just as it did at the beginning of civilization. "Use and wont" exert their force on all men always. They produce familiarity, and mass acts become unconscious. The same effect is produced by customary acts repeated at all recurring occasions. The range of societal activity may be greatly enlarged, interests may be extended and multiplied, the materials by which needs can be supplied may become far more numerous, the processes of societal cooperation may become more complicated, and contract or artifice may take the place of custom for many interests; but, if the case is one which touches the ways or interests of the masses, folkways will develop on and around it by the same process as that which has been described as taking place from the beginning of civilization. The ways of carrying on war have changed with all new inventions of weapons or armor, and have grown into folkways of commanding range and importance. The factory system of handicrafts has produced a body of folkways in which artisans live, and which distinguish factory towns from commercial cities or agricultural villages. The use of cotton instead of linen has greatly affected modern folkways. The applications of power and machinery have changed the standards of comfort of all classes. The folkways, however, have kept their character and authority through all the changes of form which they have undergone.

MORE EXACT DEFINITION OF THE MORES

We may now formulate a more complete definition of the mores. They are the ways of doing things which are current in a society to satisfy human needs and desires, together with the faiths, notions, codes, and standards of well living which inhere in those ways, having a genetic connection with them. By virtue of the latter element the mores are traits in the specific character (ethos) of a society or a period. They pervade and control the ways of thinking in all the exigencies of life, returning from the world of abstractions to the world of action, to give guidance and to win revivification. "The mores [*Sitten*] are, before any beginning of reflection, the regulators of the political, social, and religious behavior of the individual. Conscious reflection is the worst enemy of the mores, because mores begin unconsciously and pursue unconscious purposes, which are recognized by reflection often only after long and circuitous processes, and because their expediency often depends on the assumption that they will have general acceptance and currency, uninterfered with by reflection." "The mores are usage in any group, in so far as it, on the one hand, is not the expression or fulfillment of an absolute natural necessity [e.g., eating or sleeping], and, on the other hand, is independent of the arbitrary will of the individual, and is generally accepted as good and proper, appropriate and worthy."

Success, Educational Values and the American Dream

EPHRAIM HAROLD MIZRUCHI

ANTHROPOLOGISTS, SOCIOLOGISTS AND PSYCHOLOGISTS have recently begun to direct a great deal of their research efforts to the study of values, shared conceptions of the desirable. Thus, for example, the Harvard University Laboratory of Social Relations has been engaged in a long-term project known as "The Comparative Study of Values in Five Cultures."

From the viewpoint of the social scientist, in particular, the focus of attention has been on the nature of values; the role that values play in differentiating one culture from another; social change; and the maintenance of order and stability in social systems. But efforts to study values from the social scientific point of view have met obstacles which have obscured the significance of value analysis as a medium of understanding group behavior.

The late Clyde Kluckhohn, one of the leading analysts in this sphere of study, took strong issue with some of the arguments against value analysis posed by social scientists and humanists alike.

> No tenet of intellectual folklore has been so damaging to our life and times as the cliché that "science has nothing to do with values." If the consideration of values is to be the exclusive property of religion and the humanties, a scientific understanding of human experience is impossible.

But why study values in the first place? Evon Z. Vogt and John M. Roberts, in a paper describing the Harvard-Cornell project on the study of values hold that,

> The forming and choosing of values is a central concern of all men and societies. Conceptions of the desirable, the fitting and the good vary widely among the world's 3,000 or so cultures. They strongly influence the selection of the modes, the means and the ends of human behavior. The social scientist cannot view man in culture as conditioned only by economic forces and biological impulses.
>
> People see the world through cultural lenses compounded of particular combinations of values; they respond in different ways in accordance with their differing values. We must recognize that people are not just "driven" by situational pressures; they are also "pulled" by the ideals and goals of their cultures.

Our own concern with values is directed to somewhat more modest objectives than those which characterize the studies of the five cultures, referred to above.

Published for the first time in this volume.

Perhaps the most significant unknown factor in our efforts to make assessments of educational attainment is motivation. We are constantly deluged with cases of both students and teachers who fail to perform designated tasks at a level which even approximates known ability to perform.

To be sure there are personality factors which play a role in this failure to achieve. However, recent research in the area of achievement values suggest that there are elements which both inhibit and enhance performance in the educational sphere which are clearly of another stamp. Persistent exposure to group and cultural experiences strongly influence the individual's reactions to specific group occurrences.

It is to an understanding of these group and cultural experiences and their possible impact on performance in the educational sphere that the present discussion is directed.

THE COMMUNITY SURVEY

Some years ago (1956) the writer began a series of intensive interviews dealing with the conceptions of "success" and success symbols held by rural Western New York State residents.

The interview data derived from the 1956 study proved interesting enough to warrant further exploration of the nature of "success" and the values people hold. These values appeared at that time to be of some significance in understanding the motivation of Americans in their response to the cultural mandates of the American Dream of Success.

As a result, further interviews were undertaken in a small city in 1958; in three Central New York communities in 1959; and again in the small city in 1960.

THE PROBLEM

The main focus of our study is a rather widely accepted sociological theory that in American society there is a great deal of emphasis on the *goal* of success and a lack of corresponding emphasis on the *means* by which the end is to be attained. The means-ends discrepancy leads to demoralization in society which is conducive to deviant behavior, e.g., crime and delinquency. This in turn leads to more deviant behavior in those groups which have least access to the available *legitimate* means for attaining success, the lower social classes. This theory is relevant to an understanding of deviant behavior in American society in general, and criminal and delinquent behavior in particular.

Without going into too much detail, an hypothesis derived from the theory holds that there is a great deal of emphasis placed on the goal of "success" in American society but there is little emphasis upon legitimate means for the attainment of that goal. Therefore a characteristic of this society is demoralization. In short, since it is primarily the *goal* which is held to be important, *how* the goal is achieved becomes a matter of expediency rather than a matter requiring adherence to a moral code.

In an intuitive sense we experience little difficulty in finding examples of this devaluation of the means to a goal. We note that some students cheat on examinations because parents exert pressure for good grades; coaches, whose alumni watchdogs are concerned only with the won-lost statistics, exert pressure on players to win at any cost; and price-fixing scandals reflect pressures on executives to win contracts, again at any cost. All of these reflect primary concern with goals and little concern with morality.

Intuition, however, provides us with considerably less rigor in our analyses than we find desirable. As a result it became necessary to make systematic observations using respondents selected by chance factors alone, i.e., systematic sampling techniques.

Our first problem was to explore the first assumption that "success" is a goal which is uniformly adhered to in American society.

SUCCESS VALUES

Before proceeding to our analysis it would be well to comment briefly on what we mean by *value*. For our purposes we can accept Clyde Kluckhohn's definition.

> A value is a conception, explicit or implicit, distinctive of an individual or characteristic of a group, of the desirable which influences the selection from available modes, means, and ends of action.

The specific values in which we are interested, indices of which we shall attempt to analyze, are those associated with the American notion of "success." Lyman Abbott, a late 19th century clergyman who is described as "a true prophet of the success cult," describes the American concept with a great deal of clarity and succinctness,

> The ambition to succeed may be and always ought to be a laudable one. It is the ambition of every parent for his child. It is emphatically an American ambition; at once the national vice and the national virtue. It is the mainspring of activity; the driving wheel of industry; the spur to intellectual and moral progress. It makes the difference between a people that are a pool; between America and China. It makes us at once active and restless; industrious and overworked; generous and greedy. When it is great, it is a virtue; when it is petty, it is a vice.

Sociologists have also made note of the striving toward success. In their study of Middletown during the 1920's, the Lynds noted that "in season and out, regardless of such vicissitudes as unemployment, everybody who gets a living in Middletown is theoretically in process of 'getting there'; the traditional social philosophy assumes that each person has a large degree of freedom to climb the ladder to ever wider responsibility, independence, and money income."

Robin Williams described the factors associated with success in American society and commented on the relationship between money and success.

> . . . Santayana's insight has more accurately indicated the central function of money in the American value system: "It is the symbol and measure he (the American) has at hand for success, intelligence, and power; but as to money itself, he makes, loses, spends and gives it away with a very light heart." In a society of relatively high social mobility, in which position in the scale of social stratification basically depends upon occupational achievement, wealth is one of the few obvious signs of one's place in the hierarchy. Achievement is difficult to index, in a highly complex society of diverse occupations, because of the great differences in abilities and effort required for success in various fields. At the same time, the central type of achievement is in business, manufacturing, commerce, finance; and since traditionalized social hierarchies, fixed estates, and established symbols of hereditary rank have had only a rudimentary development, there is a strong tendency to use money as a symbol of success. Money comes to be valued not only for itself and for the goods it will buy, but as symbolic evidence of success and, thereby, of personal worth.

It seems clear, from these observations, that as far as a good many historians, philosophers and sociologists are concerned, success is a pervasive motivating force for the American people. Our job is to provide empirical evidence which will either lend support to or reject this thesis.

In the interviews conducted between 1956 and 1960, we were concerned, in part, with the relationship between the goal of success and the role of this goal in the American process of "getting ahead." Social class was seen as an important variable in the conceptualization of success and the attainment of this goal.

As a result we posed the question in the following manner: to what extent do members of the various classes hold values which would aid or inhibit them in their efforts to achieve success? More specifically, what is success from the viewpoint of the respondent, how is it attained and what role do his conceptions of success and its corollary values play in his opportunities for achievement?

SOCIAL CLASS AND SUCCESS SYMBOLS

One method of exploring the nature of success as perceived by Americans is to analyze the degree of importance attributed to symbols which

they associate with success. In an effort to uncover these presumably important symbols our respondents were asked, "Could you list, in order of importance, those things which you believe to be signs of success in our
society?" Six possible responses were read by the interviewer and the respondent stated an order of preference.

The symbol which was rated first in importance by the greatest proportion of our sample was home ownership which was selected by 31 percent
of the respondents. "Having a good education" was ranked most important
by 29 percent of the respondents and, "Having a good, steady job," was
ranked most important by 23 percent of our respondents.

When we view the distribution of success symbol evaluation by class
(Hollingshead's ISP) we notice certain trends. Home ownership tends to
become the most important symbol of success as class position declines.
Job security as a symbol also shows a slightly similar tendency. However,
education tended to be selected as the most important symbol of success as
the class position of the respondents rose.

A closer examination of the data suggests that these are more than
simple chance relationships. By grouping job security, home ownership and
money into one category designated as "Material-Economic Symbols" (as
contrasted with "Non-Economic-Material Symbols"), we find that class and
the type of success symbol are associated. We discover a much greater concentration of "Material-Economic" responses in the lower classes than we
would expect by chance alone. It is clear, then, from our analysis that what
symbolizes the attainment of success is differentially perceived by the respondents in the several classes. There are at least three possible interpretations of this finding which seem worthy of consideration. Many have noted
that those at the bottom of the class structure know very little about those
at the top. Therefore the data may reflect the low degree of awareness of
other goals, or the limited range of experience of respondents in the lower
classes. This is particularly true in the area of material-economic symbols.
The symbols of success among lower class respondents are limited to what
others in the same class have attained, particularly when those attainments
are concrete, easily identifiable and conspicuous.

A second possible interpretation is that people value most what they
have least. Thus on the lower levels people are still striving for the basic
necessities and only after having attained these do they look to other fields
for goals. The process of attainment then, in a society in which products
change quickly and goals are frequently being reformulated—in short, a
society which tends toward a great deal of limitless aspirations in its subgroups—is one of reaching a goal and then reaching out for still other goals
in an endless process. This has been referred to as the "escalator process."
The mass media of communication, our children and neighbors and a host
of other influentials encourage us to continue accumulating and trading-in
the old model for the new. In the middle classes the goals have shifted be-

yond the material, which presumably anyone can attain, to more abstract goals while the lower classes still focus on material goals.

Finally, Robin Williams' distinction between "achievement" and "success" provides a broad enough framework for the incorporation of our first two ideas.

Achievement refers to "valued accomplishments," the result of the application of skill and effort in attempting to reach a goal, e.g., a college degree, the establishment of one's own business enterprise. *Success* involves a focus on rewards rather than attainments. Money and prestige represent examples of success goals. Rewards come to be viewed as ends in themselves rather than concomitants of valued accomplishments. Let us attempt to view our data in relation to this achievement-success dimension.

The lower class symbols are clearly *success* symbols as contrasted with the middle and upper class *achievement* symbols. The current types of occupational pursuits in the lower class groupings, for example, are much less likely to lead to achievement. Even the skilled technician has difficulty thinking of his work in achievement terms, as does the clerk who is in the same working-class category. Contrast this with the engineer or scientist or the small business owner who constantly speaks of "building" his business and we gain a new perspective with regard to aspiration. It is not until the minimal *success* symbols have been attained that *achievement* becomes a goal in contemporary American society.

In this respect those in the lower classes do not suffer from stress as much as those in the relatively higher classes. There is relatively little of the problem of abstract, difficult to attain, goals for those in the lower classes. Their problem is the attainment of goals which are inherently more limited. By contrast, the middle class American seeks goals which are somewhat more difficult to attain—even though he often does manage to attain them— and must also concern himself with questions of the relative legitimacy of his *success* or lack of *success,* as contrasted with *achievement.*

It is on the relatively higher class levels that we observe the consequences of pressures of a different type. For certain occupational groups, the intellectuals particularly, the gap between success and achievement is wide. Thus while many have achieved some degree of prominence in their occupational sphere they have not been rewarded with adequate symbols of success. This is particularly true of intellectuals. Furthermore, there is a tendency for the opposite to occur as well. The groups which have attained *success* without having *achieved* tend to look upon themselves and be looked upon by others as not quite legitimate. Thus we are somewhat reluctant to give power to those who have wealth but have not achieved it—the prototype of this being the speculator who seeks control of a long established business enterprise—and we do not accord as much prestige to the attainers of success alone as we do to those who have success because of their achievements. In terms of our present objectives these questions are beyond the scope of this report.

EDUCATION AS A VALUE

Because education has been found to be a relatively important symbol of underlying values and because it plays a major role in opportunity for advancement we attempted to take a closer look at the part that education plays in the evaluative perceptions of our respondents. Herbert Hyman has devoted a large part of his analysis to the value placed on formal education. As he points out, the degree to which education is evaluated highly is a significant factor in differential opportunities to achieve success. As he suggests,

> Part of the ideology of American life is that important positions are not simply inherited by virtue of the wealth of one's parents, but can be achieved. Such achievement, however, requires for many types of important positions considerable formal education. One cannot, for example, become a physician or a lawyer or an engineer without advanced education. Consequently, insofar as the lower classes placed less value on higher education, this would constitute an aspect of a larger value system which would work detrimental to their advancement.

Hyman then proceeds to show that there is differential preference among the classes for college education with preference increasing with class position. Even though our data lend support to Hyman's findings and generalizations we would approach his interpretation with some caution. The use of indices of "preference for college education" as a means of assessing educational values would seem to this writer to involve a middle-class type of bias on the part of the investigator. We would hold that success relative to a lower class position can be achieved with high school education alone. The skilled technician and the shop foreman, for example, have certainly attained at least a modest degree of success in an objective sense and the need for college education in this context would seem to be superfluous, if not completely meaningless. For those of the middle classes, however, whose aspirations include professional achievement the significance of a college education may be much more meaningful.

We are dealing here with means-values rather than ends-values. In this context, a college education is thought of as a means toward other ends, one of several alternative means for achieving "success." Our earlier findings, however, as reported above, suggest that education as an *end-value* was more highly rated by the middle-classes than by the lower classes. We would hypothesize that the greater importance of education as an *end-value* for the middle class provides them with greater chances of advancement *because* they view it as an end-value.

Values can have consequences which are either compatible with or incompatible with the objectives of the actors in a social system and these consequences may or may not be known to the actor or the group members more generally. In other words there may be latent consequences of values for particular groups. In this particular case holding education as an *end-value* for the middle classes has a latent, i.e., unanticipated and unrecognized, consequence of providing relatively greater chances of attaining both success and achievement goals while for the lower classes the *lack* of education as an important *end-value* has a latent consequence of limiting the chances for reaching goals in either the skilled, commercial or professional occupations, to name only a few.

If this is so then we would expect to find that education itself is evaluated differently among the several classes. In order to test this hypothesis our respondents were asked the following question taken from Robin Williams' study. "Here are some reasons different people have given for wanting to have their children finish a certain amount of education. Which *one* of these would you say is most important?" The responses were grouped into two categories, the Instrumental Perception of Education and the Non-Instrumental Perception of Education.

The 205 respondents were almost evenly distributed with regard to the Instrumental–Non-Instrumental dimension. Thus 52 percent perceived education as a *means-value* while 48 percent perceived education in non-instrumental (*end-value*) terms. There is, however, a marked tendency for instrumental perceptions of education to increase with a decline in social class. Our statistical analysis indicates that social class and perception of education as instrumental are associated. When probed as to what is most important about receiving an education the lower class respondents clearly evaluated education in instrumental terms. Our middle class respondents tended to see education not only as a means to achieving a better job or income, but also as providing personal benefits separated from the sphere of advancement. We would speculate that our lower class respondents tended to view the significance of education, with hindsight, as something which would have helped them in adulthood had they pursued it in childhood and adolescence. Thus while it is seen as a means to success it is not evaluated as highly as are other things.

In answer to our question, to what extent do members of the various classes hold values which would aid or hinder them in their efforts to attain success in American society, we must conclude that although our lower class respondents are aware of the utility of education as a means for getting ahead, the fact that they do not place high valuation on it as an *end-value* does limit their chances for even modest advancement. We must agree, then, with Hyman that the lower class population does share a self-imposed tendency, through lack of utilizable *end-values,* to non-achievement of success goals.

DISCUSSION

What we have attempted to do in this brief report is describe one of the ways in which a systematic approach to the study of values provides data which are somewhat more conclusive than those derived from intuitive processes.

We have, in short, asked a series of questions and have gone directly to the participants in group activities for answers.

It should be clear from our analysis that value orientations differ systematically for diverse groups in the population. Furthermore, the nature of the beliefs and sentiments which characterize certain groups have consequences for individuals and groups regardless of their conscious awareness of these consequences.

Moving from a more objective analysis, the question which might be asked is, what of it?

Setting aside the question of "success" it seems to this writer that our observations with respect to educational values provide directives for the teacher, the student and the layman.

One of the most serious problems of contemporary American society is incidence of extreme instrumentalization. Our response to the arts, literature and social relationships are characterized to too great an extent by a tendency to use experiences not as ends-in-themselves but as means to other ends. Interest in art, literature and learning, in general, becomes a means for enhancing one's prestige or economic position. We take the risk of experiencing what others expect us to experience in contrast to our own unique, personal response to valued artistic and intellectual expression.

As educated citizens we are in a sorry condition if intellectual endeavors are more meaningful to us as means rather than as ends. Is scholarship a medium for the attainment of non-intellectual goals or is scholarship personally gratifying? Do we have images of ourselves as people who accept and cherish these values? Are we contributing to a society in which there will be firm commitment to meaningful values generally? Are we contributing to an image of a way of life in which values, thought and action tend to conjoin or to diverge? Where there is divergence do we contribute to responsible intellectual skepticism?

There is a maxim among the specialists in the field of marketing that a good salesman is one who really believes in the merchandise which he is selling. Are we, the formally educated, good salesmen?

Rationality in Social Relationships

BRONISLAW MALINOWSKI

IT SCARCELY NEEDS TO BE ADDED that there are also other driving motives, besides the constraint of reciprocal obligations, which keep the fishermen to their task. The utility of the pursuit, the craving for the fresh, excellent diet, above all, perhaps, the attraction of what to the natives is an intensely fascinating sport—move them more obviously, more consciously even, and more effectively than what we have described as the legal obligation. But the social constraint, the regard for the effective rights and claims of others is always prominent in the mind of the natives as well as in their behaviour, once this is well understood. It is also indispensable to ensure the smooth working of their institutions. For in spite of all zest and attractions, there are on each occasion a few individuals, indisposed, moody, obsessed by some other interest—very often by an intrigue—who would like to escape from their obligation, if they could. Anyone who knows how extremely difficult, if not impossible, it is to organize a body of Melanesians for even a short and amusing pursuit requiring concerted action, and how well and readily they set to work in their customary enterprises, will realize the function and the need of compulsion, due to the native's conviction that another man has a claim on his work.

There is yet another force which makes the obligations still more binding. I have mentioned already the ceremonial aspect of the transactions. The gifts of food in the system of exchange described above must be offered according to strict formalities, in specially made measures of wood, carried and presented in a prescribed manner, in a ceremonial procession and with a blast of conch-shells. Now nothing has a greater sway over the Melanesian's mind than ambition and vanity associated with a display of food and wealth. In the giving of gifts, in the distribution of their surplus, they feel a manifestation of power, and an enhancement of personality. The Trobriander keeps his food in houses better made and more highly ornamented than his dwelling huts. Generosity is the highest virtue to him, and wealth the essential element of influence and rank. The association of a semi-commercial transaction with definite public ceremonies supplies another binding force of fulfilment through a special psychological mechanism: the desire for display, the ambition to appear munificent, the extreme esteem for wealth and for the accumulation of food.

We have thus gained some insight into the nature of the mental and

Crime and Custom in Savage Society, London: Routledge & Kegan Paul, Ltd., 1926, pp. 29-32. Reprinted by permission of the publisher.

social forces which make certain rules of conduct into binding law. Nor is the binding force superfluous. Whenever the native can evade his obligations without the loss of prestige, or without the prospective loss of gain, he does so, exactly as a civilized business man would do. When the 'automatic smoothness' in the run of obligations so often attributed to the Melanesian is studied more closely, it becomes clear that there are constant hitches in the transactions, that there is much grumbling and recrimination and seldom is a man completely satisfied with his partner. But, on the whole, he continues in the partnership and, on the whole, every one tries to fulfil his obligations, for he is impelled to do so partly through enlightened self-interest, partly in obedience to his social ambitions and sentiments. Take the real savage, keen on evading his duties, swaggering and boastful when he has fulfilled them, and compare him with the anthropologist's dummy who slavishly follows custom and automatically obeys every regulation. There is not the remotest resemblance between the teachings of anthropology on this subject and the reality of native life. We begin to see how the dogma of mechanical obedience to law would prevent the field-worker from seeing the really relevant facts of primitive legal organization. We understand now that the rules of law, the rules with a definite binding obligation, stand out from the mere rules of custom. We can see also that civil law, consisting of positive ordinances, is much more developed than the body of mere prohibitions, and that a study of purely criminal law among savages misses the most important phenomena of their legal life.

It is also obvious that the type of rules which we have been discussing, although they are unquestionably rules of binding law, have in no way the character of religious commandments, laid down absolutely, obeyed rigidly and integrally. The rules here described are essentially elastic and adjustable, leaving a considerable latitude within which their fulfilment is regarded as satisfactory. The bundles of fish, the measures of yams, or bunches of taro, can only be roughly assessed, and naturally the quantities exchanged vary according to whether the fishing season or the harvest is more abundant. All this is taken into account and only wilful stinginess, neglect, or laziness are regarded as a breach of contract. Since, again, largesse is a matter of honour and praise, the average native will strain all his resources to be lavish in his measure. He knows, moreover, that any excess in zeal and generosity is bound sooner or later to be rewarded.

We can see now that a narrow and rigid conception of the problem—a definition of 'law' as the machinery of carrying out justice in cases of trespass —would leave on one side all the phenomena to which we have referred. In all the facts described, the element or aspect of law, that is of effective social constraint, consists in the complex arrangements which make people keep to their obligations. Among them the most important is the manner in which many transactions are linked into chains of mutual services, every one of them having to be repaid at some later date. The public and ceremonial manner in which these transactions are usually carried out, combined with

the great ambition and vanity of the Melanesian, adds also to the safeguard-
ing forces of law.

FURTHER READINGS

Davis, Kingsley. *Human Society*. New York: Macmillan, 1948.

Myrdal, Gunnar, *et al. An American Dilemma,* 2nd ed. New York: Harper &
Row, 1962.

Williams, Robin M., Jr. *American Society,* New York: Alfred A. Knopf, 1960.

4

GROUPS AND INTERACTION

Introduction

THE SMALLEST UNIT of social interaction is a two-person relationship. Similarly the typical definition of a group includes the assumption that two or more persons are in interaction. Groups vary not only in size but in type of organization, purposes and longevity. Sociologists have at one time or another distinguished between primary groups and other groups (Cooley), small groups and larger groups (Homans), in-groups and out-groups (Sumner) and, more recently, reference-groups and nonreference-groups (Merton). Groups and group structures are central to sociological study.

Groups must be thought of within the larger frameworks of social organizations of various types. Complex organizations, including bureaucracies and associations, are also included in this category. Discussions of associations and complex organizations are included in essays selected for Chapter 9, Urbanization (Little) and in Chapter 10, Bureaucratization. We select for our focus here some issues surrounding the nature of group life and social interaction from two-person situations to broader contexts.

Charles Warriner's paper provides a lucid statement describing the various approaches to group orientations as well as a strong appeal for the modern *realistic* position in sociological thought. In getting at the subtleties of the several viewpoints he suggests how the relationship between person and group might be best understood. This theme is repeated in Chapter 5, The Self.

The inclusion of some excerpts from Georg Simmel's work is in keeping with our efforts to provide the reader with as much classical sociological material as is appropriate and meaningful in a given context. Simmel's brilliant analysis of the significance of group size on the quality of interaction is unmatched in the literature of social science. In contrasting the two-person group (dyad) with the three-person group (triad) we observe a basic transformation in type of interaction. We have limited our selections here but have included the discussion of the *tertius gaudens* role in contrast to the mediator and arbitrator roles because *tertius gaudens* reflects the kind of rationality in social relationships which contrasts so sharply with our images of "normative" man.

Simmel's interest in friendship and love as role relationships emerges out of his interest in the relationship between group size and intimacy. These lead, further, into a concern with reciprocal knowledge and ignorance and its functions in maintaining interaction.

Interest in conflict has re-emerged during the past decade after a long period of slumber. A number of nineteenth-century sociological thinkers, including Sumner, Marx, Gumplowicz, Ratzenhofer, and Albion Small—whose translations of Simmel we have used here—focused on conflict. The significance of conflict theory in understanding contemporary international relations has played no small part in its rise to prominence. More complete translations of Simmel's work have become available in recent decades and are recommended for further reading (cf. Wolff and Coser).

Groups Are Real: A Reaffirmation

CHARLES K. WARRINER

THE TERM "GROUP" is an ancient one in the social sciences, but despite its antiquity there is little agreement on the nature of the reality to which it refers—or even if it refers to any reality at all. This problem has been fundamental to many of the arguments of the past. There have been times when we assured ourselves that the issues were resolved only to find that they have arisen again in somewhat different form.

Contemporary writings on the small group—research reports and theoretical statements—exhibit four major orientations to the group and to the question of its reality. Each of these orientations is here presented as a logically consistent point of view. However, it must be remembered that in their concrete representation they are not often so clearly stated or consistent. Any particular author may exhibit elements of several of these orientations.

Nominalism. The oldest, and the most extreme position in the light of contemporary knowledge, is the *nominalist* view that the group is not a real entity, but is merely a term used to refer to "an assemblage of individuals." According to this view, the term is reified if it is used to refer to anything

From *American Sociological Review*, Vol. 21, No. 5, 1956, pp. 549-554. Reprinted by permission of the publisher and author.

more than the behavior of individuals. Since individuals are the only reality, then the only thing which needs to be or can be explained is their behavior, singly or collectively. This point of view has its most favorable climate in a mechanistic type of psychological theory.

The nominalist orientation is implicit in much of the present work on the small group. A recent issue of the *American Sociological Review*, devoted to small group studies, included several research papers in which the total extra-individual phenomenon was to be found in very brief contact between "subjects" with a minimum of interaction. These papers, no doubt, deal with phenomena which have some bearing upon interpersonal relations, but by no stretch of the imagination can they be called studies of *groups*, as some purported to be.

Interactionism. Pure nominalism as an explicit theoretical doctrine has died out during the past thirty years with the rise of the *interactionist* point of view. The focus upon interaction led to a rejection of the group-individual dichotomy intrinsic to the nominalist-realist argument and to a stress upon the concrete indivisibility of the two. Wirth makes these points explicit:

> Rather than settling the issue as to whether the individual or the group is the ultimate unit in terms of which social life must be analyzed, the main stream of sociological and social-psychological thought has forgotten this issue and proceeded to analyze social phenomena as complexes of the meaningfully oriented actions of persons reciprocally related to one another.

According to this doctrine, neither the group nor the individual is real except in terms of the other: that is, you-don't-have-persons-without-a-group and you-don't-have-groups-without-persons. In addition to the stress upon the indivisibility of the two, there is an emphasis upon the study of this whole in its concrete entirety and complexity. Finally, the interactionist doctrine has placed emphasis upon the multiplicity of causative factors needed to account for what happens. It combines biological, cultural, personal, and social explanations.

In much of the interactionist literature there are ghosts of the older nominalist thoughtways, most often found as implicit assumptions of and stresses upon the individual as the greater or more basic reality, and of the more fundamental character of biological and psychological explanations of social life. On the other hand, the pure nominalist orientation could not continue unaffected in the face of the evidence on the social origins of personality and the findings on the interconnectedness of social and personal phenomena.

Neo-nominalism. However, the interest in persons and the orientation toward the individual remained and formed the basis for a revised nominalist doctrine. The *neo-nominalist* pattern of thought accepts the proposition that the term "group" refers to an objective reality, but claims that the group is less real than persons for it is, after all, made up of persons and of processes which have their locus and immediate origin in the person.

The exact character of the neo-nominalist view depends to a great extent upon the conception of interaction that is held. The most extreme rejection of the equal reality of the group is possible where the interaction is seen in stimulus-response terms. In this view the interaction itself, though being something different from individuals, is explicable only through individual psychological processes.

The basis for the explanation of group phenomena is perhaps the most clearly distinguishing characteristic of the neo-nominalist view. This is an essentially reductionist philosophy which holds that, since the individual is the more fundamental unit, the final and basic explanations of the group are obtained only when these explanations are couched in terms of individual psychology. Allport, the most persistent exponent of this view, says:

> The concept of a causal science on a purely social (non-psychological) plane is untenable, because in all science *explanation* is possible only by drawing upon the concepts of sciences at more elementary levels. . . . The true basis for sociology is the social behavior of the socialized individual, in other words, social psychology. The work of sociology is to describe collectivities of social behavior and social change resulting from it in terms of the group, and to explain these phenomena in terms of "the individual."

Realism. The antithesis of these nominalist views has been the realist argument. Realism, like nominalism, has undergone metamorphoses since Durkheim's time, but since the earlier forms of realism are seldom encountered today we shall describe merely what we have called *modern realism.*

This doctrine holds that (1) the group is just as real as the person, but that (2) both are abstract, analytical units, not concrete entities, and that (3) the group is understandable and explicable solely in terms of distinctly social processes and factors, not by reference to individual psychology. In short, modern realism is theoretical, analytical, and anti-reductionist. However, this does not mean that it is non-empirical.

There are relatively few explicit presentations of this orientation. A recent article by two "group psychologists" argues for it and there are occasional incidental papers in the sociological journals. In addition there are occasional research reports which, in an unself-conscious fashion, exhibit this kind of thinking. There are, however, many tendencies in the thoughtways which appear this author to lead toward the realist orientation.

Of the four doctrines discussed, the neo-nominalist view appears to be in the ascendency today in small group research as well as in other areas of inquiry. Even interactionism has been distorted in this direction. This stress upon the individual, upon explanations in terms of psychology or psychological processes, and upon the lesser reality and importance of the group and other social phenomena have become the sensible, common-sense point of view. Its acceptance does not need to be defended because it is common-sense and because its doctrines are congenial to a period in which there is a general cultural stress upon individualism and the importance of the person.

But progress in a discipline depends upon getting beyond the common-sense orientations of the time. The purpose here is to make this attempt by calling attention to and defending the legitimacy and validity of the realist position, and to propose that this is the most valid and potentially fruitful sociological approach to the study of the group and society. This follows a long sociological tradition: the work of Durkheim, Simmel, and Radcliffe-Brown, among others.

In order to do this within the scope of this paper it will be necessary to be elliptical and to forego the kind of documentation that might be desirable. However, the intention is not so much to prove a position as to call attention to it and to the bases upon which it can be defended. This effort seems particularly pertinent at this time when sociology, at least as far as its interest in small groups is concerned, is in danger of being displaced by psychologists, some of whom are claiming the field for their own and stressing a psychological orientation as the only valid one:

> We have . . . to establish a branch of psychology concerned with the "personality" of groups . . . in spite of much talk about 'culture patterns,' methods and concepts simply do not exist. The sociologists, recognizing that a group cannot be defined in merely political or economic terms have turned to the psychologist for a science of the living group entity. . . .

Such excesses could be forgiven if it were not for the fact that many sociologists seem to accept the premises and orientations such a statement implies.

THE ARGUMENTS AGAINST REALISM EXAMINED

There are four basic propositions in the thoughtways of contemporary social science that serve as the bases for arguments against the realist position. The propositions are thought to be self-evident and not in need of defense. Such widespread uncritical acceptance is itself reason enough for critical scrutiny, but it is our thesis that these propositions are fundamental fallacies in contemporary sociological thought and are a bar to further progress in the sociology of the group. These propositions are:

1. We can see persons, but we cannot see groups except by observing persons.
2. Groups are composed of persons.
3. Social phenomena have their reality only in persons, this is the only possible location of such phenomena.
4. The purpose for studying groups is to facilitate explanations and predictions of individual behavior.

The first proposition, that we can see persons, but not groups, has recently been criticized by several authors who suggest that the argument involves a confusion between the idea of *individual* and that of *person*. They point out that the individual and the person are different "things" and that it is only the former, the biological structure, which we see directly, while the person is observed only through a series of actions and behaviors.

We can, perhaps, define the problem more clearly by stating it as a situation in which we treat a conceptual entity as a perceptual entity. The only thing which we as humans can observe are events within a relatively limited time and space location. Any unity that is microscopic, that extends beyond the scope of our perceptual equipment in space, or whose structural processes are too slow or too fast for our perception must be inferred from partial observations made via instruments or through time series. The fact that we cannot directly perceive their unity does not detract from their essential empirical reality; it merely reflects the human limitation. This appears to be no less true of social phenomena than of physical ones.

Whenever we are dealing with a unity that exceeds our perceptual facility, we postulate that unity from the observation of sequences of events appearing to have a continuity and a degree of causal connection. We create a conceptual unit. When, as a result of the use of this concept, we become fully convinced that it refers to, and essentially coincides with, an empirical, objective unity, we then come to project that conceptual reality upon our limited observations. That is, we call to mind the total thing when we see only a part of it; we come to treat our conception as if it were perception. This appears to be exactly the same kind of process as occurs in the operation of stereotypes except that in the former case we take greater pains, presumably, to make sure that our concept has a sounder basis in empirical fact.

In any case, our argument here is that we cannot "see" persons any more than we can see groups: both are realities which extend beyond the range of human perception. Both are abstractions from and summaries of our observations of more limited aspects of the reality. The proposition that "we can see persons, but cannot see groups" is then a statement about our relative confidence in and acceptance of these concepts, *not a statement about perception or about what exists in external reality.*

We might note here that this argument is often joined with an assumption that the only *realities* are those which have physical substance. The basis for this belief is undermined by contemporary theory in physics, which proposes the interchangeability of matter and motion. As we inquire more carefully into the nature of what we believe is solid substance, we find that the solidity is more often than not the substance of our perceptual limitations.

The second proposition, that "groups are composed of persons," serves as a basic premise for two distinct conclusions about groups: (1) that they are more abstract, less real than persons, and (2) that really basic explanations of groups are in terms of their components, the persons of which they are composed.

This proposition loses its strength once we accept the idea that persons are no more concrete entities than are groups, but it is an idea that is so widely and unquestioningly accepted that it is worth examining independently of our earlier argument.

First, the proposition ignores the fact of interaction and is incompatible with the fact unless interaction is treated purely as a stimulus-response phenomenon, which can be done only through extreme contortion. There is much evidence to show that interaction results in new phenomena which are emergent in the situation and not explicable by reference to the persons as they exist prior to the interaction. The statement thus ignores the fact that in combination here, as in chemistry, the elements cease to be the same thing they were before and that the characteristics of the compound are not the results of a mere blending or mixing of the components.

There is, however, a much more fundamental problem—a problem that raises the issue of what we mean by components, elements, or units and whether there are different orders of components involved in the same concrete phenomenon.

Without going into the lengthy argument necessary we propose that *components*$_1$ (the materials from which a substance is created) have been confused with *components*$_2$ (the structural elements or members unique to and characteristic of the system or unity with which we are dealing). We can clarify the problem by an analogy from common experience. Suppose we ask, "Of what is a chair composed?" We might get this variety of answers: wood and cloth, steel and leather, metal and organic compounds, atoms and molecules, chemical compounds. Each of these is in some senses a correct statement about some chairs, i.e. about certain observable objects. None of these, however, tells us anything about chairs as chairs, as a unique class of phenomena. Rather the answers tell us about the kinds of materials from which chairs may be created or about physical substances in general. The only answer which makes sense when we are investigating chairs, *qua* chairs —rather than chairs as furniture, or as wood products, or as chemical compounds, or as physical substances—is the answer which defines chairs in terms of their common structural parts and arrangements, the parts and arrangements which set chairs off from all other objects. Thus a chair is composed of a seat, legs, back, frame, etc.

In the language of the general semanticists, we have jumped abstraction ladders when we say that chairs are composed of atoms, of metal, or of chemical compounds. These may be characteristics of some or all chairs, but are not the components of chairs.

It would seem then that the proposition that groups are composed of persons tells us nothing about groups as such, but merely says that persons are characteristic of human social life. It describes a characteristic of groups as one kind of social life, but does not indicate the structural components that are involved in groups as a particular kind of unity and reality.

Our third proposition claims that "the only existence of social phenomena is in the individual." The proposition is an ambiguous one and may have several interpretations. It is frequently taken to mean that culture and other social phenomena are distributive only through the individuals in the group. Hence, for example, culture exists only as a sum or average of the beliefs or habits of the members of the group.

This point of view is fostered by such doctrines as Cooley's that the group is one side of the coin of which the individual is the other, and the perhaps misinterpreted statements of ethnographers that one can often find out all about a primitive culture from the study of a few members. These notions suggest that society and culture are mirrored in each individual member of the group.

The fallacy is the assumption that for a social phenomenon to be real it must be internalized by the individual, and results from a failure to make the distinction between knowing and internalization. It is clear that a person may know cultural forms, beliefs, and patterns and know when they are appropriate (much in the way an anthropologist knows a culture which he studies) without these becoming an integral part of his own personality.

When we recognize this distinction, we see that it is possible for social phenomena to exist without being a part of the personalities who are the actors in the situation. Just as an anthropologist may participate in a savage rite in which he does not believe in order not to offend his hosts, so may any actor express cultural beliefs or conform to social actions he does not really believe or are not his personal habits. He may do so for a variety of motivations, but from a sociological point of view the character of the motivations is not the important thing, but the fact that he is motivated and that he knows the belief, ideology, or social act called for in the situation. Internalization or mirroring of social facts in the person is thus not a prerequisite to existence of the phenomenon. Because of this, such phenomena take on a reality independent of persons as persons. This means that we cannot discover social facts through a study of persons except in certain extremely stable and limited societies. As a result, to say that social phenomena have their location in the person is misleading. It would be much more appropriate to say that social phenomena have their reality only through expression by actors, in which case we imply the necessity not only for distinguishing person from individual, but also for distinguishing actor from person.

Support for this argument of the independent reality of social phenomena was found in my own study of a small Kansas village. We learned that there was a public, "official" morality regarding the use of alcoholic beverages that was quite different from the morality observed in other contexts. All the members of the community knew what the official morality was and they expressed it in their public behavior, but many of them did not "believe" it and conformed to other patterns in their homes, in small groups, and away from the village. There were a variety of sentiments (i.e. motivations) which led to the expression of this morality. They ranged from a few who *really believed* that drinking was wrong, to those who felt that it was *good for others* to abstain ("my brother's keeper" attitude), to those who merely felt that it was easiest not to go against the official position. Many other situations, which we now explain in terms of ambivalence of persons, bias, etc., are more easily explained by this formulation and support our conclusion.

The final proposition holds that the only purpose for studying groups is to facilitate knowledge of and prediction for persons. In the final analysis this is a value issue and is therefore not amenable to argument. It is in some ways basic to all the other arguments, however, for a thorough commitment to this value renders the realist approach superfluous. The only reason for realism as defined here is to facilitate the study of groups for their own sake. This author believes that anything which is real and observable is worth studying for itself. I am of the knowledge-for-the-sake-of-knowledge persuasion. But for those who judge knowledge and science in terms of "what good is it?" it might be pointed out that we have seldom perceived the ultimate values or applications of new developments in knowledge at their start.

CONCLUSION

In conclusion we must note that argument against the critics of a position does not prove that position. We have merely suggested that *a priori* rejection of realism is founded upon fallacy and misconception. The proof of the realist doctrine lies not so much in whether its present statement upon ultimate test will prove to be valid, but rather whether the present statement of it leads to fruitful research that would not otherwise be done.

Furthermore, the acceptance of the realist doctrine does not require that other views be rejected as wrong. They, too, reflect some aspects of reality and provide a way of approaching certain problems.

I propose that if we treat groups as real units or systems, if we cease to identify group phenomena with a particular personnel and with personality, if we cease to look for group phenomena in persons, and if we study groups for the sake of learning more about groups, only then will we begin to make real strides in a uniquely sociological problem.

On Group Size and Quality of Interaction

GEORG SIMMEL

ON THE WHOLE, it may be said that unions in pairs, as contrasted with those of larger numbers, favor a relatively higher individuality of the participants, while, on the other hand, they presuppose that the restraint of peculiarity through the social articulation to an average level is lacking. If it for that reason is true that women are the less individual sex, that their differentiations vary less from the species type than is on the average the case with men, it would help to explain the further very general opinion that they are, as a rule, less accessible to friendship than are men. For friendship is a relationship entirely founded upon the individuality of the elements, perhaps even more than marriage, which, through its traditional forms, its social fixities, its real interests, includes much that is super-individual and independent of the peculiarity of the personalities. The fundamental differentiation upon which marriage rests is, in itself, not individual, but it pertains to the species; friendship, however, rests upon a purely personal differentiation, and hence it is intelligible that in general real and permanent friendships are rare at the inferior levels of personal development, and that, on the other hand, the modern highly differentiated woman manifests notably enhanced capacity and inclination for friendships, alike with men and with women. The entirely individual differentiation has, in this case, attained decisiveness over that which pertains to the species, and we thus see the correlation formed between the sharpest individualization and a relation that at this grade is absolutely limited to duality. This, of course, does not prevent the same person from forming at the same time various relations of friendship.

That combinations of two in general have, as such, specific traits is shown not merely by the fact that the entrance of a third modifies them entirely, but still more the variously observed fact that the still further extension to four or more by no means modifies the nature of the combination to a correspondingly wide degree. For example, a marriage union resulting in a single child has a quite different character from a childless union, while there is not an equally significant difference between it and the union resulting in two or more children. To be sure, the difference in its essential nature which the second child produces is again much greater than that springing from the arrival of the third. But this simply follows the above rule; for a family with one child is still, in many respects, a relationship

Translated by Albion Small, from *American Journal of Sociology*, 2, 1896, pp. 159-160, 174-180.

between two members; namely, the parents as a unity, on the one hand, the child on the other. The second child is then in fact not merely a fourth, but, sociologically considered, at the same time also a third member in a relationship, and it exerts the peculiar influences of such third members; for within the family, so soon as the actual age of minority is passed, the parents constitute much more frequently a working unity than do the children as a totality.

Furthermore, in the realm of the forms of marriage the decisive difference is whether, on the one hand, monogamy prevails, or, on the other, the man has a second wife. If the latter is the case, the third or the twentieth wife is relatively without significance for the structure of the union. Within the boundaries of such a structure, the step to the second wife is here also, at least in *one* direction, richer in consequences than that to a still larger number, for precisely the duality of wives may give occasion, in the life of the man, to the sharpest conflicts and profoundest perplexities, which, in general, do not arise in the case of each higher number. For in the latter instance such a fundamental declassing and deindividualizing of the wives is involved, there is so decided reduction of the relationship to its sensuous basis (since every more spiritual union is always of a more individual nature), that in general it cannot lead to those profounder disturbances for the man which may flow directly and only from a dual relationship.

✿   ✿   ✿

THE TERTIUS GAUDENS

The nonpartisanship of the third element has benefited or injured the group as a whole, in the combinations thus far discussed. The mediator and the arbitrator alike wish to preserve the group unity against the danger of disruption. The nonpartisan, however, may use his relatively superior status in a purely egoistic interest. While in the former cases he acted as a means to the ends of the group, in this case, on the contrary, he makes the reciprocal occurrences between the parties and between himself and the parties a means for his own ends. Here we have to do not always with previously consolidated structures, in the social life of which this occurrence emerges by the side of others, but now the relationship between the parties and the nonpartisan is often formed *ad hoc*. Elements which otherwise constitute no reciprocal unity may come into conflict; a third, previously unattached to both alike, may seize, by means of a spontaneous action, the opportunities which this conflict gives to him, the nonpartisan, and thus may set up a purely precarious reciprocity, whose vitality and richness of forms may for each element be entirely out of proportion to the fluidity of its constitution.

I note, without further discussion, two forms of the *tertius gaudens,* because the reciprocity within the tetrad, with the typical forms of which we are here concerned, does not appear very characteristically in these instances. Rather is the significant thing in these cases a certain passivity, which rests either upon the two contestants or upon the third element. The forms are these: In the first place the advantage of the third may be produced by the fact that the two others hold each other reciprocally in check, and he can now make a gain which one of these two would otherwise contest with him. The quarrel brings about in this instance merely a paralyzing of forces which, if they could, would turn against the third. The situation in this case thus really suspends the reciprocity between the three elements, instead of establishing it, without on that account, it must be added, excluding the most appreciable results for all three. We have to treat the intentional production of this situation in the case of the next configuration of threes. In the second place, advantage may accrue to the third party merely because the action of the one contending party realizes this advantage for purposes of its own, and without the necessity of using any initiative on the part of the person reaping the advantage. The type for this form is furnished by the benefactions and the promotions which a party may confer upon a third, merely for the sake of thereby embarrassing the opposing party. For instance, the English laws for the protection of labor had their origin at first partly in the mere spite of the Tories against the Liberal manufacturers, and in the same way competition for popularity has produced very many ostensibly philanthropic actions. Strange as it is, it is a peculiarly petty and malicious temper which, for the sake of afflicting a second, confers a benefit upon a third. That indifference to the self-serving effects of philanthropy which is proper to altruism cannot more sharply appear than through such an exploiting of it. Moreover, it is doubly characteristic that one may reach the end of irritating the opponent both through the favors which one shows to his friend and through those conferred upon his enemy.

The formations of this type which are more essential at this point, result when the third party, for reasons of prudence respecting his own interests, adopts an attitude of practical support toward the one party (that is, not merely by way of intellectual decision, as in the case of the arbitrator) and from this attitude derives his mediate or immediate gain. Within this form there are two chief variations; namely, two parties are hostile to each other, and for that reason compete for the favor of a third; or two parties compete for the favor of a third, and are for that reason hostile to each other. This difference has specially important bearings upon the further development of the constellation. If an already existing hostility makes in the direction of an attempt by each party to get the favor of the third, the decision of this competition, that is, the attachment of the third to the one party, will really mean the beginning of the conflict. On the other hand, in case the two elements independent of each other seek the favor of a third, and this constitutes the ground of their hostility, of their partisanship, the final assignment of this favor, which is in this case end, not means, of the strife, will terminate the same. The decision is reached, and further hostility is therewith made meaningless. In both cases the advantage of nonpartisanship, with which the *tertius* originally stood in antithesis with the other two, consists in the fact that he can set his own *conditions* for the decision. Where, for any reason, this assignment of conditions is denied to him, the situation does not bring to him the complete advantage. Thus, in one of the most frequent cases of the second type, namely, the competition of two persons of the same sex for the favor of the same person of the opposite sex. In this case the decision of the latter does not in general depend in the same sense upon the will of the latter as that of a purchaser between competing vendors, or that of a prince dispensing favors between competing solicitors. It is rather given through existing feelings, which are not determinable by will, and to that extent do not permit the decision to depend on completely free choice. For that reason we are not here speaking of proposals, the significance of which is merely the guidance of choice, and, although the situation of the *tertius gaudens* is completely given, its specific utilization is on the whole forbidden. The most comprehensive illustration of the *tertius gaudens* is the purchasing public under a régime of free competition. The struggle of the producers for purchasers gives to the latter almost complete independence of the individual source of supply, although the purchaser is completely dependent upon the aggregate of sellers, and therefore a coalition among them would at once reverse the relationship. The former situation of independence permits the purchaser to make his purchases conditional upon satisfaction of his demands as to quality and price of the goods. His status thus has, moreover, the special advantage that the producers must even seek to anticipate these conditions, to guess the unspoken or unconscious wishes of the consumer, to suggest to him conditions that are not present, or to accustom him to desirable conditions. From the first-mentioned case of the woman between two admirers, in which, because the decision depends upon their personality, and not upon their actions, she does not set conditions, and therefore does not exploit the situation, a continuous series of phenomena leads up to the case of modern commerce, from which the element of personal characteristic is completely eliminated, and in which the advantage of the party selecting extends so far that the competing parties even relieve him of the trouble of advancing the conditions to their maximum. This last is the utmost which the situation of *tertius gaudens* can accomplish for the latter.

Of the other formation, namely, that a conflict originally entirely unrelated to the third party forces its opponents to compete for the help of the latter, the history of every alliance, from that between states to that between members of a family, usually furnishes examples. The very simple typical course of events gains, however, in such a modification as the following, a peculiar sociological interest. In order to produce this advantageous situation for the third party, the energy which he is called upon to bring to bear by no means need possess a considerable quantity in proportion to that of either party. On the contrary, the necessary amount of the energy which he must have for the purpose is determined exclusively by the relationship which the energies of the parties exhibit toward each other. Evidently all that is necessary is that the addition of his reserve force to one of these shall give to the same a preponderance. When, therefore, the quantities of force are practically equal, a minimum of addition often suffices in order to give a final decision to one of the sides. Hence the frequent influence of small parliamentary parties, an influence which they could never win by their proper significance, but only through the fact that they are able to turn the scale between the great parties. Wherever majorities decide, that is, where everything often depends upon a single vote, the possibility exists that utterly insignificant parties may set the most relentless conditions for their support. The like may occur in the relationship of smaller to larger states when the latter are in conflict. It is merely necessary that the energies of two antagonistic elements paralyze each other, in order that the never so weak position of the unattached third party may attain to unlimited strength. Elements that are strong in themselves will, of course, profit not less from this situation, and especially because it frequently spares them the real mobilization of power. The advantages of the *tertius gaudens* will accrue to him from the situation here indicated, not merely when actual conflict occurs, but even from a tension and latent antagonism between the others. He functions in such a case through the mere *possibility* of giving his adhesion to the one or to the other, even if it does not come to the serious extreme. This variation was illustrated in the case of English politics at the transition from mediæval to modern time; that is, it appeared in the fact that England no longer sought possessions and immediate power upon the continent, but always possessed a power which stood potentially between the continental governments. Already in the sixteenth century it was said: "France and Spain are the scales of the European balance; England, however, is the tongue or the holder of the balance." This case occurs, however, only when the potential capacity of the third party is *considerable*, because, if this power is transformed into a merely potential operation, it sacrifices in a very large degree its effective force, and it withdraws to a distance at which a power that is not very substantial would no longer enjoy much respect.

But the advantage which accrues to the third party from the fact that he has to the two others a relationship *a priori* equal, equally independent, and for that very reason decisive, is not solely dependent upon the fact that these two are in a relationship of hostility. It is enough, on the contrary, that between them there is only a certain degree of variation, alienation, or qualitative dualism. This is, indeed, the universal formula of the type, of which the hostility of the elements constitutes merely a special, although the most frequent, case. The following, for instance, is a very characteristic situation of advantage for a *tertius*, resulting from the mere duality:

If B is under obligation to perform for A a certain definitely limited duty, and this obligation passes from B to C and D, between whom the performance is to be divided, it is a very natural temptation for A to impose upon each of the two, if possible, a fraction more than the half, so that in the aggregate he enjoys more than before, when the duty was in a single hand. In 1751 the government of Bohemia was obliged to forbid, in the case of the division of peasant holdings by the proprietors, the imposition upon each partial holding of more than its proportional share of the burden of customary service which attached to the undivided holding. In division of an obligation between two, the impression prevails that each individual has still less to do than the former individual upon whom the whole rested. The precise balancing of the quantity consequently becomes a secondary matter, and may thus easily be omitted. While here, therefore, as it were, the mere numerical fact of the duality, instead of the unity, of the party produces the situation of the *tertius gaudens,* in the following case it arises from a duality that is determined by qualitative differences. The juridical prerogative of the English king after the Norman conquest, which was something unknown to mediæval Germany, is to be explained as follows: William the Conqueror encountered existing rights of the Anglo-Saxon population, which had to be respected in principle, and at the same time his Normans brought with them their peculiar rights; but these two legal complexes did not harmonize. They produced no unity of popular rights as opposed to the king, who could, by means of the unity of his interest, interpose between the two and to a considerable extent annul them. In the cleavage between the nations—not merely because they were in constant friction with each other, but because their very divergency forbade their uniting upon a law to be maintained in common—was the pillar of absolutism, and consequently its power steadily declined so soon as the two nationalities actually dissolved into a single one.

The favored status of the third party disappears, as a matter of course, at the moment in which the two others come together in a unity; that is, the grouping reverts in the respect that is now in question from the triad to the dyad type.

Friendship, Love and Secrecy

GEORG SIMMEL

THE IDEAL FRIENDSHIP that has come down from antique tradition, and singularly enough has been developed directly in the romantic sense, aims at absolute spiritual confidence, with the attachment that material possession also shall be a resource common to the friends. This entrance of the entire undivided ego into the relationship may be the more plausible in friendship than in love, for the reason that, in the case of friendship, the one-sided concentration upon a single element is lacking, which is present in the other case on account of the sensuous factor in love. To be sure, through the circumstance that in the totality of possible grounds of attachment one assumes the headship, a certain organization of the relationship occurs, as is the case in a group with recognized leadership. A single strong factor of coherence often blazes out the path along which the others, otherwise likely to have remained latent, follow; and undeniably in the case of most men, sexual love opens the doors of the total personality widest; indeed, in the case of not a few, sexuality is the sole form in which they can give their whole ego; just as, in the case of the artist, the form of his art, whatever it may be, furnishes the only possibility of presenting his entire nature. This is to be observed with special frequency among women —to be sure, the same thing is to be asserted in the case of the quite different "Christian love"—namely, that they not only, because they love, devote their life and fortune without reserve; but that this at the same time is chemically dissolved in love, and only and entirely in its coloring, form, and temperature flows over upon the other. On the other hand, however, where the feeling of love is not expansive enough, where the other contents of the soul are not flexible enough, it may take place, as I indicated, that the predominance of the erotic nexus may suppress not only the practically moral, but also the spiritual, contacts that are outside of the erotic group. Consequently friendship, in which this intensity, but also this inequality of devotion, is lacking, may more easily attach the whole person to the whole person, may more easily break up the reserves of the soul, not indeed by so impulsive a process, but throughout a wider area and during a longer succession. This complete intimacy of confidence probably becomes, with the changing differentiation of men, more and more difficult. Perhaps the modern man has too much to conceal to make a friendship in the ancient sense possible; perhaps personalities also, except in very early years, are too peculiarly individualized for the complete reciprocality

Translated by Albion Small, from *American Journal of Sociology*, 11, 1906, pp. 457-466.

of understanding, to which always so much divination and productive phantasy are essential. It appears that, for this reason, the modern type of feeling inclines more to differentiated friendships; that is, to those which have their territory only upon one side of the personality at a time, and in which the rest of the personality plays no part. Thus a quite special type of friendship emerges. For our problem, namely, the degree of intrusion or of reserve within the friendly relationship, this type is of the highest significance. These differentiated friendships, which bind us to one man from the side of sympathy, to another from the side of intellectual community, to a third on account of religious impulses, to a fourth because of common experiences, present, in connection with the problem of discretion, or self-revelation and self-concealment, a quite peculiar synthesis. They demand that the friends reciprocally refrain from obtruding themselves into the range of interests and feelings not included in the special relationship in each case. Failure to observe this condition would seriously disturb reciprocal understanding. But the relationship thus bounded and circumscribed by discretion nevertheless has its sources at the center of the whole personality, in spite of the fact that it expresses itself only in a single segment of its periphery. It leads ideally toward the same depths of sentiment, and to the same capacity to sacrifice, which undifferentiated epochs and persons associate only with a community of the total circumference of life, with no question about reserves and discretions.

Much more difficult is measurement of self-revelation and reserve, with their correlates intrusiveness and discretion, in the case of marriage. In this relationship these forms are among the universal problems of the highest importance for the sociology of intimate associations. We are confronted with the questions, whether the maximum of reciprocality is attained in a relationship in which the personalities entirely resign to each other their separate existence, or quite the contrary, through a certain reserve—whether they do not in a certain qualitative way belong to each other more if they belong to each other less quantitatively. These questions of ratio can of course, at the outset, be answered only with the further question: How is the boundary to be drawn, within the whole area of a person's potential communicability, at which ultimately the reserve and the respect of another are to begin? The advantage of modern marriage—which, to be sure, makes both questions answerable only one case at a time—is that this boundary is not from the start determined, as was the case in earlier civilizations. In these other civilizations marriage is, in principle, as a rule, not an erotic phenomenon, but merely a social-economic institution. The satisfaction of the instincts of love is only accidentally connected with it. With certain exceptions, the marriage is not on grounds of individual attraction, but rather of family policy, labor relationships, or desire for descendants. The Greeks, for example, carried this institution to the most extreme differentiation. Thus Demosthenes said: "We have *hetaerae* for our pleasure, concubines for our daily needs, but wives to give us lawful children and to care for the interior of the house." The same tendency to exclude from the community of marriage, *a priori*, certain defined life-contents, and by means of super-individual provisions, appears in the variations in the forms of marriage to be found in one and the same people, with possibility of choice in advance on the part of those contracting marriages. These forms are differentiated in various ways with reference to the economic, religious, legal, and other interests connected with the family. We might cite many nature-peoples, the Indians, the Romans, etc. No one will, of course, fail to observe that, also within modern life, marriage is, probably in the majority of cases, contracted from conventional or material motives; nevertheless, entirely apart from the frequency of its realization, the sociological idea of modern marriage is the community of all life-contents, in so far as they immediately, and through their effects, determine the value and the destiny of the personalities. Moreover, the prejudice of this ideal demand is by no means ineffective. It has often enough given place and stimulus for developing an originally very incomplete reciprocation into an increasingly comprehensive attachment. But, while the very indeterminateness of this process is the vehicle of the happiness and the essential vitality of the relationship, its reversal usually brings severe disappointments. If, for example, absolute unity is from the beginning anticipated, if demand and satisfaction recognize no sort of reserve, not even that which for all fine and deep natures must always remain in the hidden recesses of the soul, although they may think they open themselves entirely to each other—in such cases the reaction and disillusionment must come sooner or later.

In marriage, as in free relationships of analogous types, the temptation is very natural to open oneself to the other at the outset without limit; to abandon the last reserve of the soul equally with those of the body, and thus to lose oneself completely in another. This, however, usually threatens the future of the relationship. Only those people can without danger give themselves entirely to each other who *cannot possibly* give themselves entirely, because the wealth of their soul rests in constant progressive development, which follows every devotion immediately with the growth of new treasures. Complete devotion is safe only in the case of those people who have an inexhaustible fund of latent spiritual riches, and therefore can no more alienate them in a single confidence than a tree can give up the fruits of next year by letting go what it produces at the present moment. The case is quite different, however, with those people who, so to speak, draw from their capital all their betrayals of feeling and the revelations of their inner life; in whose case there is no further source from which to derive those elements which should not be revealed, and which are not to be disjoined from the essential ego. In such cases it is highly probable that the parties to the confidence will one day face each other empty-handed; that the Dionysian free-heartedness may leave behind a poverty which—unjustly, but not on that account with less bitterness—may so react as even to charge the enjoyed devotion with deception. We are so constituted that we not merely, as was remarked, need a certain proportion of truth and error as the basis of our life, but also a similar mixture of definiteness and indefiniteness in the picture of our life-elements. That which we can see through plainly to its last ground shows us therewith the limit of its attraction, and forbids our phantasy to do its utmost in adding to the reality. For this loss no literal reality can compensate us, because the action of the imagination of which we are deprived is self-activity, which cannot permanently be displaced in value by any receptivity and enjoyment. Our friend should not only give us a cumulative gift, but also the possibility of conferring gifts upon him, with hopes and idealizations, with concealed beauties and charms unknown even to himself. The manner, however, in which we dispose of all this, produced by ourselves, but for his sake, is the vague horizon of his personality, the intermediate zone in which faith takes the place of knowledge. It must be observed that we have here to do by no means with mere illusions, or with optimistic or infatuated self-deception. The fact is rather that, if the utmost attractiveness of another person is to be preserved for us, it must be presented to us in part in the form of vagueness or impenetrability. This is the only substitute which the great majority of people can offer for that attractive value which the small minority possess through the inexhaustibility of their inner life and growth. The mere fact of absolute understanding, of having accomplished psychological exhaustion of the contents of relationship with another, produces a feeling of insipidity, even if there is no reaction from previous exaltation; it cripples the vitality of the relationship, and gives to its continuance an appearance of utter futility. This is the danger of that unbroken, and in a more than external sense shameless, dedication to which the unrestricted possibilities of intimate relationships seduce, which indeed is easily regarded as a species of obligation in those relationships. Because of this absence of reciprocal discretion, on the side of receiving as well as of giving, many marriages are failures. That is, they degenerate into vulgar habit, utterly bereft of charm, into a matter-of-course which retains no room for surprises. The fruitful depth of relationships which, behind every latest revelation, implies the still unrevealed, which also stimulates anew every day to gain what is already possessed, is merely the reward of that tenderness and self-control which, even in the closest relationship, comprehending the whole person, still respect the inner private property, which hold the right of questioning to be limited by a right of secrecy.

All these combinations are characterized sociologically by the fact that the secret of the one party is to a certain extent recognized by the other, and the intentionally or unintentionally concealed is intentionally or unintentionally respected. The intention of the concealment assumes, however, a quite different intensity so soon as it is confronted by a purpose of discovery. Thereupon follows that purposeful concealment, that aggressive defense, so to speak, against the other party, which we call secrecy in the most real sense. Secrecy in this sense—i.e., which is effective through negative or positive means of concealment—is one of the greatest accomplishments of humanity. In contrast with the juvenile condition in which every mental picture is at once revealed, every undertaking is open to everyone's view, secrecy procures enormous extension of life, because with publicity many sorts of purposes could never arrive at realization. Secrecy secures, so to speak, the possibility of a second world alongside of the obvious world, and the latter is most strenuously affected by the former. Every relationship between two individuals or two groups will be characterized by the ratio of secrecy that is involved in it. Even when one of the parties does not notice the secret factor, yet the attitude of the concealer, and consequently the whole relationship, will be modified by it. The historical development of society is in many respects characterized by the fact that what was formerly public passes under the protection of secrecy, and that, on the contrary, what was formerly secret ceases to require such protection and proclaims itself. This is analogous with that other evolution of mind in which movements at first executed consciously become unconsciously mechanical, and, on the other hand, what was unconscious and instinctive rises into the light of consciousness. How this development is distributed over the various formations of private and public life, how the evolution proceeds toward better-adapted conditions, because, on the one hand, secrecy that is awkward and undifferentiated is often far too widely extended, while, on the other hand, in many respects the usefulness of secrecy is discovered very late; how the quantum of secrecy has variously modified consequences in accordance with the importance or indifference of its content—all this, merely in its form as questions, throws a flow of light upon the significance of secrecy for the structure of human reciprocities. In this connection we must not allow ourselves to be deceived by the manifold ethical negativeness of secrecy. Secrecy is a universal sociological form, which, as such, has nothing to do with the moral valuations of its contents. On the one hand, secrecy may embrace the highest values: the refined shame of the lofty spirit, which covers up precisely its best, that it may not seem to seek its reward in praise or wage; for after such payment one retains the reward, but no longer the real value itself. On the other hand, secrecy is not in immediate interdependence with evil, but evil with secrecy. For obvious reasons, the immoral hides itself, even when its content encounters no social penalty, as, for example, many sexual faults. The essentially isolating effect of immorality as such, entirely apart from all primary social repulsion, is actual and important. Secrecy is, among other things, also the sociological expression of moral badness, although the classical aphorism, "No one is so bad that he also wants to seem bad," takes issue with the facts. Obstinacy and cynicism may often enough stand in the way of disguising the badness. They may even exploit it for magnifying the personality in the judgment of others, to the degree that sometimes immoralities which do not exist are seized upon as material for self-advertising.

The application of secrecy as a sociological technique, as a form of commerce without which, in view of our social environment, certain purposes could not be attained, is evident without further discussion. Not so evident are the charms and the values which it possesses over and above its significance as a means, the peculiar attraction of the relation which is mysterious in form, regardless of its accidental content. In the first place, the strongly accentuated exclusion of all not within the circle of secrecy results in a correspondingly accentuated feeling of personal possession. For many natures possession acquires its proper significance, not from the mere fact of having, but besides that there must be the consciousness that others must forego the possession. Evidently this fact has its roots in our stimulability by contrast. Moreover, since exclusion of others from a possession may occur especially in the case of high values, the reverse is psychologically very natural, viz., that what is withheld from the many appears to have a special value. Accordingly, subjective possessions of the most various sorts acquire a decisive accentuation of value through the form of secrecy, in which the substantial significance of the facts concealed often enough falls into a significance entirely subordinate to the fact that others are excluded from knowing them. Among children a pride and self-glory often bases itself on the fact that the one can say to the others: "I know something that you don't know." This is carried to such a degree that it becomes a formal means of swaggering on the one hand, and of de-classing on the other. This occurs even when it is a pure fiction, and no secret exists. From the narrowest to the widest relationships, there are exhibitions of this jealousy about knowing something that is concealed from others. The sittings of the English Parliament were long secret, and even in the reign of George III reports of them in the press were liable to criminal penalties as violations of parliamentary privilege. Secrecy gives the person enshrouded by it an exceptional position; it works as a stimulus of purely social derivation, which is in principle quite independent of its casual content, but is naturally heightened in the degree in which the exclusively possessed secret is significant and comprehensive. There is also in this connection an inverse phenomenon, analogous with the one just mentioned. Every superior personality, and every superior performance, has, for the average of mankind, something mysterious. To be sure, all human being and doing spring from inexplicable forces. Nevertheless, within levels of similarity in quality and value, this fact does not make the one person a problem to another, especially because in respect to this equality a certain immediate understanding exists which is not a special function of the intellect. If there is essential inequality, this understanding cannot be reached, and in the form of specific divergence the general mysteriousness will be effective—somewhat as one who always lives in the same locality may never encounter the problem of the influence of the environment, which influence, however, may obtrude itself upon him so soon as he changes his environment, and the contrast in the reaction of feeling upon the life-conditions calls his attention to this causal factor in the situation. Out of this secrecy, which throws a shadow over all that is deep and significant, grows the logically fallacious, but typical, error, that everything secret is something essential and significant. The natural impulse to idealization, and the natural timidity of men, operate to one and the same end in the presence of secrecy; viz., to heighten it by phantasy, and to distinguish it by a degree of attention that published reality could not command.

Singularly enough, these attractions of secrecy enter into combination with those of its logical opposite; viz., treason or betrayal of secrets, which are evidently no less sociological in their nature. Secrecy involves a tension which, at the moment of revelation, finds its release. This constitutes the climax in the development of the secret; in it the whole charm of secrecy concentrates and rises to its highest pitch—just as the moment of the disappearance of an object brings out the feeling of its value in the most intense degree. The sense of power connected with possession of money is most completely and greedily concentrated for the soul of the spendthrift at the moment at which this power slips from his hands. Secrecy also is sustained by the consciousness that it *might be* exploited, and therefore confers power to modify fortunes, to produce surprises, joys, and calamities, even if the latter be only misfortunes to ourselves. Hence the possibility and the temptation of treachery plays around the secret, and the external danger of being discovered is interwoven with the internal danger of self-discovery, which has the fascination of the brink of a precipice. Secrecy sets barriers between men, but at the same time offers the seductive temptation to break through the barriers by gossip or confession. This temptation accompanies the psychical life of the secret like an overtone. Hence the sociological significance of the secret, its practical measure, and the mode of its workings must be found in the capacity or the inclination of the initiated to keep the secret to himself, or in his resistance or weakness relative to the temptation to betrayal. From the play of these two interests, in concealment and in revelation, spring shadings and fortunes of human reciprocities throughout their whole range. If, according to our previous analysis, every human relationship has, as one of its traits, the degree of secrecy within or around it, it follows that the further development of the relationship in this respect depends on the combining proportions of the retentive and the communicative energies—the former sustained by the practical interest and the formal attractiveness of secrecy as such, the latter by inability to endure longer the tension of reticence, and by the superiority which is latent, so to speak, in secrecy, but which is actualized for the feelings only at the moment of revelation, and often also, on the other hand, by the joy of confession, which may contain that sense of power in negative and perverted form, as self-abasement and contrition.

The Sociology of Conflict

GEORG SIMMEL

THAT CONFLICT has sociological significance, inasmuch as it either produces or modifies communities of interest, unifications, organizations, is in principle never contested. On the other hand, it must appear paradoxical to the ordinary mode of thinking to ask whether conflict itself, without reference to its consequences or its accompaniments, is not a form of sociation. This seems, at first glance, to be merely a verbal question. If every reaction among men is a sociation, of course conflict must count as such, since it is one of the most intense reactions, and is logically impossible if restricted to a single element. The actually dissociating elements are the causes of the conflict—hatred and envy, want and desire. If, however, from these impulses conflict has once broken out, it is in reality the way to remove the dualism and to arrive at some form of unity, even if through annihilation of one of the parties. The case is, in a way, illustrated by the most violent symptoms of disease. They frequently represent the efforts of the organism to free itself from disorders and injuries. This is by no means equivalent merely to the triviality, *si vis pacem para bellum,* but it is the wide generalization of which that special case is a particular. Conflict itself is the resolution of the tension between the contraries. That it eventuates in peace is only a single, specially obvious and evident, expression of the fact that it is a conjunction of elements, an opposition, which belongs with the combination under one higher conception. This conception is characterized by the common contrast between both forms of relationship and the mere reciprocal indifference between elements. Repudiation and dissolution of social relation are also negatives, but conflict shows itself to be the positive factor in this very contrast with them; viz., shows negative factors in a unity which, in idea only, not at all in reality, is disjunctive. It is practically more correct to say, however, that every historically actual unification contains, along with the factors that are unifying in the narrower sense, others which primarily make against unity.

As the individual achieves the unity of his personality not in such fashion that its contents invariably harmonize according to logical or material, religious or ethical, standards, but rather as contradiction and strife not merely precede that unity, but are operative in it at every moment of life; so it is hardly to be expected that there should be any social unity in which the converging tendencies of the elements are not incessantly shot through

Translated by Albion Small, from *American Journal of Sociology,* 9, 1904, pp. 490-492, 517-518, 679-689.

with elements of divergence. A group which was entirely centripetal and harmonious—that is, "unification" merely—is not only impossible empirically, but it would also display no essential life-process and no stable structure. As the cosmos requires *"Liebe und Hass,"* attraction and repulsion, in order to have a form, society likewise requires some quantitative relation of harmony and disharmony, association and dissociation, liking and disliking, in order to attain to a definite formation. Moreover, these enmities are by no means mere sociological passivities, negative factors, in the sense that actual society comes into existence only through the working of the other and positive social forces, and this, too, only in so far as the negative forces are powerless to hinder the process. This ordinary conception is entirely superficial. Society, as it is given in fact, is the result of both categories of reactions, and in so far both act in a completely positive way. The misconception that the one factor tears down what the other builds up, and that what at last remains is the result of subtracting the one from the other (while in reality it is much rather to be regarded as the addition of one to the other), doubtless springs from the equivocal sense of the concept of unity. We describe as unity the agreement and the conjunction of social elements in contrast with their disjunctions, separations, disharmonies. We also use the term unity, however, for the total synthesis of the persons, energies, and forms in a group, in which the final wholeness is made up, not merely of those factors which are unifying in the narrower sense, but also of those which are, in the narrower sense, dualistic. We associate a corresponding double meaning with disunity or opposition. Since the latter displays its nullifying or destructive sense *between the individual elements,* the conclusion is hastily drawn that it must work in the same manner upon the *total relationship.* In reality, however, it by no means follows that the factor which is something negative and diminutive in its action between individuals, considered in a given direction and separately, has the same working throughout the totality of its relationships. In this larger circle of relationships the perspective may be quite different. That which was negative and dualistic may, after deduction of its destructive action in particular relationships, on the whole, play an entirely positive rôle. This visibly appears especially in those instances where the social structure is characterized by exactness and carefully conserved purity of social divisions and gradations. For instance, the social system of India rests not only upon the hierarchy of the castes, but also directly upon their reciprocal repulsion. Enmities not merely prevent gradual disappearance of the boundaries within the society —and for this reason these enmities may be consciously promoted, as guarantee of the existing social constitution—but more than this the enmities are directly productive sociologically. They give classes and personalities their position toward each other, which they would not have found if these objective *causes* of hostility had been present and effective in precisely the same way, but had not been accompanied by the feeling of enmity. It is by no means certain that a secure and complete community life would always result if these energies should disappear which, looked at in detail, seem repulsive and destructive, just as a qualitatively unchanged and richer property results when unproductive elements disappear; but there would ensue rather a condition as changed and often as unrealizable, as after the elimination of the forces of co-operation—sympathy, assistance, harmony of interests.

❖   ❖   ❖

The deepest hatred grows out of terminated love. In this case the decisive factor is not merely the susceptibility of difference, but principally the repudiation of one's own past, which is involved in such a revulsion of feeling. A profound love—one which is not merely sexual—recognized as a mistake and a misdirection of instinct, constitutes such an exposure of ourselves to ourselves, such a break in the security and unity of our self-consciousness, that we unavoidably make the object of this incompatibility the scapegoat of the error. It is a very convenient way to cover up the secret feeling of our own fault in the transaction, by the hatred which makes it easy for us to charge the whole responsibility upon the other party.

This peculiar bitterness of conflict in relationships in which from their very nature it is supposed that peace should reign, appears to be a positive confirmation of the matter of course that relationships show their intimacy and strength by the absence of differences. This matter of course, however, is by no means without its exceptions.

That in very intimate relationships, which control, or at least affect, the whole content of life—such, for example, as marriage—no occasions for conflicts emerge, is unthinkable. Never to yield to them, but to anticipate them from a distance, to insure against them in advance by reciprocal concession, is by no means always an affair of the most genuine and profound affinity, but it occurs rather in the case of sentiments which are affectionate to be sure, virtuous, and loyal, in which, however, the ultimate unlimited devotion of feeling is lacking. The individual in such instances may be conscious of inability to offer such devotion, and may be all the more anxious to preserve the relationship free from every shadow. He may consequently manifest the most extreme kindness, self-control, consideration, in order to compensate the other for any lack. All this may also be necessary, in particular, to quiet his own conscience because of slight or serious infidelity in his own attitude. Not even the most upright, or even the most passionate will is always able to escape such affections. This is because the whole is a matter of feelings, which as such are not amenable to the will, but come or go as forces of destiny. The perceived insecurity in the basis of such relationships frequently influences us, because of our wish to preserve the relationships at all costs, to exercise quite exaggerated unselfishness, and even to use mechanical guarantees of the situation, through avoidance on principle of every threatening conflict. In case one is certain of the immovability and unreserve of his own feeling, this absolute assurance of peace is by no means necessary. One knows that no shock could penetrate to the foundation of the relationship upon which there would not always be a revival of the attachment. The strongest love can best endure a blow, and the fear which troubles lesser affections, that they will not be able to endure the consequences of such a blow, and that it must consequently be avoided at all hazards, does not suggest itself to the stronger affection. In spite of the fact, therefore, that a feud between intimate friends may have more tragic consequences than between strangers, it appears from the foregoing analysis that the most deeply rooted relationship may come much easier to such a conflict, while many another which is good and moral, but rooted in inferior depths of feeling, may to all appearances run a course that is much more harmonious and free from conflict.

❄   ❄   ❄

Women recognize, as a rule, with reference to another woman, only complete inclusion or complete exclusion from the realm of morality. There exists among them the tendency so far as possible not to concede a breach of morality by a woman—to interpret it as harmless, except where love of scandal and other individual motives work in the other direction. If this assumption, however, is no longer possible, they render an irrevocable and severe judgment of exclusion from good society. If the violation of morality must be confessed, the culprit is also eliminated radically from that unity which is held together by the common interest for morality. We have seen, therefore, that women have sometimes passed the same condemnation upon Gretchen as upon Marguérite Gauthier, upon Stella as upon Messalina. Thus, by negation of differences in degree, they have made impossible an intermediation between those within and those outside the boundaries of morality. The defensive situation of women does not permit that the wall of morality be lowered at even a single point. Their party knows, in principle at least, no compromise, but only decisive acceptance of the individual into the ideal totality of "respectable women," or the equally decisive exclusion—an alternative whose abruptness cannot by any means be justified from the purely moral standpoint. It is only intelligible when understood in connection with the above-considered demand for inviolable unity, occasioned by the need of a party firmly consolidated against an opponent.

For the same reasons it may be advantageous for political parties to suffer even the diminution of their numbers, so soon as such change would remove elements inclined to mediation and compromise. In order that this procedure should be indicated, two conditions should usually coincide: in the first place, there should be a condition of acute conflict; in the second place, the struggling group should be relatively small. The type is the minority party, and in particular in cases in which it does not limit itself to defensive action. English parliamentary history has furnished many illustrations. In 1793, for instance, the Whig party was already greatly depleted, yet it operated as a renewal of strength when another defection of all the still somewhat mediating and irresolute elements occurred. The few remaining very resolute members could then pursue a quite coherent and radical policy. The majority group does not need to insist upon such certainty of acquiescence or opposition. Vacillating and equivocal adherents are less dangerous to it, because its greater extent can endure such phenomena at the periphery without suffering any serious effect at the center. In cases of more restricted groups, where center and circumference are not far apart, every insecurity with reference to a member at once threatens the nucleus, and therewith the coherence of the whole. On account of the limited span between the elements, there is lacking that elasticity of the group which in this case is the limit of tolerance.

Consequently groups, and especially minorities, that exist in struggle and persecution, frequently rebuff approaches and tolerance from the other side, because otherwise the solidity of their opposition would disappear, and without this they could not further struggle. This, for example, has occurred more than once in the struggles over creeds in England. Both under James II and William and Mary the nonconformists, independents, Baptists, Quakers, repeatedly experienced attempted approaches on the part of the government, which they met with no sort of response. Otherwise the possibility would have been offered to the more yielding and irresolute elements among them, and the temptation would have been furnished, to build compromise parties, or at least to have modified their opposition. Every concession on the part of the government, *provided it is only partial,* threatens that uniformity in the opposition of all the members, and therewith that unity of coherence, upon which a struggling minority must uncompromisingly insist. Accordingly, the unity of groups so frequently disappears if they have no more enemies. This has often been pointed out from various directions in the case of Protestantism. Just because the protest was essential to Protestantism, the moment the opponent against whom it protested passed out of the range of active struggle, it lost its energy or its inner unity; this latter in such a degree, indeed, that in such circumstances Protestantism repeated the conflict with the enemy in its own camp, and divided itself into a liberal and an orthodox party. The same thing has occurred in the party history of the United States. More than once the complete inferiority of one of the great parties has had as a consequence the dissolution of the other in minor groups with party antipathies of their own. Moreover, it is by no means promotive of the unity of Protestantism that it has really no heretics. On the other hand, the consciousness of unity in the Catholic church is decidedly strengthened by the fact of heresy and by its hostile attitude toward the same. The various elements of the church have always been able to orient themselves by the implacability of the antithesis with heresy, and in spite of many a centrifugal interest they have been by this fact able to preserve consciousness of unity. Hence the complete victory of a group over its enemies is not always fortunate in the sociological sense, for the consequence may be a decline of the energy which guarantees the coherence of the group, and, on the other hand, proportional activity of the disintegrating forces that are always at work. The fall of the Romano-Latin empire in the fifth century has been explained by the fact that the common enemies were all subdued. Perhaps its basis—namely, protection on the one side, and devotion on the other—had for a period been no longer of a natural sort; but this came to light only after there was no longer any common enemy to offset the essential contradictions in the structure. Indeed, it may be actual political sagacity within many a group to provide for enemies in order that the unity of the elements may remain active and conscious as the vital interest.

The example last cited leads to the following additional emphasis upon the meaning of struggle as a means of cohesion in the group: namely, through struggle not merely an existing unity concentrates itself more energetically, and excludes radically all elements which might tend to erase the sharp boundary distinctions against the enemy, but further struggle brings persons and groups that otherwise had nothing to do with each other into a coalition. The energy with which struggle operates in this direction will perhaps be most distinctly visible from the fact that the relationship between the two parties is strong enough to operate also in the reverse direction. Psychological associations in general display their strength in the fact that they are also retroactive. If, for example, a given personality is represented under the concept "hero," the connection between the two conceptions proves itself to be the strongest if it becomes impossible to think the notion "hero" in general without reproducing the image of that particular personality. In the same way, the combination for the purpose of struggle is a procedure so often experienced that frequently the mere combination of elements, even if it is not formed for any aggressive or other competitive purposes, seems to other groups to be a threatening or unfriendly act. The despotism of the modern state directed itself primarily against the mediæval conception of unity. At last every association, as such, between cities, ranks, nobles, or any other elements in the state, counted in the eyes of the government as a rebellion, as a latent struggle against itself. For instance, in Moravia an ordinance of 1628 provided: "Accordingly federations or coalitions, for whatever purpose, or against whomsoever directed, are the prerogative of no one else except the king." For the particular tendencies now in question historical instances are so close at hand that it would be superfluous to make any further inquiry, except as to the degree of unification which is feasible in this particular way. In the forefront must be placed the establishment of the unified state. France owes the consciousness of its national unity essentially to struggle against the English; the Moorish war was the means of converting the Spanish subdivisions into one community. The next lower grade is marked by the confederacies and leagues of states in the order of their coherence, and of the power of their central administration in manifold gradations. The United States required its War of the Rebellion, Switzerland its struggle against Austria, the Low Countries their uprising against Spain, the Achean League its war against Macedonia; and the founding of the new German Empire furnishes a parallel instance. In all these cases the characteristic element is that the unity came into being through the struggle and for the purposes of the same, to be sure; but, over and above the struggle, this unity persists, and develops ulterior interests and combinations, that have no connection with the warlike purpose. The significance of the struggle is in these cases virtually that it is only the reagent to set the latent relationship and unity into activity; it is thus much more the occasioning cause of essentially demanded unifications than their purpose. It is the latter, at the most, in the first moment. In the degree in which the unification is grounded in some other necessity than essential needs—that is, not in the immanent qualities and affinities of the elements— in precisely that degree does the meaning of the unity reduce, of course, to the militant purpose, as the externally exploited aim, which remains the irreducible element of the collectivity. However particularistic the component parts of a confederated state or a confederation of states may be, however small may be the proportion of their individual rights and liberties which they concede to the federation, they usually transfer to it at least the prerogative of waging war. This is the *pièce de résistance* of coherence; if this should fall away, the atoms would have to assume again their completely isolated life. *Within* the collective struggle-interest there is, to be sure, a still further gradation, namely, whether the unification for purposes of struggle is offensive and defensive, or only for defensive purposes. The latter is probably the case with the majority of coalitions between already existing groups, especially between numerous groups or those that are very different from each other. The defensive purpose is the collectivistic minimum, because for each particular group, and for each individual, it is the most inevitable form of the instinct of self-preservation. The more various the elements are which unite, the smaller is the visible number of the interests in which they coincide; and in the extreme case it reduces to the primitive impulse, namely, the ultimate instinct of self-preservation. In reply to expressions of anxiety on the part of the employers over the possible unification of all English trade organizations, one of their most ardent adherents asserted that even if it should go so far, it could be exclusively for defensive purposes alone.

Among the cases in which the solidifying effect of struggle is projected beyond the moment and the immediate purpose, which may occur in the case of the above discussed minimum of the same, the extension again sinks to the cases in which the unification actually occurs only *ad hoc.* Here two types are to be distinguished, namely: the federated unification for a single action, which, however, frequently involves the total energies of the elements as in the case of actual wars. In this case an unlimited unity is formed, which, however, after attaining, or failure in attaining, the definite purpose, releases the parties again for their previous separate existence, as, for instance, in the case of the Greeks, after the removal of the Persian danger. In the case of the other type the unity is less complete, but also less transient. The grouping takes place around a purpose which is less a matter of time than of content, and which occasions no disturbance of the other sides of the elements. Thus in England since 1873 there exists a federation of associated employers of labor, founded to antagonize the influence of the trades unions. In the same way, several years later, a combination of employers as such was formed in the United States, without reference to the various branches of business, in order, as a whole, to put an end to strikes. The character of both types appears, of course, most evidently when the elements of the struggling unity are, in other periods or in other relationships, not merely indifferent, but even hostile to each other. The unifying power of the struggle-principle never shows itself stronger than when it produces a temporal or actual consensus out of relationships of competition or animosity.

The antithesis between violent antagonism and momentary comradeship in struggle may, under particular circumstances, reach such refinement that, for the parties concerned, the very absoluteness of their enmity may constitute the direct cause of their coalition. The opposition in the English Parliament has sometimes been constituted in the following manner: The ultras of the ministerial party were not satisfied by the administration, and they joined as a party with those who were their opponents on principle. This combination was held together by the common element of hostility to the ministry. For instance, the ultra-Whigs under Pulteney united with the high Tories against Robert Walpole. Thus the very radicalism of the principle which was nourished on hostility against the Tories fused its adherents with the latter. If they had not been so extremely anti-Tory, they would not have combined with the Tories in order to secure the fall of the Whig ministry which was not sufficiently Whiggish for them. This case is so vivid because the common enemy led individuals who were otherwise enemies to the point where he, in the view of each, seemed to stand too much on the side of the other. Further than this, the case is still only the clearest example of the vulgar experience that even the most bitter enmities do not hinder coalition, so soon as it may have a bearing upon a common enemy.

Finally, the lowest step in this scale, its least acute form, consists of those coalitions which are merely formed by a common tone of feeling (*Stimmung*). That is, in this case there is consciousness of belonging together only in so far as there is a similar aversion or a similar practical interest against a third; but this need not lead to a concerted struggle. In this case also we must distinguish two types. Concentrated industry, which has placed masses of laborers in opposition to a few employers has, as we know, not merely brought into existence separate coalitions of the former for struggle over the conditions of labor, but another consequence has been the quite general feeling that all wage-laborers in some way belong together, because they are all in the struggle which is radically one against the employing class. This opinion crystallizes, to be sure, at certain points in distinct actions in the way of organizing political parties, or of wage-struggle.

Yet, as a whole, this feeling cannot, by reason of its very nature, become practical. It remains the feeling of an abstract principle of community, namely, that of common hostility against an abstract enemy. While in the former case the feeling of unity is abstract, but persistent, in the second case it is concrete, but temporary. This second case occurs, for instance, when strangers who, however, belong in the same plane of culture or the same sphere of sympathy, find themselves together in company, say in a railroad car or elsewhere, with other persons of uncouth and vulgar manners. Without any outbreak or scene, without any interchange of word or look, the former have certain awareness of themselves as a party joined by common aversion against what may be regarded as, at least in the ideal sense, the aggressive vulgarity of the others. Through its highly refined and sensitive character, with accompanying unequivocalness, this unification completes the structural grades of those who are brought from the condition of completely alien elements through the community of hostility. In case the synthetic energy of the latter is not in question, so far as the number of points of interest are concerned, but with reference to the permanence and intensity of the coalition, it is an especially favorable circumstance if, instead of actual struggle, permanent threatening by an enemy is present. From the first days of the Achean League, that is, about 270, it was emphasized that Achaia was surrounded by enemies, who all, however, for the time being were otherwise occupied than with attack upon Achaia. Such a period of danger which constantly threatened, but which was as constantly postponed, is said to have been especially favorable for the strengthening of the feeling of unity. This is a case of the unique type that a certain *distance* between the elements that are to be united, on the one hand, and the point and interest that unites them, on the other hand, is an especially favorable combination for the union. This is particularly the case when somewhat extended circles are concerned. This is true of religious relationships. In contrast with the tribal and national deities, the God of Christianity, who is equally related to all the world, is immeasurably removed from the faithful. He lacks entirely those traits which are attributed to the special divinities. On the other hand, for that very reason, he can unite the most heterogeneous peoples and personalities in an unprecedented religious community. Still further, the costume characterizes always distinct social strata as belonging together; and it often appears to fulfil this social function best when it is an imported costume. To dress as they dress in Paris signifies a close and exclusive community with a certain social stratum in other lands. The prophet Zephaniah spoke already of the superior classes, which as such wore foreign garments. The very manifold meanings which the notion of "distance" covers have still many sorts of psychological relationship. An image the object of which is presented as in any way "distant" appears to work in a certain degree more impersonally, the individual reaction which follows from immediate vicinity and contact is thereby less intense, it bears a less immediately subjective character, and may consequently be the same for

a greater number of individuals. Just as the general notion which compre-
hends a number of particulars is the more abstract, that is, the more widely
distant from each of these separate particulars, the more numerous and the
more unlike each other the latter are, so also a social point of unification
appears to exercise specifically consolidating and comprehensive influences,
if it is somewhat widely removed from the elements to be combined. This
interval may be also both spatial and of other sorts. Such unifications in
consequence of a danger which, however, has rather a chronic than an acute
character, through a struggle that is not fought out, but always latent, will
be most effective in cases where a permanent unification of elements that
are in some way antithetical is in question. This was the situation in the
case of the Achean League to which I have already referred. Accordingly,
Montesquieu observed that "while peace and confidence make the glory
and the security of the monarchy, a republic needs to be in fear of somebody." Obviously the basis for this assertion is an undefined consciousness
of the before-mentioned constellation. The monarchy as such takes care for
the cohesion of elements in any wise antagonistic. Where these elements,
however, have no one above them who brings them into unity, but possess
relative sovereignty, they will easily fall apart if no common sense of danger
forces them together—a danger which evidently is not presented as a struggle
already in existence, but as a permanent threat of such a struggle which
exerts a constant menace.

   While it is more a question of degree, the principle of connection between the coherence of the collectivity and hostility calls for the following
addition: Aggressive enterprises tend much more than peaceful ones to draw
into co-operation, from their very beginnings, the largest possible number
of elements which are otherwise unrelated, and which would not of themselves have begun the undertaking. In the case of peaceful actions, it is the
rule, on the whole, to be confined to those who in other respects are somewhat nearly associated. But for "allies," to which notion verbal usage has
already imparted a martial coloring, one selects often enough elements with
which one has scarcely anything in common, nor even wishes to have. Reasons for this fact are, in the first place, that war, and not merely the political type, frequently represents a case of desperation in which in selecting reinforcements one may not be finical. In the second place, the situation
in question is likely to occur if the object of the action lies outside of the
territory or other immediate interest-sphere of the allies, so that they may
return after the end of the struggle to their former distance. In the third
place, the gain to be made by struggle, although a precarious one, nevertheless under favorable circumstances is likely to be especially rapid and intensive, and consequently exercises upon certain natures a formal attraction
which it is possible for peaceful enterprises to exert only through their
content. In the fourth place, the struggle causes the essentially personal in
the parties in conflict to take a position of relative insignificance, and thereby
permits the unification of elements that are otherwise heterogeneous. There

comes finally, in addition, the motive that hostilities are easily aroused on both sides. Even within one and the same group, if it maintains a feud with another, all sorts of hidden or half-forgotten enmities of the individual against individuals in the other group come to expression. Accordingly, struggle between two groups within a third group usually evokes in this third group all the malice and resentment against one of them which of themselves would not have come to expression; but now, while the other hostility has led the way, they are occasioned as a sort of annex to the operation of this instigating hostility. It is quite in accordance with this trait that, especially in earlier times, the unifying relationships of populations as wholes to each other were martial only, while the other assimilations, like commerce, hospitality, intermarriage, were relationships which affected merely the intercourse of individuals. Understandings between the peoples made these relationships possible, to be sure, but did not of themselves put them into effect.

FURTHER READINGS

Cooley, Charles H., *Social Organization*. New York: Charles Scribner, 1915.

Coser, Lewis. *The Functions of Social Conflict*. New York: The Free Press, 1956.

Homans, George. *The Human Group*. New York: Harcourt, Brace & World, 1950.

Simmel, Georg. *The Sociology of Georg Simmel*. Trans. and ed. by Kurt Wolff. New York: The Free Press, 1950.

Whyte, William F., Jr. *Street Corner Society*. Chicago: University of Chicago Press, 1943. Phoenix Edition, 1955.

5

THE SELF AND INTERACTION

Introduction

CONCERN WITH UNDERSTANDING the nature of the self, particularly the role it plays in binding the person to the group, has required that sociologists maintain their interests in social psychology. Even Durkheim, who is often accused of ignoring the person and his more private sentiments, dealt with aspects of child training and discipline in his later works.

Dennis Wrong brings together some major themes in sociological theory to remind us that our conceptions of man ignore significant aspects of his nature. He presents us with a means for integrating ideas discussed in Chapter 3, The Normative and The Factual.

Charles Horton Cooley is best known for his concept, "The Looking-Glass Self," which is included among our excerpts from his classic work. In our first excerpt the idea of self is defined and described in its relationship to the social environment. The second excerpt provides a description of action in the process of self-emergence. It is one of the most lucid descriptions of this process in the classical sociological literature.

George Herbert Mead, whose works are also accepted as major classics, is best known for his studies of mind and self. Focusing on language and symbols and their functions in social interaction he shows us how man's acts are interrelated with the meanings associated with the communication process and the emergence of conscience.

Two of Mead's most significant concepts are role-playing and role-taking. This distinction differentiates between mental and behavioral processes. Walter Coutu clarifies the distinctions made in Mead's works and sensitizes us to the significance of these distinctions. Some of the issues dealt with by Bolton in Chapter 2 are anticipated in this early essay.

Herbert Blumer, in our final selection in this chapter, clarifies a number of issues surrounding Mead's social psychology. This lucid discussion provides a bridge between the purely social psychological aspects of Mead's approach and the philosophical implications of these ideas. As such they aid in bridging the gap between social science and philosophy, one of the goals of our effort to include issues associated with meaning (Chapter 6).

The Oversocialized Conception of Man in Modern Sociology

DENNIS H. WRONG

GERTRUDE STEIN, bed-ridden with a fatal illness, is reported to have suddenly muttered, "What, then, is the answer?" Pausing, she raised her head, murmured, "But what is the question?" and died. Miss Stein presumably was pondering the ultimate meaning of human life, but her brief final soliloquy has a broader and humbler relevance. Its point is that answers are meaningless apart from questions. If we forget the questions, even while remembering the answers, our knowledge of them will subtly deteriorate, becoming rigid, formal, and catechistic as the sense of indeterminacy, of rival possibilities, implied by the very putting of a question is lost.

Social theory must be seen primarily as a set of answers to questions we ask of social reality. If the initiating questions are forgotten, we readily misconstrue the task of theory and the answers previous thinkers have given become narrowly confining conceptual prisons, degenerating into little more than a special, professional vocabulary applied to situations and events that can be described with equal or greater precision in ordinary language. Forgetfulness of the questions that are the starting points of inquiry leads us to ignore the substantive assumptions "buried" in our concepts and commits us to a one-sided view of reality.

Perhaps this is simply an elaborate way of saying that sociological theory can never afford to lose what is usually called a "sense of significance"; or, as it is sometimes put, that sociological theory must be "problem-conscious." I choose instead to speak of theory as a set of answers to questions because reference to "problems" may seem to suggest too close a linkage with social criticism or reform. My primary reason for insisting on the necessity of holding constantly in mind the questions that our concepts and theories are designed to answer is to preclude defining the goal of sociological theory as the creation of a formal body of knowledge satis-

From *American Sociological Review*, 26, 1961, pp. 183-193. Reprinted by permission of the publisher and author.

fying the logical criteria of scientific theory set up by philosophers and methodologists of natural science. Needless to say, this is the way theory is often defined by contemporary sociologists.

Yet to speak of theory as interrogatory may suggest too self-sufficiently intellectual an enterprise. Cannot questions be satisfactorily answered and then forgotten, the answers becoming the assumptions from which we start in framing new questions? It may convey my view of theory more adequately to say that sociological theory concerns itself with questions arising out of problems that are inherent in the very existence of human societies and that cannot therefore be finally "solved" in the way that particular social problems perhaps can be. The "problems" theory concerns itself with are problems *for* human societies which, because of their universality, become intellectually problematic for sociological theorists.

Essentially, the historicist conception of sociological knowledge that is central to the thought of Max Weber and has recently been ably restated by Barrington Moore, Jr. and C. Wright Mills is a sound one. The most fruitful questions for sociology are always questions referring to the realities of a particular historical situation. Yet both of these writers, especially Mills, have a tendency to underemphasize the degree to which we genuinely wish and seek answers to trans-historical and universal questions about the nature of man and society. I do not, let it be clear, have in mind the formalistic quest for social "laws" or "universal propositions," nor the even more formalistic effort to construct all-encompassing "conceptual schemes." Moore and Mills are rightly critical of such efforts. I am thinking of such questions as "How are men capable of uniting to form enduring societies in the first place?"; "Why and to what degree is change inherent in human societies and what are the sources of change?"; "How is man's animal nature domesticated by society?"

Such questions—and they are existential as well as intellectual questions—are the *raison d'être* of social theory. They were asked by men long before the rise of sociology. Sociology itself is an effort, under new and unprecedented historical conditions, to find novel answers to them. They are not questions which lend themselves to successively more precise answers as a result of cumulative empirical research, for they remain eternally problematic. Social theory is necessarily an interminable dialogue. "True understanding," Hannah Arendt has written, "does not tire of interminable dialogue and 'vicious circles' because it trusts that imagination will eventually catch at least a glimpse of the always frightening light of truth."

I wish briefly to review the answers modern sociological theory offers to one such question, or rather to one aspect of one question. The question may be variously phrased as, "What are the sources of social cohesion?"; or, "How is social order possible?"; or, stated in social-psychological terms, "How is it that man becomes tractable to social discipline?" I shall call this question in its social-psychological aspect the "Hobbesian question" and in its more strictly sociological aspect the "Marxist question." The Hobbesian question asks how men are capable of the guidance by social norms and goals that makes possible an enduring society, while the Marxist question asks how, assuming this capability, complex societies manage to regulate and restrain destructive conflicts between groups. Much of our current theory offers an oversocialized view of man in answering the Hobbesian question and an overintegrated view of society in answering the Marxist question.

A number of writers have recently challenged the overintegrated view of society in contemporary theory. In addition to Moore and Mills, the names of Bendix, Coser, Dahrendorf, and Lockwood come to mind. My intention, therefore, is to concentrate on the answers to the Hobbesian question in an effort to disclose the oversocialized view of man which they seem to imply.

Since my view of theory is obviously very different from that of Talcott Parsons and has, in fact, been developed in opposition to his, let me pay tribute to his recognition of the importance of the Hobbesian question—the "problem of order," as he calls it—at the very beginning of his first book, *The Structure of Social Action.* Parsons correctly credits Hobbes with being the first thinker to see the necessity of explaining why human society is not a "war of all against all"; why, if man is simply a gifted animal, men refrain from unlimited resort to fraud and violence in pursuit of their ends and maintain a stable society at all. There is even a sense in which, as Coser and Mills have both noted, Parsons' entire work represents an effort to solve the Hobbesian problem of order. His solution, however, has tended to become precisely the kind of elaboration of a set of answers in abstraction from questions that is so characteristic of contemporary sociological theory.

We need not be greatly concerned with Hobbes' own solution to the problem of order he saw with such unsurpassed clarity. Whatever interest his famous theory of the origin of the state may still hold for political scientists, it is clearly inadequate as an explanation of the origin of society. Yet the pattern as opposed to the details of Hobbes' thought bears closer examination.

The polar terms in Hobbes' theory are the state of nature, where the war of all against all prevails, and the authority of Leviathan, created by social contract. But the war of all against all is not simply effaced with the creation of political authority: it remains an ever-present potentiality in human society, at times quiescent, at times erupting into open violence. Whether Hobbes believed that the state of nature and the social contract were ever historical realities—and there is evidence that he was not that simple-minded and unsociological, even in the seventeenth century—is unimportant; the whole tenor of his thought is to see the war of all against all and Leviathan dialectically, as coexisting and interacting opposites. As R. G. Collingwood has observed, "According to Hobbes . . . *a body politic is a dialectical thing,* a Heraclitean world in which at any given time there is a negative element." The first secular social theorist in the history of

Western thought, and one of the first clearly to discern and define the problem of order in human society long before Darwinism made awareness of it a commonplace, Hobbes was a dialectical thinker who refused to separate answers from questions, solutions to society's enduring problems from the conditions creating the problems.

What is the answer of contemporary sociological theory to the Hobbesian question? There are two main answers, each of which has come to be understood in a way that denies the reality and meaningfulness of the question. Together they constitute a model of human nature, sometimes clearly stated, more often implicit in accepted concepts, that pervades modern sociology. The first answer is summed up in the notion of the "internalization of social norms." The second, more commonly employed or assumed in empirical research, is the view that man is essentially motivated by the desire to achieve a positive image of self by winning acceptance or status in the eyes of others.

The following statement represents, briefly and broadly, what is probably the most influential contemporary sociological conception—and dismissal—of the Hobbesian problem: "To a modern sociologist imbued with the conception that action follows institutionalized patterns, opposition of individual and common interests has only a very limited relevance or is thoroughly unsound." From this writer's perspective, the problem is an unreal one: human conduct is totally shaped by common norms or "institutionalized patterns." Sheer ignorances must have led people who were unfortunate enough not to be modern sociologists to ask, "How is order possible?" A thoughtful bee or ant would never inquire, "How is the social order of the hive or ant-hill possible?" for the opposite of that order is unimaginable when the instinctive endowment of the insects ensures its stability and built-in harmony between "individual and common interests." Human society, we are assured, is not essentially different, although conformity and stability are there maintained by non-instinctive processes. Modern sociologists believe that they have understood these processes and that they have not merely answered but disposed of the Hobbesian question, showing that, far from expressing a valid intimation of the tensions and possibilities of social life, it can only be asked out of ignorance.

It would be hard to find a better illustration of what Collingwood, following Plato, calls *eristical* as opposed to dialectical thinking: the answer destroys the question, or rather destroys the awareness of rival possibilities suggested by the question which accounts for its having been asked in the first place. A reversal of perspective now takes place and we are moved to ask the opposite question: "How is it that violence, conflict, revolution, and the individual's sense of coercion by society manage to exist at all, if this view is correct?" Whenever a one-sided answer to a question compels us to raise the opposite question, we are caught up in a dialectic of concepts which reflects a dialectic in things. But let us examine the particular processes sociologists appeal to in order to account for the elimination from human society of the war of all against all.

THE CHANGING MEANING OF INTERNALIZATION

A well-known section of *The Structure of Social Action,* devoted to the interpretation of Durkheim's thought, is entitled "The Changing Meaning of Constraint." Parsons argues that Durkheim originally conceived of society as controlling the individual from the outside by imposing constraints on him through sanctions, best illustrated by codes of law. But in Durkheim's later work he began to see that social rules do not "merely regulate 'externally' . . . they enter directly into the constitution of the actors' ends themselves." Constraint, therefore, is more than an environmental obstacle which the actor must take into account in pursuit of his goals in the same way that he takes into account physical laws: it becomes internal, psychological, and self-imposed as well. Parsons developed this view that social norms are constitutive rather than merely regulative of human nature before he was influenced by psychoanalytic theory, but Freud's theory of the superego has become the source and model for the conception of the internalization of social norms that today plays so important a part in sociological thinking. The use some sociologists have made of Freud's idea, however, might well inspire an essay entitled, "The Changing Meaning of Internalization," although, in contrast to the shift in Durkheim's view of constraint, this change has been a change for the worse.

What has happened is that internalization has imperceptibly been equated with "learning," or even with "habit-formation" in the simplest sense. Thus when a norm is said to have been "internalized" by an individual, what is frequently meant is that he habitually both affirms it and conforms to it in his conduct. The whole stress on inner conflict, on the tension between powerful impulses and superego controls the behavioral outcome of which cannot be prejudged, drops out of the picture. And it is this that is central to Freud's view, for in psychoanalytic terms to say that a norm has been internalized, or introjected to become part of the superego, is to say no more than that a person will suffer guilt-feelings if he fails to live up to it, not that he will in fact live up to it in his behavior.

The relation between internalization and conformity assumed by most sociologists is suggested by the following passage from a recent, highly praised advanced textbook: "Conformity to institutionalized norms is, of course, 'normal.' The actor, having internalized the norms, feels something like a need to conform. His conscience would bother him if he did not." What is overlooked here is that the person who conforms may be even more "bothered," that is, subject to guilt and neurosis, than the person who violates what are not only society's norms but his own as well. To Freud, it is precisely the man with the strictest superego, he who has most thoroughly internalized and conformed to the norms of his society, who is most wracked with guilt and anxiety.

Paul Kecskemeti, to whose discussion I owe initial recognition of the erroneous view of internalization held by sociologists, argues that the relations between social norms, the individual's selection from them, his conduct, and his feelings about his conduct are far from self-evident. "It is by no means true," he writes, "to say that acting counter to one's own norms always or almost always leads to neurosis. One might assume that neurosis develops even more easily in persons who *never* violate the moral code they recognize as valid but repress and frustrate some strong instinctual motive. A person who 'succumbs to temptation,' feels guilt, and then 'purges himself' of his guilt in some reliable way (e.g., by confession) may achieve in this way a better balance, and be less neurotic, than a person who never violates his 'norms' and never feels conscious guilt."

Recent discussions of "deviant behavior" have been compelled to recognize these distinctions between social demands, personal attitudes towards them, and actual conduct, although they have done so in a laboriously taxonomic fashion. They represent, however, largely the rediscovery of what was always central to the Freudian concept of the superego. The main explanatory function of the concept is to show how people repress themselves, imposing checks on their own desires and thus turning the inner life into a battlefield of conflicting motives, no matter which side "wins," by successfully dictating overt action. So far as behavior is concerned, the psychoanalytic view of man is less deterministic than the sociological. For psychoanalysis is primarily concerned with the inner life, not with overt behavior, and its most fundamental insight is that the wish, the emotion, and the fantasy are as important as the act in man's experience.

Sociologists have appropriated the superego concept, but have separated it from any equivalent of the Freudian id. So long as most individuals are "socialized," that is, internalize the norms and conform to them in conduct, the Hobbesian problem is not even perceived as a latent reality. Deviant behavior is accounted for by special circumstances: ambiguous norms, anomie, role conflict, or greater cultural stress on valued goals than on the approved means for attaining them. Tendencies to deviant behavior are not seen as dialectically related to conformity. The presence in man of motivational forces bucking against the hold social discipline has over him is denied.

Nor does the assumption that internalization of norms and roles is the essence of socialization allow for a sufficient range of motives underlying conformity. It fails to allow for variable "tonicity of the superego," in Kardiner's phrase. The degree to which conformity is frequently the result of coercion rather than conviction is minimized. Either someone has internalized the norms, or he is "unsocialized," a feral or socially isolated child, or a psychopath. Yet Freud recognized that many people, conceivably a majority, fail to acquire superegos. "Such people," he wrote, "habitually permit themselves to do any bad deed that procures them something they want, if only they are sure that no authority will discover it or make them suffer for it; their anxiety relates only to the possibility of detection. Present-day society has to take into account the prevalence of this state of mind." The last sentence suggests that Freud was aware of the decline of "inner-direction," of the Protestant conscience, about which we have heard so much lately. So let us turn to the other elements of human nature that sociologists appeal to in order to explain, or rather explain away, the Hobbesian problem.

MAN THE ACCEPTANCE-SEEKER

The superego concept is too inflexible, too bound to the past and to individual biography, to be of service in relating conduct to the pressures of the immediate situation in which it takes place. Sociologists rely more heavily therefore on an alternative notion, here stated—or, to be fair, over-stated—in its baldest form: "People are so profoundly sensitive to the expectations of others that all action is inevitably guided by these expectations."

Parsons' model of the "complementarity of expectations," the view that in social interaction men mutually seek approval from one another by conforming to shared norms, is a formalized version of what has tended to become a distinctive sociological perspective on human motivation. Ralph Linton states it in explicit psychological terms: "The need for eliciting favorable responses from others is an almost constant component [of personality]. Indeed, it is not too much to say that there is very little organized human behavior which is not directed toward its satisfaction in at least some degree."

The insistence of sociologists on the importance of "social factors" easily leads them to stress the priority of such socialized or socializing motives in human behavior. It is frequently the task of the sociologist to call attention to the intensity with which men desire and strive for the good opinion of their immediate associates in a variety of situations, particularly those where received theories or ideologies have unduly emphasized other motives such as financial gain, commitment to ideals, or the effects on energies and aspirations of arduous physical conditions. Thus sociologists have shown that factory workers are more sensitive to the attitudes of their fellow-workers than to purely economic incentives; that voters are more influenced by the preferences of their relatives and friends than by campaign debates on the "issues"; that soldiers, whatever their ideological commitment to their nation's cause, fight more bravely when their platoons are intact and they stand side by side with their "buddies."

It is certainly not my intention to criticize the findings of such studies. My objection is that their particular selective emphasis is generalized—explicitly or, more often, implicitly—to provide apparent empirical support for an extremely one-sided view of human nature. Although sociologists have criticized past efforts to single out one fundamental motive in human conduct, the desire to achieve a favorable self-image by winning approval from others frequently occupies such a position in their own thinking. The following "theorem" has been, in fact, openly put forward by Hans Zetterberg as "a strong contender for the position as the major Motivational Theorem in sociology":

> An actor's actions have a tendency to become dispositions that are related to the occurence [sic] of favored uniform evaluations of the actor and-or his actions in his action system.

Now Zetterberg is not necessarily maintaining that this theorem is an accurate factual statement of the basic psychological roots of social behavior. He is, characteristically, far too self-conscious about the logic of theorizing and "concept formation" for that. He goes on to remark that "the maximization of favorable attitudes from others would thus be the counterpart in sociological theory to the maximization of profit in economic theory." If by this it is meant that the theorem is to be understood as a heuristic rather than an empirical assumption, that sociology has a selective point of view which is just as abstract and partial as that of economics and the other social sciences, and if his view of theory as a set of logically connected formal propositions is granted provisional acceptance, I am in agreement. (Actually, the view of theory suggested at the beginning of this paper is a quite different one.)

But there is a further point to be made. Ralf Dahrendorf has observed that structural-functional theorists do not "claim that order *is based on* a general consensus of values, but that it *can be conceived of in terms of* such consensus and that, if it is conceived of in these terms, certain propositions follow which are subject to the test of specific observations." The same may be said of the assumption that people seek to maximize favorable evaluations by others; indeed this assumption has already fathered such additional concepts as "reference group" and "circle of significant others." Yet the question must be raised as to whether we really wish to, in effect, define sociology by such partial perspectives. The assumption of the maximization of approval from others is the psychological complement to the sociological assumption of a general value consensus. And the former is as selective and one-sided a way of looking at motivation as Dahrendorf and others have argued the latter to be when it determines our way of looking at social structure. The oversocialized view of man of the one is a counterpart to the overintegrated view of society of the other.

Modern sociology, after all, originated as a protest against the partial views of man contained in such doctrines as utilitarianism, classical economics, social Darwinism, and vulgar Marxism. All of the great nineteenth and early twentieth century sociologists saw it as one of their major tasks to expose the unreality of such abstractions as economic man, the gain-seeker of the classical economists; political man, the power-seeker of the Machiavellian tradition in political science; self-preserving man, the security-seeker of Hobbes and Darwin; sexual or libidinal man, the pleasure-seeker of doctrinaire Freudianism; and even religious man, the God-seeker of the theologians. It would be ironical if it should turn out that they have merely contributed to the creation of yet another reified abstraction in socialized man, the status-seeker of our contemporary sociologists.

Of course, such an image of man is, like all the others mentioned, valuable for limited purposes so long as it is not taken for the whole truth. What are some of its deficiencies? To begin with, it neglects the other half of the model of human nature presupposed by current theory: moral man, guided by his built-in superego and beckoning ego-ideal. In recent years sociologists have been less interested than they once were in culture and national character as backgrounds to conduct, partly because stress on the concept of "role" as the crucial link between the individual and the social structure has directed their attention to the immediate situation in which social interaction takes place. Man is increasingly seen as a "role-playing" creature, responding eagerly or anxiously to the expectations of other role-players in the multiple group settings in which he finds himself. Such an approach, while valuable in helping us grasp the complexity of a highly differentiated social structure such as our own, is far too often generalized to serve as a kind of *ad hoc* social psychology, easily adaptable to particular sociological purposes.

But it is not enough to concede that men often pursue "internalized values" remaining indifferent to what others think of them, particularly when, as I have previously argued, the idea of internalization has been "hollowed out" to make it more useful as an explanation of conformity. What of desire for material and sensual satisfactions? Can we really dispense with the venerable notion of material "interests" and invariably replace it with the blander, more integrative "social values"? And what of striving for power, not necessarily for its own sake—that may be rare and pathological—but as a means by which men are able to *impose* a normative definition of reality on others? That material interests, sexual drives, and the quest for power have often been overestimated as human motives is no reason to deny their reality. To do so is to suppress one term of the dialectic between conformity and rebellion, social norms and their violation, man and social order, as completely as the other term is suppressed by those who deny the reality of man's "normative orientation" or reduce it to the effect of coercion, rational calculation, or mechanical conditioning.

The view that man is invariably pushed by internalized norms or pulled by the lure of self-validation by others ignores—to speak archaically for a moment—both the highest and the lowest, both beast and angel, in his nature. Durkheim, from whom so much of the modern sociological point of view derives, recognized that the very existence of a social norm implies and even creates the possibility of its violation. This is the meaning of his famous dictum that crime is a "normal phenomenon." He maintained that "for the originality of the idealist whose dreams transcend his century to find expression, it is necessary that the originality of the criminal, who is below the level of his time, shall also be possible. One does not occur without the other." Yet Durkheim lacked an adequate psychology and formulated his insight in terms of the actor's cognitive awareness rather than in motivational terms. We do not have Durkheim's excuse for falling back on what Homans has called a "social mold theory" of human nature.

SOCIAL BUT NOT ENTIRELY SOCIALIZED

I have referred to forces in man that are resistant to socialization. It is not my purpose to explore the nature of these forces or to suggest how we ought best conceive of them as sociologists—that would be a most ambitious undertaking. A few remarks will have to suffice. I think we must start with the recognition that *in the beginning there is the body.* As soon as the body is mentioned the specter of "biological determinism" raises its head and sociologists draw back in fright. And certainly their view of man is sufficiently disembodied and non-materialistic to satisfy Bishop Berkeley, as well as being de-sexualized enough to please Mrs. Grundy.

Am I, then, urging us to return to the older view of a human nature divided between a "social man" and a "natural man" who is either benevolent, Rousseau's Noble Savage, or sinister and destructive, as Hobbes regarded him? Freud is usually represented, or misrepresented, as the chief modern proponent of this dualistic conception which assigns to the social order the purely negative role of blocking and re-directing man's "imperious biological drives." I say "misrepresented" because, although Freud often said things supporting such an interpretation, other and more fundamental strains in his thinking suggest a different conclusion. John Dollard, certainly not a writer who is oblivious to social and cultural "factors," saw this twenty-five years ago: "It is quite clear," he wrote, ". . . that he [Freud] does not regard the instincts as having a fixed social goal; rather, indeed, in the case of the sexual instinct he has stressed the vague but powerful and impulsive nature of the drive and has emphasized that its proper social object is not picked out in advance. His seems to be a drive concept which is not at variance with our knowledge from comparative cultural studies, since his theory does not demand that the 'instinct' work itself out with mechanical certainty alike in every varying culture."

So much for Freud's "imperious biological drives"! When Freud defined psychoanalysis as the study of the "vicissitudes of the instincts," he was confirming, not denying, the "plasticity" of human nature insisted on by social scientists. The drives or "instincts" of psychoanalysis, far from being fixed dispositions to behave in a particular way, are utterly subject to social channelling and transformation and could not even reveal themselves in behavior without social molding any more than our vocal chords can produce articulate speech if we have not learned a language. To psychoanalysis man is indeed a social animal; his social nature is profoundly reflected in his bodily structure.

But there is a difference between the Freudian view on the one hand and both sociological and neo-Freudian conceptions of man on the other. To Freud man is a *social* animal without being entirely a *socialized* animal. His very social nature is the source of conflicts and antagonisms that create resistance to socialization by the norms of any of the societies which have existed in the course of human history. "Socialization" may mean two quite distinct things; when they are confused an oversocialized view of man is the result. On the one hand socialization means the "transmission of the culture," the particular culture of the society an individual enters at birth; on the other hand the term is used to mean the "process of becoming human," of acquiring uniquely human attributes from interaction with others. All men are socialized in the latter sense, but this does not mean that they have been completely molded by the particular norms and values of their culture. All cultures, as Freud contended, do violence to man's socialized bodily drives, but this in no sense means that men could possibly exist without culture or independently of society. From such a standpoint, man may properly be called as Norman Brown has called him, the "neurotic" or the "discontented" animal and repression may be seen as the main characteristic of human nature as we have known it in history.

But isn't this psychology and haven't sociologists been taught to forswear psychology, to look with suspicion on what are called "psychological variables" in contradistinction to the institutional and historical forces with which they are properly concerned? There is, indeed, as recent critics have complained, too much "psychologism" in contemporary sociology, largely, I think, because of the bias inherent in our favored research techniques. But I do not see how, at the level of theory, sociologists can fail to make assumptions about human nature. If our assumptions are left implicit, we will inevitably presuppose of a view of man that is tailor-made to our special needs; when our sociological theory overstresses the stability and integration of society we will end up imagining that man is the disembodied, conscience-driven, status-seeking phantom of current theory. We must do better if we really wish to win credit outside of our ranks for special understanding of man, that plausible creature whose wagging tongue so often hides the despair and darkness in his heart.

Sociability

CHARLES H. COOLEY

To any but a mother a new-born child hardly seems human. It appears rather to be a strange little animal, wonderful indeed, exquisitely finished even to the finger-nails; mysterious, awakening a fresh sense of our ignorance of the nearest things of life, but not friendly, not lovable. It is only after some days that a kindly nature begins to express itself and to grow into something that can be sympathized with and personally cared for. The earliest signs of it are chiefly certain smiles and babbling sounds, which are a matter of fascinating observation to anyone interested in the genesis of social feeling.

Spasmodic smiles or grimaces occur even during the first week of life, and at first seem to mean nothing in particular. I have watched the face of an infant a week old while a variety of expressions, smiles, frowns, and so on, passed over it in rapid succession; it was as if the child were rehearsing a repertory of emotional expression belonging to it by instinct. So soon as they can be connected with anything definite these rudimentary smiles appear to be a sign of satisfaction. They soon begin to connect themselves quite definitely with sensible objects, such as bright color, voices, movements, and fondling. At the same time the smile gradually develops from a grimace into a subtler, more human expression. When a child is, say, five months old, no doubt can remain, in most cases, that the smile has become an expression of pleasure in the movements, sounds, touches, and general appearance of other people. It would seem, however, that personal feeling is not at first clearly differentiated from pleasures of sight, sound, and touch of other origin, or from animal satisfactions having no obvious cause. Both of my children expended much of their early sociability on inanimate objects, such as a red Japanese screen, a swinging lamp, a bright door-knob, an orange, and the like, babbling and smiling at them for many minutes at a time; and M., when about three months old and later, would often lie awake laughing and chattering in the dead of night. The general impression left upon one is that the early manifestations of sociability indicate less fellow-feeling than the adult imagination likes to impute, but are expressions of a pleasure which persons excite chiefly because they offer such a variety of stimuli to sight, hearing, and touch; or, to put it otherwise, kindliness, while existing almost from the first, is vague and undiscriminating, has not yet become fixed upon its proper objects, but flows out upon all the pleasantness the child finds about him, like that of St. Francis, when, in his "Canticle of the Sun," he addresses the sun and the moon, stars, winds, clouds, fire, earth, and water, as brothers and sisters. Indeed, there is nothing about personal feeling which sharply marks it off from other feeling; here as elsewhere we find no fences, but gradual transition, progressive differentiation.

I do not think that early smiles are imitative. I observed both my children carefully to discover whether they smiled in response to a smile, and obtained negative results when they were under ten months old. A baby does not smile by imitation, but because he is pleased; and what pleases him in the first year of life is usually some rather obvious stimulus to the senses. If you wish a smile you must earn it by acceptable exertion; it does no good to smirk. The belief that many people seem to have that infants respond to smiling is possibly due to the fact that when a grown-up person appears, both he and the infant are likely to smile, each at the other; but although the smiles are simultaneous one need not be the cause of the other, and many observations lead me to think that it makes no difference to the infant whether the grown-up person smiles or not. He has not yet learned to appreciate this rather subtle phenomenon.

At this and at all later ages the delight in companionship so evident in children may be ascribed partly to specific social emotion or sentiment, and partly to a need of stimulating suggestions to enable them to gratify their instinct for various sorts of mental and physical activity. The influence of the latter appears in their marked preference for active persons, for grown-up people who will play with them—provided they do so with tact—and especially for other children. It is the same throughout life; alone one is like fireworks without a match: he cannot set himself off, but is a victim of *ennui*, the prisoner of some tiresome train of thought that holds his mind simply by the absence of a competitor. A good companion brings release and fresh activity, the primal delight in a fuller existence. So with the child: what excitement when visiting children come! He shouts, laughs, jumps about, produces his playthings and all his accomplishments. He needs to express himself, and a companion enables him to do so. The shout of another boy in the distance gives him the joy of shouting in response.

But the need is for something more than muscular or sensory activities. There is also a need of feeling, an overflowing of personal emotion and sentiment, set free by the act of communication. By the time a child is a year old the social feeling that at first is indistinguishable from sensuous pleasure has become much specialized upon persons, and from that time onward to call it forth by reciprocation is a chief aim of his life. Perhaps it will not be out of place to emphasize this by transcribing two or three notes taken from life.

M. will now [eleven months old] hold up something she has found, *e.g.*, the petal of a flower, or a little stick, demanding your attention to it by grunts and squeals. When you look and make some motion or exclamation she smiles.

R. [four years old] talks all day long, to real companions, if they will listen, if not to imaginary ones. As I sit on the steps this morning he seems to wish me to share his every thought and sensation. He describes everything he does, although I can see it, saying, "Now I'm digging up little stones," etc. I must look at the butterfly, feel of the fuzz on the clover stems, and try to squawk on the dandelion stems. Meanwhile he is reminded of what happened some other time, and he gives me various anecdotes of what he and other people did and said. He thinks aloud. If I seem not to listen he presently notices it and will come up and touch me, or bend over and look up into my face.

R. [about the same time] is hilariously delighted and excited when he can get anyone to laugh or wonder with him at his pictures, etc. He himself always shares by anticipation, and exaggerates the feeling he expects to produce. When B. was calling, R., with his usual desire to entertain guests, brought out his pull-book, in which pulling a strip of pasteboard transforms the picture. When he prepared to work this he was actually shaking with eagerness—apparently in anticipation of the coming surprise.

I watch E. and R. [four and a half years old] playing McGinty on the couch and guessing what card will turn up. R. is in a state of intense excitement which breaks out in boisterous laughter and all sorts of movements of the head and limbs. He is full of an emotion which has very little to do with mere curiosity or surprise relating to the card.

I take it that the child has by heredity a generous capacity and need for social feeling, rather too vague and plastic to be given any specific name like love. It is not so much any particular personal emotion or sentiment as the undifferentiated material of many: perhaps sociability is as good a word for it as any.

And this material, like all other instinct, allies itself with social experience to form, as time goes on, a growing and diversifying body of personal thought, in which the phases of social feeling developed correspond, in some measure, to the complexity of life itself. It is a process of organization, involving progressive differentiation and integration, such as we see everywhere in nature.

In children and in simple-minded adults, kindly feeling may be very strong and yet very naïve, involving little insight into the emotional states of others. A child who is extremely sociable, bubbling over with joy in companionship, may yet show a total incomprehension of pain and a scant regard for disapproval and punishment that does not take the form of a cessation of intercourse. In other words, there is a sociability that asks little from others except bodily presence and an occasional sign of attention, and often learns to supply even these by imagination. It seems nearly or quite independent of that power of interpretation which is the starting-point of true sympathy. While both of my children were extremely sociable, R. was not at all sympathetic in the sense of having quick insight into others' states of feeling.

Sociability in this simple form is an innocent, unself-conscious joy, primary and unmoral, like all simple emotion. It may shine with full brightness from the faces of idiots and imbeciles, where it sometimes alternates with fear, rage, or lust. A visitor to an institution where large numbers of these classes are collected will be impressed, as I have been, with the fact that they are as a rule amply endowed with those kindly impulses which some appear to look upon as almost the sole requisite for human welfare. It is a singular and moving fact that there is a class of cases, mostly women, I think, in whom kindly emotion is so excitable as to be a frequent source of hysterical spasms, so that it has to be discouraged by frowns and apparent harshness on the part of those in charge. The chief difference between normal people and imbeciles in this regard is that, while the former have more or less of this simple kindliness in them, social emotion is also elaborately compounded and worked up by the mind into an indefinite number of complex passions and sentiments, corresponding to the relations and functions of an intricate life.

When left to themselves children continue the joys of sociability by means of an imaginary playmate. Although all must have noticed this who have observed children at all, only close and constant observation will enable one to realize the extent to which it is carried on. It is not an occasional practice, but, rather, a necessary form of thought, flowing from a life in which personal communication is the chief interest and social feeling the stream in which, like boats on a river, most other feelings float. Some children appear to live in personal imaginations almost from the first month; others occupy their minds in early infancy mostly with solitary experiments upon blocks, cards, and other impersonal objects, and their thoughts are doubtless filled with the images of these. But, in either case, after a child learns to talk and the social world in all its wonder and provocation opens on his mind, it floods his imagination so that all his thoughts are conversations. He is never alone. Sometimes the inaudible interlocutor is recognizable as the image of a tangible playmate, sometimes he appears to be purely imaginary. Of course each child has his own peculiarities. R., beginning when about three years of age, almost invariably talked aloud while he was playing alone—which, as he was a first child, was very often the case. Most commonly he would use no form of address but "you," and perhaps had no definite person in mind. To listen to him was like hearing one at the telephone; though occasionally he would give both sides of the conversation. At times again he would be calling upon some real name, Esyllt or Dorothy, or upon "Piggy," a fanciful person of his own invention. Every thought seemed to be spoken out. If his mother called him he would say, "I've got to go in now." Once when he slipped down on the floor he was heard to say, "Did you tumble down? No. *I* did."

The main point to note here is that these conversations are not occasional and temporary effusions of the imagination, but are the naïve expression of a socialization of the mind that is to be permanent and to underlie all later thinking. The imaginary dialogue passes beyond the thinking aloud of little children into something more elaborate, reticent, and sophisticated; but it never ceases. Grown people, like children, are usually unconscious of these dialogues; as we get older we cease, for the most part, to carry them on out loud, and some of us practice a good deal of apparently solitary meditation and experiment. But, speaking broadly, it is true of adults as of children, that the mind lives in perpetual conversation. It is one of those things that we seldom notice just because they are so familiar and involuntary; but we can perceive it if we try to. If one suddenly stops and takes note of his thoughts at some time when his mind has been running free, as when he is busy with some simple mechanical work, he will be likely to find them taking the form of vague conversations. This is particularly true when one is somewhat excited with reference to a social situation. If he feels under accusation or suspicion in any way he will probably find himself making a defense, or perhaps a confession, to an imaginary hearer. A guilty man confesses "to get the load off his mind"; that is to say, the excitement of his thought cannot stop there but extends to the connected impulses of expression and creates an intense need to tell somebody. Impulsive people often talk out loud when excited, either "to themselves," as we say when we can see no one else present, or to anyone whom they can get to listen. Dreams also consist very largely of imaginary conversations; and, with some people at least, the mind runs in dialogue during the half-waking state before going to sleep. There are many other familiar facts that bear the same interpretation—such, for instance, as that it is much easier for most people to compose in the form of letters or dialogue than in any other; so that literature of this kind has been common in all ages.

Goethe, in giving an account of how he came to write "Werther" as a series of letters, discusses the matter with his usual perspicuity, and lets us see how habitually conversational was his way of thinking. Speaking of himself in the third person, he says: "Accustomed to pass his time most pleasantly in society, he changed even solitary thought into social converse, and this in the following manner: He had the habit, when he was alone, of calling before his mind any person of his acquaintance. This person he entreated to sit down, walked up and down by him, remained standing before him, and discoursed with him on the subject he had in mind. To this the person answered as occasion required, or by the ordinary gestures signified his assent or dissent—in which every man has something peculiar to himself. The speaker then continued to carry out further that which seemed to please the guest, or to condition and define more closely that of which he disapproved; and finally was polite enough to give up his own notion. . . . How nearly such a dialogue is akin to a written correspondence is clear enough; only in the latter one sees returned the confidence one has bestowed, while in the former one creates for himself a confidence which is new, ever-changing and unreturned." "Accustomed to pass his time most pleasantly in society, he changed even solitary thought into social converse," is not only a particular but a general truth, more or less applicable to all thought. The fact is that language, developed by the race through personal intercourse and imparted to the individual in the same way, can never be dissociated from personal intercourse in the mind; and since higher thought involves language, it is always a kind of imaginary conversation. The word and the interlocutor are correlative ideas.

The impulse to communicate is not so much a result of thought as it is an inseparable part of it. They are like root and branch, two phases of a common growth, so that the death of one presently involves that of the other. Psychologists now teach that every thought involves an active impulse as part of its very nature; and this impulse, with reference to the more complex and socially developed forms of thought, takes the shape of a need to talk, to write, and so on; and if none of these is practicable, it expends itself in a wholly imaginary communication.

Montaigne, who understood human nature as well, perhaps, as anyone who ever lived, remarks: "There is no pleasure to me without communication: there is not so much as a sprightly thought comes into my mind that it does not grieve me to have produced alone, and that I have no one to tell it to." And it was doubtless because he had many such thoughts which no one was at hand to appreciate, that he took to writing essays. The uncomprehended of all times and peoples have kept diaries for the same reason. So, in general, a true creative impulse in literature or art is, in one aspect, an expression of this simple, childlike need to think aloud or *to* somebody; to define and vivify thought by imparting it to an imaginary companion; by developing that communicative element which belongs to its very nature, and without which it cannot live and grow. Many authors have confessed that they always think of some person when they write, and I am inclined to believe that this is always more or less definitely the case, though the writer himself may not be aware of it. Emerson somewhere says that "the man is but half himself; the other half is his expression," and this is literally true. The man comes to be through some sort of expression, and has no higher existence apart from it; overt or imaginary it takes place all the time.

Men apparently solitary, like Thoreau, are often the best illustrations of the inseparability of thought and life from communication. No sympathetic reader of his works, I should say, can fail to see that he took to the woods and fields not because he lacked sociability, but precisely because his sensibilities were so keen that he needed to rest and protect them by a peculiar mode of life, and to express them by the indirect and considerate method of literature. No man ever labored more passionately to communicate, to give and receive adequate expression, than he did. This may be read between the lines in all his works, and is recorded in his diary. "I would fain communicate the wealth of my life to men, would really give them what is most precious in my gift. I would secrete pearls with the shell-fish and lay up honey with the bees for them. I will sift the sunbeams for the public good. I know no riches I would keep back. I have no private good unless it be my peculiar ability to serve the public. This is the only individual property. Each one may thus be innocently rich. I enclose and foster the pearl till it is grown. I wish to communicate those parts of my life which I would gladly live again." This shows, I think, a just notion of the relation between the individual and society, privacy and publicity. There is, in fact, a great deal of sound sociology in Thoreau.

Since, therefore, the need to impart is of this primary and essential character, we ought not to look upon it as something separable from and additional to the need to think or to be; it is only by imparting that one is enabled to think or to be. Everyone, in proportion to his natural vigor, necessarily strives to communicate to others that part of his life which he is trying to unfold in himself. It is a matter of self-preservation, because without expression thought cannot live. Imaginary conversation—that is, conversation carried on without the stimulus of a visible and audible response —may satisfy the needs of the mind for a long time. There is, indeed, an advantage to a vigorously constructive and yet impressible imagination in restricting communication; because in this way ideas are enabled to have a clearer and more independent development than they could have if continually disturbed by criticism or opposition. Thus artists, men of letters, and productive minds of all sorts often find it better to keep their productions to themselves until they are fully matured. But, after all, the response must come sooner or later or thought itself will perish. The imagination, in time, loses the power to create an interlocutor who is not corroborated by any fresh experience. If the artist finds no appreciator for his book or picture he will scarcely be able to produce another.

People differ much in the vividness of their imaginative sociability. The more simple, concrete, dramatic, their habit of mind is, the more their thinking is carried on in terms of actual conversation with a visible and audible interlocutor. Women, as a rule, probably do this more vividly than men, the unlettered more vividly than those trained to abstract thought, and the sort of people we call emotional more vividly than the impassive. Moreover, the interlocutor is a very mutable person, and is likely to resemble the last strong character we have been in contact with. I have noticed, for instance, that when I take up a book after a person of decided and interesting character has been talking with me I am likely to hear the words of the book in his voice. The same is true of opinions, moral standards, and the like, as well as of physical traits. In short, the interlocutor, who is half of all thought and life, is drawn from the accessible environment.

It is worth noting here that there is no separation between real and imaginary persons; indeed, to be imagined is to become real, in a social sense, as I shall presently point out. An invisible person may easily be more real to an imaginative mind than a visible one; sensible presence is not necessarily a matter of the first importance. A person can be real to us only in the degree in which we imagine an inner life which exists in us, for the time being, and which we refer to him. The sensible presence is important chiefly in stimulating us to do this. All real persons are imaginary in this sense. If, however, we use imaginary in the sense of illusory, an imagination not corresponding to fact, it is easy to see that visible presence is no bar to illusion. Thus I meet a stranger on the steamboat who corners me and tells me his private history. I care nothing for it, and he half knows that I do not; he uses me only as a lay figure to sustain the agreeable illusion of sympathy, and is talking to an imaginary companion quite as he might if I were elsewhere. So likewise good manners are largely a tribute to imaginary companionship, a make-believe of sympathy which it is agreeable to accept as real, though we may know, when we think, that it is not. To conceive a kindly and approving companion is something that one involuntarily tries to do, in accordance with that instinctive hedonizing inseparable from all wholesome mental processes, and to assist in this by at least a seeming of friendly appreciation is properly regarded as a part of good breeding. To be always sincere would be brutally to destroy this pleasant and mostly harmless figment of the imagination.

Thus the imaginary companionship which a child of three or four years so naïvely creates and expresses, is something elementary and almost omnipresent in the thought of a normal person. In fact, thought and personal intercourse may be regarded as merely aspects of the same thing: we call it personal intercourse when the suggestions that keep it going are received through faces or other symbols present to the senses; reflection when the personal suggestions come through memory and are more elaborately worked over in thought. But both are mental, both are personal. Personal images, as they are connected with nearly all our higher thought in its inception, remain inseparable from it in memory. The mind is not a hermit's cell, but a place of hospitality and intercourse. We have no higher life that is really apart from other people.

*   *   *

Apparently, then, voice, facial expression, gesture, and the like, which later become the vehicle of personal impressions and the sensible basis of sympathy, are attractive at first chiefly for their sensuous variety and vividness, very much as other bright, moving, sounding things are attractive; and the interpretation of them comes gradually by the interworking of instinct and observation. This interpretation is nothing other than the growth, in connection with these sensuous experiences, of a system of ideas that we associate with them. The interpretation of an angry look, for instance, consists in the expectation of angry words and acts, in feelings of resentment or fear, and so on; in short, it is our whole mental reaction to this sign. It may consist in part of sympathetic states of mind, that is in states of mind that we suppose the other to experience also; but it is not confined to such. These ideas that enrich the meaning of the symbol—the resentment or fear, for instance—have all, no doubt, their roots in instinct; we are born with the

crude raw material of such feelings. And it is precisely in the act of communication, in social contact of some sort, that this material grows, that it
gets the impulses that give it further definition, refinement, organization.
It is by intercourse with others that we expand our inner experience. In
other words, and this is the point of the matter, the personal idea consists
at first and in all later development, of a sensuous element or symbol with
which is connected a more or less complex body of thought and sentiment;
the whole social in genesis, formed by a series of communications.

                          *   *   *

So far as the study of immediate social relations is concerned the personal idea is the real person. That is to say, it is in this alone that one man
exists for another, and acts directly upon his mind. My association with you
evidently consists in the relation between my idea of you and the rest of
my mind. If there is something in you that is wholly beyond this and makes
no impression upon me it has no social reality in this relation. *The immediate social reality is the personal idea;* nothing, it would seem, could be much
more obvious than this.

Society, then, in its immediate aspect, *is a relation among personal
ideas.* In order to have society it is evidently necessary that persons should
get together somewhere; and they get together only as personal ideas in the
mind. Where else? What other possible *locus* can be assigned for the real
contact of persons, or in what other form can they come in contact except
as impressions or ideas formed in this common *locus?* Society exists in my
mind as the contact and reciprocal influence of certain ideas named "I,"
Thomas, Henry, Susan, Bridget, and so on. It exists in your mind as a similar group, and so in every mind. Each person is immediately aware of a
particular aspect of society: and so far as he is aware of great social wholes,
like a nation or an epoch, it is by embracing in this particular aspect ideas
or sentiments which he attributes to his countrymen or contemporaries in
their collective aspect. In order to see this it seems to me only necessary to
discard vague modes of speech which have no conceptions back of them
that will bear scrutiny, and look at the facts as we know them in experience.

(Yet most of us, perhaps, will find it hard to assent to the view that the
social person is a group of sentiments attached to some symbol or other
characteristic element, which keeps them together and from which the
whole idea is named.) The reason for this reluctance I take to be that we
are accustomed to talk and think, so far as we do think in this connection,
as if a person were a material rather than a psychical fact. Instead of basing
our sociology and ethics upon what a man really is as part of our mental
and moral life, he is vaguely and yet grossly regarded as a shadowy material body, a lump of flesh, and not as an ideal thing at all. But surely it is
only common sense to hold that the social and moral reality is that which
lives in our imaginations and affects our motives. As regards the physical
it is only the finer, more plastic and mentally significant aspects of it that

imagination is concerned with, and with that chiefly as a nucleus or centre of crystallization for sentiment. Instead of perceiving this we commonly make the physical the dominant factor, and think of the mental and moral only by a vague analogy to it.

Persons and society must, then, be studied primarily in the imagination. It is surely true, *prima facie,* that the best way of observing things is that which is most direct; and I do not see how anyone can hold that we know persons directly except as imaginative ideas in the mind. These are perhaps the most vivid things in our experience, and as observable as anything else, though it is a kind of observation in which accuracy has not been systematically cultivated. The observation of the physical aspects, however important, is for social purposes quite subsidiary: there is no way of weighing or measuring men which throws more than a very dim sidelight on their personality. The physical factors most significant are those elusive traits of expression already discussed, and in the observation and interpretation of these physical science is only indirectly helpful. What, for instance, could the most elaborate knowledge of his weights and measures, including the anatomy of his brain, tell us of the character of Napoleon? Not enough, I take it, to distinguish him with certainty from an imbecile. Our real knowledge of him is derived from reports of his conversation and manner, from his legislation and military dispositions, from the impression made upon those about him and by them communicated to us, from his portraits and the like; all serving as aids to the imagination in forming a system that we call by his name. I by no means aim to discredit the study of man or of society with the aid of physical measurements, such as those of psychological laboratories; but I think that these methods are indirect and ancillary in their nature and are most useful when employed in connection with a trained imagination.

I conclude, therefore, that the imaginations which people have of one another are the *solid facts* of society, and that to observe and interpret these must be a chief aim of sociology. I do not mean merely that society must be studied *by* the imagination—that is true of all investigations in their higher reaches—but that the *object* of study is primarily an imaginative idea or group of ideas in the mind, that we have to imagine imaginations. The intimate grasp of any social fact will be found to require that we divine what men think of one another. Charity, for instance, is not understood without imagining what ideas the giver and recipient have of each other; to grasp homicide we must, for one thing, conceive how the offender thinks of his victim and of the administrators of the law; the relation between the employing and hand-laboring classes is first of all a matter of personal attitudes which we must apprehend by sympathy with both, and so on. In other words, we want to get at motives, and motives spring from personal ideas. There is nothing particularly novel in this view; historians, for instance, have always assumed that to understand and interpret personal relations was their main business; but apparently the time is coming when this will have to be done in a more systematic and penetrating manner than in the past. Whatever may justly be urged against the introduction of frivolous and disconnected "personalities" into history, the understanding of persons is the aim of this and all other branches of social study.

The Social Self

CHARLES H. COOLEY

It is well to say at the outset that by the word "self" in this discussion is meant simply that which is designated in common speech by the pronouns of the first person singular, "I," "me," "my," "mine," and "myself." "Self" and "ego" are used by metaphysicians and moralists in many other senses, more or less remote from the "I" of daily speech and thought, and with these I wish to have as little to do as possible. What is here discussed is what psychologists call the empirical self, the self that can be apprehended or verified by ordinary observation. I qualify it by the word "social" not as implying the existence of a self that is not social—for I think that the "I" of common language always has more or less distinct reference to other people as well as the speaker—but because I wish to emphasize and dwell upon the social aspect of it.

*   *   *

The distinctive thing in the idea for which the pronouns of the first person are names is apparently a characteristic kind of feeling which may be called the my-feeling or sense of appropriation. Almost any sort of ideas may be associated with this feeling, and so come to be named "I" or "mine," but the feeling, and that alone it would seem is the determining factor in the matter. As Professor James says in his admirable discussion of the self, the words "me" and "self" designate "all the things which have the power to produce in a stream of consciousness excitement of a certain peculiar sort."

. . . I do not mean that the feeling aspect of the self is necessarily more important than any other, but that it is the immediate and decisive sign and proof of what "I" is; there is no appeal from it; if we go behind it it must be to study its history and conditions, not to question its authority. But, of course, this study of history and conditions may be quite as profitable as the direct contemplation of self-feeling. What I would wish to do is to present each aspect in its proper light.

The emotion or feeling of self may be regarded as an instinct, doubtless evolved in connection with its important function in stimulating and unifying the special activities of individuals. It is thus very profoundly rooted in the history of the human race and apparently indispensable to any plan of life at all similar to ours. It seems to exist in a vague though vigorous form at the birth of each individual, and, like other instinctive ideas or germs of ideas, to be defined and developed by experience, becoming associated, or rather incorporated, with muscular, visual and other sensations; with perceptions, apperceptions and conceptions of every degree of complexity and of infinite variety of content; and, especially, with personal ideas. Meantime the feeling itself does not remain unaltered, but undergoes differentiation and refinement just as does any other sort of crude innate feeling. Thus, while retaining under every phase its characteristic tone or flavor, it breaks up into innumerable self-sentiments. And concrete self-feeling, as it exists in mature persons, is a whole made up of these various sentiments, along with a good deal of primitive emotion not thus broken up. It partakes fully of the general development of the mind, but never loses that peculiar gusto of appropriation that causes us to name a thought with a first-personal pronoun. The other contents of the self-idea are of little use, apparently, in defining it, because they are so extremely various. It would be no more futile, it seems to me, to attempt to define fear by enumerating the things that people are afraid of, than to attempt to define "I" by enumerating the objects with which the word is associated. Very much as fear means primarily a state of feeling, or its expression, and not darkness, fire, lions, snakes, or other things that excite it, so "I" means primarily self-feeling, or its expression, and not body, clothes, treasures, ambition, honors, and the like, with which this feeling may be connected. In either case it is possible and useful to go behind the feeling and enquire what ideas arouse it and why they do so, but this is in a sense a secondary investigation.

Since "I" is known to our experience primarily as a feeling, or as a feeling-ingredient in our ideas, it cannot be described or defined without suggesting that feeling. We are sometimes likely to fall into a formal and empty way of talking regarding questions of emotion, by attempting to define that which is in its nature primary and indefinable. A formal definition of self-feeling, or indeed of any sort of feeling, must be as hollow as a formal definition of the taste of salt, or the color red; we can expect to know what it is only by experiencing it. There can be no final test of the self except the way we feel; it is that toward which we have the "my" attitude. But as this feeling is quite as familiar to us and as easy to recall as the taste of salt or the color red, there should be no difficulty in understanding what is meant by it. One need only imagine some attack on his "me," say ridicule of his dress or an attempt to take away his property or his child, or his good name by slander, and self-feeling immediately appears. Indeed, he need only pronounce, with strong emphasis, one of the self-words, like "I" or "my," and self-feeling will be recalled by association.

As many people have the impression that the verifiable self, the object that we name with "I," is usually the material body, it may be well to say that this impression is an illusion, easily dispelled by anyone who will undertake a simple examination of facts. It is true that when we philoso-phize a little about "I" and look around for a tangible object to which to attach it, we soon fix upon the material body as the most available *locus;* but when we use the word naïvely, as in ordinary speech, it is not very common to think of the body in connection with it; not nearly so common as it is to think of other things. There is no difficulty in testing this state-ment, since the word "I" is one of the commonest in conversation and litera-ture, so that nothing is more practicable than to study its meaning at any length that may be desired. One need only listen to ordinary speech until the word has occurred, say, a hundred times, noting its connections, or observe its use in a similar number of cases by the characters in a novel. Ordinarily it will be found that in not more than ten cases in a hundred does "I" have reference to the body of the person speaking. It refers chiefly to opinions, purposes, desires, claims, and the like, concerning matters that involve no thought of the body. *I* think or feel so and so; *I* wish or intend so and so; *I* want this or that; are typical uses, the self-feeling being as-sociated with the view, purpose, or object mentioned. It should also be remembered that "my" and "mine" are as much the names of the self as "I" and these, of course, commonly refer to miscellaneous possessions.

As already suggested, instinctive self-feeling is doubtless connected in evolution with its important function in stimulating and unifying the spe-cial activities of individuals. It appears to be associated chiefly with ideas of the exercise of power, of being a cause, ideas that emphasize the an-tithesis between the mind and the rest of the world. The first definite thoughts that a child associates with self-feeling are probably those of his earliest endeavors to control visible objects—his limbs, his playthings, his bottle, and the like. Then he attempts to control the actions of the persons about him, and so his circle of power and of self-feeling widens without interruption to the most complex objects of mature ambition. Although he does not say "I" or "my" during the first year or two, yet he expresses so clearly by his actions the feeling that adults associate with these words that we cannot deny him a self even in the first weeks.

The social self is simply any idea, or system of ideas, drawn from the communicative life, that the mind cherishes as its own. Self-feeling has its chief scope *within* the general life, not outside of it, the special endeavor or tendency of which it is the emotional aspect finding its principal field of exercise in a world of personal forces, reflected in the mind by a world of personal impressions.

As connected with the thought of other persons it is always a consciousness of the peculiar or differentiated aspect of one's life, because that is the aspect that has to be sustained by purpose and endeavor, and its more aggressive forms tend to attach themselves to whatever one finds to be at once congenial to one's own tendencies and at variance with those of others with whom one is in mental contact. It is here that they are most needed to serve their function of stimulating characteristic activity, of fostering those personal variations which the general plan of life seems to require. Heaven, says Shakespeare, doth divide

> The state of man in divers functions,
> Setting endeavor in continual motion,

and self-feeling is one of the means by which this diversity is achieved.

Agreeably to this view we find that the aggressive self manifests itself most conspicuously in an appropriativeness of objects of common desire, corresponding to the individual's need of power over such objects to secure his own peculiar development, and to the danger of opposition from others who also need them. And this extends from material objects to lay hold, in the same spirit, of the attentions and affections of other people, of all sorts of plans and ambitions, including the noblest special purposes the mind can entertain, and indeed of any conceivable idea which may come to seem a part of one's life and in need of assertion against someone else. The attempt to limit the word "self" and its derivatives to the lower aims of personality is quite arbitrary; at variance with common sense as expressed by the emphatic use of "I" in connection with the sense of duty and other high motives, and unphilosophical as ignoring the function of the self as the organ of specialized endeavor of higher as well as lower kinds.

That the "I" of common speech has a meaning which includes some sort of reference to other persons is involved in the very fact that the word and the ideas it stands for are phenomena of language and the communicative life. It is doubtful whether it is possible to use language at all without thinking more or less distinctly of someone else, and certainly the things to which we give names and which have a large place in reflective thought are almost always those which are impressed upon us by our contact with other people. Where there is no communication there can be no nomenclature and no developed thought. What we call "me," "mine," or "myself" is, then, not something separate from the general life, but the most interesting part of it, a part whose interest arises from the very fact that it is both general and individual. That is, we care for it just because it is that phase of the mind that is living and striving in the common life, trying to impress itself upon the minds of others. "I" is a militant social tendency, working to hold and enlarge its place in the general current of tendencies. So far as it can it waxes, as all life does. To think of it as apart from society is a palpable absurdity of which no one could be guilty who really *saw* it as a fact of life.

Der Mensch erkennt sich nur im Menschen, nur
Das Leben lehret jedem was er sei.*

If a thing has no relation to others of which one is conscious he is unlikely to think of it at all, and if he does think of it he cannot, it seems to
me, regard it as emphatically *his*. The appropriative sense is always the
shadow, as it were, of the common life, and when we have it we have a
sense of the latter in connection with it. Thus, if we think of a secluded
part of the woods as "ours," it is because we think, also, that others do not
go there. As regards the body I doubt if we have a vivid my-feeling about
any part of it which is not thought of, however vaguely, as having some
actual or possible reference to someone else. Intense self-consciousness
regarding it arises along with instincts or experiences which connect it
with the thought of others. Internal organs, like the liver, are not thought
of as peculiarly ours unless we are trying to communicate something regarding them, as, for instance, when they are giving us trouble and we are
trying to get sympathy.

"I," then, is not all of the mind, but a peculiarly central, vigorous, and
well-knit portion of it, not separate from the rest but gradually merging
into it, and yet having a certain practical distinctness, so that a man generally shows clearly enough by his language and behavior what his "I" is
as distinguished from thoughts he does not appropriate. It may be thought
of, as already suggested, under the analogy of a central colored area on a
lighted wall. It might also, and perhaps more justly, be compared to the
nucleus of a living cell, not altogether separate from the surrounding
matter, out of which indeed it is formed, but more active and definitely
organized.

The reference to other persons involved in the sense of self may be
distinct and particular, as when a boy is ashamed to have his mother catch
him at something she has forbidden, or it may be vague and general, as
when one is ashamed to do something which only his conscience, expressing
his sense of social responsibility, detects and disapproves; but it is always
there. There is no sense of "I," as in pride or shame, without its correlative
sense of you, or he, or they. Even the miser gloating over his hidden gold
can feel the "mine" only as he is aware of the world of men over whom he
has secret power; and the case is very similar with all kinds of hid treasure.
Many painters, sculptors, and writers have loved to withhold their work
from the world, fondling it in seclusion until they were quite done with
it; but the delight in this, as in all secrets, depends upon a sense of the
value of what is concealed.

In a very large and interesting class of cases the social reference takes
the form of a somewhat definite imagination of how one's self—that is, any
idea he appropriates—appears in a particular mind, and the kind of self-

* "Only in man does man know himself; life alone teaches each one what he is."—
Goethe, *Tasso*, act 2, sc. 3.

feeling one has is determined by the attitude toward this attributed to that other mind. A social self of this sort might be called the reflected or looking-glass self:

> Each to each a looking-glass
> Reflects the other that doth pass.

As we see our face, figure, and dress in the glass, and are interested in them because they are ours, and pleased or otherwise with them according as they do or do not answer to what we should like them to be; so in imagination we perceive in another's mind some thought of our appearance, manners, aims, deeds, character, friends, and so on, and are variously affected by it.

A self-idea of this sort seems to have three principal elements: the imagination of our appearance to the other person; the imagination of his judgment of that appearance, and some sort of self-feeling, such as pride or mortification. The comparison with a looking-glass hardly suggests the second element, the imagined judgment, which is quite essential. The thing that moves us to pride or shame is not the mere mechanical reflection of ourselves, but an imputed sentiment, the imagined effect of this reflection upon another's mind. This is evident from the fact that the character and weight of that other, in whose mind we see ourselves, makes all the difference with our feeling. We are ashamed to seem evasive in the presence of a straightforward man, cowardly in the presence of a brave one, gross in the eyes of a refined one, and so on. We always imagine, and in imagining share, the judgments of the other mind. A man will boast to one person of an action—say, some sharp transaction in trade—which he would be ashamed to own to another.

It should be evident that the ideas that are associated with self-feeling and form the intellectual content of the self cannot be covered by any simple description, as by saying that the body has such a part in it, friends such a part, plans so much, etc., but will vary indefinitely with particular temperaments and environments. The tendency of the self, like every aspect of personality, is expressive of far-reaching hereditary and social factors, and is not to be understood or predicted except in connection with the general life. Although special, it is in no way separate—speciality and separateness are not only different but contradictory, since the former implies connection with a whole. The object of self-feeling is affected by the general course of history, by the particular development of nations, classes, and professions, and other conditions of this sort.

The truth of this is perhaps most decisively shown in the fact that even those ideas that are most generally associated or colored with the "my" feeling, such as one's idea of his visible person, of his name, his family, his intimate friends, his property, and so on, are not universally so associated, but may be separated from the self by peculiar social conditions. Thus the ascetics, who have played so large a part in the history of Christianity and of other religions and philosophies, endeavored not without success to divorce their appropriative thought from all material surroundings, and especially from their physical persons, which they sought to look upon as accidental and degrading circumstances of the soul's earthly sojourn. In thus estranging themselves from their bodies, from property and comfort, from domestic affections—whether of wife or child, mother, brother or sister—and from other common objects of ambition, they certainly gave a singular direction to self-feeling, but they did not destroy it: there can be no doubt that the instinct, which seems imperishable so long as mental vigor endures, found other ideas to which to attach itself; and the strange and uncouth forms which ambition took in those centuries when the solitary, filthy, idle, and sense-tormenting anchorite was a widely accepted ideal of human life, are a matter of instructive study and reflection. Even in the highest exponents of the ascetic ideal, like St. Jerome, it is easy to see that the discipline, far from effacing the self, only concentrated its energy in lofty and unusual channels. The self-idea may be that of some great moral reform, of a religious creed, of the destiny of one's soul after death, or even a cherished conception of the deity. Thus devout writers, like George Herbert and Thomas à Kempis, often address *my* God, not at all conventionally as I conceive the matter, but with an intimate sense of appropriation. And it has been observed that the demand for the continued and separate existence of the individual soul after death is an expression of self-feeling, as by J. A. Symonds, who thinks that it is connected with the intense egotism and personality of the European races, and asserts that the millions of Buddhism shrink from it with horror.

Habit and familiarity are not of themselves sufficient to cause an idea to be appropriated into the self. Many habits and familiar objects that have been forced upon us by circumstances rather than chosen for their congeniality remain external and possibly repulsive to the self; and, on the other hand, a novel but very congenial element in experience, like the idea of a new toy, or, if you please, Romeo's idea of Juliet, is often appropriated almost immediately, and becomes, for the time at least, the very heart of the self. Habit has the same fixing and consolidating action in the growth of the self that it has elsewhere, but is not its distinctive characteristic.

As suggested in the previous chapter, self-feeling may be regarded as in a sense the antithesis, or better perhaps, the complement, of that disinterested and contemplative love that tends to obliterate the sense of a divergent individuality. Love of this sort has no sense of bounds, but is what we feel when we are expanding and assimilating new and indeterminate experience, while self-feeling accompanies the appropriating, delimiting, and defending of a certain part of experience; the one impels us to receive life, the other to individuate it. The self, from this point of view, might be regarded as a sort of citadel of the mind, fortified without and containing selected treasures within, while love is an undivided share in the rest of the universe. In a healthy mind each contributes to the growth of the other: what we love intensely or for a long time we are likely to bring within the citadel, and to assert as part of ourself. On the other hand, it is only on the basis of a substantial self that a person is capable of progressive sympathy or love.

The sickness of either is to lack the support of the other. There is no health in a mind except as it keeps expanding, taking in fresh life, feeling love and enthusiasm; and so long as it does this its self-feeling is likely to be modest and generous; since these sentiments accompany that sense of the large and the superior which love implies. But if love closes, the self contracts and hardens: the mind having nothing else to occupy its attention and give it that change and renewal it requires, busies itself more and more with self-feeling, which takes on narrow and disgusting forms, like avarice, arrogance, and fatuity. It is necessary that we should have self-feeling about a matter during its conception and execution; but when it is accomplished or has failed the self ought to break loose and escape, renewing its skin like the snake, as Thoreau says. No matter what a man does, he is not fully sane or human unless there is a spirit of freedom in him, a soul unconfined by purpose and larger than the practicable world. And this is really what those mean who inculcate the suppression of the self; they mean that its rigidity must be broken up by growth and renewal, that it must be more or less decisively "born again." A healthy self must be both vigorous and plastic, a nucleus of solid, well-knit private purpose and feeling, guided and nourished by sympathy.

The view that "self" and the pronouns of the first person are names which the race has learned to apply to an instinctive attitude of mind, and which each child in turn learns to apply in a similar way, was impressed upon me by observing my child M. at the time when she was learning to use these pronouns. When she was two years and two weeks old I was surprised to discover that she had a clear notion of the first and second persons when used possessively. When asked, "Where is your nose?" she would put her hand upon it and say "my." She also understood that when someone else said "my" and touched an object, it meant something opposite to what was meant when she touched the same object and used the same word. Now, anyone who will exercise his imagination upon the question how this matter must appear to a mind having no means of knowing anything about "I" and "my" except what it learns by hearing them used, will see that it should be very puzzling. Unlike other words, the personal pronouns have, apparently, no uniform meaning, but convey different and even opposite ideas when employed by different persons. It seems remarkable that children should master the problem before they arrive at considerable power of abstract reasoning. How should a little girl of two, not particularly reflective, have discovered that "my" was not the sign of a definite object like other words, but meant something different with each person who used it? And, still more surprising, how should she have achieved the correct use of it with reference to herself which, it would seem, *could not be copied from anyone else,* simply because no one else used it to describe what belonged to her? The meaning of words is learned by associating them with other phenomena. But how is it possible to learn the meaning of one which, as used by others, is never associated with the same phenomenon as when properly used by one's self? Watching her use of the first person, I was at once struck with the fact that she employed it almost wholly in a possessive sense, and that, too, when in an aggressive, self-assertive mood. It was extremely common to see R. tugging at one end of a plaything and M. at the other, screaming, "My, my." "Me" was sometimes nearly equivalent to "my," and was also employed to call attention to herself when she wanted something done for her. Another common use of "my" was to demand something she did not have at all. Thus if R. had something the like of which she wanted, say a cart, she would exclaim, "Where's *my* cart?"

It seemed to me that she might have learned the use of these pronouns about as follows. The self-feeling had always been there. From the first week she had wanted things and cried and fought for them. She had also become familiar by observation and opposition with similar appropriative activities on the part of R. Thus she not only had the feeling herself, but by associating it with its visible expression had probably divined it, sympathized with it, resented it, in others. Grasping, tugging, and screaming would be associated with the feeling in her own case and would recall the feeling when observed in others. They would constitute a language, precedent to the use of first-personal pronouns, to express the self-idea. All was ready, then, for the word to name this experience. She now observed that R., when contentiously appropriating something, frequently exclaimed, *"my," "mine,"* "give it to *me*," "*I* want it," and the like. Nothing more natural, then, than that she should adopt these words as names for a frequent and vivid experience with which she was already familiar in her own case and had learned to attribute to others. Accordingly it appeared to me, as I recorded in my notes at the time, that " 'my' and 'mine' are simply names for concrete images of appropriativeness," embracing both the appropriative feeling and its manifestation. If this is true the child does not at first work out the I-and-you idea in an abstract form. The first-personal pronoun is a sign of a concrete thing after all, but that thing is not primarily the child's body, or his muscular sensations as such, but the phenomenon of aggressive appropriation, practised by himself, witnessed in others, and incited and interpreted by a hereditary instinct. This seems to get over the difficulty above mentioned, namely, the seeming lack of a common content between the meaning of "my" when used by another and when used by one's self. This common content is found in the appropriative feeling and the visible and audible signs of that feeling. An element of difference and strife comes in, of course, in the opposite actions or purposes which the "my" of another and one's own "my" are likely to stand for. When another person says "mine" regarding something which I claim, I sympathize with him enough to understand what he means, but it is a hostile sympathy, overpowered by another and more vivid "mine" connected with the idea of drawing the object my way.

In other words, the meaning of "I" and "mine" is learned in the same way that the meanings of hope, regret, chagrin, disgust, and thousands of other words of emotion and sentiment are learned: that is, by having the feeling, imputing it to others in connection with some kind of expression, and hearing the word along with it. As to its communication and growth the self-idea is in no way peculiar that I see, but essentially like other ideas. In its more complex forms, such as are expressed by "I" in conversation and literature, it is a social sentiment, or type of sentiment, defined and developed by intercourse, in the manner suggested in a previous chapter.

R., though a more reflective child than M., was much slower in understanding these pronouns, and in his thirty-fifth month had not yet straightened them out, sometimes calling his father "me." I imagine that this was partly because he was placid and uncontentious in his earliest years, manifesting little social self-feeling, but chiefly occupied with impersonal experiment and reflection; and partly because he saw little of other children by antithesis to whom his self could be awakened. M., on the other hand, coming later, had R.'s opposition on which to whet her naturally keen appropriativeness. And her society had a marked effect in developing self-feeling in R., who found self-assertion necessary to preserve his playthings, or anything else capable of appropriation. He learned the use of "my," however, when he was about three years old, before M. was born. He doubtless acquired it in his dealings with his parents. Thus he would perhaps notice his mother claiming the scissors as *mine* and seizing upon them, and would be moved sympathetically to claim something in the same way—connecting the word with the act and the feeling rather than the object. But as I had not the problem clearly in mind at that time I made no satisfactory observations.

I imagine, then, that as a rule the child associates "I" and "me" at first only with those ideas regarding which his appropriative feeling is aroused and defined by opposition. He appropriates his nose, eye, or foot in very much the same way as a plaything—by antithesis to other noses, eyes, and feet, which he cannot control. It is not uncommon to tease little children by proposing to take away one of these organs, and they behave precisely as if the "mine" threatened were a separable object—which it might be for all they know. And, as I have suggested, even in adult life, "I," "me," and "mine" are applied with a strong sense of their meaning only to things distinguished as peculiar to us by some sort of opposition or contrast. They always imply social life and relation to other persons. That which is most distinctively mine is very private, it is true, but it is that part of the private which I am cherishing in antithesis to the rest of the world, not the separate but the special. The aggressive self is essentially a militant phase of the mind, having for its apparent function the energizing of peculiar activities, and although the militancy may not go on in an obvious, external manner, it always exists as a mental attitude.

The process by which self-feeling of the looking-glass sort develops in children may be followed without much difficulty. Studying the movements of others as closely as they do they soon see a connection between their own acts and changes in those movements; that is, they perceive their own influence or power over persons. The child appropriates the visible actions of his parent or nurse, over which he finds he has some control, in quite the same way as he appropriates one of his own members or a plaything, and he will try to do things with this new possession, just as he will with his hand or his rattle. A girl six months old will attempt in the most evident and deliberate manner to attract attention to herself, to set going by her actions some of those movements of other persons that she has appropriated. She has tasted the joy of being a cause, of exerting social power, and wishes more of it. She will tug at her mother's skirts, wriggle, gurgle, stretch out her arms, etc., all the time watching for the hoped-for effect. These performances often give the child, even at this age, an appearance of what is called affectation, that is, she seems to be unduly preoccupied with what other people think of her. Affectation, at any age, exists when the passion to influence others seems to overbalance the established character and give it an obvious twist or pose. It is instructive to find that even Darwin was, in his childhood, capable of departing from truth for the sake of making an impression. "For instance," he says in his autobiography, "I once gathered much valuable fruit from my father's trees and hid it in the shrubbery, and then ran in breathless haste to spread the news that I had discovered a hoard of stolen fruit."

The young performer soon learns to be different things to different people, showing that he begins to apprehend personality and to foresee its operation. If the mother or nurse is more tender than just she will almost certainly be "worked" by systematic weeping. It is a matter of common observation that children often behave worse with their mother than with other and less sympathetic people. Of the new persons that a child sees it is evident that some make a strong impression and awaken a desire to interest and please them, while others are indifferent or repugnant. Sometimes the reason can be perceived or guessed, sometimes not; but the fact of selective interest, admiration, prestige, is obvious before the end of the second year. By that time a child already cares much for the reflection of himself upon one personality and little for that upon another. Moreover, he soon claims intimate and tractable persons as *mine*, classes them among his other possessions, and maintains his ownership against all comers. M., at three years of age, vigorously resented R.'s claim upon their mother. The latter was "*my* mamma," whenever the point was raised.

Strong joy and grief depend upon the treatment this rudimentary social self receives. In the case of M. I noticed as early as the fourth month a "hurt" way of crying which seemed to indicate a sense of personal slight. It was quite different from the cry of pain or that of anger, but seemed about the same as the cry of fright. The slightest tone of reproof would produce it. On the other hand, if people took notice and laughed and encouraged, she was hilarious. At about fifteen months old she had become "a perfect little actress," seeming to live largely in imaginations of her effect upon other people. She constantly and obviously laid traps for attention, and looked abashed or wept at any signs of disapproval or indifference. At times it would seem as if she could not get over these repulses, but would cry long in a grieved way, refusing to be comforted. If she hit upon any little trick that made people laugh she would be sure to repeat it, laughing loudly and affectedly in imitation. She had quite a repertory of these small performances, which she would display to a sympathetic audience, or even try upon strangers. I have seen her at sixteen months, when R. refused to give her the scissors, sit down and make believe cry, putting up her under lip and snuffling, meanwhile looking up now and then to see what effect she was producing.

In such phenomena we have plainly enough, it seems to me, the germ of personal ambition of every sort. Imagination co-operating with instinctive self-feeling has already created a social "I," and this has become a principal object of interest and endeavor.

Progress from this point is chiefly in the way of a greater definiteness, fulness, and inwardness in the imagination of the other's state of mind. A little child thinks of and tries to elicit certain visible or audible phenomena, and does not go back of them; but what a grown-up person desires to produce in others is an internal, invisible condition which his own richer experience enables him to imagine, and of which expression is only the sign. Even adults, however, make no separation between what other people think and the visible expression of that thought. They imagine the whole thing at once, and their idea differs from that of a child chiefly in the comparative richness and complexity of the elements that accompany and interpret the visible or audible sign. There is also a progress from the naïve to the subtle in socially self-assertive action. A child obviously and simply, at first, does things for effect. Later there is an endeavor to suppress the appearance of doing so; affection, indifference, contempt, etc., are simulated to hide the real wish to affect the self-image. It is perceived that an obvious seeking after good opinion is weak and disagreeable.

I doubt whether there are any regular stages in the development of social self-feeling and expression common to the majority of children. The sentiments of self develop by imperceptible gradations out of the crude appropriative instinct of new-born babes, and their manifestations vary indefinitely in different cases. Many children show "self-consciousness" conspicuously from the first half year; others have little appearance of it at any age. Still others pass through periods of affectation whose length and time of occurrence would probably be found to be exceedingly various. In childhood, as at all times of life, absorption in some idea other than that of the social self tends to drive "self-consciousness" out.

Nearly everyone, however, whose turn of mind is at all imaginative goes through a season of passionate self-feeling during adolescence, when, according to current belief, the social impulses are stimulated in connection with the rapid development of the functions of sex. This is a time of hero-worship, of high resolve, of impassioned reverie, of vague but fierce ambition, of strenuous imitation that seems affected, of *gêne* in the presence of the other sex or of superior persons, and so on.

Many autobiographies describe the social self-feeling of youth which, in the case of strenuous, susceptible natures, prevented by weak health or uncongenial surroundings from gaining the sort of success proper to that age, often attains extreme intensity. This is quite generally the case with the youth of men of genius, whose exceptional endowment and tendencies usually isolate them more or less from the ordinary life about them.

                                    *   *   *

In the presence of one whom we feel to be of importance there is a tendency to enter into and adopt, by sympathy, his judgment of ourself, to put a new value on ideas and purposes, to recast life in his image. With a very sensitive person this tendency is often evident to others in ordinary conversation and in trivial matters. By force of an impulse springing directly from the delicacy of his perceptions he is continually imagining how he appears to his interlocutor, and accepting the image, for the moment, as himself. If the other appears to think him well-informed on some recondite matter, he is likely to assume a learned expression; if thought judicious he looks as if he were; if accused of dishonesty he appears guilty, and so on. In short, a sensitive man, in the presence of an impressive personality, tends to become, for the time, his interpretation of what the other thinks he is. It is only the heavy-minded who will not feel this to be true, in some degree, of themselves. Of course it is usually a temporary and somewhat superficial phenomenon; but it is typical of all ascendency, and helps us to understand how persons have power over us through some hold upon our imaginations, and how our personality grows and takes form by divining the appearance of our present self to other minds.

So long as a character is open and capable of growth it retains a corresponding impressibility, which is not weakness unless it swamps the assimilating and organizing faculty. I know men whose careers are a proof of stable and aggressive character who have an almost feminine sensitiveness regarding their seeming to others. Indeed, if one sees a man whose attitude toward others is always assertive, never receptive, he may be confident that man will never go far, because he will never learn much. In character, as in every phase of life, health requires a just union of stability with plasticity.

There is a vague excitement of the social self more general than any particular emotion or sentiment. Thus the mere presence of people, a "sense of other persons," as Professor Baldwin says, and an awareness of their observation, often causes a vague discomfort, doubt, and tension. One feels that there is a social image of himself lurking about, and not knowing what it is he is obscurely alarmed. Many people, perhaps most, feel more or less agitation and embarrassment under the observation of strangers, and for some even sitting in the same room with unfamiliar or uncongenial people is harassing and exhausting. It is well known, for instance, that a visit from a stranger would often cost Darwin his night's sleep, and many similar examples could be collected from the records of men of letters. At this point, however, it is evident that we approach the borders of mental pathology.

Possibly some will think that I exaggerate the importance of social self-feeling by taking persons and periods of life that are abnormally sensitive. But I believe that with all normal and human people it remains, in one form or another, the mainspring of endeavor and a chief interest of the imagination throughout life. As is the case with other feelings, we do not think much of it so long as it is moderately and regularly gratified. Many people of balanced mind and congenial activity scarcely know that they care what others think of them, and will deny, perhaps with indignation, that such care is an important factor in what they are and do. But this is illusion. If failure or disgrace arrives, if one suddenly finds that the faces of men show coldness or contempt instead of the kindliness and deference that he is used to, he will perceive from the shock, the fear, the sense of being outcast and helpless, that he was living in the minds of others without knowing it, just as we daily walk the solid ground without thinking how it bears us up. This fact is so familiar in literature, especially in modern novels, that it ought to be obvious enough. The works of George Eliot are particularly strong in the exposition of it. In most of her novels there is some character like Mr. Bulstrode in "Middlemarch" or Mr. Jermyn in "Felix Holt," whose respectable and long-established social image of himself is shattered by the coming to light of hidden truth.

It is true, however, that the attempt to describe the social self and to analyze the mental processes that enter into it almost unavoidably makes it appear more reflective and "self-conscious" than it usually is. Thus while some readers will be able to discover in themselves a quite definite and deliberate contemplation of the reflected self, others will perhaps find nothing but a sympathetic impulse, so simple that it can hardly be made the object of distinct thought. Many people whose behavior shows that their idea of themselves is largely caught from the persons they are with, are yet quite innocent of any intentional posing; it is a matter of subconscious impulse or mere suggestion. The self of very sensitive but non-reflective minds is of this character.

Play, the Game, and the Generalized Other

GEORGE HERBERT MEAD

WE WERE SPEAKING of the social conditions under which the self arises as an object. In addition to language we found two illustrations, one in play and the other in the game, and I wish to summarize and expand my account on these points. I have spoken of these from the point of view of children. We can, of course, refer also to the attitudes of more primitive people out of which our civilization has arisen. A striking illustration of play as distinct from the game is found in the myths and various of the plays which primitive people carry out, especially in religious pageants. The pure play attitude which we find in the case of little children may not be found here, since the participants are adults, and undoubtedly the relationship of these play processes to that which they interpret is more or less in the minds of even the most primitive people. In the process of interpretation of such rituals, there is an organization of play which perhaps might be compared to that which is taking place in the kindergarten in dealing with the plays of little children, where these are made into a set that will have a definite structure or relationship. At least something of the same sort is found in the play of primitive people. This type of activity belongs, of course, not to the everyday life of the people in their dealing with the objects about them—there we have a more or less definitely developed self-consciousness —but in their attitudes toward the forces about them, the nature upon which they depend; in their attitude toward this nature which is vague and uncertain, there we have a much more primitive response; and that response finds its expression in taking the rôle of the other, playing at the expression of their gods and their heroes, going through certain rites which are the representation of what these individuals are suppposed to be doing. The process is one which develops, to be sure, into a more or less definite technique and is controlled; and yet we can say that it has arisen out of situations similar to those in which little children play at being a parent, at being a teacher—vague personalities that are about them and which affect them and on which they depend. These are personalities which they take, rôles they play, and in so far control the development of their own personality. This outcome is just what the kindergarten works toward. It takes the characters of these various vague beings and gets them into such an organized social relationship to each other that they build up the character of the little child. The very introduction of organization from outside sup-

Reprinted from *Mind, Self, and Society*, by George Herbert Mead, by permission of The University of Chicago Press, 1934, pp. 152-164.

poses a lack of organization at this period in the child's experience. Over against such a situation of the little child and primitive people, we have the game as such.

The fundamental difference between the game and play is that in the latter the child must have the attitude of all the others involved in that game. The attitudes of the other players which the participant assumes organize into a sort of unit, and it is that organization which controls the response of the individual. The illustration used was of a person playing baseball. Each one of his own acts is determined by his assumption of the action of the others who are playing the game. What he does is controlled by his being everyone else on that team, at least in so far as those attitudes affect his own particular response. We get then an "other" which is an organization of the attitudes of those involved in the same process.

The organized community or social group which gives to the individual his unity of self may be called "the generalized other." The attitude of the generalized other is the attitude of the whole community. Thus, for example, in the case of such a social group as a ball team, the team is the generalized other in so far as it enters—as an organized process or social activity—into the experience of any one of the individual members of it.

If the given human individual is to develop a self in the fullest sense, it is not sufficient for him merely to take the attitudes of other human individuals toward himself and toward one another within the human social process, and to bring that social process as a whole into his individual experience merely in these terms: he must also, in the same way that he takes the attitudes of other individuals toward himself and toward one another, take their attitudes toward the various phases or aspects of the common social activity or set of social undertakings in which, as members of an organized society or social group, they are all engaged; and he must then, by generalizing these individual attitudes of that organized society or social group itself, as a whole, act toward different social projects which at any given time it is carrying out, or toward the various larger phases of the general social process which constitutes its life and of which these projects are specific manifestations. This getting of the broad activities of any given social whole or organized society as such within the experiential field of any one of the individuals involved or included in that whole is, in other words, the essential basis and prerequisite of the fullest development of that individual's self: only in so far as he takes the attitudes of the organized social group to which he belongs toward the organized, co-operative social activity or set of such activities in which that group as such is engaged, does he develop a complete self or possess the sort of complete self he has developed. And on the other hand, the complex co-operative processes and activities and institutional functionings of organized human society are also possible only in so far as every individual involved in them or belonging to that society can take the general attitudes of all other such individuals with reference to these processes and activities and institutional function-

ings, and to the organized social whole of experiential relations and interactions thereby constituted—and can direct his own behavior accordingly.

It is in the form of the generalized other that the social process influences the behavior of the individuals involved in it and carrying it on, i.e.,
that the community exercises control over the conduct of its individual
members; for it is in this form that the social process or community enters
as a determining factor into the individual's thinking. In abstract thought
the individual takes the attitude of the generalized other toward himself,
without reference to its expression in any particular other individuals; and
in concrete thought he takes that attitude in so far as it is expressed in the
attitudes toward his behavior of those other individuals with whom he is
involved in the given social situation or act. But only by taking the attitude
of the generalized other toward himself, in one or another of these ways,
can he think at all; for only thus can thinking—or the internalized conversation of gestures which constitutes thinking—occur. And only through the
taking by individuals of the attitude or attitudes of the generalized other
toward themselves is the existence of a universe of discourse, as that system
of common or social meanings which thinking presupposes at its context,
rendered possible.

The self-conscious human individual, then, takes or assumes the organized social attitudes of the given social group or community (or of some
one section thereof) to which he belongs, toward the social problems of
various kinds which confront that group or community at any given time,
and which arise in connection with the correspondingly different social
projects or organized co-operative enterprises in which that group or community as such is engaged; and as an individual participant in these social
projects or co-operative enterprises, he governs his own conduct accordingly. In politics, for example, the individual identifies himself with an
entire political party and takes the organized attitudes of that entire party
toward the rest of the given social community and toward the problems
which confront the party within the given social situation; and he consequently reacts or responds in terms of the organized attitudes of the party
as a whole. He thus enters into a special set of social relations with all the
other individuals who belong to that political party; and in the same way he
enters into various other special sets of social relations, with various other
classes of individuals respectively, the individuals of each of these classes
being the other members of some one of the particular organized subgroups
(determined in socially functional terms) of which he himself is a member
within the entire given society or social community. In the most highly
developed, organized, and complicated human social communities—those
evolved by civilized man—these various socially functional classes or subgroups of individuals to which any given individual belongs (and with the
other individual members of which he thus enters into a special set of
social relations) are of two kinds. Some of them are concrete social classes
or subgroups, such as political parties, clubs, corporations, which are all

actually functional social units, in terms of which their individual members are directly related to one another. The others are abstract social classes or subgroups, such as the class of debtors and the class of creditors, in terms of which their individual members are related to one another only more or less indirectly, and which only more or less indirectly function as social units, but which afford or represent unlimited possibilities for the widening and ramifying and enriching of the social relations among all the individual members of the given society as an organized and unified whole. The given individual's membership in several of these abstract social classes or subgroups makes possible his entrance into definite social relations (however indirect) with an almost infinite number of other individuals who also belong to or are included within one or another of these abstract social classes or subgroups cutting across functional lines of demarcation which divide different human social communities from one another, and including individual members from several (in some cases from all) such communities. Of these abstract social classes or subgroups of human individuals the one which is most inclusive and extensive is, of course, the one defined by the logical universe of discourse (or system of universally significant symbols) determined by the participation and communicative interaction of individuals; for of all such classes or subgroups, it is the one which claims the largest number of individual members, and which enables the largest conceivable number of human individuals to enter into some sort of social relation, however indirect or abstract it may be, with one another—a relation arising from the universal functioning of gestures as significant symbols in the general human social process of communication.

I have pointed out, then, that there are two general stages in the full development of the self. At the first of these stages, the individual's self is constituted simply by an organization of the particular attitudes of other individuals toward himself and toward one another in the specific social acts in which he participates with them. But at the second stage in the full development of the individual's self that self is constituted not only by an organization of these particular individual attitudes, but also by an organization of the social attitudes of the generalized other or the social group as a whole to which he belongs. These social or group attitudes are brought within the individual's field of direct experience, and are included as elements in the structure or constitution of his self, in the same way that the attitudes of particular other individuals are; and the individual arrives at them, or succeeds in taking them, by means of further organizing, and then generalizing, the attitudes of particular other individuals in terms of their organized social bearings and implications. So the self reaches its full development by organizing these individual attitudes of others into the organized social or group attitudes, and by thus becoming an individual reflection of the general systematic pattern of social or group behavior in which it and the others are all involved—a pattern which enters as a whole into the individual's experience in terms of these organized group attitudes which, through the mechanism of his central nervous system, he takes toward himself, just as he takes the individual attitudes of others.

The game has a logic, so that such an organization of the self is rendered possible: there is a definite end to be obtained; the actions of the different individuals are all related to each other with reference to that end so that they do not conflict; one is not in conflict with himself in the attitude of another man on the team. If one has the attitude of the person throwing the ball he can also have the response of catching the ball. The two are related so that they further the purpose of the game itself. They are interrelated in a unitary, organic fashion. There is a definite unity, then, which is introduced into the organization of other selves when we reach such a stage as that of the game, as over against the situation of play where there is a simple succession of one rôle after another, a situation which is, of course, characteristic of the child's own personality. The child is one thing at one time and another at another, and what he is at one moment does not determine what he is at another. That is both the charm of childhood as well as its inadequacy. You cannot count on the child; you cannot assume that all the things he does are going to determine what he will do at any moment. He is not organized into a whole. The child has no definite character, no definite personality.

The gang is then an illustration of the situation out of which an organized personality arises. In so far as the child does take the attitude of the other and allows that attitude of the other to determine the thing he is going to do with reference to a common end, he is becoming an organic member of society. He is taking over the morale of that society and is becoming an essential member of it. He belongs to it in so far as he does allow the attitude of the other that he takes to control his own immediate expression. What is involved here is some sort of an organized process. That which is expressed in terms of the game is, of course, being continually expressed in the social life of the child, but this wider process goes beyond the immediate experience of the child himself. The importance of the game is that it lies entirely inside of the child's own experience, and the importance of our modern type of education is that it is brought as far as possible within this realm. The different attitudes that a child assumes are so organized that they exercise a definite control over his response, as the attitudes in a game control his own immediate response. In the game we get an organized other, a generalized other, which is found in the nature of the child itself, and finds its expression in the immediate experience of the child. And it is that organized activity in the child's own nature controlling the particular response which gives unity, and which builds up his own self.

What goes on in the game goes on in the life of the child all the time. He is continually taking the attitudes of those about him, especially the rôles of those who in some sense control him and on whom he depends. He gets the function of the process in an abstract sort of a way at first.

It goes over from the play into the game in a real sense. He has to play the game. The morale of the game takes hold of the child more than a larger morale of the whole community. The child passes into the game and the game expresses a social situation in which he can completely enter; its morale may have a greater hold on him than that of the family to which he belongs or the community in which he lives. There are all sorts of social organizations, some of which are fairly lasting, some temporary, into which the child is entering, and he is playing a sort of social game in them. It is a period in which he likes "to belong," and he gets into organizations which come into existence and pass out of existence. He becomes a something which can function in the organized whole, and thus tends to determine himself in his relationship with the group to which he belongs. That process is one which is a striking stage in the development of the child's morale. It constitutes him a self-conscious member of the community to which he belongs.

Such is the process by which a personality arises. I have spoken of this as a process in which a child takes the rôle of the other, and said that it takes place essentially through the use of language. Language is predominantly based on the vocal gesture by means of which co-operative activities in a community are carried out. Language in its significant sense is that vocal gesture which tends to arouse in the individual the attitude which it arouses in others, and it is this perfecting of the self by the gesture which mediates the social activities that gives rise to the process of taking the rôle of the other. The latter phrase is a little unfortunate because it suggests an actor's attitude which is actually more sophisticated than that which is involved in our own experience. To this degree it does not correctly describe that which I have in mind. We see the process most definitely in a primitive form in those situations where the child's play takes different rôles. Here the very fact that he is ready to pay out money, for instance, arouses the attitude of the person who receives money; the very process is calling out in him the corresponding activities of the other person involved. The individual stimulates himself to the response which he is calling out in the other person, and then acts in some degree in response to that situation. In play the child does definitely act out the rôle which he himself has aroused in himself. It is that which gives, as I have said, a definite content in the individual which answers to the stimulus that affects him as it affects somebody else. The content of the other that enters into one personality is the response in the individual which his gesture calls out in the other.

We may illustrate our basic concept by a reference to the notion of property. If we say "This is my property, I shall control it," that affirmation calls out a certain set of responses which must be the same in any community in which property exists. It involves an organized attitude with reference to property which is common to all the members of the community. One must have a definite attitude of control of his own property and respect for the property of others. Those attitudes (as organized sets of responses) must be there on the part of all, so that when one says such a thing he calls out in himself the response of the others. He is calling out the response of what I have called a generalized other. That which makes society possible is such common responses, such organized attitudes, with reference to what we term property, the cults of religion, the process of education, and the relations of the family. Of course, the wider the society the more definitely universal these objects must be. In any case there must be a definite set of responses, which we may speak of as abstract, and which can belong to a very large group. Property is in itself a very abstract concept. It is that which the individual himself can control and nobody else can control. The attitude is different from that of a dog toward a bone. A dog will fight any other dog trying to take the bone. The dog is not taking the attitude of the other dog. A man who says "This is my property" is taking an attitude of the other person. The man is appealing to his rights because he is able to take the attitude which everybody else in the group has with reference to property, thus arousing in himself the attitude of others.

What goes to make up the organized self is the organization of the attitudes which are common to the group. A person is a personality because he belongs to a community, because he takes over the institutions of that community into his own conduct. He takes its language as a medium by which he gets his personality, and then through a process of taking the different rôles that all the others furnish he comes to get the attitude of the members of the community. Such, in a certain sense, is the structure of a man's personality. There are certain common responses which each individual has toward certain common things, and in so far as those common reponses are awakened in the individual when he is affecting other persons he arouses his own self. The structure, then, on which the self is built is this response which is common to all, for one has to be a member of a community to be a self. Such responses are abstract attitudes, but they constitute just what we term a man's character. They give him what we term his principles, the acknowledged attitudes of all members of the community toward what are the values of that community. He is putting himself in the place of the generalized other, which represents the organized responses of all the members of the group. It is that which guides conduct controlled by principles, and a person who has such an organized group of responses is a man whom we say has character, in the moral sense.

It is a structure of attitudes, then, which goes to make up a self, as distinct from a group of habits. We all of us have, for example, certain groups of habits, such as the particular intonations which a person uses in his speech. This is a set of habits of vocal expression which one has but which one does not know about. The sets of habits which we have of that sort mean nothing to us; we do not hear the intonations of our speech that others hear unless we are paying particular attention to them. The habits of emotional expression which belong to our speech are of the same sort. We may know that we have expressed ourselves in a joyous fashion but the detailed process is one which does not come back to our conscious selves. There are whole bundles of such habits which do not enter into a conscious self, but which help to make up what is termed the unconscious self.

After all, what we mean by self-consciousness is an awakening in ourselves of the group of attitudes which we are arousing in others, especially when it is an important set of responses which go to make up the members of the community. It is unfortunate to fuse or mix up consciousness, as we ordinarily use that term, and self-consciousness. Consciousness, as frequently used, simply has reference to the field of experience, but self-consciousness refers to the ability to call out in ourselves a set of definite responses which belong to the others of the group. Consciousness and self-consciousness are not on the same level. A man alone has, fortunately or unfortunately, access to his own toothache, but that is not what we mean by self-consciousness.

I have so far emphasized what I have called the structures upon which the self is constructed, the framework of the self, as it were. Of course we are not only what is common to all: each one of the selves is different from everyone else; but there has to be such a common structure as I have sketched in order that we may be members of a community at all. We cannot be ourselves unless we are also members in whom there is a community of attitudes which control the attitudes of all. We cannot have rights unless we have common attitudes. That which we have acquired as self-conscious persons makes us such members of society and gives us selves. Selves can only exist in definite relationships to other selves. No hard-and-fast line can be drawn between our own selves and the selves of others, since our own selves exist and enter as such into our experience only in so far as the selves of others exist and enter as such into our experience also. The individual possesses a self only in relation to the selves of the other members of his social group; and the structure of his self expresses or reflects the general behavior pattern of this social group to which he belongs, just as does the structure of the self of every other individual belonging to this social group.

Role-Playing vs. Role-Taking: An Appeal for Clarification

WALTER COUTU

IT APPEARS that two great concepts are in imminent danger of being lost through confusion. Three recent texts in social psychology, all of them unusually good, have dangerously confused the sociological concept of role-playing with the psychological concept of role-taking.

In order to clarify the issue, let us specify the traditional meanings of the terms involved.

1. *Role.* Every person in every society holds or occupies certain positions or statuses—parent, educator, healer, public servant, etc. With every social position there are socially prescribed duties or functions to be performed, and rights to be enjoyed. These functions are called "social roles" or just "roles." Every role involves a whole system of behaviors more or less expected and enforced by various groups. We may define role, then, as a socially prescribed way of behaving in particular situations for any person occupying a given social position or status. A role represents what a person is supposed to do in a given situation by virtue of the social position he holds.

2. *Role-Playing.* This term refers to performing the above functions. It is important to note that the term refers to *behavior, performance, conduct, overt activity.* A woman occupying the position or status of parent is socially expected to *play the role* of mother, involving a whole series of behaviors—protecting the child, feeding it, dressing it, training it, loving it, etc. These are called role behaviors. People thus perform the roles of mother, father, son, daughter, milkman, policeman, cowboy, gangster, etc., in all sorts of situations.

3. *Role-Taking.* This term, unfortunately, has nothing whatever to do with playing a role as described above. Role-taking is a term instituted by George Herbert Mead years ago at a time when social psychology was hardly more than a name for Mead's course at the University of Chicago. The term role-taking meant, for Mead, a strictly mental or cognitive or empathic activity, not overt behavior or conduct. In Mead's usage the term refers to that phase of the symbolic process by which a person momentarily pretends to himself that he is another person, projects himself into the perceptual field of the other person, imaginatively "puts himself in the other's place," in order that he may get an insight into the other person's prob-

From *American Sociological Review*, 16, 1961, pp. 180-187. Reprinted by permission of the publisher and the author.

able behavior in a given situation. The purpose of this is to enable him to get the other person's "point of view" so that he can anticipate the other's behavior and then act accordingly.

It is one of the misfortunes of history that Mead used the term "role" in this connection. What he meant is easily determined by the alternate phrase he used; synonymously with the expression "taking-the-role-of-the-other" he invariably used the expression "taking-the-attitude-of-the-other." For historical reasons "role" and "attitude" had much the same meaning for Mead. No one in contemporary social psychology, however, would confuse the terms "role" and "attitude," but for Mead they represented one and the same idea. Thus the contemporary concept of role as described above has little in common with Mead's concept of "role" in his famous term "role-taking." Mead's concept means "taking" over into oneself the other's attitude, point of view, perceptual field; imagining what the other person "thinks he is supposed to do." Only in the latter sense is Mead's use of "role" related to contemporary use of the term "role."

4. *Playing-at a Role*. There is a fourth term which Mead used and which was part of common speech then as now. This term is "playing-at" a role. It represents a concept involving two processes: (1) role-taking on an elementary level and (2) *playing-at*, or pretending to *play*, some well-known role. While under certain conditions adults engage in this practice, yet the term refers almost exclusively to certain aspects of the fantasy of life of children. It refers to the activity in which a child pretends he is, say, a milkman, and in which he thinks, talks and performs *like* one. The child cannot *play* this role, since he cannot occupy the appropriate position, but he can play at it, thus learning both role-taking and role-playing. "Playing-at" thus involves both the "playing" and "taking" concepts in a make-believe, playful, fictitious or fantasy form.

The fact that these three different concepts are denoted by highly similar symbols (words) is most unfortunate, for this condition not only leads to confusion, but what is worse, it leads some people to believe that the attempt to differentiate the concepts constitutes "quibbling about words." Nothing could be further from the truth.

In order to demonstrate this, let us enumerate some of the differences between these great and increasingly useful concepts.

DIFFERENTIATING FACTORS

In the first place *role-playing* is a strictly sociological concept with a long history. *Role-taking*, however, is a strictly psychological concept, also with a long history. The symbolic process gives the human being a remarkable power; it enables him to pretend momentarily that he is another person. While he is "being" that person, i.e., acting like him verbally or empathically, or both, he gets an insight into how that person probably views a given situation. He rehearses what he believes to be the other person's attitude, point of view, perspective, perceptual field, or "role," so that when, a moment later, he returns to "being" himself, he has a good idea of how this other person will probably act in that situation, since he himself would probably have acted that way if he had continued to "be" that other person. With this new knowledge he can now sympathize with, *feel with* and as, the other person, and can thus anticipate what the other person will probably think and do, and he himself can act accordingly. *Role-taking*, then, is a psychological concept referring to a mental or cognitive process, while *role-playing* is a sociological concept referring to a social function which all people holding a particular position or status are expected to perform in overt conduct.

A second differentiating factor is that in *role-taking* one pretends he is another person; while in *role-playing* one does not pretend anything. A policeman arresting a person is not pretending; he is performing or *playing* a role expected of one holding the position of public protector.

The term "play-at" enters the confused picture in this connection. Children play-at being policemen, milkmen, mother, etc.; but they do not and cannot *play* these roles. Playing-at involves an elementary form of role-taking, the verbalized fantasy by which the child learns how to take the role of another. Here the child both imaginatively and overtly pretends he is another person—not necessarily a particular other person, but often a stereotype of some functionary. Playing-at is "make believe" or "play acting." *Playing-at* a role is not necessarily *playing-at-being* another person; it may represent playing-at performing some socially prescribed function which he cannot actually perform since he cannot at his age occupy the appropriate social position; or it may even involve playing-at being a cow pony, machine gun or airplane, with the appropriate vocalizations, sounds or noises.

A third factor differentiating the concepts of *role-taking* and *role-playing* is that role-taking is significantly and necessarily related to social distance, whereas role-playing is not. Indeed there are conditions under which certain roles can be successfully *played* only to the extent that role-taking is inhibited. Too efficient role-taking, putting oneself in the place of one's victim, might prevent a policeman from making an arrest, a soldier from bayoneting an enemy, or a surgeon from operating on a patient. In each of these instances professional training is designed to inhibit *role-taking* ability so that the role can be properly *played*. To play the roles of physician, clergyman, professor, a person must usually be a good role-taker; to play the roles of top executive, hangman, disciplinarian often requires that a person be a poor role-taker, in appropriate situations.

A fourth differentiating factor in these concepts is that role-taking concerns another's "role" (attitude, perspective), whereas role-playing concerns one's own role (social function). Role-taking means thinking and feeling like someone else—a form of projection; role-playing means acting like oneself, a form of socially expected conduct for one holding a given social position.

A fifth differentiating factor is that role-taking is primarily a communicating mechanism, whereas role-playing is only indirectly so. Role-taking involves thinking and feeling as one believes the other person thinks and feels—a form of empathy or of what might be called synconation. Role-taking is thus clearly related to sympathy, whereas role-playing bears no necessary relation to sympathy.

While there is a good deal more to these concepts than is indicated by these five points, yet these are the traditional meanings of the terms as used by Mead and as established in a large sociological literature. Despite the unfortunate similarity of symbols by which the concepts are known, they are, nevertheless, very different constructs. . . .

RECENT EVIDENCE OF CONFUSION

The three texts involved in the following criticism are among the best in social psychology, and they all represent, in one way or another, the new mode in this field. They, with the present writer's text, are the first to use these concepts in an extensive and systematic manner. That confusion of these concepts could occur in such outstanding books indicates that the concepts had not been adequately differentiated in the literature. It is hoped that this paper will contribute to this tardy differentiation.

Newcomb. Newcomb's book is the largest of the three and gives what is probably the most extensive and thoroughgoing analysis of roles and role-playing ever published. This part of his book is an excellent piece of work—but while his exhaustive analysis is concerned almost entirely with roles and *role-playing,* he mistakenly calls the process *role-taking.* In the space of 51 pages the traditional usage of the term "role-taking" is violated 65 times and observed 8 times; and in the rest of the book these figures are more than doubled. In these 51 pages the *process* of role-taking is described 7 times without being given a name, and in numerous instances one or both terms (role-taking and role-playing) are used in a context in which the proper meaning cannot be determined, since it could properly be either, but certainly not both.

The traditional usage of the term "role-taking" is violated 6 times in the following paragraph.

> *Individual Motivation to Take [Play] Roles.* No position within a group endures unless its occupants are motivated to take [play] the role associated with that position. It will not endure, furthermore, unless other group members are motivated to encourage (or at least tolerate) that role. Both of these conditions are necessary. Such motives are acquired by interaction with group members among whom norms already exist which call for certain positions and

roles. Through such interaction, individuals acquire frames of reference, respond to rewards and punishments, and learn the techniques of taking [playing] the role and of responding to others who take [play] roles. In brief, they become motivated to take [play] roles and to have others take [play] roles.

In the above quotation there is not a single instance of the use of "role-taking" in the sense in which George Herbert Mead used the term. Again the text says:

> The role prescribed for any position is necessarily defined in relation to the roles of other people, who, of course, also hold positions. A mother cannot *perform her role* except in relation to a child . . .

Here the term "perform" which is synonoymous with the traditional term "play" is used as if it were synonymous with "take" in the previous quotation, an obvious violation of Mead's usage.

In the following passage the term "take" is misused for "play," and this is followed by an accurate description of true role-taking (the italicized words) but without the use of the term "role-taking":

> In this chapter we shall examine more closely the ways in which individuals come to interiorize social norms and take [play] their roles, more or less as prescribed . . . As an end result of this development individuals become able, in varying degrees, *to put themselves in the place of those with whom they interact,* and to treat them as persons who have attitudes of their own.

This practice of discussing role-playing while calling it role-taking and then suddenly giving a description of true role-taking without using the term is rather frequent, leading the reader to believe that only one concept is involved.

In the following passage the term "plays-at" is used consistently with tradition under the heading "role-taking"; while "plays" is confusingly used for "plays-at."

> *Role-Taking Depends Upon Anticipations.* During this period of absolutism, children begin to practice the prescribed roles of others in their society. The child *plays at* being a milkman, storekeeper, or mother. Quite obviously he is copying whole patterns of behavior which he has observed. The role must be *enacted* in a certain way; there is no readier source of argument among small children than different versions of the proper way of doing it—*e.g. playing* [at] mother, or *playing* [at] milkman. . . . They are commonly *enacted* in such a way as to involve interaction between himself and milkman, storekeeper, or mother. This may be either substitutively (by getting a companion to *play the part* of the child while he *plays* [at] the adult role) or alternately (taking [playing at] each role himself, one after the other).

In the above passage the traditionally proper concept is "play-at" (a child cannot *play* these roles), but is denoted by all three terms—role-taking, playing-at, and role-playing. Furthermore, the heading of this section should be reversed, for anticipation depends on role-taking, not vice versa. One

cannot anticipate the behavior of another without first imaginatively taking his role—putting himself in the other's place. Role-playing, however, is
dependent upon anticipation, which indicates that role-playing is dependent upon role-taking, again indicating two concepts. (This point is important for learning theory in social psychology, for it means that the child
cannot perform the sociological process of role-playing until he is capable
of the psychological process of role-taking in some degree.)

It is remarkable that in one passage Mead's concept of role-taking is
accurately described and named and then immediately confused with role-
playing.

> A person who is speaking to another is also, so to speak, informing himself as
> to what the other is hearing. Thus he is able, in Mead's memorable phrase, to
> "take the role of the other"—i.e., to put himself sufficiently in the other's place
> to anticipate how the other will respond. Thus the child takes [plays] a dual
> role, presumably for the first time, when he begins to speak—i.e., he is [playing
> the roles of] both speaker to others and listener to himself.

The roles of speaker and listener are roles the child can play, so "role-
playing" is proper here, if our analysis of traditional usage is correct.

By the time he reached p. 309 Professor Newcomb apparently felt
that something was wrong, for here, finding his analysis in need of Mead's
concept of role-taking, he captures and uses the concept by giving it a
new name, "Taking the Perspectives of Others." And he does not confuse
this concept with role-playing. However, the new term is seldom used
thereafter and the term "role-taking" again comes into use for both role-
playing and role-taking. On p. 333 the term "take" is used nine times in
accordance with tradition, and once in violation of it. This inconsistent
usage, which occurs frequently, is what is so discouraging, for if the book
always used *taking* for *playing*, correction would be relatively easy.

What we have in Newcomb, then, is (1) an exhaustive analysis of role-
playing which in most instances is unfortunately called role-taking; (2) a
rather frequent reference to the role-taking process but without use of the
identifying term; and (3) a few good descriptions of the role-taking process
with proper use of the identifying term. But the uninitiated reader has no
way of knowing which is what, when or why.

Lindesmith and Strauss. Unlike Newcomb's text, which is of a more or
less eclectic pattern, that of Lindesmith and Strauss is definitely in the new
mode of symbolic interaction. Whereas Newcomb is a psychologist, these
authors are sociologists; and since they, too, confuse the concepts, it is apparent that sociologists have not in the past adequately differentiated these
concepts. Both concepts found their origin and development in sociological
literature.

These authors understand role-playing, and like Newcomb, often use
as synonyms the words enact or enacting. Yet they use the term role-playing
for role-taking, and manage to confuse the two concepts; and they often

neglect to use the term role-taking when discussing the process to which the term refers. We have the strange phenomenon that whereas Newcomb discusses role-playing and calls it role-taking, Lindesmith and Strauss discuss role-taking and call it role-playing, generally speaking, in both cases.

> The appropriateness of the projected *role-playing* is judged by imagining the proposed action from the standpoint of other persons involved in it.

What this passage says is that the appropriateness of a projected role-playing is judged by role-taking on the part of the person contemplating the particular role-playing. While there is nothing wrong in the usage here, yet there is no awareness that this passage, and most of the page, involves both concepts, and the reader is the loser. Although this description of role-taking appears on p. 170, the section entitled "Taking the Role of the Other" does not appear until p. 196, where, amazingly, the term is not used except in the section heading.

There is a remarkable section of three pages entitled "Learning to *play* roles," the context of which is concerned with learning to *take* roles.

> The most extreme and convincing empirical report of the way in which human children gradually learn to take into account the points of view of others has been given by Piaget. . . . The child is at first enclosed in his own point of view and sees all things from within it. His perceptions and judgments tend to be "absolute" or egocentric because he is unaware of any other points of view and perceptions. . . . Because perspectives other than his own are not taken into account, his own perceptions appear absolute. . . .

This is exactly what Mead meant by "role-taking"; and it is what has been called role-taking in a vast sociological literature since Mead. There are in this three-page section eight descriptive references to the role-taking process, but the identifying term is never used; the terms used are "take into account," "take a point of view," "grasp the roles of others," "assume the perspective of others," "grasp the point of view of others," all of which are, to be sure, sound synonyms of "role-taking" or "taking the role of the other," but the reader is not told this, and is not here made familiar with the traditional term. And although the title of the section is on "playing roles," not even this term appears in the section. (Incidentally, this otherwise brilliant section supports our proposition stated earlier that role-taking ability must precede role-playing ability, an important factor in a symbolic-interactionist theory of learning.)

The next section in the book has the title "The Linguistic Basis of Role-Playing," but as in the previous section the subject discussed is role-taking and not role-playing. The burden of this section is to indicate "that language is basic in the development of the ability to *play* roles," despite the fact that the long quotation from Mead given on this page points out that language is basic to role-*taking* ability, even to the extent of using the expressions "taking the roles of others" and "taking different roles." In this quotation Mead also uses the term "playing-at":

The child plays at being a mother, at being a teacher, at being a policeman. . . . He has a set of stimuli which call out in himself the sort of responses they call out in others.

As we pointed out earlier, playing-at roles involves an elementary stage of role-taking primarily concerned with the fantasy life of children, as well as the overt activity of pretending to *play* certain roles which the child could not actually play. The child is playfully acting-out his own fantasy.

The authors close this section by concluding

Through his make-believe verbal play the child learns to take the role of other persons and thus learns to see his own activity from the standpoint of these others. Role-taking in play is paralleled in real-life situations by the child's grasping of actual roles played toward him by parents and other associates, and by his incorporation of certain roles into the structure of his own personality.

Thus, despite the title of the section, nothing is said about role-playing, but an excellent analysis is given of *the linguistic basis of role-taking*. In another quotation from Mead Lindesmith and Strauss give us a clear illustration of what Mead meant by the word "role" in his expression "role-taking":

If we contrast play with . . . an organized game, we note the essential difference that the child who plays in a game must be ready *to take the attitude* of everyone else involved in that game, and that *these different roles* must have a different relationship to each other. . . . In a game where a number of individuals are involved . . . the child taking one role must be ready to take the role of everyone else. . . . He has to have an organization of these roles; otherwise he cannot play the game.

Unfortunately for contemporary social psychology *role* and *attitude* had the same meaning for Mead, and when he used the concept "role-taking" he was not speaking about roles as we understand them in the term "role-playing." It is the failure of the authors of the books under discussion to understand Mead that has led to the confusion. It should be obvious that a ball-player could not play all the "positions" or roles on a team, at least not all at once or while he is playing his own, but in this quotation Mead has the child taking-the-role of everyone on the team while playing his own. A person can, while playing shortstop, take the role of all others on the team involved in a given play. One can *take the attitude* of a gangster without *playing his role;* this is how police catch offenders. We have two concepts here, not one.

In summarizing the importance of studies of children's moral ideas, the authors enumerate several points, among them the fact that the child "moves from simple role-playing [role-taking] to generalized role-playing [role-taking], i.e., his generalized other develops." It should now be apparent that the terms in brackets are the correct ones according to traditional usage. Students of Mead are aware that the "generalized-other" in his thinking is a phenomenon of role-taking, and is irrelevant to role-playing. Generalized "role-playing" is an impossible conception.

The difference between the two concepts is illustrated by two items which the authors use in their "Materials for Discussion" which they give at the end of each chapter without comment. On p. 182 appear the following:

> Richet . . . has shown that the subject on whom a change of personality is imposed [during hypnosis] not only adapts his speech, gestures and attitudes to the new personality, but even his handwriting is modified. (A. Binet)

> There is a continual flow of agreement by the [Southern] Negro while the white man is talking, such as "yes, boss," "Sho nuff," "Well I declare," and the like. (J. Dollard)

I should interpret the first quotation as representing *role-taking*, and the second as representing *role-playing*, but the authors give the reader no cue to what is significant in these quotations.

We saw that in Newcomb's book the terms under discussion are sometimes used in accordance with tradition, and sometimes not, on the same page. This occurs also on p. 186 of Lindesmith and Strauss:

> . . . the ability of human beings to *play* [take] *roles* enables them to acquire objectivity. . . . By assuming the positions of other persons, the individual is able to turn his language upon himself and his own actions.

> The ability to take into account the view of other persons, to *take their roles,* is fundamental to the achievement of "objective" thought.

The same thing occurs on the page following this, while on p. 190 "role-taking" is properly used.

After the authors have already given this extended discussion of role-taking, sometimes properly named but usually called role-playing, there now appears on p. 196 a section entitled "Taking the Role of the Other." Although the process of role-taking is here well described, with its linguistic basis, the term "role-taking" is not used. A more proper title of this section would be "The Linguistic Basis of Role-taking"—a second instance of this.

Sargent. The third of these excellent new texts is that of S. Stansfeld Sargent. As compared with the other two this book lays considerably less stress on roles, role-playing and role-taking, but there is confusion here nevertheless. Whereas Newcomb's book stresses role-playing and calls it role-taking, Sargent's book, like that of Lindesmith and Strauss, stresses role-taking and calls it role-playing, generally speaking.

The discussion begins on p. 205 with the child's elementary role-taking —in the form of "playing-at," after Mead, and the terms follow traditional usage. It is also recognized here that the "generalized-other" emerges from this early type of role-taking, not from role-playing. On p. 206 both terms, role-taking and role-playing, are used with an apparent understanding that the two terms represent different concepts. The subject is then dropped and resumed on p. 273, where doubt begins to enter the reader's mind.

In a quotation from Cameron on p. 275 the term "playing-at" would have been appropriate instead of his using both *playing* and *taking* to denote the process. On p. 278 both terms follow traditional usage, but there appears to be no awareness that two concepts are involved. Then on p. 281 our doubts are substantiated with the violation of traditional usage of the term "take" in two instances. Using the illustration of a guest at a dinner party, the text reads:

> Our guest may, of course, be *displaying* other roles in addition to his central guest role. He may also take [play or display] the role of a man of the world, a cynic, or a prophet. . . . From a strictly psychological standpoint, *role-taking* [role-playing] is possible because the human organism can take and maintain a "mental set" which facilitates certain kinds of behavior and inhibits other responses.

Then at the bottom of the page the word "play" is traditionally used, but is assumed to have the same meaning as "taking" in the last quotation above; and on p. 283 "play" follows traditional usage three times. On p. 284, however, "playing" follows traditional usage but "taken" is used to mean the same thing.

> For the most part the individual is unconscious of the fact that he is *playing* a role. Teacher and student, employer and employee, husband and wife seldom stop to think what is the appropriate behavior. . . . In new and unusual circumstances, however, the situation must be interpreted or defined, and the role *to be taken* [played] may be consciously considered.

The term "role-taking" is again misused on p. 290; but "role-playing" is repeatedly used correctly on pages 306, 309 and 310. Later, pp. 319-320, in a quotation from Carl Rogers we are given a perfect descriptive statement of the role-taking process, even though it is not so named.

> Client-centered therapy has led us to try to *adopt the client's perceptive field* as the basis for genuine understanding.

This is exactly what Mead meant by "taking the role of the other," adopting the other's perceptive field, imaginatively and empathically putting oneself in the other's place.

CONCLUSION

In this paper we have tried to demonstrate the following propositions: (1) that tradition has given us two important concepts pertaining to two very different types of human activity, one sociological and one psychological; (2) that this tradition has also given us two different terms with which to refer to these concepts and activities—terms which, though different, yet are imprecise and inadequately differentiated in the tradition; (3) that these concepts are now in danger of being lost through confusion because recent important texts are using either or both terms to refer to either or both concepts and their relevant activities; and (4) that the corrective for this state of confusion is to use Mead's terms and concepts as Mead used them. There are several adequate synonyms for the term "role-taking," but the reader is the loser, as is the profession, when the original term is not identified with them.

Sociological Implications of the Thought of George Herbert Mead

HERBERT BLUMER

MY PURPOSE IS to depict the nature of human society when seen from the point of view of George Herbert Mead. While Mead gave human society a position of paramount importance in his scheme of thought he did little to outline its character. His central concern was with cardinal problems of philosophy. The development of his ideas of human society was largely limited to handling these problems. His treatment took the form of showing that human group life was the essential condition for the emergence of consciousness, the mind, a world of objects, human beings as organisms possessing selves, and human conduct in the form of constructed acts. He reversed the traditional assumptions underlying philosophical, psychological, and sociological thought to the effect that human beings possess minds and consciousness as original "givens," that they live in worlds of pre-existing and self-constituted objects, that their behavior consists of responses to such objects, and that group life consists of the association of such reacting human organisms. In making his brilliant contributions along this line he did not map out a theoretical scheme of human society. However, such a scheme is implicit in his work. It has to be constructed by tracing the implications of the central matters which he analyzed. This is what I propose to do. The central matters I shall consider are (1) the self, (2) the act, (3) social interaction, (4) objects, and (5) joint action.

Reprinted from *The American Journal of Sociology*, LXXI (March, 1966), pp. 535-544, by Herbert Blumer, by permission of The University of Chicago Press and the author.

THE SELF

Mead's picture of the human being as an actor differs radically from the conception of man that dominates current psychological and social science. He saw the human being as an organism having a self. The possession of a self converts the human being into a special kind of actor, transforms his relation to the world, and gives his action a unique character. In asserting that the human being has a self, Mead simply meant that the human being is an object to himself. The human being may perceive himself, have conceptions of himself, communicate with himself, and act toward himself. As these types of behavior imply, the human being may become the object of his own action. This gives him the means of interacting with himself—addressing himself, responding to the address, and addressing himself anew. Such self-interaction takes the form of making indications to himself and meeting these indications by making further indications. The human being can designate things to himself—his wants, his pains, his goals, objects around him, the presence of others, their actions, their expected actions, or whatnot. Through further interaction with himself, he may judge, analyze, and evaluate the things he has designated to himself. And by continuing to interact with himself he may plan and organize his action with regard to what he has designated and evaluated. In short, the possession of a self provides the human being with a mechanism of self-interaction with which to meet the world—a mechanism that is used in forming and guiding his conduct.

I wish to stress that Mead saw the self as a process and not as a structure. Here Mead clearly parts company with the great bulk of students who seek to bring a self into the human being by identifying it with some kind of organization or structure. All of us are familiar with this practice because it is all around us in the literature. Thus, we see scholars who identify the self with the "ego," or who regard the self as an organized body of needs or motives, or who think of it as an organization of attitudes, or who treat it as a structure of internalized norms and values. Such schemes which seek to lodge the self in a structure make no sense since they miss the reflexive process which alone can yield and constitute a self. For any posited structure to be a self, it would have to act upon and respond to itself—otherwise, it is merely an organization awaiting activation and release without exercising any effect on itself or on its operation. This marks the crucial weakness or inadequacy of the many schemes such as referred to above, which misguidingly associate the self with some kind of psychological or personality structure. For example, the ego, as such, is not a self; it would be a self only by becoming reflexive, that is to say, acting toward or on itself. And the same thing is true of any other posited psychological structure. Yet, such reflexive action changes both the status and the character of the structure and elevates the process of self-interaction to the position of major importance.

We can see this in the case of the reflexive process that Mead has isolated in the human being. As mentioned, this reflexive process takes the form of the person making indications to himself, that is to say, noting things and determining their significance for his line of action. To indicate something is to stand over against it and to put oneself in the position of acting toward it instead of automatically responding to it. In the face of something which one indicates, one can withhold action toward it, inspect it, judge it, ascertain its meaning, determine its possibilities, and direct one's action with regard to it. With the mechanism of self-interaction the human being ceases to be a responding organism whose behavior is a product of what plays upon him from the outside, the inside, or both. Instead, he acts toward his world, interpreting what confronts him and organizing his action on the basis of the interpretation. To illustrate: a pain one identifies and interprets is very different from a mere organic feeling and lays the basis for doing something about it instead of merely responding organically to it; to note and interpret the activity of another person is very different from having a response released by that activity; to be aware that one is hungry is very different from merely being hungry; to perceive one's "ego" puts one in the position of doing something with regard to it instead of merely giving expression to the ego. As these illustrations show, the process of self-interaction puts the human being over against his world instead of merely in it, requires him to meet and handle his world through a defining process instead of merely responding to it, and forces him to construct his action instead of merely releasing it. This is the kind of acting organism that Mead sees man to be as a result of having a self.[1]

THE ACT

Human action acquires a radically different character as a result of being formed through a process of self-interaction. Action is built up in coping with the world instead of merely being released from a pre-existing psychological structure by factors playing on that structure. By making indications to himself and by interpreting what he indicates, the human being has to forge or piece together a line of action. In order to act the individual has to identify what he wants, establish an objective or goal, map out a prospective line of behavior, note and interpret the actions of

[1] The self, or indeed human being, is not brought into the picture merely by introducing psychological elements, such as motives and interests, along side of societal elements. Such additions merely compound the error of the omission. This is the flaw in George Homan's presidential address on "Bringing Man Back In" (*American Sociological Review*, XXIX, No. 6, 809-18).

others, size up his situation, check himself at this or that point, figure out what to do at other points, and frequently spur himself on in the face of dragging dispositions or discouraging settings. The fact that the human act is self-directed or built up means in no sense that the actor necessarily exercises excellence in its construction. Indeed, he may do a very poor job in constructing his act. He may fail to note things of which he should be aware, he may misinterpret things that he notes, he may exercise poor judgment, he may be faulty in mapping out prospective lines of conduct, and he may be half-hearted in contending with recalcitrant dispositions. Such deficiencies in the construction of his acts do not belie the fact that his acts are still constructed by him out of what he takes into account. What he takes into account are the things that he indicates to himself. They cover such matters as his wants, his feelings, his goals, the actions of others, the expectations and demands of others, the rules of his group, his situation, his conceptions of himself, his recollections, and his images of prospective lines of conduct. He is not in the mere recipient position of responding to such matters; he stands over against them and has to handle them. He has to organize or cut out his lines of conduct on the basis of how he does handle them.

This way of viewing human action is directly opposite to that which dominates psychological and social sciences. In these sciences human action is seen as a product of factors that play upon or through the human actor. Depending on the preference of the scholar, such determining factors may be physiological stimulations, organic drives, needs, feelings, unconscious motives, conscious motives, sentiments, ideas, attitudes, norms, values, role requirements, status demands, cultural prescriptions, institutional pressures, or social-system requirements. Regardless of which factors are chosen, either singly or in combination, action is regarded as their product and hence is explained in their terms. The formula is simple: Given factors play on the human being to produce given types of behavior. The formula is frequently amplified so as to read: Under specified conditions, given factors playing on a given organization of the human being will produce a given type of behavior. The formula, in either its simple or amplified form, represents the way in which human action is seen in theory and research. Under the formula the human being becomes a mere medium or forum for the operation of the factors that produce the behavior. Mead's scheme is fundamentally different from this formula. In place of being a mere medium for operation of determining factors that play upon him, the human being is seen as an active organism in his own right, facing, dealing with, and acting toward the objects he indicates. Action is seen as conduct which is constructed by the actor instead of response elicited from some kind of preformed organization in him. We can say that the traditional formula of human action fails to recognize that the human being is a self. Mead's scheme, in contrast, is based on this recognition.

SOCIAL INTERACTION

I can give here only a very brief sketch of Mead's highly illuminating analysis of social interaction. He identified two forms or levels—non-symbolic interaction and symbolic interaction. In non-symbolic interaction human beings respond directly to one another's gestures or actions; in symbolic interaction they interpret each other's gestures and act on the basis of the meaning yielded by the interpretation. An unwitting response to the tone of another's voice illustrates non-symbolic interaction. Interpreting the shaking of a fist as signifying that a person is preparing to attack illustrates symbolic interaction. Mead's concern was predominantly with symbolic interaction. Symbolic interaction involves *interpretation,* or ascertaining the meaning of the actions or remarks of the other person, and *definition,* or conveying indications to another person as to how he is to act. Human association consists of a process of such interpretation and definition. Through this process the participants fit their own acts to the ongoing acts of one another and guide others in doing so.

Several important matters need to be noted in the case of symbolic interaction. First, it is a formative process in its own right. The prevailing practice of psychology and sociology is to treat social interaction as a neutral medium, as a mere forum for the operation of outside factors. Thus psychologists are led to account for the behavior of people in interaction by resorting to elements of the psychological equipment of the participants —such elements as motives, feelings, attitudes, or personality organization. Sociologists do the same sort of thing by resorting to societal factors, such as cultural prescriptions, values, social roles, or structural pressures. Both miss the central point that human interaction is a positive shaping process in its own right. The participants in it have to build up their respective lines of conduct by constant interpretation of each other's ongoing lines of action. As participants take account of each other's ongoing acts, they have to arrest, reorganize, or adjust their own intentions, wishes, feelings, and attitudes; similarly, they have to judge the fitness of norms, values, and group prescriptions for the situation being formed by the acts of others. Factors of psychological equipment and social organization are not substitutes for the interpretative process; they are admissible only in terms of how they are handled in the interpretative process. Symbolic interaction has to be seen and studied in its own right.

Symbolic interaction is noteworthy in a second way. Because of it human group life takes on the character of an ongoing process—a continuing matter of fitting developing lines of conduct to one another. The fitting together of the lines of conduct is done through the dual process of definition and interpretation. This dual process operates both to sustain established patterns of joint conduct and to open them to transformation.

Established patterns of group life exist and persist only through the continued use of the same schemes of interpretation; and such schemes of interpretation are maintained only through their continued confirmation by the defining acts of others. It is highly important to recognize that the established patterns of group life just do not carry on by themselves but are dependent for their continuity on recurrent affirmative definition. Let the interpretations that sustain them be undermined or disrupted by changed definitions from others and the patterns can quickly collapse. This dependency of interpretations on the defining acts of others also explains why symbolic interaction conduces so markedly to the transformation of the forms of joint activity that make up group life. In the flow of group life there are innumerable points at which the participants are *re*defining each other's acts. Such redefinition is very common in adversary relations, it is frequent in group discussion, and it is essentially intrinsic to dealing with problems. (And I may remark here that no human group is free of problems.) Redefinition imparts a formative character to human interaction, giving rise at this or that point to new objects, new conceptions, new relations, and new types of behavior. In short, the reliance on symbolic interaction makes human group life a developing process instead of a mere issue or product of psychological or social structure.

There is a third aspect of symbolic interaction which is important to note. In making the process of interpretation and definition of one another's acts central in human interaction, symbolic interaction is able to cover the full range of the generic forms of human association. It embraces equally well such relationships as cooperation, conflict, domination, exploitation, consensus, disagreement, closely knit identification, and indifferent concern for one another. The participants in each of such relations have the same common task of constructing their acts by interpreting and defining the acts of each other. The significance of this simple observation becomes evident in contrasting symbolic interaction with the various schemes of human interaction that are to be found in the literature. Almost always such schemes construct a general model of human interaction or society on the basis of a particular type of human relationship. An outstanding contemporary instance is Talcott Parsons' scheme which presumes and asserts that the primordial and generic form of human interaction is the "complementarity of expectations." Other schemes depict the basic and generic model of human interaction as being "conflict," others assert it to be "identity through common sentiments," and still others that it is agreement in the form of "consensus." Such schemes are parochial. Their great danger lies in imposing on the breadth of human interaction an image derived from the study of only one form of interaction. Thus, in different hands, human society is said to be fundamentally a sharing of common values; or, conversely, a struggle for power; or, still differently, the exercise of consensus; and so on. The simple point implicit in Mead's analysis of symbolic interaction is that human beings, in interpreting and defining one another's acts, can and do meet each other in the full range of human relations. Proposed schemes of human society should respect this simple point.

OBJECTS

The concept of object is another fundamental pillar in Mead's scheme of analysis. Human beings live in a world or environment of objects, and their activities are formed around objects. This bland statement becomes very significant when it is realized that for Mead objects are human constructs and not self-existing entities with intrinsic natures. Their nature is dependent on the orientation and action of people toward them. Let me spell this out. For Mead, an object is anything that can be designated or referred to. It may be physical as a chair or imaginary as a ghost, natural as a cloud in the sky or man-made as an automobile, material as the Empire State Building or abstract as the concept of liberty, animate as an elephant or inanimate as a vein of coal, inclusive of a class of people as politicians or restricted to a specific person as President de Gaulle, definite as a multiplication table or vague as a philosophical doctrine. In short, objects consist of whatever people indicate or refer to.

There are several important points in this analysis of objects. First, the nature of an object is constituted by the meaning it has for the person or persons for whom it is an object. Second, this meaning is not intrinsic to the object but arises from how the person is initially prepared to act toward it. Readiness to use a chair as something in which to sit gives it the meaning of a chair; to one with no experience with the use of chairs the object would appear with a different meaning, such as a strange weapon. It follows that objects vary in their meaning. A tree is not the same object to a lumberman, a botanist, or a poet; a star is a different object to a modern astronomer than it was to a sheepherder of antiquity; communism is a different object to a Soviet patriot than it is to a Wall Street broker. Third, objects—all objects—are social products in that they are formed and transformed by the defining process that takes place in social interaction. The meaning of the objects—chairs, trees, stars, prostitutes, saints, communism, public education, or whatnot—is formed from the ways in which others refer to such objects or act toward them. Fourth, people are prepared or set to act toward objects on the basis of the meaning of the objects for them. In a genuine sense the organization of a human being consists of his objects, that is, his tendencies to act on the basis of their meanings. Fifth, just because an object is something that is designated, one can organize one's action toward it instead of responding immediately to it; one can inspect the object, think about it, work out a plan of action toward it, or decide whether or not to act toward it. In standing over against the object in both a logical and psychological sense, one is freed from coercive response to it. In this profound sense an object is different from a stimulus as ordinarily conceived.

This analysis of objects puts human group life into a new and interesting perspective. Human beings are seen as living in a world of meaningful objects—not in an environment of stimuli or self-constituted entities. This world is socially produced in that the meanings are fabricated through the process of social interaction. Thus, different groups come to develop different worlds—and these worlds change as the objects that compose them change in meaning. Since people are set to act in terms of the meanings of their objects, the world of objects of a group represents in a genuine sense its action organization. To identify and understand the life of a group it is necessary to identify its world of objects; this identification has to be in terms of the meanings objects have for the members of the group. Finally, people are not locked to their objects; they may check action toward objects and indeed work out new lines of conduct toward them. This condition introduces into human group life an indigenous source of transformation.

JOINT ACTION

I use the term "joint action" in place of Mead's term "social act." It refers to the larger collective form of action that is constituted by the fitting together of the lines of behavior of the separate participants. Illustrations of joint action are a trading transaction, a family dinner, a marriage ceremony, a shopping expedition, a game, a convivial party, a debate, a court trial, or a war. We note in each instance an identifiable and distinctive form of joint action, comprised by an articulation of the acts of the participants. Joint actions range from a simple collaboration of two individuals to a complex alignment of the acts of huge organizations or institutions. Everywhere we look in a human society we see people engaging in forms of joint action. Indeed, the totality of such instances—in all of their multitudinous variety, their variable connections, and their complex networks—constitutes the life of a society. It is easy to understand from these remarks why Mead saw joint action, or the social act, as the distinguishing characteristic of society. For him, the social act was the fundamental unit of society. Its analysis, accordingly, lays bare the generic nature of society.

To begin with, a joint action cannot be resolved into a common or same type of behavior on the part of the participants. Each participant necessarily occupies a different position, acts from that position, and engages in a separate and distinctive act. It is the fitting together of these acts and not their commonality that constitutes joint action. How do these separate acts come to fit together in the case of human society? Their alignment does not occur through sheer mechanical juggling, as in the shaking of walnuts in a jar or through unwitting adaptation, as in an ecological arrangement in a plant community. Instead, the participants fit their acts together, first, by identifying the social act in which they are about to engage and, second, by interpreting and defining each other's acts in forming the joint act. By identifying the social act or joint action the participant is able to orient himself; he has a key to interpreting the acts of others and a guide for directing his action with regard to them. Thus, to act appropriately, the participant has to identify a marriage ceremony as a marriage ceremony, a holdup as a holdup, a debate as a debate, a war as a war, and so forth. But, even though this identification be made, the participants in the joint action that is being formed still find it necessary to interpret and define one another's ongoing acts. They have to ascertain what the others are doing and plan to do and make indications to one another of what to do.

This brief analysis of joint action enables us to note several matters of distinct importance. It calls attention, first, to the fact that the essence of society lies in an ongoing process of action—not in a posited structure of relations. Without action, any structure of relations between people is meaningless. To be understood, a society must be seen and grasped in terms of the action that comprises it. Next, such action has to be seen and treated, not by tracing the separate lines of action of the participants—whether the participants be single individuals, collectivities, or organizations—but in terms of the joint action into which the separate lines of action fit and merge. Few students of human society have fully grasped this point or its implications. Third, just because it is built up over time by the fitting together of acts, each joint action must be seen as having a career or a history. In having a career, its course and fate are contingent on what happens during its formation. Fourth, this career is generally orderly, fixed and repetitious by virtue of a common identification or definition of the joint action that is made by its participants. The common definition supplies each participant with decisive guidance in directing his own act so as to fit into the acts of the others. Such common definitions serve, above everything else, to account for the regularity, stability, and repetitiveness of joint action in vast areas of group life; they are the source of the established and regulated social behavior that is envisioned in the concept of culture. Fifth, however, the career of joint actions also must be seen as open to many possibilities of uncertainty. Let me specify the more important of these possibilities. One, joint actions have to be initiated—and they may not be. Two, once started a joint action may be interrupted, abandoned, or transformed. Three, the participants may not make a common definition of the joint action into which they are thrown and hence may orient their acts on different premises. Four, a common definition of a joint action may still allow wide differences in the direction of the separate lines of action and hence in the course taken by the joint action; a war is a good example. Five, new situations may arise calling for hitherto unexisting types of joint action, leading to confused exploratory efforts to work out a fitting together of acts. And, six, even in the context of a commonly defined joint action, participants may be led to rely on other considerations in interpreting and defining each other's lines of action. Time does not allow me to spell out and illustrate the importance of these possibilities. To mention them should be sufficient, however, to show that uncertainty, contingency, and transformation are part and parcel of the process of joint action. To assume that the diversified joint actions which comprise a human society are set to follow fixed and established channels is a sheer gratuitous assumption.

From the foregoing discussion of the self, the act, social interaction, objects, and joint action we can sketch a picture of human society. The picture is composed in terms of action. A society is seen as people meeting the varieties of situations that are thrust on them by their conditions of life. These situations are met by working out joint actions in which participants have to align their acts to one another. Each participant does so by interpreting the acts of others and, in turn, by making indications to others as to how they should act. By virtue of this process of interpretation and definition joint actions are built up; they have careers. Usually, the course of a joint action is outlined in advance by the fact that the participants make a common identification of it; this makes for regularity, stability, and repetitiveness in the joint action. However, there are many joint actions that encounter obstructions, that have no preestablished pathways, and that have to be constructed along new lines. Mead saw human society in this way—as a diversified social process in which people were engaged in forming joint actions to deal with situations confronting them.

This picture of society stands in significant contrast to the dominant views of society in the social and psychological sciences—even to those that pretend to view society as action. To point out the major differences in the contrast is the best way of specifying the sociological implications of Mead's scheme of thought.

The chief difference is that the dominant views in sociology and psychology fail, alike, to see human beings as organisms having selves. Instead, they regard human beings as merely responding organisms and, accordingly, treat action as mere response to factors playing on human beings. This is exemplified in the efforts to account for human behavior by such factors as motives, ego demands, attitudes, role requirements, values, status expectations, and structural stresses. In such approaches the human being becomes a mere medium through which such initiating factors operate to produce given actions. From Mead's point of view such a conception grossly misrepresents the nature of human beings and human action. Mead's scheme interposes a process of self-interaction between initiating factors and the action that may follow in their wake. By virtue of self-interaction the human being becomes an acting organism coping with situations in place of being an organism merely responding to the play of factors. And his action becomes something he constructs and directs to meet the situations in place of an unrolling of reactions evoked from him. In introducing the self, Mead's position focuses on how human beings handle and fashion their world, not on disparate responses to imputed factors.

If human beings are, indeed, organisms with selves, and if their action is, indeed, an outcome of a process of self-interaction, schemes that purport to study and explain social action should respect and accommodate these features. To do so, current schemes in sociology and psychology would have to undergo radical revision. They would have to shift from a preoccupation with initiating factor and terminal result to a preoccupation with a process of formation. They would have to view action as something constructed by the actor instead of something evoked from him. They would have to depict the milieu of action in terms of how the milieu appears to the actor in place of how it appears to the outside student. They would have to incorporate the interpretive process which at present they scarcely deign to touch. They would have to recognize that any given act has a career in which it is constructed but in which it may be interrupted, held in abeyance, abandoned, or recast.

On the methodological or research side the study of action would have to be made from the position of the actor. Since action is forged by the actor out of what he perceives, interprets, and judges, one would have to see the operating situation as the actor sees it, perceive objects as the actor perceives them, ascertain their meaning in terms of the meaning they have for the actor, and follow the actor's line of conduct as the actor organizes it—in short, one would have to take the role of the actor and see his world from his standpoint. This methodological approach stands in contrast to the so-called objective approach so dominant today, namely, that of viewing the actor and his action from the perspective of an outside, detached observer. The "objective" approach holds the danger of the observer substituting his view of the field of action for the view held by the actor. It is unnecessary to add that the actor acts toward his world on the basis of how he sees it and not on the basis of how that world appears to the outside observer.

In continuing the discussion of this matter, I wish to consider especially what we might term the structural conception of human society. This conception views society as established organization, familiar to us in the use of such terms as social structure, social system, status position, social role, social stratification, institutional structure, cultural pattern, social codes, social norms, and social values. The conception presumes that a human society is structured with regard to (a) the social positions occupied by the people in it and with regard to (b) the patterns of behavior in which they engage. It is presumed further that this interlinked structure of social positions and behavior patterns is the over-all determinant of social action; this is evidenced, of course, in the practice of explaining conduct by such structural concepts as role requirements, status demands, strata differences, cultural prescriptions, values, and norms. Social action falls into two general categories: conformity, marked by adherence to the structure, and deviance, marked by departure from it. Because of the central and determinative position into which it is elevated, structure becomes necessarily the encompassing object of sociological study and analysis—epitomized by the well-nigh universal assertion that a human group or society is a "social system." It is perhaps unnecessary to observe that the conception of human society as structure or organization is ingrained in the very marrow of contemporary sociology.

Mead's scheme definitely challenges this conception. It sees human society not as an established structure but as people meeting their conditions of life; it sees social action not as an emanation of societal structure but as a formation made by human actors; it sees this formation of action not as societal factors coming to expression through the medium of human organisms but as constructions made by actors out of what they take into account; it sees group life not as a release or expression of established structure but as a process of building up joint actions; it sees social actions as having variable careers and not as confined to the alternatives of conformity to or deviation from the dictates of established structure; it sees the so-called interaction between parts of a society not as a direct exercising of influence by one part on another but as mediated throughout by interpretations made by people; accordingly, it sees society not as a system, whether in the form of a static, moving or whatever kind of equilibrium, but as a vast number of occurring joint actions, many closely linked, many not linked at all, many prefigured and repetitious, others being carved out in new directions, and all being pursued to serve the purposes of the participants and not the requirements of a system. I have said enough, I think, to point out the drastic differences between the Meadian conception of society and the widespread sociological conceptions of it as structure.

The differences do not mean, incidentally, that Mead's view rejects the existence of structure in human society. Such a position would be ridiculous. There are such matters as social roles, status positions, rank orders, bureaucratic organizations, relations between institutions, differential authority arrangements, social codes, norms, values, and the like. And they are very important. But their importance does not lie in an alleged determination of action nor in an alleged existence as parts of a self-operating societal system. Instead, they are important only as they enter into the process of interpretation and definition out of which joint actions are formed. The manner and extent to which they enter may vary greatly from situation to situation, depending on what people take into account and how they assess what they take account of. Let me give one brief illustration. It is ridiculous, for instance, to assert, as a number of eminent sociologists have done, that social interaction is an interaction between social roles. Social interaction is obviously an interaction between *people* and not between roles; the needs of the participants are to interpret and handle what confronts them—such as a topic of conversation or a problem

—and not to give expression to their roles. It is only in highly ritualistic relations that the direction and content of conduct can be explained by roles. Usually, the direction and content are fashioned out of what people in interaction have to deal with. That roles affect in varying degree phases of the direction and content of action is true but is a matter of determination in given cases. This is a far cry from asserting action to be a product of roles. The observation I have made in this brief discussion of social roles applies with equal validity to all other structural matters.

Another significant implication of Mead's scheme of thought refers to the question of what holds a human society together. As we know, this question is converted by sociologists into a problem of unity, stability, and orderliness. And, as we know further, the typical answer given by sociologists is that unity, stability, and orderliness come from a sharing in common of certain basic matters, such as codes, sentiments, and, above all, values. Thus, the disposition is to regard common values as the glue that holds a society together, as the controlling regulator that brings and keeps the activities in a society in orderly relationship, and as the force that preserves stability in a society. Conversely, it is held that conflict between values or the disintegration of values creates disunity, disorder, and instability. This conception of human society becomes subject to great modification if we think of society as consisting of the fitting together of acts to form joint action. Such alignment may take place for any number of reasons, depending on the situations calling for joint action, and need not involve, or spring from, the sharing of common values. The participants may fit their acts to one another in orderly joint actions on the basis of compromise, out of duress, because they may use one another in achieving their respective ends, because it is the sensible thing to do, or out of sheer necessity. This is particularly likely to be true in our modern complex societies with their great diversity in composition, in lines of interest, and in their respective worlds of concern. In very large measure, society becomes the formation of workable relations. To seek to encompass, analyze, and understand the life of a society on the assumption that the existence of a society necessarily depends on the sharing of values can lead to strained treatment, gross misrepresentation, and faulty lines of interpretation. I believe that the Meadian perspective, in posing the question of how people are led to align their acts in different situations in place of presuming that this necessarily requires and stems from a sharing of common values, is a more salutary and realistic approach.

There are many other significant sociological implications in Mead's scheme of thought which, under the limit of space, I can do no more than mention. Socialization shifts its character from being an effective internalization of norms and values to a cultivated capacity to take the roles of others effectively. Social control becomes fundamentally and necessarily a matter of self-control. Social change becomes a continuous indigenous process in human group life instead of an episodic result of extraneous factors playing on established structure. Human group life is seen as always incomplete and undergoing development instead of jumping from one completed state to another. Social disorganization is seen not as a breakdown of existing structure but as an inability to mobilize action effectively in the face of a given situation. Social action, since it has a career, is recognized as having a historical dimension which has to be taken into account in order to be adequately understood.

In closing I wish to say that my presentation has necessarily skipped much in Mead's scheme that is of great significance. Further, I have not sought to demonstrate the validity of his analyses. However, I have tried to suggest the freshness, the fecundity, and the revolutionary implications of his point of view.

FURTHER READINGS

Brown, Roger. *Social Psychology*. New York: The Free Press, 1965.

Elkin, Frederick. *The Child and Society: The Process of Socialization*. New York: Random House, 1960.

Goffman, Erving. *The Presentation of Self in Everyday Life*. Garden City, New York: Doubleday Anchor Books, 1959.

Piaget, Jean. *Play, Dreams and Imitation in Childhood,* New York: W. W. Norton, 1962.

6

MEANING AND
ITS CONSEQUENCES

Introduction

ABOUT A HALF-CENTURY AGO two of the pioneers of American sociology were enmeshed in a study which was to become a classic in the theoretical and empirical literature. W. I. Thomas and Florian Znaniecki's, *The Polish Peasant in Europe and America* (1918), represents a major effort to wed empirical research with theoretical generalization at a time when only a handful of sociologists existed. That it provided a stimulus for empirical research in American sociology is beyond doubt. However, a number of important concepts were developed in this study, one of which was the "definition of the situation."

In Merton's paraphrase, included in his essay reprinted here, "if men define situations as real then they are real in their consequences." Thus the person's reaction to the elements in a given situation, whether it is in accord with the true state of affairs or not, induces acts which have consequences for him and his fellows.

Jean Paul Sartre in a Mead-like analysis of the mental state of a type of contemporary man reminds us that our response to others is a subtle and complicated process which is at the heart of man's existential problems. It makes it clear to us that there are sociological precedents which are of value in interpreting contemporary philosophical thought. In addition it is closely bound up with problems of alienation and is meaningful within the context of the essay in Chapter 13, Alienation and Anomie.

The excerpt from one of Robert MacIver's best-known works is a good example of how the definition of the situation works in a very concrete instance. It is well to note that MacIver's approach is very similar to the Thomas and Znaniecki approach.

Robert K. Merton's brilliant paper has become a classic. It is profound and practical in its applicability to societal processes. Not only do we see the direct workings of the self-fulfilling prophecy within the mind of the actor but we see how it operates on the larger social structure. No more meaningful statement on the forces contributing to the segregation and subordination of minority groups exists in the sociological literature. It can profitably be reread with the materials in Chapter 8, Institutionalization and Change; Chapter 11, Industrialization; and Chapter 12, Mass Society and Mass Culture.

Authentic and Inauthentic Man

JEAN-PAUL SARTRE

IF IT IS AGREED that man may be defined as a being having freedom within the limits of a situation, then it is easy to see that the exercise of this freedom may be considered as *authentic* or *inauthentic* according to the choices made in the situation. Authenticity, it is almost needless to say, consists in having a true and lucid consciousness of the situation, in assuming the responsibilities and risks that it involves, in accepting it in pride or humiliation, sometimes in horror and hate.

There is no doubt that authenticity demands much courage and more than courage. Thus it is not surprising that one finds it so rarely. Most members of the middle class and most Christians are not authentic, in the sense that they refuse to live up to their middle-class or Christian condition fully and that they always conceal certain parts of themselves from themselves. When the Communists set down as part of their program "the radicalization of the masses," when Marx explains that the proletarian class *ought to be* conscious of itself, what does that mean if not that the worker, too, is not at first authentic?

And the Jew does not escape this rule: authenticity for him is to live to the full his condition as Jew; inauthenticity is to deny it or to attempt to escape from it. Inauthenticity is no doubt more tempting for him than for other men, because the situation which he has to lay claim to and to live in is quite simply that of a martyr. What the least favored of men ordinarily discover in their situation is a bond of concrete solidarity with other men. The economic condition of the salaried man living in the perspective of revolution, or the condition of the member of a persecuted church, involves in itself a profound unity of material and spiritual interests. But we have shown that the Jews have neither community of interests nor community of beliefs. They do not have the same fatherland; they have no history. The

From *Anti-Semite and Jew*, by Jean-Paul Sartre. Copyright ©, 1948, by Shocken Books, Inc. Translated by George J. Becker. French Edition: *Reflexions sur la Question Juive*. ©, Editions Gallimard, 1954. Reprinted by permission of the publishers.

sole tie that binds them is the hostility and disdain of the societies which surround them. Thus the authentic Jew is the one who asserts his claim in the face of the disdain shown toward him.

The situation he wishes fully to understand and live out is, in time of social peace, almost incomprehensible: it is an atmosphere, a subtle sense of faces and of words, a menace that is concealed in things, an abstract bond that unites him to men who in all other respects are very different from him. Everything conspires actually to show him to his own eyes as a simple Frenchman. For the prosperity of his affairs depends closely upon that of his country, the fate of his sons is linked to peace, to the greatness of France, and the language he speaks and the culture that has been given him permit him to base his calculations and his reasoning on the principles common to the whole nation. He should therefore only have to let himself go in order to forget that he is a Jew, if he did not detect everywhere this almost undetectable poison—the hostile consciousness of others.

What is astonishing is certainly not that there are inauthentic Jews; it is rather that, in proportion, they are fewer than the inauthentic Christians. However, it is by taking advantage of certain aspects of the conduct of inauthentic Jews that the anti-Semite has forged his general mythology of the Jew. What characterizes the inauthentic Jews is that they deal with their situation by running away from it; they have chosen to deny it, or to deny their responsibilities, or to deny their isolation, which appears intolerable to them. That does not necessarily mean that they wish to destroy the concept of the Jew or that they explicitly deny the existence of a Jewish reality. But their gestures, sentiments and acts aim secretly at destroying this reality.

In a word, the inauthentic Jews are men whom other men take for Jews and who have decided to run away from this insupportable situation. The result is that they display various types of behavior not all of which are present at the same time in the same person but each of which may be characterized as an *avenue of flight*. The anti-Semite by collecting and assembling all these distinct and often incompatible avenues of flight has traced out a monstrous portrait which is supposed to be that of the Jew in general; at the same time he explains these free efforts at escape from a painful situation as hereditary traits, engraved on the very body of Israel and, consequently, incapable of modification.

If we wish to see the problem clearly, we must take this portrait apart, restore the autonomy of these "avenues of flight," and present them in their true character as ventures in behavior instead of innate qualities. It must be understood that the description of these avenues of flight is applied solely to the *inauthentic* Jew (the term "inauthentic" implying no moral blame, of course), and that it should be supplemented by a description of authentic Jewishness. Finally, we must grasp the idea that it is the *situation* of the Jew which must under all circumstances serve us as guiding thread. If we understand this method and if we apply it rigorously, perhaps we will be able to substitute for the great Manichaean myth about Israel a few truths which, while more fragmentary, are more accurate.

What is the first trait in the anti-Semitic mythology? It is, we are told, that the Jew is a complicated being who passes his time in self-analysis and subtle scheming. We are quick to call him a "splitter of hairs" without even asking ourselves whether this tendency to analysis and introspection is compatible with the sharpness in business and the blind aggressiveness that are also attributed to him. For my part, I recognize that the effort to escape produces in some Jews—for the most part intellectuals—an almost continuously reflective attitude. But again we must understand each other. This reflective behavior is not inherited. It is an avenue of flight, and it is we who force the Jew to flee.

Stekel, along with several other psychoanalysts, speaks of a "Jewish complex," and many are the Jews who mention their "inferiority complex." I see no harm in using this expression if we understand that this complex has not been received from the outside and that the Jew *creates this complex* when he chooses to live out his situation in an inauthentic manner. He has allowed himself to be persuaded by the anti-Semites; he is the first victim of their propaganda. He admits with them that, *if there is a Jew*, he must have the characteristics with which popular malevolence endows him, and his effort is to constitute himself a martyr, in the proper sense of the term, that is, to prove *in his person* that there are no Jews.

With him anxiety often takes a special form; it becomes a fear of acting or feeling like a Jew. We are familiar with those neurasthenics who are haunted by the fear of killing, of jumping out of a window, of uttering obscene words. Certain Jews are in some degree comparable to these people, though their anxiety rarely attains a pathological level. They have allowed themselves to be poisoned by the stereotype that others have of them, and they live in fear that their acts will correspond to this stereotype. Repeating a term used earlier, we may say that their conduct is perpetually over-determined from the inside. Their acts have not only the motives which can be assigned to those of non-Jews—interest, passion, altruism, etc.—but they seek also to distinguish themselves radically from the acts catalogued as "Jewish." How many Jews are deliberately generous, disinterested, and even magnificent simply *because* the Jew is ordinarily taken to be a man of money? That in no way signifies that they have to struggle against "tendencies" to avarice—there is no reason, a priori, for Jews to be more avaricious than Christians—it means rather that their gestures of generosity are poisoned by the decision to be generous. Spontaneity and deliberate choice are here inextricably mixed. The end pursued is to obtain a certain result in the external world and at the same time to prove to oneself, to prove to others, that there is no such thing as Jewish nature.

Thus many inauthentic Jews play at not being Jews. Several Jews have reported to me their curious reaction after the armistice. We know that the role of the Jews in the Resistance was admirable; it was they who formed the principal cadres before the Communists went into action; for four years they gave proof of a courage and a spirit of decision which it is a pleasure to acknowledge. However, certain of them hesitated a great deal before "resisting," for the Resistance appeared to them so completely in line with Jewish interests that they were reluctant at first to engage in it; they wanted to make sure they were resisting not *as Jews* but *as Frenchmen.* This scrupulousness shows sufficiently the peculiar quality of their deliberations: the Jewish factor intervenes on every occasion and it is impossible for them to make a decision based merely on the pure and simple examination of the facts. In a word, they fall naturally into a state of reflective self-consciousness.

Like the timid person, like the scrupulous person, the Jew is not content to act or think; he sees himself act, he sees himself think. We must remark, however, that Jewish reflectiveness is in itself *practical*, since it does not originate in disinterested curiosity or in the desire for moral conversion. It is not the man but the *Jew* whom the Jews seek to know in themselves through introspection; and they wish to know him *in order to deny him.* With them it is not a question of recognizing certain faults and combating them, but of underlining by their conduct the fact that they do not have those faults. Thus we may explain that particular quality of Jewish irony which exercises itself most often at the expense of the Jew himself and which is a perpetual attempt to see himself from the outside. The Jew, because he knows he is under observation, takes the initiative and attempts to look at himself through the eyes of others. This objectivity toward himself is still another ruse of inauthenticity: while he contemplates himself with the "detachment" of another, he feels himself in effect *detached* from himself; he becomes another person, a pure witness.

However, he knows that this detachment from himself will be effective only if it is ratified by others. That is why one finds in him so often the faculty of assimilation. He absorbs all knowledge with an avidity which is not to be confused with disinterested curiosity. He hopes to become "a man," nothing but a man, a man like all other men, by taking in all the thoughts of man and acquiring a human point of view of the universe. He cultivates himself in order to destroy the Jew in himself, as if he wished to have applied to him—but in modified form—the phrase of Terence: *Nil humani alienum puto ergo homo sum.**

At the same time he tries to lose himself in the crowd of Christians. We have seen that the latter have the art and the audacity to pretend before the Jew that they are not *another race*, but purely and simply *men*; if the Jew is fascinated by Christians it is not because of their virtues, which he values little, but because they represent anonymity, humanity without race. If he tries to penetrate the most exclusive circles, it is not because of that boundless ambition with which he is reproached so often—or, rather, that ambition has only one meaning: the Jew seeks to be recognized as a man

---

* "Nothing human is alien to me; therefore, I am a man."

by other men. If he wishes to slip in everywhere, it is because he cannot be at rest so long as there remains a single place which resists him and which, by resisting him, makes him a Jew in his own eyes. The principle behind this drive toward assimilation is an excellent one: the Jew is claiming his rights as a Frenchman. Unfortunately the realization of this enterprise rests on an inadequate foundation. He wants people to receive him as "a man," but even in the circles which he has been able to enter, he is received as a Jew. He is the rich or powerful Jew whom it is absolutely necessary to associate with, or the "good" Jew, the exceptional Jew, with whom one associates *in spite of* his race.

The Jew is not unaware of this, but if he admitted to himself that he was received as a Jew his enterprise would lose all meaning and he would become discouraged. He is therefore acting in bad faith: he is concealing the truth from himself, though he knows it in his heart. He conquers a position in his capacity as Jew; he keeps it with the means he has at his disposal, that is, with "Jewish" means, but he considers that each new conquest is a symbol of a higher step in the process of assimilation. It develops automatically that anti-Semitism, which is the almost immediate reaction of the circles he has penetrated, does not long permit him to remain unaware of what he would so much like to ignore. Yet the violence of the anti-Semite has the paradoxical effect of pushing the Jews to the conquest of other milieux and other groups. In short, his ambition is fundamentally a search for security, just as his snobbism—when he is a snob—is an effort to assimilate national values (pictures, books, etc.).

Thus he moves rapidly and brilliantly up through all social levels, but he remains like a hard kernel in the circles which accept him, and his assimilation is as ephemeral as it is brilliant. He is often reproached for this. According to a remark by André Siegfried, the Americans believe that their anti-Semitism originates in the fact that Jewish immigrants, in appearance the first to be assimilated, are still Jews in the second and third generations. This is naturally interpreted as meaning that the Jew does not sincerely desire to be assimilated and that, behind a feigned adaptability, there is concealed a deliberate and conscious attachment to the traditions of his race. The truth is exactly the contrary: it is because he is never accepted as *a* man, but always and everywhere as *the* Jew that the Jew is unassimilable.

The Dynamic Assessment

ROBERT MacIVER

1. BUSINESS MAN sits in his office. He has concluded an important deal. The tension under which he had been working is relaxed. He is back to the everyday routine and it has less savor than before. He is conscious of a vague restlessness. He wants a change of some sort. His days have been too slavishly devoted to the demands of business, he has been missing other things. He has been making money—why shouldn't he spend some, indulge himself a little? Why not take time off and go on a voyage? The business can get along without him for a few weeks. A steamship company's advertisement of a "luxury cruise," which he had read some days before, comes to his mind. "It is just the thing I need," he says to himself, "a complete change of scene." His wife has been warning him against overworking. His family will appreciate him more when he comes back after an absence. The air and sunshine will do him good. He will make new acquaintances. It will be pleasant to visit Rio and Buenos Aires and other places he has merely read about. The more he thinks of the idea the better he likes it. Before the day is over he "makes up his mind" and telephones the steamship company for a reservation.

What has our business man been doing? He has been assessing a situation and arriving at a decision. He has had alternatives before him and has chosen between them. He is going to travel, for recreation or health or adventure. That is the way he puts it to others—or to himself. His statement of objective is necessarily incomplete and is probably a simplification. Anyhow he has reached a decision, probably without any meticulous calculation. He cannot really tell you how he arrived at it. *It is his dynamic assessment of a situation.* Let us take it at that for the present. In the process of making a decision, some desire, some valuation, simple or complex, has become dominant for the time being, as a determinant of action within the individual's scheme of values.

2. Having made his decision, our business man reorganizes his activities in order to attain his objective. He gives instructions for the conduct of his affairs during his absence. He makes arrangements for family needs. He foresees certain contingencies and provides against them. He cancels some engagements. He buys some travelling equipment. He turns resources hitherto neutral and undirected, such as the money he pays for his transportation, into specific means, the means for his new objective.

From *Social Causation,* 1942, pp. 291-299. Reprinted through the courtesy of Blaisdell Publishing Company, a division of Ginn and Company.

In all conscious behavior there is thus a twofold process of selective organization. On the one hand the value-system of the individual, his active cultural complex, his personality, is focussed in a particular direction, towards a particular objective. (Sometimes, as we previously pointed out, the incentive to the reorganization of activity may be a dominating motive that is not attached to a specific objective.) On the other hand certain aspects of external reality are selectively related to the controlling valuation, are distinguished from the rest of the external world, are in a sense withdrawn from it, since they now become themselves value factors, the means, obstacles, or conditions relevant to the value quest. The inner, or subjective, system is focussed by a dynamic valuation; and the outer, or external, system is "spotlighted" in that focus, the part within the spotlight being *transformed from mere externality into something also belonging to a world of values*, as vehicle, accessory, hindrance, and cost of the value attainment.

3. The traveller sets out on his voyage. He enters into a new system of social relations. He is subjected to new influences. He may be deflected thereby from his original objective, he may find new additional objectives, or he may pursue exclusively the first one. Even in the last event he may fail to attain his goal. The experience of adventure may fall flat, he may not improve his health, he may not achieve whatever other end he sought. His assessment of the situation may have been faulty. He may have miscalculated the chances of success. He may have left out of the reckoning some important considerations. Or it may be that developments of an unforeseen character intervene and make his voyage nugatory.

In all conscious behavior we relate means to ends, but the process of establishing this relationship is contingent and involves an attribution of causality that may or may not be confirmed by experience. Before embarking on his ship our traveller had somehow assessed the situation. This assessment, whether superficial or thorough, involved a reckoning of alternatives. It contained, as do all decisions to act, a speculative element. A dynamic assessment weighs alternatives not yet actualized, sets what would be the consequences if this course were taken over against what would be the consequences if that course were taken. It is in this regard a causal judgment. We pointed out in a previous chapter that the attribution of social causation always contains a speculative factor of this sort. But the dynamic assessment, that is, the judgment that carries a decision to act, differs from the *post mortem* judgment of history or social science in that it is doubly contingent. In the historical attribution we imaginatively construct what would have happened if the historically presented event or act had not occurred, or at the least we postulate that certain happenings would not have occurred but for the event or act in question. One of the alternatives that must be weighed in the process of causal attribution is always imaginatively constructed. But in the practical judgment that unleashes action *both* of the final alternatives are constructs, for both refer to the future. The voyager chose what he thought likely to happen if he travelled in preference to what he thought likely to happen if he stayed at home.

4. Our traveller set out on his voyage without reckoning all the contingencies. No one does or could calculate all the possible combinations of circumstance that may conspire against—or in favor of—his enterprise. When a man decides to act he generally has two or three alternatives before him and he assesses these alternatives in the light of a few expectancies. These alone come within the focus of decision. But "there's many a slip 'twixt the cup and the lip." We can perhaps distinguish three types of contingency that may frustrate the attainment of an objective once decided upon. Two of these we have already suggested. The traveller may "change his mind" while he travels and be diverted to another quest. Or he may carry through his project and at the end find that he had miscalculated the means-end nexus—if he travels for health the voyage may not restore him. The first contingency occurs in the structure of the inner or subjective system; the second in the relationship of the inner and the outer—the relation of means to ends was conceived to be such and such and it turned out to be different. But there is a third type of contingency which has reference to the dynamics of the external order alone. Our traveller probably did not consider the chance that his ship might strike a rock or founder in a storm. He certainly did not consider the chance that he might fall on a slippery deck and break his leg. He thought of the ship as an instrument of his ends and since most ships make the port they sail for he gave no consideration to the fact that the ship, as physical reality, is subjected to forces that are oblivious of its instrumental quality. It enters, like all instruments, into two causal systems, the means-end system of the conscious realm and the neutral system of physical nature. The adjustment of the dependent causality of the first system to the independent causality of the second is imperfect, and thus a new set of contingencies arises. Our traveller did not concern himself with these contingencies. He was content to assess a certain routine of experience that he expected would continue if he stayed at home and a certain alternative to that routine that he expected would occur if he took the voyage. He foresaw, under the impulse of the emotions congenial to his temperament, a preferable train of consequences as likely to occur if he decided to travel—and decided accordingly.

In all conscious behavior the situation we assess, as preliminary to action, is in no sense the total objective situation. In the first place it is obviously not the situation as it might appear to some omniscient and disinterested eye, viewing all its complex interdependences and all its endless contingencies. In the second place it is not the situation as inclusive of all the conditions and aspects observable, or even observed, by the participant himself. Many things of which he is aware he excludes from the focus of interest or attention. Many contingencies he ignores. The situation he assesses is one that he has selectively defined, in terms of his experience, his habit of response, his intellectual grasp, and his emotional engrossment. The dynamic assessment limits the situation by excluding all the numerous aspects that are not apprehended as relevant to the choice between alternatives. At the same time it includes in the situation various aspects that are not objectively given, that would not be listed in any merely physical inventory. For in the first place it envisages the situation as impregnated with values and susceptible of new potential values; and in the second place the envisagement is dependent on the ever-changing value-system of the individual, charged with memory of past experience, moulded by the impact of previous indoctrination, responsive to the processes of change within his whole psycho-organic being. Thus no two individuals envisage and define a situation in exactly the same way, even when they make a seemingly identical decision and even although social influences are always powerfully at work to merge individual assessments into a collective assessment.

Our simple instance of the traveller has brought out a number of points, which we recapitulate as follows:

1. A preliminary to conscious activity is a decision between alternatives —to do this or to do that, to do or not to do. In the process of decision-making the individual assesses a situation in the light of these alternatives. A choice between values congenial to the larger value-system of the individual is somehow reached.

2. The decision once taken, the other purposes or valuations of the individual are accommodated to it. Preparatory actions follow. In this orientation certain external factors are selectively reorganized and given subjective significance. They are construed as means, obstacles, conditions, and limitations, with reference to the attainment of the dominant desire or value. The dynamic assessment brings the external world selectively into the subjective realm, conferring on it subjective significance for the ends of action.

3. The dynamic assessment involves a type of causal judgment that differs from the *post factum* attribution of causality characteristic of the social sciences, in that it is doubly speculative. It rests always on a predictive judgment of the form: if this is done, this consequence will (is likely to) follow *and* if this is not done or if this other thing is done, this other consequence will (is likely to) follow. We may observe in passing that even the most simple-seeming choice may conceal a subtle and unfathomed subjective process.

4. The selectivity of the dynamic assessment, as it reviews the situation prior to decision and as it formulates the alternatives of action, makes it subject to several kinds of contingency and practical hazard. First, the dominant objective registered in the decision to act may not persist throughout the process leading to its attainment. Second, the means-ends nexus envisaged in the decision to act may be misapprehended. Third, the physical order assumed to be under control as the means and conditions of action may "erupt" into the situation in unanticipated ways. All conscious behaving is an implicit reckoning of probabilities, which may or may not be justified by the event.

Before we take leave of our simple case we may point out that the analysis of it contains already the clue to our main problem. What has particularly troubled us is that the various factors we causally relate to any socio-psychological phenomenon belong to different orders of reality. Yet they must somehow get together, they must somehow become comparable and co-ordinate, since they must operate with or against one another in the determination of the phenomenon. But how does, say, a moral conviction "co-operate" with an empty stomach in determining whether or not a man will steal? How does the prevalence of a particular religion combine with rural conditions in determining a high birth-rate? How does the decline of religious authority combine with urban congestion and the improvement of contraceptives in the lowering of the birth-rate? The suggested answer is that *in the dynamic assessment all the factors determining conscious behavior are brought into a single order.* The external factors enter not as such, but as considerations affecting or relative to the pursuit of ends. A change of religious attitudes and the expense of bringing up children both affect the value-system of the individuals concerned. At every moment of deliberation or decision the individual is faced with alternatives. He has not one desire but many, and they are not independent but inter-dependent. He seeks attainment not of one value but of a system of values, for that is what it means to have, or be, a personality. What choice he will make, what end he will here and now pursue, depends on the urgency of particular desires, the intensity or depth of particular valuations, relative to the variant conditions of attainment. The intensity and depth of particular valuations will in turn register a recognition of the different possibilities of attainment. The change in religious attitudes is not wholly independent of the conditions of urban living. In any event, it introduces a change in the individual's scheme of values. But so, indirectly, does the fact of urban congestion. It makes some values easier of attainment, and some harder. Values are values only as calling for attainment or for maintenance—there would be no values in a static world; conditions and means are such only as they make for or against the attaining or the maintaining of values.

The Self-Fulfilling Prophecy

ROBERT K. MERTON

IN A SERIES OF WORKS seldom consulted outside the academic fraternity, W. I. Thomas, the dean of American sociologists, set forth a theorem basic to the social sciences: "If men define situations as real, they are real in their consequences." Were the Thomas theorem and its implications more widely known more men would understand more of the workings of our society. Though it lacks the sweep and precision of a Newtonian theorem, it possesses the same gift of relevance, being instructively applicable to many, if indeed not most, social processes.

THE THOMAS THEOREM

"If men define situations as real, they are real in their consequences," wrote Professor Thomas. The suspicion that he was driving at a crucial point becomes all the more insistent when we note that essentially the same theorem had been repeatedly set forth by disciplined and observant minds long before Thomas.

When we find such otherwise discrepant minds as the redoubtable Bishop Bossuet in his passionate seventeenth-century defense of Catholic orthodoxy; the ironic Mandeville in his eighteenth-century allegory honeycombed with observations on the paradoxes of human society; the irascible genius Marx in his revision of Hegel's theory of historical change; the seminal Freud in works which have perhaps gone further than any others of his day toward modifying man's outlook on man; and the erudite, dogmatic, and occasionally sound Yale professor, William Graham Sumner, who lives on as the Karl Marx of the middle classes—when we find this mixed company (and I select from a longer if less distinguished list) agreeing on the truth and the pertinence of what is substantially the Thomas theorem, we may conclude that perhaps it's worth our attention as well.

To what, then, are Thomas and Bossuet, Mandeville, Marx, Freud and Sumner directing our attention?

The first part of the theorem provides an unceasing reminder that men respond not only to the objective features of a situation, but also, and at times primarily, to the meaning this situation has for them. And once they have assigned some meaning to the situation, their consequent behavior

Reprinted from *The Antioch Review*, Volume VII, Number 2, copyright, 1948, by The Antioch Press.

and some of the consequences of that behavior are determined by the ascribed meaning. But this is still rather abstract, and abstractions have a way of becoming unintelligible if they are not occasionally tied to concrete data. What is a case in point?

A SOCIOLOGICAL PARABLE

It is the year 1932. The Last National Bank is a flourishing institution. A large part of its resources is liquid without being watered. Cartwright Millingville has ample reason to be proud of the banking institution over which he presides. Until Black Wednesday. As he enters his bank, he notices that business is unusually brisk. A little odd, that, since the men at the A.M.O.K. steel plant and the K.O.M.A. mattress factory are not usually paid until Saturday. Yet here are two dozen men, obviously from the factories, queued up in front of the tellers' cages. As he turns into his private office, the president muses rather compassionately: "Hope they haven't been laid off in midweek. They should be in the shop at this hour."

But speculations of this sort have never made for a thriving bank, and Millingville turns to the pile of documents upon his desk. His precise signature is affixed to fewer than a score of papers when he is disturbed by the absence of something familiar and the intrusion of something alien. The low discreet hum of bank business has given way to a strange and annoying stridency of many voices. A situation has been defined as real. And that is the beginning of what ends as Black Wednesday—the last Wednesday, it might be noted, of the Last National Bank.

Cartwright Millingville had never heard of the Thomas theorem. But he had no difficulty in recognizing its workings. He knew that, despite the comparative liquidity of the bank's assets, a rumor of insolvency, once believed by enough depositors, would result in the insolvency of the bank. And by the close of Black Wednesday—and Blacker Thursday—when the long lines of anxious depositors, each frantically seeking to salvage his own, grew to longer lines of even more anxious depositors, it turned out that he was right.

The stable financial structure of the bank had depended upon one set of definitions of the situation: belief in the validity of the interlocking system of economic promises men live by. Once depositors had defined the situation otherwise, once they questioned the possibility of having these promises fulfilled, the consequences of this unreal definition were real enough.

A familiar type-case this, and one doesn't need the Thomas theorem to understand how it happened—not, at least, if one is old enough to have voted for Franklin Roosevelt in 1932. But with the aid of the theorem the tragic history of Millingville's bank can perhaps be converted into a sociological parable which may help us understand not only what happened to hundreds of banks in the '30's but also what happens to the relations between Negro and white, between Protestant and Catholic and Jew in these days.

The parable tells us that public definitions of a situation (prophecies or predictions) become an integral part of the situation and thus affect subsequent developments. This is peculiar to human affairs. It is not found in the world of nature. Predictions of the return of Halley's comet do not influence its orbit. But the rumored insolvency of Millingville's bank did affect the actual outcome. The prophecy of collapse led to its own fulfillment.

So common is the pattern of the self-fulfilling prophecy that each of us has his favored specimen. Consider the case of the examination neurosis. Convinced that he is destined to fail, the anxious student devotes more time to worry than to study and then turns in a poor examination. The initially fallacious anxiety is transformed into an entirely justified fear. Or it is believed that war between two nations is "inevitable." Actuated by this conviction, representatives of the two nations become progressively alienated, apprehensively countering each "offensive" move of the other with a "defensive" move of their own. Stockpiles of armaments, raw materials, and armed men grow larger and eventually the anticipation of war helps create the actuality.

The self-fulfilling prophecy is, in the beginning, a *false* definition of the situation evoking a new behavior which makes the originally false conception come *true*. The specious validity of the self-fulfilling prophecy perpetuates a reign of error. For the prophet will cite the actual course of events as proof that he was right from the very beginning. (Yet we know that Millingville's bank was solvent, that it would have survived for many years had not the misleading rumor *created* the very conditions of its own fulfillment). Such are the perversities of social logic.

It is the self-fulfilling prophecy which goes far toward explaining the dynamics of ethnic and racial conflict in the America of today. That this is the case, at least for relations between Negroes and whites, may be gathered from the fifteen hundred pages which make up Gunnar Myrdal's *An American Dilemma*. That the self-fulfilling prophecy may have even more general bearing upon the relations between ethnic groups than Myrdal has indicated is the thesis of the considerably briefer discussion which follows.

SOCIAL BELIEFS FATHER SOCIAL REALITY

As a result of their failure to comprehend the operation of the self-fulfilling prophecy, many Americans of good will are (sometimes reluctantly) brought to retain enduring ethnic and racial prejudices. They experience these beliefs, not as prejudices, not as prejudgments, but as irresistible products of their own observation. "The facts of the case" permit them no other conclusion.

Thus our fair-minded white citizen strongly supports a policy of excluding Negroes from his labor union. His views are, of course, based not upon prejudice, but upon the cold hard facts. And the facts seem clear enough. Negroes, "lately from the non-industrial South, are undisciplined in traditions of trade unionism and the art of collective bargaining." The Negro is a strikebreaker. The Negro, with his "low standard of living," rushes in to take jobs at less than prevailing wages. The Negro is, in short, "a traitor to the working class," and should manifestly be excluded from union organizations. So run the facts of the case as seen by our tolerant but hard-headed union member, innocent of any understanding of the self-fulfilling prophecy as a basic process of society.

Our unionist fails to see, of course, that he and his kind have produced the very "facts" which he observes. For by defining the situation as one in which Negroes are held to be incorrigibly at odds with principles of unionism and by excluding Negroes from unions, he invited a series of consequences which indeed made it difficult if not impossible for many Negroes to avoid the role of scab. Out of work after World War I, and kept out of unions, thousands of Negroes could not resist strikebound employers who held a door invitingly open upon a world of jobs from which they were otherwise excluded.

History creates its own test of the theory of self-fulfilling prophecies. That Negroes were strikebreakers because they were excluded from unions (and from a large range of jobs) rather than excluded because they were strikebreakers can be seen from the virtual disappearance of Negroes as scabs in industries where they have gained admission to unions in the last decades.

The application of the Thomas theorem also suggests how the tragic, often vicious, circle of self-fulfilling prophecies can be broken. The initial definition of the situation which has set the circle in motion must be abandoned. Only when the original assumption is questioned and a new definition of the situation introduced, does the consequent flow of events give the lie to the assumption. Only then does the belief no longer father the reality.

But to question these deep-rooted definitions of the situation is no simple act of the will. The will, or for that matter, good will, cannot be turned on and off like a faucet. Social intelligence and good will are themselves *products* of distinct social forces. They are not brought into being by mass propaganda and mass education, in the usual sense of these terms so dear to the sociological panaceans. In the social realm, no more than in the psychological realm, do false ideas quietly vanish when confronted with the truth. One does not expect a paranoiac to abandon his hard-won distortions and delusions upon being informed that they are altogether groundless. If psychic ills could be cured merely by the dissemination of truth, the psychiatrists of this country would be suffering from technological unemployment rather than from overwork. Nor will a continuing "educational campaign" itself destroy racial prejudice and discrimination.

This is not a particularly popular situation. The appeal to "education" as a cure-all for the most varied social problems is rooted deep in the mores of America. Yet it is nonetheless illusory for all that. For how would this program of racial education proceed? Who is to do the educating? The teachers in our communities? But, in some measure like many other Americans, the teachers share the same prejudices they are being urged to combat. And when they don't, aren't they being asked to serve as conscientious martyrs in the cause of educational utopianism? How long the tenure of an elementary school teacher in Alabama or Mississippi or Georgia who attempted meticulously to disabuse his young pupils of the racial beliefs they acquired at home? Education may serve as an operational adjunct but not as the chief basis for any but excruciatingly slow change in the prevailing patterns of race relations.

To understand further why educational campaigns cannot be counted on to eliminate prevailing ethnic hostilities, we must examine the operation of "in-groups" and "out-groups" in our society. Ethnic out-groups, to adopt Sumner's useful bit of sociological jargon, consist of all those who are believed to differ significantly from "ourselves" in terms of nationality, race, or religion. Counterpart of the ethnic out-group is of course the ethnic in-group, constituted by those who "belong." There is nothing fixed or eternal about the lines separating the in-group from out-groups. As situations change, the lines of separation change. For a large number of white Americans, Joe Louis is a member of an out-group—when the situation is defined in racial terms. On another occasion, when Louis defeated the nazified Schmeling, many of these same white Americans acclaimed him as a member of the (national) in-group. National loyalty took precedence over racial separatism. These abrupt shifts in group boundaries sometimes prove embarrassing. Thus, when Negro-Americans ran away with the honors in the Olympic games held in Berlin, the Nazis, pointing to the second-class citizenship assigned Negroes in various regions of this country, denied that the United States had really won the games, since the Negro athletes were by our own admission "not full-fledged" Americans. And what could Bilbo or Rankin say to that?

Under the benevolent guidance of the dominant in-group, ethnic out-groups are continuously subjected to a lively process of prejudice which, I think, goes far toward vitiating mass education and mass propaganda for ethnic tolerance. This is the process whereby "in-group virtues become out-group vices," to paraphrase a remark by the sociologist Donald Young. Or, more colloquially and perhaps more instructively, it may be called the "damned-if-you-do and damned-if-you-don't" process in ethnic and racial relations.

IN-GROUP VIRTUES AND OUT-GROUP VICES

To discover that ethnic out-groups are damned if they do embrace the values of white Protestant society and damned if they don't, we have first to turn to one of the in-group culture heroes, examine the qualities with which he is endowed by biographers and popular belief, and thus distill the qualities of mind and action and character which are generally regarded as altogether admirable.

Periodic public opinion polls are not needed to justify the selection of Abe Lincoln as the culture hero who most fully embodies the cardinal American virtues. As the Lynds point out in *Middletown*, the people of that typical small city allow George Washington alone to join Lincoln as the greatest of Americans. He is claimed as their very own by almost as many well-to-do Republicans as by less well-to-do Democrats.

Even the inevitable schoolboy knows that Lincoln was thrifty, hard-working, eager for knowledge, ambitious, devoted to the rights of the average man, and eminently successful in climbing the ladder of opportunity from the lowermost rung of laborer to the respectable heights of merchant and lawyer. (We need follow his dizzying ascent no farther.)

If one did not know that these attributes and achievements are numbered high among the values of middle-class America, one would soon discover it by glancing through the Lynds' account of "The Middletown Spirit." For there we find the image of the Great Emancipator fully reflected in the values in which Middletown believes. And since these are their values, it is not surprising to find the Middletowns of America condemning and disparaging those individuals and groups who fail, presumably, to exhibit these virtues. If it appears to the white in-group that Negroes are *not* educated in the same measure as themselves, that they have an "unduly" high proportion of unskilled workers and an "unduly" low proportion of successful business and professional men, that they are thriftless, and so on through the catalogue of middle-class virtue and sin, it is not difficult to understand the charge that the Negro is "inferior" to the white.

Sensitized to the workings of the self-fulfilling prophecy, we should be prepared to find that the anti-Negro charges which are not patently false are only speciously true. The allegations are "true" in the Pickwickian sense that we have found self-fulfilling prophecies in general to be true. Thus, if the dominant in-group believes that Negroes are inferior, and sees to it that funds for education are not "wasted on these incompetents" and then proclaims as final evidence of this inferiority that Negroes have proportionately "only" one-fifth as many college graduates as whites, one can scarcely be amazed by this transparent bit of social legerdemain. Having seen the rabbit carefully though not too adroitly placed in the hat, we can only look askance at the triumphant air with which it is finally produced. (In fact, it is a little embarrassing to note that a larger proportion of Negro than of white high school graduates goes on to college; obviously, the Negroes who are hardy enough to scale the high walls of discrimination represent an even more highly selected group than the run-of-the-high-school white population.)

So, too, when the gentleman from Mississippi (a state which spends five times as much on the average white pupil as on the average Negro pupil) proclaims the essential inferiority of the Negro by pointing to the per capita ratio of physicians among Negroes as less than one-fourth that of whites, we are impressed more by his scrambled logic than by his profound prejudices. So plain is the mechanism of the self-fulfilling prophecy in these instances that only those forever devoted to the victory of sentiment over fact can take these specious evidences seriously. Yet the spurious evidence often creates a genuine belief. Self-hypnosis through one's own propaganda is a not infrequent phase of the self-fulfilling prophecy.

So much for out-groups being damned if they don't (apparently) manifest in-group virtues. It is a tasteless bit of ethnocentrism, seasoned with self-interest. But what of the second phase of this process? Can one seriously mean that out-groups are also damned if they *do* possess these virtues? One can.

Through a faultlessly bisymmetrical prejudice, ethnic and racial outgroups get it coming and going. The systematic condemnation of the outgrouper continues largely *irrespective of what he does*. More: through a freakish exercise of capricious judicial logic, the victim is punished for the crime. Superficial appearances notwithstanding, prejudice and discrimination aimed at the out-group are not a result of what the out-group does, but are rooted deep in the structure of our society and the social psychology of its members.

To understand how this happens, we must examine the moral alchemy through which the in-group readily transmutes virtue into vice and vice into virtue, as the occasion may demand. Our studies will proceed by the casemethod.

We begin with the engagingly simple formula of moral alchemy: the same behavior must be differently evaluated according to the person who exhibits it. For example, the proficient alchemist will at once know that the word "firm" is properly declined as follows:

> I am firm,
> Thou art obstinate,
> He is pigheaded.

There are some, unversed in the skills of this science, who will tell you that one and the same term should be applied to all three instances of identical behavior. Such unalchemical nonsense should simply be ignored.

With this experiment in mind, we are prepared to observe how the very same behavior undergoes a complete change of evaluation in its transition

from the in-group Abe Lincoln to the out-group Abe Cohen or Abe Kuro-
kawa. We proceed systematically. Did Lincoln work far into the night? This
testifies that he was industrious, resolute, perseverant, and eager to realize
his capacities to the full. Do the out-group Jews or Japanese keep these same
hours? This only bears witness to their sweatshop mentality, their ruthless
undercutting of American standards, their unfair competitive practices. Is
the in-group hero frugal, thrifty, and sparing? Then the out-group villain is
stingy, miserly and penny-pinching. All honor is due the in-group Abe for
his having been smart, shrewd, and intelligent and, by the same token, all
contempt is owing the out-group Abes for their being sharp, cunning, crafty,
and too clever by far. Did the indomitable Lincoln refuse to remain content
with a life of work with the hands? Did he prefer to make use of his brain?
Then, all praise for his plucky climb up the shaky ladder of opportunity.
But, of course, the eschewing of manual work for brain work among the
merchants and lawyers of the out-group deserves nothing but censure for a
parasitic way of life. Was Abe Lincoln eager to learn the accumulated wisdom of the ages by unending study? The trouble with the Jew is that he's a
greasy grind, with his head always in a book, while decent people are going
to a show or a ball game. Was the resolute Lincoln unwilling to limit his
standards to those of his provincial community? That is what we should
expect of a man of vision. And if the out-groupers criticize the vulnerable
areas in our society, then send 'em back where they came from. Did Lincoln,
rising high above his origins, never forget the rights of the common man and
applaud the right of workers to strike? This testifies only that, like all real
Americans, this greatest of Americans was deathlessly devoted to the cause
of freedom. But, as you examine the recent statistics on strikes, remember
that these un-American practices are the result of out-groupers pursuing
their evil agitation among otherwise contented workers.

Once stated, the classical formula of moral alchemy is clear enough.
Through the adroit use of these rich vocabularies of encomium and opprobrium, the in-group readily transmutes its own virtues into others' vices.
But why do so many in-groupers qualify as moral alchemists? Why are so
many in the dominant in-group so fully devoted to this continuing experiment in moral transmutation?

An explanation may be found by putting ourselves at some distance
from this country and following the anthropologist Malinowski to the Trobriand Islands. For there we find an instructively similar pattern. Among the
Trobrianders, to a degree which Americans, despite Hollywood and the confession magazines, have apparently not yet approximated, success with
women confers honor and prestige on a man. Sexual prowess is a positive
value, a moral virtue. But if a rank-and-file Trobriander has "too much"
sexual success, if he achieves "too many" triumphs of the heart, an achievement which should of course be limited to the elite, the chiefs or men of
power, then this glorious record becomes a scandal and an abomination.
The chiefs are quick *to resent any personal achievement not warranted by*

social position. The moral virtues remain virtues only so long as they are jealously confined to the proper in-group. The right activity by the wrong people becomes a thing of contempt, not of honor. For clearly, only in this way, by holding these virtues exclusively to themselves, can the men of power retain their distinction, their prestige, and their power. No wiser procedure could be devised to hold intact a system of social stratification and social power.

The Trobrianders could teach us more. For it seems clear that the chiefs have not calculatingly devised this program of entrenchment. Their behavior is spontaneous, unthinking, and immediate. Their resentment of "too much" ambition or "too much" success in the ordinary Trobriander is not contrived, it is genuine. It just happens that this prompt emotional response to the "misplaced" manifestation of in-group virtues also serves the useful expedient of reinforcing the chiefs' special claims to the good things of Trobriand life. Nothing could be more remote from the truth and more distorted a reading of the facts than to assume that this conversion of in-group virtues into out-group vices is part of a calculated deliberate plot of Trobriand chiefs to keep Trobriand commoners in their place. It is merely that the chiefs have been indoctrinated with an appreciation of the proper order of things, and see it as their heavy burden to enforce the mediocrity of others.

Nor, in quick revulsion from the culpabilities of the moral alchemists, need we succumb to the equivalent error of simply upending the moral status of the in-group and the out-groups. It is not that Jews and Negroes are one and all angelic while Gentiles and whites are one and all fiendish. It is not that individual virtue will now be found exclusively on the wrong side of the ethnic-racial tracks and individual viciousness on the right side. It is conceivable even that there are as many corrupt and vicious men and women among Negroes and Jews as among Gentile whites. It is only that the ugly fence which encloses the in-group happens to exclude the people who make up the out-groups from being treated with the decency ordinarily accorded human beings.

SOCIAL FUNCTIONS AND DYSFUNCTIONS

We have only to look at the consequences of this peculiar moral alchemy to see that there is no paradox at all in damning out-groupers if they do and if they don't exhibit in-group virtues. Condemnation on these two scores performs one and the same social function. Seeming opposites coalesce. When Negroes are tagged as incorrigibly inferior because they (apparently) don't manifest these virtues, this confirms the natural rightness of their being assigned an inferior status in society. And when Jews or Japanese are tagged as having too many of the in-group values, it becomes plain that they must be securely controlled by the high walls of discrimination. In both cases, the special status assigned the several out-groups can be seen to be eminently reasonable.

Yet this distinctly reasonable arrangement persists in having most unreasonable consequences, both logical and social. Consider only a few of these.

In some contexts, the eliminations enforced upon the out-group—say, rationing the number of Jews permitted to enter colleges and professional schools—logically imply a fear of the alleged superiority of the out-group. Were it otherwise, no discrimination need be practiced. The unyielding, impersonal forces of academic competition would soon trim down the number of Jewish (or Japanese or Negro) students to an "appropriate" size.

This implied belief in the superiority of the out-group seems premature. There is simply not enough scientific evidence to demonstrate Jewish or Japanese or Negro superiority. The effort of the in-group discriminator to supplant the myth of Aryan superiority with the myth of non-Aryan superiority is condemned to failure by science. Moreover, such myths are illadvised. Eventually, life in a world of myth must collide with fact in the world of reality. As a matter of simple self-interest and social therapy, therefore, it might be wise for the in-group to abandon the myth and cling to the reality.

The pattern of being damned-if-you-do and damned-if-you-don't has further consequences—among the out-groups themselves. The response to alleged deficiencies is as clear as it is predictable. If one is repeatedly told that one is inferior, that one lacks any positive accomplishments, it is all too human to seize upon every bit of evidence to the contrary. The in-group definitions force upon the allegedly inferior out-group a defensive tendency to magnify and exalt "race accomplishments." As the distinguished Negro sociologist, Franklin Frazier, has noted, the Negro newspapers are "intensely race conscious and exhibit considerable pride in the achievements of the Negro, most of which are meagre performances as measured by broader standards." Self-glorification, found in some measure among all groups, becomes a frequent counter-response to persistent belittlement from without.

It is the damnation of out-groups for "excessive achievement," however, which gives rise to truly bizarre behavior. For, after a time and often as a matter of self-defense, these out-groups become persuaded that their virtues really are vices. And this provides the final episode in a tragi-comedy of inverted values.

Let us try to follow the plot through its intricate maze of self-contradictions. Respectful admiration for the arduous climb from office boy to president is rooted deep in American culture. This long and strenuous ascent carries with it a two-fold testimonial: it testifies that careers are abundantly open to genuine talent in American society and it testifies to the worth of the man who has distinguished himself by his heroic rise. It would be invidious to choose among the many stalwart figures who have fought their way up, against all odds, until they have reached the pinnacle, there to sit at the head of the long conference table in the longer conference room of The Board. Taken at random, the saga of Frederick H. Ecker, chairman of the board of one of the largest privately managed corporations in the world, the Metropolitan Life Insurance Company, will suffice as the prototype. From a menial and poorly paid job, he rose to a position of eminence. Appropriately enough, an unceasing flow of honors has come to this man of large power and large achievement. It so happens, though it is a matter personal to this eminent man of finance, that Mr. Ecker is a Presbyterian. Yet at last report, no elder of the Presbyterian church has risen publicly to announce that Mr. Ecker's successful career should not be taken too seriously, that, after all, relatively few Presbyterians have risen from rags to riches and that Presbyterians do not actually "control" the world of finance—or life insurance, or investment housing. Rather, one would suppose, Presbyterian elders join with other Americans imbued with middle-class standards of success to felicitate the eminently successful Mr. Ecker and to acclaim other sons of the faith who have risen to almost equal heights. Secure with their in-group status, they point the finger of pride rather than the finger of dismay at individual success.

Prompted by the practice of moral alchemy, noteworthy achievements by out-groupers elicit other responses. Patently, if achievement is a vice, the achievements must be disclaimed—or at least, discounted. Under these conditions, what is an occasion for Presbyterian pride must become an occasion for Jewish dismay. If the Jew is condemned for his educational or professional or scientific or economic success, then, understandably enough, many Jews will come to feel that these accomplishments must be minimized in simple self-defense. Thus is the circle of paradox closed by out-groupers busily engaged in assuring the powerful in-group that they have not, in fact, been guilty of inordinate contributions to science, the professions, the arts, the government, and the economy.

In a society which ordinarily looks upon wealth as a warrant of ability, an out-group is compelled by the inverted attitudes of the dominant in-group to deny that many men of wealth are among its members. "Among the 200 largest non-banking corporations . . . only ten have a Jew as president or chairman of the board." Is this an observation of an anti-Semite, intent on proving the incapacity and inferiority of Jews who have done so little "to build the corporations which have built America"? No; it is a retort of the Anti-Defamation League of B'nai B'rith to anti-Semitic propaganda.

In a society where, as a recent survey by the National Opinion Research Center has shown, the profession of medicine ranks higher in social prestige than any other of ninety occupations (save that of United States Supreme Court Justice), we find some Jewish spokesmen manœuvered by the attacking in-group into the fantastic position of announcing their "deep concern" over the number of Jews in medical practice, which is "disproportionate to the number of Jews in other occupations." In a nation suffering from a notorious undersupply of physicians, the Jewish doctor becomes a deplorable occasion for deep concern, rather than receiving applause for his hard-won acquisition of knowledge and skills and for his social utility. Only when the New York Yankees publicly announce deep concern over their eleven World Series titles, so disproportionate to the number of triumphs achieved by other major league teams, will this self-abnegation seem part of the normal order of things.

In a culture which consistently judges the professionals higher in social value than even the most skilled hewers of wood and drawers of water, the out-group finds itself in the anomalous position of pointing with defensive relief to the large number of Jewish painters and paper hangers, plasterers and electricians, plumbers and sheet-metal workers.

But the ultimate reversal of values is yet to be noted. Each succeeding census finds more and more Americans in the city and its suburbs. Americans have travelled the road to urbanization until less than one-fifth of the nation's population live on farms. Plainly, it is high time for the Methodist and the Catholic, the Baptist and the Episcopalian to recognize the iniquity of this trek of their co-religionists to the city. For, as is well known, one of the central accusations levelled against the Jew is his heinous tendency to live in cities. Jewish leaders, therefore, find themselves in the incredible position of defensively urging their people to move into the very farm areas being hastily vacated by city-bound hordes of Christians. Perhaps this is not altogether necessary. As the Jewish crime of urbanism becomes ever more popular among the in-group, it may be reshaped into transcendent virtue. But, admittedly, one can't be certain. For in this daft confusion of inverted values, it soon becomes impossible to determine when virtue is sin and sin, moral perfection.

Amid this confusion, one fact remains unambiguous. The Jews, like other peoples, have made distinguished contributions to world culture. Consider only an abbreviated catalogue. In the field of creative literature (and with acknowledgment of large variations in the calibre of achievement), Jewish authors include Heine, Karl Kraus, Börne, Hofmannsthal, Schnitzler, Kafka. In the realm of musical composition, there are Meyerbeer, Felix Mendelssohn, Offenbach, Mahler, and Schönberg. Among the musical virtuosi, consider only Rosenthal, Schnabel, Godowsky, Pachman, Kreisler, Hubermann, Milstein, Elman, Heifetz, Joachim, and Menuhin. And among scientists of a stature sufficient to merit the Nobel prize, examine the familiar list which includes Beranyi, Mayerhof, Ehrlich, Michelson, Lippmann, Haber, Willstätter, and Einstein. Or in the esoteric and imaginative universe of mathematical invention, take note only of Kronecker, the creator of the modern theory of numbers; Herman Minkowski, who supplied the mathematical foundations of the special theory of relativity; or Jacobi, with his basic work in the theory of elliptical functions. And so through each special province of cultural achievement, we are supplied with a list of pre-eminent men and women who happened to be Jews.

And who is thus busily engaged in singing the praises of the Jews? Who has so assiduously compiled the list of many hundreds of distinguished Jews who contributed so notably to science, literature and the arts—a list from which these few cases were excerpted? A philo-Semite, eager to demonstrate that his people have contributed their due share to world culture? No, by now we should know better than that. The complete list will be found in the thirty-sixth edition of the anti-Semitic handbook by the racist Fritsch. In accord with the alchemical formula for transmuting in-group virtues into out-group vices, he presents this as a roll call of sinister spirits who have usurped the accomplishments properly owing the Aryan in-group.

Once we comprehend the predominant role of the in-group in defining the situation, the further paradox of the seemingly opposed behavior of the Negro out-group and the Jewish out-group falls away. The behavior of both minority groups is in response to the majority-group allegations.

If the Negroes are accused of inferiority, and their alleged failure to contribute to world culture is cited in support of this accusation, the human urge for self-respect and a concern for security leads them *defensively* often to magnify each and every achievement by members of the race. If Jews are accused of "excessive" achievements and "excessive" ambitions, and lists of pre-eminent Jews are compiled in support of this counter-accusation, then the urge for security leads them *defensively* to minimize the actual achievements of members of the group. Apparently opposed types of behavior have the same psychological and social functions. Self-assertion and self-effacement become the devices for seeking to cope with condemnation for alleged group deficiency and condemnation for alleged group excesses, respectively. And with a fine sense of moral superiority, the secure in-group looks on these curious performances by the out-groups with mingled derision and contempt.

ENACTED INSTITUTIONAL CHANGE

Will this desolate tragi-comedy run on and on, marked only by minor changes in the cast? Not necessarily.

Were moral scruples and a sense of decency the only bases for bringing the play to an end, one would indeed expect it to continue an indefinitely long run. In and of themselves, moral sentiments are not much more effective in curing social ills than in curing physical ills. Moral sentiments no doubt help to motivate efforts for change, but they are no substitute for hard-headed instrumentalities for achieving the objective, as the thickly populated graveyard of soft-headed utopias bears witness.

There are ample indications that a deliberate and planned halt can be put to the workings of the self-fulfilling prophecy and the vicious circle in society. The sequel to our sociological parable of the Last National Bank provides one clue to the way in which this can be achieved. During the fabulous '20's, when Coolidge undoubtedly caused a Republican era of lush prosperity, an average of 635 banks a year quietly suspended operations. And during the four years immediately before and after The Crash, when Hoover undoubtedly did not cause a Republican era of sluggish depression, this zoomed to the more spectacular average of 2,276 bank suspensions annually. But, interestingly enough, in the twelve years following the establishment of the Federal Deposit Insurance Corporation and the enactment of other banking legislation while Roosevelt presided over Democratic depression and revival, recession and boom, bank suspensions dropped to a niggardly average of 28 a year. Perhaps money panics have not been institutionally exorcized by legislation. Nevertheless, millions of depositors no longer have occasion to give way to panic-motivated runs on banks simply because deliberate institutional change has removed the grounds for panic. Occasions for racial hostility are no more inborn psychological constants than are occasions for panic. Despite the teachings of amateur psychologists, blind panic and racial aggression are not rooted in "human nature." These patterns of human behavior are largely a product of the modifiable structure of society.

For a further clue, return to our instance of widespread hostility of white unionists toward the Negro strikebreakers brought into industry by employers after the close of the very first World War. Once the initial definition of Negroes as not deserving of union membership had largely broken down, the Negro, with a wider range of work opportunities, no longer found it necessary to enter industry through the doors held open by strikebound employers. Again, appropriate institutional change broke through the tragic circle of the self-fulfilling prophecy. Deliberate social change gave the lie to the firm conviction that "it just ain't in the nature of the nigra" to join co-operatively with his white fellows in trade unions.

A final instance is drawn from a study of a bi-racial housing project which I have been conducting with Patricia J. Salter, under a grant from the Lavanburg Foundation. Located in Pittsburgh, this community of Hilltown is made up of fifty per cent Negro families and fifty per cent white. It is not a twentieth-century utopia. There is some interpersonal friction here as elsewhere. But in a community made up of equal numbers of the two races, fewer than a fifth of the whites and less than a third of the Negroes report that this friction occurs between members of *different* races. By their own testimony, it is very largely confined to disagreements *within* each racial group. Yet only one in every twenty-five whites initially *expected* relations between the races in this community to run smoothly, whereas five times as many expected serious trouble, the remainder anticipating a tolerable, if not altogether pleasant, situation. So much for expectations. Upon reviewing their actual experience, three of every four of the most apprehensive whites subsequently found that the "races get along fairly well," after all. This is not the place to report the findings of the Lavanburg study in detail, but substantially these demonstrate anew that under *ap-*

propriate institutional and administrative conditions, the experience of interracial amity can supplant the fear of interracial conflict.

These changes, and others of the same kind, do not occur automatically. *The self-fulfilling prophecy, whereby fears are translated into reality, operates only in the absence of deliberate institutional controls.* And it is only with the rejection of social fatalism implied in the notion of unchangeable human nature that the tragic circle of fear, social disaster, reinforced fear can be broken.

Ethnic prejudices do die—but slowly. They can be helped over the threshold of oblivion, not by insisting that it is unreasonable and unworthy of them to survive, but by cutting off their sustenance now provided by certain institutions of our society.

If we find ourselves doubting man's capacity to control man and his society, if we persist in our tendency to find in the patterns of the past the chart of the future, it is perhaps time to take up anew the wisdom of de Tocqueville's 112-year-old apothegm: "What we call necessary institutions are often no more than institutions to which we have grown accustomed."

Nor can widespread, even typical, failures in planning human relations between ethnic groups be cited as evidence for pessimism. In the world laboratory of the sociologist, as in the more secluded laboratories of the physicist and chemist, it is the successful experiment which is decisive and not the thousand-and-one failures which preceded it. More is learned from the single success than from the multiple failures. A single success proves it can be done. Thereafter, it is necessary only to learn what made it work. This, at least, is what I take to be the sociological sense of those revealing words of Thomas Love Peacock: "Whatever is, is possible."

FURTHER READINGS

Mead, George Herbert. *George Herbert Mead On Social Psychology,* ed. by Anselm Strauss. Chicago: University of Chicago Press, 1964.

Tiryakian, Edward. *Sociologism and Existentialism.* Englewood Cliffs, New Jersey: Prentice-Hall, Inc., 1962.

Thomas, W. I. and Znaniecki, Florian. *The Polish Peasant in Europe and America.* Chicago: University of Chicago Press, 1918.

Volkart, Edmund H., ed. *Social Behavior and Personality: Contributions of W. I. Thomas to Theory and Research.* New York: Social Science Research Council, 1951.

7

DEVIANCE AND

CONFORMITY

Introduction

O NE OF THE AREAS which seems to have always been most stimulating to college students has been deviance. Included in the general category are the study of crime, delinquency, problem drinking, aberrant sex behavior, bohemianism, suicide, drug addiction, and mental disorders, to name a selected few.

A major problem for the sociologist has been the difficulty encountered in organizing the concepts in the field. Some types of deviant behavior are also medical problems or perceived social problems while others are purely evasive acts. Merton clarifies some of these issues in a paper in Merton and Nisbet (1961).

Anomie has become a fashionable concept in this sphere and much twisting and straining has characterized some research in this field to try to fit data into a conceptual scheme that includes Merton's anomie hypothesis. A paper dealing explicitly with this concept is not included here. However, the concept of anomie makes its way into the essay by Deutscher, and Mizruchi and Perrucci and is central to other papers by Mizruchi in Chapters 3 and 13. Radcliffe-Brown deals with anomie briefly in his paper in Chapter 8, Institutionalization and Change.

Another idea of Durkheim's which is of major significance is that crime is the price that society pays for creativity. Social systems require a degree of flexibility in order to operate, and too much pressure to conform leads to stagnation. Although there are a number of theoretical and philosophical issues surrounding this notion we reprint this excerpt because it provides a stimulus to serious thought about dealing with perceived social problems.

Deutscher's article provides a concrete example of how sociological ideas provide insight into what are often viewed myopically and it makes a lucid distinction between social and personal factors in the nexus surrounding deviant behavior.

The article by Mizruchi and Perrucci represents an attempt to systematize previously gathered data into a meaningful theoretical scheme. It illustrates how theoretical analysis based on empirical research yields testable hypotheses.

Simmons in his paper on stereotypes of deviant behavior describes the reactions of several groups of respondents to images of social acts. His study is a clear reminder that much of the research associated with deviant behavior approaches this phenomenon from the perspective of the group response to the act rather than the quality of the act alone. Thus deviant behavior analysis is often informed by the approach associated with the concept of the definition of the situation, refered to earlier, which was an implicit idea in the work of both Durkheim and Sumner.

The Normal and the Pathological

ÉMILE DURKHEIM

IF THERE IS ANY FACT whose pathological character appears incontestable, that fact is crime. All criminologists are agreed on this point. Although they explain this pathology differently, they are unanimous in recognizing it. But let us see if this problem does not demand a more extended consideration.

We shall apply the foregoing rules. Crime is present not only in the majority of societies of one particular species but in all societies of all types. There is no society that is not confronted with the problem of criminality. Its form changes; the acts thus characterized are not the same everywhere; but, everywhere and always, there have been men who have behaved in such a way as to draw upon themselves penal repression. If, in proportion as societies pass from the lower to the higher types, the rate of criminality, i.e., the relation between the yearly number of crimes and the population, tended to decline, it might be believed that crime, while still normal, is tending to lose this character of normality. But we have no reason to believe that such a regression is substantiated. Many facts would seem rather to indicate a movement in the opposite direction. From the beginning of the [nineteenth] century, statistics enable us to follow the course of criminality. It has everywhere increased. In France the increase is nearly 300 per cent. There is, then, no phenomenon that presents more indisputably

Reprinted with permission of The Free Press from *The Rules of Sociological Method*, edited by G. Catlin, trans. by S. Solovay and J. Mueller, pp. 65-75. Copyright, 1938, by The University of Chicago.

all the symptoms of normality, since it appears closely connected with the conditions of all collective life. To make of crime a form of social morbidity would be to admit that morbidity is not something accidental, but, on the contrary, that in certain cases it grows out of the fundamental constitution of the living organism; it would result in wiping out all distinction between the physiological and the pathological. No doubt it is possible that crime itself will have abnormal forms, as, for example, when its rate is unusually high. This excess is, indeed, undoubtedly morbid in nature. What is normal, simply, is the existence of criminality, provided that it attains and does not exceed, for each social type, a certain level, which it is perhaps not impossible to fix in conformity with the preceding rules.

Here we are, then, in the presence of a conclusion in appearance quite paradoxical. Let us make no mistake. To classify crime among the phenomena of normal sociology is not to say merely that it is an inevitable, although regrettable phenomenon, due to the incorrigible wickedness of men; it is to affirm that it is a factor in public health, an integral part of all healthy societies. This result is, at first glance, surprising enough to have puzzled even ourselves for a long time. Once this first surprise has been overcome, however, it is not difficult to find reasons explaining this normality and at the same time confirming it.

In the first place crime is normal because a society exempt from it is utterly impossible. Crime, we have shown elsewhere, consists of an act that offends certain very strong collective sentiments. In a society in which criminal acts are no longer committed, the sentiments they offend would have to be found without exception in all individual consciousnesses, and to them. Assuming that this condition could actually be realized, crime would not thereby disappear; it would only change its form, for the very cause which would thus dry up the sources of criminality would immediately they must be found to exist with the same degree as sentiments contrary open up new ones.

Indeed, for the collective sentiments which are protected by the penal law of a people at a specified moment of its history to take possession of the public conscience or for them to acquire a stronger hold where they have an insufficient grip, they must acquire an intensity greater than that which they had hitherto had. The community as a whole must experience them more vividly, for it can acquire from no other source the greater force necessary to control these individuals who formerly were the most refractory. For murderers to disappear, the horror of bloodshed must become greater in those social strata from which murderers are recruited; but, first it must become greater throughout the entire society. Moreover, the very absence of crime would directly contribute to produce this horror; because any sentiment seems much more respectable when it is always and uniformly respected.

One easily overlooks the consideration that these strong states of the common consciousness cannot be thus reinforced without reinforcing at the same time the more feeble states, whose violation previously gave birth to mere infraction of convention—since the weaker ones are only the prolongation, the attenuated form, of the stronger. Thus robbery and simple bad taste injure the same single altruistic sentiment, the respect for that which is another's. However, this same sentiment is less grievously offended by bad taste than by robbery; and since, in addition, the average consciousness has not sufficient intensity to react keenly to the bad taste, it is treated with greater tolerance. That is why the person guilty of bad taste is merely blamed, whereas the thief is punished. But, if this sentiment grows stronger, to the point of silencing in all consciousnesses the inclination which disposes man to steal, he will become more sensitive to the offenses which, until then, touched him but lightly. He will react against them, then, with more energy; they will be the object of greater opprobrium, which will transform certain of them from the simple moral faults that they were and give them the quality of crimes. For example, improper contracts, or contracts improperly executed, which only incur public blame or civil damages, will become offenses in law.

Imagine a society of saints, a perfect cloister of exemplary individuals. Crimes, properly so called, will there be unknown; but faults which appear venial to the layman will create there the same scandal that the ordinary offense does in ordinary consciousnesses. If, then, this society has the power to judge and punish, it will define these acts as criminal and will treat them as such. For the same reason, the perfect and upright man judges his smallest failings with a severity that the majority reserve for acts more truly in the nature of an offense. Formerly, acts of violence against persons were more frequent than they are today, because respect for individual dignity was less strong. As this has increased, these crimes have become more rare; and also, many acts violating this sentiment have been introduced into the penal law which were not included there in primitive times.

In order to exhaust all the hypotheses logically possible, it will perhaps be asked why this unanimity does not extend to all collective sentiments without exception. Why should not even the most feeble sentiment gather enough energy to prevent all dissent? The moral consciousness of the society would be present in its entirety in all the individuals, with a vitality sufficient to prevent all acts offending it—the purely conventional faults as well as the crimes. But a uniformity so universal and absolute is utterly impossible; for the immediate physical milieu in which each one of us is placed, the hereditary antecedents, and the social influences vary from one individual to the next, and consequently diversify consciousnesses. It is impossible for all to be alike, if only because each one has his own organism and that these organisms occupy different areas in space. That is why, even among the lower peoples, where individual originality is very little developed, it nevertheless does exist.

Thus, since there cannot be a society in which the individuals do not differ more or less from the collective type, it is also inevitable that, among these divergences, there are some with a criminal character. What confers this character upon them is not the intrinsic quality of a given act but that definition which the collective conscience lends them. If the collective conscience is stronger, if it has enough authority practically to suppress these divergences, it will also be more sensitive, more exacting; and, reacting against the slightest deviations with the energy it otherwise displays only against more considerable infractions, it will attribute to them the same gravity as formerly to crimes. In other words, it will designate them as criminal.

Crime is, then, necessary; it is bound up with the fundamental conditions of all social life, and by that very fact it is useful, because these conditions of which it is a part are themselves indispensable to the normal evolution of morality and law.

Indeed, it is no longer possible today to dispute the fact that law and morality vary from one social type to the next, nor that they change within the same type if the conditions of life are modified. But, in order that these transformations may be possible, the collective sentiments at the basis of morality must not be hostile to change, and consequently must have but moderate energy. If they were too strong, they would no longer be plastic. Every pattern is an obstacle to new patterns, to the extent that the first pattern is inflexible. The better a structure is articulated, the more it offers a healthy resistance to all modification; and this is equally true of functional, as of anatomical, organization. If there were no crimes, this condition could not have been fulfilled; for such a hypothesis presupposes that collective sentiments have arrived at a degree of intensity unexampled in history. Nothing is good indefinitely and to an unlimited extent. The authority which the moral conscience enjoys must not be excessive; otherwise no one would dare criticize it, and it would too easily congeal into an immutable form. To make progress, individual originality must be able to express itself. In order that the originality of the idealist whose dreams transcend his century may find expression, it is necessary that the originality of the criminal, who is below the level of his time, shall also be possible. One does not occur without the other.

Nor is this all. Aside from this indirect utility, it happens that crime itself plays a useful role in this evolution. Crime implies not only that the way remains open to necessary changes but that in certain cases it directly prepares these changes. Where crime exists, collective sentiments are sufficiently flexible to take on a new form, and crime sometimes helps to determine the form they will take. How many times, indeed, it is only an anticipation of future morality—a step toward what will be! According to Athenian law, Socrates was a criminal, and his condemnation was no more than just. However, his crime, namely, the independence of his thought, rendered a service not only to humanity but to his country. It served to prepare a new morality and faith which the Athenians needed, since the traditions by which they had lived until then were no longer in harmony with

the current conditions of life. Nor is the case of Socrates unique; it is repro-
duced periodically in history. It would never have been possible to establish
the freedom of thought we now enjoy if the regulations prohibiting it had not
been violated before being solemnly abrogated. At that time, however, the
violation was a crime, since it was an offense against sentiments still very
keen in the average conscience. And yet this crime was useful as a prelude
to reforms which daily became more necessary. Liberal philosophy had as
its precursors the heretics of all kinds who were justly punished by secular
authorities during the entire course of the Middle Ages and until the eve of
modern times.

From this point of view the fundamental facts of criminality present
themselves to us in an entirely new light. Contrary to current ideas, the
criminal no longer seems a totally unsociable being, a sort of parasitic element, a strange and unassimilable body, introduced into the midst of society.
On the contrary, he plays a definite role in social life. Crime, for its part,
must no longer be conceived as an evil that cannot be too much suppressed.
There is no occasion for self-congratulation when the crime rate drops notice-
ably below the average level, for we may be certain that this apparent progress is associated with some social disorder. Thus, the number of assault cases
never falls so low as in times of want.* With the drop in the crime rate, and
as a reaction to it, comes a revision, or the need of a revision in the theory
of punishment. If, indeed, crime is a disease, its punishment is its remedy
and cannot be otherwise conceived; thus, all the discussions it arouses bear
on the point of determining what the punishment must be in order to fulfill
this role of remedy. If crime is not pathological at all, the object of punishment cannot be to cure it, and its true function must be sought elsewhere.

It is far from the truth, then, that the rules previously stated have no
other justification than to satisfy an urge for logical formalism of little practical value, since, on the contrary, according as they are or are not applied,
the most essential social facts are entirely changed in character. If the foregoing example is particularly convincing—and this was our hope in dwelling
upon it—there are likewise many others which might have been cited with
equal profit. There is no society where the rule does not exist that the punishment must be proportional to the offense; yet, for the Italian school, this
principle is but an invention of jurists, without adequate basis.

For these criminologists the entire penal system, as it has functioned
until the present day among all known peoples, is a phenomenon contrary

* Although crime is a fact of normal sociology, it does not follow that we must not
abhor it. Pain itself has nothing desirable about it; the individual dislikes it as society
does crime, and yet it is a function of normal physiology. Not only is it necessarily derived
from the very constitution of every living organism, but it plays a useful role in life, for
which reason it cannot be replaced. It would, then, be a singular distortion of our thought
to present it as an apology for crime. We would not even think of protesting against such
an interpretation, did we not know to what strange accusations and misunderstandings
one exposes oneself when one undertakes to study moral facts objectively and to speak of
them in a different language from that of the layman.

to nature. We have already seen that, for M. Garofalo, the criminality peculiar to lower societies is not at all natural. For socialists it is the capitalist
system, in spite of its wide diffusion, which constitutes a deviation from the
normal state, produced, as it was, by violence and fraud. Spencer, on the
contrary, maintains that our administrative centralization and the extension
of governmental powers are the radical vices of our societies, although both
proceed most regularly and generally as we advance in history. We do not
believe that scholars have ever systematically endeavored to distinguish the
normal or abnormal character of social phenomena from their degree of
generality. It is always with a great array of dialectics that these questions
are partly resolved.

Once we have eliminated this criterion, however, we are not only exposed to confusions and partial errors, such as those just pointed out, but
science is rendered all but impossible. Its immediate object is the study of
the normal type. If, however, the most widely diffused facts can be pathological, it is possible that the normal types never existed in actuality; and if
that is the case, why study the facts? Such study can only confirm our
prejudices and fix us in our errors. If punishment and the responsibility for
crime are only the products of ignorance and barbarism, why strive to know
them in order to derive the normal forms from them? By such arguments the
mind is diverted from a reality in which we have lost interest, and falls back
on itself in order to seek within itself the materials necessary to reconstruct
its world. In order that sociology may treat facts as things, the sociologist
must feel the necessity of studying them exclusively.

The principal object of all sciences of life, whether individual or social,
is to define and explain the normal state and to distinguish it from its opposite. If, however, normality is not given in the things themselves—if it is, on
the contrary, a character we may or may not impute to them—this solid foot-
ing is lost. The mind is then complacent in the face of a reality which has
little to teach it; it is no longer restrained by the matter which it is analyzing,
since it is the mind, in some manner or other, that determines the matter.

The various principles we have established up to the present are, then,
closely interconnected. In order that sociology may be a true science of
things, the generality of phenomena must be taken as the criterion of their
normality.

Our method has, moreover, the advantage of regulating action at the
same time as thought. If the social values are not subjects of observation but
can and must be determined by a sort of mental calculus, no limit, so to
speak, can be set for the free inventions of the imagination in search of the
best. For how may we assign to perfection a limit? It escapes all limitation,
by definition. The goal of humanity recedes into infinity, discouraging some
by its very remoteness and arousing others who, in order to draw a little
nearer to it, quicken the pace and plunge into revolutions. This practical
dilemma may be escaped if the desirable is defined in the same way as is
health and normality and if health is something that is defined as inherent

in things. For then the object of our efforts is both given and defined at the same time. It is no longer a matter of pursuing desperately an objective that retreats as one advances, but of working with steady perseverance to maintain the normal state, of re-establishing it if it is threatened, and of rediscovering its conditions if they have changed. The duty of the statesman is no longer to push society toward an ideal that seems attractive to him, but his role is that of the physician: he prevents the outbreak of illnesses by good hygiene, and he seeks to cure them when they have appeared.

෧෬ ෬෫

The Social Causes of Social Problems:
From Suicide to Delinquency

IRWIN DEUTSCHER

IN THINKING ABOUT SOCIAL PROBLEMS and their causes it is easy to forget that social problems are indeed social—that, although they reflect themselves through the behavior of individuals, the sources, the origins, the causes lie outside of individuals. One may be able to cope with problematic behavior in an individual by treating that individual, but the problem will remain to reflect itself in hundreds of thousands of other individuals until the external pressures in the society which are creating the problem can be identified and modified.

Social problems will ultimately be solved when we learn where to intervene in the ongoing processes of the society. They will not be solved by treating the individual whose behavior is merely symptomatic of difficulties which transcend him and which are outside of him. This is what I mean when I say that social problems are social.

When we forget this, and start thinking of social problems as personal or individual, we begin to become enmeshed in the fallacious line of reasoning which has been called reductionism. Thus, if we reduce the social problem (crime, delinquency, divorce, or what have you) to a personal problem and observe the individual as our unit of study rather than the society, why not continue? Why not observe only the brain rather than the whole complex individual? Or why not study just a brain cell? Or, better still, let us isolate a molecule of matter from that cell, put it under an electron microscope, separate out an atom, and then carefully observe the nature of the atomic particles in order to really get at the ultimate sources of crime, delinquency,

From *Publications of the Youth Development Center,* Syracuse University, Syracuse, 1962. Reprinted by permission of the publisher and author.

divorce or what have you? This is reductionism carried to its extreme and its absurdity is apparent. Although less apparent, this same absurdity is present at any point in the process of reduction, including the first step when one reduces the social problem into a personal problem.

All of this is not to deny such things as idiosyncratic individual or personality problems. I am simply stressing the point that social problems are social and individual problems are individual and that the distinction should be kept clear. It is no more reasonable to expect to eliminate social problems by treating individuals than it is to expect to eliminate some kinds of personality problems by treating the society. Historically, man has always attempted to place blame or responsibility on the individual. At one time we thought he was taken with evil spirits or the devil, and that explained why he behaved so badly. Later we decided he had bad genes, and that explained why he behaved so badly. More recently we have decided that he is "sick," and that explains why he behaves so badly. I can see no basic difference in defining, say, a delinquent boy, in terms of the devil, the genes, or mental illness. The shift in words tends only to make us more condescending, more tolerant, more "understanding" of the deviant behavior. Whatever you call it, it remains reductionism.

This perspective is hardly original with me. I am standing on the shoulders of giants who stood on the shoulders of other giants before them. The giant who most clearly formulated this position, both in terms of its logic and in terms of its empirical demonstration, was a turn-of-the-century Frenchman named Emile Durkheim. As a concrete example of how a social problem can be understood in terms of social phenomena, let's take a look at a classic study conducted by Durkheim. The problem he chose to explore was suicide—on the surface one of the most individualistic, personal, nonsocial kinds of acts a person can commit.

In one of the first attempts to work with mass statistics, Durkheim was able to demonstrate convincingly that suicide rates were very stable. In places and among groups where the rates were high they tended to remain high over a considerable period of time, while in places and among groups where the rates were low they tended to remain low over a considerable period of time. In addition, he was able to show that when these rates were related to external events, changes were consistent no matter where they occurred. For example, under conditions of sudden economic or political upheavals suicide rates declined. Durkheim actually demonstrated that suicide rates were more stable than mortality rates. Thus, one could predict the expected number of suicides in any segment of the population with greater accuracy than one could predict the number of deaths.

Durkheim did not stop with a simple description of variation in suicide rates. The uniformity and regularity he found in those rates suggested to him that suicide was not a whimsical individual matter, but rather was a reflection of the kind of society in which people lived. He went on to demonstrate that wherever people were collectively enmeshed in something bigger than themselves, wherever they were well incorporated into one or more major institutions of the society, wherever they felt themselves bound by strong external controls, wherever they lived under the shadow of what Durkheim called a "collective conscience"—under these conditions people were much less likely to take their own lives. And where these conditions did not exist, the suicide rates were higher. For example, with the breakdown of family solidarity by widowhood or divorce, suicide rates went up: for married men in Prussia the rate was four per 10,000, for widowed men it was fifteen, and for divorced men it jumped to nineteen. For women it went from one to two to three. And the figures were remarkably similar in other European countries.

But the family is not the only major social institution. Looking at religion, he showed that where religious ties were strong and collective, as with Catholics and Jews, the rates of suicide were considerably lower than where religious ties were either weak or individualistic, as among Protestants. The same held when community ties were considered; in the French provincial rural villages the rates were not nearly as high as they were in the burgeoning prefectures of Paris.

Durkheim's general conclusions, based on both his data and a logical critique of other explanations, was that suicide was a social fact and that it could be explained in terms of other social facts. He concluded that when people felt that they were an integral part of a larger collectivity and that collectivity maintained a degree of reasonable order in their world, then there would be significantly less alienation from the society. And what could be a more perfect index of alienation than the rate at which people deliberately took their own lives? When people cease to believe that there are any rules worth abiding by because it doesn't do any good when you do abide by them, then suicide can be expected to increase.

There are some holes in all of this. Some of them were recognized by Durkheim and handled by him. Others are the result of more extensive knowledge that has accumulated in the half-century since *Suicide* was written. One of the big problems which Durkheim recognized was that the word "suicide" was a popular, or at best, a legalistic term which tended to be either loose or arbitrary. He tried to clarify the concept by defining it as the voluntary taking of one's own life, but realized that even this included some very different kinds of behavior which resulted from very different motives. As a result of his historical research he classified suicide into three distinct types, to which he gave the names "anomic," "altruistic," and "egoistic."

Briefly, the anomic suicide is most prevalent where people find themselves frustrated by the kind of society in which they live. It occurs when people perceive disharmony between the desired goals of life and the right or proper means of achieving those goals. The potential anomic suicide has the desire to get somewhere but no matter how hard he tries he can't make it. This is indeed a nightmare situation.

The egoistic suicide occurs when people, rather than seeing anything wrong with the society, see themselves as outside of it. They don't want to get anywhere. The egoistic suicide has nothing to live for; he is completely malintegrated in what may be a well-integrated society.

The altruistic suicide is the polar opposite of the egoistic. It occurs when people are so well integrated that the demands and loyalties of the society are more meaningful than life itself; for example, the man who dies for his family, his church, or his country. He may deliberately and knowingly give up his own life, but his "suicide" is indeed in a different category from the others.

I mention all this not because I think we should be more familiar with esoteric sociological treatises, but because Durkheim has provided us with a model that gives a new perspective to the understanding of social problems in general. Let me illustrate by attempting to apply the model to a second case: juvenile delinquency.

Durkheim addressed himself to three basic questions in his efforts to understand suicide: (1) What is the logical status of popular causal explanations of the phenomenon? (Although I have not discussed this, he analyzed the weaknesses of arguments explaining suicide in terms of psychopathy, race, heredity, imitation, etc.); (2) Can the phenomenon be described as a social fact? (If it can, we must avoid the reductionist fallacy and pursue understanding in terms of other social facts); (3) Is the phenomenon actually unitary or does the concept need to be broken down into distinct classes which require different explanations?

What is the logical status of popular causal explanations of delinquency? Pick up your daily newspaper, talk to a neighbor, read a magazine, or ask your best friend and you will discover *the cause of* delinquency. Depending on whom you ask or where you look, it may be television, "bad" schools, inability to read properly, poverty, lack of recreation facilities, comic books, alcohol, divorce, working mothers, mental illness, mental retardation, school dropouts, habits of dress, or even physical stature—to mention only a few. Although it is probably true that at some time, in some place, each of these factors has been a major contributing element in the delinquency of some child, it is also true that no one of these factors is associated with most of the behavior which we label "delinquent."

The late Edwin H. Sutherland, noted criminologist, liked to tell the story of the two slum youths who were being chased by a policeman after committing an act of vandalism. One was a tall fellow with long legs who ran fast, leaped over a high fence, and escaped. The other was a short fellow whose stubby little legs just wouldn't carry him fast enough or far enough. He was caught by the policeman and sent to the reformatory. For our short-legged fellow, this was the beginning of a long career in crime, while the long-legged fellow continued in school and eventually became a priest. Moral of the story: short legs cause crime!

The story, although absurd, points up the weakness of the causal logic associated with all arguments relating specific factors to delinquency, whether the factor is physical stature, television, or whatever. Television provides a good general example. Certainly there were delinquents before TV was invented; most children who watch television do not become delinquents; there is no evidence that most delinquents are addicted to television.

As a matter of fact, while working as a volunteer probation officer I encountered a case where TV might have had the opposite effect. Orville, my twelve-year-old charge, had been apprehended for breaking into the homes of five neighbors. Counting the fountain pen he ruined, the footstool he damaged while standing on it in search of treasure in high places, and the thirty-five cents he discovered in Mrs. Polanski's sugar bowl, Orville did damage and stole property amounting to $8.35. But the point of this story has to do with the technique of entry rather than the amount of loot. In his confession, Orville stated that he entered the first home by using the key to the back door. The key was obtained by inserting a newspaper under the door and pushing the key (which had been left in the keyhole on the inside) onto the paper. The paper was then removed along with the key.

When I asked Orville where he had acquired this clever technique, he replied that he had seen it on TV. Evidence that television is a "cause" of delinquency? Probably not, because what really got Orville into trouble wasn't the first door; *it was the other four.* Since the householders in these cases did not leave keys inside their back doors, Orville had no alternative but to take an axe to those doors. In assessing restitution against Orville father, the court ordered that the following amounts be paid (Orville's father earns fifty-five dollars a week on the shipping dock of a downtown department store and supports a wife and two other children in addition to Orville):

DAMAGE INSIDE OF PREMISES	$ 8.00
CASH STOLEN	.35
REPLACEMENT OF FOUR DOORS @ $78.50	314.00
TOTAL	$322.35

Orville was to remain on probation until this amount had been fully paid at the rate of ten dollars per week—approximately eight months. The technique he had picked up from television saved him nearly eight weeks probation and considerably reduced the risk of failure to meet restitution payments and the institutionalization which would probably result from such failure. Had all of the neighbors been so thoughtful as to leave keys inside of their back doors, Orville might well have gotten off with a simple reprimand after his father paid the $8.35. I could go on and remind you of the thousands of boys who saw the same TV program and did not attempt to demonstrate the technique to their own satisfaction.

I might even suggest that the hundreds of boys who get caught breaking into homes each year would be better off had they seen this program.

Again, although true, the story is told with tongue-in-cheek. The serious conclusion is that it is difficult to defend the position that television causes delinquency. The same is true of comic books, which I want to mention briefly before moving on to other things. Although the same arguments hold in reference to comic books that hold for all of the other attempts to explain delinquency in terms of simple factor causes, there is an additional argument that can be made in this case; that is, that things are no different than they have ever been in this respect.

I once made an attempt to introduce my four-year-old to classic children's literature. I thought *Cinderella* would be a nice starting place and obtained the original version of Grimm's. I began worrying right from the start, and by the time we got to the part where one of the wicked sisters was whittling her heel off with a kitchen knife in order to make the slipper fit, I closed the book on the pool of blood and eventually managed to calm my horrified daughter. *Gulliver's Travels* didn't work out much better; fortunately, I read a little ahead and managed to suggest something else before we got to the part where Gulliver attempts to drown the cute little Lilliputians in his urine. *Jack and the Beanstalk* worked the final cure. This story of a deceitful boy who spends the family's last penny for a colored bean, who betrays the kindly and generous Mrs. Giant by stealing everything of value in her home, and tops it off by murdering her husband when he attempts to retrieve what is rightfully his—this story convinced me that my daughter was better off with Disneyesque comic books, and certainly no worse off with other types where at least right is clearly delineated from wrong and justice always prevails.

Enough said concerning the logic of currently popular causative arguments. Turning to Durkheim's second question, is there evidence that delinquency is a social fact which shows some regularity in the rate of its appearance, as well as exhibiting consistent rate differences between various collectivities in the society? Or is it an idiosyncratic phenomenon, whose range of appearance varies as widely as the range of personality structure? I could tell you of the hundreds of studies which show that urban rates are higher than rural ones, and incidentally relate to you the problems of my colleague, Professor Jerome Himmelhoch, who undertook a delinquency study in the state of Vermont and after three years is still frantically trying to find a delinquent. Or I could describe the classic study of delinquency areas conducted twenty years ago in Chicago by Clifford Shaw and Henry McKay. This study showed that delinquency rates were always high in one section of the city regardless of which ethnic group happened to be migrating through it at the time. Poles, Italians, Irish, Negroes—it made no difference what the nativity of the population was; that area always had high delinquency rates.

But rather than describe ancient studies conducted in far-away places, let's take a look at Syracuse, N. Y., right now. Professor Robert Hardt of the Youth Development Center staff has been gathering and analyzing data on delinquency for Syracuse and Onondaga County since 1957. He has published three *Delinquency Profiles;* one reporting the distribution of apprehensions for 1957-1958, another for 1959-1960 and the third for 1961. These data reveal that for the county as a whole the rates have been stable over the five-year period, varying between 18 and 22 apprehensions per thousand children. When we separate the city from the rest of the county we also find stability, but of a different order. Apprehension rates in the city vary, not between 18 and 22, but between 28 and 34 apprehensions per thousand children. And what of the rest of the county? Here too we find stability, not in the range of 28-34, but with only 10 to 13 children out of every thousand in the county apprehended each year. Actually, the difference between city and county appears to be even more constant than the relatively stable year-to-year picture: apprehensions in the city remain very close to two-and-a-half times greater than those in the county every year.

There are differences by sex, with boys being apprehended four to five times more frequently than girls every year. There are diffrences by age, with the rates for fourteen and fifteen year-olds being eight times greater than those for seven to nine year-olds. Putting these two facts together, we find that for each seven to nine year-old girl apprehended, 73 fourteen to fifteen year-old boys are apprehended. There are also differences within the city—very marked and very stable differences. Comparing economic areas of the city, we find that no matter what the year, the rates consistently go up as the average income of the area goes down. In the highest income area the rates of apprehension are from 10 to 14 per thousand, while in the lowest they are from 74 to 79 per thousand. For boys only in the lowest income area the rates range between 113 and 123 over the years, and for fourteen to fifteen year-old boys in that area they are a phenomenal 243 apprehensions per thousand. Contrast this with girls in the high income area, where apprehension rates vary only between one and four per thousand.

Since practically all of Syracuse's non-white residents are concentrated in the lowest income ghetto, the only comparisons which can be made by race are within this low-income area. In the urban slum—roughly the 15th Ward—where the rates are high for everyone, there is no difference between Negro and white boys. Today 75 per cent of the children in that area are Negro. Yet a study conducted twenty years ago, when only 13 per cent of the children were Negro, shows that this area had the highest delinquency rates in the city at that time, too. Apparently what Shaw and McKay discovered in Chicago is also true of Syracuse, and there is little doubt but that it is true of most cities. There are areas of the city which consistently reflect high rates of delinquency as well as a wide range of other sociopathic behaviors.

It is, of course, clear that migrant Negro families do not move out of these ghettoes in a generation or two, as did the Germans, Poles, Italians, Greeks, Irish, and others. To the extent that a Negro is compelled by external constraints to remain in such an area generation after generation, the Negro will manifest all of the symptoms created by the pressures of this kind of living and will manifest those symptoms generation after generation: crime, delinquency, vice, gambling, high rates of infant mortality, illegitimacy, desertion, dependency—the whole range. When a community refuses to allow this particular group the same opportunities to move up and out which other groups had before it, then the community should be aware of the great price to be paid for such a luxury—both in the economic and in the social sense. It is not my purpose to preach about race relations; I just want to remind you that, like the man says, "you pays your money and you takes your choice." What can be done about this situation is a problem to which we will return shortly.

Studies such as those done in Chicago and Syracuse indicate that there are forces external to the individual which act consistently and uniformly in a manner which is either encouraging or permissive of delinquency. Delinquency is indeed in large part a social fact. I must emphasize the "in large part" because, low though they may be, there are delinquency rates in all parts of the city and county, in both sexes, in all age groups, and in all economic areas. Where rates are low, as where rates are high, we have a social fact which must be explained by other social facts. But other levels of explanation may be required to understand why we find some delinquent youngsters in low-rate groups and some non-delinquent youngsters in high-rate groups. Such aberrations do not appear explainable by social facts.

The Durkheimian model would lead us to seek explanation in the various agencies of social control, those constraining institutions in the society which imbue young people with the norms and values of the large community: the family, religion, the neighborhood, the school. The Durkheimian model would lead us to suspect that these agencies are either ineffective in their socializing functions (that is, in a state of breakdown) or are effectively operating counter to the norms of those in the larger society. Thus, on the basis of his Boston studies, Walter Miller argues that the lower class represents a cultural solidarity in itself and what is defined by agents of the middle class as "delinquency" is not viewed as anti-social behavior by the lower class family and neighborhood. Richard Cloward and Lloyd Ohlin consciously adapt the Durkheimian framework in their analysis of delinquent gangs in large cities. They suggest that such gangs represent various types of adaptations to what Durkheim called a state of *anomie* in the society—a condition under which the normative structure has deteriorated to such an extent that people see little hope of achieving success by legitimate means. Cloward and Ohlin recommend that the apparently blocked opportunity systems be opened for these youngsters so that they can see themselves as having the same chances for success as do middle-class youth. Of special importance are the opportunities provided for meaningful education and for work.

Turning to Durkheim's third question, is the phenomenon just one thing or does the concept need to be broken down into distinct classes which require different explanations? Even a casual observer can recognize the lack of precision in the notion of "juvenile delinquency." In a sense it refers to any kind of behavior on the part of a young person which older people strongly disapprove. If we try to pin delinquency down to legalistic terms, the situation remains messy. Not only does the legal definition of a young person vary from one jurisdiction to another and from one time to another, but the kinds of acts included in the definition present a spectrum of misdeeds, many of which bear no relationship to each other. For example, the sharp differences in rates between sexes noted above may be explained in part by the fact that for girls the external controls operate with greater force and provide fewer opportunities for delinquency. But it is also true that what is called delinquency among girls is generally not the same phenomenon as what is called delinquency among boys. In Syracuse the great majority of apprehended girls are defined as delinquent because of behavior which is thought to endanger their own morals. The great majority of boys, on the other hand, are apprehended because of threat or damage to other people or their property.

As another example of the inadequacy of legal definitions, let me point out that New York State will have a large decline in the number of adjudicated delinquents beginning September 1, 1962. This decline has nothing to do with the changing behavior of young people, only with the changing behavior of legislators. The new Family Court legislation defines a delinquent as a juvenile who commits an act which would be a crime if committed by an adult. The older law included many other things in its definition: habitual truancy, ungovernable behavior, willfully deporting oneself in such a manner as to endanger the health or morals of oneself or others, etc. With such items as these excluded from the court's delinquency jurisdiction, not only will rates go down all over the state but adjudicated girl delinquents will practically disappear. (Under the new law, youngsters involved in these behaviors are defined as juveniles in need of supervision.) I suppose it can be argued that this is one way to solve the delinquency problem.

We must be continually aware that "delinquency" is really more than one kind of thing and therefore will require more than one kind of explanation. Cloward and Ohlin have applied the Durkheim theory with some success to an explanation of juvenile gang behavior in large cities. But it is unlikely that such an explanation is appropriate when we try to understand why nice Johnny Jones from that respectable Jones farm family shot his father's head off with a shotgun. This is a different phenomenon in spite of the deceptive sameness of the label. Even the same overt acts are not necessarily a result of the same causes. Some boys steal cars for joy rides and then abandon them; others steal cars, strip them of everything removable, make contact with a fence, and sell their loot. These are not the same kinds of behavior.

I believe that the perspective on social problems that I have been discussing enables us to take a more level-headed look at social problems. I also believe that as this perspective is more systematically applied to contemporary problems, with the sophistication of contemporary techniques, we will begin to learn considerably more about the causes of such problems. There have been recent efforts: Ohlin and Cloward in the field of delinquency and Charles C. Hughes and his associates in the field of mental health provide two examples. Perhaps the most promising aspect of this perspective is that it strikes at the roots of the problem rather than at the symptoms which manifest themselves in the behavior of one individual or another. If we can learn how to alter the agencies of social control, to reinforce the collective conscience, to intervene in the organization of the society, then we will have cut off the mainsprings of the problem and automatically relieved the pressure on many little dams we must currently build in the form of individual treatment and therapy.

Most people would agree that if we could find a way to do away with delinquency, this would be better than finding a way to cure delinquents. Further, most would agree with the assertion that our current therapeutic methods are designed to deal with people who are psychologically disturbed in one way or another. However, many, if not most, so-called delinquents do not fall in this category. When the problems are not internal—that is, not personality problems—but are the result of external pressures—that is, social problems—then personality treatment is inappropriate. In addition, there is no conclusive evidence regarding the extent to which and the conditions under which current therapeutic methods are effective. Finally, even assuming for the moment that individual treatment is effective, it must be a losing battle since trained psychotherapists, psychiatrists, and caseworkers cannot be produced at nearly as rapid a rate as can delinquents. This problem is further confounded by the slow process of such treatment—it may take many months or even years to complete a therapeutic program with one delinquent boy. At best, treatment and correction programs provide only a holding action. Those agencies which are fighting this discouraging holding action should be encouraged and supported, but we know that the war is not to be won on that battleground. It is for such reasons as these that I prefer to think in terms of prevention.

When we state that we are concerned with prevention, we have made a policy choice and, I think, a wise one. The alternative is to be primarily concerned with programs of treatment, therapy, correction, cure, or whatever you want to call it. These represent two distinct and different kinds of problems. Prevention means getting at the roots of the problem, intervening in the processes that lead to it, providing young people with the stimulus, encouragement, and opportunity for healthy productive adolescent careers *before* delinquent careers can become crystallized. Prevention means keeping people from becoming delinquent; treatment means working with delinquents in an effort to redirect their life careers.

If we are going to "prevent," where do we begin? It seems that a prevention target area and target population will emerge from a careful study of delinquency rates in almost any city. But having identified such target areas, what does one do with them or to them? If you will agree that the delinquency problem in such areas—as well as many other problems—is a social problem, that it is a consequence of external pressures in the areas themselves rather than of internal pressures which arise within individual young people, then you will also agree that prevention means somehow altering the nature of the external pressures in those areas rather than altering the personalities of individuals. Unlike the skid row to which homeless and frequently alcoholic men tend to gravitate, the high delinquency area is one which creates the problems which characterize it.

We know, then, what part of the city it is necessary to focus our efforts upon and we know that those efforts must be directed at altering the community rather than altering individual personalities. But the question remains, what does one do to such a community to alter its complexion—to change its impact on the behavior of the people who live in it? I suggested earlier that the Durkheim model leads us to look at the sources of the collective conscience—at those agencies in the community which exercise constraints upon their members. Behavioral constraints are conveyed to the individual and enforced by a limited number of entities in the community which we call social institutions. Among these are the family, the neighborhood, the church, the school, the political establishment, and the economic order. These, in effect, make a community what it is. Each is responsible for conveying to young people certain standards of behavior, and further, for conveying the consequences of not living up to those standards.

It follows, then, that efforts must be directed at altering these social institutions, not toward altering the physical quality of the area. Altering social institutions is seldom a simple matter. Because of its difficulty and complexity, I would suggest that if it were to be attempted attention be directed toward those institutions over which there is some collective control by the larger community: the school and the neighborhood. Through public schools, public housing, urban relocation, and slum clearance we find an opening wedge—a point at which we can exert some leverage. But to build a new school building is no more the answer than to build a new public housing project. These are things of brick and mortar, not social institutions. In effect, we have used such brick and mortar construction to ease our middle-class consciences while tightening the noose around our ghettos. The slum school is a demoralized, custodial institution wherever it is found and regardless of how pretty it may appear. Public housing does indeed provide people with the opportunity to move out of crowded, rat-infested, unsanitary housing into clean, new, and relatively roomy living facilities, but the social world is the same—a world of gin mills, numbers rackets, whore houses, and economic exploitation from outside as well as from within. It remains the social world of the slum and the rates of socio-pathic behavior do not change.

In wrestling with the problems of such areas, I would like to think that there is some way of helping to mobilize the apathetic, frustrated, depend-ent, defeated people who live in them to organize themselves—to stand up on their own collective legs and demand to be heard. In this way, regard-less of what the issue is, they might establish a degree of hope, of collective strength, of collective self-respect. We have several members on the staff of the Youth Development Center who think this is possible and are willing to make the effort. But it may be that the task of reorganizing such areas is too gigantic. It may be that the best public policy is one which permits urban renewal to move in the direction of converting these demoralized areas into uses other than residential. The alternative is to destroy them. It may be that the most effective public policy is one which enables the peo-ple of the slum to be assimilated into the larger city, as other generations were before them—before the doors were closed.

Why, for example, should we continue to build low-income public housing in such areas when we know what it does to people to live in such areas? Why, for that matter, should we build big, expensive public housing projects anywhere when it would probably be much cheaper and certainly more effective to move potential tenants into scattered houses, purchased on the open market wherever they might appear in the city? In effect, why not absorb the eight or nine per cent of the population who live in high-delinquency areas into other areas of the city where the collective conscience is supported by existing strong institutions and where rates of delinquency as well as other sociopathic behavior are not high? What would happen? There is evidence that the behavior of these people would begin to ap-proximate that of their neighbors. Alan Wilson and Robert Hardt have both reported data indicating that children from low-income families who attend schools in middle-income areas tend to approximate middle-income children in school performance and aspirations for college education. In Rochester a limited experiment in scattered-site housing shows a drastic decline in police calls, marital conflict, and drunkenness on the part of problem slum families who were placed in the scattered houses.

As you can see, I have shifted ground from an emphasis on strengthen-ing indigenous institutions to a suggestion that the slum be allowed to die—to be voided of its people. At the same time opportunities must be opened up to permit those people to be incorporated into the larger social world of the American city where they can benefit from the same collective con-science which supports, constrains, and motivates the rest of us.

Norm Qualities and Deviant Behavior

EPHRAIM H. MIZRUCHI and ROBERT PERRUCCI

A MAJOR PROBLEM for contemporary sociologists revolves about the issue of long range vs. short range goals in the solution of perceived social problems. Should the sociologist concern himself primarily with abstract theory which is of a level of generality capable of application to many social settings, once developed and refined? Or, should he apply himself to a particular question yielding more immediate rewards for the process of solving seemingly urgent societal problems? In reality we find only a small number who clearly espouse either one position or the other. More typical of contemporary research is an effort to study the particular in order to cast light on the general.

The present paper attempts to illustrate how the study of normative and deviant drinking behavior yields hypotheses which are explicitly tied to more abstract generalizations which are applicable to a variety of social settings. Thus, research in the sphere of alcohol and society can make simultaneous contributions to the solution of immediate social problems and to the development of general theories of societal processes.

Our data in this paper are analyzed within a broad framework which embodies questions about the nature of normative integration, deviance, group reactions to deviance and social change.

The organizing concepts emerged both from a study of the data on cultural factors in drinking behavior and further induction into an appropriate theoretical model. The process includes the establishment of ideal type aspects of norms; providing data illustrating the significance of distinguishing these aspects from other norm qualities; and deriving *explicit* empirically testable hypotheses for the assessment of the original typology. Thus what is being attempted, in addition, is a study of how ideal-type method can be directly integrated with more formal empirical analysis.

NORMS AND NORMATIVE INTEGRATION

A fundamental notion embodied in the functional approach to social systems is that certain tasks must be performed in order that a given system may persist. Among the various tasks, or functional prerequisites, is the maintenance of a system of order. Many of the traditional dichotomies associated with the names of eminent forerunners of contemporary sociology

From *American Sociological Review*, 27, 1962, pp. 391-399. Revised and extended.

reflect explicit and implicit concern with order. Durkheim's mechanical and organic solidarity, Tönnies' Gemeinschaft-Gesellschaft, Redfield's Folk-Urban, and, more recently, Becker's Sacred-Secular, to name only a few, indicate a concern with the fundamental question of how society is organized and changed.

Though there are great divergences of viewpoint among contemporary sociologists regarding which factors are most significant in contrasting relatively simple and complex social organizations, few would disagree that the process of group adherence to shared norms represents an important dimension of order. Thus Durkheim and, more recently, Freedman *et al.* have focused their attention on the contrast between normative and functional integration. These two dimensions as conceived by these writers are to be found in all group structures and represent ideal-typical states of systems. Thus contemporary urban communities, for example, would be expected to be integrated not only in terms of functional integration, i.e., integration based on the interrelated activities of heterogeneous groups, but normatively as well. The norms, consequently, represent crucial mechanisms in the process of maintaining order.

Relatively little attention has been paid to the qualitative nature of the norms themselves as contrasted with the great concern associated with the direct effect of norms in controlling the activities of individuals in groups. This is particularly the case with regard to the role played by the qualitative characteristics of norms in the process of normative integration and the utility of this dimension in empirical analysis.

In terms of the sociocultural system, the problem of order may be analyzed with respect to the particular characteristics of the norms themselves, and not necessarily with respect to the control mechanisms associated with the norms. In other words, the stability or integration of a system is not insured simply because the normative system is effectively transmitted (socialization) or collectively controlled (sanctions). The qualities of the norms themselves provide an inherent potential for system maintenance and system mal-integration.

PROSCRIPTIVE AND PRESCRIPTIVE DIMENSIONS OF NORMS

Richard T. Morris, in a paper published a decade ago, suggested a classification of norms which focused on four significant aspects: (1) their distribution; (2) the mode of enforcement associated with a given norm; (3) the transmission of norms; and (4) the process of conformity to given norms. Robin M. Williams, Jr. has recently incorporated this scheme in his systematic study of American society. Though there is no shortage of classificatory schemes in this important area of sociological theory, it would seem to the present writers that still another dimension is worthy of consideration as a possible addition to Morris' classification.

Indeed, Morris himself has suggested that "probably the most striking omission . . . [in his typology of norms] . . . is the content of the norms."

"Content" is used here in two senses: classification of norms according to the area of behavior regulated . . . , or classification of norms according to the nature of action called for by the norms. . . .

It is the latter to which we are addressing ourselves in this paper.

Our specific objective will be to present an additional typology, to illustrate its potential value by making reference to several sets of data related to the typology, and to suggest how greater attention to this dimension may prove fruitful in assessing the functional significance of certain aspects of norms in social systems.

In discussing norms in general, Williams points out that ". . . norms always carry some prescriptive or proscriptive *quality* . . ." Talcott Parsons, in discussing the integration of social systems, has also directed attention to the significance of the proscriptive-prescriptive dimension. He states,

It is this integration by common values, manifested in the action of solidary groups or collectivities, which characterizes the partial or total integrations of social systems.

Social integration, however much it depends on internalized norms, cannot be achieved by these alone. It requires also some supplementary coordination provided by explicit *prescriptive* or *prohibitory* role-expectations (e.g., laws).

This particular dimension appears worthy of further exploration on the level of system-maintenance analysis. A preliminary ideal-typical description should prove sufficient for the first step in our analysis.

Norms in which the *proscriptive* element is most predominant are those which direct participants in the social structure to avoid, abstain, desist, and reject all forms of behavior associated with a particular potential type of activity. Examples of this dimension are the "thou shalt not" directives of the Ten Commandments and abstention from the pleasures of the flesh as directed by ascetic Protestantism.

The *prescriptive* dimension, on the other hand, directs participants to act in a particular way, spelling out the forms of behavior to which group members must conform. Typical of prescriptive directives are the norms requiring periodical church attendance and confession among Roman Catholics and the elaborate directives associated with the consumption of alcoholic beverages among the Orthodox Jews.

Thus the mandate of the predominantly proscriptive norm is "do not" while the mandate of the predominantly prescriptive norm is "do this" or "do that." The former provides only a goal viewed negatively; the latter provides a goal viewed positively, as well as a set of means for its attainment.

Whether this scheme is worthy of serious attention as a possible addition to the body of theory on norms would seem to depend upon its usefulness as an analytical tool, particularly as a means of organizing empirical findings. We have, with this in mind, selected some studies which help illustrate the possible utility of these notions in the process of relating theory to concrete data.

At least one area of patterned activity which particularly lends itself to analysis in this context has undergone extensive investigation. The several sociological studies of the relationship between sociocultural factors and the consumption of alcoholic beverages should provide us with a "goodness of fit" criterion for our conceptual analysis. The specific studies to which we refer are those of Straus and Bacon, Snyder, Skolnick, and, more recently, Mulford and Miller. All represent a high order of methodological procedure in terms of sampling, question design and data analysis. All of these studies focus on variations in drinking behavior among various social strata and ethnic groups, and provide a broad range of data on norms, beliefs, and sentiments concerning the uses of alcohol. Thus they are particularly valuable for codification. Our first problem, then, is to demonstrate whether any differences between prescriptive and proscriptive dimensions of norms are of significance in the analysis of concrete data.

The above studies report significant differences among the various groups with regard to pathological reactions resulting from differential patterns of alcohol consumption. By "pathological" we mean the extent to which these behaviors represent deviations which are defined by the group's members as either a threat to the existing institutional system, e.g., the kinship or religious system, or as threats to the personal well-being of group members, e.g., problem drinking or psychosis. We are suggesting that the extent to which these levels of pathology are present in a given system is directly related to problems of system maintenance although as we suggest below, these threats may also play a role in attaining greater short-run integration.

CULTURAL NORMS AND DRINKING PATHOLOGY

Three sets of data have been selected to demonstrate the existence of a relationship between types of normative system and drinking pathology. Snyder's study shows that intoxication is related to religio-ethnic group affiliation for college students. As contrasted with the rates for the Jewish students, whose behavior is presumably directed by prescriptive norms, for example, the intoxication rate is much higher for the ascetic Protestant and Mormon groups, for whom the drinking of alcoholic beverages is proscribed. Snyder holds that,

> These data should not be construed as representing the comparative overall effectiveness of the norms of these groups in minimizing intoxication. The percentages . . . are based on the numbers of students in each group who have had some experience in using alcoholic beverages. They, therefore, do not re-

flect the large numbers of abstainers, especially in the Protestant group, who have never been intoxicated.

We would hold that Snyder's interpretation is most meaningful within the context of the relationship between group affiliation and overall drinking behavior. However, it is precisely the question of the "overall effectiveness of the norms" for those who drink which concerns us here; this is the sphere in which the fundamental difference between our concern and that of the various analysts of drinking behavior manifests itself. While their focus is on the relationship between norms and specified features of the social structure, ours is on the qualitative nature of the norms themselves.

Skolnick's data reveal even more sharply some of the consequences of normative deviation. When one compares the degree of social complications associated with religio-ethnic group affiliation, one finds that social complications tend to increase for selected groups of students. While social complications for the Jewish students are minimal, there is a marked increase for the ascetic Protestant groups. Thus, the data again reflect a relationship between ascetic Protestant affiliation and drinking pathology with respect to the extremities of deviant reactions for these groups.

Still other results that are significant in the context of the present study are the findings of Mulford and Miller in one of the most elaborate and extensive studies of the drinking behavior of an adult population. They approach questions similar to those posed by the other researchers from a social psychological viewpoint. Differentiating between drinking behavior that is directed by normative systems and that which involves idiosyncratic decisions regarding alcohol consumption, they developed a scale of "personal-effects definitions," which makes a distinction between relatively normative and non-normative drinking behavior.

Mulford and Miller's interpretation of their findings is consistent with those of Straus and Bacon and Snyder with regard to the lack of norms which characterizes the drinking behavior of respondents with abstinence backgrounds. From their results, it seems clear that the focus on "personal-effects" on the part of the drinker as contrasted with a more normative orientation is associated with problem drinking. An extensive statement by Mulford and Miller with regard to their findings reflects some points of convergence between their viewpoint and our own.

> The heavier consumption by the personal-effects drinker may also be a reflection of the *relative absence of social norms* in the situations where he does much of his drinking. Persons who drink primarily for social effects may be presumed to do most of their drinking in more intimate group situations, involving family and friends, where restrictive norms are relatively effective; although, of course, the party norms may permit considerable latitude. The personal-effects drinker who attends parties probably is the one most likely to exceed the party norms, but as he does so repeatedly, he may find that he is not welcome and is then 'forced' to do more of his drinking alone and in public places where there is relative freedom from intimate group-norm restrictions.

Finally, the heavy drinking of the individual who is drinking mainly for the personal effects of alcohol may also reflect the likelihood that he does not carry in his mind a conception of *how many drinks* it takes to attain the desired effect, especially since such *prescriptions* are presumably not general in our culture. . . .

We can conclude from the above studies that normative systems play a role in the consumption of alcoholic beverages, and that pathological reactions to drinking tend to be greater for certain ascetic Protestant and Mormon groups, as compared with other religious groups. We would hold, in general, that pathological drinking behavior is associated with a relative absence of directives for the act of drinking alcoholic beverages itself. The important question then is: What is there about the nature of the normative systems of the ascetic Protestant and Mormon groups that predisposes their deviants to greater pathological reactions and, consequently, their structure to greater strain?

SIGNIFICANCE OF PRESCRIPTIVE AND PROSCRIPTIVE DIMENSION

We have indicated above that there is an absence of directives regarding drinking behavior among the ascetic Protestant and Mormon groups. In contrast to the prescriptive norms associated with drinking by Jews, for example, the ascetic Protestant and Mormon norms may be characterized as primarily *proscriptive*. Total abstinence is the norm for these groups. Hence, deviation from the abstinence pattern, even in what is ordinarily recognized as socially approved drinking in the larger society, e.g., before dinner, at parties, and like occasions, is associated with an almost complete absence of directives. As Straus and Bacon have pointed out in discussing the drinking behavior of Mormons, "If drinking behavior is adopted, variation must be the rule since there is no norm. Extremes are likely since the behavior itself represents rejection of social rules."

Jewish drinking, as Snyder has shown, is patterned by an elaborate system of explicit directives as to what, when, where, with whom, how much, and why one is expected to consume alcoholic beverages. The norm is predominantly *prescriptive* in nature, and deviation from the drinking norms is associated with gradual and predictable patterns of deviant behavior. Thus Snyder's statistics show that tendencies to alcohol pathology increase in "step like" fashion from Orthodox Jewish drinking, which is associated with the relative absence of signs of pathology, to the Reform and Secular drinking pattern in which pathology is relatively high. Nevertheless, the highest rate still tends to remain lower than rates for the Protestant group.

We would hold that it is inherent in the nature of the two sets of norms, the ascetic Protestant and Mormon norms, on the one hand, and the Jewish norms, on the other, that they predispose group members to different kinds of deviant reactions. The consequence of the differential deviant reactions is differential strain for the two sub-systems. Alcohol pathology represents not only personal problems, but problems for the group as well. The various efforts to cope with problems of alcohol on the part of different groups—governmental agencies, private welfare organizations, and religious groups, to name only a few—suggest that strain exists not only for the sub-systems in which they occur, but for larger social systems as well. In general, it can be noted that at least four types of group reactions to system strain can be isolated as indices of the extent of perceived threat to the system or its members. Group reactions may take the form of: (1) *Retrenchment,* in which all deviants are cast out of the group, leaving only a small hard core of adherents; (2) *Regeneration,* in which there is an attempt to revitalize the norm through a cultural renaissance; (3) *Rational-Scientific Innovation,* which includes efforts on the part of persons outside of the group as well as enlightened group participants to adapt new normative patterns to the pre-existing cultural system; and (4) *Permissiveness,* which involves individual determination of limits. Examples of these types of reactions may be found reflected in behavior associated with deviant drinking activities. *Retrenchment* has manifested itself in the strong reactions to public intoxication on the part of the Chinese in the United States, who, in the past, forced alcoholics and problem drinkers to return to the Chinese mainland if they failed to mend their ways, at the same time reinforcing the norms of individual responsibility to the group. *Regeneration* is reflected in the abstinence movement in the United States. *The Rational-Scientific Innovation* reaction is exemplified in Mulford and Miller's suggestion that prescriptive drinking norms should replace proscriptive drinking norms for the ascetic Protestant groups in the United States. And the persistence of patternless drinking in a good many American social contexts is a manifestation of *Permissiveness.*

A TYPOLOGY OF NORMS

We have suggested above that the proscriptive and prescriptive dimensions of norms do make it possible for us to attain greater understanding of the dynamics of social pathology. We have, up to this point, discussed the two dimensions in very broad terms. To what extent can we specify the nature of these dimensions and place them in a context of social system analysis? With this perspective in view, norms may be classified ideal-typically in terms of the following descriptive characteristics which have emerged from our review of the various studies cited above: (1) the degree of elasticity; (2) the degree of elaboration; (3) the degree of pervasiveness; and (4) the degree of functional interrelatedness.

Table 1 describes those aspects of norms which make them classifiable

Table 1

QUALITATIVE CHARACTERISTICS OF PRESCRIPTIVE AND PROSCRIPTIVE NORMS

Characteristic of Norm	Proscriptive	Prescriptive
Elasticity	Inflexible: Behavior is defined as either compliant or deviant and there are no directives for action	Flexible: Behavior is defined in degree of conformity and directives for how to act are explicit
Elaboration	No ritual, no embellishment associated with act	Great deal of embellishment in ritualized and symbolic acts
Pervasiveness	Focus on a specific act applying to any and all contexts	Focus on a variety of similar acts in specified contexts
Functional interrelatedness	Norm tends to have few or no convergences with other norms in the larger system	Norm tends to converge with other norms in the larger system

as either proscriptive or prescriptive. Table 2 shows how these factors are related, by way of illustration, to drinking behavior. The extent to which these factors, in varying degree, manifest themselves in given normative systems represents, in our judgment, a measure of the relative degree of predisposition to normative mal-integration with respect to a given norm.

THE NORMATIVE AND THE FACTUAL

As we have suggested above, the over-all effectiveness of norms in the process of system maintenance can be attributed to at least two characteristics: (1) the extent to which both internal and external sanctions

Table 2

DRINKING NORMS FOR SELECTED GROUPS BY QUALITATIVE CHARACTERISTICS AND PRESCRIPTIVE-PROSCRIPTIVE DIMENSION

	Elasticity	Elaboration	Pervasiveness	Functional Interrelatedness	
Prescriptive					
	++	++	++	++	Jews
	+	+	+	++	Italians
	−	−	−	+	Mormons
Proscriptive					

effectively direct the behavior of group members; and (2) the nature of the norms themselves. It is the latter to which we have addressed ourselves in this paper. Though the two are undoubtedly related, we would hold that the qualitative nature of the norm is analytically distinct from the strength of sanctions attached to the norm. Thus, whether controls are internalized or externalized, or whether the sanctioning agents are informally or formally designated does not concern us here. The above data are consistent with our hypothesis that predominantly proscriptive norms are more likely than predominantly prescriptive norms to lead to extreme degrees of pathological reactions when deviation occurs.

It is possible to treat the whole matter of the relationship between norms and social pathology in terms of the relationship between the normative and factual orders. While we have indicated that our focus is on the qualitative nature of the norms themselves, our ultimate concern is with social control and group integration. The normative-factual orders lend themselves to analysis within the framework of the prescriptive-proscriptive dimension. Thus, one could interpret our discussion as an attempt to explore the consequences of situations in which the normative order and the factual order are more or less convergent or divergent. Rather than assume that it is simply the divergence between these two orders which is productive of strain, we would hold that it is still primarily the quality of the normative order which determines the extent of strain. The following suggestive scheme provides an illustration of a possible systematic approach to these dimensions. Thus, the following table describes a factual order, given a certain prescriptive-proscriptive normative order. The examples represent approximate empirical referents with regard to drinking norms.

	NORMS	
	Jewish *Italian*	*Mormon* *Methodist*
Normative Order	Highly Prescriptive	Highly Proscriptive
Factual Order	Deviation	Deviation
Level of Pathology	Low Level of Pathology	High Level of Pathology (Anomie)

As this preliminary scheme suggests, the following propositions can be formulated with respect to the aspects of norms referred to above:

   [1] Given a situation in which there is *proscription* on the *normative* level and *deviation* on the factual level, pathology will be *high*.

   [2] Given a situation in which there is *prescription* on the *normative* level and *deviation* on the factual level, pathology will be *low*.

The above discussion implies that under certain normative conditions behavior which deviated from the norm does not threaten the system of order, while under other conditions it does. It should be added that the present analysis does not include a discussion of the relative effectiveness of each type of norm under conditions of normative integration without strain. Presumably, pathology is minimized as a result of conformity to both the predominantly proscriptive and prescriptive norms referred to above. Stated as a third proposition:

> [3] Given a situation in which there is *either* prescription or proscription on the *normative* level and *conformity* on the *factual* level, pathology will be *low*.

Thus, this approach is systematic and directly lends itself to empirical analysis.

PERMISSIVENESS AND ANOMIE

A third general aspect, to which we referred only briefly, is permissiveness. Although the evidence with respect to this pattern or lack of pattern is scanty, permissiveness appears to be characteristic of periods of normative transformation. Thus, in the United States the shift from proscription among Protestant abstentionist groups *without the provision of a corresponding set of clear directives* for drinking behavior appears to represent a period of *anomic* behavior which will, in time, become organized into a new pattern. In this context directives tend to be vague injunctions to avoid immoderate drinking and to "stay out of trouble." That this condition may persist over very long periods of time without becoming organized, thus enhancing the anomic condition and consequent deviant behavior, is illustrated by studies of Finnish drinking.

In Finland, where religious groups preach proscription and where the sale and distribution of alcohol is carefully controlled, the arrests for drunkenness rate in 1959 was 72.0 per 1000 inhabitants compared with 26.0 for Norway, 17.2 for Sweden and 6.3 for Denmark. Finland and Norway, it should be noted, are countries which had prohibition laws following World War I in contrast to Sweden which rejected prohibition as a solution to drinking problems and Denmark which did not even entertain the question of prohibition. Assuming that the behaviors associated with efforts to solve problems reflects underlying differences in normative orientations, it seems clear that arrests for drunkenness as a reflection of deviant behavior are higher where a background of proscription is greater.

Straus and Bacon and Mulford and Miller as we noted above, held that when those who were reared as abstainers drink there are no directives for how, when, how much and with whom to drink. Allardt explored the intensity of attitude toward drinking in his Finnish sample and found what he described as an intensive negative attitude toward drinking (proscriptive) as contrasted with "an ambivalent one."

> The finding agrees very well with the intuitive picture one gets of the attitudes toward drinking in Finnish society. There are certain people with a strong negative attitude towards drinking, while most other people may show a very positive verbal attitude towards drinking and towards the functions of drinking, but this attitude is not consistent, and it is often expressed in a jocular way.

Permissive attitudes toward drinking in Finland are also associated with acceptance of the value of occasional unrestrained drinking, suggesting still another link between permissiveness and deviance. Thus the study of drinking in Finnish culture lends support to our original assumption regarding permissiveness and deviance.

We suggested above that permissiveness represents a condition of unresolved anomie. Recent research in the area of deviant behavior has focused on Merton's hypothesis that strains in social systems lead to deviant behavior and consequent anomie. More specifically, in American society the discrepancy between the American desire for success and differential opportunity for the attainment of success goals leads to deviant reactions and, ultimately, to anomie.

Although a thorough discussion of Merton's approach to anomie is beyond our primary concern here, it is well to comment briefly at this point since permissiveness and anomie represent aspects of the same phenomenon.

Our usage of anomie suggests that the source of the weakening of social controls on drinking is a reflection of general societal transformation related to industrialization and urbanization which were the foci of attention of the sociologists to whom we referred at the outset—Durkheim, Tonnies, Redfield and Becker. Given the kind of rapid transformation which characterizes the responses of sub-systems to increase in population, change in type of production and modification of family functions, to suggest only a few consequences of industrialization, there is a simultaneous change in group attitudes toward the normative order. Thus, although there still tends to be an awareness of the rules limiting and directing man's desires, there is somewhat less certainty regarding whether or not adherence to these norms should be enforced. As social structures undergo change, so do normative systems. During periods of uncertainty a wider range of deviance is tolerated in the form of permissiveness, which, as we suggested above, allows the person rather than the group to determine the range of appropriate conduct. While all societies and groups must provide for flexibility in order to persist, periods during which permissiveness predominates do not always result in a reinforcement of the original normative system, as we noted above. Thus the uncertainty, i.e., anomie, associated with some of these periods is often the prelude to the emergence of new *normative patterns.*

With respect to drinking behavior in particular, however, the flexibility associated with change, if we are correct in our analysis of deviance, has more profound effects in systems undergoing change from proscription to other normative forms.

Similar to Merton's approach which deals with the group's response to deviance is our concern with what we have called permissiveness.

Recently several analysts of deviant drinking behavior, following Merton, have suggested that problem drinking represents a *retreatist* reaction to the strain associated with the discrepancy between success goals and opportunity to attain them. Thus the retreatist, having failed to reach his goal, withdraws from the race and turns to excessive drinking and, finally to problem drinking. This in turn leads to more deviant drinking on the part of others who observe the toleration of deviance. Given the paucity of empirical data on this aspect of anomie it is not possible to draw any conclusions at this time. If, however, patterns of deviant drinking can be linked to more general societal processes and their impact on normative systems then our objectives in this paper will have been served.

We have suggested that proscriptive and prescriptive dimensions are to be found in the analysis of other normative systems and data other than those dealing with alcohol pathology alone. We would suggest that sex behavior may be a fruitful area of investigation. Some specific examples of other problems that would seem to lend themselves to this type of analysis would be studies of norms proscribing aggression among Jews; norms proscribing female pre-marital intercourse among Italians; and norms proscribing the acquisition of material luxuries among the Old Order Amish.

Finally, although we have abstracted norm qualities as our focus of attention and hold that they are an essential aspect of the processes enhancing and inhibiting deviance and pathology we do not feel that this approach is alone sufficient to understand these phenomena. Thus the subsequent experiences of persons reared in proscriptive cultures and subcultures play an important role in decisions to conform or deviate. Ernest Campbell in a recent study, for example, presents data which indicate that college students who have internalized proscriptive drinking norms are more likely to form peer group associations that encourage personal abstinence and non-drinkers are less likely to pledge fraternities and sororities than drinkers. The study of the effects of drinking norms on behavior, then, also provides entree into the sphere of group formation studies. In short, the study of drinking behavior is not only significant because it contributes directly to the solution of social problems but also for its contribution to the understanding of basic societal processes.

Public Stereotypes of Deviants

J. L. SIMMONS
With the assistance of Hazel Chambers

THE IDEA THAT publics "create" deviance through the same symbolic processes by which they invent "baseball," "flags," and "niggers" existed *passim* in the writings of Durkheim [1] and has recently been set forth in a more explicit and systematic manner by Lemert,[2] Erikson,[3] Kitsuse,[4] and Becker,[5] among others. Put simply, the assertion is that "deviance" is not an intrinsic attribute of any behavior, but is instead the distilled result of a social process of labelling.[6]

One of the most provocative outgrowths of this approach is that it has focused attention upon the labelling and imputing social audience as well as on the deviate himself. But the approach still remains a promising orientation rather than a full-blown theory.[7] With a few notable exceptions,[8] there has been remarkably little explicit investigation of public attitudes toward deviant behavior. And for almost all the questions arising from this perspective, we have little more than intelligent guesses as answers.

This paper is a report on four pilot studies which were carried out as an attempt to provide a more empirical grounding for the perspective sketched above. The aim was to explore this labelling process and its consequences by modifying techniques previously developed for studying attitudes toward racial and cultural minorities. These studies yielded some preliminary and "soft" data on the following questions: 1) How much agreement is there about what is deviant? 2) Does the public hold stereotyped images

This research was carried out under a grant from the University Research Board, Graduate College, University of Illinois. The writer is indebted to Daniel Glaser for his advice and constructive criticism. From *Social Problems*, 13, Fall, 1965, pp. 223-232. Reprinted by permission of the publisher and author.

[1] See, especially, Émile Durkheim, *The Rules of Sociological Method*, New York: The Free Press, 1938.

[2] Edwin Lemert, *Social Pathology*, New York: McGraw-Hill, 1951, pp. 3-101.

[3] Kai Erikson, "Notes on The Sociology of Deviance," *Social Problems*, 9 (Spring, 1962), pp. 307-314.

[4] John Kitsuse, "Societal Reactions to Deviant Behavior," *Social Problems*, 9 (Winter, 1962), pp. 247-257.

[5] Howard S. Becker, *Outsiders*, New York: The Free Press, 1963.

[6] This does not mean there is "really" no such thing as deviance, or that society is the villain and the deviate an innocent bystander.

[7] This is, of course, also true of most other "theories" in sociology. Cf. Hans Zetterberg, *On Theory and Verification in Sociology*, Totowa, N.J.: Bedminster Press, 1963.

[8] Kitsuse, *op. cit.*, and Thomas Sheff, "The Societal Reaction to Deviance: Ascriptive Elements in the Psychiatric Screening of Mental Patients in a Midwestern State," *Social Problems*, 11 (Spring, 1964), pp. 401-413.

of deviants? 3) If so, what are some of the consequences? Some differences between those who stereotype and those who don't will also be noted.

PUBLIC CONSENSUS ON WHAT IS DEVIANT

In the first pilot study the following question was asked of one hundred and eighty subjects selected by a quota formula designed to produce variation in age, sex, education, occupation, religion, race, and census region within the sample: [9]

In the following spaces please list those things or types of persons whom you regard as deviant.

In response, the 180 subjects listed a total of 1,154 items (mean of 6.4 responses per subject). Even with a certain amount of grouping and collapsing, these included no less than 252 different acts and persons as "deviant." The sheer range of responses included such expected items as homosexuals, prostitutes, drug addicts, beatniks, and murderers; it also included liars, democrats, reckless drivers, atheists, self-pitiers, the retired, career women, divorcees, movie stars, perpetual bridge-players, prudes, pacifists, psychiatrists, priests, liberals, conservatives, junior executives, girls who wear makeup, and know-it-all professors.

Table 1

MOST FREQUENT RESPONSES TO THE QUESTION
"WHAT IS DEVIANT"
N = 180

Response	%
Homosexuals	49
Drug Addicts	47
Alcoholics	46
Prostitutes	27
Murderers	22
Criminals	18
Lesbians	13
Juvenile Delinquents	13
Beatniks	12
Mentally Ill	12
Perverts	12
Communists	10
Atheists	10
Political Extremists	10

[9] The questionnaires were administered by members of an advanced research methods class who had been previously trained in interviewing.

The most frequently mentioned acts or persons, together with the per cent of respondents who mentioned them, are given in Table 1. No type was mentioned by as many as half of the subjects, and only 14 of the 252 different types were mentioned by as many as 10% of the sample. Examination of the percentages in Table 1 shows, further, that the proportion *spontaneously* subscribing to a given thing as deviant falls off sharply.

But the data from this study must be interpreted in the light of the weaknesses inherent in all open-ended responses. We can more or less assume that the respondent means what he *says*, but we can assume nothing about what he happened *not* to say. For instance, we can assume that at least 47% of the subjects regard drug addiction as deviant, but it does not follow that the other 53% do not. Given a list, we would expect 80% or 90% of a sample to check drug addiction as deviant.[10] When you ask persons to list "what is deviant," you get primarily the denotative definition of a word.

In light of this qualification, the data from this study suggest that there is wide consensus that some types of acts and persons are deviant, but also that a tremendous variety of things are considered deviant by at least some people.

The respondents were subdivided by age, sex, and education but there were few significant differences between these subgroups in frequency of mentioning types. Thirty-six per cent of the females, as opposed to 18% of the males, mentioned prostitute; 54% of those with some college, as opposed to 34% of those who had finished high school or less, mentioned drug addicts; and 19% of those over 40 years old, as opposed to 7% of those under 40, said beatniks were deviant. But all other subgroup variations were too slight to be reliable. Thus, no clear between-group differences emerged, at least with these variables, and within-group variations remained very high.

Because of sample inadequacies [11] the data from this pilot study must be regarded as tentative and exploratory, but they do suggest and lend support to the following generalizations. The facts that even this small number of respondents—all contemporary Americans—named so many different things as deviant, and that there was much within-group variation even among those with the same social background, suggest that almost every conceivable dimension of human behavior is considered deviant from the normative perspective of some existing persons and groups. A fascinating corollary of this is that most individuals would be labelled deviant from someone's point of view.

The range of items mentioned seems to defy content analysis; that is,

[10] A further study using a list to be checked deviant-nondeviant would be useful in providing more accurate data on percentages of respondents who regarded various acts as deviant.

[11] Actually, since such quota samples almost always underrepresent the heterogeneity of the population from which it is drawn, a representative sample would, almost certainly, produce even greater variation of response on what is deviant. Also, response biases— tendencies not to write down "unspeakable" things and tendencies to omit one's more idiosyncratic dislikes—would lead to a spurious reduction in variation of response.

the items do not seem to have any characteristics in common except that they are regarded as deviant by someone. Thus, *there may be only one sense in which all deviants are alike: very simply, the fact that some social audience regards them and treats them as deviant.*

A further implication of the above variation in responses is that, by embracing and conforming to the normative standards of some groups, the individual will *automatically* be violating the standards of other groups and persons. To the extent that this is true, questions of deviance and conformity become questions of inter-group divergence and conflict. And to the extent that the individual is mobile, he will tend to experience normative cross-pressures. Hence, as mobility rates increase within a pluralistic society, the amount of such cross-pressures and the amount of ambivalence resulting from it will likely increase. As one of our informants said: "I'm not sure what's right anymore so how can I say who's doing wrong?"

This may indeed be one important sense in which our society and perhaps other modern industrial societies are "pluralistic." It seems that there are not one but several publics and normative standards. As a result, societal definitions of deviance become somewhat blurred and standards of right and wrong become issues in themselves. This would seem to call into question the assumption, so pervasive among "social structure" theorists, that American society is composed of a large majority who more or less conform to a broad normative standard and a fraction of "boat-rockers" who deviate grossly from this standard. "Social system" is a devised abstraction, several steps removed from concrete social life, and when we observe conflicts and accommodations among groups and cliques in every milieu, the degree of normative integration within society seems quite problematic.

STEREOTYPED CONCEPTIONS OF DEVIANTS

The "overcategorization" of objects seems to be a necessary and ubiquitous aspect of human thought processes—a necessary means of organizing the infinite detail and complexity of the "outside" world.[12] But such coding is necessarily a simplification of incoming stimuli, a *selective* simplification in which information is lost, and misinformation may be added. It must be emphasized that such stereotypes about people and things often contain some freight of truth. But they lead to distorted appraisals because they overestimate within-group similarity and between-group differences, and they tend to be unresponsive to objective evidence.

The other three pilot studies were designed to explore the content of public stereotypes of several kinds of deviants, the extent of consensus on these stereotypes, and some possible corollaries of tendency to stereotype.

---

[12] For an excellent summary of this process see Jerome Bruner, "Social Psychology and Perception," in Eleanor Maccoby, *et al.* (eds.), *Readings in Social Psychology* (3rd ed.), New York: Holt, Rinehart and Winston, 1958, pp. 85-94.

The types chosen were those usually considered deviant by social scientists and laymen, and they were further picked to represent something of a range of behaviors. The research designs were an elaboration of techniques developed by Katz and Braly to explore stereotypes of racial and ethnic groups.[13]

First, we asked a sample of 89 students enrolled in a social problems class to write a description of homosexuals, beatniks, adulterers, and marijuana smokers:

In response, more than half of the students wrote a highly stereotyped characterization of every deviant type. The responses of those who presented stereotypes were remarkably similar in content; the only major variation among the student protocols was between those who stereotyped and those who didn't. This variation appeared to be something of a natural dichotomy; the former group expressing an image of the deviate as a dark haunted creature beyond the pale of ordinary life, the latter describing deviates as just people. Illustrative of the stereotyped response is the following description of the marijuana smoker by a male sociology major.

> . . . a greasy Puerto Rican boy or the shaky little Skid Row bum . . . As for the life led, it is shiftless, unhappy, dog eat dog for survival. I guess marijuana is used as a means of avoiding reality. The pleasure that comes from the drug outweighs the pleasure of life as it really is.

The following portrayal of homosexuals by a female sophomore illustrates the nonstereotyped responses.

> As far as I know the homosexual is not like anything. They are merely people who have different ideas about sex than I do. They probably lead lives which are normal and are different only in the way they receive sexual gratification. They have no distinguishing characteristics.

Emotional reactions toward the deviants ranged from revulsion to benevolent contempt among the stereotyping group, and from mild sympathy to no apparent reaction among the nonstereotypers. The only exceptions were in the responses to beatniks, in which a moderate fraction of both groups expressed some ambivalence.

The two groups of respondents were not distinguishable by any of the social category variables included in the questionnaire. Some other facets of the open-ended responses will be drawn upon in the final section of this paper, dealing with the consequences of stereotypes.

Following the procedures developed by Katz and Braly and similar studies of racial and ethnic stereotypes, we constructed a second questionnaire listing 70 traits extracted from content analysis of the first open-ended questionnaire. The list included a variety of positive, negative, and neutral attributes from which respondents could choose in building their portraits.

[13] Daniel Katz and Kenneth Braly, "Racial Stereotypes of One Hundred College Students," *Journal of Abnormal and Social Psychology* (October-December, 1933), pp. 280-290.

Respondents were asked to select those words and phrases they considered necessary to adequately characterize each of the following groups: marijuana smokers, adulterers, beatniks, homosexuals, and political radicals. They were encouraged to add any words they considered descriptively important, but only a very few did so. They were asked then to go back and encircle those five words which they considered the most important in describing each group. As with earlier studies, our analysis is based largely on the encircled words, although as a reliability check we analyzed the entire lists chosen, with comparable results.

The questionnaire was administered to a sample of 134 subjects selected again on the basis of a quota sampling formula designed to guarantee variation in age, education, census region, sex, occupation, and race.

The most frequently chosen traits and the proportion who encircled them for each of the five deviant types are presented in Table 2. Examination of the table shows that, for each deviant type, a handful of traits accounts for a large proportion of the responses and that a large number of traits were chosen not at all or only once or twice. Thus, as in the open-ended questionnaire, a fair degree of stereotyping is evidenced.

From further examination of the table, we see that the stereotypic portrait of each deviant type is somewhat distinct in content. The marijuana smoker stereotype emerges as an insecure escapist, lacking self-control and looking for kicks; the beatnik is a sloppy, immature nonconformist; the adulterer is immoral, promiscuous, and insecure; the homosexual is perverted and mentally ill; the political radical is ambitious, aggressive, stubborn, and dangerous. The only characteristic imputed frequently to all five types was irresponsible, lacking self-control. All but the radicals were described as lonely and frustrated. Immaturity was encircled by at least some fraction of respondents for each of the types.

The word portraits are almost unequivocally negative for the marijuana smokers, homosexual, and adulterer. The only differences of opinion seem to revolve around whether they should be pitied or condemned. Characterizations of the beatnik and political radical were more ambivalent and respectful. Each was considered clearly beyond the pale of the ordinary citizen, but a number of positive and neutral traits were imputed to each with a good deal of frequency. The beatnik image included artistic, imaginative, and happy-go-lucky, and the radical was considered imaginative and intelligent. Both were conceived as individualistic by over one-fourth of the respondents. But the preponderant image of both these types was also negative; the positive and neutral imputations were only an attenuation of a basically pariah image.

In order to get a more quantitative idea of the degree of agreement among the respondents in imputing traits to the deviant types, we calculated what proportion of the total encirclings was covered by the one most frequent, by the five most frequent, and by the ten most frequent traits for each deviant type. When there was no agreement, any one word received

Table 2

TRAITS ENCIRCLED AS DESCRIPTIVELY MOST IMPORTANT
FOR EACH OF THE FIVE DEVIANT GROUPS

N = 134

Marijuana smokers	%	Beatniks	%	Adulterers	%	Homosexuals	%	Political Radical	%
Looking for kicks	59	Sloppy	57	Immoral	41	Sexually abnormal	72	Ambitious	61
Escapist	52	Non-conformist	46	Promiscuous	36	Perverted	52	Aggressive	47
Insecure	49	Escapist	32	Insecure	34	Mentally Ill	40	Stubborn	32
Lacking self-control	41	Immature	28	Lonely	32	Maladjusted	40	Non-conformist	32
Frustrated	34	Individualistic	27	Sinful	31	Effeminate	29	Impulsive	28
Excitement seeking	29	Lazy	27	Self-interested	29	Lonely	22	Dangerous	28
Nervous	26	Insecure	26	Lacking self-control	28	Insecure	21	Individualistic	26
Maladjusted	24	Irresponsible	20	Passionate	24	Immoral	16	Self-interested	23
Lonely	22	Self-interested	18	Irresponsible	22	Repulsive	14	Intelligent	22
Immature	21	False lives	16	Frustrated	21	Frustrated	14	Irresponsible	21
Weakminded	17	Artistic	16	Immature	16	Weakminded	12	Conceited	15
Irresponsible	15	Maladjusted	14	Sensual	14	Lacking self-control	12	Imaginative	14
Mentally Ill	13	Harmless	13	Over-sexed	13	Sensual	11	Excitement-seeking	9
Pleasure-loving	11	Imaginative	12	Sexually abnormal	12	Secretive	11		
Dangerous	11	Lonely	11	Pleasure-loving	11	Over-sexed	10		
		Imitative	10	False lives	11	Dangerous	10		
		Frustrated	10	Maladjusted	11	Sinful	10		
		Happy-go-lucky	9			Sensitive	10		

less than 2% of the responses; any five words accounted for 7% of the responses; and any ten words, for 14%. When there was a completely consensual image, every respondent encircled the same five words, and these would account for 100% of the responses. The results are presented in Table 3.

Table 3

AMOUNT OF AGREEMENT AMONG RESPONDENTS IN
IMPUTING TRAITS TO DEVIANTS
N = 134

	% of All Responses Covered By:		
Deviant Type	Most Frequent Trait	Five Most Frequent Traits	Ten Most Frequent Traits
Marijuana Smokers	12	47	71
Adulterers	8	35	60
Beatniks	11	38	59
Homosexuals	14	47	64
Political Radicals	12	40	64
Expected by Chance	1.5	7	14

This table shows a fair degree of consensus among the respondents in imputing traits to each deviant type. One-twelfth to one-seventh of all responses were accounted for by the first trait; from a third to half of all responses were covered by the five most frequent traits; and the ten most frequent traits accounted for three-fifths or more of the encirclings. Since a number of the words overlap each other in meaning, the actual degree of consensus among the sample is somewhat higher. That is, if the traits were distinct, the consensus figures would have been even higher.

It appears that the deviant types are far more similar than different in the degree to which a consensual stereotype of them exists. Hence an attempt to rank the types on amount of consensus would be exaggerating the significance of slight variations.

In summary, the data lend preliminary support to the contention that discernible stereotypes of at least several kinds of deviants do exist in our society and that there is a fair amount of agreement on the content of these stereotypes.

SOME CORRELATES OF TENDENCY TO STEREOTYPE

Like the respondents on the open-ended questionnaire, the subjects of the third pilot study seemed to fall into a natural dichotomy of those who stereotyped and those who didn't. We therefore classified the subjects into this high-low dichotomy by the extent to which their encircled words corresponded with the group of most frequently chosen words (those negative words chosen by at least 10% of the respondents). This classification was then run against the other variables in the questionnaire and a fourth pilot study, using exactly the same procedures and base on a judgment sample of 78 students, was conducted to explore the possible correlates of tendency to stereotype deviants.[14]

To see the extent to which stereotyping was a generic tendency, we computed the associations between scores on each possible pairing of deviant types. All ten of the resulting associations (Q) were significant beyond the .001 level, and positive, suggesting that tendency to stereotype deviants is a general characteristic of the appraiser himself. The associations ranged from .80 to .22 and eight of them were above .50.

There was also a rather marked relationship between educational level and tendency to stereotype deviants. When the high-low dichotomy was run against an education trichotomy (less than high school grad, high school grad, some college) the resulting associations (gamma) ranged from .38 to .64. When respondents' scores for each of the five deviant types were summed, the relationship between these composite stereotype scores and education was .63. Thus a strong inverse association between amount of education and tendency to stereotype was found.

But this finding cannot be taken at face value. For one thing, the associations are largely one-way. The majority of even the most highly educated group expressed unequivocally negative stereotypes toward most or all of the deviant types. The associations were produced by the fact that *none* of those low in education scored low in tendency to stereotype. The "success" of education in teaching more thoughtfulness in appraising social objects is therefore only relative.

In the second place, the response protocols suggest that the more educated groups expressed what might be termed a "secondary stereotype" of each deviant type, derived from the currently fashionable psychiatric explanations of human behavior so rampant in the high- and middle-brow mass media. Albeit, these images are more liberal than the traditional stereotypes and psychoanalytic pity is a softer stance than rigid rejection; these protocols suggest that many of the educated are merely more subtle in their stereotyping.

Sex, age, and the other background variables bore no significant relationship to tendency to stereotype deviants.

In the fourth pilot study, stereotyping tendencies were compared with a number of attitudinal variables. Since this study was also a pre-test of

---

[14] As a reliability check, we "intuitively" coded tendencies to stereotype and ran this variable against the others. All associations were as high or higher than those here reported. For example, the gamma between education and this intuitive coding was .75.

other measures and since the sample size was small, analysis problems are complex and only one of the associations will be presented here.[15]

For this student sample, a moderate inverse relationship was found between tendencies to stereotype and a composite liberalism scale.[16] The associations (gamma) between these scores and stereotyping of the specific deviant types ranged from .22 to .58 and the relation between composite liberalism and composite stereotyping tendency was .57. These associations are fairly modest, but unlike the education findings they are more reliable because they are two-way. Liberals stereotyped less and conservatives stereotyped more often than moderates.

CONSEQUENCES OF PUBLIC STEREOTYPES OF DEVIANTS

The major generalization suggested by the data from these pilot studies is that empirically discernible stereotypes of at least several major types of deviance do exist among the populace. But this finding is important only to the extent that it has consequences for deviants or for society, or both. The finding that stereotypes exist immediately poses the question, what effects do they have?

In the first place, it should be noted that stereotypes may provide useful information for evaluating and behaving toward deviants. To the extent that they contain some descriptive validity, they may provide the same kind of utility as generalizations like "policemen can be trusted to help when you're in trouble" or "wildcats are vicious and unfriendly." Stereotypes of deviants probably do contain some fraction of truth; certainly the populace does better than chance in recognizing deviants and predicting their behavior. However, as Merton and others have pointed out,[17] even those aspects of the stereotype which have some *descriptive* validity may be the self-fulfilling result of the stereotype in the first place.

Second, as Becker has suggested,[18] the stereotype is a major mechanism of social control. The baleful image, learned in socialization, prevents a large proportion of the populace from engaging in that type of deviance or even seriously contemplating it. Becker pointed out that this negative stereotype must be overcome before an individual will become a marijuana smoker. And in our open-ended questionnaire, three-fourths of the respondents—enrolled in an advanced sociology course—characterized the marijuana smoker as physiologically enslaved by the drug.

[15] The other findings and many details from the other pilot studies will be presented in J. L. Simmons, *The Deviant in Society,* forthcoming.

[16] The liberalism scale is a composite index including questions pertaining to politics, economics, international affairs, sex, divorce, child rearing, and religion. Copies will be sent upon request.

[17] Robert Merton, "The Self-fulfilling Prophecy," in *Social Theory and Social Structure* (revised ed.), New York: The Free Press, 1957, pp. 421-439.

[18] Howard S. Becker, *op. cit.,* pp. 41-78.

Third, the negative stereotype results in a virtual *a priori* rejection and social isolation of those who are labelled, wrongly or rightly, deviant. In this sense the person so labelled is literally prejudged and is largely helpless to alter the evaluations or treatment of himself. The force of such negative stereotypes is not necessarily attenuated even when the individual is aware that his image is a stereotypic one. As one student wrote in the open-ended questionnaire:

> I realize that this is a stereotypical picture, but nevertheless it is my conception. For me homosexuality is repulsive. It is inconceivable to me how anyone can physically love someone of the same sex.

The negative stereotype may imprison or freeze the individual so labelled into willy-nilly adopting and continuing in a deviant role. This "role imprisonment" occurs because the stereotype leads to social reactions which may considerably alter the individual's opportunity structure, notably, impeding his continuation or re-adoption of conventional roles. The reaction of others, based on stereotypes, is thus a major aspect of the link between performing deviant acts and systematically adopting deviant roles.

It should be noted that this reaction may be somewhat realistic in terms of the self-interests of those reacting. Even the enlightened reformer is realistic in hesitating to let his children become involved with youths who have delinquent records, and we cannot entirely damn a businessman for hesitating to hire an ex-mental patient on an important deadline job. But the sum of these personal behavioral decisions—many of them made by liberal and kindhearted people—is to make it more than ordinarily difficult for one labelled deviant to perform conventional roles.

Finally, among those known to have committed deviant acts, stereotypes have a selective influence upon who is labelled "deviant." Studies have shown [19] that a sizeable proportion of the populace has committed deviant acts, yet only a small fraction of this proportion is labelled deviant. The fraction so labelled is not a random subset of the larger group. With type and frequency of offense held constant, it has been shown that minority groups, lower class persons, and men, for most offenses, are differentially susceptible to the labelling process.[20] Among those who are known to have committed a deviant act, those who seem to possess additional qualities concurring with the stereotypic image of that kind of deviance are far more likely to be labelled and processed a deviate. Again, to the extent that the stereotype is a valid generalization about a class of elements, this labelling by stereotype may have diagnostic and prognostic value. But to the extent that the stereotype is invalid, it serves no useful purpose and

[19] For example, see James Wallerstein and Ckennebt Wyle, "Our Law-abiding Law Breakers," *Probation* (April, 1947), pp. 107-112.

[20] For a summary discussion of this point, see the monograph by Donald Cressey, "Crime," in Robert Merton and Robert Nisbet (eds.), *Contemporary Social Problems*, New York: Harcourt, Brace & World, 1961, pp. 21-76.

does positive damage by imprisoning innocent people, and people no more guilty than a large proportion of the populace, in deviant roles.

We noted earlier that stereotyping, in the broad sense of building up inferential generalizations about classes of phenomena, is an inherent aspect of perception and cognition. In the light of this, an injunction to eliminate stereotypic thinking is facile and impossible, and it is based, if you will, on stereotyped thinking about stereotypes. We are, it would seem, stuck with stereotypes. But stereotypes are variable: at one extreme they may be myths invented from superstition and misinformation; at the other, verified scientific generalizations. They may be rigid prejudgments immune to reality testing, or they may be tentative appraisals with the built-in notion that their validity and applicability to all class members is problematic.

Rather than try to eliminate stereotypes about deviants and other social objects, it would seem, then, that social scientists should aim at gathering and communicating valid knowledge, in the hope that this knowledge will form the basis for future public attitudes.

FURTHER READINGS

Becker, Howard. *Outsiders: Studies in the Sociology of Deviance*. New York: The Free Press, 1963.

Merton, Robert K. *Social Theory and Social Structure*, rev. ed. New York: The Free Press, 1957.

————, and Nisbet, Robert A., eds. *Contemporary Social Problems*. New York: Harcourt, Brace & World, Inc., 1961.

Mizruchi, Ephraim H. *Success and Opportunity: A Study of Anomie*. New York: The Free Press, 1964.

8

INSTITUTIONS, INSTITUTIONALIZATION AND CHANGE

Introduction

ALTHOUGH THE CONCEPT of institution is funda-
mental in the social sciences, no concept enjoys a greater variety of
definition. Because there is much variance in this sphere we will
avoid a general definition in an effort to avert a meaningless gesture.
Instead we provide a variety of materials in breadth and depth which
should help clarify a number of aspects of institutional change and
behavior.

Sumner's conception of an institution as being composed of a
structure and an idea is considered a classic one. It is placed squarely
within the framework of the normative although he makes it clear
that group processes are organized about usages.

The general statement by Hamilton provides us with a broad
descriptive analysis which gives us a background into the basic aspects of institutional organization. As in Sumner the emphasis is upon
the normative. However there is in this case an example of the risks
involved in too inclusive a definition.

The central idea that *purpose* and *result* must be set apart from
one another in our thoughts is found throughout the sociological literature. The late A. R. Radcliffe-Brown's essay on function helps
clarify some of the issues in this sphere as well as a valuable analysis
of the processes associated with social pathology and anomie.

Schneider and Dornbusch's paper provides us with a description
and analysis of manifest and latent functions within a concrete institutional setting. As such it brings together many of the ideas scattered
throughout our other essays. A careful review of the Mizruchi paper
on values in Chapter 3 and a careful reading of Sumner's essay in this
section will add still other institutional contexts within which manifest
and latent functions are analyzed.

Perrucci describes the activities of patients on a psychiatric ward using an institutional framework. Focusing on the relationship between the normative and the factual he assesses the value of applying a revision of the Merton anomie hypothesis to the study of organizations and ties his interpretation in with both Schneider and Dornbusch's ideas and the anomie literature.

While changes in institutions occur very slowly it is also possible to observe veritible revolutions in institutional patterns. Leonard Koppett's fascinating account of the impact of mass society and increasing rationality on professional baseball in the United States is an example of remarkable transformation in so brief a time period.*

That change does occur in patterns is the principle developed by S. N. Eisenstadt. Viewed within a dynamic framework the concepts of contemporary functionalism are of significant value in understanding the processes of transformation. Eisenstadt directs his interest in this analytical scheme to still another institutional context in his essay in Chapter 10, Bureaucratization.

The Mores and Institutions

WILLIAM GRAHAM SUMNER

INSTITUTIONS AND LAWS are produced out of mores. An institution consists of a concept (idea, notion, doctrine, interest) and a structure. The structure is a framework, or apparatus, or perhaps only a number of functionaries set to cooperate in prescribed ways at a certain conjuncture. The structure holds the concept and furnishes instrumentalities for bringing it into the world of facts and action in a way to serve the interests of men in society. Institutions are either crescive or enacted. They are crescive when they take shape in the mores, growing by the instinctive efforts by which the mores are produced. Then the efforts, through long use, become definite and specific. Property, marriage, and religion are the most primary institutions. They began in folkways. They became customs. They developed into mores by the addition of some philosophy of welfare, however crude. Then they were made more definite and specific as regards the rules, the prescribed acts, and the apparatus to be employed. This produced a structure and the institution was complete. Enacted institutions are products of rational in-

* I am indebted to my friend Professor Milton Mayeroff for bringing this paper to my attention [Editor].

From *Folkways*, 1906. Reprinted through the courtesy of Blaisdell Publishing Company, a division of Ginn and Company.

vention and intention. They belong to high civilization. Banks are institutions of credit founded on usages which can be traced back to barbarism. There came a time when, guided by rational reflection on experience, men systematized and regulated the usages which had become current, and thus created positive institutions of credit, defined by law and sanctioned by the force of the state. Pure enacted institutions which are strong and prosperous are hard to find. It is too difficult to invent and create an institution, for a purpose, out of nothing. The electoral college in the constitution of the United States is an example. In that case the democratic mores of the people have seized upon the device and made of it something quite different from what the inventors planned. All institutions have come out of mores, although the rational element in them is sometimes so large that their origin in the mores is not to be ascertained except by an historical investigation (legislatures, courts, juries, joint stock companies, the stock exchange). Property, marriage, and religion are still almost entirely in the mores. Amongst nature men any man might capture and hold a woman at any time, if he could. He did it by superior force which was its own supreme justification. But his act brought his group and her group into war, and produced harm to his comrades. They forbade capture, or set conditions for it. Beyond the limits, the individual might still use force, but his comrades were no longer responsible. The glory to him, if he succeeded, might be all the greater. His control over his captive was absolute. Within the prescribed conditions, "capture" became technical and institutional, and rights grew out of it. The woman had a status which was defined by custom, and was very different from the status of a real captive. Marriage was the institutional relation, in the society and under its sanction, of a woman to a man, where the woman had been obtained in the prescribed way. She was then a "wife." What her rights and duties were was defined by the mores, as they are today in all civilized society.

Institutions

WALTON H. HAMILTON

INSTITUTION IS A VERBAL SYMBOL which . . . describes a cluster of social usages. It connotes a way of thought or action of some prevalence and permanence, which is embedded in the habits of a group or the customs of a

Reprinted with permission of The Macmillan Company, from *Encyclopedia of Social Sciences*, Vol. VII, 1937. Copyright, 1932, The Macmillan Company; copyright renewed, 1960, by The Macmillan Company.

people. In ordinary speech it is another word for procedure, convention or arrangement; in the language of books it is the singular of which the mores or the folkways are the plural. Institutions fix the confines of and impose form upon the activities of human beings. The world of use and wont, to which imperfectly we accommodate our lives, is a tangled and unbroken web of institutions.

The range of institutions is as wide as the interests of mankind. Any simple thing we observe—a coin, a time table, a canceled check, a baseball score, a phonograph record—has little significance in itself; the meaning it imparts comes from the ideas, values and habits established about it. Any informal body of usage—the common law, athletics, the higher learning, literary criticism, the moral code—is an institution in that it lends sanctions, imposes tabus and lords it over some human concern. Any formal organization—the government, the church, the university, the corporation, the trade union—imposes commands, assesses penalties and exercises authority over its members. Arrangements as diverse as the money economy, classical education, the chain store, fundamentalism and democracy are institutions. They may be rigid or flexible in their structures, exacting or lenient in their demands; but alike they constitute standards of conformity from which an individual may depart only at his peril. About every urge of mankind an institution grows up; the expression of every taste and capacity is crowded into an institutional mold.

Our culture is a synthesis—or at least an aggregation—of institutions, each of which has its own domain and its distinctive office. The function of each is to set a pattern of behavior and to fix a zone of tolerance for an activity or a complement of activities. Etiquette decrees the rituals which must be observed in all polite intercourse. Education provides the civilizing exposures through which the potential capacities of individuals are developed into the abilities for performance, appreciation and enjoyment which are personality. Marriage gives propriety to the sex union, bestows regularity upon procreation, establishes the structure of the family and effects such a mediation as may be between personal ambition and social stability. A number of institutions may combine and compete to impress character upon and give direction to the mass of human endeavor. The state claims primary obedience and imposes a crude order upon the doings of mankind; the law of punishing offenses and settling disputes determines the outmost limits of acceptable actions; morality with neater distinctions and more meticulous standards distinguishes respectable from unconventional conduct. The community is made up of such overlapping provinces of social government. It is the institution in its role of organizer which makes of this a social and not a monadic world.

It is impossible to discover for such an organic complex of usages as an institution a legitimate origin. Its nucleus may lie in an accidental, an arbitrary or a conscious action. A man—savage or civilized—strikes a spark from flint, upturns the sod, makes an image of mud, brews a concoction, mumbles a rigamarole, decides a quarrel or helps himself to what he may require. The act is repeated, then multiplied; ideas, formulae, sanctions and habits from the impinging culture get attached; and gradually there develops a ritual of fire, a hoe and spade agronomy, a ceremonial for appeasing the gods, a cult of healing, a spell for casting out devils, a due process of law or a sound business policy. Even if it is deliberately established an institution has neither a definite beginning nor an uncompromised identity. A religious creed or a legislative statute is compounded of beliefs and ideas which bear the mark of age and of wear; a paper charter and a document engrossed upon parchment are not insulated against the novelties in usage which attend the going corporation and the living constitution. It is impossible even in the most rudimentary culture to find folkways which are simple and direct answers to social necessities. In all societies, however forward or backward, the roots of the most elementary of arrangements—barter, burial, worship, the dietary, the work life, the sex union—run far back into the unknown past and embody the knowledge and ignorance, the hopes and fears, of a people.

In fact as an aspect of a continuous social process an institution has no origin apart from its development. It emerges from the impact of novel circumstances upon ancient custom; it is transformed into a different group of usages by cultural change. In institutional growth the usual may give way to the unusual so gradually as to be almost unnoticed. At any moment the familiar seems the obvious; the unfamiliar appears but a little revealed—an implication in a convention which is itself taken for granted, a potentiality slowly quickening into life. So it is that the corporation is still a person, the work of the machine is manufacture, the labor contract concerns masters and servants and industrial accidents are personal wrongs. It often happens that new arrangements spring up under the cloak of an established organization. Thus the empire of the Caesars emerged behind the forms of the republic, the holy Catholic church is nominally the episcopal see of Rome and the British Commonwealth does its business in the name of His Majesty. In like manner in the domain of ideas the novelty in doctrine usually appears as a gloss upon the ancient text; systems of theology are commentaries upon the words of Scripture; Coke and Cooley set down their own understanding of the law upon the authority of Littleton and Blackstone. Thus too so intangible a thing as a social theory or a public policy may emerge from the practical commitments of the moment. A mere expediency, such as the abolition of the corn laws, is abstracted from cause and occasion and becomes a generalized policy of free trade; or a comprehensive scheme of railway regulation, such as obtains in the United States, appears as a by-product of the empirical elimination of specific abuses. In the course of events the fact arrives before the word and new wine must be put up in old bottles. Novelties win a tacit acceptance before their strangeness is noticed and compel before their actuality is appreciated. In institutional life current realities are usually to be found behind ancient forms.

As an institution develops within a culture it responds to changes in prevailing sense and reason. A history of the interpretation of Aristotle or St. Paul or Kant at various periods indicates how easily a document lends itself to successive systems of ideas. The public regulation of business has consistently even if belatedly reflected the prevailing winds of doctrine upon the relation of the state to industry. The pages of the law reports reveal the ingenuity with which, in spite of professions that the law remains the same, old rules and standards are remade to serve changing notions of social necessity. An institution which has enjoyed long life has managed to make itself at home in many systems of thought. The classic example is the Christian Gospel. The simple story of the man Jesus presently became a body of Pauline philosophy; the Middle Ages converted it into an intricate theological system and the rationalization of a powerful ecclesiastical empire; at the individualistic touch of the Reformation it became a doctrine of the personal relationship between man and his maker; it is today patching up a truce with Darwinism, the scientific attitude, relativity and even religious skepticism. In this continuous process of the adaptation of usage and arrangement to intellectual environment an active role is assumed by that body of ideas taken for granted which is called common sense. Because it determines the climate of opinion within which all others must live it is the dominant institution in a society.

In an even broader way an institution is accommodated to the folkways of a culture. As circumstances impel and changing ideas permit, a usage in high esteem, like piracy, may fall from grace; while another under tabu, such as birth control, may first win tolerance and in time general acceptance. As one social system passes into another and the manner of living and the values of life are transformed, one institution gives way to another better adapted to the times. It required a number of changes in use and wont to convert the ordeal by combat into the trial by law; the prestige of the family tie, of blood vengeance, of the magical ritual and of might made right had to decline and a consciousness of the waste and injustice which attended legalized conflict had to become prevalent. An institution that survives, such as matrimony, responds surely even if stubbornly to cultural change. While the basis of Christian marriage is no more than the primitive custom of monogamy, the rigid lines of the institution bear the marks of the mediaeval order. It gave support to a caste system resting upon landed property, elevated the social values of family above the individual values of love, was blessed with the ascetic ideal of otherworldliness and became a sacrament. Companionate marriage is emerging from a different world of fact, appreciation, habit and belief. It reduces to usage an attempt to escape the rigors of matrimony without resort to casual relationships; it reflects the condition of an urban society where blood is no longer blue, life is impersonal, children are a luxury and women must earn their own livings. In a culture which develops slowly enough to allow a graceful accommodation folkways may be drawn together into rich and intricate institutional patterns. In the Middle Ages the usages of the church—the trinity, the creed, the litany, the ecclesiastical empire—were all fused into a single conventional whole, to which unity was given by the idea of the death of the god as a vicarious atonement. In the late eighteenth century politics, law, economics, ethics and theology in separate domains alike attempted to superimpose a symmetrical system of mechanical principles upon the mass of human behavior; the common element was an analogue borrowed from physical science. In the social process the life of an institution depends upon its capacity for adaptation. But always amid the whirl of change elements of disorder are present; and long before a harmony is achieved between unlike conventions disintegration has set in.

Nor is an institution introduced from an alien society immune to this process of development. The act of borrowing merely gives the opportunity for its transformation. The nucleus is liberated from its cultural matrix and takes on the character of the usages among which it is set down. In their native habitat the books of the Old Testament were the literature of a people; in the strange world of the mediaeval schoolmen they became a collection of verses inviting dialectical exposition. In England "the higher law" was invoked to justify a popular revolution against an irresponsible monarchy; in America it has become the sanction for a judicial review of legislative acts. In appropriating the machine process Russia stripped away the enveloping business arrangements and made of it an instrument to serve a national social economy. The act of transplantation may at first retard but eventually is likely to promote growth. It introduces into a culture an unknown usage but allows it to emerge as an indigenous institution.

Its very flexibility makes an institution a creature of social stress and strain. In a stable or slowly changing society it fits rather neatly into the cultural pattern; amid the disorder which change brings its office may be compromised by the inflexibility of its structure. As necessity changes, tradition and inertia may stand in the way of the performance of new duties. A group of usages, for all the new demands upon it, may never quite escape slavery to its past. The shadow of ordeal by combat still hangs heavy over trial by law; the jury decides the contest, the judge is the umpire, the procedures are the rules of the game, the witnesses are clansmen armed with oaths and the attorneys are the champions; an appeal court orders a new trial not primarily for want of justice but because of error in the conduct of the ordeal. The United States Supreme Court has come to be the official interpreter of the constitution; yet by tradition its function is judicial, and it is only as an issue is germane to the disposition of a case that it can declare the meaning of the higher law. Almost every institution—from the superfluous buttons on the sleeve of a coat to the ceremonial electors in a presidential contest—bears the vestigial mark of a usage which is gone.

But its elements of stability may be powerless to prevent the conversion of an institution to a service for which it was never intended. Its existence and repute give it value; it may adventitiously or by design assume a new character and play a new role in the social order. Equity, once an informal method of doing justice, now possesses all the appurtenances of a system of law. The principle of "no liability without fault" was once the basis of an individualistic law of torts; in our times the rules of recovery are being socialized, as, for example, in workmen's compensation, by a mere extension of "fault" to acts involving no personal blame. An institution may even fall into the hands of the enemy and be used to defeat its reputed purpose. Thus a community of ascetics develops into a wealthy monastic establishment; a theory of social contract invented as a justification of monarchy is converted into a sanction for its overthrow; a party dedicated to personal freedom becomes the champion of vested wealth; and a philosophy contrived to liberate thought remains to enslave it. As time and chance present their problems, men meet them with expediencies as best they can; but those who contrive rules and formulae cannot control the uses to which they are put. The proneness of an institution, like a lost sheep, to go astray, has been caught in the sentence: "Saint Francis of Assisi set out to bring people to sweetness and light, and left in his wake a plague of gray friars." The folkways are marked by a disposition of event to belie intent.

In the course of time the function of an institution may be compromised by or perhaps even be lost in its establishment. The spirit may become the letter, and the vision may be lost in a ritual of conformity. In time a way of intellectual inquiry may become a mere keeping of the faith; a nice propriety in social relations may decay into a code of etiquette; or a morality intended to point the way toward the good life may come to impose the duty of doing right. Thus ceremonial replaces purposive action and claims a vicarious obedience. The existence of an informal institution gets buttressed about by prevailing opinion and by personal interest. In legislative "deliberation" statesmen cherish their stock in trade of time-honored argument and resent the appearance of unfamiliar issues; scholars of repute defend the established ways of inquiry and the accepted verities; and social lights conserving the older proprieties against feminism "entrench themselves behind their tea-cups and defend their frontiers to the last calling-card." The persons immediately concerned have their stakes in arrangements as they are and do not wish to have personal position, comfort of mind or social prestige disturbed. As it crystallizes into reputable usages an institution creates in its defense vested interest, vested habit and vested ideas and claims allegiance in its own right.

If an institution becomes formal, an even greater hazard to its integrity is to be found in its organization and its personnel. A need for order finds expression in a government or the demand for justice in a legal system or the desire for worship in a church; and various groups become interested in its structure and offices, its procedures and emoluments, its ceremonials and consolations. A host of officials great and small comes into being, who are as solicitous about the maintenance of the establishment to which they are committed. They possess preferences and prejudices, are not immune to considerations of prestige and place and are able to rationalize their own interests. As the scheme of arrangements grows rigid, "the good of the nation"—or the church or the party or the lodge or whatever it is—tends to become dominant. The lines of activity may be frozen into rigidity and ecclesiasticism, legalism, constitutionalism and ritualism remain as fetishes to be served. An institution when once accepted represents the answer to a social problem. In the maze of advantage, accommodation, sense and reason which grows up about it lies a barrier to the consideration of alternatives. Its successor for better or for worse is likely to prevail only through revolution or by stealth.

In its ideal likeness an institution usually creates its apology. As long as it remains vital, men accommodate their actions to its detailed arrangements with little bother about its inherent nature or cosmic purpose. As it begins to give way or is seriously challenged, compelling arguments for its existence are set forth. The picture-as-it-is-painted is likely to be rather a work of art than a representation of fact, a product rather of rationalization than of reason; and, however adventitious its growth, disorderly its structure or confused its function, the lines of its defense lack nothing of trimness and purpose. The feudal regime was an empirical sort of affair; men of iron lorded it over underlings as they could, yielded to their betters as they were compelled and maintained such law and order as the times allowed; but with its passing its sprawling arrangements and befuddled functions were turned into office and estate ordained of God. In the days of the Tudors kings were kings without any dialectical to-do about it; the overneat statement of the theory of divine right had to await the decadent monarchy of the Stuarts. The tangled thing called capitalism was never created by design or cut to a blueprint; but now that it is here, contemporary schoolmen have intellectualized it into a purposive and self-regulating instrument of general welfare. If it is to be replaced by a "functional society," the new order will emerge blunderingly enough; but acquisition of a cleancut structure and clearly defined purpose will have to wait upon its rationalizers. An assumption of uniformity underlies all apologies; invariably they impose simple, abstract names, such as monarchy, democracy, competition and socialism, upon a mass of divergent arrangements.

In this endowment with neatness and purpose an institution is fitted out with the sanctions and trappings of ancient usage. Republican government harks back to Greece and Rome; the "liberties" for which seventeenth century Englishmen fought were the ancient rights of man. Magna Carta, a feudal document, was remade to serve the cause of Parliament against king; a primitive folk government was discovered in the dim twilight of the German forests to give to English democracy a fountainhead which was neither French nor American; and "the spirit of '76" grew up long after the event to serve the patriotism of another century. In the courts it is a poor rule which cannot find a good reason in former decisions and fit itself out with an ancient lineage. But law does not invoke the sanction of precedent more often than other institutions; the openness of its written records merely makes more evident the essential process. A succession of usages stretching from Aristotle to Calhoun has been justified as expressions of the natural order. Even—or above all—in the church the prevailing dogma is set down as interpretations of the creed of the apostles; and Christian marriage "was instituted by God in the time of man's innocency." As tradition leaves its impress upon fact, fact helps to remake tradition. The thing that is is the thing that always was.

It is only as stability gives way to change that the lines of an institution stand out in sharp relief. So long as a people is able to do as its fathers did it manifests little curiosity about the arrangements under which it lives and works; the folk of the South Sea Islands can administer justice after their ways, but they can neither give answers to hypothetical cases nor tell in abstract terms what they do. So long as the procedure of a group or a school is unquestioned it is little aware of the conventions and values which give character even to outstanding achievement: Scott had little conscious appreciation of the distinctive qualities of the English novel; Jowett could never have put in terms the peculiar features of Oxford education; and Kant might not have been able to place his own philosophy in time and opinion. But the break of usage from usage within a culture and the resulting maladjustment lead to a discovery of the detail which makes up an institution. A number of crises were required to reveal the customs which are the British constitution; it took a Civil War to make clear the nature of the union between the American states. The appearance of social unrest was essential to an appreciation of the difference between competition and laissez faire and between industry and business. An aesthetic revolt marked by a riding into almost all the winds that blow was requisite to a realization of the distinctive modes and values in classical music and in Gothic architecture and to an appreciation of the molds imposed by acceptable form upon creative effort. For such casual glimpses of the intricacies of social institutions as men are permitted to see they are indebted to the stress and strain of transition.

It follows almost of course that institutional development drives a fault line between current fact and prevailing opinion. Men see with their ideas as well as with their eyes and crowd the novel life about them into outmoded concepts. They meet events with the wisdom they already possess, and that wisdom belongs to the past and is a product of a by-gone experience. As new institutions gradually emerge from the old, men persist in dealing with the unfamiliar as if it were the familiar. A national legislature by the enactment of antitrust laws tries to superimpose the competitive pattern upon the turbulent forces of a rising industrialism; a trade union uses the traditional device of a strike to advance wages in an industry in which the unorganized plants can easily supply the total output; a group of elder statesmen approaches the problems of war debts and reparations with the old formula of protection versus free trade. At a time when a depression bears witness to economic disorder the institution of business is discussed in the outgrown vocabulary of private property, liberty of contract, equality of opportunity and free enterprise; and rugged American individualism is invoked as a way of order for a system which has somehow become an uncontrolled and unacknowledged collectivism. Even the Protestants as often as not turn belief into denial; and heresy shackled to an inherited ideology is merely a reverse orthodoxy. In the flux of modern life the various usages which with their conflicting values converge upon the individual create difficult problems that demand judgment; and in the course of very human events it is the fate alike of individual, group and society to have to meet emerging fact with obsolescing idea.

Thus an institution like the living thing it is has a tangled identity. It cannot be shown in perspective or revealed in detail by the logical method of inclusion and exclusion. It holds within its actuality the vestiges of design and accident, the stuff of idea and custom, from many ages, societies, civilizations and climates of opinion. In any important group of institutions, such as marriage, property, the market or the law, there are to be discovered as inseparable aspects of an organic whole notions, procedures, sanctions and values hailing from cultural points far apart. Each holds within its being elements in idea and in form drawn from the contemporary era of relativity, the rational universe of the eighteenth century, the mediaeval world of absolutes and verities and the folkways of some dim far off era. An institution is an aspect of all that it has met, a potential part of all that it will encounter. It holds many unknown possibilities which a suitable occasion may kindle into life. It may continue to hold sanctions which we think have departed; it may already have come to possess compulsions of which we are still unmindful. The discovery of its meaning demands an inquiry into its life history; but even the genetic method will tell much less than we should like to know of how a thing which cannot for long abide came to be.

Moreover, the way of knowledge is itself an institution. The physical world, natural resources and human nature may be elementary things; but we can learn about them only in terms of and to the extent allowed by our prevailing methods of inquiry. The little we understand of the universe is a function of the size of the telescope, the sensitiveness of the photographic plate and the bundle of intellectual usages called astronomy. Our national resources are a product of technology, and their catalogues at different times reflect the contemporary states of the industrial arts. It was the steam engine and the machine which made of coal and iron potential wealth; it was not until Faraday and Edison had done their work that electricity became potential energy. The little we understand or think we understand about human nature is an institutional product. The inquiries called physiology, anatomy and neurology—each of them a bundle of intellectual usages —reveal no more than the raw material of personal character; the stuff has ripened into individuality within the matrix of the prevailing folkways.

Man and woman are so much creatures of custom and belief that the word innate is most treacherously applied to masculine and feminine traits. In various societies the stages upon which peoples must play their parts are set so differently by social heritage that we can as yet speak with little certainty about racial characteristics. The physical world and the human nature we know are aspects of the prevailing state of culture. In matter and in the chromosome may lie limitless possibilities, the actualities which appear are creatures of social institutions.

Among the ways of knowing is "the institutional approach." Institutes as the ordained principles of a realm of learning or of life have long existed; they are known to theology, law, education and all subjects ruled over by dialectic. About the turn of the last century a genetic study of the folkways began to win academic respectability. It could make little headway so long as the Newtonian concept was dominant; inquirers went in search of laws and uniformities, explanations were set down in mechanical formulae and the end of the quest was an articulate and symmetrical body of truths. The institutional method had to wait until the idea of development was incorporated into academic thought and the mind of the inquirer became resigned to the inconsistency which attends growth. The analogy with a biological organism had to be renounced and a basis in ideology had to be discovered before it could become a fruitful method of study in economics, history, philosophy, law and politics. The practical impulse toward its use came with a change in public opinion; so long as laissez faire dominated our minds, dialectic served well enough to turn out explanatory apologies for the existing social arrangements; when we began to demand that order and direction be imposed upon an unruly society, a genetic study of how its constituent usages had grown up into an empirical organization seemed proper. An inquiry into institutions may supply the analytical knowledge essential to a program of social control or it may do no more than set adventures for idle curiosity. In either event the study of institutions rests itself upon an institution.

Accordingly an institution is an imperfect agent of order and of purpose in a developing culture. Intent and chance alike share in its creation; it imposes its pattern of conduct upon the activities of men and its compulsion upon the course of unanticipated events. Its identity through the impact of idea upon circumstance and the rebound of circumstance upon idea is forever being remade. It performs in the social economy a none too clearly defined office—a performance compromised by the maintenance of its own existence, by the interests of its personnel, by the diversion to alien purpose which the adventitious march of time brings. It may like any creation of man be taken into bondage by the power it was designed to control. It is a folkway, always new yet ever old, directive and responsive, a spur to and a check upon change, a creature of means and a master of ends. It is in social organization an instrument, a challenge and a hazard; in its wake come order and disorder, fulfillment, aimlessness and frustration. The arrangements of community life alike set the stage for and take up the shock of what man does and what he leaves undone. Institutions and human actions, complements and antitheses, are forever remaking each other in the endless drama of the social process.

On Function and Social Institutions

A. R. RADCLIFFE-BROWN

THE CONCEPT OF FUNCTION applied to human societies is based on an analogy between social life and organic life. The recognition of the analogy and of some of its important implications is at least as old as Protagoras and Plato. In the nineteenth century the analogy, the concept of function, and the word itself appear frequently in social philosophy and sociology. So far as I know the first systematic formulation of the concept as applying to the strictly scientific study of society was that of Émile Durkheim in 1895.

Durkheim's definition is that the "function" of a social institution is the correspondence between it and the needs of the social organism. This definition requires some elaboration. In the first place, to avoid possible ambiguity and in particular the possibility of a teleological interpretation, I would like to substitute for the term "needs" the term "necessary conditions of existence," or, if the term "need" is used, it is to be understood only in this sense. It may here be noted, as a point to be returned to, that any attempt to apply this concept of function in social science involves the assumption that there *are* necessary conditions of existence for human societies just as there are for animal organisms, and that they can be discovered by the proper kind of scientific inquiry.

For the further elucidation of the concept it is convenient to use the analogy between social life and organic life. Like all analogies it has to be used with care. An animal organism is an agglomeration of cells and interstitial fluids arranged in relation to one another not as an aggregate but as an integrated whole. For the bio-chemist, it is a complexly integrated system of complex molecules. The system of relations by which these units are related is the organic structure. As the terms are here used the organism *is not* itself the structure; it is a collection of units (cells or molecules) arranged in a structure, i.e., in a set of relations; the organism *has* a structure. Two mature animals of the same species and sex consist of

From "On the Concept of Function in Social Science," *American Anthropologist*, 37, 1935, pp. 394-402. Reprinted by permission of the publisher and author.

similar units combined in a similar structure. The structure is thus to be defined as a set of relations between the entities. (The structure of a cell is in the same way a set of relations between complex molecules, and the structure of an atom is a set of relations between electrons and protons.) As long as it lives the organism preserves a certain continuity of structure although it does not preserve the complete identity of its constituent parts. It loses some of its constituent molecules by respiration or excretion; it takes in others by respiration and alimentary absorption. Over a period its constituent cells do not remain the same. But the structural arrangement of the constituent units does remain similar. The process by which this structural continuity of the organism is maintained is called life. The life-process consists of the activities and interactions of the constituent units of the organism, the cells, and the organs into which the cells are united.

As the word function is here being used the life of an organism is conceived as the *functioning* of its structure. It is through and by the continuity of the functioning that the continuity of the structure is preserved. If we consider any recurrent part of the life-process, such as respiration, digestion, etc., its *function* is the part it plays in, the contribution it makes to, the life of the organism as a whole. As the terms are here being used a cell or an organ has an *activity* and that activity has a *function*. It is true that we commonly speak of the secretion of gastric fluid as a "function" of the stomach. As the words are here used we should say that this is an "activity" of the stomach, the "function" of which is to change the proteins of food into a form in which these are absorbed and distributed by the blood to the tissues. We may note that the function of a recurrent physiological process is thus a correspondence between it and the needs (i.e., necessary conditions of existence) of the organism.

If we set out upon a systematic investigation of the nature of organisms and organic life there are three sets of problems presented to us. (There are, in addition, certain other sets of problems concerning aspects or characteristics of organic life with which we are not here concerned.) One is that of morphology—what kinds of organic structures are there, what similarities and variations do they show, and how can they be classified? Second are the problems of physiology—how, in general, do organic structures function; what, therefore, is the nature of the life-process? Third are the problems of development—how do new types of organisms come into existence?

To turn from organic life to social life, if we examine such a community as an African or Australian tribe we can recognize the existence of a social structure. Individual human beings, the essential units in this instance, are connected by a definite set of social relations into an integrated whole. The continuity of the social structure, like that of an organic structure, is not destroyed by changes in the units. Individuals may leave the society, by death or otherwise; others may enter it. The continuity of structure is maintained by the process of social life, which consists of the activities and interactions of the individual human beings and of the organized groups into which they are united. (The social life of the community is here defined as the *functioning* of the social structure.) The *function* of any recurrent activity, such as the punishment of a crime, or a funeral ceremony, is the part it plays in the social life as a whole and therefore the contribution it makes to the maintenance of the structural continuity.

The concept of function as here defined thus involves the notion of a *structure* consisting of a *set of relations* amongst *unit entities,* the *continuity* of the structure being maintained by a *life-process* made up of the *activities* of the constituent units.

If, with these concepts in mind, we set out on a systematic investigation of the nature of human society and of social life, we find presented to us three sets of problems. First, the problems of social morphology—what kinds of social structures are there, what are their similarities and differences, how are they to be classified? Second, the problems of social physiology—how do social structures function? Third, the problems of development—how do new types of social structure come into existence?

Two important points where the analogy between organism and society breaks down must be noted. In an animal organism it is possible to observe the organic structure to a large extent independently of its functioning. It is therefore possible to make a morphology which is independent of physiology. But in human society the social structure as a whole can only be *observed* in its functioning. Some of the features of social structure, such as the geographical distribution of individuals and groups, can be directly observed, but most of the social relations which in their totality constitute the structure, such as relations of father and son, buyer and seller, ruler and subject, cannot be observed except in the social activities in which the relations are functioning. It follows that a social morphology cannot be established independently of a social physiology.

The second point is that an animal organism does not, in the course of its life, change its structural type. A pig does not become a hippopotamus. (The development of the animal from germination to maturity is not a change of type since the process in all its stages is typical for the species.) On the other hand a society in the course of its history can and does change its structural type without any breach of continuity.

By the definition here offered "function" is the contribution which a partial activity makes to the total activity of which it is a part. The function of a particular social usage is the contribution it makes to the total social life as the functioning of the total social system. Such a view implies that a social system (the total social structure of a society together with the totality of social usages, in which that structure appears and on which it depends for its continued existence) has a certain kind of unity, which we may speak of as a functional unity. We may define it as a condition in which all parts of the social system work together with a sufficient degree of harmony or internal consistency, i.e., without producing persistent conflicts which can neither be resolved nor regulated.

This idea of the functional unity of a social system is, of course, a hypothesis. But it is one which, to the functionalist, it seems worthwhile to test by systematic examination of the facts.

There is another aspect of functional theory that should be briefly mentioned. To return to the analogy of social life and organic life, we recognize that an organism may function more or less efficiently and so we set up a special science of pathology to deal with all phenomena of dysfunction. We distinguish in an organism what we call health and disease. The Greeks of the fifth century B.C. thought that one might apply the same notion to society, to the city-state, distinguishing conditions of *eunomia*, good order, social health, from *dysnomia*, disorder, social ill-health. In the nineteenth century Durkheim, in his application of the notion of function, sought to lay the basis for a scientific social pathology, based on a morphology and a physiology. In his works, particularly those on suicide and on the division of labor, he attempted to find objective criteria by which to judge whether a given society at a given time is normal or pathological, eunomic or dysnomic. For example, he tried to show that the increase of the rate of suicide in many countries during part of the nineteenth century is symptomatic of a dysnomic or, in his terminology, anomic, social condition. Probably there is no sociologist who would hold that Durkheim really succeeded in establishing an objective basis for a science of social pathology.

In relation to organic structures we can find strictly objective criteria by which to distinguish disease from health, pathological from normal, for disease is that which either threatens the organism with death (the dissolution of its structure) or interferes with the activities which are characteristic of the organic type. Societies do not die in the same sense that animals die and therefore we cannot define dysnomia as that which leads, if unchecked, to the death of a society. Further a society differs from an organism in that it can change its structural type, or can be absorbed as an integral part of a larger society. Therefore we cannot define dysnomia as a disturbance of the usual activities of a social type (as Durkheim tried to do).

Let us return for a moment to the Greeks. They conceived the health of an organism and the eunomia of a society as being in each instance a condition of the harmonious working together of its parts. Now this, where society is concerned, is the same thing as what was considered above as the functional unity or inner consistency of a social system, and it is suggested that for the degree of functional unity of a particular society it may be possible to establish a purely objective criterion. Admittedly this cannot be done at present; but the science of human society is as yet in its extreme infancy. So that it may be that we should say that while an organism that is attacked by a virulent disease will react thereto, and, if its reaction fails, will die, a society that is thrown into a condition of functional disunity or inconsistency (for this we now provisionally identify with dysnomia) will not die, except in such comparatively rare instances as an Australian tribe overwhelmed by the white man's destructive force, but will continue to struggle toward some sort of eunomia, some kind of social health, and may, in the course of this, change its structural type. This process, it seems, the "functionalist" has ample opportunities of observing at the present day, in native peoples subjected to the domination of the civilized nations, and in those nations themselves.

Space will not allow a discussion here of another aspect of functional theory, viz., the question whether change of social type is or is not dependent on function, i.e., on the laws of social physiology. My own view is that there is such a dependence and that its nature can be studied in the development of the legal and political institutions, the economic systems and the religions of Europe through the last twenty-five centuries. For the preliterate societies with which anthropology is concerned it is not possible to study the details of long processes of change of type. The one kind of change which the anthropologist can observe is the disintegration of social structures. Yet even here we can observe and compare spontaneous movements towards reintegration. We have, for instance, in Africa, in Oceania, and in America the appearance of new religions which can be interpreted on a functional hypothesis as attempts to relieve a condition of social dysnomia produced by the rapid modification of the social life through contact with white civilization.

The concept of function as defined above constitutes a "working hypothesis" by which a number of problems are formulated for investigation. No scientific inquiry is possible without some such formulation of working hypotheses. Two remarks are necessary here. One is that the hypothesis does not require the dogmatic assertion that everything in the life of every community has a function. It only requires the assumption that it *may* have one, and that we are justified in seeking to discover it. The second is that what appears to be the same social usage in two societies may have different functions in the two. Thus the practice of celibacy in the Roman Catholic Church of to-day has very different functions from those of celibacy in the early Christian church. In other words, in order to define a social usage, and therefore in order to make valid comparisons between the usages of different peoples or periods, it is necessary to consider not merely the form of the usage but also its function. On this basis, for example, belief in a Supreme Being in a simple society is something different from such a belief in a modern civilized community.

The acceptance of the functional hypothesis or point of view outlined above results in the recognition of a vast number of problems for the solution of which there are required wide comparative studies of societies of many diverse types and also intensive studies of as many single societies as possible. In field studies of the simpler peoples it leads, first of all, to a direct study of the social life of the community as the functioning of a social structure, and of this there are several examples in recent literature. Since the function of a social activity is to be found by examining its effects upon individuals, these are studied, either in the average individual or in both average and exceptional individuals. Further the hypothesis leads to attempts to investigate directly the functional consistency or unity of a social system and to determine as far as possible in each instance the nature of that unity. Such field studies will obviously be different in many ways from studies carried out from other points of view, e.g., the ethnological point of view that lays emphasis on diffusion. We do not have to say that one point of view is better than another, but only that they are different, and any particular piece of work should be judged in reference to what it aims to do.

If the view here outlined is taken as one form of "functionalism," a few remarks on Dr. Lesser's paper become permissible. He makes reference to a difference of "content" in functional and non-functional anthropology. From the point of view here presented the "content" or subject matter of social anthropology is the whole social life of a people in all its aspects. For convenience of handling it is often necessary to devote special attention to some particular part or aspect of the social life, but if functionalism means any thing at all it does mean the attempt to see the social life of a people as a whole, as a functional unity.

Dr. Lesser speaks of the functionalist as stressing "the psychological aspects of culture." I presume that he here refers to the functionalist's recognition that the usages of a society work or "function" only through their effects in the life, i.e., in the thoughts, sentiments and actions of individuals.

The "functionalist" point of view here presented does therefore imply that we have to investigate as thoroughly as possible all aspects of social life, considering them in relation to one another, and that an essential part of the task is the investigation of the individual and of the way in which he is moulded by or adjusted to the social life.

Turning from content to method Dr. Lesser seems to find some conflict between the functional point of view and the historical. This is reminiscent of the attempts formerly made to see a conflict between sociology and history. There need be no conflict, but there is a difference.

There is not, and cannot be, any conflict between the functional hypothesis and the view that any culture, any social system, is the end-result of a unique series of historical accidents. The process of development of the race-horse from its five-toed ancestor was a unique series of historical accidents. This does not conflict with the view of the physiologist that the horse of to-day and all the antecedent forms conform or conformed to physiological laws, i.e., to the necessary conditions of organic existence. Palaeontology and physiology are not in conflict. One "explanation" of the race-horse is to be found in its history—how it came to be just what it is and where it is. Another and entirely independent "explanation" is to show how the horse is a special exemplification of physiological laws. Similarly one "explanation" of a social system will be its history, where we know it—the detailed account of how it came to be what it is and where it is. Another "explanation" of the same system is obtained by showing (as the functionalist attempts to do) that it is a special exemplification of laws of social physiology or social functioning. The two kinds of explanation do not conflict, but supplement one another.

The functional hypothesis is in conflict with two views that are held by some ethnologists, and it is probably these, held as they often are without precise formulation, that are the cause of the antagonism to that approach. One is the "shreds and patches" theory of culture, the designation being taken from a phrase of Professor Lowie when he speaks of "that planless hodge-podge, that thing of shreds and patches called civilization." The concentration of attention on what is called the diffusion of culture-traits tends to produce a conception of culture as a collection of disparate entities (the so-called traits) brought together by pure historical accident and having only accidental relations to one another. The conception is rarely formulated and maintained with any precision, but as a half unconscious point of view it does seem to control the thinking of many ethnologists. It is, of course, in direct conflict with the hypothesis of the functional unity of social systems.

The second view which is in direct conflict with the functional hypothesis is the view that there are no discoverable significant sociological laws such as the functionalist is seeking. I know that some two or three ethnologists say that they hold this view, but I have found it impossible to know what they mean, or on what sort of evidence (rational or empirical) they would base their contention. Generalizations about any sort of subject matter are of two kinds: the generalizations of common opinion, and generalizations that have been verified or demonstrated by a systematic examination of evidence afforded by precise observations systematically made. Generalizations of the latter kind are called scientific laws. Those who hold that there are no laws of human society cannot hold that there are no generalizations about human society because they themselves hold such generalizations and even make new ones of their own. They must therefore hold that in the field of social phenomena, in contradistinction to physical and biological phenomena, any attempt at the systematic testing of existing generalizations or towards the discovery and verification of new ones, is, for some unexplained reason, futile, or, as Dr. Radin puts it, "crying for the moon." Argument against such a contention is unprofitable or indeed impossible.

Inspirational Religious Literature: From Latent to Manifest Functions of Religion [1]

LOUIS SCHNEIDER and SANFORD M. DORNBUSCH

INSPIRATIONAL RELIGIOUS LITERATURE is known to be enormously popular. The books of Norman Vincent Peale today, of Bruce Barton a generation ago, and of numerous of their close intellectual relatives and imitators have achieved staggering sales.[2] Sociologists have left comment on the literature to journalists or theologians or gifted outsiders.[3] But it is of significance for the analysis of "cultural drift," with broad general implications. In this article, a brief survey of the literature and a summary of its dominant trends and themes, attention is given to a special phase which is of considerable sociological import.[4]

The literature is by no means entirely unitary, but strains or trends in it exhibit prominent elements of unity.[5] Ralph Waldo Trine's *In Tune with the*

Reprinted from *The American Journal of Sociology*, Vol. LXII, No. 5, March 1957, pp. 476-481, by permission of The University of Chicago Press. Copyright 1957 by The University of Chicago.

[1] Grateful acknowledgment is made to the Center for Advanced Study in the Behavioral Sciences, Inc., and to the Laboratory of Social Relations of Harvard University for their support of the project which this paper reports in part. We are also grateful to Miriam Gallaher, Margaret Swenson, David Feldman, and Bruce Finney.

[2] A two-page advertisement in the *New York Times Book Review* (April 8, 1956) announces that Peale's *The Power of Positive Thinking*, "the best-loved inspirational book of our times, reaches its 2,000,000 copy anniversary." A generation ago it could be remarked that "few realize that the field of religious books often furnishes the most spectacular and continuing records in book sales. While novelists may vie with each other for records of a hundred thousand, there are continually springing up in the field of religious books titles that go far beyond that, and even into the million" (*Publisher's Weekly*, February 19, 1921, p. 513).

[3] See, however, Everett C. Parker, David W. Barry, and Dallas W. Smythe, *The Television-Radio Audience and Religion* (New York: Harper & Row, 1955), for a sociological analysis of the output of inspirational religion on television and radio in New Haven. Other discussions are: William Lee Miller, "A Passionate Faith in the Great Whatever" (review of Edward R. Murrow's *This I Believe*), *The Reporter*, X (April, 1954), 46-48, and "Some Negative Thinking about Norman Vincent Peale," *ibid.*, XII (January, 1955), 19-24; and Gustave Weigel, "Protestantism as a Catholic Concern," *Theological Studies*, XVI (June, 1955), 214-32.

Detailed statistical verification of some points made here will be provided in a forthcoming paper, "American Inspirational Religious Literature, 1880-1955."

[4] The article reports part of a study of a sample of over thirty best-sellers published since about 1880.

[5] Individual writers differ; e.g., there are marked differences between Peale and Harry Emerson Fosdick and between them and Bruce Barton or between all three and British writers who have found a sizable American public, like Harold Begbie, who in *Twice-born Men* (Boston: F. H. Revell, 1909) praised the "inspiration" afforded the poor of the London slums by the Salvation Army more than a generation ago, or like Daphne du Maurier, who ranges herself, in *Come Wind, Come Weather* (New York: Doubleday,

Infinite, Bruce Barton's *The Man Nobody Knows,* Henry C. Link's *The Return to Religion,* and Peale's *A Guide to Confident Living* and *The Power of Positive Thinking* suggest for purposes of definition four criteria to which the items of literature should conform: (*a*) they assume the general validity of the Judeo-Christian religious tradition; (*b*) they aim to inspire with the hope of salvation here or in an afterlife; (*c*) they recommend use of techniques to achieve salvation, in whatever sense salvation might be understood; and (*d*) they address themselves to the "everyday problems" or "everyday people." The books vary in the balance among the four points.

The general validity of the Judeo-Christian tradition is assumed in these works with significant vagueness. Specific theological doctrines, such as of Christ's soteriological mission, or specific theological discussions, as of Christ's status as a member of the Trinity, are hard to find. More likely, there will be found discussion of a transcendent "something" about which a professed theologian could say practically nothing. Daniel Poling confesses, "I began saying in the morning two words, 'I believe'—those two words with nothing added." [6]

The literature also holds forth the hope of some kind of salvation. In the seventy-five years covered in the survey eschatological interest has declined. But, while concern with the next world fades increasingly, salvation comes quite conclusively to mean salvation in this world: release from poverty or handicapping inhibition in personal relations or from ill health or emotional disequilibrium. But salvation in this secular sense is held forth as a definite hope and even a promise.[7]

The inspirational literature bristles with techniques to attain peace and power which range from putting one's self "in tune with the infinite" by some intuitive twist of the psyche to sensing a deity in the chair by one's bed at night; from reconstructing failures as trifles or even as successes to whispering to one's self a promise of good things to come. These practices, finally, are represented as helpful to ordinary men and women in solving their everyday problems, but this point needs no elaboration here.

& Co., 1940), with the followers of Frank Buchman. Catholic writers, like Bishop Sheen, are in quite a different universe, to which the characterization below will not apply well. This should not, however, suggest that there are no important resemblances between Catholic and other writers; many, for example, share the view that "social salvation" or social reform is to be achieved more or less exclusively through the reform of the individual and increased numbers of reformed individuals. Thus, Bishop Sheen, who avers that "world wars are *nothing but* macrocosmic signs of the psychic wars waging inside microcosmic muddled souls" (*Peace of Soul* [New York: Permabooks, 1954], p. 8) (italics ours), allies himself on this point with Daphne du Maurier and Henry C. Link.

[6] Quoted from *Parade: The Sunday Picture Magazine,* September 19, 1954, by Will Herberg, *Protestant—Catholic—Jew* (New York: Doubleday & Co., 1956), p. 282.

[7] So Emmet Fox: "If only you will find out the thing God intends you to do, and will do it, you will find that all doors will open to you; all obstacles in your path will melt away; you will be acclaimed a brilliant success; you will be most liberally rewarded from the monetary point of view; and you will be gloriously happy" (*Power through Constructive Thinking* [New York: Harper & Row, 1932]), p. 23.

Elements of this kind may be found in a variety of other places, for example, in Augustine's *Confessions* or Thomas à Kempis' *Imitation of Christ*. But these documents differ in affirming faith unequivocally. Moreover, the salvation they envisage is not of this world. The ends they set out lack the concrete, tangible quality of such goals as business success or emotional "adjustment," and, consequently, they hardly bristle with the techniques with which the modern literature is filled. True, in a certain sense there is some overlap, as, for instance, in the case of prayer, which is often recommended; but there are obvious differences between devotional prayer and prayer that, not very subtly, is instrumental.[8] On the other hand, the literature, not only on its own recognizances, is in some sense "religious." Advertisements that promise to add six inches to the chests of scrawny men are "inspirational" in tone, but they make no pretensions to being religious and cannot qualify as inspirational religious literature.

A dominant trend in the literature through the decades is secularization; for instance, suffering has lost its "meaningfulness" and more and more is described as senseless misery, best gotten rid of. No longer divinely or transcendentally significant, suffering figures as a pathological experience calling for a psychiatrist or a minister trained in counseling. Again, the deity as represented in the literature is in process of transformation: his existence in some objective sense is no longer insisted upon, and he often approximates a consciously useful fiction. The "hero" appears more and more as the "well-adjusted" man, who does not question existing social institutions and who, ideally successful both in a business or in professional sense,[9] feels no emotional pain. Finally, there is a strong bias against the "unscientific" and for equating religion and "science." [10]

---

[8] A qualification rather unusual in the literature is: "Too often the whole value of a prayer is judged by emotional awareness of change in one's inner states, and if one does not feel differently after having prayed, he begins to wonder if there is anything to it." The writer adds, in even more unusual vein, that "to make such a test is to forget that prayer is directed toward God, not toward ourselves" (Georgia Harkness, *Prayer and the Common Life* [Nashville: Abingdon-Cokesbury Press, 1948], p. 66).

[9] Bruce Barton in one strategic sentence sets off two dominant strains in the literature in speaking of the life of Christ: "Stripped of all dogma, this is the grandest achievement story of all" (*The Man Nobody Knows* [Indianapolis: Bobbs-Merrill Co., 1925], p. 9). Surprisingly little attention has been given by sociologists to the success theme and the support for it in American religion, especially in view of the leads given by Weber and Tawney. The Reverend Russell H. Conwell's "Acres of Diamonds" speech, with its forthright assertion that "the foundation principles of business success and the foundation principles of Chrstianity, itself, are both the same" (*Acres of Diamonds* [New York: Modern Eloquence Corp., 1901], pp. 138-68 at p. 148) is a pertinent and well-known item, but Weber would also have been interested in numerous cognate items, such as the contention of Mrs. Stetson, the Christian Scientist, that poverty is a form of evil and error, while prosperity is both symbol and consequence of spirituality (see E. S. Bates and J. V. Dittemore, *Mary Baker Eddy: The Truth and the Tradition* [New York: A. A. Knopf, 1932], p. 381).

[10] Perhaps simply an exaggeration of an already fundamental strain in Protestant philosophy of religion and theology (cf. George F. Thomas, *Protestant Thought in the Twentieth Century*, ed. Arnold S. Nash [New York: Macmillan Co., 1951], pp. 99-100).

In American thought William James,[11] in effect, substituted, "I believe because it is useful" for "I believe because it is so"—or even, with Tertullian, "because it is impossible"—an idea which abounds in the inspirational religious literature. Or the best is made of both worlds in a combination such as, "I feel it is absurd; but, since it is useful, I shall insist that it is true." Thus, Henry Link avers, "I believe in God because I have found that without the belief in someone more important than themselves, people fail to achieve their own potential importance." And he adds later: "Agnosticism is an intellectual disease, and faith in fallacies is better than no faith at all." [12] Writers like Harry Emerson Fosdick will go only a certain distance in this direction. Fosdick asserts:

> The explanation of the rise of cults like Christian Science and New Thought is obvious. While the old-line churches were largely concerning themselves with dogma, ritual, and organization, multitudes of folk were starving for available spiritual power with which to live. These cults arose to meet this need, and with all their mistaken attitudes . . . they have genuinely served millions of people by *translating religion into terms of power available for daily use*.[13]

But if Fosdick is willing to go only thus far, others are willing to go beyond him. The literature consistently emphasizes "God-power" as divine flow into men, sustaining and aiding them in some materially useful sense to the point where the deity often becomes simply a psychological device. The strain toward instrumentalization is so strong in Peale, for example, that one must by inference from his work assign to God as a primary function the dispensing of divine vitamins to men eager for health and wealth.

A kind of spiritual technology has also been developed, inseparable, of course, from the instrumental element. Standard religious procedures like prayer are constantly recommended, although often with a characteristic twist, as in Peale when he urges: "Learn to pray correctly, scientifically. Employ tested and proven methods. Avoid slipshod praying." [14] Self-exhortation, another frequently suggested procedure, undoubtedly has affinities with more "classical" religious procedures, as in: "I do believe," "Christ is with me," "In everything I do God helps," "I cannot lose." Again, stress is placed on special psychic states, perhaps with physical props simultaneously suggested—for example, a state of receptivity to "God-power." A notable set of

[11] Cf. his *Varieties of Religious Experience* (New York: Longmans, Green & Co., 1902) and *Essays on Faith and Morals* (New York: Longmans, Green & Co., 1949). From James comes, apparently, much of whatever intellectual stock in trade the inspirational literature manifests. "Believe," he says, at one point, "that life *is* worth living, and your belief will help create the fact" (*Essays on Faith and Morals*, p. 31). However, the literature, taking the stance that "faith is the answer," hardly bothers with instances in which the most devoted faith has not brought emotional calm or brought it only after long struggle, such as are often found in James.

[12] *The Return to Religion* (New York: Macmillan Co., 1936), pp. 34, 63. This may also be simply an exaggeration of trends found throughout American Protestantism (cf. Willard L. Sperry, *Religion in America* [New York: Macmillan Co., 1947], pp. 153-54).

[13] *As I See Religion* (New York: Harper & Bros., 1932), pp. 17-18 (italics ours).

[14] *A Guide to Confident Living* (Englewood Cliffs, N.J.: Prentice-Hall, Inc., 1948), p. 114.

recommendations depends upon converting spiritual principles into magic. Thus, as in some of the work of Lloyd Douglas, which is frequently only a fictional transcript of inspirational religious literature, he who gives without letting anyone know it is repaid a thousandfold, both magically and materially; he becomes a great success. An outcome not only of impossible physics but—in the light of the principle, "cast your bread upon the waters" and cognate exhortations—of a dubious spirituality, this can be described as spiritual technology.

Other trends include, as the quotation above from Fosdick illustrates, a definitely antiritualistic,[15] antidogmatic, antiinstitutional (antiorganizational) strain. The stress is most emphatically on religious "experience," as might be expected.

In marking the transition from latent to manifest functions of religion, one must distinguish between a *primary* and a *secondary* religious sequence. A good enough text for the primary sequence is afforded by the biblical prescription and promise, "Seek ye first the Kingdom of God, and all these things shall be added unto you." "Faith" is thus urged, but it is urged as primary; its possible "fruits" are only hinted at. The notion that Job might have been seeking to be "well adjusted" simply on the basis of the Book of Job is incongruous. The primary religious sequence may be roughly rendered, then, as follows: Faith → Action → "Results" (for example, emotional equanimity).[16]

But the modern inspirational literature more or less deliberately reverses this sequence. It starts from the observation (here assumed to be correct) that what is loosely called "faith" *can* bring about "peace of mind" and cognate desired ends. It does not, so to say, start with "the Kingdom of God," that is, with what may be called "classical" religious belief, because the belief is thought to be *true*. (Of course, it may incidentally hold out for the truth of such doctrine as it happens to retain.) It relies on a secondary sequence that begins with a projection or presentation of the desirability of all manner of "good things," mainly wealth and emotional or physical health. This secondary sequence becomes, then, "Results" (in prospect) → Action → Faith (or, possibly, also "Results" → Faith → Action), "action" being largely on the lines of spiritual technology. The modern spiritual technology may in a number of ways be a substitute for older religious ritual. If it is acknowledged that at times, when men have believed sincerely and devotedly, serenity or calm has come to them, it has clearly often come as a

---

[15] Cf., e.g., E. Stanley Jones: "Nothing is essential but God, and no rite or ceremony is essential in finding him" (*The Christ of Every Road* [Nashville: Abingdon Press, 1930], p. 150).

[16] An anthropologically or psychologically simplistic view is not being suggested. If "faith" can lead to "action," under "action" including ritual or ceremonial behavior, there is no implication that this is a *necessary* sequence. It is quite possible for "action" to reinforce "faith" or for each to reinforce the other. Moreover, it is not suggested that a *necessary* outcome of "faith" is "peace of mind"; merely that this is *sometimes* the outcome.

by-product. Serenity, calm, and the like have been latent functions of religious faith and devotion. It is not necessary to claim that they have been *unqualifiedly* latent; differences of degree may well be crucial. But the inspirational religious literature makes these latent functions of religion manifest and pursues them as aims.

The shift from latent to manifest raises the question: Can the same "results" be obtained? A task facing sociological theory is the classification and explanation of cases in which the transition has different kinds of results. If, say, factory workers can be inspired by a demonstration of the full nature and final uses of the product to which their seemingly disjointed individual efforts have led, it does not follow that an analogous service will always be performed by a demonstration to the religious that their efforts to "find God" afford them "peace of mind." Nor is there any reason to think that faith will be enhanced if it is also shown, directly or by implication, that gaining peace of mind is the point of religious practice in the first place. Here, too, differences of degree are important. That the inspirational religious literature does not always make an outright and unqualified shift from latent to manifest but often stops short of an uninhibited assertion that the *object* of faith is to attain power or peace of mind is of sociological interest.

But the sheer fact that there has been a shift on the lines indicated is easily documented and, for that matter, not only in the inspirational religious literature. Thus, Marshall Sklare notes a similar development in Conservative Judaism:

> According to tradition, the Jew should observe the Sabbath because it is God's will that he do so. In appealing for a reinvigoration of the holiday, Conservatism, however, speaks in terms of *social utility*—in this case the potential contribution of observance to better mental health. Only secondarily is it suggested that the Sabbath may have something more than therapeutic significance, and, furthermore, no Divine sanctions are inferred. The performance of a religious obligation becomes a technique for achieving personality adjustment.[17]

Thus, curiously, the religious begin to look on their own activity in the manner of functionally oriented sociologists and psychologists. The question is whether, in doing so, they do not endanger the religious function; or perhaps these are all signs that faith has already lapsed, the efforts to exhibit its virtues being proof. In this connection it is pertinent to look back to a recent paper by William Kolb, who poses a "moral dilemma" for sociologists of religion who affirm the "integrating" function and necessity of belief in ultimates while themselves holding that belief to be illusory:

> To spread the idea that a belief in ultimate validity of values is necessary but illusory would be to destroy society through destroying or confusing this be-

---

[17] *Conservative Judaism* (New York: The Free Press, 1955), pp. 121-122. Sklare also quotes from a wall poster that avers the Sabbath has afforded the Jew "a blessed opportunity for personality adjustment" and the opportunity, furthermore, "to preserve our psychological, physical, and spiritual equilibrium" amid the tensions of daily stress (*ibid.*, p. 122).

lief. Yet to urge people to accept the idea that there is an ontic realm of values while believing oneself that such an idea is false is deliberately to deprive people of the knowledge necessary for their freedom and dignity.[18]

Many of the purveyors of inspirational religion may represent a kind of halfway house. At one extreme we would find followers of the "old-time religion," unreserved believers that their creed has objective validity, who, at times, incidentally reap material benefits from it. At another extreme, are "positivistic" functional sociologists, quite prepared to find religion increasing the solidarity of the group, drawing the deviant individual back to it, and so on, while unconvinced themselves. Inspirational religion is somewhere between these extremes, somewhat fluctuating and unsure, yet with a powerful instrumental bent. Faith, again, is "the answer"—enjoined in the first instance not because the religious content that it affirms is above all "true," but just because it is "the answer." The concentration on "the answer," the results, already half-suggests an "illusion." The presumed primary "truth," put into the background from the very absence of attention to it, becomes the more dubious the less stress it receives and the vaguer it gets. The impulse to make religion "useful" is understandable, but the deliberate effort to do so may be self-defeating.

Heroes and Hopelessness in a Total Institution: Anomie and Collective Disturbance *

ROBERT PERRUCCI

THE STUDY OF INTERNAL DISORDERS and the breakdown of social control in institutional settings has long provided an excellent opportunity for an analysis of the sources of strain and stability in a system. Studies maintaining this focus have been concerned with what they have called a "collective disturbance" or a "riot." These terms have been used to denote the fact that the phenomenon under consideration is not an individual disturbance or an aggregate of individual disturbances, but a disturbance which has a contagious element that is transmitted in an interpersonal

    [18] W. L. Kolb, "Values, Positivism, and the Functional Theory of Religion: The Growth of a Moral Dilemma," *Social Forces*, XXXI (May, 1953), 309.
    * Robert Perrucci, "Heroes and Hopelessness: Anomie Theory Applied to a Collective Disturbance," from Donald A. Hansen (ed.), *Counseling, Therapy and Sociology*, Boston: Houghton Mifflin Company, 1967. In preparation. Copyright © by Houghton Mifflin Company. Reprinted by permission of the publisher and author.

context. As Stanton and Schwartz describe it, . . . "the collective disturbance involves the participation of a number of people in such a way that *the disturbance of one patient is integrated with the disturbance of many other patients.*" [1]

In seeking to locate the elements involved in a collective disturbance on a psychiatric ward, Stanton and Schwartz have focused primarily upon covert staff disagreements and disruptions of normal communication channels.[2] The consequences of these internal disruptions were increased disturbances of many patients, the magnification of staff problems such as errors in technique, distorted messages, increased absenteeism, and the partial withdrawal of staff members from normal participation on the ward. Similarly, Caudill focused attention on the strains created by an imbalance between affective and cognitive communication among staff members.[3] This, in turn, led to staff disagreements which were still, for the most part, covert and unexpressed. That is, the disagreements tended to "attach themselves" to discussions of plans for individual patients, who then became the vehicles through which the disagreements were expressed. A later stage in the disturbance was characterized by the mutual withdrawal of staff groups which cut the channels of communication between patients and staff, and within staff groups. The still covert nature of the disagreements led to the formation of various support-seeking coalitions, which Caudill labels as "paired role group responses." The final "restitution" phase, or the return to equilibrium, occurred when the "real" disagreements between staff members were openly discussed.

Looking at prison riots, Bates suggests that one of the direct causes of the tensions which burst forth in riot and disorder are due to the enforced idleness of the inmates.[4] His hypothesis suggests that a certain amount of free-floating tension will, from time to time, manifest itself in various types of disturbances.

What we find lacking in these discussions of collective disturbances is any explicit analysis of the disturbances in light of the sociological concept of anomie. That is, there is relatively little discussion of the disturbance in terms of the state of the system as it operates as a mechanism of social control. For example, the Stanton and Schwartz definition of a collective disturbance could very well include the case of an individually disturbed patient who upsets other patients by her presence and behavior. Thus, the contagion aspect of the disturbance might only be that other patients get upset by the mere fact of having a patient in their midst who is extremely

[1] Alfred H. Stanton and Morris S. Schwartz, *The Mental Hospital*, New York: Basic Books, 1954.

[2] *Ibid.*, Chapter 17.

[3] William Caudill, *The Psychiatric Hospital As a Small Society*, Cambridge, Massachusetts: Harvard University Press, 1958.

[4] Sanford Bates, *A Statement Concerning Causes, Preventive Measures, and Methods of Controlling Prison Riots and Disturbances*, New York: American Prison Association, 1953.

disturbed, hostile, or critical of others. This possibility is strongly suggested in both the Stanton and Schwartz and Caudill studies, in that each of them presents the situation of an especially disturbed or obnoxious patient or patients as key figures in the overall collective disturbance.

What we shall focus upon in this paper, is an explanation of the collective disturbance as a condition of a social system. That is, a *chronic* condition of a system in which various aspects of its social and cultural structure are likely to produce a breakdown of social control. A condition where the parts of the system are arranged in such a fashion as to continually contain the "seeds" of its own disequilibrium. In this analysis, emphasis will be put on an aspect of Durkheim's concept of anomie which, we believe, has received relatively little attention.

MEANS, ENDS AND ANOMIE

When the normative systems of a society no longer influence and direct the behavior of its members we may say that there is an absence of social control. Individual behavior is no longer a response to collective definitions of the "appropriate," but is, rather, a case of individual determination of behavior. Perhaps the single most important study dealing with the breakdown of normative control is Durkheim's *Suicide*.[5] Durkheim was primarily concerned with analyzing the situation in which the means and ends of individual behavior no longer correspond to the normative definitions of means and ends. When the ends of individual action are no longer subject to normative definitions, that is, a state of *de-regulation* of behavior exists, society is said to be characterized by a state or condition of anomie.

Durkheim identified two general conditions in the means-ends system of behavior that give rise to a state of de-regulation. The first refers to a condition where due to acute changes in society, e.g., economic crises, the means and ends of a system of action that existed *prior* to the crises no longer work. That is, the connection or link between the means-ends action system are inappropriate in a new social context; behavior which once "paid off," i.e., yielded a desirable end state, is no longer applicable to the new situation. With economic crises, both booms and depressions, Durkheim suggests that "something like a declassification occurs." [6] In describing this he states:

> Then, truly, as the conditions of life are changed, the standard according to which most needs are regulated can no longer remain the same. . . . The scale is upset; but a new scale cannot be immediately improvised. Time is required for the public conscience to reclassify men and things. So long as the social forces thus freed have not regained equilibrium, their respective values are unknown and so all regulation is lacking for a time. The limits are un-

---

[5] Émile Durkheim, *Suicide*, translated by John A. Spaulding and George Simpson, New York: The Free Press, 1951.

[6] *Ibid.*, p. 252.

known between the possible and the impossible, what is just and what is unjust, legitimate claims and the hopes of those which are immoderate. Consequently, there is no restraint upon aspirations.[7]

The second condition discussed by Durkheim refers only to the ends or goals of action. Here we find a description of goals which can never be attained; a condition of unattainability of goals because the goals are by definition unattainable.[8] Referring to this point, he wrote:

Appetites, not being controlled by public opinion become disoriented, no longer recognize the limits proper to them. . . . But then their very demands make fulfillment impossible. Overweening ambition always exceeds the results obtained, great as they may be, since there is no warning to pause here. Nothing gives satisfaction and all this agitation is uninterruptedly maintained without appeasement. Above all, since this race for an unattainable goal can give no other pleasure but that of the race itself, if it is one, once it is interrupted the participants are left empty-handed. At the same time the struggle grows more violent and painful, both from being less controlled and because competition is greater.[9]

Therefore, it is not a case where the means and ends of action are out of joint and must be readjusted, it is a case where the goals could not be attained by *any* goal-directed means.

Durkheim's analysis of anomie received its fullest elaboration in the now well known essay by Merton entitled, "Social Structure and Anomie." [10] In addressing himself to the social and cultural sources of deviant behavior, Merton has focused upon the first condition of anomie raised by Durkheim: when the means and ends of action are distributed in society in such a way as to make certain sought-after ends unattainable. As Merton states,

Anomie . . . is a breakdown in the cultural structure, occurring particularly when there is an acute disjunction between the cultural norms and goals and the socially structured capacities of members of the group to act in accord with them. In this conception, cultural values may help to produce the behavior which is at odds with the mandates of the values themselves.[11]

Thus, the emphasis by Merton is on the pressure for deviant behavior which is the result of the selection of normatively *proscribed* means for the attainment of cultural goals. This outcome of anomie results in a disruption of the normative system in its effectiveness in ensuring "conforming" behavior. However, it should be noted that the pressures for deviant behavior produce the deviant adaptations primarily within the lower classes. Thus, it is possible that the existence of deviant adaptations may in fact *reinforce* the legitimacy of the normative system for the larger society precisely be-

[7] *Ibid.*, pp. 252-253.
[8] *Ibid.*, p. 248.
[9] *Ibid.*, p. 253.
[10] Robert K. Merton, *Social Theory and Social Structure*, New York: The Free Press, 1957, Chapter IV.
[11] *Ibid.*, p. 162.

cause compliance with *prescribed* means does result in the attainment of desired goals. Put differently, we are suggesting that the existence of deviant adaptations which are the result of the way the system is organized, does not necessarily question the legitimacy or moral fiber of the system. Clearly, the deviant has not utilized the appropriate means for attaining his ends, and as long as the system contains examples that appropriate means are available and *do work,* the action of the deviant can only deserve the moral disapproval of the society. For example, even though it may be recognized that the lower strata are economically disadvantaged and have fewer chances to attain higher education, there is a sufficient masking overlay from the open class ideology and from examples of the rags to riches success story.[12]

The question we are raising here, in a roundabout way, is under what conditions is the legitimacy of the normative system questioned. When will the actors in the system no longer comply with the normative definitions of acceptable means and ends governing behavior? This involves a broader type of normative disruption than concerns Merton. We are thinking here of the kind of moral sickness or *malaise* described by Durkheim. Individual reactions to such a condition are best described by terms like demoralization or disenchantment. Under such conditions, the legitimacy of norms is discredited, and the usefulness of the existing institutionalized system is questioned.[13]

We suggest that the system will be blamed, so to speak, for failures to attain cultural goals primarily under conditions where *prescribed and culturally appropriate means have been utilized and the expected ends are still not forthcoming.* It is under these conditions that the normative system is put to the test and found to be lacking, while in the Merton paradigm, the normative system is not *necessarily* shaken. Here is where we see the second condition of anomie discussed by Durkheim; namely, where the goals are unattainable because of the *nature of the goal,* and irrespec-

---

[12] It is also possible that those who do follow the deviant adaptations are also unable to blame the system for their personal difficulties. Since they have probably had some exposure to examples of "those who have made it" via appropriate means, they can turn to such adaptations as self-blame, withdrawal, transferring aspirations to children, stressing luck, chance and fatalistic ideologies, and out-group hostility. Each of these adaptations functions to blame everything but the existing institutional structure.

[13] It should be noted, that the discussion here is very close to Merton's "Rebellion" mode of adaptation. He states: "when the institutional system is regarded as a barrier to the satisfaction of legitimized goals, the stage is set for rebellion as an adaptive response." (*Social Theory and Social Structure,* p. 156.) The precise question we are asking is: *when is the institutional system regarded as a barrier?* We suggested earlier, that under Merton's means-ends paradigm the legitimacy of the existing system need not be questioned. Merton implies that the prerequisite for rebellion is a stage of "awareness" or "consciousness" of the faults of the system. In this sense, then, our question resembles the Marxian concern of looking for the specific social conditions which are necessary for the proletariat to "see" the factors influencing his class situation. Differences between Merton's and Durkheim's anomie are discussed in Ephraim H. Mizruchi, *Success and Opportunity,* New York: The Free Press, 1964.

tive of the means of attainment utilized. However, we are primarily concerned here with the situation where the means used and the goal pursued are *both* culturally approved, yet they do not work when they become part of an individual's behavioral system. Several sources of evidence in existing sociological literature may illustrate more clearly the idea we are concerned with here; some are explicitly developed, while others are only suggestions of evidence which seem to fit our framework.

The analysis of inspirational religious literature by Schneider and Dornbusch [14] focuses in large part upon the process of "de-religionization." Aside from the fact that the authors identify a strong secular bent in popular religion, they also describe a "de-religionizing" process which they link to what they call a "spiritual technology." This process involves the conscious pursuit of certain goals as expected results or benefits of religious activity. As the authors put it:

> These desired ends [Health, wealth, happiness and "peace of mind"], however, time after time have come to realization in the form of *latent* functions of religion, that is, in the form of not-deliberately-sought consequences of religious activity undertaken, again, for reasons having little or nothing to do with the consequences themselves or with any foresight thereof.[15]

Thus, we find the pursuit of goals which are by definition unattainable put within the framework of instrumental means. The implication of this process is that to turn religious activity into an expectation of certain ends, through an explicit means-ends system of action, is to "eat away" at the very foundations of religious commitment when these ends are not forthcoming. As Schneider and Dornbusch indicate:

> It is an intriguing speculation that, when faith lapses, the things it may ordinarily achieve for us without any particular thought or effort on our part become objects of technologically oriented behavior. The speculation is of interest both within and outside of religion. It has been suggested that preoccupation with the technology of sexual intercourse is likely to occur when love has become a problematic and dubious matter, as well as that technologies of child-rearing appear to flourish when "natural" love for children is no longer an easy and spontaneous thing. Similar considerations may apply in the field of religion. If this speculation has any merit, then the emergence of a technological orientation in certain fields of human concern may be interpreted as in some sense a sign of "degeneration." Unfortunately, our knowledge of these matters is exceedingly meager.[16]

Additional suggestive evidence can be found in Mizruchi's study dealing with a test of the Merton hypothesis on social structure and anomie.[17]

[14] Louis Schneider and Sanford Dornbusch, *Popular Religion,* Chicago: University of Chicago Press, 1958.

[15] *Ibid.,* p. 67.

[16] *Ibid.,* p. 70.

[17] Ephraim H. Mizruchi, "Social Structure and Anomia in a Small City," *American Sociological Review,* 25 (October, 1960), pp. 645-654; and Mizruchi, *op. cit.,* pp. 82-90 and 93-94.

In one part of the study, Mizruchi explored the relationship between scores on Srole's anomia scale and income (above or below $5000) with education held constant. For grade school graduates, no association between anomia and income was found. However, for those who attended high school and college significant associations are found. This suggests that for those persons who utilize appropriate institutionalized means (education) *without* attaining the expected cultural rewards (increased income) the consequence of disenchantment with the system (i.e., high anomia scores) is more likely. For those who have not used the appropriate institutionalized means (grade school and high school graduates) there is not the expectation of certain ends, and hence no disenchantment when rewards are not forthcoming.

Similarly, research done on the relationship between social class origins and intra-occupational mobility of professional engineers suggests that attainment of goals after the utilization of appropriate means is associated with the social origins of the engineers.[18] Engineers of lower class origins are more likely to experience limitations on the extent to which they can "move up" in their own profession. A social structure which imposes what Drake and Cayton [19] have called "the job ceiling" on occupational opportunities for persons who *have not* used the appropriate means for "moving up" may be legitimized; but a social structure which imposes such restraints on certain groups of persons (e.g., the engineers of lower class origin) who *have* utilized the appropriate means, would seem less likely to provide support for the inequities.

What we have suggested then, is that the Merton paradigm for anomie focuses upon structural constraints which lead to *deviation* from normative patterns of behavior. When, as Merton states, "the technically most effective procedure for the attainment of culture goals, whether culturally legitimate or not, becomes typically preferred to institutionally prescribed conduct," a state of anomie or normlessness will result.[20] However, while these socio-cultural conditions may lead to deviant adaptations, it is not necessarily true that it will result in a general rejection of the "moral rightness" of acting in accord with the normative system, i.e., the legitimacy of the system. For as Merton himself has indicated, these deviant adaptations tend to become *localized* to various segments of the social structure; a feature which may, in turn, serve to further reinforce the existing normative system.

Thus, we would offer the hypothesis that *conformity* to a culturally legitimized and approved set of institutionalized means and culture goals,

[18] Robert Perrucci, "The Significance of Intra-Occupational Mobility: Some Methodological and Theoretical Notes, Together With a Case Study of Engineers," *American Sociological Review*, 26 (December, 1961), pp. 874-883.

[19] St. Clair Drake and Horace R. Cayton, *Black Metropolis*, New York: Harcourt, Brace & World, 1962, Chapter 9.

[20] Merton, *op. cit.*, p. 135.

when the goals are not realized, will be more likely to result in disenchantment with and/or rejection of the institutionalized system than will *deviation* from the normative prescriptions as evidenced in the selection of the
most effective means, whether culturally legitimate or not. We shall try
to illustrate the relevance of this hypothesis in a discussion of a collective
disturbance on a psychiatric ward.[21]

SOME PRECONDITIONS FOR THE DISTURBANCE

A good many of the patients on the study ward have been through the
"treatment mill." During their present hospitalization and in previous ones,
they have been exposed to one or another of the physical, chemical, mechanical, or analytic therapies available in psychiatric practice. It is by no
means unusual to find patients who have had insulin shock, electro-shock,
lobotomy, group therapy, individual therapy, drugs and assorted occupational and recreational therapies. Given the considerable amount of existing treatment that has already been received by most patients, what can
one expect of the ward physician who has the responsibility of trying to
provide some therapeutic program for these patients? As might be expected,
the ward physician, in large part, adopts the pose of the surgeon who has
just completed a difficult operation saying, "I've done all I can, it's out of
my hands now." The responsibility for getting "well" again somehow winds
up in the hands of the patients themselves. As one physician put it, in
speaking of the patients: "A lot of them here are somewhere between the
hospital and the community, but they won't get off the seat of their pants.
If they don't make a move, there's nothing we can do for them." Similarly,
the ward physician, in response to the numerous questions such as, "When
can I go home," or "Am I getting any better," or "Do you think I'm ready
to go to staff," will generally respond, "I can't tell you that, Mary; you've
got to tell me when you're ready to go home."

In many respects, then, the patient is thrown back on her own resources to get estimates of just how well she is or isn't doing. Patients thus
become overly sensitive to the little nuances of staff behavior which they
take to be signs full of various meanings. For example, in an attempt to
cheer up a patient who had been very depressed for several days, the
ward attendant called her into the office and offered her a relatively new
winter coat that a volunteer worker had donated (it was late July at the
time). While the patient tried on the coat, the ward nurse and attendant
both commented on how well the coat fitted her and how nice she looked

[21] The data reported in this section were collected by the author during a one-year
field study of a psychiatric hospital. For a report on procedures and additional findings
see the author's, "Social Distance Strategies and Intra-Organizational Stratification: A
Study of the Status System on a Psychiatric Ward," *American Sociological Review,* 28
(December, 1963), pp. 951-962; and "Social Distance, Bargaining Power, and Compliance With Rules on a Hospital Ward," *Psychiatry,* 29 (February, 1966), pp. 42-55.

in it. After listening to them for a few moments, the patient turned to them and said, "In other words, I'll be here this winter."

Thus, in this setting, we find a fertile ground for the emergence of various belief systems dealing with the problem of obtaining various indications of one's therapeutic position on the ward. If we may be permitted the analogy, the patients are similar to Durkheim's Protestants, who must, through their own resources and free inquiry, come to terms with their maker.[22] In response to this situation, what we find is the emergence of what we will call a "release ideology," or a collection of beliefs referring to available means for obtaining a release from the hospital.

THE CONSTRUCTION OF A RELEASE IDEOLOGY

Every socio-cultural system which persists long enough to develop a "history" generally creates "culture heroes." These figures, either real or fictitious, are thought to reflect the most highly valued qualities of the culture; and as such they often become, in a vague sort of way, a potential source of culturally approved aspirations for group members. In this respect, the mental hospital also creates its culture heroes. On the study ward in particular, these heroes tend to be patients who "have made it," who have been released from the hospital. Thus, these culture figures may be viewed as reflecting the most highly valued patient aspiration, namely, getting out of the hospital.

The creation of culture heroes, however, does not occur only among the patients. Ward staff are also quite instrumental in influencing the patient's concern with exemplary heroes. For example, ward attendants are repeatedly telling and retelling the success stories of patients who went from incontinents on a back ward to rehabilitated members of society. It is a clear counterpart to the Horatio Alger myth, only in a psychiatric setting. The main reason why attendants seem to retell these success stories is primarily due to the paucity of cases in which the attendants can illustrate how they helped patients to recover. Thus, in the success stories, the attendants can indicate the role they themselves played in the rehabilitation process.

With this impetus from ward staff toward a focus on patients who have made successful recoveries, the patients themselves also tend to focus upon these ex-patients. For one thing the patients probably hope they can enjoy some of the praise which attendants heap upon the heroes for real or alleged behavioral or personality characteristics. For another, it becomes a tangible piece of evidence from which they may judge their own stage of progress in the hospital; a piece of evidence which, as we indicated earlier, is not easily obtained from the ward physician.

[22] Durkheim, *op. cit.*, pp. 157-159.

In the actual "putting together" of the ideology, the patients tend to focus upon the most prominent features of the culture hero's life in the hospital; especially in the period of time just prior to discharge. These prominent features of exemplary heroes that patients seemed to isolate most often were:

(1) Working with Companion Service—this involves a patient-organized and patient-run service to the hospital (with staff supervision) whereby the participating patients provide an escort service to all wards of the hospital. They escort single patients or groups of patients to and from activities, appointments, and the like, thereby releasing considerable time for the regular hospital staff to turn to more important work. This program has received much publicity both within and outside the hospital, and is considered a very desirable position by most patients.

(2) Coming off medication—as this implies, it simply means a ward physician's decision to take a patient off any mood-elevating or tranquilizing drug program.

(3) Becoming a patient leader—what we generally find here is the recognition of the formal patient leader, in terms of the elected ward president or vice president. Thus, the leadership role would exclude informal leaders, since they would not have the recognition and approval of the hospital staff members.

(4) Getting along well with ward staff—This is the loosest or vaguest characteristic of the culture heroes which the patients recognize. It generally means that a patient "talks well" with staff members; that they engage in extended conversations on topics which transcend the patient-staff role relationships. For example, the freedom to walk into the nurse's office and sit down and chat with the attendants, or more important, to be taken into the confidence of a ward staff member.

These are the four main factors that the patients tend to isolate in reflecting upon the pre-release behavior of the culture heroes. In most cases, these four factors quite accurately characterize the pre-release behavior of discharged patients. We would suggest that the reason these four characteristics are manifested by the culture heroes is that they are the *results* or *consequences* of a poorly understood process of "getting better." That is, the patient who is making good progress "putting himself together again," will be very likely to go on Companion Service, to come off medication, to become a patient leader, and to get on well with ward staff. However, in the creation of the release ideology, these four characteristics are viewed as *things to be done in order to get better*. The patients on the ward take the behavioral manifestations of the "getting better" process and make them the causes of the process. In the language of Schneider and Dornbusch, the patients have taken certain "latent" functions of the recovery process and made them "manifest" by pursuing them as goals.[23]

[23] Schneider and Dornbusch, *op. cit.*, pp. 58-77.

What had previously been realized as a by-product is now "instrumental-ized" as a means for attaining mental health.

THE CONCRETIZATION OF THE IDEOLOGY

The release ideology described above allows the patients to maintain the belief that there is a clear-cut way to get better and get out of the hospital. The actual reality of the belief system is never an issue, since it has been created out of rather reliable evidence (i.e., discharged patients), and also since it has never been shown not to be true. That is, the only patients who have ever embodied these four ideological characteristics have been the culture heroes. Aside from them, several patients may have one or two of the characteristics, e.g., work or Companion Service, and get on well with ward staff, but never all four characteristics.

In this part of the process of the collective disturbance, we will de-scribe the case of the patient who did embody all four characteristics, i.e., the "concretization" of the ideology. This is the case of Marie I., a patient who represented the unfolding of the ward's "Horatio Alger" myth. Marie I. came on Ward X during the last week in May. She came to the ward with what might be considered "poor credentials." That is, she was not the most desirable type of patient for an open ward. The ward attendant upon hear-ing of Marie I.'s transfer made the following comment:

> Well, we're getting two new girls. Dr. Powell said we're getting one good one and one of the other kind. The good one is Connie Green; the other girl is Marie I. She's coming from a back ward, a real fighter. I don't know how they expect us to help her on this ward.

On the ward two days later, the day attendant pointed out Marie I. to the observer:

> That's Marie. She came over from the disturbed ward. You better watch out for her; when she blows she really blows. I feel sorry for the night attendant. She can sure have trouble sometimes, especially with girls like Marie.

The first two weeks on the ward for Marie I. were rather uneventful. She was immediately assigned to a job doing housework in one of the hospital buildings, which she did without difficulty. Her medication pro-gram included two depressants (Thorazine and Equanil) which she took without incident. Aside from a few minor evening complaints of inability to sleep, and several physical complaints requiring absence from work, Marie was a good patient. She was good in the sense of being unobtrusive, keeping to herself, and causing no difficulties for other patients or ward staff.

On June 20, Marie had her first extended contact with the ward physi-cian during office hours. The interview was a pleasant one, with the doctor indicating his interest in Marie's condition, and the importance, to Marie, of this move to an open ward. The doctor stressed the fact that this was probably an important turning point in her illness. Marie was clearly pleased with the doctor, and repeatedly stated how much she liked the ward, the staff and the other patients.

At this point Marie was observed to have become much more out-going. She established a close friendship with Mary G., one of the very well-liked patients on the ward. The ward staff also became sensitive to the fact that Marie was "coming out of her shell." On June 29, Mrs. Talbot, the day attendant, made the following reply to Dr. Powell's inquiry concerning Marie:

> She's getting along real fine. She fits in well, and most of the girls really like her. Just the other morning she went by the office door and said, Hi, Tommy (*nickname*). Well, my head just shot up. She came back and apologized because she thought I was mad. Well, I wasn't; it was just a surprise to hear her say that. A lot of the old timers call me that, but a new girl usually won't.

On July 1, the ward president received a six-months leave of absence. A special election was held, and Marie I. was elected the new president. The ward staff, and by extension, the patients, made quite a bit of "noise" about it. At attendant lunches or coffee breaks, Marie became a living testimonial to the therapeutic atmosphere of the ward. "A little over a month ago she was fighting and scratching on a back ward, and now she's president at the ward council," was the comment of the day attendant.

On July 12, the evening shift attendant wrote the following unsolicited progress note on Marie:

> This patient has shown a wonderful improvement on my time since she first came on this ward. She is no longer a sleeping problem. She sleeps all night. She gets up very bright and cheerful at 5:30 a.m.

During this time, Marie made a definite effort to convince the ward attendants and ward physician that she no longer needed her medication. Each time the ward physician came for office hours Marie managed to see him and repeat her request. On July 20, the following note appeared in Marie's chart:

> Patient asked doctor to have her medication discontinued again. Discontinue Thorazine and Dulcolox. Reduce Equanil to 200 mg.

At this point in Marie I.'s stay on the ward she had managed to exhibit the four most highly valued factors which made up the release ideology. She was an escort for Companion Service; she was ward president; she was off medication; and she got along very well with ward staff. Regardless of the "workability" of the ideology in actually yielding the desired result of a release from the hospital, a patient who exhibited these four characteristics should carry a rather favorable prognosis. For Marie I., however, we find a very rapid process of deterioration setting in; a transition even more marked than her meteoric rise from a back ward to ward hero. We will now turn to Marie's individual "breakdown," and the manner in which it affected the other patients on the ward.

THE IDEOLOGY PUT TO THE TEST

The rapid decline of Marie I. made its first appearance with the news that two patients on the ward were in the planning stage for a release from the hospital. While plans were apparently in progress for some time through the Social Service Department, it now became public ward information that Carla W. was being considered for a six-month leave of absence, and Lizzie S. was under consideration for a work placement. Neither of these two patients was very popular on the ward. In fact, Lizzie S. was one of the patients receiving the highest number of negative sociometric choices on the ward.[24] In addition, the news of these plans was not met with the wholehearted approval of the ward attendants. As Mrs. Talbot put it:

> I can't understand it. Neither Carla nor Lizzie is ready to leave here; they're both very disturbed. Not that I'm not glad to get rid of them, but they'll never make it. They shouldn't even be considered for leaves.

This news became public on July 26. On July 27, Lizzie S. was put on additional medication (Reserpine). On July 28 and 29, the following notes were written in Marie I.'s chart:

> Patient came to office with a thin blouse on and a pair of jeans. Told her to go get a brassiere and slip on because you could see through the blouse. Said she was alright, no one could see through her. Just stood and stared at me. After a while she finally put on a dress. Said she didn't like to be told about her clothes. Patient seems very nervous. First complaining of constipation and was given laxative. This patient stated bowels acted some. Stayed on ward this p.m. saying didn't feel well. Is trying hard to get upset. Is disturbed at times. Is irritable and very unreasonable. Patient came to office saying she might as well go back to work for she had to listen to Celine's radio. Tried to talk with patient but she became very sullen and held her mouth open running her tongue around the inside of her mouth and stared into space. Patient went to room to rest up.

On July 31, the following note was written on Carla W.:

> Patient given medication for upset stomach. Patient restless, found her crying. Stated she was having bad dreams. Was very unhappy all evening.

The following three notes were written on Lizzie S. for July 30, 31 and August 1 respectively:

> This patient has been getting up for last week complaining of pains in stomach. States she has a lot of diarrhea.

[24] See Perrucci, "Social Distance Strategies . . . . . ," op. cit.

Patient has been very talkative several times during night. Very restless.

Patient put on Equanil to relieve anxiety.

On August 3, the following note was written on Marie I.:

Patient is very strong against Elsa P. sleeping next to her. She is continually calling her names to this attendant. States Elsa watches her all the time.

On August 6, both Carla W. and Lizzie S. were released from the hospital on a leave of absence and a work placement respectively. The departure of these two patients was discussed by the ward attendant and ward nurse in the following manner:

ATTENDANT: Well, Carla went out, but was she high. She went around demanding that things be done for her. She said to me, "I demand that you call [*social worker*] about me going home." I don't know how they let her go. Just two days ago the doctor gave orders to seclude her or send her to [*closed ward*] if she acted up, and today they let her out.

NURSE: Lizzie was just as disturbed. Monday she told me that Beth L. was threatening to kill her, and she started crying. Anyway, I'm glad to see her go.

With the release of these two patients we find a move into the acute stage of the disturbance. For up to this point (July 29 to August 6), what we found was primarily the individual upset of Marie I. The rest of the patients on the ward were apparently affected only to the extent that there appeared to be a marked increase in complaints about physical ailments.[25] Thus, the acute phase of the disturbance involved the "complete breakdown" of Marie I. (by staff definitions, this involves a psychotic episode and the return to a closed ward), as well as a number of extreme upsets of other patients that were presumably related to Marie's disturbance. We will relate each incident by the day of occurrence and the patient involved:

August 7: Marie I., nursing note, day shift.

Patient has burning sensation when she urinates. Patient said she felt stuffy, and needed a bowel movement.

August 8: Marie I., day shift, observations on the ward:

MARIE: Could I have a soda mint or bicarb?
NURSE: Why?
MARIE: So I can belch.

---

[25] It is interesting to note in this context that the one and only case of incontinence on the ward (during the field study) occurred during the disturbance phase. On August 3 and 4, Joan B. became incontinent. At this time she was "specialed" by the evening and night attendants. That is, she was awakened periodically during the night and taken to the bathroom. She was generally awakened at 11 p.m. and 3 a.m. This solved the bed wetting problem, but then Joan became a "problem sleeper," i.e., it was very difficult getting her up in the morning.

NURSE: Are you under tension at work, Marie?

MARIE: (Laughs) Who isn't under tension here. Can I have a soda mint?

NURSE: Well, Marie, you know what we are trying to do here is to get you people off medications. You can't always be running for a soda mint or a bicarb when you get out.

MARIE: Well, I'm sure I can get a bicarb if I need it.

Marie walked away from the office into the day room and out to the loggie. She spoke of the incident to a group of patients who were smoking on the loggie.

MARIE: She told me, "we don't want you to get used to the medication" (in a mimicing voice). I'll get my own stuff to burp. I can spend a dime on a coca cola so she won't have to chart a soda mint. They don't worry about shock treatments becoming habit forming, but they worry about soda mint.

August 9: Marie I., nursing note, evening shift:

Patient very disturbed. Was restless and fault-finding all evening. Attendant talked with her at 7 p.m. She quieted down for a while. Later came in office while supervisor was here. She walked up to medicine cabinet and tried to open it. She was very angry to find it locked. Threatened the supervisor. Attendant talked with her again. She threatened her life; also stated she would run away if doctor did not transfer her to ward ___. Was very insulting to some of the other patients. Seemed to think she was as well or even better than two of the patients that had been sent out on work placement. Patient was watched very close.

August 10: Marie I., day shift, observations on the ward:

Marie went to work on Companion Service at 8:30 a.m. At 10:15 a.m. Marie was brought back to the ward by the attendant in charge of the service. The patient was very upset and crying. Mrs. Talbot, the ward attendant, asked Marie what was the matter. Marie stated, "If we'd get rid of Beth L. and Betty L. (two other patients on the ward) things would go a lot better on this ward." Mrs. Talbot helped Marie to her room to lie down.

Dr. Powell was called and he came right over. Marie was asked to come to the nurses' office and talk with him.

DR. POWELL: I understand you've been a little upset, Marie. You want to tell me about it.

MARIE: It's this whole goddamn place. You ask for a soda mint and they make a big deal out of it. I tried to get some powder from the medicine cabinet and the attendant and the supervisor jump on me. They told me that the office was for the nurses and attendants and that I should stay out.

DR. POWELL: You have to understand that there are some rules around here, Marie. Don't you think you have to abide by the rules?

MARIE: Yes, I know there are rules, I've been following them for weeks.
              I was the good Marie, the sweet Marie. I worked hard to go on
              Companion Service and to get along without my medicine, and
              what did it get me. (Patient starts crying at this point) You
              let Carla and Lizzie go out, and I was better than either of
              them. Lizzie even went on medicine before she went out.

DR. POWELL: Well, what do you want me to do, Marie? You think I should
              let you go home?

MARIE: I want to go to Ward O (*closed ward*). At least over there I
              can cry and no one looks at you as if something's wrong.

DR. POWELL: I'll tell you what. Why don't you go lie down and rest for a
              while. I'll give you something to help you rest and we can
              talk again later.

MARIE: I don't give a shit for your medicine or your hospital.

Marie gets up and walks out of the office. Mrs. Talbot goes after her and
gets her to lie down in her room. Mrs. Talbot returns to the office.

MRS. TALBOT: You think we should send her over to O (*closed ward*). She's
              going to blow any minute.

DR. POWELL: Let's hold her here for now. She's made such great strides
              these past months; I'd hate to set her back without a good try.
              Keep her in her room and keep an eye on her once in a while.
              I'll talk to her again tomorrow.

That noon at lunch time, Marie did not go to lunch with the ward but
remained in her room. The ward attendant escorted the patients from the
study ward and the upstairs ward to the dining room. The attendant from
the upper ward was to keep an eye on the patients who do not go to
regular lunch. When the attendant and the observer returned to the ward,
the following incident was reported by the upstairs attendant:

> I was upstairs in the office when all of a sudden I heard a big racket coming
> from below. There was some yelling and screaming. I ran downstairs and
> there at the end of the hall were Marie I. and Beth L. rolling around and
> fighting on the floor. It was a job getting them apart, but I finally got them
> in their own rooms. I couldn't get anything out of Marie because she'd been
> crying all this time. Beth told me that she was in her room minding her own
> business when Marie walked in and called her a "goddam whore" and started
> hitting her and pulling her hair. Marie picked on the wrong one this time,
> because Beth was really giving it to her when I got down here.

Mrs. Talbot called Dr. Powell and reported the incident. Marie was
immediately sent over to a closed ward. Later that evening, and through
the night, a number of additional incidents occurred. However, it becomes
most difficult to establish anything like a causal link between Marie I.'s
disturbance and the subsequent upsets of several other patients. At this
point, we will only relate the incidents and then attempt to establish their

relationship to Marie's disturbance. Reported below is the statement made by the day attendant to the observer on August 11, the day after Marie I. was sent to a closed ward:

> Last night it was really a madhouse here. You knew that Marie "blew" yesterday, didn't you. Well, that's not the all of it. About 8:00 last night, Mary G. went psychotic. She was running up and down the hall yelling and singing hymns. Then she started talking to God, saying how sorry she was and all that. Minton (evening attendant) said it was a real mess. They sent her over with Marie I. on O (*closed ward*). Then to top it all off, Elizabeth K. tried to choke Julia T. in the middle of the night. Julia started yelling and practically woke up the whole ward. They moved Elizabeth to the empty room at the end of the hall, and they're going to keep her door locked at night.

Aside from these remarks by the day attendant, the observer also noted some additional incidents which may or may not be relevant to the disturbance. However, their occurrence at this particular time, i.e., the acute stage of the disturbance, makes them potentially relevant. The incidents simply involve three patients who did not go to work on August 11. Wanda R., Bertha G., and Betty L. all claimed that they were not feeling good, for one reason or another, and wished to be excused from work.

As we stated above, the causal connection between Marie I.'s disturbance and the subsequent upsets of other patients is difficult to establish. The one common element in all these events is their occurrence in a certain time sequence. Aside from this, we would be hard put to explain the connections among *all* these events. Nevertheless, the following explanation is offered.

The psychotic episode of Mary G., which followed very closely the disturbance of Marie I., is most interesting in view of the fact that Mary G. and Marie I. were very close friends on the ward. On the sociometric questionnaire, they were among the few pairs of mutual friendship choices made by patients. Thus, there does seem to be some likelihood that the two disturbances were connected. The other significant feature of all of the disturbances which followed Marie I.'s is the fact that they occurred among relatively active patients holding significant status positions within the patient group. For example, of the six patients involved in these upsets, five were patients who were either very popular or very unpopular according to our sociometric questionnaire. Mary G., Elizabeth K., and Wanda R. were all among the patients most frequently chosen for potential roommates; Julia T. was one of the two ward leaders; and Betty L. and Lizzie S. were two of the four most frequently negatively selected patients on the ward. Thus, it is quite possible that due to the fact that they were all active patients, they were perhaps more sensitive to the symbolic meaning of the breakdown of Marie I. That is, that her disturbance represented a breakdown of the release ideology. It is with respect to the release ideology that we would expect the active patients to be concerned, since they would be more likely to be cognizant of the presumed utility of the ideology in attaining a release from the hospital.

UNATTAINABLE GOALS AND THE COLLECTIVE DISTURBANCE

The collective disturbance described in this paper was seen to be the result of a release ideology which provided a framework of instrumental means for the attainment of a hospital release. The ideology, however, was badly constructed, in that the specific means isolated by the patients were not necessarily related to the indicators used by staff to establish a patient's release prognosis.[26]

The existence of the strong ideological factors found among the patients raises some questions concerning the persistence of magic within the rationalized framework of the hospital. The combination of uncertainty in treatment technology, and anxiety concerning one's personal prognosis leads to a dependence upon a belief system that makes institutional life bearable. Since patients are "kept in the dark" as to expectations regarding treatment effectiveness and release prognosis, the patients build an explanatory system which provides this information and allows them to accept the constraints imposed upon them by legitimizing the authority of those above them in the hospital hierarchy. The functions of magic in a social system are examined by Parsons in discussing Malinowski's work on magic.

> Malinowski, however, went beyond this in attempting to understand the functional necessity for such mechanisms as magic. In this connection, he laid stress on the importance of the emotional interests involved in the successful outcome of such enterprises. *The combination of a strong emotional interest with important factors of uncertainty, which on the given technical level are inherent in the situation, produces a state of tension and exposes the actor to frustration.* This, it should be noted, exists not only in cases where uncontrollable factors, such as bad weather or insect pests in gardening result in "undeserved" failure, *but also in cases where success is out of proportion to reasonable expectations of the results of intelligence and effort.* Unless there were mechanisms which had the psychological function of mitigating the sense of frustration, the consequences would be unfavorable to maintaining a high level of confidence or effort, and it is in this connection that magic may be seen to perform important positive functions. . . . It would follow that wherever such uncertainty elements enter into the pursuit of emotionally important

[26] The criteria for releasing patients developed by the psychiatric staff is often vague and unrelated to estimates of "wellness" and patients' behavior in the hospital. For an analysis of staff release decisions, see Robert Perrucci, "Social Processes in Psychiatric Decisions," in D. Hansen, ed., *Counseling and Therapy in Contemporary Society: Sociological Perspectives,* Boston: Houghton Mifflin, 1967. In preparation.

goals, if not magic, at least functionally equivalent phenomena could be expected to appear.[27]

Thus, while both Parsons and Malinowski point out the functional significance of magic in coping with uncertainty, it is quite clear that the magical beliefs *coexist* with the rational knowledge rather than seeking to *replace* the rational knowledge in a system of goal directed activity. As Parsons points out:

> Side by side with the system of rational knowledge and technique, however, and specifically not confused with it, was a system of magical beliefs and practices. . . . *Correspondingly, the practices were not rational techniques* but rituals involving specific orientation to this world of supernatural forces and entities.[28]

It appears in this interpretation that the contribution, i.e., functional significance, which the magical system makes to maintaining order in the system, comes primarily from the fact that the belief system stands *outside* of any expectation of results in goal directed behavior. This is also quite similar to Durkheim's distinction between the sacred and profane in religious activity, where one of the major sources of strength for the religious system is that it exists apart from the utilitarian orientation of rational techniques.[29]

The psychiatric setting seems to generate pressure for converting magical beliefs into rational, technical means designed to achieve certain goals. This pressure can be traced to the complete absence of intermediate goals for patients, which may be pursued in their own right, and which may be related to a hospital release as a consequence of involvement with such intermediate goals.[30]

[27] Talcott Parsons, "The Theoretical Development of the Sociology of Religion," in *Essays in Sociological Theory,* New York: The Free Press, 1949, pp. 203-204, italics ours. It should be noted that in a footnote to the quoted statement, Parsons explicitly refers to the importance of these ideas on magic in the field of health and medicine.

[28] *Ibid.,* p. 202.

[29] Émile Durkheim, *The Elementary Forms of the Religious Life,* New York: The Free Press, 1947. For an extended discussion of this point in Durkheim's work, see Talcott Parsons, *Structure of Social Action,* New York: The Free Press, 1937, pp. 411-429.

[30] For a discussion of the mechanisms of "gain by indirection" and "attractiveness of intermediates," see Louis Schneider, "The Category of Ignorance in Sociological Theory," *American Sociological Review,* 27 (August, 1962), pp. 492-508.

The Ex-National Sport Looks to Its Image

LEONARD KOPPETT

MAJOR LEAGUE BASEBALL, a mass spectator sport still steeped in its 19th-century origins, is suffering today from that most modern of 20th-century maladies: "bad image."

The illness has occurred relatively recently. Until a decade ago few people bothered to challenge baseball's right to a place alongside Mom, apple pie and freedom of assembly. There were those who didn't care, but not many who did failed to accept baseball as a peculiar, indigenous and vaguely defined "special" element in the fabric of American culture.

Today this favored position is not merely challenged—it has disappeared. While millions of people still feel a passionate interest in every sort of baseball news, fewer and fewer regard it as essentially different from other forms of entertainment. Even baseball's own hierarchy admits that the aura has gone, or is going. Commissioner Ford C. Frick, in a top-secret report to the 20 major-league club owners last month in Phoenix, spelled out the "bad image" problem and blamed the owners for it. As with most top-secret stories in baseball, this one made headlines right away. At the regular winter meetings of the majors and minors, however, held in Houston two weeks ago, officials occupied themselves with other matters and gave Frick's "image" warning only passing notice.

The chances are that the issue will not escape the loquacious attention of the hot-stove leaguers this winter as they relive past seasons and speculate on those to come. What, indeed, has happened to bring about the change? What was the baseball of the "old days" like, before the "image" got tarnished? Well, a generation ago it would have sounded sacrilegious to identify the sport as "part of the *entertainment* industry." (Today, of course, that very phrase is used to justify the purchase of the New York Yankees by the Columbia Broadcasting System.) A fan attended an event, not a performance. He had as little interest in—and awareness of—the commercial background of the goings-on on the field as the audience at a concert or opera has of the financial problems involved in a musical evening.

The supply of heroes seemed endless: Mathewson, Johnson, Cobb, Ruth. These, and a hundred others slightly less famous, were not merely great ball players; each had a distinct character in the eye of the fan. This character did not always coincide with the man in real life, but it was clear-cut, consistent, identifiable and human.

The fan, a generation ago, believed that victory on the field was the most important thing in the world to all those concerned with baseball. And he was deeply loyal to locale. He knew that the players who wore, let's say, a Brooklyn uniform were recruited from all over the country, but as long as they wore it, they were part of Brooklyn.

To a great extent the prominent players did become a part of the community they played in. They settled in the residential neighborhoods that surrounded the ball parks built in the early years of the century; they frequented local restaurants, shops (yes, bars, too); they mingled with the fans entering and leaving the park.

Consider, for example, Ebbets Field. The structure was small, the stands close to the foul lines and the sense of intimacy very great. A fan yelling "Throw him a fish!" when Lonnie Frey booted a ball at shortstop could be heard clearly throughout the park. Players' shouts at one another could be heard, too.

When a man came to a game—a *day* game—he brought his children, who became converts. Older children could come by themselves—after school in spring and fall, to double-headers in summer. Relatively few seats were boxes and almost any location in the park was available the day of a game.

In such surroundings, the Dodgers could, and did, become national as well as civic celebrities. Their "daffiness," their overpopulation of third base, their brushes with death from fly balls to the head were known to baseball fans everywhere. When they got into a fight (which Red Barber, their radio announcer, established once and for all as a "rhubarb"), no one could help taking sides.

A personal rivalry, like the one between John McGraw, supreme dictator of the New York Giants, and Uncle Wilbert Robinson, kindly but often bumbling manager of the Dodgers, helped divide Brooklyn from New York as sharply as Scotland from England. No mere political unity could erase the lines drawn.

An incident in the early life of Casey Stengel illustrates the communal atmosphere in which baseball players used to live. When Casey played for the Dodgers, he used to commute by trolley car to a boardinghouse. One day, after a game, he was riding the trolley when he saw one of his teammates on the sidewalk. The teammate, who had gone hitless that day, had caught one of his children swiping some fruit and was applying discipline and education with sharp smacks.

Stengel leaned out of the speeding trolley car, hanging on by one hand, and yelled: "When you go oh-for-four, you take it out on the kid, eh?"

The point is that everyone around knew who the players were and what they were talking about.

Later, when the Dodgers had earned the affectionate title of "Bums," they started to win pennants. They became the epitome of the successful underdog. The love lavished on Pee Wee Reese, Jackie Robinson, Gil

Hodges, Roy Campanella and the others of the postwar era was a beautiful thing.

In 1948, when Leo Durocher switched from managing the Dodgers to managing the Giants, the sense of shock was as real as if an Englishman had been suddenly elected Premier of France. When the lights were turned out at Ebbets Field and 30,000 fans lit matches to simulate a birthday cake for Pee Wee Reese, it was a press-agent-instigated idea, yes, but instigated by a press agent in tune with the populace.

When the Dodgers won the 1941 pennant, their first in 21 years, fans marched across Brooklyn Bridge and stood for hours on West 42d Street, booing the darkened offices of the Yankees, whom they would play in the World Series.

And what is it like today? The Dodgers have ceased to exist, although there is a team by that name playing in a place called Los Angeles. At the new Dodger Stadium, almost half the seats are boxes. A man is more likely to bring a client than a son. (This is even more true at Yankee Stadium today.) The players, having become members of the upper middle class, live in suburban communities 20 and 30 miles away; they are scattered, and the community life in which they take part is suburban, not *local* in the fans' sense of the term.

Inside the Los Angeles park, the customer can get dinner, plenty of liquor, souvenirs by the dozen, a host of special services—all far removed from the hot dogs and peanuts that used to represent the limit of ball park fare. This makes him more comfortable, and probably overweight, and it also drives home the point that his money is being sought at every turn.

Where have the fans' illusions that baseball was "something special" gone? How could they be maintained for half a century, then eroded in the last five years? The steps are easy to identify.

First, by yielding to the pressure (perhaps unavoidable) for unlimited night games, the majors gave up one of their distinctive characteristics. The difference between a night game and a day game may be hard to define, but it's easy to feel: the one connotes sport, the other performance; one belongs to the young of all ages, the other to seekers of entertainment. A few night games were attractive galas, like extra Sundays or holidays; a steady diet undermined one psychological prop of the "something special" illusion.

Then, by jumping franchises in all directions for the avowed purpose of making more money, baseball destroyed the very stability, statistical validity and competitive integrity that made the game so attractive.

Between 1903, when the American League solidified and won major status, and 1953, when the Braves moved from Boston to Milwaukee, the major league structure stood as a monument to security in a frightening, changing world. The same 16 teams, located in only 11 cities with fairly compact travel connections, played a similar schedule pattern year after year, creating records that could be compared and discussed. What changes occurred were few, minor and easily understood.

The first few franchise shifts did not have an immediately disastrous effect. But then, in 1957, the point of no return was reached when, after months of rumors and denials, the Dodgers and Giants were moved to Los Angeles and San Francisco.

The moving of these teams to new towns tore the fabric of stability beyond repair. If Brooklyn could be deprived of its Dodgers, if the Giants of McGraw could leave Broadway, if all the accumulated tradition could be brushed aside, the fan could feel no more sure of his baseball than of anything else in a bewildering universe.

And again, details were disturbing. All sorts of regulations had to be rewritten to make the shifts legal, even in baseball terms. The Dodgers had to play (for four years, it turned out) in a football stadium with 90,000 seats but no suitable playing field. The Pacific Coast League, highest of the minor leagues, had its status summarily destroyed. Coast-to-coast travel was required of players with no essential change in schedule patterns. In other words, honorable business dealings and decent conditions for playing the games had to be sacrificed for potential profit.

The next step was expansion. In the fall of 1960, the American League decided to go to 10 teams immediately; the National League would do so in 1962.

This was organized baseball's answer to a proposed third major league, to be called the Continental. After tossing up roadblocks of one sort and another, the majors finally decided to take in what appeared to be the strongest members of the developing league. This killed third-league talk. Only one of the Continental groups—the New York Mets—actually wound up with a franchise.

To stock the four new clubs, the existing teams supplied 100 of the least desirable players on their rosters for a total of about $8,000,000. In other words, the initiation fee for each newcomer was something over $2,000,000; the profit for each existing club was about $600,000. And, competitively speaking, the talent supplied, with few exceptions, was practically worthless.

All this, of course, received extensive press coverage, and its effect on baseball's image as a sport need not be belabored.

Expansion also meant 10-team leagues, playing 162-game schedules, with back-breaking travel. There were two serious drawbacks to this scheme. One is that a 10-team league is bottom-heavy with also-rans; a contending team can play only two-ninths of its games with other contenders (that is, the top three teams in the standings at any given time).

The other is that all the records and statistics, so precious a part of baseball lore, were compromised, and events conspired to underline this point immediately. In 1961, Roger Maris of the Yankees hit 61 home runs, breaking Babe Ruth's record; but instead of being hailed as the most glamorous of all baseball feats, this only generated arguments about the validity of records made in 162-game schedules vs. 154-game schedules.

Meanwhile, the players themselves were doing their share to disillusion the fan. When they achieved a fabulous pension plan, financed by World Series television income, most fans identified with them and cheered; when they foisted a second all-star game on the public to increase pension funds, they revealed themselves in a mercenary light.

More and more players complained of the hardships of travel and night ball—and the fans read their remarks. More and more, players made plain their concern with business connections, post-baseball careers, income from endorsements and personal appearances and other "I play baseball just for the money" attitudes. Whether or not expressing such feelings is an expression of honesty, it certainly dispels illusion.

Baseball's increasing dependence on radio and television income has also helped prevent the creation of illusion, especially in children. Messages selling beer and cigarettes, delivered 20 times per game day after day, may or may not be desirable from any of a dozen points of view; they definitely do not, however, instill an image of pure sport.

Radio had been a help to baseball, whetting the appetite of the true fan, keeping him informed and making new addicts. Television, however, was a short-term bonanza leading to long-term disaster which is only now beginning to be recognized.

The trouble with television is that it exists. It creates a demand for the one big thing, seen now, by everybody, everywhere, and makes any sort of minor-league operation difficult. The major leagues, however, were not content to let attrition take its course, let alone develop a plan for combating it: they piped major league games into minor league territories and promptly killed off the minors then and there.

The main thing is that a baseball game on television remains a television show: it may make some baseball addicts, but it certainly makes more television addicts. Thus, one more distinguishing feature of baseball is removed and it becomes "just another entertainment."

Other problems, which the fan did not seek out, were thrown into his illusion-making machinery.

The Congressional hearings about whether or not baseball (and other sports) should be granted specific antitrust exemptions contributed a great deal of illusion-wrecking information and speculation. Congress still hasn't taken any action, but exactly how much business and how little sport there is in today's corporate-structure, tax-conscious, peripheral-income-oriented baseball "clubs" has been spelled out too often to be ignored.

And the unprecedented increase in shifting of players, stimulated by expansion, corroded much fan identification. By June, 1962, the turnover of personnel on all major league rosters in the preceding 12 months exceeded 50 per cent.

All these factors, then, bruised baseball's image and robbed it of its special status. The events of 1964 knocked the image flat on its back.

Chief among them was the purchase of the Yankees in August by C.B.S.

for $14.2 million. There was talk of conflict of interest; antitrust action seemed possible; for weeks the papers were full of stories about why the deal might be a bad thing. Aside from anything else, it certainly tied base-ball closer to the "entertainment industry"; in fact, both the Yankees and C.B.S. boasted of this.

In October, the Braves decided to move to Atlanta, having milked Mil-waukee dry. (Attendance, after an average of 2,000,000 a year for seven years, had dropped to under 1,000,000 in the last three.) The avowed rea-son: Atlanta had a better TV-market area potential!

Milwaukee authorities went to court to make the Braves stay. The National League ordered them to stay, then approved the move for 1966, and a lease with Atlanta's new stadium was signed. Milwaukee citizens in-sist they'll find another big league team to come to Milwaukee by then. (It might be Cleveland, which after much consideration of Seattle, Oakland and Dallas, decided to stay in Cleveland "for one more year," and perhaps longer, if the citizens bestir themselves to buy enough tickets.)

It is no wonder, then, that in November even Frick, who had never before shown the slightest inclination to rock a boat, told the owners off, stating that "baseball people are unwilling to abide by the rules which they themselves make" and that "expediency is permitted to replace sound judg-ment." It was, in a sense, a farewell gesture. He will retire from his $65,000-a-year job next October after 14 years.

Can anything be done? Not really. Public relations consultants may be called in (they have been called in before, without effect), and Frick's sug-gestion that the commissioner be given greater powers—like those possessed by the late Judge Kenesaw Mountain Landis, who ruled baseball with an iron hand until 1945—was adopted at the winter meetings. However, the effectiveness of any such change in powers will be wholly dependent on how strong a man the owners choose—in other words, want—as their next commissioner.

The only real change on the horizon is further expansion. Within a few years, the leagues will probably expand to 12 teams, playing in six-team subdivisions. Thus, six teams in the Western half of the National League may play one another 20 times each, and the six in the Eastern half nine times a year, with all games counting in the standings, but with two sepa-rate standings. This would mean a 154-game schedule, with two divisional pennant races and no team ever lower than sixth. The divisional winners would play off for the right to go into the World Series against the Ameri-can League winner, determined the same way.

This particular case of expansion will help. It will cut travel, heighten fan interest in pennant races, remove the bottom layer of dead weight and improve statistics.

But it will not restore baseball to the unique position it once held. Nothing will. Times, as even the owners and Frick have finally admitted, change.

Baseball seems destined to remain a profitable, respected, important segment of the mass entertainment industry, a growing field. It will still command a certain number of fanatics. But it must share billing with pro football, and with television it simply cannot compete.

For the average fan, something has gone out of the game; or rather, come into it: a wariness that makes total emotional commitment difficult. Years ago, a columnist commented on the coldly efficient, perpetually victorious Yankees: "Rooting for the Yankees is like rooting for U. S. Steel." Now the joke has become a reality, and it's pretty hard to root for a business—especially a business that may move away when a better offer comes along.

The old fan's motto might have been "My ball club, right or wrong, but right or wrong, my ball club still." Today's fan had better feel: "Eat, drink (beer), smoke (the right brand) and make merry—for tomorrow they may move the franchise." And if that be bad image, perhaps baseball had better make the most of it.

Institutionalization and Change

S. N. EISENSTADT

I

THIS PAPER ILLUSTRATES the combination of systematic institutional analysis with the analysis of change, showing that the explication of change is inherent in the systematic analysis of concrete societies or parts thereof.

Claims have long been made that structural or "structural-functional" analysis, with its stress on systems, equilibrium, common values and boundary-maintenance, not only neglects problems of change, but is analytically incapable of dealing with them. In response, many sociologists have recently asserted that not only is there no necessary contradiction between structural analysis and the analysis of change, but that on the contrary the two are basically compatible.

As formulated, for instance, by Moore, the argument is that every society (or social system) is inherently predisposed to change because of basic problems to which there is no overall continuous solution. These problems include uncertainties of socialization, perennial scarcity of resources relative to individual aspirations, and contrasting types of social orientation or prin-

From *American Sociological Review*, Vol. 29, No. 2, pp. 235-247. Reprinted by permission of the publisher and author.

ciples of social organization (e.g., *Gemeinschaft* vs. *Gesellschaft*) within the society. While this general view has been accepted to some extent, it has given rise to the contrary claim that it is couched in terms too general to explain the specific directions of change in any concrete society, that such specificity is beyond the province of "structural" analysis, and that such analysis can explain any concrete change only by reference either to very general and hence inadequate causes, or to forces external to the system.

These difficulties can be at least partially overcome by recognizing that the general "predilections" to change inherent in any social system become "concretized" or "specified" through the process of institutionalization. Our major point is that the institutionalization of any social system—be it political, economic or a system of social stratification or of any collectivity or role—creates in its wake the possibilities for change. The process of institutionalization is the organization of a societally prescribed system of differentiated behavior oriented to the solution of certain problems inherent in a major area of social life.

The organization of such systems of behavior involves the creation and definition of norms to regulate the major units of social behavior and organization, criteria according to which the flow of resources is regulated between such units, and sanctions to ensure that such norms are upheld. All these involve the maintenance of the specific boundaries of the system, i.e., the maintenance of the units that constitute it, of its relations with outside systems, and of the norms that delineate its specific characteristics.

And yet the very attempt to institutionalize any such system creates in its wake the possibility for change. These are possibilities not only for general, unspecified change but for more specific changes, which develop not randomly but in relatively specific directions, to a large extent set by the very process of institutionalization. Hence a systematic structural analysis is a prerequisite for an adequate analysis of change.

II

We shall illustrate this general point by analyzing the process of institutionalization in one type of political and one type of religious system, drawing on recent work on the social and political structure of the historical centralized bureaucratic Empires, i.e., the Sassanid, Roman, Byzantine, Chinese, Caliphate and Ottoman Empires and the European states in the period of absolutism, and on the development of religious institutions within them.

The majority of these Empires developed from (a) patrimonial empires such as Egypt or the Sassanid Empire; (b) dualistic nomadic-sedentary empires (necessarily sharing many characteristics with the patrimonial ones); (c) feudal systems, such as the European absolutist states; or (d) city-states (the Roman and Hellenistic Empires). Despite the great variety in historical and cultural settings, we may designate some common features in the first stages of establishment of such polities.

The Empires were first established through interaction between the political goals of the rulers who established them, and the broader conditions prevailing in their respective social structures. The initiative for the establishment of these polities came, in all cases, from the rulers—emperors, kings or members of a patrician ruling elite (like the more active and dynamic element of the patrician elite in Republican Rome). These rulers came, in most cases, from established patrician, patrimonial, tribal or feudal families. Some were usurpers, coming from lower-class families, who attempted to establish new dynasties or to conquer new territories, and some were conquerors who attempted to establish their rule over various territories.

In most cases such rulers arose in periods of strife and turmoil during dismemberment of the existing political system or during acute strife within it. Usually their aim was to reestablish peace and order. They did not, however, attempt to restore the old order in its entirety, although for propagandist reasons they sometimes upheld such restoration as political ideology or slogan. They sought to establish a more centralized, unified polity in which they could monopolize and set the political goals, without being bound by traditional aristocratic, tribal or patrician groups. Even the conquerors—as in the Roman, Islamic or Spanish American Empires—had some vision of distinctly political goals and attempted to transmit it to at least part of the conquered population. These aims were very often oriented against, and opposed by, various social and political groups. However great the turmoil, unrest and internal strife, some groups always either benefited from it (or hoped to do so) or aimed to reestablish the "old" order in which they held positions of power and influence.

To implement their aims against aristocratic patrician forces, the rulers found allies, active or passive, among the strata whose interests were opposed to those of the aristocratic groups and who could benefit from weakening the aristocracy and establishing a more unified polity. These allies were, basically, of two kinds. The first were the more active (mostly urban) economic, cultural and professional groups who, by origin or by social interest and orientation, or both, were opposed to the traditional aristocratic groups. The second were the larger, politically and socially more passive strata, including especially peasants and also lower urban groups who could benefit, even if indirectly, by the weakening of the aristocratic forces.

To implement their aims the Emperors attempted to establish a relatively centralized administration and to mobilize the resources needed for the neutralization, weakening or destruction of their enemies.

III

The successful institutionalization of the organizations through which the rulers could realize their aims was thus dependent first on the emergence of political entrepreneurs, the Emperors and their immediate entourage, who had the vision and ability to create new political entities.

Second, it depended on the existence, within the broader society, of certain specific conditions. Briefly, the most important of these conditions was the development, in all major institutional spheres, of a certain level of differentiation, i.e., the development of specific collectivities and roles in the major institutional spheres, such that the activities and resources of large parts of the population were freed from ascriptive (kinship, lineage, aristocratic) commitments and thus could be made available to the rulers.

These different social groups were willing to provide resources and support mostly because they perceived these Emperors as the best available choice among the various existing possibilities (as compared to more traditional aristocratic pretenders or to a state of continuous disorder). They may have identified themselves to various degrees with the goals and symbols of the Emperors; they may have hoped that the Emperors would help them attain some of their own goals, and in maintaining their values, establish norms and organizations to help regulate some of their internal problems, or they may have seen these Emperors as the least evil among the available choices.

To the degree that both sets of conditions developed in a given society, the possibility that a new imperial political system would be institutionalized was relatively great.

These conditions developed, for instance, though in varying degrees, in China from the beginning of the Han dynasty, in Byzantium and the Roman Empire in their formative stages, and in the Caliphates at the initial stages of their development.

In the Greek City States, on the other hand, while the broader social conditions did develop, there arose no group of leaders or entrepreneurs capable of forging a new polity. In other historical cases—e.g., those of Charlemagne or Genghis Khan—such leaders did arise but the broader social conditions were lacking.

IV

But even when such conditions were propitious, and the new political leaders could obtain enough support, such support was of varying quality and intensity.

Several basic attitudes of the major strata toward the premises of the political systems of these Empires and toward the rulers' primary aims can be distinguished. The first attitude, evinced chiefly by the aristocracy, was one of opposition to the premises of the political systems. The second, passivity, was manifested mainly by the peasantry and sometimes also by other groups interested only in maintaining their limited local autonomy and their immediate economic interests.

The third attitude, found mostly in the bureaucracy, in some urban groups and in part of the professional and cultural elite, consisted of basic identification with the premises of the political system and willingness to fight for their interests within the framework of existing political institutions. The fourth attitude, developed mainly by the more differentiated urban groups and by the professional and intellectual elite, favored changes in the scope of the political system.

These attitudes often overlapped in concrete instances, and the attitudes of each group and stratum varied in different societies and periods. Moreover, the attitudes of any one group were never homogeneous and stable, and they could change according to the conditions or the demands made by the rulers. The concrete constellations of these various political attitudes of the major social groups greatly influenced the extent of their political participation.

V

Out of the interaction between these goals of the rulers on the one hand, and the broader social conditions and the varied attitudes of the various social strata on the other, the specific characteristics of these Empires became institutionalized.

Whatever the differences between the aims of various rulers and whatever the attitudes of the various groups, once the major contours of the Empires were institutionalized, various organizations developed within them—mostly through the efforts of the rulers—to implement policies designed to maintain the specific external and internal boundaries of the system, that is, its specific institutional contours and characteristics.

The most important characteristic of these Empires was the coexistence, within the same political institutions, of traditional, undifferentiated political activities, orientations and organizations with more differentiated, specifically *political* goals. Or in more general terms, the autonomy of the political as a distinct institutional sphere was limited. Autonomy of the political sphere was manifest first in the tendency toward political centralization, second, in the development by the rulers of autonomous political goals and third, in the relatively high organizational autonomy of executive and administrative organs and activities.

But the differentiation of political activities, organizations and goals was, in these political systems, limited by several important factors. First, the rulers were usually legitimated in terms of basically traditional-religious values, even where they stressed their own ultimate monopoly of such values. Second, the subject's political role was not fully distinguished from other basic societal roles—such as, for instance, membership in local communities; it was often embedded in local groups, and the citizen or subject did not exercise any direct political rights through a system of voting or franchise. Third, many traditional ascriptive units, such as aristocratic lineages or territorial communities, performed crucial political functions and served as units of political representation. As a consequence, the scope of political activity and participation was far narrower than in most contemporary political systems.

Let us briefly analyze the policies of the rulers. First, they were interested in the limited promotion of free resources and in freeing them from commitments to traditional aristocratic groups. Second, the rulers wished to control these resources, to commit them, as it were, to their own use. Third, they tended to pursue various goals—e.g., military expansion—that could, in themselves, have exhausted many of the available free resources.

Perhaps the most interesting example of these policies is the rulers' attempts to create and maintain an independent free peasantry with smallholdings and to restrict the big landowners' encroachments on these smallholdings, in order to assure both the peasants' independence and the provision of resources to the rulers.

Of special importance too was the establishment of colonies and settlements of peasant soldiers, to make certain that the state would have sufficient military manpower. These colonies were not necessarily state-owned: they were closely associated with more complicated economic measures and policies, like various types of taxation. The policy of establishing such colonies evolved particularly in societies whose problems of frontier defense were of paramount importance. In Byzantium one purpose of the famous system of themes, supposedly evolved by the Emperor Heraclius (A.D. 610-641), was to provide adequate manpower for frontier garrisons. This was achieved by starting colonies of free peasants from which soldiers were involuntarily recruited. A similar pattern was established in the Sassanid Empire by Khousru the Great. The T'ang Emperors of China also organized the peasant militia on similar lines.

VI

But the initial institutionalization of these political systems did not, in itself, assure their continuity. The very process of institutionalizing these Empires created new problems—mainly because maintaining the conditions necessary for these institutions became a more or less continuous concern of the rulers, so that special policies, activities and organizations had to be set up to ensure their perpetuation. Because the rulers had to pursue continuously certain policies oriented against some social groups and in favor of others, the contradictions among their various goals and in the attitudes of various groups to the basic premises of the system were evoked, and the negative orientations of certain groups were intensified. Though not always consciously grasped by the rulers, these contradictions were nevertheless implicit in their structural positions, in the problems and exigencies with which they dealt, and in the concrete policies they employed to solve these problems.

These internal contradictions developed in almost all the major institutional spheres, but perhaps especially in the sphere of legitimation and stratification. As we have seen, the rulers often attempted to limit the aristocracy's power and to create new status groups such as the free peasantry, a non-aristocratic officialdom, and so on. But these attempts faced several obstacles. Regardless of the number of new titles created or of the degree to which new or lower strata were encouraged, the symbols of status used by the rulers were usually very similar to those borne by the landed, hereditary aristocracy or by some religious elites. To create an entirely new secular and "rational" legitimation based on universalistic social principles was either beyond their capacities or against their basic political interest, or both. To do so would necessarily have enlarged the sphere of political participation and consequently increased the influence of various strata in the political institutions. The rulers therefore were usually unable to transcend the symbols of stratification and legitimation represented by the very strata whose influence they wanted to limit.

Thus the ability of the rulers to appeal to the lower strata of the population was obviously limited. Even more important, because of the emphasis on the superiority and worth of aristocratic symbols and values, many middle or new strata and groups tended to identify with them and consequently to "aristocratize" themselves.

Contradictions in the rulers' policies and goals developed in another direction as well. However tradition-bound the ruling elite may have been, its policies required the creation and propagation of more flexible "free" resources in various institutional fields, and the propagation of free resources gave rise to or promoted many religious, intellectual and legal groups whose value orientations differed from the traditional ones. Although in many societies all these groups were weak and succumbed to the influence of more conservative groups, in other cases—as in Europe—they developed into relatively independent centers of power, whose opposition to the rulers was only stimulated by the latter's conservative policies.

Similar contradictions also existed in the military, economic, and cultural spheres. Thus, for example, the growing needs of the Sassanid and Byzantine Empires in the last centuries of their respective Empires, for military manpower and economic resources, caused them to weaken the independent peasantry through mobilization and taxation, and to increase the power of the landed aristocracy. These policies undermined the very bases of their Empires.

VII

But contradictions in the activities of the rulers and in the attitudes of the various strata did not constitute the only important foci of potential change in these political systems. Of no less importance was the possibility that the very organs created to implement the goals and policies of the rulers could develop goals and activities opposed to the basic premises of these political systems. The most important problem of this kind arose from the tendency of members of the bureaucratic administration to develop autonomous political orientations and activities.

First, the power that these bureaucracies acquired in societies in which there were usually but few "constitutional" limits on power and in which access to power was relatively limited, put the members of the bureaucracy in an especially privileged position. Second, the great emphasis, in these societies, on ascriptive symbols of status, necessarily "tempted" the members of the bureaucracy to use their power to acquire such symbols or to convert their positions into ascriptive, often hereditary status symbols. Third, the relatively low level of economic development and social differentiation permitted only limited development of special professional roles and only inadequate remuneration for them. The fact that in most of these societies the sale of offices was a very common expedient fully attests to this.

As a result of these conditions, members of the bureaucracies often tended to distort many of the customary or explicit rules and to divert many services to their own benefit or to that of some social groups with whom they were identified, and they tended to be both alienated from other groups in the society and oppressive toward them. In other words, they displaced the goal of service to the rulers and the various social strata, emphasizing goals of self-interest and aggrandizement instead.

On the other hand, the relative weakness of many political groups, and the great dependence of the bureaucracy on the rulers, often weakened and undermined the relative autonomy of the bureaucracy and brought about its total subjugation to the rulers. The latter could divert all the activities of the bureaucracy to their own exclusive use and prevent it from upholding any general rules for providing services to other strata in the society.

Thus the bureaucratic administration in these societies could, potentially, develop political orientations which were to some extent opposed to the basic premises of these polities and which generated changes that could not be contained within the institutional framework of the polity.

VIII

In these ways the very process of institutionalizing the political systems of these Empires created the possibility of change—change that could be absorbed within the institutional structures as well as change that undermined them.

The concrete reasons for these changes were usually series of events closely related to the various contradictions described above, the impingement of external events (such as wars, invasions, or fluctuations of trade routes), or interaction between internal and external processes.

In more concrete terms, the main factors generating processes of change in these Empires were (a) the continuous needs of the rulers for different types of resources and especially their great dependence on various "flexible" resources; (b) the rulers' attempts to maintain their own positions of control, in terms of both traditional legitimation and effective political control over the more flexible forces in the society; (c) the development in most of these societies, of what has been called *Primat der Aussenpolitik* and the consequent great sensitivity of the internal structure of these societies to various external pressures and to international political and economic developments; (d) the development of various autonomous orientations and goals among the major strata and their respective demands on the rulers. These changes were more intensive so far as the rulers emphasized very "expensive" goals that exhausted the available economic and manpower resources, or different strata developed strong, autonomous political orientations.

In such situations, the rulers' tendency to maintain strong control over the more differentiated strata could become predominant, thus increasing the power of traditional forces and orientations and sharpening the conflicts between the traditional and the more flexible, differentiated strata, so that the latter were destroyed or alienated from the rulers. The excessive demands of the rulers in such situations, the growing public expenditures and the consequent increase of taxation and inflation, if not checked, often struck hardest at those groups whose economic organization was based on more flexible resources.

At such times, a continuous flux of foreign elements—mercenaries, hirelings and personal helpers of the rulers—often invaded the centers of the realms. With the depletion of the native strata and the growing external and internal exigencies, they succeeded in infiltrating some of the most important political posts (such as those of eunuchs, military commandments and viziers) and finally in totally usurping the ultimate power. Foreign merchants sometimes played a similar role, as in Byzantium or the Ottoman Empire, where they gradually succeeded in monopolizing all the tradeposts abandoned by the depleted indigenous merchants.

Where, as in Europe, these economically and socially more active strata were not depleted, they became alienated from the rulers, their policies and the political institutions of the society, becoming hotbeds of revolt and change.

Such developments usually intensified the great sensitivity of the rulers and the society to various external economic and political changes (in trade routes or in international price movements, or through the intrusion of foreign elements). Usually, some combination of external and internal pressures and exigencies precipitated changes in the political systems of these Empires. Hence, the greater the intensity of these internal contradictions and the greater the pressure of external exigencies that could not be dealt with by internal forces, the more quickly changes accumulated in these societies.

IX

Some salient features of these changes were: First, interaction between internal and external events was greatly dependent on the special systemic characteristics of these political systems. While naturally enough many external events, such as invasions, were entirely beyond the control of any given Empire, each polity constituted part of a relatively "international" environment. Because of its basically expansionist goals and its great dependence on free economic resources, each Empire was especially sensitive to various specific developments in its broader environment. Moreover, external events and influences could very easily become closely interwoven with many of the internal problems of these Empires.

Second, while some such exigencies and problems are common to all political systems, their *specific* nature depends on the structure of the institutional system. Thus, the special sensitivity of the centralized bureaucratic Empires to such exigencies and pressures and to international economic fluctuations was rooted first, in their rulers' great emphasis on military and expansionist goals and second, in their need for various "free" resources, the availability of which depended on the international economic situation.

Similarly, while all political systems are influenced by and dependent on the efficiency and political loyalty of their administrative personnel, these Empires were especially sensitive to the possibility that the bureaucracy might become "aristocratized," "parasitic," and inflated. This sensitivity was due first to the fact that the bureaucracy was the ruler's main instrument for implementing his goals and overcoming his political opponents, and second, to the constant danger that the free resources so necessary for the implementation of his goals might be depleted by the encroachments of various aristocratic or traditional groups and by the aristocratic tendencies of the bureaucracy.

These specific sensitivities also determined the location of the foci from which the impetus to change developed. Such foci tended to develop, in these political systems, mainly though certainly not only, in two basic spheres. One was that of economic and social organization. The level of differentiation of this sphere and the nature of its internal, autonomous organization was crucial to the development of different levels of resources on the one hand and different levels of political demand on the other.

The other sphere was that of values, or "culture." This sphere encompassed the legitimation of the system and of the ruler and, because the active cultural elites regulated many aspects of communication in the society, it greatly influenced the level of demands made on the central political institutions. While in many cases cultural values kept the level of such demands within the confines of the system, in other cases, as in the Islamic or European countries, values became a very important focus of charismatic innovations that might easily have undermined the existing system and created entirely new perceptions of the political sphere among many social groups.

Both economic organization and special cultural values strongly influenced the specific sensibilities of these systems and the generation of change within them. And when the two developed simultaneously, in the direction of either increasing or diminishing differentiation, their impact on the destiny of these political systems was of crucial importance.

Finally, the directions of change and the outcomes of the processes of change were to a very large extent set by the nature of the institutional systems of these Empires and by their internal problems. The range of political systems that arose on the ruins, as it were, of these Empires was relatively limited. Short of total disorganization, they could either "recede" into some type of relatively uncentralized patrimonial or feudal system (but not, for instance, into a city-state or a primitive system) or become a relatively more differentiated oligarchic modern system (but not a mass democracy or a "canton-democracy").

X

The preceding analysis has drawn on illustrations only from the political sphere. But the same problems of institutionalization are found in any other major social sphere. We shall briefly illustrate this by analyzing the problems of institutionalization of religions and religious organizations in the Empires analyzed above.

The religions that developed within the confines of these Empires were among the major world religious systems: the Mazdean religion in Iran, Confucianism, Taoism and Buddhism in China and India, Islam, Eastern Christianity in Byzantium, Catholicism in Europe and Spanish America and, later in Europe, Protestantism. These religions were usually developed through the activities of great religious innovators—either outstanding individuals or small groups of intense religious devotees—who attempted to create new cults and doctrines, and to spread and establish them in their respective societies.

Despite the great variety among these religions, they share important characteristics in some aspects of their value orientations, especially in their orientations to social reality.

The first such aspect is the breadth of the "group referent" of these religions; in most cases it was wider than any ascriptive or territorial group in these Empires. The basic religious group referents were the total society as the bearer of religious values, the specific religious community, and such wider potential religious collectivities as "all believers" or "all mankind."

The second major characteristic of these religious value orientations is their emphasis on individual moral or religious activism, stressing the devotee's commitment to certain religiously prescribed tenets and lines of action and to the endeavor to implement them in social life.

Third, each of these value systems developed relatively independent ideological systems, attempting to organize and evaluate, in terms of ultimate values, the social reality in which they grew up, to shape the world in terms of religious values and purposes, and to convert others to the same endeavor. The commitments imposed by these ideological systems were not simply embedded in ritual and religious acts but implied the development of more specific social or political activities.

All of these orientations denote the detachment of religious orientations from basic ascriptive symbols and communities. They were developed mainly in the centers of religious activity by the more active religious leaders and innovators. Among the broader strata the differentiation of religious activities and organizations was much more limited. Nevertheless these orientations did develop to some extent, constituting the basis for the potential willingness of these groups to join the new religions and for the possibility of their institutionalization.

From the interaction of the major religious orientations with the religious leaders' concrete goals and with the broader social and religious conditions prevalent in the society, as well as from the more specific relations with the rulers and other groups, developed the specific institutional characteristics of these religions, their organization into churches, orders and sects or the more diffuse organizational patterns characteristic of China.

But in all these Empires, the distinctiveness of the religious sphere was limited. On the one hand, there were many specialized religious organizations, such as temples, religious "foundations," priestly associations, sects, churches, and monastic orders, many of which were organized in a bureaucratic manner, and, in conjunction with these, many specialized religious roles—priests, preachers, monks, and occupants of different positions in ecclesiastical organizations and hierarchies. On the other hand, however, the worshipping community was, to a very large extent, either identical with local groups or closely related to them. Only within the various sects and monastic orders did a special type of religious community develop.

Neither the institutionalization nor the continuity of these religious systems was assured. The religious leaders who aimed to establish and institutionalize them within their respective societies faced several basic problems. The most general problem stemmed from the existence of relatively free-floating cultural and religious orientations and activities which were not embedded in ascriptive units. To maintain their place in the cultural order, religious organizations had to shape and direct these resources. They not only had to ensure the loyalty and adherence of their members, but they also had to compete for economic resources, manpower, allegiance and support, both with other religious groups and with other social spheres, especially the political and economic ones.

Thus, the leaders of these religions were faced with the internal problems of formulating and formalizing their creeds and traditions so as to articulate and organize them on a relatively differentiated cultural level, and also with the necessity of regulating and channelling the diverse dynamic orientations and elements that could develop within them.

In connection with these internal problems several policies and patterns of activity were developed by the religious elites and organizations in these societies. Perhaps the most important of these was the very extensive formalization and codification of religious traditions, as manifested in the codification of sacred books, in the development of schools devoted to interpretation of the texts, in the growth of special educational organizations for the spread of religious knowledge and in the elaboration of comprehensive ideologies.

The religious leaders also faced more concrete organizational and external problems. Because they depended, in all their endeavors, on both the rulers and the broader strata in the society, they developed several basic aims. The first was to gain full official recognition and protection from the State as the established religion or, at least as a secondary but recognized and protected one. The second aim was to maintain independence and autonomy in the performance of the major religious functions, especially in internal government, organization of activities, and recruitment of members. This meant relative autonomy in the propagation of the creed and the maintenance of shrines, temples, and educational institutions, as well as independent determination and transmission of the major religious values and dogma. The demands for autonomy were directed mainly against the rulers and the bureaucracy who, as we have seen earlier, usually aspired to control the activities of the religious elite and to incorporate them into the general framework of their administrative activities.

The third major political objective of the religious elite, closely related to the first, was to preserve and extend the material bases (i.e., property) of the religious groups and institutions and to enhance their general social positions. A fourth objective, at least for some members of the religious elite, was to obtain positions of political and administrative influence.

XI

Whatever the success of the religious leaders in achieving these aims, the very institutionalization of these religions within the framework of their respective societies and polities could create continuous tension and give rise to several new problems.

The religious organizations needed the protection and help of the political institutions to establish and maintain their positions, organizations, and property, just as the political institutions needed the basic legitimation and support that could be provided only by the religious elite. This mutual dependence of relatively autonomous spheres could easily create many tensions, since each aimed to control the structural positions of the other and thus provide for its own needs. But whatever the scope of such conflicts and tensions, some *modus vivendi* was usually established, constituting a basic aspect of the institutionalization of these religions.

Thus in all of the societies studied, the religious elite upheld both the traditional legitimation of the rulers and supported, in principle, at least some of their political orientations and policies, despite the numerous conflicts over concrete issues arising between themselves and the political elite. Moreover, in most of the societies studied, the political participation of religious groups was, at least for certain periods of time, contained well within the basic framework of bureaucratic policy and institutions. In such cases these groups furthered the development of legitimate political struggle and contributed in this way to the continuity of the regime. The Mazdean Church in Persia, the Byzantine Church, and especially the Confucians and Buddhists in the Chinese Empire actively participated in politics and cooperated with the rulers. Thus they contributed, directly or indirectly, to the continuity of these systems. At the same time, the State provided important protection for the religious organizaions.

But whatever the concrete *modus vivendi* between the rulers and any given religious elite or organization, in almost none of these societies—with the partial exception of Confucianism in China—did such mutual accommodation persist throughout the life of the Empire or of the religious organizations.

The very institutionalization of any such *modus vivendi* created the possibility for change both within the religions themselves and in their relations with other institutional spheres. The process of institutionalizing these religions and the necessity for continuous maintenance through varied policies and accommodations could easily enhance the contradictions inherent in the orientations of the religious leaders.

These contradictions were of several, often overlapping, kinds. One was between a "conservative" orientation that accepted the existing social order and the place of religion within it, on the one hand, and, on the other hand, a more radical orientation aiming to extend the autonomy of religious orientations and activities. Another was between an "other-worldly" emphasis stressing the perfection of purely religious attitudes and activities, and a more active, this-worldly orientation aiming at the transformation of the world.

Such contradictions were rooted in the relative autonomy and independent historical origins of the religious sphere, in its continuous interaction with the political sphere and in the nature of its value orientations. All these characteristics could serve as foci of crystallization for new religious groups—sects, groups of devotees, or "free-lance" religious intellectuals upholding one or another of these orientations in its purity as against the more "compromise-ridden" activities of the established religious leaders and organizations. The religious elites, in the course of working out and implementing their various *modi vivendi* with the rulers, and in attempting to maintain their own interests, tended to alienate some of the religiously active elements as well as some of the broader strata.

Moreover, the relatively complex organizations of these religions, and the great importance of a formal written tradition and its exegesis, were fertile ground for the rise of various sectarian movements and orders. The possibility of sectarian development was also enhanced by the fact that in many of these societies several religious bodies and organizations competed with one another for predominance.

Hence within all these religions there developed many processes of change, which created new forms of religious organization. Some of these could be contained within the established religious framework, while others completely undermined it.

The same factors frequently also predisposed some of the religious groups and elites to develop more extreme political orientations and to participate—as in China, Persia, or Byzantium—in radical political and social movements, such as peasant uprisings, urban movements, and conspiracies. Co-operation between popular movements and leaders of religious secret societies was a common characteristic of rebellions in China and to some extent Byzantium and of peasant uprisings in France.

In still other cases—or in the same societies under changing circumstances—these religious organizations could also influence processes of change in the political system by instigating or furthering the withdrawal of active social and political support from the ruling elites. In this way they undermined the political frameworks of the Empires and indirectly also the bases of the *modus vivendi* between political and religious institutions.

The exact strength and direction of these processes of change depended greatly on the basic value orientations and institutional characteristics of the religions and on the nature of their struggles and accommodations with the rulers and other centers of power in the society.

But the direction of these changes was not random, nor were these changes limitless. Organizationally, religious institutions could either undergo what might be called the "ossification" and "indrawing" of existing churches, as in the case of the Eastern Church after the fall of the Byzantine Empire, or, through the development of various sects and more independent religious activities, be transformed into less homogeneous and monolithic, more differentiated structures, as was the case in Western Christianity, especially in Protestantism, and to a lesser extent in early and "middle" Islam.

The effect of these changes on religious orientations is either to enhance the tendency towards "other-worldliness," social passivity, withdrawal and mysticism, or to encourage more active and differentiated this-worldly activity.

XII

The preceding analysis of the processes of change in the centralized Empires and in the major religions that developed within them is intended to illustrate the ways in which the institutionalization of a political, a religious, or any other social system in itself creates the potentialities and directions of change.

The institutionalization of any social system means that certain norms, sanctions and organizations must be set up, and that policies through which these norms can be upheld and applied to a relatively large and complex variety of social situations must be implemented. These things are done by people who are placed in or attempt to achieve strategic positions and who aspire to certain goals. The new norms regulate the provision of various resources from other parts of the society to these power positions and to the new organizations, some of the relations among the different groups in the society, and the obligations of the occupants of these positions toward various groups in the society.

While the occupants of these positions naturally attempt to set up norms in accord with their own values, goals and interests, they also define certain norms shared by a number of groups. Very often they legitimize these norms by values that are purportedly shared, to some extent, by a large part of the society and symbolized by themselves. Hence, such values tend to be binding on the rulers themselves.

But whatever the success of such attempts to establish common norms and legitimize them in terms of common values and symbols, these norms are probably never fully accepted by the entire society. Most groups within any society or collectivity tend to exhibit some autonomy in terms of their attitudes toward any such institutionalization, and they vary greatly in the extent of their willingness or ability to provide the resources demanded by the system. While for very long periods of time a great majority of the members of a given society may be to some degree identified with the values and norms of the system and willing to provide it with the resources it needs, other tendencies also develop. Some groups—like the aristocracy in the case of the Empires discussed above—may be greatly opposed to the very premises of the institutionalization of a given system, may share its values only to a very small extent, and may accept these norms only as the least among evils and as binding on them only in a very limited sense.

Others may share these values and accept the norms to a greater degree but, like the cultural and economic elites or sects, may look on themselves as the more appropriate repositories of these same values, may oppose the concrete level at which the norms are institutionalized by the elite in power, and may attempt to interpret them in different ways. Others again may develop new interpretations of existing values and strive for a change in the very bases of the institutional order. Hence any institutional system is never fully "homogeneous," that is, fully accepted or accepted to the same degree by all those participating in it, and these different orientations all may become foci of conflict and of potential institutional change.

Even more important, from the point of view of our analysis, is that whatever the initial attitudes of any given group to the basic premises of the institutional system, these may greatly change after the initial institutionalization of the system. Any institutionalization necessarily entails efforts to maintain the boundaries of the system, through continuous attempts to mobilize resources from different groups and individuals, and to maintain the legitimacy of the values, symbols and norms of the system. But continuous implementation of these policies may affect the positions of different groups in the society, giving rise to continuous shifts in the balance of power among them and in their orientations to the existing institutional system and its values.

Moreover, the institutionalization of any system usually creates new collectivities and organizations, such as the bureaucratic organizations in the centralized Empires. These organizations necessarily develop needs, interests, and orientations of their own which may impinge on various other groups and institutional spheres.

Similarly, changes in the balance of forces within the system also facilitate the development and "maturation" of certain inherent tendencies in the structure and orientation of key groups and elites, as in the tendencies of some religious groups to develop and establish wider universalistic orientations and membership units, which may then develop beyond the basic premises of the system.

These processes may be intensified by the systematic relations between any given institutional framework or sphere and other spheres within the society. Whatever the degree of integration of the "total" society, systemic relations between, e.g., the political and the economic, or the political and the kinship systems, are inherent in any ongoing society. But as has been so often pointed out, the basic or predominant orientations and norms regulating each of these institutions differ to some extent. For example, family and kinship units tend to emphasize particularistic, diffuse, and ascriptive orientations while economic units emphasize universalism and achievement.

These different institutional spheres, represented by the structurally patterned activities of occupants of the major positions within them, attempt to maintain their autonomy and tend to make contradictory demands on different groups to provide them with the necessary resources. Each may look for support from different groups in the society, thus exacerbating potential conflicts among the various groups, changing their relative strengths and possibly undermining the premises of a given institutional system.

These contradictions, conflicts and shifts in the balance of power may lead to the depletion of the resources needed to maintain a given system or give rise to the crystallization of new foci of resources and orientations which may in turn seek to create a new institutional system.

Events leading to different processes of change, as has been pointed out before, also affect the relations between any given institutional system and its external environment. Each institutional system is especially sensitive, in terms of dependence on resources and maintenance of its own boundaries, to certain aspects of its relations with its environment.

XIII

Thus we conclude that the institutionalization of a system creates the possibility that "anti-systems," or groups with negative orientations toward its premises, will develop within it. While the nature and strength of such anti-systems may vary, as between different institutional (i.e., religious, political) systems and between different types within each, and while they may often remain latent for very long periods of time, they also constitute important foci of change, under propitious conditions.

The existence of such contradictions or conflicts among the different institutional spheres and among different groups does not, of course, preclude the possibility that the system will maintain its boundaries more or less continuously, through a hierarchy of norms and accommodation or partial insulation of different subsystems, and that a definite order and stable relations among the system's parts will persist. But the possibility of conflict and potential change is always present, rooted in the very process of institutionalization, and the direction and occurrence of change depend heavily on the nature of this process.

Just as the predilection for change is necessarily built into any institutional system, so the direction and scope of change are not random but depend, as we have shown in discussing the processes of change in the Empires and in the great religions, on the nature of the system generating the change, on its values, norms and organizations, on the various internal forces operating within it and on the external forces to which it is especially sensitive because of its systemic properties. These various forces naturally differ between religious and political institutions and among different societies, but sensitivity to these forces and the tendency to change are inherent in all of them.

The analysis presented above does not pretend to solve all the problems in analyzing social change; we have not discussed the mechanisms of change, nor the relations between changes at different institutional levels of a given society. But at least we have indicated that for conceptual tools adequate to the analysis of change we need not necessarily go beyond systematic sociological analysis; rather, a full explication of systematic sociological concepts can provide a fruitful initial step for the analysis of change.

FURTHER READINGS

Feibleman, James K. *The Institutions of Society*. London: George Allen & Unwin, 1956.

MacIver, Robert M. and Page, Charles H. *Society*. New York: Holt, Rinehart, and Winston, 1949.

Merton, Robert K., *Social Theory and Social Structure*. New York: The Free Press, 1957. Rev.

Williams, Robin M., Jr. *American Society*, 2nd ed., New York: Alfred A. Knopf, 1960.

9

URBANIZATION AND
SOCIAL CHANGE

Introduction

THREE MAJOR PROCESSES are central to the societal revolutions which have been transforming the nature of group life the world over: urbanization, bureaucratization, and industrialization. To suggest that one of these processes preceded and is thus causal in the emergence of another is to obscure the fact that they have at times grown at uneven rates, sometimes simultaneously, but, probably, never independently.

In discussing phenomena associated with urban processes it is well to keep in mind the distinction between *urbanism*, which refers to the life-ways of city dwellers, and *urbanization*, which is related to the process by which the urban patterns are diffused to previously non-urban areas. In contemporary American society urbanization is often synonymous with the process of the spread of mass culture, dealt with in Chapter 12.

The paper by Raymond Mack and Dennis McElrath deals with urbanization in relation to three dimensions of urban differentiation: occupational; ethnic, and migrant; and life-style. Not only does it provide an overview of factors influencing urban behavior but it has implications for our concern over homogenization of tastes and general behavior patterns dealt with in our discussions of deviance and conformity in Chapter 7, and mass society and mass culture in Chapter 12.

Kenneth Little's oft cited essay on an interesting aspect of urbanization in West Africa is very descriptive and concrete. It gives us a glimpse of total societal transformation in the process of analyzing the functions of a type of group structure, the association. The description of what occurs in West African cities is reminiscent of similar phenomena in the United States during the periods of mass immigration preceding World War I. From similarities to the early *Landsmanschaften* to ethnically dominated unions the affinities are remarkable.

An interesting aspect of the transformation of behavior patterns under urbanization is the impact it has on highly specialized institutional systems. S. Kirson Weinberg's insightful description and analysis of the changing occupational culture of mental healers provides us with a picture of a non-Western type of psychiatric role. It also gives us a glimpse into the activity of the social psychiatry branch of medical sociology, a new but increasingly important area of sociological research.

Urbanization and Differentiation

RAYMOND W. MACK and DENNIS C. McELRATH

URBANIZATION IS THE DEVELOPMENT of a social and spatial organization within which both the valued and the deplored products of a complex and elaborate society are allocated. The urban mode of distribution has been built upon a folk, peasant, feudal, and industrializing past. These backgrounds influence the present state of urbanization and the system of distribution in contemporary societies throughout the world. They are the foundation upon which this process of urbanization has developed.

URBANIZATION

Is it possible to look at this process in broad enough terms to specify its impact on the distribution of choice and constraint; of ideas and products wherever it occurs? We believe so: to do this we shall first sketch the process of urbanization and then link it to its corresponding mode of distribution.

SCALE

Urbanization involves the transformation of a total society. Only in the past century and a half has the world approached truly urban *societies*, in which a high proportion of the total population live in cities. As recently as 1800, only 2.4 percent of the world's population lived in cities of 20,000 or more; today over one-fifth of the people live in such cities. Furthermore, the proportion of people living in large cities has risen even more dramati-

From "Urban Social Differentiation and the Allocation of Resources," *The Annals of the American Academy of Political and Social Science,* 358, 1964, pp. 26-32. Reprinted by permission of the publisher and authors.

cally. By 1950 the proportion of people in the world living in cities was higher than that in even the most urbanized country before modern times.

Between 1800 and 1850, the total population of the world increased only 29 percent, but the population living in cities of 5,000 or more grew by 175 percent, that in cities of 20,000 or more by 132 percent, and the population in cities of 100,000 or more increased by 76 percent. Then, from 1850 to 1900, the impact of scientific technology began to be felt in rapid industrialization. During this period, the total population of the world increased by 37 percent. But, in this span of time, cities of 5,000 or more increased by 192 percent, those of 20,000 or more by 194 percent, and those of 100,000 or more by 222 percent. During the next half century, from 1900 to 1950, cities expanded at an even more accelerated rate. While the population of the world increased by 49 percent, the three size categories of urban population grew, respectively, 228, 240, and 254 percent.

If this trend continues at its present rate, more than a fourth of the world's people will be living in cities of 100,000 or more by the year 2000, and more than half by 2050. If the present rate of urbanization continues to the year 2050, over 90 percent of the world's people will live in cities of 20,000 or more.

Today, we have whole societies which can be called "urbanized." Over four-fifths of the people in England live in urban places; nearly 40 percent of them live in cities of over 100,000. In societies such as our own, with radio, television, rapid transportation, and an industrial distribution system, what is a fad on Manhattan Island today is a fad in Manhattan, Kansas tomorrow.

Even if the present rate of urbanization should slow, the prospect is that the future will see an ever-increasing proportion of the world's people living in urbanized societies.

The most obvious change associated with urbanization is the development of a far-reaching network of interdependent activities. This network usually proceeds from the loose linking of peasant villagers to the city through tangential interdependence with urban commercial, religious, political, or military centers to the almost complete interdependence of an urbanized world. This change in the scale of society obviously affects the ways in which the products of civilization are allocated. For example, most of the world's population lives in little communities on the fringes of urban society where interdependence with distant urban centers is slight and limited in scope. Redfield has noted the special place of "hinge people" in these communities. These representatives of limited areas of interdependence—the schoolteacher, the village priest, the merchant-traders, or the representatives of distant political and military authority—have special access to the benefits of urban civilization. They act as filters or transmitters in the system of allocation centered in the city. Their power derives from limited interdependence between village and city. Their role is important today and likely to become increasingly so as interdependence increases.

This description of the process of urbanization leans heavily on the aggregation of people in cities. This aggregation is one important sociological change which defines the process of urbanization. But, in addition to this increase in scale, urbanization is characterized by the accretion of control and co-ordination activities in cities and by the development of a network of urban centers.

CO-ORDINATION AND CONTROL

Urbanization involves locating co-ordination and control functions in cities. Wide-ranging activities are originated in, funneled through, or transformed by the urban posts of command and co-ordination. This centralizing function is evidenced by the presence in all modern cities of a substantial tertiary labor force. It is a truism that the city is the home of workers whose major functions involve co-ordinating and controlling wide-ranging economic, political, military, and religious activities.

The urban mode of distribution, thus, always places the city dweller at the hub of the distribution system. Through his hands and mind pass the products of an urban society. His access to these products is built into a society where cities are the accumulators and distributors of the products of civilization.

NETWORK OF URBAN SITES

Finally, the process of urbanization involves the development of a system of urban sites, a network of cities which jointly house a myriad of urban activities. This system varies widely in contemporary societies. Students have attempted to describe it in such terms as: primacy and a hierarchy of cities; functional specialization of cities; regional networks of dominant and subdominant centers; sheer relative aggregation of the population; cities vis-à-vis their hinterlands or vis-à-vis a peasant foreland. Clearly, this variety is crucial to the way in which the products of civilization are distributed. If, for example, a society contains a single, multifunctioned primary city with all other centers being much smaller, one would expect the flow of products and access to this flow to be quite different from those in societies with a lower level of primacy or a flattened hierarchy of cities. In the high primacy situation, the flow of ideas, beliefs, and products of civilization would be highly centralized in every institutional area. Control personnel and initiators of action within the major institutional arenas might well overlap. How different this is from the society where religious centers are separate from the economic and these from the political seats of power! Here, in a society with several large and specialized cities, one is likely to find centralization within each institutional area, but little overlapping and substantial insulation.

Increasing scale, centralizing control and co-ordination, and developing a network of urban sites—these describe the process of urbanization.

Any society may be situated at a given scale, with a certain degree of co-ordination and control, and characterized by a particular system of urban locations. Each of these facets of the urbanization of that society influences the way in which products are, or could be, allocated.

DIFFERENTIATION AND ALLOCATION

The pattern of distribution which emerges in societies with relatively advanced levels of urbanization is characterized by three broad systems of distribution and deprivation: (1) occupational differentiation, (2) ethnic and migrant differentiation, and (3) life style or familial differentiation.

OCCUPATIONAL DIFFERENTIATION AND CLASS ACCESS

Until the past couple of centuries, there has been relatively little differentiation of the labor force beyond that based on age and sex. Only within the last 200 years, with the technological applications of the discoveries of scientists, have societies existed in which a large proportion of the population learned occupational roles differentiated from one another on other grounds.

Other consequences of the growth of science and technology are elaborate occupational specialization and an increase in the content of culture. Bushmen do not have much more to transmit than one Bushman can know. Americans have so much more shared, learned behavior to transmit than one American could know that the task of organizing a program of general education becomes staggering.

A complex division of labor through a whole society leads to what some sociologists have called "situses"—sets of related occupational specialties arranged hierarchically parallel to and separate from other sets of related roles, which also are arranged in hierarchies. Each situs, or family of related occupations, builds up a set of norms peculiar to it. These occupational subcultures insulate their participants from the members of another situs. Doctors and nurses hold values not shared by railroaders and truck drivers; the occupational norms of the longshoreman are not those of the laboratory worker.

Occupational specialization contributes a good share to what we call the impersonality of urban life. People in urban-industrial societies have segmentalized roles. One may be an assembly-line worker, a Methodist, a Grand Vizier at the lodge, a father, a member of the bowling team. No one of these bears the same necessary relationship to another that the roles filled by a tribesman in an unspecialized society do. In a society which has not felt the impact of technology, one need only know a man's clan membership to predict his occupation, his religion, his educational attainment. Among the segmentalized roles which a man plays in an urban-industrial society, occupation is crucial. It is more specialized than most of his roles; he has an enormous investment in it. An adult male in our labor force spends more of his waking hours at work than at home; his work is likely to be a powerful factor in shaping his view of the world.

Societies with elaborate occupational differentiation, therefore, while bound together by a common culture, are at the same time fragmented by occupational subcultures. People who share an occupational history develop norms, enforce an in-group ideology, and come to serve as a reference group for each other. We see this at its extreme when physicists from the Soviet Union and from the United States have more to talk about with each other than either group has with the farmers from its own country.

But let us remember that role segmentalization is not synonymous with a fragmented social structure. The stuff of occupational subcultures can serve as the specialized urban-industrial worker's social substitute for community. Occupational codes can contribute to what Durkheim called organic solidarity; they can help replace the mechanical solidarity of the rural village. Occupational groups, with their shared values, can contribute to the sense of purpose which formerly was a function of the small community.

Various occupations, incomes, and amounts of education lead people to share different norms and to behave differently. In other words, the existence of a class structure leads to the development of class subcultures. And, in time, the subcultures themselves become criteria of placement in the class structure. Not just one's income but the way he spends it, not just his occupational status but his attitude toward it—these become factors partially determining his class status.

The evidence of differences in access to and enjoyment of the products of civilization includes variations by class in family pattern, religious participation, and many other culture patterns. People in the lowest income strata spend nearly three-fourths of their total income for food, while those in the higher strata spend less than one-fourth of their income for food. Obviously, this leaves lower-class families with not only less money but a lower proportion of their total incomes available for education and other expenditures which might improve their class position. The smaller amount of money available for purposes other than groceries is reflected in the fact that a sample of lower-class people exceeded those in wealthier classes both in symptoms of illness and in the proportion of those symptoms which were not being treated by a physician. Lack of money is likely to be only one of the factors accounting for this situation; lower education levels would make it less likely that the lower-income classes would be aware of the need for treatment of some symptoms.

The basic variables of class structure reinforce each other through the medium of life chances. People who have high incomes and college educations are more likely than those who do not to be able to afford to send their children to college.

A person's occupation, with its concomitant income, education, and class status, affects greatly the likelihood that certain things will happen to him. An individual's position in the class structure alters everything from the chance to stay alive during the first year after birth to the chance to view fine art, the chance to remain healthy and grow tall, and, if sick, to get well again quickly, the chance to avoid becoming a juvenile delinquent—and, very crucially, the chance to complete an intermediary or higher educational grade. It is easy to dismiss many factors which are really life chances with the notion that the individual controls his own destiny: the statement, for instance, that class status influences one's chances to view fine art can be brushed aside with the retort that museums are free and that, if a person does not take advantage of them, it is his own fault. Such an attitude fails to take into account the power of subculture. A child reared in a slum area who does not even know about the existence of museums or who has been social-ized to believe that painting is for "sissies" has different chances for art ex-perience than one brought up in a wealthy home and taught that all respectable people know something about art.

The significance of class consciousness for social mobility lies in the fact that attitudes and values have consequences in behavior patterns. If one believes he can be mobile, he will try to be. One's level of aspiration depends on what he has been taught to believe about his present status and the changes and desirability of altering it. Research has shown that manual workers are aware that most of them are not going to rise to managerial posi-tions and that, reconciled to the status in which they find themselves, they do not plan upward mobility for themselves but project their ambitions onto their children. But we also know that the ones most likely to be upwardly mobile are those who actively seek to achieve upward mobility. This being so, there is an element of the self-fulfilling prophecy in vertical mobility.

Thus, just as race can become an ascribed status through the social definition imposed by the culture, so can class subcultures make education and occupation, and hence income, tend to be ascribed.

Access to the products of civilization in an urban society is structured, then, largely by class position, and, for many, this position is likely to persist for generations. Underlying this system is occupational differentiation built upon the requirements of large-scale enterprise which has become the domi-nant pattern in each institutional area. Big government, big military, big business, big church, big medicine and welfare are the *leit motif* of a society characterized by wide-ranging interdependence and centralized co-ordina-tion and control housed in a web of urban locations. As other societies move toward this kind of social organization and as peripheral societies become enmeshed in it, they, too, may be expected to generate similar patterns of occupational differentiation and a corresponding way of distributing the social products.

ETHNIC AND MIGRANT DIFFERENTIATIONS

Building an urban society requires a massive movement of peoples; the process of urbanization involves a redistribution of the population in space. Since urban fertility rates are never as high as those in the hinter-land, a growing *proportion* of the total population can be settled in cities only by a net migration balance from rural to urban areas. Further, as the scale of society increases, the concentration of population as well as other resources brings people into cities from an ever-widening geographic base. This means that the cities of large-scale societies not only are composed of a substantial proportion of migrants but of migrants from widely dispersed origins. Thus, both the *rate* and *level* of urbanization are reflected in the ethnic composition of city populations. Rates of urbanization affect the relative volume of migration, and levels are reflected in the dispersion of origins of migrants.

At a given rate and level of urbanization, cities are composed of a proportion of migrants from a particular web of recruitment bases. This compositional change, when compounded with the selective character of migration, provides a basis for ethnic and migrant differentiation in every urban society: the establishment of a socially defined ethnic and migrant pecking order.

Excellent studies of the "newcomers" have been carried out in New York, Yankee City, London, and from Durban to Dallas. They all point to differential allocation patterned along the dimensions of ethnicity and migrancy.

The fastest *rates* of urbanization now are occurring in societies with relatively low *levels* of urbanization. Under this condition, the cities of these developing nations will be composed of a high proportion of migrants, but these migrants are likely to be recruited from a fairly narrow hinterland. *Migrant* differentiation is important in these areas today. As they increase in scale and widen their recruitment base, *ethnic* differentiation is likely to become more important to the distribution of life chances. More advanced societies, on the other hand, with existing high levels of urbanization, are now experiencing declining rates of urbanization. Here, ethnic differences are likely to persist for some time while migrancy declines as a basis for differentiation and allocation.

LIFE-STYLE DIFFERENTIATION

A third dimension along which variation in access to facilities and rewards occurs is emergent in the urban sectors of advanced societies. This dimension appeared first among fairly wealthy city dwellers. It is a variation in style of life which we often associate with suburban growth and the development of familistic orientation. Recent urban developments, including advances in transportation technology, decentralized production location, opportunities for women to work outside the household, and a widening array of housing opportunities, permit variations in life style. By now, in most American cities, all except the central-city ethnics and recent migrants have generally become distributed along a life-style continuum. At one end of this continuum lie the fertile, familistic plains of suburbia. At the other are the more centrally located, small family or aged apartment dwellers oriented to career or consumption.

Access to the benefits of advanced societies is distributed along this continuum as well. Benefits available to the familistic consumer are in some instances constrained and in other cases widened by the demands of his orientation and location. Opportunities for neighboring, local acquaintances and local area participation may be high. He may find a limited but intense local community. He has access to the patio or rumpus-room culture and the creative pursuits of a garage or basement workshop. For him, the benefits of civilization are likely to revolve around family, school, and the local area.

Much of this is not available to the career- and consumption-oriented urbanite, but just beyond his elevator lie all the resources of the old central city. All the variety, liveliness, and sophistication of modern society are stored at this stoop, and much of it available in a stroll or a short commute. These products are available not only because of location but also as a consequence of the way in which he may allocate his scarce time, resources, and social capital. He has neither the choices nor the constraints of familism.

Increasing concern has been expressed about the durability of this variation. In recent years, thoughtful critics have suggested that rampant familism and the apparent popular association of it with suburban location may lead to the destruction of the advantages of central-city urban life style. Jane Jacobs, for example, has deplored the systematic destruction of urban liveliness. Others have questioned the ability of the institutions in the core city to survive in the midst of growing sprawl.

The evidence seems to support the optimists, however. Variation in life style can and does persist even in the most sprawling metropolitan areas. Marked variations in orientation and consumption have been observed even within the white middle class in Los Angeles.

A close look at these newer cities and the fringes of the old preautomobile cities suggests that several changes are likely to occur in the near future. The first is that life style will become less bound to a locality. Familism can and probably will return to the central area, and urbanism may spread to the suburbs and exurbs. At the same time, many of the advantages of the old urban core will be made more available to a diffused populace. This view does not deny the fact that the central city is likely to contain self-imposed ghettos of lively urbanites for some time nor deny that the suburbs will generally hold the familistically oriented community. Rather, we suggest that the differences will be less dramatic and that a much finer gradation will occur along the life-style continuum.

CONCLUSION'

Our thesis has been that the process of urbanization arrays a populace along three major dimensions. Most of the cultural resources of an urban society are allocated via occupational, ethnic and migrant, and life-style differentiation. These three dimensions of differentiation develop and become effective at different points in the urbanization process. The occurrence of and persistence of ethnic and migrant differentiation apparently are contingent upon the rate and level of urbanization. Life-style differentiation appears to develop fairly late in this process of urbanization, while occupational differentiation arises quite early in the process and persists to relatively advanced levels.

Urbanization thus initiates a variety of systems of allocation. Ever since David Reisman added "inner-directed" and "other-directed" to the American lexicon, we have been asking one another whether there is too much conformity in American life. We worry that there is not enough encouragement of individualism, that we are too much a herd. We have, of course, a tradition of concern for fear we are too much bounded by social expectations; it has found expression from Henry David Thoreau to Sinclair Lewis. Still, each new analysis of "the Organization Man" or of "mass culture" brings a fresh rash of sermons, seminars, and soul-searching.

It is, perhaps, a healthy sign that so many Americans worry about whether there is too much conformity in our society, but there is something wryly amusing about it, too. The people of the United States tolerate a range of behavior in their fellow citizens which the people of most societies throughout human history would have found simply incredible. Our society defines as acceptable a wide range of behavior and will tolerate an enormous amount of deviance in familial roles, educational policy, economic behavior, political participation, and religious beliefs.

Urbanization gives rise to a great heterogeneity in the population. Urban life leads to ethnic and migrant differentiation and allows people with a different skin color or language or religion to pass relatively unnoticed in a way that could never be possible in the primary organization of a folk community. In addition, the occupational specialties associated with the complex division of labor create differences in the population: variations in training, values, work hours, recreation patterns, and, ultimately, differentiation in style of life.

The Role of Voluntary Associations in West African Urbanization

KENNETH LITTLE

INTRODUCTION

TAKEN AS A WHOLE, the West African region was relatively unaffected by the modern world until the end of the 19th century. Modern development of the hinterland began with the British adoption of trusteeship as colonial policy and with the British and French realization that these territories constituted an expanding market for imported goods as well as important sources of mineral and raw materials needed by the metropolitan country. The French were also concerned with the question of military manpower. These factors were finally crystallized by World War II and the events following it. The British war effort demanded greatly increased supplies of palm kernels, cotton, cocoa, and other locally grown products as well as hides, tin, iron ore, etc., which the colonial governments concerned were required to stimulate. Since the War there have been resettlement schemes, new industries and constructional projects have been instituted, and there has been a general improvement in communications by road, rail, and air. With the strategic implications of West Africa in the struggle against Communism also becoming manifest, political development has also gone on very rapidly, and there has been a corresponding expansion of education and the social services.

The consequence of all these technical and other changes is that there are now many more different modes of life and ways of earning a living than existed in West Africa some fifty years ago. It also goes without saying that its inhabitants have acquired a taste for the material elements of Western civilization, including consumer goods of every possible kind. In addition to new economic incentives, Western interests ranging from Christianity and nationalism to football and ballroom dancing have also been generated on a wide scale. In short, there has been produced the kind of phenomenon which anthropologists have customarily studied under the heading of culture contact, or acculturation. This term, however, is not precise enough for purposes of present analysis. First, many of the principal agents of cultural change nowadays are Africans themselves, and second, many Western ideas, practices, and procedures have already been fully assimilated to African culture. Africans became important as "acculturative agents" about

From *American Anthropologist*, Vol. 59, No. 4, Aug. 1957, pp. 579-594. Reprinted by permission of the publisher and author.

the middle of the 19th century when Western-educated Creoles from Sierra Leone went off evangelizing and trading down the Coast. All the way from the Gambia in the west to the Congo in the south they constituted, in many cases, little oases of westernized culture. Consequently, although much of the traditional life has disintegrated, new forms of social organization have arisen out of the older structure. There are, moreover, considerable differences in the extent to which given peoples and groups of Africans have undergone so-called detribalization, and it is rare to find whole communities which have completely severed all traditional loyalties and obligations. More often is it the case, as I propose to show, that the African individual moving out of the tribal area continues to be influenced by tribal culture. In other words, instead of viewing the contemporary West African situation in terms of the juxtaposition of two entirely different cultures, we shall do better to conceive it as a process of adaptation to new circumstances and conditions. Cultural contacts still go on, but between westernized Africans and other Africans, as well as between Westerners and Africans; so that the changes occurring are no different in kind from those within a single society.

THE URBANIZATION OF WEST AFRICA

What, in effect, this transformation of West Africa involves is a social process somewhat analogous to the social changes that resulted in the urbanization of Western Europe during the 19th century. Western contact with Africa, like the Industrial Revolution in Europe, has created new social and psychological needs which life in the countryside is rarely able to satisfy. The consequence is a tremendous migration of men and women to the towns, and to places where money can be earned to pay taxes, to provide bridewealth, and to buy manufactured goods and appliances.

Many of these people are in search of a higher standard of living in the shape of the more up-to-date amenities and better housing as well as the higher income that the town can offer. But this is not the only motivation. A large number of the younger men are looking for further educational opportunities, or are hoping to start a fresh career. Others move as a means of escaping from the restrictions of village life, and some of the younger girls, as well as the boys, out of love of adventure and desire for fresh experiences As Fortes has written in reference to the Gold Coast: "Labour, enterprise, and skill are now marketable in their own right anywhere in the country. . . . People feel that there is little risk in moving about, especially if, as appears to be the case with most mobile elements, their earning capacity is low. A clerk getting £2.10 a month feels that he cannot go much lower if he moves." The development of motor transport, in the shape of the ubiquitous lorry, is an important factor in these respects. Not only has it greatly increased local mobility between town and town, and between town and surrounding countryside, but it has created a new and influential social role—that of the lorry-driver, as a go-between between the urban labor market and the rural village.

Most of this migration is in the direction of towns already established as large centers of Western commerce and administration, of the rapidly growing ports, and of places where mining and other industries are being developed. Its effect has been to swell the population of such places far beyond their previous size, as well as to convert a good many villages into urban areas. For example, the principal towns of Senegal in French West Africa increased their populations by 100 percent between 1942 and 1952 and those of the French Ivory Coast by 109 percent during the same decade. In the Gold Coast there was an increase of 98 percent in the populations of the five largest towns between 1931 and 1948. Cotonou in Dahomey grew from 1100 in 1905 to 35,000 in 1952 and Lunsar, in Sierra Leone, which was a village of 30 inhabitants in 1929, has a population today of nearly 17,000.

Although urbanism in terms of "a relatively large, dense, and permanent settlement of socially heterogeneous individuals" is not a general characteristic of traditional life, it is far from being a unique phenomenon in West Africa. In 1931, some 28 percent of the Yoruba population of Western Nigeria lived in 9 cities of over 45,000 inhabitants, while a further 34 percent lived in cities of over 20,000 inhabitants. However, what distinguishes the "new" African city—"new" in the sense, as Georges Balandier points out, that they were built by European colonists—from traditional urbanism is that a large part of its population is industrial, depending upon the labor market for a living. This is particularly evident in the case of towns of recent growth. In Cotonou, for example, some 10,000 persons out of a population of some 35,000 are in wage employment.

A further point is that the modern town is much more heterogeneous. It has groups of professionals, office workers, municipal employees, artisans, etc., and in addition to its indigenous political and social segmentation, it also accommodates a large proportion of "strangers." Not only do the latter frequently outnumber the native inhabitants of the town, but they include a wide diversity of tribes. For example, Kumasi, although the capital of Ashantiland, contains as many non-Ashantis as Ashantis; Takoradi-Sekondi contains representatives of more than 60 different tribes; and less than 10 percent of the inhabitants of Poto-Poto, one of the three African towns of Brazzaville, were born in that city. In the Gold Coast, as a whole, more than two-thirds of the inhabitants of the big towns have been there for less than five years. A further significant characteristic of these urban populations is the numerical preponderance of young people over old and, to a less appreciable extent, the preponderance of men over women. For example, only 2.4 percent of the population of Cotonou are over 60 years of age. In 1921, men considerably outnumbered women, but by 1952 the masculinity rate had dropped to 111. In an area of Poto-Poto, on the other hand, where the average age of the population is about 25, there are only 515 females to every 1000 males.

VOLUNTARY ASSOCIATIONS

(a) TRIBAL UNIONS

From the point of view of social organization one of the most striking characteristics of these modern towns is the very large number and variety of voluntary associations. These include a host of new political, religious, recreational, and occupational associations as well as the more traditional mutual aid groups and secret societies out of which some of these more recent organizations have developed. What generally distinguishes the latter kind of association is its more formal constitution and the fact that it has been formed to meet certain needs arising specifically out of the urban environment of its members. It is also more "modern" both in respect to its aims and the methods employed to attain them. One of the best illustrations of these points is provided by certain tribal associations of an extraterritorial kind, known in Nigeria and the Gold Coast as Tribal Unions.

These tribal unions range from little unions, consisting of a few members of the same extended family or clan, to much larger bodies like the Ibo State Union which is a collection of village and clan unions. In Nigeria, these associations were originally formed by Ibo and other migrants from Eastern Nigeria to protect themselves from the hostile way in which they were received when they took jobs as policemen, traders, and laborers in the towns of the West and the North. Their aim is to provide members with mutual aid, including support, while out of work, sympathy and financial assistance in the case of illness, and the responsibility for the funeral and the repatriation of the family of the deceased in the case of death. The main raison d'être, however, is that of fostering and keeping alive an interest in tribal song, history, language, and moral beliefs, and thus maintaining a person's attachment to his native town or village and to his lineage there. In furtherance of this sentiment, money is collected for the purpose of improving amenities in the union's home town and to provide its younger people with education. Social activities include the organization of dances on festival days and of sports meetings and games for their young people. Some of these unions also produce an annual magazine, called an Almanac, in which their members' activities are recorded.

Associations based upon membership of the same ethnic group also exist in French and Belgian Africa where they perform somewhat similar functions. In Cotonou, for example, such groups welcome and look after persons newly arrived from the country. They provide a means whereby both the old people and the "evolué" can keep in touch with their rural relatives and friends. Each such association has an annual feast and celebration which brings together everyone from the same region. It is also a means of helping the needy and aged members of the group.

In Nigeria there have also been developed home branches of the tribal union abroad; and as a final step, State unions have been created, comprising every union of members of the same tribe. It is not surprising, therefore, that these Nigerian tribal unions have obtained a power and influence far beyond their original objectives. The larger unions have played an important part in the expansion of education. They offer scholarships for deserving boys and girls and run their own schools. In some places, the monthly contributions of members for education are invested in some form of commercial enterprise, and appeals for money to build schools seem to meet with a particularly ready response. One observer claims that he saw an up-country union raise in six hours and in a single meeting over £16,000 for such purposes. Some higher education overseas has also been provided, and several leading members of the Nigerian Eastern House of Assembly owe their training in British universities to State union money. Even more ambitious plans have included the building of a national bank where people can obtain loans for industrial and commercial purposes. In this connection, some unions have economic advisers who survey trade reports for the benefit of members. These tribal unions also serve a number of important political purposes and are recognized as units for purposes of tax collection. In addition to pressing local authorities for better roads, dispensaries and hospitals, and other public amenities, they have been a powerful force in the democratizing of traditional councils; in the multitribal centers they were for many years the recognized basis for representation on Township Advisory Boards or Native Authority Councils. They have also provided a forum for the expression of national politics and for the rise to positions of leadership of the younger educated element.

(b) FRIENDLY SOCIETIES

In addition to the tribal union, there are also a large number of tribal societies where objectives are limited to mutual aid and benefit. One of the most complicated of these organizations is run by the wives of Kru immigrants in Freetown. This kind of society is divided into three classes. A member pays an admission fee of one guinea and enters the class of least importance. He or she may subsequently be promoted to a higher class and in this event will be expected to make members of that class a present of several pounds. On his or her death, the relatives receive a sum of money commensurate with the deceased person's status. These societies endeavor to develop a high esprit de corps and have been known to impose fines of as much as £20 on members guilty of unfriendly conduct toward each other.

Kru men go to sea for a living and so the members of their societies are divided into "ships," named after various recent additions to Messrs. Elder Dempster's fleet, instead of classes. The Kru also have so-called "family societies" comprising the migrant members of a particular class, or *dako* (a small local federation of patriclans). These groups also provide bereavement benefits. In Freetown there are also a number of traditional organizations, including so-called secret societies and dancing groups, which provide funeral expenses, presents, and entertainment for members when they marry. The congregations of mosques, too, usually have what is loosely called a *Jama Compin* (Compin = Krio, "Company") whose members help each other over funerals. Up country, another Moslem group, composed of women, endeavors to intervene in domestic quarrels and to reconcile man and wife. In this case, a sixpenny subscription is collected every Sunday, and persons joining as new members have to pay the equivalent of what a foundation member has already paid in subscriptions. Some of this money is disbursed as alms, but most of it is used to provide sickness and funeral benefits.

A different kind of mutual aid group is the *esusu*, which is of Yoruba origin. Members of the group pay in at regular intervals a fixed sum and the total is given each time to one of the members. This is an important method for buying trading stock, expensive clothing, etc. In southeastern Nigeria, a somewhat similar kind of "contribution club" is divided into seven sections, each under a headman. Each member pays one or more weekly subscriptions. The headmen are responsible for collecting the shares from their members, and when the shares have all been collected, the money is handed over to a member nominated by the headman in turn. The recipient has a number of obligations, including that of supplying a quantity of palm wine for the refreshment of club members.

A further organization serves all three functions—providing funeral benefits, charity, and helping its members to save. This is the *Nanamei Akpee*, or "mutual help" society. It has its headquarters in Accra and branches in several other Gold Coast towns, including Keta. The Keta branch has well over 400 members, the great majority of whom are educated or semiliterate women traders. There is a monthly subscription of one shilling and when a member dies, the surviving relatives are given at least £10 towards the cost of funeral expenses. Money for loans is raised at weekly collections which begin with community singing. All the women present give as much money as they feel they can afford, and their contributions are written down in a book which also contains a list of the society's members, in order of seniority. When the collection is finished, all the money is given to the member whose name takes first place; the following week it is given to the second, then to the third, and so on. Eventually, all members will in this way receive a contribution, though the process as a whole naturally takes a very long time. However, the man or woman receiving a collection is also given a list showing the amount of money contributed by other members. This determines, during later weeks, the amounts he must contribute himself. For example, if A has given B two shillings then B must raise the same amount when eventually A's turn arrives to receive a weekly collection. In effect, this arrangement means that senior members, i.e., those who have joined early, receive an interest-free loan, which they repay weekly by small contributions; those on the bottom of the list, on the other hand, are saving in a small way, for their own ultimate benefit. In a period of rising prices, those at the top of the list naturally have the advantage, but on the other hand those who wait longer may receive more because the society's membership will in the meantime have increased. There is an element of chance in all this which adds spice to the normally dull business of saving, and this partly explains the society's popularity. Finally, when a member falls ill he is visited in the hospital, given small gifts of money, and so on. At times the society also gives presents and small sums of money to old and sick people even if they are not members.

(c) Occupational Associations

In addition to raising loans through such organizations as *Nanamei Akpee,* African market women also form associations in order to control the supply or price of commodities in which their members trade. Some of the larger markets have a woman in charge, and each of the various sections which women monopolize, such as the sale of yams, gari, cloth, etc. is also headed by a woman, who represents them in relation to customers and the market authorities. In Lagos market each such section has its own union, which discourages competition between women trading in that particular commodity. Another women's association is the Fish Sellers Union at Takoradi-Sekondi. The members of this association may club together to raise money to buy fishing nets. The group then sells the nets to fishermen on agreed terms. A fisherman who receives a net sells his catches during the fishing season to the creditor group, and the value of the fish is reckoned against the net. In this way, the members are able to obtain the fish on which their livelihood depends. Women also associate for industrial purposes. In southern Nigeria, for example, there are women's societies which run a bakery, a laundry, a calabash manufactory, and a gari mill. One of the most interesting of these associations, the Egba Women's Union in Abeokuta, claims a membership of 80,000 women, paying subscriptions of 13 shillings a year. It operates as a weaving co-operative, and runs a maternity and a child welfare clinic as well as conducting classes for illiterate women.

Other occupational and professional associations are concerned with the status and remuneration of their members as workers. Such groups include modern crafts such as goldsmiths, tinkers, gunsmiths, tailors, and barbers, as well as certain trade unions which, unlike Government-sponsored trade unions, have come spontaneously into being. One example of these is the Motor Drivers Union at Keta which is now a branch of a nationwide union which negotiates freight rates, working conditions, and so on. Unlike European trade unions, this Motor Drivers Union is an association of small entrepreneurs owning their own vehicles rather than an association of employees. Its main purpose is to look after the interests of drivers generally and in particular to offer them legal assistance and insurance. When a driver is convicted, the Union tries as far as possible to pay his fine; and when a driver dies the Union provides part of the funeral expenses. There are also smaller sickness and accident benefits. The entrance fee is 14 shillings and there is a monthly subscription of one shilling. In addition, the Union organizes meetings and dances.

The organization of modern crafts, on the other hand, takes on the form of guilds resembling those of medieval Europe. The first rule of all these guilds in Yoruba towns, where many of them have developed, is that every craftsman, whether master, journeyman or apprentice, must be registered with the guild, must attend meetings, and must pay his dues. One of the guild's prime functions is to maintain a reasonable standard of work in the craft. It determines the rules of apprenticeship; fixes prices of workmanship; and settles disputes, whether between master and apprentice or between craftsman and customer. On the other hand, the guild does not undertake to care for its members in sickness or old age; neither does it function as a bank, lending money to members for tools. Most forms of social security are still organized by the lineage—in which the guild members still retain full membership—and not by the guild.

Unions of a different kind which are also concerned with the status and remuneration of their members are associations of prostitutes. These have been reported from Takoradi and also from Brazzaville. In the latter city, the members of such organizations try to improve their own social and economic position by insisting on a high standard of dress and deportment, and by ostracizing other women who are too casual or too free with their sexual favors. Each group has its own name, such as *La Rose, Diamant,* etc. and is under a leader, an elderly woman, who can set a pattern of elegance and sophistication. Membership is limited and is regulated by a committee. There is also a common fund out of which members in financial straits are helped and their funeral expenses paid should they die. In the latter event, the association behaves as if it were the family of the deceased. Every girl goes into mourning, giving up her jewelry and finer clothes for six months, at the end of which there is a night-long celebration in some "bar-dancing" establishment hired for the occasion.

(d) Entertainment and Recreational Associations

A large number of associations are concerned with dancing and musical forms of entertainment. Many of these, such as the drumming companies found in Ewe villages in the Gold Coast, still retain much of their traditional character. A number of groups in Brazzaville also perform traditional music, but on a commercial basis. These societies consist of young men who have formed themselves into an orchestra under the presidency of an older man whose compound they use for the purpose of staging an evening's "social" on Saturdays and Sundays. The public is charged for admission on these occasions and the "band," which goes by such appropriate titles as *Etoile, Jeunesse, Record de la Gaieté,* etc. undertakes outside engagements. The receipts are divided among the members according to their position in the society and anything left over goes toward the purchase of new instruments and the provision of further conviviality. Other such associations, which began as simple dancing societies, have developed under urban conditions into a relatively complex organization and set of modern objectives. A striking example of this kind of phenomenon is the dancing *compin* of Sierra Leone. This is a group of young men and women concerned with the performance of "plays" of traditional music and dancing and with the raising of money for mutual benefit. The music is provided mainly by native drums, xylophones, and calabash rattles, and is accompanied by singing. The dancing which, like the drumming, shows signs of Western influence, is somewhat reminiscent of English country dancing. A "play" is generally given in connection with some important event, such as the close of Ramadan, or as part of the ceremonies celebrating a wedding or a funeral. The general public as well as the persons honored by the performance are expected to donate money to the compin on these occasions. Money is also collected in the form of weekly subscriptions from the members.

In one of these organizations, which are particularly numerous among Temne and Mandinka immigrants in Freetown, this amount goes into a general fund to cover corporate expenses of the society's activities—rent of yard, provision of lamps, replacement of drum skins, etc. Then, when any member is bereaved, a collection is held to which all must contribute. However, quite an elaborate procedure is necessary before the money can be paid. The bereaved person must first notify the Reporter with a reporting fee. This is passed on to the company's Doctor, who investigates the circumstances of death, for the company will fine any member who has not notified them of a relative's illness so that they can see that the sick person receives attention. The Doctor washes the body and sends the Prevoe (Provost) round to the other members, telling them to gather that evening when they must pay their contributions. When anyone avoids payment without good cause, the Bailiff may seize an item of his property of equal value. The evening's meeting is organized by the Manager. He will bring the company's lamps, for members are under an obligation to take part in a wake which will last into the early hours. At the wake the bereaved person will provide cigarettes, kola nuts, bread, and coffee, and will employ a singer. Another duty of the Doctor is to examine members before admission, and to attend them if sick. The Commissioner or Inspector is the disciplinary officer and he can arrest or eject trouble makers, the Prevoe acting on his orders. The Clerk or Secretary keeps accounts and writes letters, and the Cashier receives from the Sultan for safe keeping any money accruing to the society. The Sultan is the chief executive; his female counterpart, who has charge of the women members, is the Mammy Queen. For the dancing there is a leader who directs it, and a Conductor who supervises the band. There is also a Sister in charge of the Nurses, young girls who bring round refreshments at dances, often in white dresses with a red cross on the breast and the appropriate headgear. If there is no woman Doctor, an older Nurse or Sister may assist the Doctor with the invalids, or the washing of the corpse. There may also be further officials, such as an Overseer, an M. C., a Solicitor, a Lawyer, Sick Visitor, etc. Many of these titles involve no work, but they can be given to honor even the least deserving member and to strengthen his identification with the group's company.

Other groups concerned with recreation range from Improvement Leagues and Women's Institutes to cricket and football clubs. Some of the latter are characterized by such colorful titles as Mighty Poisons, Hearts of Oak, Heroes, etc. Football teams are also run by associations of the former pupils of certain schools, known as Old Boys Association, which also organize receptions and "send-offs" and sometimes hold evening classes. Most organizations of the latter kind are modeled rather closely on European lines, particularly the so-called "social club." This is constituted for dining and drinking purposes as well as for tennis, whist, billiards, ballroom dancing, amateur dramatics, and other European recreational and cultural activities. For the latter reasons, "social clubs" are mainly confined to the most Westernized section of the population, including well-to-do professionals and businessmen as well as teachers, clerks, and other white-collar workers. Such clubs are open to persons of any tribe, but members are expected to conform to European patterns of social etiquette. Europeans themselves are frequently admitted either as members or as guests. Examples of this kind of institution are the Rodgers Club in Accra, the Island Club in Lagos, and the Bo African Club in Sierra Leone. In the latter association, all official business and proceedings, including lectures, debates, etc., are conducted in English. At the weekly dance, which is one of the club's principal activities, the general rule is for the women to wear print or silk dresses (without the head tie), and the men open-necked shirts with a blazer or sports jacket. On special occasions evening dress is worn by both sexes. In addition to its ordinary activities, this club undertakes a number of public functions, including special dances to honor visiting notables. It also entertains the teams of visiting football clubs, and its premises are used for such purposes as political meetings and adult education classes.

Women, too, have their social clubs which broadly complement those under the control of men. These are very often known as Ladies' Clubs and Women's Institutes. Many of the latter have been formed under the auspices of churches. A large number of literate husbands have nonliterate wives, and some of these women's clubs reflect the sociological situation in that they are divided into "literate" and "illiterate" sections which hold separate meetings. "Literate" activities consist mainly in sewing and crochet work, in practicing the cooking of European and native dishes, and in listening to talks about household economy. Individual literate women give instruction in these arts to the "illiterate" meeting, and in return nonliterate women sometimes teach the literate group native methods of dyeing, spinning, basketry, and traditional songs and dances.

Women's Institutes are primarily the result of the initiative of educated women. For example, the President and leading officers of the Keta Women's Institute in the Gold Coast are teachers, although the bulk of its membership consists of market women. It is principally a social club, but it has certain other more important interests. For example, it has acted as a "pressure group," intervening with the Urban Council in support of a plan for improving amenities at the local markets. Among other local changes, the women achieved the provision of ambulance services, and the employment of a larger number of female nurses at the Keta hospital.

THE ORGANIZATION OF VOLUNTARY ASSOCIATIONS

Before we attempt to generalize about these voluntary associations, it is necessary to distinguish between three rather different types. The first is still basically concerned with traditional activities, although with some slight modification; in the second type, traditional activities have been deliberately modified or expanded to suit modern purposes; and the third type is wholly modern in organization and objectives. It will be convenient to term these three types respectively "traditional," "traditional-modernized" and "modern."

The function of the "traditional" association is generally limited to the organization of some particular religious, occupational, or recreational interest, such as a cult, a trade, or some form of dancing or drumming. Space unfortunately prevents description of religious associations in general. These exist alongside Islam and the ancestral cult, and according to Hofstra (1955) they may be divided into four categories: (1) Christian churches organized by missionaries, (2) so-called African churches, (3) looser, smaller groups of a syncretistic character, (4) irregularly organized movements of a messianic or prophetic kind. In the traditional type of association some provision may be made for mutual benefit, but this is incidental to the main purpose of the society. Membership in the group is usually confined to persons belonging to the same village or ward of a town and is often related to other traditional institutions, such as an age set. For example, drumming companies among the Ewe are organized on a ward basis, and usually there are three in every ward. The first comprises children up to the age of about fifteen; the second consists of the so-called "young men," ranging in age from about fifteen to thirty; and the third comprises "elders," i.e. the male population over thirty or so. The senior companies usually give themselves names such as "Patience" or "U.A.C." (abbreviation for United Africa Company), and some of these are, in effect, associations of semi-professional entertainers who travel about the country in search of engagements. Although the organization of such "traditional" associations is generally quite simple and informal, a number of them have adapted to modern conditions by incorporating literate persons as officials and by widening the scope of their function. In the traditional economy of the Gold Coast, for example, each trade or occupation normally had a chief-practitioner who settled disputes and represented his associates in relation to outsiders. This is largely true today, but in addition some of these groups have turned themselves into local branches of a nation-wide union. In the case of the goldsmiths, this involved appointing its chief-practitioner as Life-Chairman of the association, while an educated man who could deal adequately with its business affairs was elected President. Similarly, the semiliterate president of the Carpenters Union now has a literate secretary and treasurer to help him.

It goes without saying that the great majority of people who belong to "traditional" associations are unlettered. The number of persons who can read and write or speak a European language is larger in the "traditional-modernized" association, but what mainly distinguishes the latter is its syncretistic character, its relatively formal organization, and the variety of its functions. A particularly striking example of the latter point is *La Goumbé*, a Moslem and predominantly Dioula youth organization for both sexes in the Ivory Coast. This combines the functions of emancipating young women from family influence; assisting the process of marital selection; providing, on a contributory basis, marriage and maternity benefits (including perfume and layettes for the newborn); preserving the Dioula tribal spirit; running an orchestra; and acting as the local propaganda agent for *Rassemblement Démocratique Africain*. It also maintains its own police force. In addition to a written constitution which embodies the declared aims and rules of the society, this kind of association sometimes has its own name and a special uniform of its own, and generally follows such Western practices as the holding of regular meetings, keeping of minutes, accounts, etc. The wearing of a uniform type of dress is probably more characteristic of women's societies than those formed by men. The women members of *Nanemei Akpee*, for example, all dress in white for meetings, and the practice of appearing in the same kind of dress, including head-tie, necklace, and sandals, is followed by other women's groups on formal occasions. Finance plays an important part in its affairs, and there is a regular tariff of entrance fees; weekly or monthly dues are collected and fines are sometimes levied. These funds are administered by a Treasurer or Financial Secretary, sometimes supervised by a committee which also conducts the everyday business of the association, including the sifting of fresh applications for membership, settlement of disputes, etc. Related partly to the wide diversity of functions performed is the large number of persons holding official positions in some of these societies. Many of these office-bearers, as exemplified by the dancing compin, have European titles, or, as in the case of the Kru women's societies, are known by the native equivalents of such titles. This enactment of European roles, as in the dancing compin, is a fairly common feature of associations of the "traditional-modernized" type. It has been termed "vicarious participation in the European social structure" by J. Clyde Mitchell, but as Michael Banton points out (1956), this possibly places too much emphasis on the process of westernization and too little on the independent process of change in the tribal group. An assistant official sometimes has the duty of conveying information about the society's activities to the general public as well as to members. *La Goumbé*, for example, has a number of town criers, members of the *griot* caste, to carry news through the town.

The organization of the "traditional-modernized" association is also rendered more elaborate by a tendency toward affiliation. This ranges all the way from a fully centralized organization of individual branches to a loose fraternal arrangement between entirely autonomous branches of the same movement. Affiliation of individual branches sometimes seems to be the result of traditional conditions. Thus, the "village-group union" of the Afikpo Ibo of Nigeria is apparently modelled largely upon the indigenous age-set structure of the people concerned. The *Goumbé* movement comprises a number of local "cells" co-ordinated by a central committee, which settles disputes between them and lays down general policy. The dancing compin movement, on the other hand, consists of a large number of separate societies which occasionally exchange visits and information and extend hospitality to each other's members, but are otherwise entirely independent. Finally, although membership of these associations tends to be tribally or regionally circumscribed, this is not invariably so. Even tribal unions sometimes have persons from more than one tribe among their members. The Benin Nation Club (Nigeria), for example, provides facilities for all natives of the Benin Province. Several occupational and other groups recruit their members on an intertribal basis, and this also applies to some of the societies run by women.

The "modern" association has already been briefly described in terms of the "social club," and so it will suffice merely to add that its organization is broadly the same as that of any European association of a comparable kind. Like its European counterpart, it is often a medium for social prestige.

Despite their wide variety, one objective common to all types of voluntary association is that of sociability and fraternity. Not only is the serving of refreshments, including such beverages as tea, palm wine, beer, or stronger drink, an integral part of any formal gathering of members, but the latter are expected and encouraged to visit each others' homes, especially in the event of illness or bereavement. Again, although some groups, including certain guilds and occupations, are confined to persons of the same sex, it seems to be a fairly common practice for women to be admitted into associations under the control of men, and for men to be members of certain associations in which women predominate. Some associations organized by men deliberately encourage the recruitment of female members but have them under a more or less separate administration, with the women's leader responsible to the head of the society. A further fairly common feature of all kinds of voluntary associations is the fact that most of their personnel are young people. Indeed, some societies expect their members to retire at the age of thirty, and it is rare for persons over middle age to play an active part in their affairs. This, however, is less typical of the "traditional" organizations than it is of the other types of association which, nevertheless, quite often like to have an elderly man or woman as an honorary president. The role of such a person is to uphold the association's reputation for respectability and to help its relations with the wider commmunity. The fact that he is not infrequently a person of importance in tribal society is indicative of the desire of such associations to keep on good terms with the traditional authorities. The size of membership is a more variable factor. It ranges from a mere handful of individuals to several hundred or even thousands, in the case of the larger tribal associations. In the smaller societies, which are often very ephemeral, the amount of support given is probably bound up as much with the personality and personal influence of the leader as it is with the popularity of the institution.

VOLUNTARY ASSOCIATIONS AS AN ADAPTIVE MECHANISM

It was suggested earlier that the social changes resulting from culture contact may be seen as an historical process of adaptation to new conditions. Adaptation in the present context implies not only the modification of African institutions, but their development to meet the demands of an industrial economy and urban way of life. In effect, as Banton has shown in reference to Temne immigrants in Freetown, this sometimes amounts to a virtual resuscitation of the tribal system in the interests of the modernist ambitions and social prestige of the younger educated element concerned. The unpublished findings of Jean Rouch seem to give even greater emphasis to this kind of phenomenon, which he has labelled "super-tribalization." Some of the immigrants into the Gold Coast, whom he has studied, have gained sufficient solidarity through their associations and cults to dominate over the local population, achieving monopolies in various trades. A further important effect of this kind of development, as both Busia and Banton have pointed out, is to inhibit the growth of civic loyalty or responsibility for the town concerned. Modern urbanism, in other words, is the conditioning factor in contemporary African society as well as the culmination of so-called acculturation. West African urbanism of course differs from comparable Western situations in being less advanced, although it is probably more dynamic. It involves a particularly rapid diffusion of entirely new ideas, habits, and technical procedures, and a considerable restructuring of social relationships as a consequence of the new technical roles and groups created.

Voluntary associations play their part in both these processes through the fresh criteria of social achievement that they set up and through the scope that they offer, in particular, to women and to the younger age groups. Women, and younger people in general, possess a new status in the urban economy, and this is reflected in the various functions which these associations perform as political pressure groups, in serving as a forum for political expression, and in providing both groups with training in modern methods of business. Equally significant is the fact that women's participation in societies with a mixed membership involves them in a new kind of social relationship with men, including companionship and the opportunity of selecting a spouse for oneself. In particular, voluntary associations provide an outlet for the energies and ambitions of the rising class of young men with a tribal background who have been to school. The individuals concerned are debarred by their "Western" occupations as clerks, school teachers, artisans, etc. and by their youth from playing a prominent part in traditional society proper; but they are the natural leaders of other young people less Westernized and sophisticated than themselves. This is largely because of their ability to interpret the "progressive" ideas they have gained through their work and travel, and through reading newspapers and books, in terms that are meaningful to the illiterate rank and file of the movement.

It is, in fact, in relation to the latter group, particularly the urban immigrant, that the significance of voluntary associations as an adaptive mechanism is most apparent. The newly arrived immigrant from the rural areas has been used to living and working as a member of a compact group of kinsmen and neighbors on a highly personal basis of relationship and mutuality. He knows of no other way of community living than this, and his natural reaction is to make a similar adjustment to urban conditions.

This adjustment the association facilitates by substituting for the extended group of kinsmen a grouping based upon common interest which is capable of serving many of the same needs as the traditional family or lineage. In other words, the migrant's participation in some organization such as a tribal union or a dancing compin not only replaces much of what he has lost in terms of moral assurance in removing from his native village, but offers him companionship and an opportunity of sharing joys as well as sorrows with others in the same position as himself. (Probably an important point in this regard is the large number of offices available in some associations, enabling even the most humble member to feel that he "matters.") Such an association also substitutes for the extended family in providing counsel and protection, in terms of legal aid; and by placing him in the company of women members, it also helps to find him a wife. It also substitutes for some of the economic support available at home by supplying him with sickness and funeral benefits, thereby enabling him to continue his most important kinship obligations. Further, it introduces him to a number of economically useful habits and practices, such as punctuality and thrift, and it aids his social reorientation by inculcating new standards of dress, etiquette, and personal hygiene. Above all, by encouraging him to mix with persons outside his own lineage and sometimes tribe, the voluntary association helps him to adjust to the more cosmopolitan ethos of the city. Equally significant, too, is the syncretistic character of associations of the "traditional-modernized" type. Their combination of modern and traditional traits constitutes a cultural bridge which conveys, metaphorically speaking, the tribal individual from one kind of sociological universe to another.

The latter point is also indicative of various ways in which these voluntary associations substitute for traditional agencies of social control. Not only are positive injunctions to friendly and fraternal conduct embodied in the constitution by which members agree to bind themselves, but many associations have rules proscribing particular misdemeanors and what they regard as antisocial behavior. In this respect, the frequent inclusion of sexual offenses, such as the seduction of the wife or the daughter of a fellow member, is very significant. The association also sets new moral standards and attempts to control the personal conduct of its members in a number of ways. For example, the Lagos branch of *Awo Omama* Patriotic Union resolved not to marry any girl of their town so long as the prevailing amount of money asked for bridewealth was not reduced. The dancing compin will withhold its legal aid from a member unless the company's officials examining the case feel that he is in the right. Also, there are women's groups concerning themselves specifically with the settlement of domestic quarrels, which expel members who are constant troublemakers in the home and among other women. More frequently, punishment takes the form of a fine, but the strongest sanction probably lies in the fact that every reputable association is at pains to check fresh applications for membership. In other words, a person who has earned a bad name for himself in one organization may find it difficult to get into another; and this form of ostracism may in some cases be as painful as exile from the tribe.

A final important point is the extent to which disputes of a private or domestic nature, which would formerly have been heard by some traditional authority such as the head of a lineage, are now frequently taken to the head of an association, even when the matter is quite unconcerned with the life of that particular body.

CONCLUSION

Theorists of Western urbanism have stressed the importance of voluntary associations as a distinctive feature of contemporary social organization. Wirth, in particular, has emphasized the impersonality of the modern city, arguing that its psychological effect is to cause the individual urbanite to exert himself by joining with others of similar interests into organized groups to obtain his ends. "This," wrote Wirth (1938), "results in an enormous multiplication of voluntary organizations directed towards as great a variety of objectives as are human needs and interests." However, this thesis has not been strongly supported by empirical enquiry. According to Komarovsky, who studied voluntary associations in New York, the old neighborhood, the larger kin group, might have broken down, but they have not been replaced by the specialized voluntary groups to the extent usually assumed. Floyd Dotson, who conducted a similar investigation in Detroit, also failed to find a wholesale displacement of primary by secondary groups. He concludes that the majority of urban working class people do not participate in formally organized voluntary associations. Perhaps more significant for the present context is the fact that the same writer found even less participation in voluntary organizations among the working class population of Guadalajara, the second largest city of Mexico.

The quantitative methods used in obtaining the latter results have not as yet been employed in African towns, so it is impossible to make exact comparisons. Also, the investigations concerned appear to have been made among relatively stable populations. Further study is therefore needed of the two factors which seem to be largely instrumental in the growth of these African voluntary associations. The first of these factors is the existence of an urban population which is largely immigrant, unstable, and socially heterogeneous. The second is the adaptability of traditional institutions to urban conditions. Possibly, it is the existence and interrelationship of these two factors rather than "anomie" which creates the essential conditions for the "fictional kinship groups," which, according to Wirth, substitute for actual kinship ties within the urban environment.

"Mental Healing" and Urbanization in West Africa

S. KIRSON WEINBERG

THE INDIGENOUS TREATMENT of mental disorders in Ghana, West Africa, despite its continuity with a tribal past, is in process of change by the pressures of urbanization. Although retaining a dominant position in the therapy of mental disorders, it is challenged increasingly by Christian faith healing and Western psychiatry. Our aim in this paper is to analyze 1) the meaning of illness from perspective of the patients, 2) the diagnostic and therapeutic procedures of the native doctor as components of a sub-culture, and 3) the

From *Social Problems*, Vol. XI, Winter, 1964, pp. 257-269. Reprinted by permission of the publisher and author.

mode of change in the position of this profession as compared with that of Christian faith healing and Western psychiatry.

I. RATIONALE OF METHOD

This sociological study of a changing occupational culture in a non-Western, urban society differs from the characteristic anthropological study of the traditional heritage of a static, territorially contiguous tribe into which the individual is born and becomes socialized. This study investigates instead the changing culture of dispersed urban practitioners into which a socialized novice is recruited and becomes acculturated. From this perspective it aims specifically to ascertain not only the diagnostic and therapeutic orientations and techniques of the native doctors and the effectiveness of their skills, but also the extent to which they enforced standards of practice, communicated and shared their professional lore, and selected competent recruits to sustain their craft. Since these native doctors were members of several groups, we had to sift their professional ideas and techniques from those which are idiosyncratic or peculiar to their tribe. Although we emphasized the shared facets of this occupation, we recognized too that manifest differences existed in the professional knowledge and skills of the members. Some native doctors had knowledge of herb mixtures which others lacked; some doctors were more effective than others in their psychotherapeutic procedures and in their handling of patients.

This inquiry emerged from a study of hospitalized schizophrenics in the state hospital in Accra. We found that the characteristic lower class, non-violent schizophrenics, who were so numerous in state hospitals in the United States, were relatively scarce in this hospital. From further inquiry we found that some persons whose symptoms were those of schizophrenics were treated by native doctors or faith-healers, and other persons with these symptoms were in the villages and in the marketplaces of the city. As we continued this tangential search we realized that these native doctors were the indigenous psychiatrists in this society and that their orientations and procedures differed somewhat from those of their counterparts in the villages as described by Rattray and Field. We then concentrated upon the characteristics and direction of this changing occupational culture.

Our first informants were two native doctors and one college student who described in detail the orientation and theoretical framework of the medicine man. These informants presented us to sixteen native doctors and five faith-healers whom we interviewed at length. For validating information concerning this occupational culture we interviewed mental hospital patients and other persons who had been treated by native doctors or faith-healers.

We gathered information concerning the official characteristics of the native doctors from the records at two towns near Accra, Amasaman and Prampram, where the doctors were licensed. Information about the mental hospital was obtained from our interviews with the staff and patients, from direct observation and from hospital records. Although our findings concerning the workings of the diverse forms of healings are circumscribed to and around Accra, Ghana, the relative similarity of conditions to other parts of West Africa means that our conclusions could pertain with minor variations to the urban sectors of West Africa generally.

II. CONCEPTIONS OF ILLNESS AND THE TYPES OF PATIENTS

Since the native doctor treats psychological and organic difficulties, his role approximates that of the Western physician and psychiatrist. His dual therapeutic role results from the African's conception of illness and health. In a holistic sense he considers illness or ill-being in polarity to well-being, so that it connotes not only (1) physical ailments but also (on a temporal and psychological dimension) (2) present and (3) future personal misfortune, and finally, (4) social deviation. The African interprets deviant behavior both as a symptom and cause of illness, because deviant behavior can weaken the kra or kla, the vital spiritual source of well-being. Since the patient does not distinguish between organic and personality difficulties, he may seek treatment from a native doctor because of an organic ailment such as a stomach-ache or sexual impotency, or because of a personal problem such as marital difficulties or unemployment. He regards physical illness and emotional disturbances as supernaturally caused and as manifestations of his personal destiny. He does not consider infection by germs or agitation by conflict as the bases of his malady or misfortune.

The African consistently regards healing as a religio-psychological process, involving the spiritual triumph of the idol, i.e., the "juju," and/or the medicine or the spirit of the native doctor over the spirit of the illness. The patient defines treatment as symptom-removal and as an invocation to spirits who can remove the supernatural sources of the symptom. Some doctors and faith-healers do not consider the removal of symptoms possible without placating or vanquishing the proper spirits. When confronted with personal difficulties, the patient, lacking a developmental perspective, does not attribute past influences in childhood to his present condition. Instead he perceives his condition as a result of animistic influences. Nonetheless, he may also have a trial and success empirical naturalism so that, for example, he can relate his recovery to specific herbs.

Personality and mental disorders range in severity from minor situational and personality difficulties to chronic psychoses. For example, an individual who seeks a job or a promotion or who strives to avert future misfortune visits the native doctor to correct his condition. When he incurs a physical ailment which resists medication, or when he is gripped by compulsive addictions such as alcoholism, and drug-addiction, he believes that he is influenced by witches, by black magic or juju, by ancestral or other spirits which obscure his will and obstruct his destiny, and he believes that only the native doctor can help him. Why does the African interpret his condition in this way?

Apart from the concepts of well-being or ill-being, of spirit possession or spirit-belief, his thought categories of personality and for introspective analysis are simple and few. His conception of himself is simpler than his knowledge and his skills in mechanical, political and clerical pursuits.

Even though an urbanized person becomes relatively individualized and in the process of detribalization changes his value scheme from family-centered status to bureaucratic-centered status, he still may interpret his tensions and inter-personal conflicts as well as his misfortunes in terms of spirits, juju and witchcraft. His conceptions used in introspective analysis of his predicament are not those of Western psychology. Instead he resorts to folk beliefs to appraise his behavior, beliefs which seem to be compartmentalized from his rational orientation towards his work and mechanical pursuits.

From this supernatural vantage point, the African believes that a witch or literally a released spirit—in Twi, called oba-yi—can harm him. By thinking harmful thoughts a witch can project her spirit onto his destiny and thereby affect his present or future fortunes. An idol or the black magic of juju also can affect his personal condition. Consequently, when an African with this perspective encounters misfortune, he does not seek explanations in terms of natural causes but rather contemplates the intervention of supernatural forces which contributed to his particular misfortune. With this frame of mind he would seek help from the native doctor who shares his frame of reference and the idiomatic aspects of his personal expressions.

Hence persons in nearly all strata of society would visit the native doctor when personal stress impelled psychological help. According to one survey, however, the proportion of persons in a given social stratum declined with the amount of schooling. Of those persons who "had no schooling," 20.3 per cent admittedly visited the native doctor, 13.8 per cent of those who attended primary school, 2.9 per cent of those who attended middle school and 1.2 per cent of those who had commercial and technical training or higher visit the native doctor. Although these figures demonstrate that as people acquired more education fewer of them visited the native doctor, these figures must be viewed in a more complete social perspective. First, the majority of people in Accra (especially women), had little or no schooling. Hence most sick or emotionally distressed people would visit the native doctor or a faith healer. Second, some educated people would visit the native doctor furtively and would hesitate to divulge their visits. Third, some people who were treated by the Western-trained doctor for physical maladies would prefer the native doctor for help in their personal problems. Thus it appears that more people would use the services of the native doctor than the results of this survey imply.

The widespread visits of people to the native doctor are consistent with the beliefs of the people towards supernatural processes. In an exploratory survey of 40 college students, we asked them to estimate the percentage of people in their range of contacts who believed in spirits, juju and witchcraft. Their estimates of the persons in their scope of social relations who believed in the influence of supernatural forces upon personality ranged from 65 to 99 per cent, with an average of 85 per cent. The native doctor who could communicate with these people in their frame of reference could provide the kinds of psychotherapy and its resultant emotional security which many Africans in nearly all strata of Ghanaian society would appreciate and seek.

III. THE ORIENTATIONS AND TECHNIQUES OF NATIVE DOCTOR AS "MENTAL HEALER"

The African's holistic, bio-psychological conception of illness permits the native doctor to apply two broad points of departure to therapy. The first is bio-medical, emphasizes the healing properties of herbs, veers towards a quasi-naturalism and represents the specialty of the herbalist. The second is religio-psychological, emphasizes the therapeutic force of prayer, sacrifice and incantation, is supernaturalistic and is the specialty of the fetish priest. In an analysis of 108 records of native doctors who applied for licenses from 1951 to 1960, we found that 49 per cent regarded themselves primarily as herbalists, 43.5 per cent considered themselves herbalist-soothsayers, and 7.5 per cent regarded themselves as fetish priests (including individual and cultistic priests, such as the Tigare). These records from the local councils where the licenses are granted reveal the marked decline of the fetish priests who were cult leaders, and the marked increase of individual practitioners who combined herbalist and priest-like functions in their adaptation to the shifting needs of the urban populace. This meant that the native doctor tended to perform religious rituals as well as to administer herbs. Although a few herbalists confined their practice to those with physical maladies mainly, most native doctors did attempt to treat mental disorders and emotional disturbances.

The native doctor, whether predominantly herbalist or fetish priest, used a sequence of therapeutic procedures to remedy personality disorders. When the native doctor initially encountered the patient, he found it incumbent upon himself to diagnose the illness as well as to prescribe the remedy in so impressively convincing a manner that the patient would return for additional treatment. For example, one native doctor claimed that his intuitive judgment had an empathic basis for his diagnosis. When he shook hands with the patient he noted the firmness of his grasp, observed his appearance, modes of expression, and quality of speech. He pursued his observations by asking pointed questions until he felt that he had discerned the patient's condition.

The native doctor usually had a particular diagnostic procedure which became virtually a trademark and which was sometimes quite flamboyant. One doctor deciphered handwriting which he claimed to have learned from Spanish Moroccans. Another used what he called "Jacob's stone pillow," which he supposedly acquired in Egypt. A third looked into a mirror as if he were peering into the patient's present and future condition. A fourth used Egyptian sand-writing by counting the strung beads flung into a designated space of sand by the patient. A fifth doctor shook cowry shells and made squealing noises. All the doctors seemed to emphasize a certain mystery in their techniques and strived to impress the patient as well as to diagnose his condition.

The knowledgeable medicine man or fetish priest could apply the following characteristic psychotherapeutic techniques in handling his patient. First, the doctor could impress the patient that he had the spiritual power to protect him from witches, juju and other hostile spirits. Second, he could "immunize" the patient from future injury or misfortune by a given protective medicine; this protective medicine was effective presumably as long as the patient himself conformed so he was motivated not to deviate. On the other hand, the patient felt secure in the belief that the culprit who tried to harm him would get "caught" by the medicine and become sick. Third, the medicine man could persuade a guilt-ridden person to relieve himself by confession and to become "purified" by the sacrifice of an animal. For example, in one ritual, he could cut the throat of a chicken and fling it towards the shrine. If the bird died breast upward, it signified that the gift was accepted by the gods and the patient had been purified. If the bird died breast downward, it meant that that patient had sins which he must confess. But some medicine men did not ask the patient to confess when the bird died breast downward, but merely repeated the ritual until the bird died breast upward. Apparently they felt that the ritual was sufficient. Fourth, the medicine man could resort to exorcism to dispel an evil spirit from a disturbed patient who felt that an intruding spirit compelled him to behave bizarrely. Fifth, he could try to offset by suggestive techniques the influence of a supposed witch when a person's illness was very sudden, resisted medication or recurred. On this level, he recognized and emphasized a psychosomatic view of illness. Sixth, he could apply various devices to test a person charged with witchcraft with the intent of either accusing or clearing him of the charge. If the patient did admit witchcraft, the medicine man could use exorcism and other suggestive techniques in an effort to rid the patient from the alien or perverse spirit. Seventh, the medicine man who treated a psychotic had the knowledge and means to restrain him—usually by chains or rope—and to quiet him by sedation. His treatment consisted of making incisions on the patient's arm or shoulders to emit the evil spirits, to prescribe emetics and to inject varied substances in the patient's nose in order to clear his brain. Eighth, some medicine men had private hospitals where they kept patients on an in-treatment and custody basis and, in effect, were administrators of small hospitals.

When evaluated from a social-psychological viewpoint, how meaningful and effective were these modes of therapy? Since many techniques of therapy were learned by rote and in blind conformity to traditional belief, the effective workability of the techniques and the medicines were not tested and were of dubious value—except perhaps to impress the patient. For example, one patient recounted his experience with a medicine man as follows:

> My mother took me to one herbalist and I followed like a sheep because I did not know what was the matter with me. I stayed at this herbalist's place for six months and wasn't helped at all. He made cuts on my arm and chest. He put an awful mixture of eggs and herbs over my body and that didn't help. He put some stuff in my nose and later poured a libation of schnapps on a stone while praying in a loud voice. I left after six months and was not improved.

Since the medicine man and the patient shared a supernatural orientation to illness, they could communicate and the medicine man could reach and influence the patient. On a psychological level, the medicine man could provide emotional security and reassurance to the anxious and harassed patient who was troubled by supposedly hostile spirits and people who might harm him. He could relieve the guilt-ridden by permitting confession and by the purification of a designated sacrifice. He could reduce the intensity of an enraged person by permitting the confessional, and he could reduce the tension within a family by testing whether a person was or was not a witch, which could mean that this person may be harming others. On the other hand, the native doctor could actually harm a person by labelling him a witch and, in effect, condemning the person in the eyes of the family. He could enhance a person's confidence by protective reassurance and encouragement; and he could arouse diffidence in a person by the knowledge that black magic or juju is being practiced on him. Although the medicine man might deny that he would try to harm a person by juju, he would claim that other medicine men did practice this type of juju for a suitable fee.

Since the medicine man was concerned more with the pragmatic workability of his procedures and medicines than with the rationale of his techniques, his capacity to explain the reasons behind his practices was very inadequate. In general, his theories of mental disorder represented a composite of superstitious animism, mystical and biological ideas of personality from the West which sometimes were as antiquated as those from the 18th century. For example, he believed that piles affect the veins of the brain and cause emotional disorders. His recourse to incisions for bleeding and his use of emetics were medical procedures of the 19th century. Since he seemed to lack the knowledge of even the traditional lore of psychodynamics of personality, he seemed unaware of the traditional recognition and practice of confession as was institutionalized in the Apo ceremony of the Ashanti. Rattray has reported an account of a high priest concerning the rationale of this eight-day holiday, the name of which means "to speak harshly to":

> You know that every one has a sunsum (soul) that may get hurt or knocked about or become sick, and so make the body ill. Very often, although there may be other causes, e.g. witchcraft, ill-health is caused by the evil and the hate that another has in his head. Again you may have hatred in your head against another because of something that person has done to you, and that causes your sunsum to fret and become sick. Our forebears knew this to be the case and so they ordained a time once every year when every man and woman, free and slave, should have the freedom to speak out just what was in his head, to tell the neighbors just what they thought of them, and of their actions and not only their neighbors but also the king or chief. When a man has spoken freely his sunsum is cool and quieted, and the sunsum of the other person against whom he has spoken openly will be quieted also.

Since the native doctor appraised his therapeutic prowess by the improvement of the patient, he tended to rely upon this criterion as the rationale for his techniques and as the basis for his spiritual "power" in coping with the patient's illness. Furthermore, he might publicize his successes and overlook his failures in treatment. Although some doctors were discreet and modest about their successes, others promoted their successes in treatment by written testimonials from the patient or his relatives. For example, one doctor publicized the following letter:

> I have known Mr. O. as Divine Healer and Herbalist of no mean order. In support of my recommendation I would like to mention that my niece had a complete mental breakdown and after having failed to her normal state of health, I approached Mr. O. who was able to cure her within a couple of months which is really a remarkable achievement on his part.

These testimonials were used by the native doctor as evidence of his prowess and as means to convince other and prospective patients of his spiritual "power."

These native doctors varied considerably in their knowledge, procedural effectiveness and scope of their practice. On the one extreme, some doctors had a very extensive practice, owned several offices, a shrine and a hospital and were known for their "power." On the other extreme, many doctors hardly earned a living and were forced to turn to other occupations for supplementary income, or to abandon the profession entirely. Their mobility away from the practice of native medicine was indicative of a more profound disorganization within the occupation itself.

IV. THE DECLINING POSITION OF THE NATIVE DOCTOR AS "MENTAL HEALER"

The native doctor's declining if still dominant role of "mental healer" was influenced by the indifferent and discouraging attitude of the government, by the lack of professional authority to control the practitioners and to enforce standards of practice, by the adverse reaction of the people to the abuses of some practitioners and by the spread of competing therapies.

Although the government has encouraged the rise of Western medicine, it has either ignored or discouraged native medicine. The government has required examinations for licensing Western-trained doctors but it has permitted the regional councils to grant licenses to native doctors on the recommendation of a chief herbalist and without an examination. The government has hoped that eventually the indigenous medicinal and psychotherapeutic practices would become extinct and be replaced and its best features incorporated by Western practices. The implicit contrast between the two forms of therapy was noted unwittingly by a native doctor who referred to a Western-trained doctor as a "qualified doctor," implying that the other type was not.

But the profession itself because of its inability to authoritatively set and maintain standards and to control its members has become disorganized or even unorganized. In 1946, the Ga Medical Association was formed and in 1955 had 155 members, but its founders and leaders were unable to sustain standards. When it lapsed, the profession had no controls over the activities of its members. The traditional controls which existed for the native doctor in the villages were reduced amidst the anonymity of the urban community, and by the changing and tribally diverse clientele. In addition, the native doctor had no formal standards for recruiting and training novices. Traditionally, and in the present, he strived to interest a son or nephew or an enthusiastic youth in his craft and then to train him. But the native doctor found that few competent youths were attracted to his occupation and instead wanted more modern jobs, such as clerking in the ministries. A successful practitioner could induce a son or relative to be trained as a partner and eventual successor, but in this instance the entrepreneurial as well as the therapeutic interests become rewarding considerations. With the decrease in the recruitment of competent novices the continuity of the profession was being disrupted.

Furthermore, the ease with which the aspirant for native doctorhood secured a license not only lessened the need for training but also reduced the standards of practice. In the past, the apprentice to the native doctor was trained for about three years and thus acquired the lore for his specialty. But some native doctors who claimed to have been inspired by the "call" to become native doctors evidently lacked this training and were not competent even in terms of folk standards.

The native doctor lacked the formal means for acquiring new formulas and techniques from other native doctors unless he solicited formulas from them for a given payment or for herb formulas of his own. Although some friendly native doctors exchanged formulas and ideas, the profession lacked any institutionalized means for such exchange. Moreover, the native doctor seemed to distrust and avoid many of his colleagues some of whom he regarded as scoundrels.

Furthermore, because they dealt with an unknown clientele of diverse tribes in a changing urban society and aspired for monetary success, some native doctors were not bound by professional restraints and resorted to sharp practices. Intermittently, a few native doctors were charged with criminal practices, such as in an extreme instance conspiring to murder a given victim by black magic or juju. These practices, of course, adversely affected the image of and confidence in the whole profession.

But the native doctor encountered a crucial conflict from the competing therapies. On the one hand, he saw that Western medicines and techniques were more effective than his. On the other hand, he perceived that Christian faith-healing frequently was more attractive in the realm of faith than his appeals to jujus and deities. He noted that patients were being drawn increasingly to these other therapies. But his dominant role as mental healer was sustained by the inherent weaknesses of the competing therapies. Western psychiatry lacked the supernatural orientation which would enable the psychiatrist to share the patient's conflicts in his own idiom, which the native doctor understood. Christian faith-healing lacked any knowledge of medicines which the patient frequently wanted and which the native doctor could provide. Thus the native doctor's combined supernatural orientation and knowledge of herbs sustained him against the intensified competition of the two other therapies.

V. THE EFFECTIVE BUT LIMITED ROLE OF THE WESTERN-TRAINED PSYCHIATRIST

Psychiatric therapy was limited almost exclusively to the in-patient treatment of the state mental hospital and was largely organic in orientation. The three psychiatrists in this hospital used drugs and electric shock as their modes of therapy although they did practice some form of group therapy for the educated, volunteer patients. Out-patient treatment was negligible or virtually non-existent. But the spreading acceptance of Western psychiatry was evidenced by the increasing number of resident patients in the hospital. Thus in 1955, the state mental hospital had an excess of 8.1 per cent over capacity of 1100 patients. In 1960, the excess rose to 54.5 per cent (see Table I).

The two major types of hospitalized patients were 1) the volunteer "paying" patients and 2) the violently insane. The "paying" patients were the educated persons who tired of or discarded native treatments and sought Western therapies. These paying patients were frequently detribalized and Western-oriented. By contrast, the tribally and animistically oriented African suspected the mental hospital. In fact, Field observed that rural patients were rarely committed to the mental hospital because mental

Table I

EXCESS OF RESIDENT PATIENTS OVER HOSPITAL CAPACITY IN STATE
MENTAL HOSPITALS ACCRA GHANA: 1955-1960 *

Year	Resident Patients	Excess of Capacity Per cent.**
1955	1189	8.1
1956	1287	17.0
1957	1362	23.8
1958	1495	35.9
1959	1555	41.3
1960	1700	54.5

* Data from auditing office of State Mental Hospital, Accra Ghana.
** Capacity equals 1100 patients.

illness was considered supernaturally determined and outside the scope of the hospital.

On the other hand, news of the successful treatment of patients spread so that increasingly people began to accept the hospital as an institution to which they could commit their psychotic relatives for custody as well as therapy. But the hospitalization of patients became complicated by the stigma of defective heredity which was associated with insanity. In this respect, the family of the patient also became suspect of the hereditary "taint." Educated persons were especially sensitive about this point. When psychotics were reluctant to be sent to the mental hospital, their relatives felt a similar hesitation. Thus they were caught in the dilemma of seeking effective treatment and of being stigmatized. Some sought out the native doctor for initial treatment as a way out, but soon recognized the futility of this procedure and as a last recourse turned to the state mental hospital.

Western psychiatry, despite its effective modes of physical therapy for the several types of psychoses, was a very circumscribed form of therapy in Ghana. It was limited mainly to in-patient treatment and to psychotics. Biological in its emphasis, it also lacked the frame of reference for treating on a psychological level the supernaturally oriented African. But news of its effectiveness in treating psychotic cases spread so that more people sent relatives to the hospital for treatment, although these people encountered the complicating fact of prejudice towards the insane by many urban people.

VI. THE SPREADING INFLUENCE OF CHRISTIAN
FAITH-HEALER

The Christian faith-healer's influence has spread because of the declining influence of the native doctor, the decline of tribal animism as manifested in fetish cults, and the search for more powerful gods. As a central facet of an indigenous religion, Christian faith-healing has been consistent with the African's form of orgiastic and emotional worship and with his version of the function of religion in healing. Its central tenets have been expressed by one of the Christian cults, "The Lord is There," as follows: "Jesus Christ is not only the Savior of the soul but the Healer of the body, the great and perfect Physician." Because of this emphasis upon healing, indigenous Christianity thus differed from missionary Christianity which is more restrained and rational in its method of worship and far more concentrated upon education and social service.

The African's acceptance of indigenous Christianity contributed to his sense of social purpose while his reaction to its faith-healing sustained his emotional security. Some followers of healing cults lived in colonies so that their religious credo was the basis for a complete way of life not just a response to a mode of therapy.

But the faith healer also used specific forms of psychotherapy many of which were similar to and perhaps imitations of the native doctor. But he incorporated these techniques within the general framework of his belief system. One prevalent form of crude group psychotherapy which was peculiar to the faith healer's technique was the revival. During a revival, the faith healer could arouse the audience to pitches of emotional intensity which would lead to deep emotional catharses and to seizures. These revivals were not only verbal but had the deep rhythmic pulse of the drumming, the effects of which were unavoidable. These revivals were especially effective for hysterical persons and for suggestible, social marginal followers.

Since the faith healer compelled his followers to manifest their belief in Christ, he could also demand that they disavow their belief in witchcraft and juju as spiritual forces, and even surrender their idols. He could elicit confessions or restrain them. Sometimes, his inadequate training in psychotherapy led to strange uses of these techniques. For example, one faith healer restrained his followers from uninhibited confessions, perhaps not to arouse his own anxieties. His rationalization was the following:

> Confessing disease is like signing for a package that the Express Company has delivered. Don't accept anything that Satan brings. A spiritual law that few recognize is that our confession rules us. It is what we confess with our lips that really dominates our inner being. Make your lips do their duty.

The faith healer also forbade the use of medicines for physical ailments, and the newer cult leader proscribed medicine even for serious physical diseases. Instead, he advocated the use of "holy water" as a healing potion for emotional as well as physical disorders. He also distributed a protective symbol such as the "holy handkerchief" to avert misfortune from evil persons and spirits.

The faith healer in the established cult seemed more trained, more responsible and milder in manner than the faith healer from the newer and "wilder" cults. The faith healer in the newer cults frequently felt that a "divine call" was almost enough for his vocation. Hence he relied upon informal training, inspirational improvising and copying from other healers for his psychotherapeutic procedures. Since these indigenous faith-healing cults lacked an association, the faith healer had no professional restraints upon his practices. The extreme type of faith healer was both flamboyant and unscrupulous. His chief emphasis in his varied healing procedures was faith in God and faith in his own prowess, which from his claims approached omnipotence. His exaggerated emphasis upon his healing prowess was presumably "verified" by testimonial letters and statements from his patients and their relatives. Even the faith-healer of the more established cult presented an exaggerated version of his healing prowess, as can be seen from the following account by the Pastor-prophet James K. Nkansah:

> At Teppa in Ashanti I prayed and 50 blind persons, 693 devil-possessed persons were healed on Sunday the 26th of March, 1961. At Kukuom, I prayed and 47 blind persons, 592 devil possessed persons were healed on the 2nd day of April, 1961. Last Sunday when you came here and departed 9 blind persons got their sight.

As head of a religious movement, the faith healer solicited gifts and money from his followers and his patients, which sometimes left room for unscrupulous practices.

The faith healer had a widespread appeal for many persons who, in the anomie of the urban community, were in search of new gods for spiritual protection and craved the social purpose that a cohesive religious movement provided. Although his repertoire of psychotherapeutic techniques did not differ markedly from that of the native doctor, and included counseling, exorcism and even environmental manipulation, the faith healer also had the impetus of a social movement to reinforce his individual forms of therapy. Thus the cathartic expressions in the revivals and drummings and the emotionally supportive therapy of group approval were implicit psychotherapeutic processes which the native doctor lacked. But just as there were no enforced standards of treatment for the native doctor, the faith healer also had no associational restraints upon his practices, so that the unscrupulous and deceptive practitioner diminished the confidence and aroused the suspicions of initially trusting followers. Nonetheless, his aggressive recruiting practices and a flamboyant manner have continued to attract many followers, especially women. These followers have turned to the faith healer not only for religious guidance but for counsel and psychotherapy when in distress over their personal problems.

VII. CONCLUSIONS AND IMPLICATIONS

The native doctor in Ghana, West Africa has a heritage of orientations, practices and rituals for the diagnosis and treatment of mental disorders as components of an occupational culture. This culture is suitable peculiarly to the treatment of the African's disordered behavior because it provides a frame of reference and perspective to illness generally and mental disorders particularly which the patient and native doctor, as indigenous psychiatrist, share. Both conceive of disordered behavior as a supernatural phenomenon and as determined by spirits, black magic or juju and witches and not as naturalistic products of conflicts or germs. Hence the native doctor can communicate with and influence the patient. Although ineffectual in treating many mental disorders as well as physical ailments, the competent native doctor can provide reassurance to the anxious patient who fears harm or misfortune from spirits or witches, can reduce the intensity of the guilt-ridden patient, can soften the individual afflicted with silent rage and can quiet the agitated psychotic by restraints, sedation and relevant conversation.

But amidst the rapid changes of the urban community, his profession, though conforming superficially to the needs of the urban populace, has become disorganized and its prestige has begun to decline. This decline has been facilitated by the pressures within the urban community and has been focused mainly in the lack of enforcement of standards, the inadequate communication and exchange of ideas and techniques, the inability to recruit competent personnel to sustain the profession, the ease of obtaining a license from the regional council, and the increase of untrained, incompetent and unscrupulous practitioners who have damaged the confidence which the people have had in the native doctor. The outward forces which have contributed to the declining influence of the native doctor are the negative attitude of the government towards this profession as an instance of tribalism and the challenge of competing therapists such as the Western psychiatrist and the Christian faith healer. In spite of these pressures, the native doctor remains the dominant healer of mental disorders because of the limitations underlying the strengths of the competing therapists.

The Western psychiatrist has confined his practice largely to the in-patient treatment in the state mental hospital, so that out-patient treatment is definitely negligible. In addition, his emphasis on organic and physical therapies and his naturalistic orientation to behavior would deter him from effective and therapeutic communication with his supernaturally oriented patients. Although his physical therapies within the hospital have been successful and have attracted an increasing number of people who are becoming agreeable to committing their psychotic relatives to this institution, his influence as therapist remains circumscribed, and on an out-patient, psychotherapeutic basis would be effective mainly with Western-oriented, educated Africans.

The Christian faith-healer, however, represents a formidable, but not necessarily enduring, challenge to the native doctor as counselor and improvised psychotherapist. His widespread appeal as a religious leader provides him with the impetus of a social movement to bolster his individual psychotherapy as well as his crude group therapy in the revivals and the drummings. But the faith healer, like the medicine man, lacks professional restraints upon his behavior and his exaggerated claims; this lack of inherent professional controls enables the new and "wild" faith healers to indulge in grandiose pretensions and in unscrupulous practices. In this light, it remains to be seen whether the indigenous Christian cult with its central tenet of healing is not a tentative recourse resulting from the declining prestige of the native doctor and the retardation in the training of Western trained doctors and Western trained psychiatrists.

The trend of the future is revealed partly by the increasingly educated youth who are turning away from supernatural versions of healing and relying increasingly upon the naturalistic practices of the Western doctor. For example, in a survey of 100 primary and middle school children we found that 92 percent preferred Western-trained doctors to the indigenous doctor for treatment. Although some may have concealed their attitudes and preferences for the native doctor, still the evidence showing changed attitudes towards healing is definite. On the other hand, we do not know whether this trust in the Western-trained doctor will carry over into the amelioration of their personal difficulties.

In view of the urgent mental health needs of the people amidst the rapidly changing position of the native doctor in the urban context, the following implications suggest themselves from this inquiry. First, on the level of social action, it means that a concerted program is necessary to fulfill the urgent mental health needs of the people and that this program can be facilitated by training competent native doctors as well as educated youth who can implement the treatment of disordered behavior within the supernatural framework of their patients but by the use of modern psychotherapeutic techniques. Second, on the level of social control, it indicates that more effective vigilance by the government is necessary to deter unscrupulous practitioners (whether native doctors or Christian faith healers) from harming unsuspecting patients. Third, on the level of social change, it means that a transplanted occupational group from a rural to an urban environment can become quickly disorganized by the pressures of urban processes. Fourth, and finally, it reveals on the level of historiography the need to record and document these and other facets of change in the transition from village tribalism to urban nationalism before these facets of urban life in West Africa dissipate and are lost to further inquiry.

FURTHER READINGS

Gans, Herbert J. *The Urban Villagers*. New York: The Free Press, 1962.

Lerner, Daniel. *The Passing of Traditional Society*. New York: The Free Press, 1958.

Stein, Maurice R. *The Eclipse of Community*. Princeton, New Jersey: Princeton University Press, 1960. Harper Torchbook, 1964.

Vidich, Arthur and Bensman, Joseph. *Small Town in Mass Society*. Princeton, New Jersey: Princeton University Press, 1958. Doubleday Anchor Books, 1960.

10

BUREAUCRATIZATION AND SOCIAL CHANGE

Introduction

HARDLY A PERSON EXISTS in the Western World who is not directly affected by the process of bureaucratization. We find examples of bureaucracy in literature describing societies at only primitive levels of industrialization and urbanization like Nicolai Gogol's, *The Overcoat,* about a Russian government clerk or at more advanced levels as in Guy De Maupassant's, *A Family Affair,* whose principal character is a clerk in the French naval office. For Americans a frequently voiced comment is, "You can't beat the system."

S. N. Eisenstadt discusses some approaches to the study of bureaucratization, the factors influencing and enhancing the development of this process and the conditions giving rise to debureaucratization. As in his other essay reprinted in Chapter 8 there is a concern with flexibility as an important aspect of social systems. This relates back to our discussion of Durkheim in particular and deviance and conformity, more generally, in Chapter 7.

The societal structure of modern Germany represents an extremely bureaucratic type of social system. It is hardly surprising that sociological analysis of bureaucratic structure reached a high point in the work of the late Max Weber who was a participant in German bureaucratic structures at the turn of the century. Ralf Dahrendorf describes a type of perspective in contemporary German life which is illustrative of a highly bureaucratized society. At the same time we get a glimpse of the German situation we learn something about the fundamental requirements of a democratic political system.

Finally, Selo Soemardjan provides us with a discussion and description of bureaucratic organizations undergoing change during a revolution. Focusing on his observations as a participating bureaucrat in the Indonesian government he shows us how political, economic, historical and cultural forces shaped the process of transformation.

Bureaucracy, Bureaucratization and Debureaucratization

S. N. EISENSTADT

IN THE LITERATURE dealing with bureaucracy we can often discern a continual shift between two points of view. The first point of view defines bureaucracy mainly as a tool, or a mechanism created for the successful and efficient implementation of a certain goal or goals. Bureaucracy is seen as an epitome of rationality and of efficient implementation of goals and provision of services.

The second point of view sees bureaucracy mainly as an instrument of power, of exercising control over people and over different spheres of life, and of continuous expansion of such power either in the interests of the bureaucracy itself or in the interests of some (often sinister) masters. This point of view tends mainly to stress the process of bureaucratization, i.e., the extension of the power of a bureaucratic organization over many areas beyond its initial purpose, the growing internal formalization within the bureaucracy, the regimentation of these areas by the bureaucracy, and in general a strong emphasis by the bureaucracy on the extension of its power.

This twofold attitude toward bureaucracy can be discerned, although in differing degrees, in most of the basic literature on the subject, whether that of the classical sociological approaches (Max Weber, Mosca, Michels) or that of public administration and the theory of organization. This twofold approach has in fact run through most of the discussions about bureaucracy since the end of the last century.

Although the awareness of this problem of the twofold aspect of bureaucracy can be found in most of the literature dealing with bureaucracy, it is significant that these two points of view rarely converge. For those persons, as for instance the students of public administration, who see bureaucracy as a tool for implementation of goals, the power element is mainly seen as a stumbling block in the process of rational and efficient implementation of such goals. For those who see in bureaucracies mainly instruments of power and bearers of a continuous process of bureaucratization and of growing power of oligarchies, the implementation of the official or purported goals of the bureaucracy is but a secondary aspect, sometimes only an empty ideology.

And yet the very fact that these two points of view can be found in

From *Administrative Science Quarterly*, 4, 1960, pp. 303-320. Reprinted by permission of the publisher and author.

almost all the literature on bureaucracy seems to indicate that they are not two entirely separate and contradictory points of view, but rather that they point to various possibilities, all inherent in the very nature of bureaucracy. Thus the main problem seems to be not which point of view is right in itself, but rather the conditions under which each of these tendencies becomes actualized and predominant in any given bureaucratic organization.

It is the purpose of this paper, first, to show that both these tendencies are indeed inherent in the basic conditions of growth and development of any bureaucracy by its very nature as a social organization; and, second, to propose some preliminary hypotheses about the conditions under which each of these tendencies may become predominant in a given bureaucracy. In this way we hope to demonstrate that the convergence of various types of studies of bureaucracy and organizations that have developed recently can enable us to overcome the dichotomy developing between these two different points of view and some of the problems of the "metaphysical pathos" in the discussion of bureaucracy.

CONDITIONS OF DEVELOPMENT OF BUREAUCRATIC ORGANIZATIONS

We shall start with an analysis of the conditions of development of bureaucratic organizations and see to what extent these conditions can explain the existence of different inherent tendencies in their development and their patterns of activities.

Although since Weber there have been relatively few systematic studies of the conditions responsible for the development of bureaucratic organizations and processes of bureaucratization that could serve as a basis for a systematic comparative anlaysis, there exist numerous concrete historical analyses of the development and functioning of different bureaucratic organizations. On the basis of these materials and of current research it is possible to specify, tentatively, the conditions under which bureaucratic organizations tend to develop and which apply both to historical (Chinese, Byzantine, and Egyptian) bureaucratic societies and to modern societies or sectors of them.

The available material suggests that bureaucratic organizations tend to develop in societies when:

1) There develops extensive differentiation between major types of roles and institutional (economic, political, religious, and so forth) spheres.

2) The most important social roles are allocated not according to criteria of membership in the basic particularistic (kinship or territorial) groups, but rather according to universalistic and achievement criteria, or criteria of membership in more flexibly constituted groups such as professional, religious, vocational, or "national" groups.

3) There evolve many functionally specific groups (economic, cultural, religious, social-integrative) that are not embedded in basic particularistic groups, as, for example, economic and professional organizations, various types of voluntary associations, clubs, and so forth.

4) The definition of the total community is not identical with, and consequently is wider than, any such basic particularistic group, as can be seen, for instance, in the definition of the Hellenic culture in Byzantium or of the Confucian cultural order.

5) The major groups and strata in the society develop, uphold, and attempt to implement numerous discrete, political, economic, and social-service goals which cannot be implemented within the limited framework of the basic particularistic groups.

6) The growing differentiation in the social structure makes for complexity in many spheres of life, such as increasing interdependence between far-off groups and growing difficulty in the assurance of supply of resources and services.

7) These developments result to some extent in "free-floating" resources, i.e., manpower and economic resources as well as commitments for political support which are neither embedded in nor assured to any primary ascriptive-particularistic groups, as, for example, monetary resources, a relatively free labor force, and a free political vote. Consequently, the various institutional units in the society have to compete for resources, manpower, and support for the implementation of their goals and provision of services; and the major social units are faced with many regulative and administrative problems.

The available material suggests that bureaucratic organizations develop in relation to such differentiation in the social system. Bureaucratic organizations can help in coping with some of the problems arising out of such differentiation, and they perform important functions in the organization of adequate services and co-ordination of large-scale activities, in the implementation of different goals, in the provision of resources to different groups, and in the regulation of various intergroup relations and conflicts. Such bureaucratic organizations are usually created by certain elites (rulers, economic entrepreneurs, etc.) to deal with the problems outlined and to assure for these elites both the provision of such services and strategic power positions in the society.

Thus in many historical societies bureaucratic administrations were created by kings who wanted to establish their rule over feudal-aristocratic forces and who wanted, through their administration, to control the resources created by various economic and social groups and to provide these groups with political, economic, and administrative services that would make them dependent on the rulers.

In many modern societies bureaucratic organizations are created when the holders of political or economic power are faced with problems that arise because of external (war, etc.) or internal (economic development, political demands, etc.) developments. For the solution of such problems they have to mobilize adequate resources from different groups and spheres of life.

Obviously, these conclusions have to be tested and amplified through detailed application to various societies and different institutional spheres. But even at this preliminary stage of our analysis they are of interest in relation to tendencies of development inherent in bureaucratic organizations.

In sum, the development of bureaucratic organizations is related to certain social conditions, the most important of which are, first, the availability of various fluid, "free-floating" resources; second, the necessity for large-scale organizations; and, third, the development of several centers of power that compete for such resources. Thus two conclusions are indicated.

First, as a result of the very conditions that give rise to a bureaucratic organization, it is, almost by definition, obliged to compete for resources, manpower, legitimation within the society, general support and clientele, and, to some extent also, patrons and protectors.

The classical theories of bureaucracy recognized that a bureaucracy is always dependent on the outside world for its resources. Unlike traditional ecological, family, or kinship groups, the incumbents of its office do not receive direct remuneration from their clients nor do they own their means of production. But because many of these theories referred chiefly to governmental bureaucracies, they took the supply of the requisite resources for granted and only emphasized the fact that dependence on external resources assures the relative segregation and independence of the bureaucrat's role. In reality, however, the need to compete for legitimation and resources faces governmental departments also and can be considered a basic aspect of every bureaucracy.

Thus from the very beginning a bureaucratic organization is put in what may be called a power situation, in which it has to cast its influence and to generate processes of power on its own behalf and in which it is under pressure from different centers of power in the society that would control it.

Second, this basic power situation in which a bureaucratic organization develops and functions is strongly underlined by the fact that any bureaucracy, not only implements different political and social goals and provides different services, but also necessarily performs regulatory and mediating functions in the society. This is because the rules governing implementation of goals and provision of services by a bureaucracy necessarily affect the distribution of power and allocation of resources to different groups in the society. These regulative and mediating functions enhance the potential power position of any bureaucracy, increase the competition of other groups for its services and for control over it, and generate many pressures both emanating from it and impinging on it.

Thus from its inception a bureaucratic organization is in a state of constant interaction with its environment and has to develop different ways of maintaining a dynamic equilibrium in this environment. The equilibrium results from adjustment of its own goals, structure, and interests in relation to the major forces in its social environment and to the power processes generated by each of them.

THE BUREAUCRATIC ORGANIZATION AS A SOCIAL SYSTEM

To understand more fully how different types of equilibrium are developed by different bureaucratic organizations, it is necessary to examine more closely some of the major characteristics of the internal structure of bureaucracies. A systematic approach to this problem is facilitated by the extensive data in the literature dealing with the problems of bureaucracy and of organization. The major insights to be gained from these materials and analyses seem to be as follows:

1) Any bureaucratic organization constitutes a social system of its own; therefore its internal division of labor is determined not only by the technical problems of implementation of goals, but also by other needs and problems. Since special roles and activities geared to the provision of these needs exist within it, there can be no purely rational bureaucratic organization free from personal, primary, or power elements. On the contrary, some such elements (like primary groups of workers or identification between different participants) perform functionally important tasks in the organization.

2) Each of the roles existing in any bureaucratic organization is systematically related to the outside world. The organization must manipulate several aspects of its external environment (e.g., directors must deal with boards of trustees and legislative committees, the sales managers with buyers and sellers, the manager with trade unions and labor exchanges). The necessary contact between the incumbents of such roles and parallel role incumbents in other organizations may establish professional, solidarity, or conflict relations and various reference orientations and identifications. The relations resulting from such contact may cut across any given organization and at the same time greatly influence the behavior of the incumbents in their organizations, consequently affecting the performance of these organizations. These contacts also distinguish the incumbents' bureaucratic roles within the organization from their other social roles in the family or community, especially the type of motivation for performance of their bureaucratic role that they bring from their social background. Finally, the relations with different types of clients and sections of the general public with which the incumbent of a bureaucratic role comes into selective contact might put him under pressure with respect to the performance of his bureaucratic roles. Such pressure may be exerted either by means of various professional or community roles and organizations in which both the bureaucrat and the client may participate, by specific organizations of the public or clients, or through direct interaction in the bureaucrat-client role.

3) Within each organization there develop various subgroups and sub-

systems (workmen, foremen, professional groups, departmental units, and so forth), and the organization is faced with the problem of co-ordinating these subgroups, of regulating their relations with each other and with the organization as a whole. Such subgroups may have different conceptions of and attitudes toward the organization's goals and needs, and these differences must be taken into account when studying the functioning of any bureaucratic organization.

4) Thus the interaction between the different subgroups or subsystems in any bureaucratic organization should be viewed as a continuous process of communication, of allocation of rewards, of mutual perception, a process by which some—but only some—fusion (the extent of which necessarily varies) is effected between the motives and goals of individuals and subgroups and the over-all organizational goals.

5) The multiplicity of any organization's external relations and internal subgroups may lead to the development of many different types of activity that transcend the specific bureaucratic roles and relations both within and without the organization. Thus an organization interested in improving its internal human and public relations may help its members and their families integrate their activities with those of other social groups—all this to improve performance of the bureaucratic role.

Such activities, in turn, bring the incumbents of the bureaucratic role into various relations with other persons that may go beyond the basic relationship of the bureaucratic role. These might consequently lead (a) to development of new goal orientations by the organization and to processes of bureaucratization or debureaucratization; (b) to attempts on the part of the bureaucrats to impose the bureaucracy's conceptions and goals on these external activities and groups, or (c) to pressures of these groups on the goals of the organization and performance of the bureaucratic roles within it. These pressures may be directed toward changing or supervising the goals and activities of the bureaucratic organization, limiting their application, adding new dimensions to them, or taking over of the organization.

Here we are confronted with an aspect of the bureaucratic organization that is of major importance to our analysis, namely, the potential flexibility of its goals. We have seen that any bureaucratic organization evolves as a means of implementing a specific goal or goals. However, the very conditions responsible for its development, the multiplicity of its internal subgroups, its continuous dependence on external groups, and the numerous pressures to which it is subjected facilitate or perhaps even necessitate modification of at least some of its goals. Such flexibility is, as Thompson and McEwen have rightly stressed, almost a condition (especially in modern society) of the bureaucratic organization's survival.

It is largely through incorporating new (mostly secondary) goals and attempting to assure the requisite resources for their implementation that a bureaucratic organization maintains its equilibrium with its environment. It thus exerts its influence on this environment, establishes various rules which influence the training of people aspiring to be enrolled into it, and indirectly may influence general educational standards and impose its own specific orientation on parts of its environment. It is through such processes, as well as those of competition for resources and power, that the different types of interaction and equilibrium between the bureaucratic organization and its social environment develop.

BUREAUCRATIZATION AND DEBUREAUCRATIZATION

It is through such continuous interaction with its environment that a bureaucratic organization may succeed in maintaining those characteristics that distinguish it from other social groups. The most important of these characteristics, common to most bureaucratic organizations and often stressed in the literature, are specialization of roles and tasks; the prevalence of autonomous, rational, nonpersonal rules in the organization; and the general orientation to rational, efficient implementation of specific goals.

These structural characteristics do not, however, develop in a social vacuum but are closely related to the functions and activities of the bureaucratic organization in its environment. The extent to which they can develop and persist in any bureaucratic organization is dependent on the type of dynamic equilibrium that the organization develops in relation to its environment. Basically, three main outcomes of such interaction or types of such dynamic equilibrium can be distinguished, although probably each of them can be further subdivided and some overlapping occurs between them.

The first type of equilibrium is one in which any given bureaucratic organization maintains its autonomy and distinctiveness. The basic structural characteristics that differentiate it from other social groups and in which it implements its goal or goals (whether its initial goals or goals added later) are retained and it is supervised by those who are legitimately entitled to do this (holders of political power, "owners," or boards of trustees).

The second main possibility is that of bureaucratization, as it has been already defined earlier. This is the extension of the bureaucracy's spheres of activities and power either in its own interest or those of some of its elite. It tends toward growing regimentation of different areas of social life and some extent of displacement of its service goals in favor of various power interests and orientations. Examples are military organizations that tend to impose their rule on civilian life, or political parties that exert pressure on their potential supporters in an effort to monopolize their private and occupational life and make them entirely dependent on the political party.

The third main outcome is debureaucratization. Here there is subversion of the goals and activities of the bureaucracy in the interests of different groups with which it is in close interaction (clients, patrons, interested parties). In debureaucratization the specific characteristics of the bureaucracy in terms both of its autonomy and its specific rules and goals are minimized, even up to the point where its very functions and activities are taken over by other groups or organizations. Examples of this can be found in cases when some organization (i.e., a parents' association or a religious or political group) attempts to divert the rules and working of a bureaucratic organization (school, economic agency, and so forth) for its own use or according to its own values and goals. It makes demands on the members of bureaucratic organizations to perform tasks that are obviously outside the specific scope of these organizations.

Each of these possibilities entails a specific development of the bureaucratic role in relation to other social roles with which it has to interact—whether other social roles of the incumbents of the bureaucratic roles or other "client," public, or similar roles. Thus in the maintenance of a bureaucracy's autonomy and of its goal and service orientation the bearers of the bureaucratic roles maintain their distinctiveness from closely related roles but at the same time fully recognize the distinctiveness of these other roles.

In the case of bureaucratization the bureaucratic roles tend to dominate the other roles (both of the incumbents and of those with whom they interact) and to impose on them the bureaucratic criteria, so as to minimize the autonomy and distinctiveness of these other roles and maximize their own power over them.

In the case of debureaucratization the various outside non-bureaucratic roles impinge on the bureaucratic role to an extent which tends to minimize the specificity of the bureaucratic roles and the relative autonomy of the bureaucratic rules in the implementation of goals and in the provision of services.

Each of these possibilities may also involve, in different ways and degrees, the bureaucracy's orientation to new goals, its incorporation of new goals, and its diversion of activities to the implementation of such new goals. Many overlappings between these various tendencies and possibilities may, of course, develop. The tendencies toward bureaucratization and debureaucratization may, in fact, develop side by side. Thus, for instance, a growing use of the bureaucratic organization and the extension of its scope of activities for purposes of political control might be accompanied by deviation from its rules for the sake of political expediency. The possibility of these tendencies occurring in the same case may be explained by the fact that a stable service-oriented bureaucracy (the type of bureaucracy depicted in the Weberian ideal type of bureaucracy) is based on the existence of some equilibrium or *modus vivendi* between professional autonomy and societal (or political) control. Once this equilibrium is severely disrupted, the outcome with respect to the bureaucracy's organization and activity may be the simultaneous development of bureaucrati-zation and debureaucratization in different spheres of its activities, although usually one of these tendencies is more pronounced.

We thus see that the problem of what kind of equilibrium any bu-reaucratic organization will develop in relation to its environment is inher-ent both in the conditions of the development of a bureaucratic organization and in its very nature as a social system, in its basic components and its interrelation with the external environment in which it functions. Thus the dilemma of viewing a bureaucracy either as an instrument for the im-plementation of goals or as a power instrument is in a way resolved.

But this poses a new problem or question as to the conditions that influence or determine which of these tendencies will become actualized or predominant in any given case.

SOME VARIABLES IN THE STUDY OF BUREAUCRACY

It is as yet very difficult to propose any definite and systematic hy-pothesis about this problem since very little research is available that is specifically related to it.

What can be done at this stage is, first, to point out some variables that, on the basis of available material and the preceding discussion, seem central to this problem, and then to propose some preliminary hypotheses, which may suggest directions in which research work on this problem may be attempted.

On the basis of those discussions we would like to propose that (a) the major goals of the bureaucratic organization, (b) the place of these goals in the social structure of the society, and (c) the type of depend-ence of the bureaucracy on external forces (clients, holders of political power, or other prominent groups) are of great importance in influencing both its internal structure and its relation with its environment. These dif-ferent variables, while to some extent interdependent, are not identical. Each brings into relief the interdependence of the bureaucratic organization with its social setting from a different point of view.

The bureaucracy's goals, as has been lately shown in great detail by Parsons, are of strategic importance, because they constitute one of the most important connecting links between the given organization and the total social structure in which it is placed. That which from the point of view of the organization is the major goal is very often from the point of view of the total society the function of the organization. Hence the various interrelations between a bureaucratic organization, other groups, and the total society are largely mediated by the nature of its goals. This applies both to the resources needed by the organization and to the prod-ucts it gives to the society.

But it is not merely the contents of the goals, i.e., whether they are mainly political, economic, cultural, and so forth, that influence the relation of the organization with its environment, but the place of the goals in the institutional structure of the society as well. By the relative place of the specific goals of any given bureaucratic organization within the society we mean the centrality (or marginality) of these goals with respect to the society's value and power system and the extent of legitimation it affords them. Thus there would obviously be many differences between a large corporation with critical products and a small economic organization with marginal products; between a political party close to the existing government performing the functions of a "loyal opposition" and a revolutionary group; between established churches and minority or militant sects; between fully established educational institutions and sectarian study or propaganda groups.

A third variable which seems to influence the bureaucracy's structural characteristics and activities is the extent and nature of its dependence on external resources and power. This dependence or relation may be defined in terms of:

1) The chief function of the organization, i.e., whether it is a service, market, or membership recruitment agency. (This definition is closely related to, but not necessarily identical with, its goals.)

2) The extent to which its clientele is entirely dependent upon its products, or conversely, the type and extent of competition between it and parallel agencies.

3) The nature and extent of the internal (ownership) and external control.

4) The criteria used to measure the success of the organization as such and its members' performance, especially the extent of changes in the behavior and membership affiliation of its clients (as, for instance, in the case of a political party).

5) The spheres of life of its personnel that the activities of a given bureaucratic organization encompass.

6) The spheres of life of its clientele that the activities of a given bureaucratic organization encompass.

It is not claimed that this list is exhaustive, but it seems to provide some preliminary clues as to the possible direction of further research on the problem.

All these variables indicate the great interdependence existing between the bureaucratic organization and its social environment. Each variable points to some ways in which a bureaucratic organization attempts to control different parts of its environment and to adapt its goals to changing environment or to different ways in which groups outside the bureaucracy control it and direct its activities. The outcome of this continuous interaction varies continuously according to the constellation of these different variables.

CONDITIONS OF BUREAUCRATIZATION
AND DEBUREAUCRATIZATION

On the basis of the foregoing considerations and of current research like that of Janowitz, of historical research on which we have reported already, and research in progress on the relations between bureaucratic organization and new immigrants in Israel, we propose several general hypotheses concerning the conditions that promote autonomy or, conversely, bureaucratization or debureaucratization. In these hypotheses we deal with the influence, first, of the structure, organization, and distribution of different goals in the bureaucracy's immediate social environment and, second, of the types of dependency of a bureaucracy on its clientele. As already noted, these are only preliminary hypotheses that do not, as yet, deal with all the variables previously outlined.

The first of these hypotheses proposes that the development of any given bureaucratic organization as a relatively autonomous service agency is contingent upon the following conditions obtaining in its social setting:

1) Relative predominance of universalistic elements in the orientations and goals of the groups most closely related to the bureaucracy.

2) Relatively wide distribution of power and values in the economic, cultural, and political spheres among many groups and the maintenance of continuous struggle and competition among them or, in other words, no monopoly of the major power positions by any one group.

3) A wide range of differentiation among different types of goals.

4) The continuous specialization and competition among different bureaucratic organizations and between them and other types of groups about their relative places with regard to implementation of different goals.

5) The existence of strongly articulated political groups and the maintenance of control over the implementation of the goals by the legitimate holders of political, communal, or economic power.

Thus a service bureaucracy, one that maintains both some measure of autonomy and of service orientation, tends to develop either in a society, such as the "classical" Chinese Empire or the Byzantine Empire from the sixth to the tenth century, in which there exist strong political rulers and some politically active groups, such as the urban groups, aristocracy, and the church in the Byzantine Empire, or the literati and gentry in China, whose aspirations are considered by the rulers. It also tends to develop in a democratic society in which effective political power is vested in an efficient, strong, representative executive. In both cases it is the combination of relatively strong political leadership with some political articulation and activity of different strata and groups (an articulation which necessarily tends to be entirely different in expression in historical empires from modern democracies) that facilitates the maintenance of a service bureaucracy.

In some societies a group may establish a power monopoly over parts of its environment and over the definition and establishment of the society's goals and the appropriation of its resources. This group may use the bureaucracy as an instrument of power and manipulation, distort its autonomous function and service orientation, and subvert some of its echelons through various threats or inducements for personal gratification. Historically the most extreme example of such developments can be found in those societies in which the rulers developed political goals that were strongly opposed by various active groups that they tried to suppress, such as in Prussia in the seventeenth and eighteenth centuries, in many conquest empires such as the Ottoman, or in the periods of aristocratization of the Byzantine Empire. Modern examples of this tendency can be found in totalitarian societies or movements. Less extreme illustrations can also be found in other societies, and it should be a major task of comparative research to specify the different possible combinations of the conditions enumerated above and their influence on the possible development of bureaucratic organizations.

The development of a bureaucratic organization in the direction of debureaucratization seems to be connected mainly with the growth of different types of *direct* dependence of the bureaucratic organization on parts of its clientele. At this stage we may propose the following preliminary hypotheses about the influence that the type of dependency of the bureaucracy on its clients has on some of its patterns of activity. First, the greater its dependence on its clientele in terms of their being able to go to a competing agency, the more it will have to develop techniques of communication and additional services to retain its clientele and the more it will be influenced by different types of demands by the clientele for services in spheres that are not directly relevant to its main goals. Second, insofar as its dependence on its clients is due to the fact that its criteria of successful organizational performance are based on the number and behavior pattern of the organization's members or clients (as is often the case in semipolitical movements, educational organizations, and so forth), it will have to take an interest in numerous spheres of its clients' activities and either establish its control over them or be subjected to their influence and direction. Finally, the greater its *direct* dependence on different participants in the political arena, and the smaller the basic economic facilities and political assurance given by the holders of political power—as is the case in some public organizations in the United States and to some extent also in different organizations in Israel—the greater will be its tendency to succumb to the demands of different political and economic pressure groups and to develop its activities and distort its own rules accordingly.

As already indicated, in concrete cases some overlapping between the tendencies to bureaucratization and debureaucratization may occur. Thus, for instance, when a politically monopolistic group gains control over a bureaucratic organization, it may distort the rules of this organization in order to give special benefits to the holders of political power or to maintain its hold over different segments of the population. On the other hand, when a process of debureaucratization sets in because of the growing pressure of different groups on a bureaucracy, there may also develop within the bureaucratic organization, as a sort of defense against these pressures, a tendency toward formalization and bureaucratization. This shows that the distinctive characteristics of a specific bureaucratic organization and role have been impinged upon in different directions, and one may usually discern which of these tendencies is predominant in different spheres of activity of the bureaucracy. It is the task of further research to analyze these different constellations in greater detail.

CONCLUSIONS

The hypotheses presented above are necessarily both very general and preliminary and have as yet to be applied in detail to different types of societies and to their institutional spheres. Nevertheless, they make it possible to identify at least some of the major variables responsible for the development of bureaucratic organizations and to relate them systematically to the factors that determine the internal structure of such organizations and to types of equilibrium developing between bureaucracies and their environment. The preceding discussion points out that the type of dynamic equilibrium established at a given time depends largely on the forces in the immediate environment of the organization on the one hand and the type of power processes it generates in its environment on the other.

The interaction between these forces and processes engenders the continuous development of bureaucratic organizations and of processes of bureaucratization and debureaucratization. Whether a given bureaucracy will maintain its relative autonomy, whether at the same time it will be subject to effective "external" control, or whether it will develop in the direction of bureaucratization or debureaucratization is not precisely predeterminable but is largely contingent upon the concrete constellation of these various forces.

It is hoped that the preceding discussion—although preliminary—indicates possible ways of investigating various structural aspects of bureaucratic organizations and the nature of the processes of bureaucratization and debureaucratization. It has shown that with the development, systematization, and convergence of different fields of research it is possible to avoid the dichotomy of viewing bureaucracy as a service instrument or viewing it as an instrument of power. It is also possible to identify the conditions under which the autonomy of a bureaucratic organization and its service orientation is maintained or the conditions under which processes of bureaucratization and debureaucratization develop, and to relate them systematically to the analysis of the structure of bureaucratic organizations.

Conflict and Liberty: Some Remarks on the Social Structure of German Politics

RALF DAHRENDORF

IF ANYONE TRAINED IN the English tradition of legal thought came to follow the preparation and conduct of a German criminal case, he would notice a number of telling differences. In fact, each of the three principal characters involved in the great drama of the trial—judge, counsel for the defense, and counsel for the prosecution—differs in important details, both in the theory and practice of criminal law, from its English counterpart. The judge, far from being the referee in a contest of parties or, in Erving Goffman's delightful description of this role, a chairman who, as 'go-between', provides his audience (in this case: the jury) with cues as to their appropriate reactions to the evidence and arguments presented, is in fact more like a 'player-manager'—and one, of course, who is always on the winning side. A German judge not only guards the rules of the game, but takes an active hand in the examination of witnesses and, above all, withdraws with the jury and guides its deliberations throughout. The judge is a civil servant (*Beamter*), so is counsel for the prosecution, but counsel for the defense is usually a private citizen. In both the general social and the specific legal context this status tends to become a disadvantage which is aggravated by the fact that often counsel for the defense does not have access to all the evidence before the trial. He is thus hardly an equal opponent of the prosecutor, but rather a beggar for clemency (and indeed the most frequent plea of the defense is that of extenuating circumstances). It is symptomatic that until quite recently counsel for the defense was physically placed, in many German courtrooms, somewhat below counsel for the prosecution whose official title of state attorney (*Staatsanwalt*) connotes an air of authority. The state attorney's is clearly the crucial role in a German criminal case; it is indeed two roles which may be regarded as barely compatible. Before the trial opens, the state attorney represents what a widely used legal commentary describes without irony and indeed with some justification as 'the most objective authority in the world'. He has every available means—files and witnesses, laboratory tests and police information, etc., etc.—at his disposal in order to work out 'the truth'. Evidently, this usually takes a long time—which is one of the reasons why many months, and sometimes years elapse between the original arrest and the opening of the trial in Germany. Evidently also, the trial itself loses in importance, if 'the truth' has been

From *British Journal of Sociology*, 1963, pp. 197-211. Reprinted by permission of the publisher and author.

worked out beforehand—which explains in part why it is often felt by critics of German criminal-law procedure that the accused is assumed guilty once the trial has been opened at all. Above all, the state attorney undergoes a curious change of character when, on the day the trial begins, he slips from the role of an impartial 'objective' investigator of 'the truth' into that of a naturally partisan counsel for the prosecution.

It is evident that brief descriptions of this kind cannot do justice to complex legal traditions; they ignore, moreover, the actual similarities of seemingly widely divergent institutions: a clever defense counsel may transform a German criminal trial into a contest of the English type, just as a clever English judge may influence the course of the trial far beyond his role of referee. Rather than as a starting point for the analysis of legal systems as such, this brief sketch of criminal-law procedure can however serve as a useful metaphor for a feature of German social structure which seems worth exploring a little more fully: Wherever opposing interests meet in German society, there is a tendency to seek authoritative and substantive rather than tentative and formal solutions. Many institutions of German society have been and still are set up in such a way as to imply that somebody or some group of people is 'the most objective authority in the world', and is therefore capable of finding ultimate solutions for all issues and conflicts. In this manner, conflict is not regulated, but 'solved'; and it appears worth examining some of the social patterns, political implications, historical causes and philosophical bases of this procedure.

The problem underlying these remarks seems no less important for its obviousness. For the German social scientist, the failure of liberal democracy in Germany continues to be a challenge of far more than antiquarian interest. While we all hope that history will not repeat itself, we can clearly not be certain that another 1933 is going to be impossible in Germany—and we know that representative government has proved precarious in many other countries as well. Thus it may be suspected that the pathology of liberty in Germany involves features which can, at other times and in other combinations, be found elsewhere as well, and that therefore—if for no other reason—an analysis of the conditions of illiberty in Germany is of more than local importance.

The failure of German democracy in 1933 has been attributed to numerous causes, ranging from the Treaty of Versailles to the national character of the Germans as described by Tacitus, from the unique personality of Hitler to the prevalence of authoritarian personalities throughout the country, from the depression of 1929 to the extremist desires of the German middle class. While some of these causes are likely to have something to do with the breakdown of the Weimar Republic, they constitute a curiously unsystematic medley of history and metaphysics which fails to amount to a convincing and controllable analysis of the situation. Perhaps the sociologist is capable here to go a step or two beyond previous attempts at explanation. Political institutions are anchored in social structure—or if they are not, they are likely to remain paper constitutions, of which admittedly we have come to see many since that 'most perfect democratic constitution ever' (as some historians still describe the Weimar Constitution of 1919). But what is it in societies that guarantees, or, more modestly, helps the success of a given set of political institutions? What are, more particularly, the social bases of the liberal (as against the totalitarian) version of political democracy? Evidently, it would be presumptuous to try and provide more than a very partial and tentative answer to this large question. In the following considerations I am guided by what may be called a theory, or, more modestly, a hope that liberal democracy presupposes four sets of social conditions: first, the effective realization of an equal status of citizenship for all participants in the political process; secondly, the presence of competing élites and interest groups none of which is capable of monopolizing the roads to power; thirdly, the prevalence of a set of values which, by contrast to the private virtues of withdrawal and non-participation, may be described as public virtues; and, finally, the acceptance of differences of opinion and conflicts of interest as an inevitable and indeed creative element of social life. These reflections will be confined to the fourth factor, i.e. to conflict and its treatment in Germany. Our main question is therefore: What is it in the ways in which conflict is dealt with in the institutions of German society that can help to explain the apparent impossibility to establish successful and lasting democratic political institutions?

Let us return for a moment to the example of criminal-law procedure. A criminal case, and in particular the drama of the trial, may be thought of in terms of a conflict of interests. In its crudest interpretation, it involves a clash between the interest of the prosecution to prove and that of the defense to disprove the guilt of the accused. In German criminal law, the task of finding out who was guilty is accomplished by setting up an elaborate machinery of research and investigation—the position and office of the state attorney. In this manner, what might be regarded as a situation of conflict is in fact conceived as one of a concerted search for truth. As a consequence, the function of the trial is less that of a contest for the judgment of common sense as embodied in the jury than one of making 'the truth' public, considering extenuating circumstances and drawing the conclusions stipulated by the legal code. In the place of debate and argument, an agency is set up to find the ultimate solution: 'the most objective authority in the world'.

In an important sense, however, the example of criminal law is merely a metaphor for social modes of dealing with conflicts. There is a fundamental difference between the clash of interests in a criminal case—for civil-law suits this would not be equally true—and, say, the clash of interests in a wage dispute or an election campaign. In the legal situation, there is no unavoidable uncertainty about the issue at hand: 'The truth' is in principle available in the sense that the crime has been committed, and that somebody has committed it. In industrial or political conflicts, on the other hand, 'the truth', i.e. the good or right solution of particular issues is fundamentally uncertain, because its proof lies in the future. For this reason, it could be said that English legal procedure has borrowed the ethics of uncertainty from other areas—from the methodology of science or the constitution of politics—in which it is more clearly appropriate. For this reason also, we have to turn now from the legal system to other social institutions.

Conflict begins at home. The family, like any other institution, may be regarded as a system of conflict regulation. Now, the authoritarian character of the German family has become a favourite with most political and literary critics of German society ever since Heinrich Mann's novels and Max Horkheimer's collection of studies on *Authorität und Familie*. Occasionally, one encounters the notion that the German father is, or at least used to be a combination of judge and state attorney: presiding over his family, prosecuting every sign of deviance and settling all disputes by his supreme authority. It is debatable, however, whether one can draw as sweeping conclusions from this alleged observation as has been done by some, including the authors of the *Authoritarian Personality*. Today, German legislation goes further than that of almost all other countries in guaranteeing equal rights to women; and so far as earlier periods are concerned, it would appear at least open to question whether the father in Wilhelminian Germany was really so much more authoritarian than his counterpart in Victorian England or in any other society of the *fin de siècle*.

A rather more pertinent illustration of the ways in which discussion and debate are dealt with in German society may be found in the educational system. When Max Weber advanced his thesis of the desirability of a value-free approach to social science, and in particular his demand for a complete abstention from value judgments in academic teaching, one of his main points was that 'in the lecture-room where one sits in front of one's listeners, they have to be silent and the lecturer has to speak'. For this reason (so Weber argued) it would be irresponsible to exploit the situation by mixing values with facts. But may it not be that the educational situation envisaged by Weber is as dated (and placed) as, say, Freud's notion of the super-ego as the internalized father? Is it not conceivable that academic teaching could be conducted in such a way that the students do not 'have to be silent', and that the lecturer is exposed to questions, objections, debate and discussion? It would be rewarding to explore the implications of these —rhetorical—questions for the demand of a value-free social science. As far as attitudes to debate and conflict are concerned, they point to a conception of the educational situation which is characteristic of German society. The institution of the *Vorlesung* in the universities, which effectively protects the lecturer from all uncomfortable questions and objections, is clearly— and, by the way, in contrast to Humboldt's idea of the *universitas magistrorum et scholarium*—based on a definition of the situation according to which teaching is not a process of exchange and dialogue, but one in which 'the truth' is passed on by its professed possessors to ignorant children. Once again, we find a situation of debate and contest reinterpreted in hierarchical terms.

With all due caution and without trying to overstate the case it might also be pointed out in this context that in the past liberal democracy seems to have flourished in countries in which there was also a fairly widespread interest in so-called non-conformist churches and sects. It is evidently more than daring to offer generalizations about the large number of such religious groups which exist in the present world. With this grain of salt, however, it may be argued that while some non-conformist groups are more dogmatic in their theology, many of them tend to be more democratic in their organization than established churches. By 'democratic' in this rather loose sense is meant the influence of the lay element in church affairs, the ways in which dignitaries are elected and controlled, the amount of discussion permitted, and the like. Before this background it may therefore be relevant to remark that German Protestantism has always, and especially in the Eastern provinces, tended to the established type, and that non-conformist groups have never played a significant part at all. Even today —at a time, that is, when they are under no public pressure and when interest in some of them is growing—only about 3 per cent of the population of Western Germany are not members of the two great churches, Protestant and Roman Catholic (and of this minority many do not belong to any church at all).

The general pattern of conflict regulation—or, more appropriately, of conflict evasion—which is characteristic of the legal and educational systems, the family and the church, reappears in the German system of industrial relations. Here too the search for ultimate and authoritative solutions prevails over the establishment of rules of the game which would regulate the disputes between management and labour. Since 1918, if not before, the history of industrial relations in Germany has been marked by two related features: first, by a tendency for industrial affairs to be settled by state intervention—whether legislative, executive, or judicial—rather than the autonomous operation of the private organizations of management and labour; and secondly, by a tendency on the part of both management and labour to devise new types of industrial organization (a new 'constitution of the enterprise', as it is generally called) rather than find a *modus vivendi* with respect to their contradictory interests. By many representatives of labour and management, the state is considered an authority that provides ultimate solutions for industrial disputes; the unbroken chain of ideologies of structural change—of workers' councils and a 'community of the enterprise' (*Betriebsgemeinschaft*), of co-determination and partnership—documents the hope that such ultimate solutions can be found.

But the case of industrial relations is of particular interest in our context, because here, more clearly than in other institutional orders, it becomes apparent that the attempt to evade or eliminate conflict by finding ultimate solutions, does not succeed. Despite the expectations attached by many to legislative measures of industrial re-organization both after the First and the Second World Wars, there was no noticeable decrease in industrial conflict in Weimar Germany, and today, after the admittedly comparatively peaceful years of reconstruction, there are signs that disputes between labour and management are growing rather than decreasing in intensity. What is more, it appears that the very measures devised to take the sting out of industrial disputes and create a state of lasting industrial peace in fact have the opposite consequence. Why this should be so, can be demonstrated by a brief analysis of the two great institutional changes effected in German industry since 1918—both legislative acts, and both affecting the constitution of the enterprise: the establishment of works councils in 1920, and the introduction of co-determination in 1951.

Consider first the German works councillor, whose functions differ so significantly from those of his English equivalent, the shop steward. He is the only living heritage of the brief triumph of the Council, or Soviet Movement after 1918, and his construction bears the traces of this ideology. Works councillors in Germany have no formal relations to the trade unions (who are represented in the enterprise by their own officials); they occupy their place with reference to the individual enterprise alone. Here, the law of 1920 ascribes to them the task of 'representing the common economic interests of the employees (manual and clerical workers) vis-à-vis the employer *and of supporting the employer in realizing the purposes of the enterprise'*. The new and extended law of 1952 (*Betriebsverfassungsgesetz*) documents by a long list of control and decision-making functions of the works council (most of them in that most sensitive sphere of the exercise of authority which concerns the hiring and firing, promotion and supervision of personnel) that 'realizing the purposes of the enterprise' is a managerial job, and that therefore the works council is at least in part an extension of management. Under these conditions the explicit stipulation is not surprising that 'employer and works council have to abstain from every measure that might endanger the work and peace of the enterprise. In particular, employer and works council must not carry out any measures of industrial conflict against each other.'

Now more than forty years old, the works council has of course long found its place in the German industrial scene. Many useful and necessary tasks are performed by works councils in many firms. But occasionally, especially in the last years, the general public was shocked by the news that in a large and well-known enterprise the majority of works councillors elected were known Communists. It is at such points that the apparent incompatibilities in the role of the works councillor become evident. More than the foreman, he must be a master and is the victim of double talk; indeed his is an 'institution on the borderline' (as Fürstenberg has described it) of at least three not altogether friendly countries: management, labour, and the unions. Whatever the works councillor does, he must do injustice to one of his groups of reference. Since his existence neither eliminates the causes nor settles the issues of industrial conflict, it complicates the fronts of dispute and therefore leads to uncontrolled outbursts of resentment and protest.

All this is *a fortiori* the case with the creature of the co-determination law of 1951, the labour manager (*Arbeitsdirektor*). As a consequence of this law, workers are accorded the right to participate, by their representatives, in the management of enterprises in the coal, iron and steel industries. This right takes two institutional forms. On the one hand, the supervisory boards (*Aufsichtsräte*) in these industries are composed of equal numbers of owners' and workers' representatives (with a 'neutral' chairman, the famous 'thirteenth man'); on the other hand a labour manager appointed in agreement with the labour representatives on the supervisory boards joins the managing directors (*Vorstand*). As with the works councils, industrial practice has on the whole led to workable solutions for these constructions. For the supervisory boards, this often means that, in clear deviation from their original legal functions, they have become bargaining bodies of a kind; as far as the labour managers are concerned, they have (as Pirker predicted soon after the enactment of the law) more or less taken over the functions of personnel managers—a position previously unknown in German industry. But since these workable solutions have evidently little relation to the great expectations attached to the law by its Christian Democratic and Social Democratic promoters, they too complicate and thereby aggravate the conflicts between labour and management. As if the problem of oligarchic rule in trade unions were not enough, resentment of the elected representatives in the enterprise is added, for many workers, to resentment of union bosses and, of course, management. It is always difficult to interpret wildcat strikes (of which Germany has seen quite a few in recent years); but it may be suspected that at least some of them are spontaneous and undirected expressions of the sense of frustration with their own representatives that emerges from all recent studies of workers' evaluation of co-determination.

The preceding sketch obviously presents a highly simplified picture of German industrial relations. There are many points at which the German scene differs little from that of Britain or other industrial countries. In so far as the institutional treatment of industrial conflict in Germany does differ from that elsewhere, it seems however to bear out my thesis. In its most distinct aspect, the history of industrial relations in Germany is a history of ultimate solutions. The fact that as such it is also a history of failures has not deterred management, or labor, or the great political parties from continuing their search for the perfect constitution of the enterprise. But whoever tries to evade or eliminate open conflict, risks guerrilla warfare, and that means, the impossibility of rational conflict regulation. The study of German industrial relations shows that industrial conflict cannot be either wished or legislated away—and that therefore, by implication, the interests of those concerned as well as of the community at large are probably better served by an effective machinery of industrial conciliation and arbitration than by a perfect constitution of the enterprise.

The attitude to conflict inherent in various institutions of German society has of course a long and in part distinguished history in political and legal history. Probably the most significant and certainly, in our context, the most relevant representative of this tradition was Hegel. In his dialectics of substantive morality (*Sittlichkeit*), the third and final part of his *Philosophy of Law*, he introduces the three categories which form the terminological arsenal of every defender of the attitude in question here: family, civil society, and the State. Hegel of course does not simply 'introduce' these categories; he presents them as that necessary sequence of both qualitative preference and historical development which is meant by his version of the term 'dialectics'. The family—the thesis of this dialectical structure—is for Hegel the primary, original community of men, a kind of *Gemeinschaft* in which the individual disappears as such, and exists (as Hegel says) 'not as a person for itself, but as a member'. But the family is neither systematically nor historically the final form of social and political organization. Rather, *Gemeinschaft* has to give way to *Gesellschaft*, the family to civil society—the antithesis of substantive morality. Hegel's analysis of civil society is justly famous; it is one of the brilliant accounts of the new society emerging from the French revolution as well as one of the intellectual roots of the work of at least the young Marx. But those who praise this analysis often overlook the fact that for Hegel the world of interests and needs, conflicts and antagonisms that is civil society is merely a step in a dialectical process, and that, as antithesis or opposition, it is the negative step, i.e. the one which throughout his constructions he always liked least. Thus, family and civil society are *aufgehoben* in the triple sense of this German word—abolished, conserved and lifted to a higher level—in the State. Above the interests and conflicts of civil society, the State acts as ultimate, tranquil, impartial authority. Hegel's statements to this effect have often been quoted: 'The State is the reality of the moral ideal. . . . The State, as the reality of the substantial will . . . is the reasonable in and for itself. This substantial unity is absolutely unmoved purpose for itself within which freedom achieves its highest right, just as this ultimate purpose has the highest right against the individuals, whose highest duty it is to be members of the State.'

Quoting Hegel as extensively as this is more than a lapse from sociological analysis to intellectual history. Through legal and political theory, Hegel has influenced German politics more than any other thinker. But even where no such direct influence can be demonstrated, his dialectics of substantive morality is a perfect description of many features of political organization in Germany (and perhaps, in other continental countries, past and present, as well).

If one was looking for a formula to describe the constitution of Bis-

marck's German Empire, none could be more appropriate than the dialectics of State and civil society. There was a parliament within which the
various and often divergent interests of civil society, organized in political
parties, were represented. But the debates of the *Reichstag* were not regarded as either legal or factual sources of legislation or of the control of
the executive. Decisions were made elsewhere by authorities which looked
upon themselves and were looked upon by others as impartial adjudicators
of right and wrong ('the reality of the moral ideal') above the petty disputes and conflicts of the parties.—In the structure of the executive, this
notion of the State as the ultimate authority and source of law and morality
was and is clearly expressed by the preferential position accorded to civil
servants (and within the civil service to lawyers as the institutional interpreters of substantive morality). The Prussian 'civil service ethos' of duty,
incorruptibility, loyalty and disinterestedness is a direct consequence of the
moral ideal as embodied in the State.—One of the most striking features of
recent German history is the extent to which the labour movement, and above
all the Social Democratic Party has taken over this suspicion of interests
and the belief in the impartial authority of the State. Lassalle, of course,
was a Hegelian, and in his *Workers' Programm* he tried to convince his
audience that the State was so clearly the embodiment of the moral ideal
that not even Bismarck's Empire could be really bad. But Lassalle did not
remain alone. All great Social Democratic leaders—Bebel, Ebert, Schu-
macher above all—believed in the privileged position of the State versus
the comparative pettiness of civil society, i.e. of interests, parties, parlia-
ments, conflicts, and the like.—That the invidious distinction between the
State and civil society, or authority and conflicts of interest, went far beyond political philosophers and party leaders, has only recently been demonstrated again by Kurt Sontheimer in his study of anti-parliamentary cur-
rents in the Weimar-Republic. In so far as parliamentary government was
ever accepted in Weimar Germany, it was accepted as a second best solution, often indeed as a mere mechanism for finding the right man or men,
i.e. him or those who know all the right answers. Thus, for many, elections
and parliamentary debates seemed acceptable as a procedure of personnel
selection, but not as a method of government. Throughout the years from
1918 to 1933 there was widespread antipathy against 'party strife', 'the rule
of interests', 'the politics of bargaining' and the whole 'system' which did
not manage to rise from the grime of civil society to the splendour of the
State.

To English ears, the usage of the word 'state' imported here from
everyday German must sound decidedly odd. Statements like 'The State is
the ultimate source of authority' or indeed 'The State is the reality of the
moral ideal' seem to provoke, if phrased in English, a question which to
many Germans would seem almost sacrilegious: Who is it who represents
this State and hides behind the personified abstraction? Which groups do in
fact dominate government and determine, directly or indirectly, the course

of the country? These questions lead directly to an historical explanation of the prevalence of the attitude to conflict under discussion. But before I follow this lead, it seems appropriate to try and state the thesis of this analysis as it is implied by the title of *Conflict and Liberty*.

In political debate, if not in political theory, the claim is often heard today that political democracy presupposes the 'total democratization of society'. The word offends the ear; but, more than that, it involves a very imprecise notion of both democracy and society. Following Schumpeter's well-known definition, parliamentary democracy may be described as 'that institutional arrangement for arriving at political decisions in which individuals acquire the power to decide by means of a competitive struggle for the people's vote'. But it can be shown that this distinctive arrangement is strictly appropriate for the political community only. It is hard to see how an army could serve its purpose if its officers had to campaign for office among their soldiers. However liberal a school system may be, the election of teachers and professors by pupils and students would probably not help the quality of teaching. While some children may dream of electing their parents, the resulting kinship system would be a novelty even for the most widely travelled anthropologist. Even in enterprises, industrial or otherwise, it would seem that the fact of ownership—whether private or public—and the requirement of continuity forbid the introduction of strictly democratic institutions. As a matter of fact, many attempts to 'democratize' these and other institutions have been undertaken in this century of large-scale social experiments, but so far as can be judged they have all failed and been abandoned, thereby providing empirical confirmation of the apparent impossibility to extend the procedures of political democracy to other institutions of society.

There is, however, implicit in the institutions of parliamentary democracy, an attitude to conflicts of interest as they emerge from the differential placement of people in society, which can be applied in other institutional areas as well. In its abstract core, this attitude involves (1) the acceptance of differences of opinion and interest as inevitable; (2) concentration on the modes rather than the causes of conflict; (3) the setting-up of institutions which provide conflicting groups with binding channels of expression; (4) the development of rules of the game by which the conflicting parties abide. What these rules of the game, and the context within which they operate, are like in detail, depends largely on the specific requirements of the institutions concerned. Thus, a system of conciliation and arbitration in industry, teaching procedures based on discussion and dialogue in universities, a machinery for lodging and hearing complaints in the army, and many other detailed modes of channelling differences of interest, may be fully appropriate equivalents of parliamentary government in the polity. While there may thus be a wide variety of institutional arrangements in the various spheres of social organization, it is the thesis of this paper that parliamentary democracy cannot work except in the context of a society the institutions of which are everywhere based on the acceptance and rational canalization of conflict.

Wherever there is social life, there is conflict. But while this sociological law—if such it is—would suggest that the liberal attitude to conflict sketched before is also the only realistic one, human history has seen more violation than acceptance of this law. Techniques of suppressing conflict are older than the word 'totalitarian' with which we describe them today. Not infrequently, such techniques are embellished by ideologies of conflict resolution, according to which there can be disinterested authorities and organizational solutions eliminating the causes of conflict. I suggest that neither the totalitarian nor the authoritarian approach to social conflict can work, but that both tend to their own supersession by revolutionary upheavals or, more frequently, by the unplanned emergence of patterns which in fact if not in theory amount to the rational regulation of conflict. But this is a statement about that 'long run' which renders so many sociological generalizations faintly irrelevant. Looking back into history and looking round in the present, it is hard to deny that there was and is rather less rationality than we might hope for.

What is the relevance of these different approaches to conflict for the cause of liberty? It may be said that in the sense in which the rational attitude to conflict regulation is a pragmatic implication of parliamentary government, it is also a precondition of that liberty of the individual which is guaranteed by representative democracy. But this is only part of what is meant here. Different attitudes to conflict involve different views of the human condition. If one is prepared to accept the existence of opposing views and use their conflict as a stimulus to social development, this implies the notion that man is living in a world of constitutional uncertainty. In the terms of the economist, we are always, and not just accidentally, lacking some of the information that would be required to decide what is true and what is good. Since no human being knows all the answers, the only way to avoid the dictatorship of wrong answers is to see to it that at all times and in all areas it remains possible to give more than one answer. Conflict is liberty, because it is the only adequate expression of the multiplicity and incompatibility of human interests and desires in a world of uncertainty.

At least in the past, however, this has not been—to quote the title of Leonard Krieger's important study—*The German Idea of Freedom.* The suspicious ties of freedom and necessity or freedom and authority in German political thought have often been noticed; Krieger adds to these the historical connection of the ideas of freedom and the sovereignty of the numerous provinces and principalities before the establishment of the Empire. In a sense, what some would describe as a Baconian view of man was and is prevalent in Germany: Perhaps, not all of us are living in a world of certainty, but it is possible for some, by hard work or by calling, to acquire certain knowledge about truth and justice. What is needed in politics as in all other social institutions is therefore not the freedom of accepted conflict, but the search for those who are in the possession of certain knowledge. Authority is for them, and they are made for the possession of authority.

At this point, the abstract discussion of attitudes to conflict and their implications meets the analysis of German social institutions. Once again we may ask: who are the select few whose claim to certain knowledge is accepted by the many, and who are evidently the secret of that abstract personality, the State? And since in this form the question still contains a strong element of ideological distortion of reality: How is it that in Germany, in a modern, industrial society, this notion of the State and of the chosen few—or indeed, the chosen one—continued to be accepted for so long?

Thorstein Veblen was one of the first authors to point out, in his spirited if sloppy study of *Imperial Germany and the Industrial Revolution,* that industrialization is by no means as great a unifying force of societies as many seem to think even today. While the rapid expansion of industrial production in Imperial Germany has certainly resulted in profound changes in German society, its more striking feature is how this process was incorporated in the earlier traditions of German society. Today, we tend to describe these traditions as 'pre-industrial.' But in fact, the German case was the first to prove that the social relations characteristic of feudal conditions everywhere need not disappear either immediately or entirely as industrialization sets in. The authoritarian welfare state and the industrial feudal society may appear contradictions in terms, but in Germany they were not contradictions in reality (unless one wants to regard the very explosiveness of these combinations as one of the sources of the instability of German politics after 1871).

Due to her peculiar version of the process of industrialization and modernization, Germany failed to develop for a long time any one of the four conditions of democracy mentioned earlier. The hidden truth of the State as the reality of the moral ideal was an established ruling class of Prussian, Protestant civil servants, soldiers, diplomats and landed aristocrats. The process of dissolution and dislodgement of this group took more than half a century, and was finally accomplished only by the intense, and often overlooked, struggle of the Nazis against Prussia and her tradition. Equality of participation was long restricted not only by formal privileges such as the three-class electoral law of Imperial Prussia, but above all by equally effective informal restrictions of political participation including the influence of local economic and religious powers. In this manner, the attitude of non-participation, of withdrawing to the family as the appropriate unit of social membership, of private rather than public virtues, remained the predominant value of German society, praised in German literature and practiced in German politics alike. For this is the other side of the assumption that some are in possession of certain knowledge: that the many are resigned to their impotence and renounce any claim to participation or even protest.

Evidently, in this context social conflict appears as a rather ugly concomitant of civil society which has to be superseded. In the ideology of feudal society there is no conflict between lords and subjects. For the lords, the subjects are but children who need a mixture of paternal severity and paternal care. The seemingly contradictory combination of the most advanced system of social welfare of the time, and the outlawing of the socialist parties and unions in Bismarck's Germany is symbolic of an attitude to conflict according to which formal antagonisms are unnecessary since there is an authority capable of settling their issues once and for all.

It would be presumptuous to claim that this analysis provides an explanation of the specific events of 1933, much less of those of 1938 and after. Indeed, one of the melancholy failings of sociological analysis seems to be that specific events escape its crude generalities altogether. But it may be suggested that one of the underlying reasons why liberal democracy failed to gain a sure foothold in German society can be found in an attitude to social conflict which is informed by an authoritarian belief in the capacity of some to gain certain knowledge about truth and justice. It is before this background that the vanity of the political venture of the Weimar Republic becomes apparent and its failure understandable.

No task seems more difficult than to conclude these observations with a few remarks about the present. But since the question of the future of liberty is asked no less anxiously inside as outside Germany, the attempt to venture, however briefly and tentatively, into this uncertain territory may be excused.

In the first place, there are of course many indications that the social substratum of German politics has changed rather less than the more visible political institutions themselves. It is true, one of the leading opinion research institutes which has asked a national sample annually since 1951, 'Do you believe that it is better for a country to have several parties, so that different opinions can be expressed freely, or but one party, so that there is as much unity as possible?' has found a consistent decrease in the proportion of those who favoured a one-party system from over 20 per cent to about 10 per cent. But perhaps the question is phrased in too rational a manner. In fact there are many Germans who favour several parties, so that there can be as much unity as possible between them; or, in other words, the multi-party system seems to be popular to the extent to which it does not function as such, but leads to all-party coalitions and unanimous decisions. Such tendencies to a new exclusion of parliament and establishment of a kind of presidential regime—sometimes called 'chancellor democracy'—as there are, have perhaps been exaggerated; but undoubtedly the State is still a very prominent institution in the Federal Republic (to say nothing of the German Democratic Republic of East

Germany). In other social institutions, analogous conclusions might be drawn. My exemplary analyses of the legal and educational systems, the family and the church, apply to the present no less than to the past; and in industrial relations both unions and management are still busy devising new constitutions of the enterprise.

On the other hand, this is clearly a very one-sided picture. There is always more continuity in social than in political history; the inertia of social institutions is greater than that of political constitutions. It is not surprising therefore that he who looks for the past in contemporary Germany in fact finds many traces of it. But there are indications of new departures as well: in the legal system where substantive and procedural reforms of considerable consequence have been worked out and in part introduced (*'Grose Strafrechtsreform'*); in the field of family relations by legislation as well as unplanned developments to a condition of partnership; in the schools and universities where the older authoritative type of teaching is today clearly on the defensive; in industrial relations where American criticisms and experience are beginning to bear fruit; in the organization of the political executive where the old 'civil service ethos' is increasingly being replaced by an economic ethos deplored by many, but possibly indicative of a less privileged place of the State in a society which is more nearly capitalist in character than the industrial feudalism of Imperial Germany.

It is too early to say with any degree of confidence which direction German social and political development is going to take. For one matter, there is the fundamental instability of the political and social systems of both Germanies of the present caused by the fact of the division of the country which remains a latent source of nationalist revival. But even apart from the re-unification issue, developments in the Western part of Germany are in the balance. While I feel that the social condition of the Federal Republic holds out more hope for the maintenance of liberty than there has ever been in German history, all that can safely be concluded from these remarks is that one of the developments to watch is that of the attitude to conflict implied by Germany's social and political institutions.

Bureaucratic Organization in a Time of Revolution

SELO SOEMARDJAN

THIS PAPER WILL DESCRIBE the situation of bureaucratic organizations in a country undergoing a revolutionary change in its political, economic, and social order. The writer will rely upon memory about events he personally observed and experienced in Indonesia as a member of the country's civil service during the time such changes took place.

A brief summary of the most important relevant political events during the last years of the prewar period is necessary as background information. Before World War II, Indonesia was a colony of the Netherlands. At the top of the colonial government was a Governor General holding administrative power delegated by the Netherlands government. The colony was divided into a number of provinces, each headed by a governor who administered the province on behalf of the Governor General. The main goal of the colonial administration was to maintain political, economic, and social control. A general pattern of bureaucratic organization was set up throughout the colony. Executive positions in governmental and private bureaucracies were in the hands of persons from the Netherlands, while native personnel occupied only minor executive positions. A colonial system of education provided elementary and high schools for native youths. One university was available in the colony, providing college education for only the wealthiest members of the native upper class.

In the first year of World War II the colonial government capitulated to the Japanese, who imposed a new, more rigid, and totalitarian colonial regime. With the exception of a few Germans and Italians, every European in the existing bureaucracies was replaced by a Japanese officer. Many of these officers were untrained for their bureaucratic duties; they ignored existing laws and rules; they made decisions arbitrarily; and as a consequence of their great mobility continuity of policy was lacking. Only with the power of arms and threat of the feared Secret Military Police (*Kenpeitai*) could the native workers be kept working under the Japanese military government.

As a direct result of the Hiroshima explosion the Japanese Emperor (*Tenno Heika*) ordered all Japanese armed forces to end hostilities. The order was promptly carried out; the Japanese military government declared itself no longer entitled to run the administration, and every responsibility was formally passed to the Allied Powers, which at that time, however,

From *Administrative Science Quarterly,* Volume 2, pp. 182-199. Reprinted by permission of the publisher.

had no representative in the colony. This vacuum in the existence of a formal colonial government gave the people of Indonesia a unique chance to proclaim their independence and to establish a new sovereign nation-state.

The transition period, lasting five years after this proclamation until the international recognition of the country as an independent and sovereign state, was marked by revolutionary changes. The influence of those changes upon bureaucratic organizations during this period is the subject of this paper.

THE GENERAL SITUATION

In connection with the bureaucratic organizations of Indonesia at this time, the following generalizations may be made:

1. An intense reaction against all people belonging to the former colonizing powers swept over the country; none was allowed to hold any kind of office.

2. Independence, proclaimed after many years of suppression and sacrifice, aroused a country-wide movement to defend the newly gained freedom at all costs. This desire led to serious efforts to put every institution and organization on a nationalistic basis; that is, they were to be led and run by natives for goals defined by the national interest. A Central National Committee was set up in the capital city of the country as a temporary body to serve as the national legislature and to guide the people in its political and social revolution. Local national committees were organized on the provincial level as a two-way avenue between the Central Committee and the people.

3. Appropriately educated, trained, and experienced persons to occupy policy- and decision-making positions in the various bureaucracies were very scarce.

4. Relations between public and private agencies and their central organizations in the Netherlands were deliberately cut off. The public agencies were proclaimed parts of the new national government, and the private agencies found themselves free both from government control and from their foreign head offices.

5. Though formally proclaimed valid until legally abolished or changed, the old colonial laws and rules were no longer acceptable to the people.

6. The war had caused considerable damage and disorder to the economic life and to the communication system of the country.

7. Under these unfavorable circumstances, the existing bureaucratic organizations had to be maintained and new ones to be established.

THE CIVIL SERVICE

The day after the order to end hostilities was promulgated, the Japanese military governor proclaimed the provincial government no longer responsible for administration. All Japanese officers holding positions in the government and private bureaucracies in the province resigned simultaneously and remained inactive, waiting for shipment back to Japan.

A decree was soon passed that the highest ranking native member in every bureaucracy was authorized to take over leadership in each organization to replace the Japanese officer who had resigned. Where there was only one such native member who enjoyed prestige among his fellow members, this decree posed only minor problems, since there was no competition for the leading positions. But in many bureaucracies there were two or more officials who stood on about the same level in the hierarchy, were of about the same capacity, the same age, and had approximately the same length of service. Competition thus demanded a higher authority to make the decision, but in most cases the members of the bureaucracies were reluctant to appeal for a decision to the new native governor or to the local National Committee for fear that they would be considered incapable of solving their own problems or that in order to overcome the internal competition an outsider would be introduced as head of the bureaucracy.

By this time the ideals of freedom, democracy, independence, peoples' sovereignty, and other antidictatorial slogans were very popular as a reaction to the many years of authoritarian colonization and suppression. These new ideas seemed to show the way to the solution of the problem of choosing leaders: all the members of the bureaucracy were assembled, and under the chairmanship of a neutral member a new head was selected. Other open positions were filled in this same way. By and large the choice was not guided by considerations of the ability of the candidates to perform the duties of the position; for the most part it was the result of general likes and dislikes toward the candidates. The people in new positions were therefore not always the most capable or the best trained and most experienced.

Thus rationality, one of the fundamental elements of modern bureaucracy, was consciously or unconsciously put aside. This lack of rationality turned out to be decisive during the time following this novel policy of bureaucratic election. As a logical consequence, the small community of members of the bureaucracy was split into factions. This had a disruptive effect because such factions continued even after a new head had been elected.

The first thing the new head had to do was to determine the way in which he could exercise the formal authority of his position, knowing that he owed his triumph to the faction which was supporting him and which now logically expected him in some way to exercise his authority in their favor. The contrafaction naturally was not eager to work under his formal leadership. Here again a central assumption of a typical bureaucracy was replaced as the basis of formal authority changed from one of skill to one resting on various subjective considerations, such as personal acceptability, the reputation of resistance to the Dutch, or rhetorical ardor. *Capability* was thus replaced by *acceptability*, and these two symbols, which were formerly not included in the Indonesian language, became current in the public service.

Thus, finding themselves insecure in their formal and responsible positions, most of the elected heads of bureaucracies built cliques around themselves. In extreme cases this practice caused a deep cleavage in many bureaucracies. For example, it often damaged lines of communication. The upward flow of communications was sometimes cut off because certain data which would have been forwarded to the head in normal times were purposely held back. On the other hand, orders and information from the head to his subordinates which were incongenial to the contrafaction were ignored, or they were implemented at a slow-down pace. Rules or guides were lacking in many bureaucracies. Where rules existed, they had lost actual validity because no sanctions were available to enforce them.

The heads of the bureaucracies were not in a position to apply administrative sanctions because of the great changes taking place in the society. Political leaders were trying to set up parties as a preparation for the coming elections for representative legislative bodies. Youth organizations and labor movements were combined with political activities in a confusing way. Meanwhile the first troops of the Allied Forces had embarked in the country and were trying to restore with armed force the prewar political order. The hatred of the people, initially directed only to members of the former colonizing power, began to extend to natives who were known as collaborators of the former alien government. The Allied troops were met with spontaneously organized people's armies defending the national independence in guerilla warfare.

Many new heads of bureaucracies had achieved their high positions in the colonial days because they were loyal to the colonial government; for the moment it was a good policy for them to keep quiet and not to attract attention outside the bureaucracy. One of the best ways to do this was to exercise indulgence toward all the members of the bureaucracy rather than to irritate them by applying administrative sanctions which could be easily called "colonial sanctions." As a result, one of the specific goals of every bureaucracy, survival, was unduly emphasized. One of the ways to do this was by maintaining internal calm.

Unlike the bureaucratic changes described above, where Japanese officers were replaced by members of the same bureaucracies, a different kind of replacement was effected in the provincial Bureau of General Affairs, a bureau of the provincial government which handled various matters which did not belong to the jurisdiction of the other provincial bureaus. Spread out in the most important towns in the province were branches of this bureau which carried orders from the central bureau and acted as contact media between it and the population. The Bureau of General Affairs was one of the very few bureaucracies which the Japanese had left to the leadership of a native official, since they were not aware of its importance. This native head was a man of great capability. He was relatively well educated, and he had had about thirty years of experience in handling many and various affairs which required direct contact with the public. He had succeeded in establishing a well-disciplined and loyal staff.

Contrary to the opinion that had been held by the Japanese military government, the local committees considered this Bureau of General Affairs very important from a political point of view and deemed it necessary, therefore, to give it a new executive head who could represent the majority of the newly established political and labor organizations. In a society 80 per cent of which were peasants, the majority was consequently a peasants' majority, so a peasants' representative had to be appointed head of the bureau. Since there were virtually no educated members among the peasants (the greater part of them were illiterate or had enjoyed only elementary-school education), the best available candidate was a peasant's son who happened to work in the executive staff of the Bureau of General Affairs. Unfortunately, in comparison with his fellow staff members, this man was of minor ability and had achieved only a relatively low rank in the hierarchy. As disciplined government officials, however, the members of the Bureau of General Affairs accepted the new head, who then formally superseded all his fellow members, including the former head of the bureau.

Immediately after his promotion the new head of the bureau moved from his little room deep in the office building to the big and well-furnished room of the former head, who became from that moment on his secretary. This sudden formal change from minor subordinate to boss in the same bureaucracy seemed not to be followed by as rapid a change in the informal relations between the new head and his secretary. Both were still convinced that by any intrinsic standard the new head was inferior to his secretary and to many of his former colleagues. Possessed by this conviction, the new head refused to sit at the large and "representative" table of the secretary and chose instead a small table located in the least conspicuous corner of the room. As the basis of his internal policy he declared to his secretary, "Please, you go on with your work, I will sign everything that you consider good!"

Under this policy no significant change was introduced in the process of work in the bureau. There was no communication at all between the new head and his staff; the only communication he had was with his secretary. The staff members recognized him as their formal head, but they overtly considered the secretary as their actual head. The staff forwarded its communications to the secretary; it discussed problems with the secretary; it expected and accepted decisions from the secretary; and many times it exercised his decisions in anticipation of the signature of the formal head of the bureau.

The local national committee, however, and particularly the peasants' organization, seriously recognized their political representative as the formal and actual head of the Bureau of General Affairs; they deliberately refused to contact the secretary. In their eyes he was an official who had no political orientation at all, because he was not a member of the new political and labor organizations.

The confusing consequences soon became obvious. Orders and decisions from the Bureau of General Affairs, officially signed by the head, which had as usual an impact upon the entire community, were explained by the head in meetings of the local national committee and the peasants' organization. But his explanations were many times quite different from the content and spirit of the written orders and decisions. Though he could maintain the confidence of the relatively less educated members of the peasants' organization, the new head was easily disarmed in debate with other members of the local national committee. Eventually a new system was introduced, assigning to the political representative not the duties of an executive head of the bureaucracy but giving him instead the position of nontechnical supervisor, which was higher in hierarchical rank but had less responsibility. This was a happy solution because the elected official and the peasant party retained their prestige, while the bureau was permitted to function adequately.

THE MILITARY ORGANIZATION

At the time Indonesia was proclaimed independent and sovereign, the new nation had no regular armed forces of its own. The military organization of the first colonial government was destroyed by the Japanese navy and army, its members imprisoned, and their arms taken by the conquerors. During the Japanese occupation the occupying military government had trained many native youths in warfare and the handling of light firearms. This training was intended to provide the Japanese army with trained manpower reserves in case of necessity. A number of young men were organized into military and semimilitary units, but when the military leaders in the top echelons realized the impossibility of victory over the Allied forces, they ordered these units to be dissolved and the arms, if any, to be withdrawn.

The national political leaders of the country were well aware that the new nation-state could not possibly survive without an adequate military force. An appeal to the national youth resulted in the formation of military units, initially uncontrolled and not well organized and only slowly growing into a structured national organization, recognized and ruled by the government. In order to obtain arms, the troops attacked Japanese military units; later, in combat with the Allied forces, more arms were taken as prizes.

In response to an appeal by the political leaders that the whole nation was expected to join the national revolution and defend independence, many youth organizations fought side by side with the official recognized military troops against both the Japanese and the Allied forces. Captured arms went to the various official and unofficial fighting organizations, resulting in the establishment of private armed forces along with the government's troops. These private organizations differed from the official units only in their formal relations with the government; they were entirely similar in organization, goals, power, and social conduct.

A military organization is usually considered to be the most perfect example of bureaucratic hierarchy. Lines of communication, functional authority, superordination and subordination, impersonality of activities according to established, explicit rules, institutionalized leadership, loyalty to the common goal, and discipline to higher rank and rules are among the typical elements it demonstrates. These characteristics may be indispensable for modern, well-trained, and well-equipped armed forces, but they may not be expected in newly formed armed units in a newly proclaimed country which had barely time to organize itself before it was faced with the necessity to fight its way to international recognition of its sovereignty.

Since we are concerned with bureaucratic organizations in a transitional period, we will first examine the stereotype of the military units before they were merged into one national military organization. This stereotype unit was the company, which did not pretend to meet the international standards of a military company; each company differed from other companies in point of members, equipment, and armament. What was then called a company was a relatively loosely organized unit of about 40 to 120 members with an average armament of no more than one firearm for five members. There was no other military equipment.

The company was divided into three or four smaller units according to the number of its men. Aside from the common duty to fight the enemy, members were assigned for duty as couriers, for food supply, for combat intelligence services, and for administrative work. Only a few had enjoyed military training before joining the unit. Owing to the manner of the company's establishment, everyone knew everyone else in the organization, since they were formerly fellow members of the same village or community, or members of the same religious organization, or students of the same school (most of them had been high-school students). Informal relations were very well cultivated, and the organization was well integrated. The leader of the company did not always have the best military training, nor was he necessarily the most able member, but he was undoubtedly the one with natural leadership. Loyalty from the members to their leader was complete in both formal and informal ways. Personal and direct communication between the leader and every one of his subordinates irrespective of rank was a common characteristic. In this stage of organizational development the company called itself a "family" and acted accordingly. The company commander was called "father" (*bapak*) and he in turn called members of the company "child" (*anak*) or "brother" (*saudara*) depending on their age and the "distance" between them. (This practice was introduced during the revolution as a reaction to the formality and stratification of bureaucratic relations under the colonial system. It is now used throughout the entire state bureaucracy. Although the lack of discipline characteristic of the revolution has been overcome, the forms of address that symbolized this social upheaval have remained.)

It was actually impossible for a higher authority (the armed-forces headquarters) to separate a company commander or even a single member from the company. The company was a real unit, one and indivisible. Communication between the members was so close and frequent that one could scarcely distinguish formal and informal relations. All ate together, the food was the same, they slept in the same room or in the same open space, and they fought together; military orders were given while private talks were going on at the same time and in the same place. There were no secrets in the company; everything was known by all the members, even operational secrets. Decisions were made by the commander, usually without a formal discussion with the commanders of the subunits because the commander had a continuous contact with them and the other members, keeping himself in this way well informed about what was going on physically and psychologically in his company. Only on a very few occasions, when a concerted attack was planned for the company as a whole, did the commander call the subunit commanders into a staff meeting. Frontal attacks on the better-equipped and better-armed enemy were seldom attempted; poor armament and lack of equipment forced the troops to use guerrilla warfare, using units of never more than ten members to attack or to mislead the enemy.

There were no written rules for the members of the company. All that was done within the company was based upon the commander's orders and upon common consensus. Norms grew rapidly during continuous interactions between the members when in battle as well as during their leisure times. A tacit norm existed that every member had to fulfill orders from his superior, though not always unquestioningly. The refusal of loyalty to the commander and indifference toward his orders were in themselves considered a sin. All the members of the company had to seek to extirpate such sins and either bring the sinner into the fold or persuade him to leave the company.

The tremendous mobility of guerrilla warfare required a considerable amount of flexibility of operation, a rapid and almost instinctive action responding to the battle situation of the day and sometimes of the hour. Written rules would have been highly inappropriate and would have hampered military movements. The newly proclaimed country itself had only a temporary constitution and no other laws than the colonial ones to meet the rising political, economic, social, and military problems. Under these circumstances it was not only unwise but impossible to draw up written rules for the armed forces.

For purposes of coordination a central national military organization, the armed-forces headquarters, was set up by the government, but owing to the number of relatively independent armed troops and the general disorder of the time, headquarters authority was only slowly accepted by the companies. Orders from this central bureaucratic organization were usually criticized by the company and were carried out only when they were not inconsistent with the local military situation it faced.

Payment to the members of the company was inconsistent with the general concept of the independence movement: it was felt that payment would degrade them to the status of hired soldiers and would seriously damage the individual's esteem as a fighter for a sacred interest, national independence. The only necessity supplied from outside was food, and it was the task of the supply officer to relate with the many "behind-the-front" people's organizations to get it. The company, which had no money at all, did not buy the food; an appeal to every village chief in the rural areas or to the president of the local neighborhood associations in the towns never failed.

An organization, in this case a military organization, is a social organization and as such is a part of the existing society. This characteristic is of particular significance for a guerrilla troop; it must be recognized by the society as its own, a resource the society has to support spiritually and materially and which it has to keep in constant good condition to fight for a goal determined by the society itself. A guerrilla troop which loses support of the society is doomed to fail and vanish. The society itself holds direct and actual control over the company through its food supply and its spiritual influence. These were always more effective than the formal control from the armed-forces headquarters.

THE FOREIGN-OWNED FACTORIES

Private enterprises owned by natives underwent no direct change as a result of the revolution; the impact upon them was indirect, and the changes, if any, depended upon the willingness of the owners to adjust to the new situation. But there were many factories owned by industrial companies in the former European motherland of the colony. The Netherlands was considered to be at war with the newly proclaimed independent country; as the motherland-colony relations were cut off, the native personnel of the motherland-owned factories consequently considered the factories to be free from their former owners. Moreover, since the factories were not owned by the motherland's government but by private bodies, the new national government was denied any right to control them.

An example of private bureaucratic organization in transition is a sugar factory, located about ten miles from the capital city of Jogjakarta Province. This factory was one of many owned by a Dutch industrial company. This company had determined the general rules for production in conformity with a broad economic policy for all its factories. The executive director of the factory, the first and second engineer, the first and second plantation supervisor, and other "European positions" in the director's technical staff were appointed by the company, whereas the director had the authority to hire native workers. Sugar was produced in the factory from sugar cane, grown by the company on land rented from farmers. Accordingly, the factory's personnel was divided into factory workers who did their work on the factory premises and field workers who were responsible for the sugar-cane plantation. During the Japanese occupation the factory was kept in operation by the replacement of the European personnel with Japanese private businessmen who worked under the direction of the occupying military government.

When at the end of the war the Japanese in the factory stopped working and left the factory to the native workers, the same problem described in the case of the civil service's bureaucracies had to be solved: how to replace the Japanese in the leading and decision-making positions. A meeting of all the native factory and field workers was called to decide upon the status of the factory and to determine the way in which the open positions should be filled. The meeting unanimously decided not to recognize the foreign company as owner of the factory, but no decision was reached as to its future ownership. A second decision was made that the workers then present should run the factory and the cane plantation. Use of the profits was to be determined by a board, its composition reflecting the former technical staff and its head to be the director. In overwhelming majority, a man who had been the assistant of a former European sugar analyst and who had chaired the meeting was elected director; he was the only one who had any specialized education in sugar production (actually only a one-year training period). The other open positions were to be occupied by the highest-ranking and oldest native worker in each branch.

In contrast to the practice of the civil-service offices, the factory director could not dispense with technically trained personnel. The machines in action during a milling campaign (in which harvested ripe canes were transported into the factory to be milled to sugar) had to run continuously from the start until the very last sugar cane had been processed. This was necessary to prevent a decrease of the sugar cane's gravity, which could be caused by too long a storage time. During this milling period of two or three months, the factory had to hire new workers from the community on a contract covering that period of time; the number of such workers was usually about twice the number of "steady workers." In the two- or three-month interval the workers had to work day and night to keep the machines in action. This required a well-timed coordination of the work within the factory premises as well as a careful timing of the work in relation to the cane transportation from the fields. The transfer of authority from the Japanese to the native workers coincided with the cane harvest time and the technical preparations for the August milling campaign.

Well aware of his inability to lead the campaign and unwilling to bear the responsibility alone, the new director conferred with the board almost every day to discuss the work and to plan further activities. Routine work could be determined with relative ease, but managerial problems caused many tensions among the board members in their efforts to find solutions. But the tensions never developed into personal cleavages or conflicts because the milling campaign exercised considerable pressure upon the board to solve every problem without delay.

The director and the board, not knowing to whom they owed responsibility, communicated every important decision to their fellow workers by written announcements upon the communication boards. As an additional incentive for the workers, the board decided to distribute a part of the sugar product to them, everyone receiving an amount of sugar according to the position he held in the hierarchy. Another part of the sugar product was put aside to support the guerilla troops. Relations with others outside the factory were carried out by the director, assisted by the members of the board. In this way the factory for several months acted as an autonomous organization, resisting any interference from outside. Even control by the provincial government was rejected on the ground that the private status of the factory made it not responsible to the government for its activities. This anarcho-syndicalism (as the provincial government called the situation) prevailed in almost every foreign-owned factory in the province during the first months of the national revolution.

As long as the milling campaign pressed for action by the director, the board, and the other workers, equilibrium and integration in the internal organization of the bureaucracy could be maintained. In some way the silent hope was fostered that some time a legal decision would be passed transferring ownership to the workers. But as soon as the campaign was over, the workers had more leisure time to discuss various problems and to criticize the mistakes of the director and the board. Meanwhile another problem arose: the workers who were hired for the campaign period only refused to quit after the campaign was over; they too were hoping to share in the ownership of the factory.

The problems presented to the director and his board were beyond their capability to solve. Since no superior authority was recognized to whom they could appeal, they finally called upon the government to help them solve the problems. The government exercised its authority and decided as follows:

1. No decision about ownership should be made until political and economic relations between the new country and the former motherland were stabilized.

2. The director and the board of the factory were authorized to continue management but were to be held responsible to the government for the good and sufficient exercise of the work.

3. The factory had to work under regulations drawn up by the government in conformity with the general national economic policy.

SUMMARY

Four types of bureaucracies in Indonesia are described in this paper with the emphasis on the relations of each with the surrounding society, which was engaged in a political and social revolution.

The first one is a well-established office of the civil service, which was faced with the necessity to fill vacancies in the management with the available native personnel; the vacant statuses were formerly monopolized by members of the alien colonial administration. In conformity with the sweeping wave of democracy, the bureaucracy resorted to election of its personnel, thus consciously or unconsciously putting aside one of the fundamental elements of modern bureaucracy, rationality.

The second bureaucracy is a well-run public office, the able and experienced native head of which was to be subordinated to a less able, but politically acceptable, official. Since this new political head failed in his responsible status in the executive bureaucracy, a modus vivendi was sought which kept both the bureaucracy and the society-in-revolution in a well-balanced position.

In the third case a people's military organization is described; the more or less informal company was entirely dependent upon the society at large for its food supply and spiritual stimuli.

The fourth case is concerned with a foreign-owned factory, which was taken over by the workers in the name of a misunderstood democracy. The anarcho-syndicalism which prevailed in the organization during a few months of hectic milling activities had finally to give way to the authority of a better trained, better organized, and competent government agent.

All the cases suggest that no bureaucratic organization can be maintained unless it is in conformity with the society in which it exists. In Indonesia the confused and unstable situation during the revolution was reflected in the civil-service bureaus, in the military organizations, and in the foreign-owned factories. The impact of the revolution on the bureaucracies, however, took place in different ways.

The civil-service office experienced only an indirect influence from the changing social situation. The prerevolutionary internal organization of the office was maintained; the only innovation was in the procedure of selecting people for the leading positions; the factor of capability was replaced by acceptability to the office's personnel, as expressed in the election of the office head.

In the case of the sugar factory not only an election procedure was adopted in lieu of appointment by a higher authority, but the structure of the managing body was—intentionally or perforce—democratized. The one-man decision-making authority was replaced by a collective body, the director with the board. The communication of every important decision to the factory workers may be seen as a device to express the management's responsibility to the workers.

With regard to the ramifications of election in a bureaucracy, we may refer to Max Weber's statement that

> bureaucratic authority is carried out in its purest form, where it is most clearly dominated by the principle of appointment. There is no such thing as a hierarchy of elected officials in the same sense as there is a hierarchical organization of appointed officials. In the first place, election makes it impossible to attain a stringency of discipline even approaching that in the appointed type. For it is open to a subordinate official to compete for elective honors on the same terms as his superiors, and his prospects are not dependent on the superior's judgment.[1]

The local national committee, which was entirely political in scope and spirit, considered the Bureau of General Affairs a lifeless apparatus for routine work only. It was thought incapable of channeling the revolutionary zeal to its ultimate goal. The political revolutionists, represented in the national committee, perceived themselves as the only carriers of the new ideals of freedom and democracy. Hence their desire and their decision to bring the revolutionary temper into the bureau by making the former head subordinate to a new politically minded head. Following Mannheim, we can say that the failure of the new head suggests that politics and bureaucratic administration are supplementary parts in a larger organization; they cannot be merged into one, but they have to be kept separate, though interrelated. Politics must confine itself to the role of giving directions and exercising corrective supervision over the bureaucratic organization; the motivation for an action, the specific significance of the action in the entire whole of political activities, the goal, and finally the timing of the action—all are to be determined on the political level. But the "how" of the action, which includes the technical preparation and operation of the action through the organization of material and human factors, belongs to the exclusive competence of the experienced and trained bureaucrat. The discontinuities committed by the new head as a consequence of bu-

---

[1] Max Weber, "The Essentials of Bureaucratic Organization: An Ideal-type Construction," in Robert K. Merton et al., Reader in Bureaucracy (Glencoe, Ill., 1952), pp. 21-22.

reaucratic considerations on the one hand and political pressures on the other led unwillingly to the separation of the double role. Politics and bureaucratic administration were put in its proper place again.

As to the military organization, this was entirely a product of the society-in-revolution; it sprang from the society to carry out the society's will and can be considered an effective tool which was organized and operated by the society.

In general, the changes in the bureaucracies as described in this paper were also influenced by the lack of trained personnel to replace the foreign workers. Thus the bureaucracies were forced to deviate from the standard requirements for rationality and competence. Tensions in the bureaucracies which were not adequately dealt with by those responsible tended to result in deterioration in the quality of production. A related element that deserves attention is that the *pressure for action* upon the members of a bureaucratic organization (in this case the military company and the factory) may be favorable to maintain internal equilibrium. On the other hand, lack of such pressure easily creates opportunities for the workers to deviate from administrative rules, bringing tensions unfavorable to the organization. After the international recognition of Indonesia's independence as a nation-state, the society regained its equilibrium, and consequently the bureaucratic organizations also became stable again. Control was restored; rationality returned and was accepted by the workers.

Finally, it has been said that "the bureaucratic machine will ordinarily continue to operate essentially unchanged even in the face of revolutionary changes in the society." [2] The events described in this paper suggest a modification of this view. Revolution means a deliberate and widespread movement aiming at the rapid change of fundamental values and institutions in a society. In the sweep of revolution no bureaucratic organization can remain unchanged.

FURTHER READINGS

Gerth, Hans H. and Mills, C. Wright, eds. *From Max Weber: Essays in Sociology.* New York: Oxford University Press, 1946.

Gouldner, Alvin. *Patterns of Industrial Bureaucracy.* New York: The Free Press, 1954. Paperback, 1964.

March, James, ed. *Handbook of Modern Organizations.* Chicago: Rand, McNally and Company, 1965.

Presthus, Robert. *The Organizational Society.* New York: Alfred A. Knopf, 1962.

Whyte, William H. *The Organization Man.* Garden City, New York: Doubleday Anchor Books, 1957.

[2] Robert K. Merton, "The Essentials of Bureaucratic Organization," in Merton *et al., op. cit.,* p. 18.

11

INDUSTRIALIZATION AND
SOCIAL CHANGE

Introduction

LIKE BUREAUCRATIZATION AND URBANIZATION, industrialization is a universal phenomenon whether we think of factory production or agricultural technology. Industrialization is the process of diffusing modern techniques of mechanical production. In the process both machines and social patterns are transmitted creating new categories of workers, new social classes and new cultures.

Paul Meadows describes what he calls "a kind of permanent revolution" which transforms not only productive processes but total societies as well. He sensitively portrays the impact which these new forms have on the human condition and warns us of the possibility of serious discontent while concluding on a more optimistic note.

Industrialism as a behavior pattern has been the focal point of a variety of sociological studies in both the United States and Europe. Georges Friedmann reviews some of these studies in the process of suggesting what kinds of research need to be done "on the eve of [the] third industrial revolution." In addition to his coverage of Western Europe his observations in the Soviet Union add to his perceptions of the diverse patterns affecting all societies undergoing industrialization.

While Meadows and Friedmann look directly at the human experiences associated with industrialism, thus placing these issues into the context of our discussion of alienation and anomie in Chapter 13, Irving L. Horowitz reviews and analyzes aspects of the ideas used to describe industrial development. Distinguishing between concepts of change and concepts of development he reviews ideas from antiquity to the present analyzing some sources of "ideological struggle" and concludes with suggestions for the social scientist's role in describing processes and clarifying alternatives.

S. M. Miller and Martin Rein's short paper places some of the problems of poverty within the context of social change generally and industrialization, more specifically. Thus it provides us with a direct focus on one of America's most serious problems at the same time illustrating what industrialization can mean to a large segment of a population. They conclude with the suggestion that we consider changing social values, a suggestion also made by Mizruchi in our Epilogue, Chapter 13.

Industrial Man

PAUL MEADOWS

I

"INDUSTRIAL TECHNOLOGY" is the latest in a long series of human technologies. The phrase describes man's tool-using behavior at the level of machine technics. Industrial technology centers around the use of the machine in the production, transportation, and exchange of goods and services. As I see it, however, the essence of the machine is not the instrument itself, is not merely power applied to an end-tool. The machine is a historically novel method of transforming random energy into disciplined power and utility. Industrial technology, then, is a matter of technical and social strategy. Technically, there must be some mechanism for performing a useful task. This mechanism is characteristically an engine and an end-tool. For industrial purposes, the productive task must be routinized and specialized, and the necessary operations must be arranged in orderly series. Any task which is repetitive can be mechanized and serialized. In this manner the productive organization establishes the means for regularity in the flow of production. Socially, there must be an organization of human relations in which human energy is accommodated to the demands of the mechanical equipment. Based on the principles of science and focussing on the machine as a system of controlled efficiency, industrial technology seeks the conversion of physical and human resources for human use by means of mechanical standardization and quantity production.

Historians commonly speak of the emergence of industrial technology as "The Industrial Revolution". Actually, as I see it, industrialism is a kind of

This article has made use of materials appearing in the present writer's articles: "The Industrial Way of Life," *The Technology Review*, XLVIII, 5, March, 1946; "Modern Man Is Vulnerable," *Unity*, CXXXVIII, 3, September-October, 1952; "Technological Change and Human Conflict," *The Personalist*, Autumn, 1948; "Culture Theory and Industrial Analysis," *Annals of the American Academy of Political and Social Science*, 274, March, 1951. Reprinted by permission of the author.

permanent revolution, perhaps the most important one of contemporary history, still reconstructing life even in Western societies and revolutionizing human relations in ever new ways in non-Western cultures. Indeed, we may actually argue, correctly I believe, that industrial technological change is a generic social process, a mechanical and social transformation of human environments which is likely to continue for a very long time. In fact, industrialism creates, wherever it invades, a culture which is dynamic in spirit, in technics, and in form. Let us note briefly what these changes mean.

The *spirit* of an industrializing society is a questing drive for increasing productivity through heightening rationality. Rationality we may define as strict adaptation of means to ends. As an example of what is meant here by rationality, consider the case of functionalism. Functionalism—a word which describes a philosophy and a method popular in such various areas as anthropology, architecture, biophysics, and zoology—may be thought of as the intellectual counterpart of the machine in technology. The machine has become a commanding model of human behavior, a model of rationality, and because of that model there develops in an industrializing society a psychocultural compulsion, a compulsion for efficiency, for an economic calculus of gains and losses, for scientific management and inventory control, for specializing and division of labor, for a well-disciplined labor force, for aptitude testing and personnel management, for market analyses and market predictions.

Industrial technology,—in other words, calls for a new kind of human discipline. It calls for a regimentation of the human spirit, a regimentation which must be austere, in order to command respect. The discipline must be this-worldly, so the daily task will not be neglected. It must be empirical, so that new learnings will issue. And industrial discipline must be exacting, so that obedient self-sacrificing will be generously forthcoming. This pattern of motivation rests—at least in the industrial West—on the self-interested and omniscient individual who has status and is legitimate because he has been "called" to the job,—the sacredness of industrial work. This new man is justifiably acquisitive and industrious because he is, after all, a steward of the Great Manager-Mathematician. He must, in other words, be rational and efficient, like the machine itself. He ought to be leisure-less, for his time is hired,—and time, moreover, is money; unhired time is indulged, however, because it possibly can, and certainly ought to, increase the productivity of the working hours. He ought, above all, to be money-minded, for else how can he be related to the machine, his products disposed of, his machined commodities secured, the imponderables of his existence "controlled"? A society of self-acting machines; such is the utopia of the philosophers and apologists of industrialism.

We have said that industrialism creates, wherever it invades, a culture dynamic in technics and in form as well as in spirit. Notice, then, that industrial technology brought together—and this was indeed a technical revolution—new sources of power, on the one hand, and functionally adapted end-tools, on the other. Techniques and skills, once used for the fortuitous fashioning of implements and weapons, as Oswald Spengler pointed out, were, under industrialization, routinized, mechanized, and serialized. So it was that a new goal-condition, a new normative orientation for human behavior emerged; with mechanization the things which count are continuity of functions, regularity of performance, accuracy in action, rapidity in flow, and volume in production.

Such a system of production had to have a parallel system of institutions. Thus, production had to be organized; and so at different times and places the entrepreneurial function had to be exercised by individuals, families, partnerships, the joint-stock company, and finally the public corporation (including the public-as-a-corporation, as in Russia). Again, markets had to be formed; and so in time self-regulating and self-adjusting exchanges of goods and services have given way to group-controlled exchanges and these in turn yielded to socially regulated or (again as in Russia) socially operated exchanges. These two illustrations make, it seems to me, a very important point, which is that in industrial culture fixity is a device, not a generic trait. Social forms are functionally defined, and limits are dynamically conceived. And so local markets become linked with national markets, and world markets become an economic unit. Raw materials become the subject-matter of a planetary ecology. Intercontinental and trans-oceanic movements of goods, capital, persons, and knowledge across national boundaries create pressures on political interests and alignments, bringing them in line, ultimately at least, with the long-run logic of technology.

What is being suggested here, then, is the fact, simple but Procrustean, that industrialism not only means the appearance of a new system of technology; it also spells transformation in the system of human relations and of beliefs of a society. The matter may be put this way, although, I must confess, a bit dramatically. Industrial technicways—to use Howard Odum's famous and effective phrase—establish suzerainty over the folkways and stateways of an industrializing society. With industrialization the folk cultures of primitives and peasants surrender their citadels of custom and tradition to the dominion of technologically organized institutions. The aftermath of industrial conquest is, thus, the creation of new dimensions of social existence. Specifically, new patterns and new problems of status, new problems in human collaboration, new problems of cultural integrity,—these are part of the legacy as well as genius of an industrializing culture.

II

It is impossible, in brief space, to spell out all of the aspects and implications of these new dimensions of social existence thus created by industrialism. Here, then, are only a few, but an important few.

Industrialization reshapes the pattern of human obligation and position, the social organization and social structure of a people. This point can be expressed in the following proposition. The transition from a pre-industrial to an industrial culture causes a shift in the status system of a people: a shift from inherited or ascribed status to one that is achieved or acquired. Status achieved through skill establishes the *modus operandi* and the *modus vivendi* of industrial societies. Industrial culture, in other words, recognizes and rewards individuals in terms of achieved skills. It extends to individuals, regardless of color, class or creed, an opportunity for acquiring and exercising skills. It promotes among the masses a competition and rivalry for scarce values. It organizes the masses into skill groups, and it expands the scope and power of skill organizations. It phrases human motivation in terms of skill. It encourages the emergence of new judicial and legislative criteria of human justice, criteria which center in the democracy of skill.

Such a status system obviously is going to precipitate, wherever it penetrates, crucial problems of human collaboration, on the job and indeed in all interpersonal relations. These problems of collaboration rarely appear in primitive and peasant cultures, for there tradition ascribes one's status and custom defines his functions. The life adjustments of pre-industrial peoples are prefabricated for them. But the life adjustments of industrial peoples must be fabricated for them as they go along. Just as the routines of machine production must be invented, so likewise must the routines of human collaboration. Unhappily, the atmosphere of social invention—the inevitable and essential counterpart of machine invention in an industrial civilization—has little of the calm and controlled and studied environment of machine invention. The stormy political history of every industrial nation of the West shows this. Thus, almost two generations ago a great religious leader, Pope Leo XIII, sensed this mood and temper of human relations in industrial society. In his justly famous *Rerum novarum* he pointed out: "The elements of a conflict are unmistakable. We perceive them in the growth of industry and the marvelous discoveries of science; in the changed relations of employers and workingmen; in the enormous fortunes of individuals and the poverty of the masses; in the increased self-reliance and the closer mutual combination of the labor population; and, finally, in the general moral deterioration."

Leo XIII was by no means the first to feel the leaderless drift of the twin forces of isolation and opposition within industrialism. David Ricardo had spoken of the conflicts of landlord and tenant, of agriculture and manufacturing. Karl Marx had systematized the oppositions in his terrific ideological onslaught. The utopian socialists of the nineteenth century, as well as the humanitarians, had been sorely perplexed by them. Today, whatever else industrial culture may contain by way of peace and human fulfillment, it rests uneasily upon the mobile foundations of isolated and opposed interests. Industrialism has both atomized and organized human relations, and this contradiction makes it tragically mercurial, volatile, and almost unmanageable.

What we are saying may be expressed this way. Much of the discontent

—and of the problem of human collaboration—of industrial peoples springs from the manner in which a status system based on skill is often and easily distorted and perverted by status-values which have little or nothing to do with skill, as Thorstein Veblen pointed out many years ago and as David Riesmann has said in recent years. In fact, in industrial cultures we have observed the appearance of strategists of mass discontent, themselves products of a new skill, the skill of probing, inflaming, and exciting the pathologies which may exist in an industrial culture of status based on skill. All of us can point to vested and ideological groups which, while promoting and protecting their skills (or lack of them), have frequently blocked a technologically sensible solution to problems of human collaboration by irrational resort to reaction, rumor, threat, character assassination, neurotic withdrawal, and pseudo-legislative confiscation of constitutional rights.

What is happening in the area of human collaboration—among and between individuals and groups—is also happening in the area of human motivation, within individuals and groups. The fast-growing literature on industrial relations is constantly elaborating an insight which was common enough among primitives and peasants alike: the theme that men cannot be loyal to that which they have not experienced. Conversely, the strongest and most predictable loyalties of men are to those things with which they have had the most satisfying experiences. Here, then, is the touchstone of industrial motivation: the discovery and nourishment of human satisfactions—and thereby of human loyalties.

This is no easy task, for it is a task which must be worked out in mass terms for a mass society. Modern man lives by mass measures, and every aspect of his life has a mass measure: mass production, mass education, mass communication, mass unemployment, mass armies, mass populations. The scale of our lives is a large scale. When new directions emerge, they are sure to take a mass form. Social change can never, in our mass age, be confined to miniature universes. In a mass age one can seldom predict the routes of social innovation, and it is virtually impossible to quarantine or immunize against all social infections. The vulnerability of modern man is a mass vulnerability. All our advances in the arts of human society are defended and have been hailed as new bulwarks of human security. And yet in daily fact they cast dark, long shadows across the future edges of our experience. The more intricate the organization, the more easily it is disrupted; the more massive the scale, the more sweeping the telltale consequences. In organization we have tried to protect and promote our individualities, and we find them engulfed by the demands and exactions of our collectivities. Mass has assumed the significance which once dwelt in the individual, and shrunken egos must find solace in swollen coffers and momentous issues. It is easy to attack the integrity of nations, to descry the inconsistencies of corporations, to castigate the contradictions of groups, but the quiet integrity of a man's own life seldom can withstand the shocks of the tiniest and most timid assertion of personal conscience. The inspired protest becomes lost in the labyrinths of administrative protocol and hierarchical disavowals. Form must substitute for feeling, and the priestly rituals of collective self-interests quench the fires of prophetic judgment. The artist in obscurities replaces the armed vision. Where men were once persons, they are now members, and they must, according to the pathetic irony of human involvements, live within walls that always shut out far more than they shut in.

Consider in this respect the problem of human loyalty.

Among tribal peoples loyalty is simply and easily defined—to the tribal gods, rituals, mores, routines, and lineage group. But in what ways can modern industrial people, living in a social universe which always turns out to be a pluriverse, lay claim freely and honorably on their loyalties? We know we should be able freely and honorably to stake them out and declare them. Indeed, we experience the greatest security of our living in the loyalty that stands unimpeachably and imperishably clear and firm. But where and how can we discover such free and honorable loyalties? If we join this group, we cannot share in that; if we hold this faith, then we must not share in that; if we cherish this value, then we must reject that; if we prize this way, then we must spurn that. Nor is that all. By affirming our loyalty to this or that principle or program or cause, we usually find that semantic subterfuges, legal technicalities, judicial sonorities, legislative "Whereases," and administrative procrastination have repudiated, where they have not humiliated, our loyalties.

A case in point is the McCarran Act. Bureaucratic predilection and inclusive but ambiguous law make a farce of group membership. Admitted membership, concealed membership, past membership in a part or in a group now under bureaucratic stigmata are no less censured and actionable than assumed membership, or likely membership, or reputed membership, membership in a group with sympathies supposedly paralleling at some past or present or possible future points the sympathies of a hated group.

But the anomaly of modern loyalties goes far beyond our contemporary secularized witchcraft. In an organized society modern man protects and promotes his particular interests, we have said, through organized groups. But now any loyalty can be defined as disloyalty, any conscience as the lack of it. The only conformity that can survive the merciless fire of privileged criticism can be only the most universal, the most flattened out, the least assertive, the most innocuous and mediocre conformity. Heresy, we are told, is the idea hated by men who have no ideas. Bigotry becomes the *deus ex machina* of a machines-processed acquiescence. And in an age of conformity, bigotry—"the appalling frenzy of the indifferent," as Chesterton called it— slashes out at the "heretical" novelty, the "traitorous" sensitivity, and "untraditional" criticism. In numbers, it seems, there is safety for very little— save numbers!

We have indeed industrialized our vulnerability; we have mass-produced it, standardized it, serialized it, streamlined it, mass-merchandised it. And in such a society every bounding line becomes a boundary, every affection an alienation, every inclusion an exclusion, every approach a withdrawal, every sympathy a suspicion, every faith a heresy.

We have been in the last few minutes trying to dramatize some of the problems of human motivation in an industrial society. We have sought to put the theme in these terms: that the strongest and most predictable loyalties of men are to those things with which they have had the most satisfying experiences. This idea was expressed many years ago by Ordway Tead in these words: "Interest is an attitude of continuing attention induced where the individual finds that the activity gives him a sense of self-expression." Whenever an industrial people seek to recognize and realize this fact, they seek to create and universalize favorable opportunities for finding, learning, exercising, and being rewarded in the use of a skill or of skills.

But skill is not to be understood merely as an economic achievement. All human activities yield up pleasure and loyalty in terms of skill. Perhaps the most ignoble illusion in the history of industrialism was the myth that industrial men are concerned only with the satisfaction of economic skills. Few people have known how utterly shallow and false that myth is than Whiting Williams who a generation ago did a restless trek through mines and mills, factories and shipyards, everywhere talking person to person, laborer to laborer, with working people. A Welsh miner told Williams: "We must all 'ave the chaunce to play the mon." Generalizing over his experiences in industries in two continents, Williams felt that here, in the "chaunce to play the mon," is "the thread of self-respect and standings and statuses . . . that ties the world of modern society together." The integrity of a culture as well as of an individual within that culture is contained in this fact.

III

Much of what I have been saying centers on the problem and prospect of human collaboration under conditions of industrialization. Now collaboration is a process which intertwines with conflict. We have here been accenting the ambivalent impact of technology on human relations, have been emphasizing the twin movements of isolation and association, of approach and withdrawal, of individualization and socialization which it seems to encourage. Specifically, has industrial technology increased or decreased the probability of conflict in human relations? If increased, under what circumstances? With what results? In the closing portion of this discussion I should like to essay an answer, of a general sort, to these questions.

Human conflict is a process: this is to say, it is a series of stages leading from one condition to another. These stages can be typically denoted and expected. They emerge in any and all of the occasions of human interaction, in industrial relations quite as easily as in race relations. I should like to assert this proposition about conflict in our kind of society: that industrial technology has radically changed the character of each of the steps in the conflict process. In order to make this point clearer, let me remind you that human behavior from contact to conflict is typically somewhat as follows:

1. Contact
2. Emergence of differences
3. Awareness of differences
4. Belief in the exclusive (irreconcilable) nature of differences
5. Decision to eliminate, or coerce, the opposing differences (By this time now called "interests")
6. Action calculated to realize this definition of the situation
7. Establishment of a new, mobile equilibrium

Industrial technology, with its progressive development, has broken down the walls of human isolation. Immobility—induced by the barriers of space, time, fear of the unknown, dread of the stranger, love for the past or for the next world—has yielded to the technicways of mechanical invention in communication and transportation. "Men on the move" are the dramatic symbols of an age which has given wings to feet and speech.

This breaking-up of vicinal isolation, together with the mental mobility which it created, has sent men on great voyages of discovery of their world. The 16th century discovered the environment. The 17th and 18th centuries explored it. The 19th century harnessed it. The 20th century promises to exploit it. Like a spring thaw, this release of the human mind has outpoured in many directions. Technology has lent expressiveness to the human spirit. It has overcome the time factor in human contacts. It has achieved incredible swiftness through space. It has become the companion of the masses and a servant diffusing the intentions and the contentions of human minds to all men. The frequency and the variety of human contacts respond to the tempo set by technological culture. Who can say that this process will cease, or even slow down.

Socially, human differences have not been diminished by increased contact but have been multiplied. It is true, of course, that the basic types of human interests and functions are fairly stable. Men have always and everywhere been religious, economic, familial, political, esthetic, and so on. But within these areas of human expression they have exhibited tremendous uniqueness and variability. Modern technology is an impressive monument to this human uniqueness, this human variability. The craftsmanship of the human species, unapproached by even the most intelligent of man's infrahuman poor relations, is the very genius of his cultural prowess. The whole, wide, rich range of culture bears witness to this "instinct of craftsmanship." We call the human craftsman by such names as discoverer, inventor, technological expert, technician, sage, technological adviser, artist; the words change, the song does not.

All the talk of human standardization as a result of machine technology must be qualified by this fact. For machine technology has incredibly multiplied the specialization of human functions, the division of labor, the variability of interests, the extent of differences. Technology has put the human species on a thousand revolving stages, there to enact its dramatic rendezvous with meaningfulness. The world is a factory; but it is also a playhouse, a hospital, a laboratory, a church, a school, a home. Moreover, the technological differentiation of human interests and functions has pulled us out in many directions. It has shifted us from localism to cosmopolitanism; from the sacred to the secular; from the provincial to the national and international; from locality and blood groups to special-interest groups. Man has become under industrialism a highly multi-valued creature. Only the destruction of his technological culture can change the involvements of that fact.

But in all this shuffling and reshuffling of the cards of human destinies, the stakes have become higher and higher and deliberately so. Men made different, act differently. They become aware of these differences, justify them, sentimentalize them, strive to make them irreconcilable and immortal. They come to see their differences through the glasses of exclusion. They set their sights on the far hills of exclusive realization.

This shift in human thinking is less the product of technology, more the work of ideology. Just as the provincial conflicts of the medieval and early modern period had their mercenaries, so the world conflicts of our own day have their paid hirelings. Janizaries have been replaced by ideologists. Fragmented world-views become supported by segmental rationalizations, and the towering spires of passionate imperialisms are strengthened and adorned by the flying buttresses of idea-systems, slogans, and stereotypes. Unfortunately, advancing technology requires sophistication, but it does not canalize sophistication; instead if anything it is given impetus to move in every direction. In so doing the conflicting ideologies of man move from violence, through intimidation and fear, to fraud: from force to fraud, as Lester F. Ward many years ago predicted. In a world of differences, we refine our philosophies of difference, and we call them ideologies. Henceforth, ideological irreconcilability is wedded to the strategy and the tactics of group annihilation, or more simply, to the strategy of terror.

Unfortunately, we pay a terrific price for this behavior—not in terms of other men's costs, for they do not matter (so we think), but in terms of our own. The conflicts of the external social universe become the mirror of the self, and the personal imbalances of insecurity and fear are the tribute money we pay for the privilege of technological exploitation of our physical and social worlds. At any rate, few people can deny the great increase in human anxiety, whether it results in psychosis or not. "Be not anxious about tomorrow" was an injunction of an agricultural society which knew little about business cycles, cut-throat competition, iron-curtain containment and isolation, imperialistic rivalries, race riots, and cultural integration. Certainly it is hardly a fitting social philosophy for the vast, congested, poorly articulated, diseased, impersonal, swift, expensive, wasteful, megalopolitan culture-centers of the twentieth century!

IV

I have no particular need to end this discussion, after the manner of a Hollywood movie, on a happy note. But there is such a note, and in all honesty it must be sounded. Let us accept the fact that the days are gone when the "time for decision" or action was an occasion for individual human action. The forces of industrial society are, as we have been saying, collective, institutional forces working within giant frames of thought action, such as "business," "industry," "labor," "agriculture," "markets," "nations," "races," "classes," "ideologies," and so on. Now if this be true, then the future of industrialism, partly because it is tied to these mass patterns of life, is likely to be more emotional, less rational, less a matter of cold, calculating determination than some of us would prefer.

However, there is "a point of no return," beyond which industrial people, nourished by the Western way of life, cannot afford to go. It is the point which we may call the free man: the free producer, the free human being, the free human group. For the first time in human history a whole culture structure has, within this theme, been built around the conviction and the custom of human integrity; the dignity and the worth of the human personality through whose free exercise of rights and powers both the stability and the expansion of a balanced culture take place. Such a conception of civilized human behavior, however imperfectly realized, a technological age dare not lose. The structure of industrial technology was raised in the West by men who had won for themselves the rights and powers of a free society. Their language at first was one of "liberty," because their need was the removal of restraints upon action. Later, their speech became positive, filled with the words of "freedom," because their need had changed to one oriented around the mobilization of resources for action. "Liberty" and "freedom": the absence of restriction and the capacity to act: the rights and the powers of free men; such was the stuff of the technological expansion which produced Western industrialism. It was not a thin, watery stuff: it was indeed a revolutionary faith, and it burned high in revolts against the Church in revolutions against the State, in protest movements even against its own society. From it came a free market, a free labor, a free enterprise, a free conscience, a free science, a free legal and political system. In a free industrialism all men have the power to act: that is the genius—the troubled genius to be sure—and the eternal heritage of our technology. And if there is leadership anywhere in industrial culture, it lies within this focus of idea and ideal.

Technological Change and Human Relations

GEORGES FRIEDMANN

IN SEVERAL COUNTRIES OF EUROPE and in the U.S.A., the study of technological change in its connections with social evolution, human relations and
human values attracts more and more attention.

This interest is justified: the studies involve a complex problem embracing many others of our time, social, ethical, and—at least, so I believe—
philosophical. It often slips out of your grasp when you try to seize it.
Roughly speaking, it could be defined as the relations between technical
and moral progress.

For my part, I firmly believe that before we rise to general ideas,
before we judge, we must be prepared to go through a long period of inquiry, of methodical observation in various types of factories, in dock-yards,
in offices. We must spend a long time observing and collecting data concerning the behavior of modern men at work and at play, and the evolution of
machines and techniques of all types which permeate and transform man's
environment in an industrial civilization.

I

I used the words "industrial civilization". What do they mean? What
historical and technological justification is there for this expression?

My first point is that there are different phases or stages in the so-called
"Industrial Revolution", which have their own particular features, each of
them showing technical, social, economic and cultural aspects which are
closely inter-related.

(a) The first industrial revolution is characterized by the supremacy of
the steam-engine and consequently, of coal, which has rightly been called
the "first bread of industry". It marks the transition from cottage industry
to the factory. Following the rather primitive inventions of Newcomen, the
appearance of James Watt's steam-pumps in the English collieries, the introduction of the first steam-looms in the weaving industry mark the beginning
of this phase in the last two decades of the eighteenth century. As shown
in Charles Ballot's classic, *L'introduction du machinisme dans l'industrie
française* (Paris, 1923), this movement reached France after a delay of about
twenty years, and, spreading through Western Europe, reached Belgium and,

From *British Journal of Sociology*, 1952, pp. 95-116. Reprinted by permission of the
publisher and author.

later, the countries of Central Europe. In the United States its beginnings were rather slow. They can be traced to the last years of Jefferson's presidency, after the conclusion of the Napoleonic Wars.

(b) Gradually, however, discoveries in physics and chemistry and their application to industrial processes put an end to the supremacy of the alternating steam-engine, whose essential characteristic was the role of the piston.

During the last three decades of the nineteenth century striking technological changes occurred. A new and original set of techniques changed the face of West European and North American communities.

To the steam-engine, hardly modified since the days of Watt, was now added, or rather substituted, a whole complex set of techniques, accompanied by economic transformations of which I can only mention here a few of the most striking features:

The appearance in industry of new combustibles and fuels, liquid and gaseous: the use of lighting gas in the machines of the Belgian, Jean Lenoir, from the 1860's, being an important stage of a movement leading to the progressive use of all kinds of petroleum oil in motor engines and, later, Diesel engines.

The revolution, more and more complete, in communications, by rail, road, and sea.

The readaptation of the steam-engine owing to the technical discoveries of Parsons, in the 1880's, and his steam-turbine.

New types of metal-cutting machines made of toughened steel, adding speed to greater precision and, moreover, involving several different tools, co-ordinated in their action: this being a stage on the road towards progressive automatization.

The invasion of industry and agriculture by chemistry.

And, last but by no means least, overshadowing and dominating all these changes, penetrating them, and setting its seal on the second industrial revolution: the universal use of electricity. Although the theoretical findings of the physicists date back a long way, only at the end of the nineteenth century do the practical applications of this new form of energy begin to transform the workshop and the use of man-power. Electricity deserves to be called the new "bread" of industry.

Closely linked with these technological changes, with the tremendous increase of total production and the necessity, henceforth, of a more rational use of man-power, are the first attempts at scientific management which can be observed during this period. The active years of the life of F. W. Taylor are between 1880 and 1914: and this is not a mere coincidence. It is permissible to say that the second industrial revolution is also distinguished by the appearance of mass production and industrial rationalization—in the U.S.A. at first, in Western Europe a little later.

(c) The second industrial revolution continued and developed at the opening of the twentieth century and during the period between the two World Wars.

To-day, we are on the eve of a third industrial revolution, whose characteristic will be the liberation of atomic energy and, as it appears from already advanced research, its application to industry in the fairly near future.

Such, if we had the space to describe it in more detail, would be the historical background of the industrial revolutions.

Under their influence, various machines have appeared and constantly increased in number. They play different and sometimes very numerous roles, and have different effects on man's activity and sensibility.

II

(1) Into the first category fall *production* machines used in industry, agriculture and offices. As for the latter, I am thinking in particular of accounting machines and of those connected with the preparation of work in the workshop. The huge international growth of a concern like the International Business Machines shows how important this field of technological development has already become.

(2) Into the second category fall the various machines *for transport* on land, sea, and in the air.

The social effects of these techniques are most important, as it appears from recent studies. The pioneering contribution of American sociology is, on this subject, remarkable, and particularly the work of Professor W. F. Ogburn and his assistants at the University of Chicago.

But I must emphasize that this part of the field is only just beginning to be explored and that very much has still to be investigated and to be said, especially concerning the motor-car. I remember my joy when, a few years before the war, I read, in a list of American Ph.D. theses, the following title: "The automobile, a sociological study." I regret to say that the contents of the work did not come up to my expectations. Yet, this field—the effects of the motor-car on society, psychology, family and even current ethics— is immense and practically untouched.

The U.S.A. has been defined as "a nation on wheels" and in Europe we observe the same trend rapidly developing. There is another definition which was given to me three years ago, in Detroit, by an executive in a big motor-car factory: "The family is the place where the son waits for the return of the automobile." I pointed out to this gentleman that another important firm of motor-car manufacturers had just put into mass production a car furnished with twin-beds, so that the inter-connections between car and family were even more tight than he seemed to believe.

(3) Into a third category fall machines of *communication*: telegraphs, telephones, radio, television. Some of the younger members of our staff are particularly interested in research in this field. For instance, a book will appear next spring, by M. Roger Veillé who has had a fairly long experience in the French broadcasting system and is also connected with our centre of

sociological studies in Paris. This book is entitled: *La Radio et les Hommes*.

(4) In our fourth category we will place the *techniques of leisure*. In an industrial civilization, mechanization of leisure accompanies mechanization of work and is closely mingled with it.

Here we find once more, though in quite different patterns, some of the transport and communication techniques previously mentioned.

For instance, the motor-car is, at different times, an instrument of work or an instrument of leisure for the doctor or the business man. For the society woman whose car wanders between the beauty-parlour, the dress-maker's shop and the fashionable seaside resorts, this double function does not occur.

Here we find also the gramophone techniques and what can be called *"the Big Two"* of mechanized leisure: the cinema and the radio, coupled with television.

III

This short classification leads us to a third point: the more and more pronounced appearance, due to the effect of these technological changes, of a new environment of man: "the technical environment".

These numerous techniques have transformed and daily continue to transform the living conditions of modern societies, and, consequently, the relations between individuals. Every moment of life, every aspect is more and more affected. We are confronted here by a phenomenon of vast proportions, invading working hours, life in the street, in the home, leisure both by day and by night.

Let us compare our life with the life of men and women in pre-industrial societies.

Let us take, for example, a man living at the "eleventh hour" of these communities and himself an industrialist. Buffon, the great French scientist, forerunner of Darwin, born in 1707, died in 1778. He was iron-master at Montbard, a town in Burgundy on the main road to Dijon. The machines he used were worked by wind and water, energy coming directly from Nature. When travelling, he could not exceed the speed of a galloping horse. For Buffon and his contemporaries, most of the stimuli to which they were submitted came from beings and things which were not artificial but natural.

For this natural environment the industrial revolutions have substituted an environment which is more and more technical: the "technical environment". This environment daily thickens, becomes more dense, more permeated, so to speak, with all the techniques we have mentioned, and envelopes on all sides, the men and women of our time. Each day we are submitted to thousands of stimuli which, until quite recently, were unknown.

A few comments are necessary concerning this technical environment.

(1) The difference between the "technical environment" and the "natural environment":

It is absolutely essential to avoid any misunderstanding as to what we mean by "natural environment". It is not our intention at all to give it the meaning of a *purely* natural environment. Such a conception would be abstract and unrealistic.

(*a*) There were techniques in all pre-industrial societies where agriculture was far more developed than industry. Concerning these techniques we must emphasize that, in these societies or communities, work included many repetitive and highly monotonous tasks, such as the millstone, the mortar, the spinning wheel and so forth.

There is no question of an idealized view of the past which would coincide with a metaphysics of the "good old days".

(*b*) Therefore, we must bear in mind that, ever since the origins of prehistory, the "natural environment" is a relatively "technical" environment. Modern ethnologists are giving more and more attention to studying the efforts by which man seeks to defend, feed, shelter and clothe himself, and the gradual development of the related techniques. Among the recent French contributions in this field, I refer here to the interesting works of M. André Leroi-Gourhan, one of the best disciples of Professor Paul Rivet, and Deputy Director of the Musée de l'Homme and Reader in the University of Lyons. And also, on the anthropo-geographical side, to the very important works published since 1945 by Professor Max Sorre under the title: *Les fondements biologiques et techniques de la Géographie humaine* (4th volume is in the press); the works of M. Sorre are in the intellectual tradition of Vidal de la Blache, the founder of the French School of human geography which is so closely connected with our sociological preoccupations.

(*c*) Does all this mean that the opposition between "technical environment" and "natural environment" is only superficial, and that it disappears on more careful examination?

We do not think so.

The term "natural environment" seems justified when applied to societies of the past or the present which use machines propelled exclusively by natural energy (animal force, wind, water). In these societies, technical change is not due to the industrial revolutions.

On the other hand, in the phase of the industrial revolutions entered upon by the Western World since the end of the eighteenth century, there is an enormous multiplication of techniques, a huge increase in the technical power of man. Motors propelled by natural energy are quickly replaced by motors and engines propelled by thermic, electric, and, in the near future, atomic energy.

For the past hundred and fifty years, technical change has shown an *acceleration* hitherto unknown. This acceleration can be measured and attempts have been made in that direction, from a sociological point of view, by Ogburn in the U.S.A., and, from an economic point of view, by Colin Clark, and in France, by my colleague Jean Fourastié in his recent works.

The impact of this accelerated technological change on the environment of man is one of the main themes of social psychology and sociology. Here we can use the famous Hegelian concept: the transformation of *quantity* into *quality*. The *quantity* of these new techniques gives birth to new forms, to a new *quality*, of civilization. In this sense, and whatever may have been the technical achievements of mankind, before the industrial revolution, the end of the eighteenth century, shall we say, constitutes a break or even a jump: it marks the beginning of a new era in the psycho-sociological conditioning of man by his environment, and the beginning of what we call the *technical environment*.

(2) My second comment on this point would be this:

Is the "technical environment" a universal phenomenon? Marcel Mauss, whose works are read and appreciated in England by social anthropologists and sociologists, studied the spread of techniques in various societies. In 1929, at the first "Semaine internationale de synthèse" held in Paris, which offered an interesting symposium on civilization, he read a very thoughtful paper, in which he emphasized the importance of what he called "les faits de civilisation" ("constitutive facts of civilization").

The techniques, their changes by development and borrowing from one society to another, are amongst the "constitutive facts of civilization." Marcel Mauss, with his extremely wide ethnogeographical knowledge, gave numerous and very convincing examples. He himself suggested the application of these ideas to the most advanced communities and especially to contemporary industrialized societies.

According to these views, we lay down that a sufficient number of these "facts of civilization" create a common pattern of civilization. They define and constitute a certain type of civilization. This happens to-day with the development of the second industrial revolution.

In this evolution the U.S.A. is the leading country. But, on the whole, the same technological changes have occurred or are occurring in Britain, France, Germany, in small but highly industrialized countries like Belgium, and recently, in Soviet Russia.

I do not underestimate (a) the differences in the speed and progress of this common evolution, (b) the role of ethical and cultural differences and, consequently, the variety of reactions to technological change, due to what Ralph Linton and other authors call the "basic structure of personality", (c) the role, and impact on these reactions, of economic, social, and political structures (for example between the U.S.A. and the U.S.S.R.).

In spite of these differences, everywhere, the same technological changes that we have outlined above control the same double process of mechanization in leisure and in work, and provide the same "constitutive facts" of civilization.

This would suggest that there is a common "technical civilization" developing in all countries subjected to the second industrial revolution.

(3) As a third comment, and in further support of these views, I would like to emphasize that valuable observations suggest the existence of com-

mon factors in industrialized areas of different countries, and refer, here, to a few points:

(*a*) The common trends in mechanization of leisure which strike the impartial observer in such industrialized cities as New York, Paris, London, Chicago and even Moscow.

Concerning Soviet Russia, these trends were already noticeable on the eve of the 2nd World War and I have noted them down, after three trips devoted to the study of the impacts of technological change in the U.S.S.R., in a book published in 1938 under the title *De la Sainte Russie á l'U.R.S.S.* ("From Holy Russia to the U.S.S.R.")

Incidentally, and in the same line of thought, an interesting problem is suggested by the reactions of newly industrialized communities to the forms of leisure of a mass society, and to the new types of values and habits which these create.

This is the case of the industrial Negro communities which have considerably increased in the U.S.A., and particularly in Chicago, Detroit and St. Louis, since the beginning of the 2nd World War. The process of their adaptation to their new environment is being studied in the field by research teams under the direction of Everett Cherrington Hughes and W. Lloyd Warner, both of the University of Chicago.

As far as France is concerned, studies in progress, undertaken by teams from the "Centre d'Études Sociologiques" and led by P. Chombart de Lauwe, in Paris, reveal interesting facts about these trends. These studies are devoted to the social ethnography of the Paris area, mainly in six districts of the city or the immediate suburbs; the first volume, which forms an ecological introduction, is now being prepared for the press.

(*b*) In the light of the development of the social psychology of personality as shown, for instance, by such works as those of Kardiner, Linton, Erich Fromm and Karen Horney, I am personally interested in the observation and definition of certain human types common to these different societies and characteristic of the technical environment. A brief mention, a rapid outline is all I can give them here.

Kayserling (whom, of course, I do not quote as a scientific authority but, in this case, he did hit the nail on the head), in one of his best books, *Die entstehende Welt* ("The Rising World"), gives the symbolic name of "chauffeur", "the driver",) to the men, who, in modern societies, use the techniques, and sometimes very powerful ones, without having any technical knowledge or any strong cultural background.

May I state that this is no special attack on motor-car drivers: it would be an attack against most of us—and against myself.

A number of observations suggest, and this is the point, that technical power, when not balanced by culture, tends to shape the whole personality: this is the case of the type called here the "chauffeur".

(*c*) There is another type, perhaps even more interesting: that is the man who considers all problems of his daily activity, of his profession (including the human problems) only from the point of view of technique and its requirements. We call this type "the technicist".

Here again I do not want to indulge in hasty generalizations and impeach a whole profession. But, being an industrial sociologist who, for years, has had the opportunity to observe many engineers inside factories and out of them in several different countries, I consider that it is a fact that a great number of production engineers, production experts and also advisers in scientific management have something of this type of personality.

Incidentally, the second Industrial Revolution has bred the most interesting type of technicist, F. W. Taylor, who can be regarded as a kind of technical genius. But his system of "scientific management" is characterized by the omission of the non-technical factors in the study of industry and of its human problems.

As I just defined him, a man who considers all the problems of his daily activity (including the human ones) from an exclusively technical point of view is a technicist. One of the usual characteristics of the technicist in offices and factories is that, when faced with a problem, he begins by making a draft, writing down figures and, if possible, formulating an equation.

But misunderstandings must be carefully avoided: the traits characteristic of the personality of the technicist are not peculiar to any particular occupation and can be found outside the professions which are considered to be specifically technical: they can be found not only in business, amongst managers and executives, but in military careers, and also amongst University professors and scholars of all descriptions, including sociologists.

Coming back to the engineer and managers, those who know France are aware that our famous "École Polytechnique," whose merits are, in many respects, considerable, has bred and is still breeding a great number of these men, who occupy important posts in public as well as private administration.

The spread of the "technicist" type and the recognition of its weaknesses are now more and more freely acknowledged. New trends in scientific management tend more and more to give importance to human relations, and influence the programmes of Engineering Colleges and High Schools. It is worthwhile to point out here as very significant, the creation and development in the U.S.A., at the Massachusetts Institute of Technology, of a section called "Economics and Engineering", which should enable a certain number of engineers to acquire broader ideas about the human factor in industry.

In France, as in other countries, there is a struggle in this matter, but I regret to say that the greater strength rests still on the side of the "technicist" managers and engineers. It so happens that, thanks to research which will be published at the end of 1953, we have had the experience of that struggle in a big French motor-car concern. A new department, supported by some of the highest executives in the firm, is trying to impose itself. It is headed by men who, in every respect, both from the point of view of vocational selection, training of supervisors, mental and physical comfort of the workers, are experienced and well-intentioned. The reaction of the technicist engineers, in the workshops as well as in the technical departments, is often negative and takes the form of scepticism and passive (or even active) resistance. In other cases, the technicist manager, who has had trouble with his employees (decrease of output and quality, turnover, absenteeism, or even strikes) suddenly discovers the magic formula: "human relations" and accepts panaceas which, he naïvely hopes, will, in a few weeks, change the whole morale of his personnel.

May I add that, in an entirely different occupation, that of medicine, we are beginning to collect data on the evolution of this profession, which show the rise and spread of a technicist type of physician (not to speak of the surgeon).

This new type seems to be closely differentiated from the former type. The abundance and perfection of technical equipment, the common use of X-rays and other kinds of laboratory analysis tend to lessen the importance of direct auscultation, to lessen also the practitioner's use of his senses of sight, hearing and touch. It changes, as far as the physician is concerned, what can be called the "feeling for the sick" (*le sens du malade*) and consequently the psychological attitude of the physician towards the patient and vice-versa. We all know (I mean all of us who have been ill)—and this has been confirmed by our interviews amongst various social strata—that the moral tact of the physician, his comprehension and sympathy, his psychological presence are important factors in his knowledge of the patient and, often, in the success of the treatment. Here are the words of Professor Schoemaker at the opening of the 1st International Congress of Gastroenterology, held in Brussels in 1935: "L'idéal que chacun de nous doit avoir dans son cœur, c'est d'être pour nos malades le médecin moderne avec ses appareils compliqués, son laboratoire chimique, ses rayons X, ses instruments à endoscopie, sa technique opératoire, et aussi le médecin ancien qui prenait la main de ses malades en disant: 'Ayez confiance, je suis avec vous.'" A well-expressed thought of which, I fear, my English will not convey all the meaning and feeling: "This is the ideal which all of us should keep in our hearts: to be, for our patients, the modern physician, with his complicated equipment, his chemical laboratories, his X-rays, his endoscopic instruments, his operative techniques, and *also*, the old-world practitioner who would take the hand of his patient and say: "Don't lose heart, I am with you." By observing methodically the evolution of the medical profession, psycho-sociological research in this field will show us if this noble ideal *is* and *can* be attained by the technicist type of physician.

Before concluding this part of my subject, may I emphasize that the evolution towards the technicist attitude is bringing us face to face with an international type of individual, the product of the technical environment.

Observations made during my trips to Soviet Rusia in 1932, 1933 and 1936, and in France in 1944 and 1945, when I had occasion to meet a number of Soviet citizens, plus the analysis of Soviet literature and recent Soviet films, have convinced me that the same evolution, expressed through different social institutions and national traits, is taking place in the U.S.S.R., where, for instance, heads of firms, engineers, Red Army officers, scientists, managers and so forth, show all the characteristics of technicist attitudes towards their tasks and the problems they involve.

In short, I think that in spite of ethnical, economic and political differences and variety in degree and expression, we must admit the "technical environment" as a universal phenomenon of our industrialized societies.

The consequences of such a statement are that:

(i) There is no scientific reason to speak (as do many distinguished writers and essayists in Western Europe) of a so-called "Americanism".

The U.S.A. is ahead of the rest in the evolution towards a "technical environment", and it is important to remember that other countries in Europe and Asia have stronger and older traditions, homogeneous social and cultural patterns which delay this evolution.

But in this path the U.S.A. has no "privilege" (if this can be called a privilege); it is only at the head of a universal trend which is leading to the construction of a "new environment".

(ii) In opposition to the scheme of orthodox Marxism there are important features which are common to capitalist and non-capitalist societies. In other words, there are important human problems, and especially problems concerning human relations, which *cannot* be solved automatically by the overthow of the capitalist system, as is dogmatically asserted by Marxist theorists. To put it in Marxist terms, the dialectic of technological change is not identical with the dialectic of the class struggle.

IV. TECHNICAL ENVIRONMENT AND THE EVOLUTION OF HUMAN SENSIBILITY

If the views which we express above are correct; if, corresponding to the technological change which has been developing rapidly since the end of the eighteenth century, there is a deep transformation of the environment of a great part of mankind; if there is such a change in the stimuli to which the individual is submitted, then there must also be a transformation of

$$\left. \begin{array}{c} \text{emotional} \\ \text{mental} \end{array} \right\} \text{ attitudes of ways of } \left\{ \begin{array}{c} \text{feeling} \\ \text{thinking} \\ \text{acting} \end{array} \right.$$

(1) This transformation has been very strongly emphasized by Lucien Febvre, the eminent French historian and co-founder, with Marc Bloch, professor at the Sorbonne and heroic Resistance leader, shot by the Germans in June 1944, of the journal, *Annales d'Histoire Economique et Sociale*, which has developed, in close connection with sociological research, into

a broad movement, highly significant of contemporary French social science, and known as the "Annales movement".

Shortly after the collapse of France, M. Febvre published in the *Annales* of January–June 1941, an article on "La sensibilité et l'histoire" (Sensitivity and History), a manifesto as well as a programme of work, which, because of the date of publication, has remained unknown to many whose attention it would certainly have attracted under normal circumstances.

This theme, concerning the evolution of emotional and mental attitudes in their relation to changes in the social and technical environment, is also the basic thesis running through his admirable book: *La Religion de Rabelais et le problème de l'incroyance au XVIᵉ Siècle* ("The religion of Rabelais and the problem of unbelief in the sixteenth century"). I would like to draw attention to a chapter of this work which contains an interesting and, I believe, quite original line of research into the history of literature in its connections with the sociology of knowledge. In it M. Febvre gives the conclusion to a careful analysis of the works of a number of poets and writers of the French Renaissance. He points out that the poetic images and comparisons which they use are, more often than not, related to the senses of smell, taste or hearing. Visual images are, in comparison, very rare. Particularly striking is the fact that, to the men of this type of civilization, living in its particular environment, hearing seems at every instant to precede and, if I may say so, supersede sight. Amongst the great writers of this period, Rabelais is the only one who can make a character-study, paint a portrait. In connection with this point it is to be noticed that sight is the most abstract of the senses, the geometrical sense, *par excellence.* Life in the natural environment, the permanent contact with natural elements, natural beings and rhythms tends to develop a more concrete form of sensibility than in our "technical environment".

(2) This same theme runs also very deeply through the works of Huizinga, the Dutch historian, professor at Leyden university, who died during the German occupation, and in my opinion one of the greatest humanist scholars of our time.

I refer here especially to his famous book, *The Decline of the Middle Ages,* and will allow myself to stress one observation which is supported by several facts mentioned at different places by Huizinga and corroborated by the works of M. Febvre and his disciples. It is the violent contrast of day and night imposed on all inhabitants of the countryside and of many of the towns. The techniques of housing and of lighting, which were still very primitive, the conditions of urban life explain this sudden transition from the labour and noise of the day to the total silence of the night. Is it, therefore, exaggerated to believe that these conditions, mainly due to the level of technological development, influenced the sensibility of men living in this environment, a sensibility which the most authoritative historians describe as full of contrasts and sharp oppositions? It is precisely what Huizinga points to, namely, that, in these men, there are violent contrasts in feelings, emotions, in the whole sensibility, and that they are accompanied by a sort of oscillation between extremes. The religious emotions especially were more violent and correspond to forms of the imagination different to the average of our time; representations of Sin, Hell, the Devil, Paradise, as observed in the plastic art of the period do not have an equivalent to-day.

The works of the above-mentioned historians suggest to the social scientist a new way of studying religion in connection with the evolution of man's environment: for instance, religious sensibility, so far as it can be reconstructed from all that we know through writings and works of art, at the time of Pope Leo X was not the same as the religious sensibility of the modern Catholic, contemporary of Pius XII. How could it be the same?

(3) The same attempt to connect the total environment and, in particular, the technical environment with the evolution of the human mind, feelings, and behaviour, appears in the more recent works of Lucien Lévy-Bruhl, and having had the privilege of seeing him fairly frequently and of consulting him in the last years of his life, I know how anxious he was to promote research in that direction. His scientific standpoint had considerably changed since the publication, in 1910, of the *Fonctions mentales dans les sociétés inférieures,* the first of his series on primitive mind, and he was perpetually criticizing his own findings, becoming more prudent in his interpretations, recasting his main theories, as has been quite recently revealed by the posthumous publication, in 1949, of his *Carnets* ("Notebooks"). One of his main preoccupations was to investigate the relations between primitive ways of thought and behaviour and the state of techniques in the environment. His study of the traditional French fairy tales, for example, *Puss in Boots* ("Le Chat botté"), *The Sleeping Beauty* ("La Belle au Bois dormant"), *Beauty and the Beast* ("La Belle et la Bête"), led him to regard these fairy tales as survivals of very ancient attitudes in the minds of modern men, living in a transformed cultural and technical environment.

(4) The comparative study of perception in the "natural environment" and the "technical environment" points to a new field of research. How could perception, the relations between space and time, be the same in men who knew of nothing quicker than the gallop of a horse or, more often, their own pace or the pace of an ox pulling a plough, and in men who live in our great European and American cities? It seems, as has been pointed out by the analysis of literary documents, that they did not observe their surroundings from the same mental standpoint as we do.

The senses of man, in the modern "technical environment" are, from childhood, subjected to the influence of new techniques, such as photography, which accustom him to seeing things from the most varied angles, to rapid vision from fast-moving vehicles, and more and more to aerial vision: these influences have been emphasized by one of our best experimental psychologists, Professor Henri Wallon, since his pioneering article published in 1935 in the *Journal de Psychologie* and entitled "Psychology and Techniques".

(5) I would like to say a few words here about the transformation of the feeling of *presence* in the "technical environment".

Piaget has analyzed the importance of the feeling of presence in the young child and the way in which it is constructed. According to the classical scheme of things, the feeling of the presence of a human being is created in the child's consciousness by a process of association. The child associates, after a time, the visual image (the external features of his mother, for example) with an auditive image (her voice) and eventually, with images of touch. By this means, he feels that the same person is present; he thus constructs the feeling of a human presence.

Is this scheme still valid in the "technical environment" where, to-day, a great number of children, often, as soon as they can speak, are accustomed by other members of the family to hear and speak on the telephone, which can be described as a technique of hearing without vision?

As far as the radio is concerned, I have personally observed the reactions of children and noticed how deeply impressed they were the first time they heard the voice of a person well known to them, for instance their father, coming out of the wireless set whilst this same person was sitting near to them in the same room. Here, also, the classical scheme, according to which the feeling of presence is constructed, is completely upset.

Television, which is rapidly spreading, will have a similar effect by giving at the same time hearing and vision without the feeling of presence.

This evolution of the role and feeling of human presence is one of the most important and profound features of the trend which I am trying to define.

A review of the techniques of work and leisure, of the constructive techniques as well as of the destructive ones used in war, would show a weakening of the feeling of human presence as it was felt and lived in the "natural environment".

In industry, mechanization and gradual automatization have, for centuries, progressively and constantly decreased the part man plays in production. The history of technological change shows us the existence of different stages in the evolution of the machine. The Egyptian potter, as it appears from figures in documents, used his two arms and his two legs to move the different parts of his machine, to hold the tool and to work on the product. His body and his mind were, so to speak, wholly absorbed by the machine which was, on the other hand, strictly dependent on man. In further stages of this technological development, machines have become *semi-independent*, as, for example, the lathes invented at the end of the eighteenth century by the famous French engineer, Vaucanson, or the textile machines designed by Edmund Cartwright, and far more still, the turret-lathes which appeared in the last decades of the nineteenth century. To-day the rapid spread of automatization has made extremely common, in modern workshops, *fully independent* machines which render unnecessary the presence of man. This trend can only be strengthened by the application to industry, in the near future, of atomic energy. In our century, a vast lay-off, a universal dismissal of man by the machine is more and more frequent. From a psycho-technical point of view, this evolution has been admirably summed up by the German industrial psychologist, Otto Lipmann, in his communication to the 4th International Congress of Psychotechnics, under the title: "Der Anteil des Menschen am Produktionseffekt" ("The part of man in production"), which was later translated and published in the *Journal de Psychologie,* in January 1928.

If we turn to the techniques of leisure, we see that a psycho-sociological study of the cinema and the radio has much to investigate about the feeling of presence. I am not one of those who question the dignity of the cinematographic art. Nevertheless, the film, as compared to the stage-play, to dramatic art, is characterized by a certain absence of man: absence of active participtaion on the part of the spectator, and, on the other hand, absence of the actor, of the human being in the flesh, with his direct action on those who see and hear him, with the direct impact of complex psychological influences. Especially when considered from the point of view of human relations, the theatre involves a kind of reciprocal action, of creative complicity between the stage and the audience, which are relatively absent from the cinema and the radio.

The radio allows millions of people, sitting by their fireside with their feet in their slippers, to be "present" at a football match, a meeting, a music hall performance, a lecture, a symphony concert. But would it not be more true to say that the radio allows, in many cases, a *certain form of absence?* Television, though adding visual to auditive images, deserves the same description.

I strongly believe that the film, the radio, and television, have enormous and splendid cultural possibilities and that they are capable, under certain conditions, of creating other kinds of human participation and *presence.* But these are still unknown, uninvestigated and, I fear, are to-day being abused.

V

In the "natural environment", man was obliged to participate, to be present, in all his activities; in production, in art, in leadership, in war. The "technical environment" is characterized by the decline of that kind of participation.

Furthermore, and this is my last point and an important one, it is also characterized by a decline in knowledge of the materials on the part of the men who work on them in industry and agriculture.

Formerly, and until quite recently, work was of an artisan nature and knowledge of the materials in which the worker operated played an important part in his skill. Much of the apprenticeship consisted in acquiring experience in the use of materials: leather, wood, paper, glass, metal, and so on; the properties of the materials, their reactions to tools, to shaping, etc., were of prime importance.

In the "technical environment" this knowledge becomes gradually less and less necessary as a result of the progress of mechanization.

And this phenomenon has, as will be seen, repercussions not only on the transformation of the working conditions of the individual, but also on the shaping of human relations in industry and agriculture.

I do not want to embark on a purely technical discussion. But, after all, examples of this evolution are very numerous. Most of the facts given here have been observed or corroborated in the course of our research in this field.

The textile industry.—Knowledge of the textile fibre, before the introduction of semi-automatic or automatic machines in the spinning mills was an important part of the skill of the workers, and particularly of carders. They had to know the varying reactions of the fibre (cotton, wool, hemp, flax, silk, etc.) to different degrees of humidity and temperature.

This knowledge is to-day considerably reduced, if not entirely eliminated, by the use of the modern machines, for instance, of the carding machines called "gills" in the textile area of Northern France (Lille-Roubaix-Tourcoing). In most cases, these machines are operated by women whose whole period of training does not exceed six months: six months which are required for them to become familiar with the machines, to acquire the psycho-motory automatisms involved by their tasks, and the last remnants of a knowledge of the fibre.

As for knowledge of the machines themselves, here, as elsewhere in most mechanized industrial processes, it is nowadays the monopoly of the *setters* who do not need any knowledge of the materials (in this case, textiles) but merely of the machine, which incidentally requires fairly high qualifications.

The skilled weavers, capable of turning out a complete article, had a very good knowledge of the materials, of the structure of the cloth and of its qualities. It so happened that, after visiting a number of weaving sheds just before the outbreak of the last war, I had, during the occupation of France by the Germans, the unexpected opportunity of making comparative observations. As a result of the abnormal economic circumstances during the years 1941 to 1945, old looms were revived and put into operation by old skilled weavers, particularly in the upper valleys of the Pyrenees. Compared with the knowledge which their work revealed, knowledge of the materials, of the role of the warp, of the structure of the cloth in its minutest details, knowledge of the materials shown by workers who are responsible for a group of fifteen to twenty-five automatic looms is practically *nil*. The devices and gadgets, which automatically give a signal as soon as the least thing goes wrong, have become both numerous and common. The workers do not know the most elementary characteristics of the materials on which they are working or of the product to which their work finally leads.

Let us now point out how the meaningless character of work in the eyes of the worker affects the individual and relations within the working group of which he is a member.

This absence of meaning is due in particular, following the mechanization of industrial processes, to the extremely tight reduction of the total work cycle and of the unit of work cycles. Light has been thrown on the psychological aspect and on some of the social aspects of these problems by an inquiry sponsored by the Human Factors Panel of the committee on social productivity, and undertaken by the National Institute of Industrial Psychology. Two members of the staff, Mr. David Cox and Miss Dyce Sharp, have recently given a first report in the journal *Occupational Psychology*.

In the metallurgical industry, knowledge of the metal, of the varieties of steel and iron, of their properties and reactions to the tool according to the different temper, knowledge of sharpening, etc., are all related to knowledge of the materials. They are now the privilege of the tool-makers, the maintenance staff and, to some extent, of the fitters and setters, who constitute a very small fraction—not more than 10 per cent as shown by our findings—of production workers in metallurgical plants with modern equipment, and form a sort of new technical aristocracy. The outstanding majority, including 90 per cent of the workers, accomplish tasks which have, in most cases, no significance for them beyond that of satisfying immediate needs.

Comparable observations have been made in the ready-made clothing industry.

It must be stressed that the manufacture of clothing has, for centuries, been a handicraft and has called for accurate and skilled knowledge of all the materials used. A large proportion of clothing—and nowadays even clothing for the middle classes—is turned out on highly mechanized lines and the unit of the work cycle has been most strikingly reduced.

As far as the shoe industry is concerned, a knowledge of leather was, until recent times, very important. The least mistake, the least flaw in that knowledge could spoil a whole product. In the case of the highly skilled shoemaker, who knows how to make a whole shoe to measure, and to adapt it carefully to the foot, the major qualification lies in a knowledge of the materials. In the average mechanized modern boot and shoe factory, the last remaining possessor of that knowledge is the "cutter," and even he, in the most up-to-date factories, as I have observed in the big shoe concerns of the State of Tennessee, is losing this privilege through the introduction of a new type of automatic machine.

The same observations are relevant in the glove industry, which has been deeply transformed by mechanization, as in the Grenoble area of France. In the paper industry producing writing paper, envelopes, etc., knowledge of paper is disappearing amongst the workers. Before leaving this topic I would like to quote a curious example taken from an industry which one could have expected to remain unaffected by this trend: the confectionery trade.

Shortly before the war, we studied a highly mechanized factory making biscuits and pastries in Paris. It was equipped with very modern and very beautiful Dutch and Swiss machines. These machines did all the work: measuring the flour, egg-powder, sugar, syrup, cooking the mixture and dividing and wrapping the biscuits.

On our first visit we found that out of a total of 80 workers, 20 were traditional, skilled French pastry-cooks. They had been kept on by the management only to take care of unforeseen incidents. We interviewed these men. They told us: "The machines are excellent. There are no mishaps. We are bored and are sorry we are not back at Deauville, Dinard or Nice, working for the season or creating ourselves, as skilled artisans, magnificent birthday or wedding-cakes at a pastry-cook's." The management finally realized the position, and when we returned for further study, these skilled workers had been dismissed. The management kept only three of them, not as you keep in museums survivals of an extinct species, but because they had acquired, in the meantime, a good mechanical knowledge of the manufacturing processes. May I here mention that, in a famous sweet factory which I visited in November 1948 in the suburbs of Chicago, the training of the men who were introduced to me by the Personnel Department as being "the best cooks" in the factory did not exceed six weeks! Needless to say, their knowledge of the materials was rather primitive and that they were, in fact, semi-skilled or highly specialized operators.

We can say then that the decline in the knowledge of materials is a universal trend connected with technological change. Of course, there still remain branches where craftsmanship survives. But satisfaction in work when the job involves the completion of a whole product lies very largely in knowledge and mastery of the materials. By jeopardizing that kind of satisfaction in work, technological change is greatly altering the human relations which were linked with it both in industry and in agriculture. We will return later to this point.

As we have mentioned agriculture, we should bear in mind that there is, in the European peasantry, an evolution similar to the one which we have outlined in industry.

In the case of France, in industrialized agricultural areas which have been greatly extended in the last three decades, traditional working processes are being rapidly transformed by mechanization. Resistance to this change must not, however, be overlooked and a recent interesting document on this question has been provided by the monograph of M. Garavel, entitled: *Les paysans de Morette, Un siècle de vie rurale dans une commune du Dauphiné,* published in 1948 in the series of the Fondation Nationale des Sciences Politiques, Paris.

An important consequence of these technological changes in the French countryside is the decrease in the number of rural craftsmen: wheelwrights, blacksmiths, harness-makers, etc. Some of these men, rather than leave their home, prefer to transfer themselves to new kinds of jobs or to readapt their old ones; for example, by becoming mechanics, maintenance men or agents for agricultural machines and equipment. We have collected some facts on this aspect of technological change and its consequences, in a brief field study made in 1947 in the Vexin district, north-west of Paris. One of the features of this evolution and its psychological repercussions is that the men who are transferred to modern mechanical jobs do not play, in the life of the villages, country towns and rural communities generally, the same role as did the old artisans. This is also shown by an interesting field study undertaken with the help of country schoolmasters under the direction of M. Varagnac, the author of an interesting book: *Civilisation traditionnelle et genres de vie.* The aim of this inquiry was to investigate the relations, in the French countryside, between recent technological change and traditional creeds and ways of behaviour. Examination of the documents has shown how greatly these creeds and ways of behaviour are influenced by the change in what we call the "technical environment". The subject tackled here is related to an important and, I would say, practical problem of modern culture: how far is it possible to maintain, in a technologically transformed world, traditional dress, traditional expression of feelings through dance, song and other forms of popular art? Is the rural folklore which was so rich up to recent times, in many French provinces, irrevocably condemned to disappear?

If we turn now from the rural artisan to the small peasant proprietor raising a number of different types of crops, as is often the case in France, it is clear that his work calls for a substantial and varied knowledge of Nature, seasons, animals, elements, plants. This knowledge is the equivalent of knowledge of materials in the industrial worker.

The peasant is a man of several techniques, a craftsman who must be able to turn his hand to widely varying tasks, including repair work. To-day, technological change has brought all sorts of machines to the farms, from the small motor tractor and the milking machine to the huge combined harvesters and threshers, and is substituting them, to a large extent, for traditional individual knowledge of Nature and the elements.

The new forms of mechanized labour in industry and in agriculture, owing to the nature of the tasks and the conditions of work which they entail, do not provide the same kind of emotional wealth or the same sources of satisfaction as the traditional jobs consisting in the creation of a complete article. Moreover, and without embarking here on an ethical discussion, we may incidentally ask ourselves the question whether the loss of intimate contacts with Nature in the "technical environment" does not imply fundamental social consequences and especially striking changes in human relations.

By splitting up the unity of traditional occupations and by decreasing knowledge of materials and the significance of the task, technological change has upset the ancient crafts inherited from the guilds and the human relations which they involved. But it would be a great mistake to leave things at that point. Indeed, after having, for a while, the effect of individualizing work by multiplying isolated machines, technological change tends nowadays to create "lines", groups, teams of workers depending on one another. This phenomenon is particularly noticeable in the many forms of work involving conveyor belts. Conveyor work increases the number of interdependent teams, and gives to each a number of complementary tasks. The teams are composed of workers who, in their work, must rely on each other. Further, in many American and certain European factories, substitutes, called "relief men", are added to the personnel of the groups. They specialize in a section of the conveyor work and know several operations. Their job consists in replacing fellow-workers during brief absences and so ensure continuity in the work.

Moreover, the use of new equipment such as secondary belts or "tool conveyors", moving floors and revolving seats for the lateral displacement of workers standing or sitting, introduces into what, until quite recently, was a rigid type of rhythm, a certain degree of fluidity. The worker has, at his disposal, a certain margin of freedom which is sometimes relatively great and can be still further increased by the introduction of "buffer stocks" of semi-finished products, placed between the workers. In these circumstances, the workers can organize their own work within the limits allowed by the rhythm of the conveyor system, and thus a certain freedom is introduced into the otherwise cramped rhythm of work.

We have observed on many occasions (and have mentioned this fact in a sketch of the psycho-sociology of conveyor work, published at the beginning of this year) that the collective structure of the work and this margin of freedom make for the creation of social relations between individuals at the place of work. These social relations are further encouraged by the fact that semi-automatic tasks can hardly be said to absorb one's attention. Men and women meet every morning at the same group of machines, at the same assembly section or inspection point and a certain social life is engendered, lending colour to the hours of work which, in the eyes of the outside observer, seem monotonous. This social life gives the operator the benefit of a conscious activity which surrounds and envelops, so to speak, the process of reflex action, of medular tasks characteristic of the repetitive, fragmentary nature of work in mass production.

It is therefore possible to speak of "social" conveyor work groups. Good understanding between members of the team, emotional and mental harmony play an important role in the creation and maintenance of this "sociability'. Thus, the selection of individuals who are destined to meet one another, to work side by side, day after day, month after month and year after year, ought not to be left to chance or to methods of a hit-and-miss nature, the results of which are often disastrous. I go so far as to say that, in a more advanced and rational stage of human relations, people will be amazed that industrial organization in the middle of the twentieth century still accepted the haphazard throwing together of individuals constitutionally unfitted to work together and, particularly, individuals whose working rhythms are very different.

The importance of *rhythm* in the working group created by technological change since the 1920's and the rise of mass production has been emphasized by recent psycho-physiological research, particularly by the work of Professor Léon Walther of Geneva. He is pursuing certain long-term projects, strongly influencing working conditions, for example, in an important food industry (Suchard's) and in a watch and clock factory in the Bernese Jura, employing 1,200 workers and which is highly rationalized and equipped with the most modern machines. I have visited him there several times. M. Walther has set out his ideas in a book, published in 1947, entitled *Psychologie du travail,* and in various recent articles. I will only mention those points arising from M. Walther's research which concern our subject, namely the repercussions of technological change on human relations and, particularly, the rhythm of working groups.

Rhythm is profoundly and specifically characteristic of the individual. Each of us has his natural "rhythm" which he can neither ignore nor transgress. One of the main tasks of the science of human work is to detect the natural rhythm of the individual in his economic activity. From a physiological point of view, rhythm can be defined as a pause inserted between muscular contractions, a pause which allows for the recuperation of spent energy. Rhythm thus increases the amplitude of a movement without increasing the initial effort, and has the effect of delaying the appearance of fatigue. Its connections with the feeling of satisfaction in work and interest in work are narrow and permanent.

M. Walther has conceived a method for determining the rhythm which is "natural" to each operative. This method is remarkably simple and has proved effective, as I have seen for myself, but I cannot enter here into technical details.

Thanks to a knowledge of the rhythms, it becomes possible to form groups of workers which are what might be called "physiologically homogeneous", that is to say, composed of individuals who have very similar, if not identical, rhythms, and for whom there is a stable satisfaction in working together.

M. Walther remembers the famous words of Bacon: "Natura non aliter quam parendo vincitur." I have heard him say, after a demonstration of his method: "After all, rhythm is stronger than sociology!" What does he mean by that? This deserves to be clarified.

Innovations, inspired by the famous experiments made at the Western Electric (Hawthorne Works, Chicago) between 1927 and 1939, and applied in a methodical and intelligent manner by certain American and European firms, tend to create, in the production lines, working groups with good understanding between their members and good relations between these groups and the supervisors; in short, to create a healthy "climate" of industrial relations. These steps, according to M. Walther, are quite insufficient if the individuals composing the groups do not possess common features in their "natural rhythm", by means of which the homogeneity of the whole group is ensured. Thus it must be considered as a heresy, from a scientific point of view, and a barbaric practice, from a human point of view, to throw together, higgledy-piggledy, into repetitive tasks with a collective and rigid cadence, men and women whose "natural rhythm" has not been previously investigated with a view to constituting homogeneous groups, thus depriving them of a cadence suited to their individual aptitudes.

Here we find the core of the fundamental opposition between the physiological and the psycho-sociological points of view, entailing important practical consequences. This dispute can be cleared up only by long, patient and methodical experiments. But we must recognize and measure its full significance. Scientific management, largely inspired by American theory and practice, is nowadays mostly directed towards the psychological factors influencing the working groups within the factory. In the near future it will undoubtedly have to admit the importance of the "natural rhythm" element and take it into account in formulating the strategy of industrial relations. At the same time, we must point out that the "primacy of physiological rhythm" is in contradiction to the principles of the "Industrial Relations" movement, at present predominant in the United States, as well as being in contradiction to the doctrine underlying the Stakhanovite movement and its recent developments in the U.S.S.R., namely that individual output is "plastic" and can be determined to a considerable degree by the economic and political structure.

I would add, finally, on this point, that the constitution of physiologically homogeneous groups should be studied in relation to the establishment of *emotionally* homogeneous groups, as understood in the sociometric tests of Moreno and the "Nominating technique" of Jenkins.

FINAL REMARKS

I am conscious of having tackled, in this short outline, a large number of problems and of having, in fact, presented here the programme of a course which might be spread over a whole year. If I have made a mistake I am now going to make my case worse by confessing that this was intentional. Nevertheless, I hope that, out of this synthetic approach, a few important lines can be selected for further reflection and concrete research.

Observation of technological change, from the point of view of its psycho-sociological consequences, presents us with facts, all of which are not likely—far from it—to strengthen our faith in the immediate future of critical thought and human dignity, those indispensable conditions of a truly democratic society.

It is a great temptation (and many have succumbed to it) for men of our time, especially intellectuals, to adopt an egocentric attitude, to indulge in a deep mistrust of the progress of technology and its social consequences, to retire into an "ivory tower" and to seek shelter in the values of art, philosophy or various kinds of mystical escape.

In my opinion this is a great mistake.

The "technical environment" is challenging us; we must accept that challenge. Techniques can work two ways; they can be used against the dignity and the life of man, but they can also be reversed and made to serve man's dignity and life. Many of the concrete problems, arising from technological change in the Machine Age, are not, whatever many people may imagine, purely individual or ethical problems. They are, in fact, also economic and social problems. For instance, it can be forcibly asserted that the cultural value of "mass media" is linked with an improved social structure, with the creation of more rational economic, social and, particularly, educational institutions.

On the other hand, these social changes, however well conceived, would not, alone, be sufficient to carry us to the goal and to solve the dramatic problems of which only a few have been outlined. The creation of really human relations in the "technical environment" calls also, on the part of the individual, for an effort towards a more acute consciousness of the situation and a greater self-control, because no good institution can remain good without being actively supported and made a living thing by upright men. This is the concrete and realistic meaning which I would, for my part, give to the famous and beautiful lines of Henri Bergson: "Le corps de l'humanité, démesurément agrandi par la technique, attend un supplément d'âme" ("The body of mankind, increased out of all proportion by technology, awaits an increase of soul").

Sociological and Ideological Conceptions of Industrial Development

IRVING-LOUIS HOROWITZ

SINCE TWENTIETH-CENTURY THINKERS began to "expose" the romantic and utopian fancies of inevitable progress, the social sciences have been plagued with the problem of accounting for "progress." Historians like Arnold Toynbee and Oswald Spengler tend to see in every kind of change the force of historical destiny.

Perhaps as a reaction to the concept of an inevitable succession of stages social scientists have turned "anti-historical"—erecting a barrier between social change and social development. This is the counterpart of the fact-value dualism in methodology. Change can be conveniently linked to "matters of fact" and hence studied, while social development entails matters of judgment and "statements of value" and hence cannot be scientifically valid. Given such a methodological injunction, it is no wonder that contemporary efforts in the field of social development do not compare with such "nineteenth century" works as Bury's *The Idea of Progress* or even Lecky's *History of European Morals*. Instead, current textbooks treat social change as an "area" of sociological investigation. This tendency toward compartmentalization violates the essential nature of change, which occurs in *all aspects of social life*.

The reasons for neglecting the question of change as human development are manifold. First, sociology has so sundered history from the social sciences that development is considered an accoutrement rather than a necessary aspect of the study of any society. Second, empirical sociological studies tend to focus on internal structure and consistency, stressing pattern maintenance, models of equilibrium, consensus systems, structural hegemony, etc. This approach leaves little place for conflict situations, forms of radical change, spontaneous and unstructured behavior, and other "unstable" forces producing change and development alike. Third, there is a fear that to discuss human development leaves one open to charges of utopianism. This is an age which takes forward strides self-consciously. Fourth, there is a widespread doubt that the concept of development is scientifically definable since it has for so long exclusively been the rallying cry of political ideologists.

In our age the struggle for social development takes place in the con-

From *American Journal of Economics and Sociology*, October, 1964, pp. 351-374. This article was slightly revised for publication in this volume. Reprinted by permission of the publisher and author.

text of a developing social struggle. The question of what constitutes social development has itself become part of the general ideological struggle. Facts and figures on everything from consumer production to rates of capital re-investment now serve as "evidence" for the superiority of capitalism over socialism or socialism over capitalism. In such circumstances the social scientist hesitates to leap into the controversy over what constitutes development. This is the most important single reason why sociology has been so tentative about the question of human development.

Before examining differences between ideological and sociological definitions of human development, we can look briefly to historical concepts of change. Ancient Greeks provide some anchor-points. Correlated to the rather sophisticated Platonic and Protagorean notion of the basic unreality of change, is the concept that changes take place in "appearances" only, while a "substratum" remains essentially one and unchanging. For Plato change in space or time meant decadence, and objects which changed were intrinsically worthless. His identification of the good and the true with a changeless state represented the conservative position, which opposed all forms of development as threats to the established order.

The Aristotelian tradition removed the pejorative connotations from things which change. Thus, while Aristotle also held that there is an essentially unchanging substratum or reality (the categories of logic and mathematics), there exists an empirical reality, which is not quite as worthwhile, subject to laws of birth, growth, maturity, and decay. From a social point of view, Aristotle shared Plato's mistrust of things subject to alteration and progression. Empirical change was thought to "actualize" the "potentialities" inherent in all things rather than to create new phenomena.

Among the pre-Socratics, Heraclitos was the first to express a general theory of change. Several cardinal principles are offered in his dialectical picture of the world: (1) change is real, and therefore all reality must be defined in terms of change; (2) there is no aspect of physical, biological, or social life that can resist the general process of change—birth, development, and decay; (3) change is patterned and proceeds in accordance with well-defined general "laws"; (4) these general laws are "dialectical," that is, they proceed in a struggle of contrary and internal forces until a new stage of reality is achieved. Contrary to the Protagorean-Platonic view, Heraclitos placed exclusive emphasis on change and growth as the essential elements of reality.

Democritus took another approach to the problem of change. He considered atomic particles the ultimate stuff of the universe. All complex organisms are built up from these atoms, with the type and level of clusters determining the characteristics of the object. Change takes place through the combination and dissolution of basic atomic entities. The Epicureans advocated "reductionism," or an explanation of change in terms of uncomplicated material entities. Change was authentic and development feasible. But the basis of social change was still considered "physical" in essence;

social laws were extensions, albeit complex, of principles of atomism and mechanics.

Although the ancient Greeks developed some highly refined and imaginative general theories of change and development, they evolved no working set of principles to account for social change and social progress. Until the start of the Industrial Revolution, concepts of human development remained highly theoretical. There evolved a variety of notions of what constitutes development: in one conception development signifies innovative possibilities of discovery. Development is also viewed as the unfolding in definite stages of the new in place of the old. There is also the "aesthetic" approach which views development as the working out of a theme or of variations on a theme. Finally, in the humanist tradition, development depended on knowledge and the bringing to light of new information.

The variety of these developmental theories should caution the social scientists from viewing development merely as a matter of "common sense." Such an attitude, which sociologists call "self-definition" or "autoperception" of change, is dangerously limited—witness the endless multiplications and sub-divisions in the "self-definition of social class." [1] Human development involves factors which are definite and can be studied—such as quantity and quality of education, level of welfare, and the gap between attitude and actions, membership and commitment, costs and benefits—not mere arbitrary and capricious feelings of individuals or groups.

The rise of modern industrial society gave a new and robust dimension to the concept of development. Raw materials were turned into finished artifacts *en masse;* machines replaced human labor as the essential agency of production; organic, e.g. feudal, societies gave way to consensus, e.g. capitalistic, societies. The perception of change quickly followed the fact of change. There was an intense interest in new forms of social production, ownership, and consumption to fit the changing circumstances in the industrial world. Standards of "normal" life-span and infant mortality were no longer accepted; hygienic measures to guarantee maximum growth and life were demanded. Salvation became naturalized, and "man's lot" was no longer necessarily synonymous with "man's fate." The feudal contentment with the *status quo* crumbled before the onslaught of the capitalist world's concern with how things might and ought to be. Capitalist society fostered new standards of achievement no less than new forms of production.

Development becomes a general human concern only at the point of dramatic changes in the material culture. With the Industrial Revolution

---

[1] See Ruth R. Kornhauser, "The Warner Approach to Social Stratification," *Class, Status and Power: A Reader in Social Stratification,* edited by Reinhard Bendix and Seymour M. Lipset. Glencoe: The Free Press, 1953; and also C. Wright Mills, "The Social Life of a Modern Community," *Power, Politics and People,* edited by Irving L. Horowitz. New York: Oxford University Press, 1963, pp. 39-52.

population burgeoned, inventions proliferated, and colonization began in earnest. The new social forces of production and the economic reorganization of life affected the whole mass of English people as had no prior political or religious event.[2] There was a great shift from rural to urban life, a change of emphasis from agricultural to commercial production, and a general change from relative scarcity to relative abundance.

Clearly, the precondition for the scientific study of social development is the fact of social change, just as a theory of progress can only arise in a changing world. These social changes wrought by industrialism turned traditional men into pragmatic risk-takers. Though the advantages were not the same for all men, opportunities for all were greater than ever before. The Industrial Revolution also highlighted problems and obstacles to change. Thus, Protestantism, Enlightenment, Liberalism, and Socialism can each be viewed as responses, at the ideological and philosophical levels, to the problems made evident by the facts of industrial development.

Weber's classic studies of the inter-relations between the Protestant ethic and the capitalist economy attempted to show how the traditional bourgeois belief in the curative power of work and the Protestant notion of "a calling" were fused into a monumental frontal assault against traditionalism.[3] This fusion of industry and religion was not made solely on grounds of abstract principles (e.g. the need of capitalism for integrity and honor in contract relations and the parallel need of Protestantism to link salvation to a practical work-ethic). It was based on a shared belief that if the individual as an active agent were to count at all, there would have to be a break with feudal "collectivism," which assumed that the things which could be changed were not worth changing, while the things worth changing were unchangeable.

The pietistic puritan and the worldly ascetic each saw development as apocalyptical rather than historical. Nonetheless, development was deemed necessary for grace. Man's redemption became more important than man's fate. The bourgeois consciousness likewise viewed development in apocalyptical terms—i.e. "windfalls," "good fortune," "business shrewdness," or just plain "luck." But even though the Lutheran concept of the calling remained traditional and the capitalist view of success remained utilitarian, both strongly hinted at a scientific view of change. In place of supernatural intervention as a means of attaining either Divine Grace or Nature's Wealth came a stress upon hard work, patient effort, and slow and tedious results. Such attitudes paved the way for the establishment of a doctrine of social change in place of the stratified and stultified view of the medieval feudal and religious world.

[2] See Gordon Childe, *Man Makes Himself*. London: Watts & Co., 1941, pp. 12-14.
[3] Cf. Max Weber, "The Religious Foundations of Worldly Asceticism," *The Protestant Ethic and the Spirit of Capitalism*. New York: Scribner's and Sons, 1930; also "The Protestant Sects and the Spirit of Capitalism," From *Max Weber: Essays in Sociology*. New York: Oxford University Press, 1946, pp. 302-22.

The concept of human development could not emerge until apocalyptic and capricious notions of change were discarded and development could be seen as a natural process proceeding independently of providential design. The French Enlightenment, characterized by Turgot's *Tableau philosophique successif de l'esprit humain,* Helvetius' *De l'esprit,* and Condorcet's *L'Esquisse d'un tableau historique des progrès de l'esprit humain,* gave the industrial world its first fully articulated theory of social development. This theory incorporated both Protestant and bourgeois modes of social explanation. The *philosophes* expounded a new humanism, extending the concept of development to include every department of human activity and every class of people.

The Enlightenment thus established a new view of social realities. History was no longer to be written in terms of "great men" or "individual genius" but in terms of the flow and the thrust of humankind. By conceiving of development as social, philosophers like Diderot and historians like Michelet fashioned a theory of change which was simultaneously "scientific" and "moral"; from illiteracy to universal education; from the rule of autocracy to a democratically oriented oligarchy and universal suffrage; from a law based on power and prestige to equality of all before the law; from *pax romana* to national sovereignty; from concentration to rational distribution of wealth; from women as slaves to women as partners. In this new humanism history became the story of man's progress, and true morality was said to consist of a radical critique of the present.

Some noted historians [4] have presented us with a sophisticated denigration of Enlightenment achievements, claiming that the philosophers confused religious belief and rational faith and muddled the idea of progress with that of redemption. But we still owe the Enlightenment the first significant formulation of a general theory of social development. The social scientists continue to frame the question of what constitutes development in Enlightenment terms. The Enlightenment not only took seriously the realities of development but predicted that the problem of development would become increasingly urgent. For example, Condorcet anticipated an era in which statistical and scientific methods would be enlisted to support the cause of progress.

While the French Enlightenment produced a theory of *social* development, it did not evolve a causal basis, an historical accounting, by which social science could be liberated from arbitrary forms of utopianism. French formulations viewed development as essentially a matter of *esprit, Zeitgeist,* and moral imperatives. Thus it tended to ignore the concrete, historical locus of development. Historically there has been decline as well as growth, decay as well as achievement. Rather than face the problem of decline, the Enlightenment chose to cast development in anti-historical terms, pitting

---

[4] Cf. Carl Becker, *The Heavenly City of the Eighteenth Century Philosophers.* New Haven: Yale University Press, 1932; and also, Crane Brinton, *The Anatomy of Revolution.* New York: W. W. Norton & Co., 1938.

human will against the dead hand of the past. The French *philosophes* in particular were troubled by discrepancies between the fact of inequality and the idea of equality. Unable to resolve this divergency empirically, they resorted to a moral posture. The progress of mankind was said to culminate in the final fusion of reason and self-interest—in short, in hedonistic utopianism.

The German Enlightenment tradition of Lessing, Herder, and Nicolai managed to fuse the Protestant doctrine of millennialism and the rationalist faith in progress into an historical theory of development. This was made possible by a concerted effort to connect reason and revelation into a general theory. Revelation is a moment in time which takes on meaning only through a painstaking process whereby reason connects one great moment with another. By framing laws governing both the continuities and discontinuities in social life, the German theorists supplied the missing link to the French Enlightenment theory of development. In the highest stage reached in pre-sociological discourse on the problem of development, change is seen as linked to the religion of humanity. The theory of development as progress became one with the religious base of human evolution. With this, "philosophical anthropology" was born. Change was no longer an accidental property of society but its very essence. Feuerbach, by bringing about materialistic theology, gave the summation of this entire tradition and, more important, the first glimmer of the critical spirit upon which nineteenth-century scientific theories of progress came to rest.[5]

The socialists, from Saint-Simon to Marx, connected the concept of development with that of particularized class interests and thus introduced the first full-fledged ideological (in contrast to religious) note to development. Progress in human affairs was no longer a total undertaking of society but a class enterprise. The "great man" was transformed into a "great class" and history became collectivized. The agencies and the bearers of change became the hitherto anonymous proletarian collectivity.

If Marxian and socialist tradition represents the substitution of ideology for religion, it no less represents the replacement of philosophy with science. By viewing development as a social question, a secular question, and insisting on the specific, interest-laden dimensions of the problem, Marxism made it unfeasible to consider development in terms of Hegelian historical categories. Marx himself developed a parallel theme: one side of development is seen as occurring in the "natural society" in which "man's own act becomes an alien power opposed to him, which enslaves him instead of being combatted by him"; development takes place also in "civil society" and actually constitutes the history of class society, the history of the division of human labor. These lines of development are resolved and synthesized in socialism; the communism of "natural society" is joined to the material achievements of "civil society." Marx waxed rhapsodic on this

[5] Cf. Irving L. Horowitz, "Lessing and Hamann: Two Views on Religion and Enlightenment," *Church History*, Vol. 30, No. 3, September 1961, pp. 334-48.

theme; through socialism, man's nature is "restored to himself." [6] Marx, however, clearly saw the problem of development as one which must account for both continuities and discontinuities in social life; and more specifically at the political level, development signified the replacement of state power with social authority.

At the same time Marx sought to enunciate principles of development in terms of the natural history of socio-economic production. The concept of an inexorable progression from slavery to feudalism, capitalism, socialism, and ultimately to communism arose out of Marx's conviction that social development is the key to prediction and explanation in the social sciences. Just as the appearance of capital announces a new age in the process of social production, the appearance of labor (and the laborers as a class affiliate) signifies the next higher stage of development—socialism.

Marx's was the first system of social science framed primarily (if not exclusively) in terms of developmental models; particularly important is the fact that by relating development to social interests this system fed the streams of both modern political ideology and modern sociological inquiry. Marx asked the scientific question: What is development? But he did so in the context of ideology, and he tried to promote specific agencies to stimulate development. Under the impetus of Marxism, development became a class task; hence development did not proceed harmoniously or mechanically, since there were always classes which depended for their existence upon the *status quo*. Only after the downfall of bourgeois society and bourgeois consciousness could there be national, and even international, development as a general, social phenomenon. It should be mentioned that, with the discovery that power and status are independent variables that continue to divide men, the vision of a general harmonious development has receded to an ever more distant future.

Until now we have discussed general orientations toward the question of social development. But the metaphysical orientation loses relevance when we make a clear distinction between sacred and profane. When analysis hinges upon specific problems—e.g. who progresses, at what rate, and at what costs—we leave behind such questions as how do we know we have progressed or how should we progress.

It should be understood that we do not view the ideological approach as bad and the sociological as good; indeed, sociology often lags behind ideology in the promotion of useful and beneficial goals. The ideological approach, which rests on the standpoint of particularized interests, has generally asked the right questions.[7] The difficulty is that it asks such questions in a biased way, with specific ends in view, irrespective both of the in-

[6] Cf. Karl Marx, *The German Ideology*, ed. by Roy Pascal. New York: International Publishers, 1939; and also his *Economic Philosophic Manuscripts of 1844*, trans. by M. Milligan. Moscow: FLPH, 1957.

[7] Cf. Irving L. Horowitz, *Philosophy, Science and the Sociology of Knowledge*. Springfield, Ill.: Charles C Thomas, 1961.

strumentalities employed and of any contravening evidence. If sociology followed the reverse approach—i.e. were unbiased, not influenced by personal or social interest factors, and always operated according to scientific canons of evidence—then our problem would be considerably eased. The fact is, both sociological and ideological discussions of development contain many unscientific and sometimes even anti-scientific formulations. Thus, while in theory it is clearly superior to argue from a sociological rather than an ideological standpoint, these two modes of thought interpenetrate to a significant degree.

Sociology confronts a human complex which is of two minds on the issue of development. Public attitudes are split not only on the worth of development but on its facts. If we distinguish between change and progress, we can see more clearly why this split has occurred. In defining human development it is important to distinguish social development from change in the physical sense of movement in space and in time, and from growth in the biological sense of alteration in the nature of an organism. For the sociologist, simple physical or biological processes do not constitute development, for such changes occur *de rerum natura* and are not subject to alteration by human decision. The orbiting of the Earth about the Sun, the growth of a fetus or of a human being—these are indeed changes, but not development processes. Human development, however, reflects at some level culture and consciousness and factors which are "unnatural" (electricity to defy the night, airplanes to defy gravity, machines to defy the limits of human labor-power, etc.). In human development alternative forms of social structure are not only possible but almost inevitable. But to conclude from these facts, as some sociologists have, that it is impossible to arrive at a scientific statement of human development is simply to abandon the major question posed for social science. The separation of "facts" and "values" is not a mandate restricting the sociologist to the former "realm" alone—but only a methodological caution for avoiding undue subjectivity. When this separation becomes a sanction for avoiding the problems of human development, it is no longer a heuristic tool but a positive hindrance.

The sociologist confronts social forces which are contradictory or at the very least ambivalent. For every utopian dream of a world of technological innovation, social justice, and material abundance, there is the sober warning of those who envision the same future as a robot-age, inhabited by technological idiots and political scoundrels.[8] To further complicate matters, the sociologists themselves are divided in their judgments of the content and meaning of human development. One current commentary indicated that "recent developments in technology suggest heretofore unimagined possibili-

[8] Cf. Irving L. Horowitz, "Formalización de la Teoría General de la Ideología y la Utopía," *Revista Mexicana de Sociología*, Vol. 24, No. 1, Jan.-April 1962, pp. 87-100; and also, "Formalization of the Sociology of Knowledge," *Behavioral Science*, Vol. 9, No. 1, January 1964, pp. 45-55.

ties in the way of human well-being." [9] Though the author pauses to indicate the dangers of such developments, he concludes "that we are only on the threshold of the possibilities and problems occasioned by these technological developments." For another contemporary sociologist the dangers far out-weigh the advantages of technological achievement, which has "degraded man to the level of a mere reflex mechanism, a mere organ motivated by sex, a mere semimechanical, semiphysiological organism, devoid of any divine spark, of any absolute value, of anything noble and sacred." [10]

Nor should it be imagined that only sociologists differ in their attitudes toward development. The industrial world itself exhibits similar confusions and dichotomies. Managerial attitudes toward automation are often dictated by a blithe optimism: "Guided by electronics, powered by atomic energy, geared to the smooth, effortless workings of automation, the magic carpet of our free economy heads for distant and undreamed of horizons." In con-trast is the conclusion drawn recently by a labor leader:

> I am not reassured by those who tell us that all will work out well in the long run because we have managed to live through radical technological changes in the past. Human beings do not live long enough for us to be satisfied with assurances about the long-run adaptation of society to automation. And while it is true that radical technological improvements have been introduced in the past, it is well to remember that they were accompanied by vast social dis-locations, recurring depressions and human suffering.[11]

Even within the social sciences development is variously defined. The demographer may measure development in terms of gross population growth or declining rates of infant mortality; in geriatrics the problem may be con-sidered primarily in terms of human longevity; the economist may use indices of industrial reinvestment, or consumer goods produced and bought, etc.; the psychiatrist may see the situation in terms of increasing the proportion of "normal" people or decreasing mental illness; and for the criminologist development may mean either the care and treatment of criminals or the abolition of the causes of crime. If there were a harmonic coalescence of all of these developmental elements, then there would be no problems. But this is not the case. The uneven distribution of wealth in the affluent society is often coupled with a high incidence of mental sickness and criminal be-havior, especially among the poor. Therefore it is the maldistribution of

[9] J. O. Hertzler, *American Social Institutions: A Sociological Analysis.* Boston: Allyn & Bacon, 1961, p. 220.

[10] Pitirim A. Sorokin, "Social and Cultural Dynamics," in *The Making of Society: An Outline of Sociology,* ed. by Robert Bierstedt. New York: Random House, 1959, p. 481.

[11] Both statements are contained in Robert P. Weeks (ed.), *Machines and the Man: A Sourcebook on Automation.* New York: Appleton-Century-Crofts, 1961, pp. 171-6 and 202-17.

wealth, rather than the absolute annual earnings, which most significantly affect "deviant" patterns.

The alternative approaches to human development are not necessarily mutually exclusive. Indeed, these various approaches all contribute to an overall definition. There are certain fundamentals common to a scientific notion of development.

Development can be seen as an aspect of human will. It can be viewed as a particular kind of planning aimed at transforming an underdeveloped country into one which will eventually resemble either the First or Second World or some combination of the two. According to this viewpoint, all planning is done by a dedicated development-oriented elite supported by loyal, self-sacrificing masses.

Another approach emphasizes the products of advanced technology, or some concrete evidence that development is taking place. These products can be the types of social structures, levels of technologies, and life styles found in the First or Second Worlds. Mass production, for example, can yield intermediary forms of social structures, technologies, and life styles. Specifically, these intermediary consequences of mass production can produce a dedicated elite, can stimulate a self-sacrificing mass, and can change handicraft activities into large-scale automated factories.

From this perspective, total social planning is not a necessary condition for development. The intermediary products of the development process, as well as the "terminal" products or stages, may or may not be produced by a dedicated elite. This open-ended view of development allows us to consider as a developing nation one which has little central planning by a dedicated elite but a plethora of modern factories and well-clothed, well-fed citizens who are politically, economically, and socially mobilized. This viewpoint makes it possible to distinguish between a "modernizing" country, with few or even no factories, and a "mobilizing" nation. This "product" way of looking at the developmental process forces us to say that Venezuela is a modernizing nation, since it has shown a marked degree of industrial development, particularly in the oil industry. It is possible that Venezuela will ultimately surpass Cuba's economic development. At the present time, however, Cuba is further along the road of development than Venezuela, for Cuba has the political forms and a mobilized dedicated mass suitable for sustained development. Thus far, Venezuela has neither.

Countries may remain underdeveloped for opposite reasons. Guinea, for example, has a dedicated elite which has done an extraordinary job of mobilizing the population politically. While the elite has tried and is still trying desperately to develop the country economically, it is unlikely to succeed. Poorly endowed in resources and population and with little to offer her own people or the world, Guinea is little more than an unfortunate accident of imperialistic map-making. Only if it can unite with richer nations will Guinea become part of a developed state. Venezuela, on the other hand, is rich in both mineral resources and population, but it may never develop if it is not successful in producing a dedicated elite supported by self-sacrificing, loyal masses.

The basic elements in a definition of development must focus on the main features of the Third World but still must not lose sight of the measurements which distinguish one nation or territory from another.

First. A developed society is one made up of the social structures, technologies, and life styles that exist today in the First and Second Worlds. In other words, these two worlds, represented by the United States and the Soviet Union in particular, will be used in this work as models of developed nations. There are obvious "pitfalls" in treating these two countries as models. But unless the development analyst makes the value judgment as to what a developed society is he will not be able to determine which changes are part of the developmental process. In short, the taboo against making value judgments has little place in the study of social and economic development.

Second. The concept "developmental process" refers to those planned and unplanned activities which produce the social structures, technologies, and life styles found in the First and Second Worlds, or else the means for obtaining these advanced forms. The developmental process includes those social and economic changes which tend to make the nations of the Third World more closely resemble the nations of the First or Second Worlds or some combination of the two.

Third. Whatever form development may take, it is universally an asynchronous process. The political, economic, and social sectors of a nation do not advance at the same rate. The economic sector of a Third World country such as Brazil or India may be rapidly approximating the economic sector of the First World, while the masses continue to live in a state of poverty unknown to the lowest classes of the United States.

Fourth. The asynchronous nature of the developmental process makes it extremely difficult to determine whether a nation is developing or stagnating. Such a judgment assumes that the investigator has measures for determining the degree of development in the various sectors which make up the nation as well as some kind of technique for weighting the "development scores" assigned to each sector. The techniques for measuring economic development are fairly adequate; those for measuring political and social development are relatively crude. While we cannot be precise, we can still speak with a fair degree of certainty as to whether a particular sector of a nation is developing. However, no generally accepted method exists for weighting and averaging the "scores" accorded to each sector. Consequently, any judgment as to whether a nation rather than a sector is developing or stagnating, while not entirely arbitrary, ultimately rests on the technique the investigator sees fit to use.

Fifth. The ideological viewpoint of development attempts to determine in advance not simply the goals but the instruments, tactics, and strategies of planning social change. The sociological viewpoint, while readily granting ends-in-view, does not have a determined scheme for the realization of such ends. It contains a pragmatic dimension which enables it to shift its theoretical focus if plans do not work out in practice. Developmental ideologies tend to compel types of change along pre-directed channels.

These are modest steps in the clarification of meaning. But if the issue of development is raised within a perspective which recognizes both a common humanity and diverse culture patterns, then this can serve as a starting point for constructive social action. Under certain conditions there is a relative absence of any perception, much less conception, of social development. An understanding of developmental processes is inhibited by two factors:

1. An absence of comparative criteria, between nations and a period of time. Under conditions of social or group isolation within a large community spatial comparisons between social sub-systems become difficult. Similarly, the absence of historicity or self-consciousness blocks a society from judging itself in terms both of past and future goals.
2. Extended periods of structural equilibrium without external, counterbalancing challenges. Since primitive societies neither retrogress nor progress, they maintain a belief in the fixity of social relations. Thus, while what we term underdeveloped societies change slowly, traditional societies lack not only the fact but the very idea of human development; that is, they do not possess a plan, a direction, or a goal.

This distinction between traditional and underdeveloped societies is pivotal. The traditional society is characterized by little change from generation to generation; a behavioral pattern governed almost exclusively by custom; status determined almost entirely by inheritance (ascriptive); low economic productivity; and a social organization and life style grounded on the principle of hierarchical command. The underdeveloped society has a great deal in common with the developed society; the phrase "underdeveloped" is used as a measure of technical and technological inferiority vis-à-vis the developed society. This society exhibits rapid change; behavior governed by law as well as custom; status based on achievement as well as on inherited patterns; low economic productivity in some sectors of the economy, high productivity in other sectors; and a life style geared to rapid social mobility, despite intensive stratification though not defined by it.

Conceptions of social development depend therefore both upon the facts and upon consciousness of change. These in turn owe their existence to a consciousness of being different, i.e. an awareness that shared values do not necessarily represent shared wealth. The rise of rapid, universal communication and transportation systems is fast transforming traditional societies into "underdeveloped" societies—if not through structural shifts, then certainly through the rise of consciousness and the growth of spatial and temporal comparisons.[12]

[12] For a dissection of the problem of change in relation to traditional societies, see Everett E. Hagen, On the Theory of Social Change: How Economic Growth Begins. Homewood, Ill.: The Dorsey Press, 1962, esp. pp. 55-8.

We can turn now to the "developed" society in which change is first and foremost a social fact. In considering the theories advanced for or against development, we become involved in the effect of ideology on the theory and practice of development. Ideology is not concerned with the ethical aspects or the morality of development. The ideological posture naturally assumes a general dissatisfaction with the present and the necessity and feasibility of change. Though the ideologist does not consider the ethical question whether development is worthwhile or needed, he must still evaluate the worth of available types of development. Ideological debates over such slogans as "revolutionary socialism" and "evolutionary socialism," or in American society over "government control" versus "laissez-faire," take on a strong ethical flavor. It is patently clear, however, that there is a huge difference between those arguing the worth of change (the moralists) and those arguing the types of change which are worthwhile (the ideologists).

What should not be lost in the fog of competing political loyalties is the similarity between capitalist and Communist industrial ideologies: material abundance, rapid urbanization, educational facilities, military strength —these indices define both American and Soviet notions of development. This is not to say that all differences between capitalist and Communist ideologies have been eliminated or that this would be advantageous. The similarities do, however, far outweigh the dissimilarities. The Russians and the Americans must face a similar set of social questions: Are large-scale changes best accomplished spontaneously or through planning? What mixture of persuasion and coercion most facilitates progress? How can the growth of a particular society be turned into a model for "underdeveloped" areas?

The ideologists tend to obfuscate and distort fundamental similarities between systems for the sake of preserving the separateness of their own, whether it be called "The American Way" or "The Communist Road." Ideologists tend also to assume a world of total voluntarism, as if human development were dictated exclusively by choice and consensus, without limitation imposed by national boundaries, traditions, political systems, or economic potential. If the sociologist is not himself to become an ideologist, he must cut through the ideological rhetoric and search out areas of convergence as well as differentiation. At the same time, due recognition must be accorded the role of ideology in defining developmental goals.

We are now in an age dominated by a common industrial ideology which is just as much the property of the Soviet Union as it is of the West. Industrial demands are sufficiently potent eventually to win out over traditional political forms. This may not be obvious in the short run, since Soviet and American societies share not only an emphasis on technological and scientific achievements but they also share a willingness to absorb the human losses which will insure them world leadership. A cardinal feature of any definition of "Western culture" is anchored to the notion that human development results from scientific achievement. The present competition between Russia and the West comes about precisely because there is so much (rather than not enough) common ground. A statement by Sorokin seems particularly relevant: [13]

> Both nations are fairly similar in scientific knowledge and technological progress. In normal conditions, without the misuse and. abuse of scientific and technological achievements by the governments and militarists, both countries would have mutually profited from scientific discoveries and inventions of each other. This means that science and technology as values do not give any ground, any reason, any justification for continuation of the belligerent policies "for Salvation of Science and Technology from the Destruction by the Russians (or the American) Barbarians." The scientists of both countries are quite successfully taking good care of scientific and technical progress, especially if they are not hindered by governmental interference in their highly important research.

The definition of economic development in terms of per capita output and rates of capital investment has become standard currency for both "Marxian" and "Keynesian" economists.[14] The convergence of East and West has proceeded so rapidly and at so many levels since World War Two that there remains an ideological lag. Apologists for capitalism expand their energies discussing the pre-revolutionary *political* ideology of Marxism instead of the functioning Soviet system.

In terms of the concept of development, the ideological struggle is not between East and West but between two styles of Western thought.

> We must not forget that Marxism and communism are also Western ideas, and that modern Russia is also culturally, intellectually, and socially in the Western tradition. Indeed, the Russian Revolution can be seen, in part, as the Westernization of a formerly "Eastern" peasantry . . . In their general drift into the mainstream of Western history, the leaders of the underdeveloped world will have a choice between divergent currents of Western development: the one represented by the free-enterprise, free-dissent nations of the Atlantic, and the other by the planned enterprise, limited or no-dissent nations of the Soviet orbit.[15]

The choice for other nations is not between capitalism and Communism —or perhaps between oligopoly and state capitalism—(the growth of the economic "mix" in both societies makes a choice implausible if not entirely impossible), but rather between the industrial ideology shared by Americans and Soviets and the pre-industrial ideology of the Third World countries.

[13] Pitirim A. Sorokin, "Mutual Convergence of the United States and the U.S.S.R. to the Mixed Sociocultural Type," *International Journal of Comparative Sociology*, Vol. 1, No. 2, Sept. 1960, pp. 143-76.

[14] Compare, for example, the capitalist apologetics of John K. Galbraith, *American Capitalism*. Boston: Houghton Mifflin Co., 1952, with the socialist apologetics of Paul A. Baran, *The Political Economy of Growth*. New York: Monthly Review Press, 1957.

[15] Robert L. Heilbroner, "The Revolution of Economic Development," *The American Scholar*, Vol. 31, No. 4, Autumn 1962, pp. 541-9.

This choice may be singularly unpleasant for those reared in inherited political ideologies. But nostalgia, while comfortable, simply does not face up to the realities of functional and ideological convergence.

The accent on development is ingrained in technological societies exhibiting high degrees of social mobility. For an American trade union leader turned businessman this signifies "self-development for everybody, everywhere." [16] For a Soviet engineer turned manager such self-development involves "the radical improving of the management of enterprises and institutions through the extensive automation and mechanization of engineering and administrative jobs." [17] In each case, the price of change is a disruption of older norms and even older patterns of culture, and development is justified in terms of the same goals, e.g. higher productivity, shorter working hours, increased leisure time, more goods to consume at lower prices. What emerges is a twofold typology of value preferences which sharply demarcate the industrial ideology of spending from the political ideology of savings. The situation in both the United States and the Soviet Union demonstrates that a technological society requires, and usually gets, an ideology built upon expertise. That the "debate" over inherited political ideologies such as liberalism and Marxism is most furious in the traditional nations merely supports the contention that Russia and the United States represent alternative means for reaching the same industrial goals. Nonetheless, it might be kept in mind that even when an ideology is built upon some well-defined principle, that principle does not necessarily dominate behavior. The "experts" do not completely dominate in the United States, and the same is undoubtedly the case in the Soviet Union. The ability to allocate and distribute wealth is still in the hands of the politicians.

It has been particularly painful for the "American way of life" to come to terms with the problem of the costs of development, and to understand that traditional patterns are not necessarily and always inimical to development.[18] For the American, for the proponent of the liberal rhetoric, the idea of progress through science has become, as Robin Williams noted, "a slogan to defend the course of technological innovation and economic rationalization and concentration. If small entrepreneurs, farmers, or urban workers felt economic distress, their condition could be considered a regrettable but necessary and temporary by-product of the triumphant march of progress." [19]

Given the combination of provincial ingenuousness, Puritan piety, and a technological definition of progress, which in large measure defines the present American mood of self-congratulation, a sociological study of the

[16] F. J. Roethlisberger, "Introduction" to Elton Mayo, The Human Problems of an Industrial Civilization. New York: Viking Press, 1960, p. xi.

[17] A. I. Berg, "Cybernetics and Society," The Soviet Review, Vol. I, No. 1 (1960), pp. 43-4.

[18] Ralph J. Braibanti and Joseph J. Spengler, Tradition, Values, and Socio-Economic Development. Durham, N.C.: Duke University Press, 1961.

[19] Robin M. Williams, Jr., American Society. New York: Alfred A. Knopf, 1960 (2nd rev. edition), p. 433.

negative aspects of social change borders on a subversive reading of American history.

W. F. Cottrell's brilliant analysis of the death of a railroad town in the southwestern United States illustrates the costs of development and the potential social consequences of technological changeover. In this town of "Caliente" everything was predicated on the railroad's need for continued growth.

> Men built their homes there, frequently of concrete and brick, at the cost in many cases of their life savings. The water system was laid in cast iron which will last for centuries. Business men erected substantial buildings which could be paid for only by profits gained through many years of business. Four churches evidence the faith of Caliente people in the future of their community. A twenty seven bed hospital serves the town. They believed in education. Their school buildings represent the investment of savings guaranteed by bonds and future taxes. There is a combined park and play field which, together with a recently modernized theatre, has been serving recreational needs. All these physical structures are material evidence of the expectations, morally and legally sanctioned and financially funded, of the people of Caliente. This is a normal and rational aspect of the culture of all "solid" and "sound" communities.[20]

"Rational" economic forces and laws of technological development worked to undermine this well-defined urban structure. When the railroad converted from steam to diesel power, Caliente, totally dependent on its water and repair facilities, was shorn of its reason to exist. The victory of technology, of the very industrial ideology of progress which the citizenry of Caliente espoused—since they were by all standards good Americans—paradoxically substantially destroyed their carefully nurtured social structure.

Development, in other words, is often preceded by social disorganization. There is a dialectic to socialization, namely privatization. The end of the parochial rural and semi-urban standards leads to Jean Gottmann's *Megalopolis*. But it also feeds a collective *anomie*, a drive for escapism and frenetic leisure-time activities, and a nihilist attitude about the future, as described in Leo Srole's *Metropolis*. The overdeveloped society is tentative about the future and cynical about the present—characteristics to which the Third World societies would do well to pay closer attention.

The enormous increase in the types and rates of technological growth has created other immense problems. Even if we accept the business ideology that technological change does not create large-scale unemployment, the problem of mass mis-employment remains. As one writer recently stated:

> The underlying assumption is that one job equals another, that income is the sole criterion and it makes no difference what you do or become in order to

[20] W. F. Cottrell, "Death by Dieselization: A Case Study in the Reaction to Technological Change," *American Sociological Review*, Vol. 16, 1951, pp. 358-65.

get it. Technological unemployment may be a myth, but what about technological mis-employment? From 1880 to 1940, the percentage of Americans who were self-employed declined sharply. The percentage employed in clerical work, or in more or less parasitical service activities, rose sharply. The percentage employed in actually making useful articles declined; and even among the productive workers, millions were downgraded from skilled craftsmen to mass-production hands, with little skill or responsibility. It may be that these changes were not, in the long run, harmful. It may be—as Henry Ford insisted—that a worker gains from the transformation into a kind of zombie, if that transformation leads to so great an increase in production that the worker can acquire a car, a refrigerator, and other objects he could not otherwise possess. But it is absolute nonsense to pretend that there is no problem, that a job is a job.[21]

The problem for the sociologist, one which the ideologist dares not recognize, is to discover the forms of creativity possible in a highly impersonal and mechanized society. The real failure of industrial ideology is that it provides a false alternative to traditionalist-conservative ideologies. For while the latter seem solely preoccupied with the costs, the former is exclusively concerned with the benefits of industrial change. The sociologist must deal with the problem of the price of change and who has to pay this price. The decision to orient a society toward rapid industrial and technical development is basically a value decision, most often made by an elite group for the mass of people.

Sociology should caution us against any "iron laws" of industrialization. Such "laws" are pernicious as well as unscientific. A decision in favor of industrial expansion may entail large-scale and long-range hardships, and short-run costs may well outweigh long-term results. An agricultural-export economy, which satisfies consumer demands by buying rather than making automobiles, television sets, washing machines, etc., does not necessarily have to be reoriented toward industrialism. Often industrialization is demanded in the name of nationalism, the common assumption being that affluence and greatness are synonymous with industrialism. Doing without the products of General Electric or General Motors because they come from an imperialist nation may be materially damaging to a nation which could trade wheat for radios and beef for cars. The problem exists not only in capitalist economies; the dogmatic application of the industrial ideology, of the assumption that home-grown goods are always cheaper to make than imported goods are to obtain, has boomeranged in Yugoslavia, Hungary, Poland, China, and Cuba.

This is not to be construed as a nostalgic critique of industrial society. To recognize the weaknesses in industrial ideology is not to condemn industrial values. A modern and efficient agricultural system must basically

[21] Geoffrey Ashe, "Technological Mis-Employment," in Machines and the Man, ed. by Robert P. Weeks. New York: Appleton-Century-Crofts, 1961, pp. 200-202.

have industrial values. It does point up the need to distinguish between absolute underdevelopment, when the basic tools whereby a citizenry can survive are lacking, and relative underdevelopment, when rates of social change are slower than in developed societies. Surely, there is a vast difference between a form of underdevelopment which witnesses mass starvation (as in parts of India) and a form of underdevelopment in which industrial capacity is low while everyone is essentially well-fed and well-clothed (as in Argentina and even peacetime Vietnam). Precisely because the word underdevelopment is charged with emotive meanings, it is doubly necessary to distinguish the actual, empirical contents of "underdevelopment" in any given society.

It should be noted that the nineteenth-century liberals' prophecies of progress through science were, indeed, realized. The extent of modern creativity would surprise and delight even an Edward Bellamy. Why then should there be such widespread disillusionment and dismay in the developed societies? Clearly, it is because the very giganticism of our achievements has made it possible for the individual to be overwhelmed and for whole populations to be annihilated. In short, technical and industrial development is not total development and does not settle the major problems of politics, economics, war and peace, etc., but only raises such issues to a new pinnacle of desperation. For human development we still require some kind of "science of values," some analytical tools for expressing the new situation in meaningful terms.

Development will take place. For an overwhelming majority of people the costs of development are well worth the price. Most "backward" tribal associations—such as the Sironis in Bolivia, the Guayaki in Paraguay, the Macu of Brazil—join with their brothers in La Paz, Asunción, and São Paulo to demand entrance into the gateways of tomorrow. But development will have its price. The task of the sociologist is not only to indicate the dangers of social dislocation but to anticipate and work out solutions for potential problems. This requires some courage. Traditional relations between parents and obedient children and between male and female may likewise have to be altered. The idea of the state as a dispenser of welfare may indeed supplant the older notion that a government governs best which governs least. The sociologist must become a physician of society.

The sociologist considers the problem of development in terms of various methods, rates, directions, and consequences, while the ideologist thinks of development as a matter of national pride, and is mainly concerned that his society reach development before others. Mills made a very pointed statement in this connection.

When we think about the "underdeveloped society" we must also think about the "overdeveloped society." There are two reasons for this: first, if we do not do so, we tend to think of everything as moving towards *the developed*. It is the old notion of nineteenth century evolutionism. And this is no longer a

ften by as much as 50 per cent—except during wartime periods. Agricul-
ural underproduction is encouraged to keep market prices inflated, federal
ubsidies given for not planting certain key crops, and tax write-offs for
ailing business enterprises.[23] Nor can we leave out of this inventory the
military build-up. Military expenditures have most often been measured
xclusively in terms of the benefits to labor and management, without a
orresponding regard for the ultimate social costs involved. Galbraith has
ut the risk of overdevelopment clearly.

As matters now stand, we have almost no institutions that are by central design and purpose directed to participation in modern scientific and technological progress and its large-scale application. We have no organization capable,
for example, of taking on the large-scale development of atomic power gen-
erators or radically new departures in passenger-carrying aircraft in advance
of knowledge that these will be commercially feasible. Much has been accomplished by research and development, not immediately subject to a commercial
criteria, under the inspiration of military need. This has done more to save us
from the partial technological stagnation that is inherent in a consumers' goods
economy than we imagine. But it is also a narrow and perilous prop, and it
has the further effect of associating great and exciting scientific advances with
an atmosphere of fear and even terror.[24]

What this should teach the newly emerging nations is that the problem
development is not exclusively one of technological or natural resources
exclusively one of sociological or human resources, but rather the inter-
f tion and interpenetration of the two. Indeed, the more "mature" a so-
ty becomes, the more it needs instruments for orderly social change, but
e less does it provide for such agencies. Similarly, the greater the tech-
logical achievement, the more the social system is pressured to accommo-
te such achievements. Any prolonged and exaggerated imbalances be-
een the social and technical sectors lead to stagnation. And the pressures
development are such that stagnation is intolerable over a long period.
is is what revolutions are all about.

[23] See L. N. Naggle, "Scylla and Charybdis of Engineering Education," *Proceedings*
he 1961 Syracuse University International Conference on Electrical Engineering Edu-
on. Syracuse, N.Y.: 1961, pp. 52-3.
[24] John K. Galbraith, *The Affluent Society*. Boston: Houghton Mifflin Co., 1958, pp.
-5.

very fruitful idea. Second, to think of the polar types leads u
a third type—an ideal which we should always keep in mind:
veloping society. We need all three types, not just two.[22]

Mills indicates that the underdeveloped society is chan
limited standard of living, whereas in the overdeveloped
style is dominated by the living standards. The fetish of prod
a fetish for consumption. And without adding a theologic
science should maximize human possibilities by helping to
than understand, the proximate future. It is this maximiza
considers to be the substance of "proper" development.

We know considerably more about the differences be
ment and underdevelopment than we do about differenc
velopment and overdevelopment, or what may just as re
mis-development. The latter is a more recent phenomenon.
to describe the sociology of scarcity than of affluence, sin
many illustrations of the former and so few of the latter.
need for a clear view of overdevelopment is urgent; for otl
be providing instruments to developing nations which ca:
worst rather than the best features of modern civilizations

As a general rule, overdevelopment can be defined as
dition in which material wealth is maldistributed and t
available are not used to a maximum extent. This occurs
social impediments—for instance, when there exist radica
tween social classes; or when there are organizational
instance, when available energy and power sources are not
An overdeveloped society is furthermore one in which fai
social and technical levels lead to breakdowns in produc
tribution and create a perennial crisis in the political inst
cational establishments. Like underdevelopment, overdev
tive to a given type of social-economic organization, one t
nical capacity to satisfy basic human needs but is lacking
mentalities to utilize such a capacity.

Thus, while the United States can by no stretch of
simply be relegated to the realm of overdevelopment—by
criteria at least—it does reveal certain properties of overdev
if not curbed, could lead to exaggerated mis-developme
there has been a vast slowing down in the development of
trical power for rural regions. There has been no follow
(Tennessee Valley Authority) and MVA (Missouri Valle
gional planning continues to be viewed as something the
in times of economic crisis. Similarly, despite an upward ti
United States industries continue to operate below ma

22 C. Wright Mills, "The Problem of Industrial Development,"
People: The Collected Papers of C. Wright Mills, edited by Irvir
York and London: Oxford University Press, 1963.

Poverty and Social Change

S. M. MILLER and MARTIN REIN

THE REDISCOVERY of the once invisible poor has rapidly captured public interest. Poverty is sloganized into political glamor by the use of military metaphor. The gaping needs of today rivet attention so that a way of thinking about poverty does not seem necessary. Unfortunately, narrow perspectives lead to narrow programs.

The concept of poverty is neither fixed nor precisely measured. As society advances, the notions of need, adequacy and subsistence must be looked at in new ways. Nor can the concepts of inequality and dependency be ignored. The inadequate conceptualization of poverty leads to an inadequate formulation of action alternatives in the present "war on poverty."

A brief review of the American experience is useful here. Economic theories of the 18th century assumed that real wages were fixed by a natural law and helped earn for economics the unhappy name of "the dismal science." Man was caught in limited possibilities; improvement of the position of the poor was impeded by the inexorable requirements of the economy. But by the mid-20th century, everyone's income was increasing, and the poor's most rapidly of all. Kuznets seemed to provide statistical proof that the income pyramid was being flattened. In a spirit of "dazed euphoria," American social scientists formulated a new natural law of income equalization.

This theory went as follows: The expansion of production and productivity resulted in a much greater economic pie. The graduated income tax, expanded welfare services, and education were more equitably distributing this larger pie. Continued increase in aggregate economic wealth would invariably filter down, more or less equitably, to all income groupings. Marginal economic groups, it was assumed, would in time "gracefully succumb" to continued economic growth and that small residual group not covered by expanding welfare and social security programs would be handily cared for by the traditional public dole.

Facts seemed to bear the theory out. The standard of living had substantially increased during the post-World War II era. The G.I. Bill provided many working-class youth, who would never have achieved technical and advanced education, an opportunity for upward occupational mobility. Indeed, the traditional income pyramid seemed to be slowly changing into a giant barrel-shaped distribution. The residual groups also seemed to be

Reprinted by permission of the publisher from March, 1964 issue of *The American Child*, quarterly journal of the National Committee on Employment of Youth, 145 East 32 St., New York, N.Y. 10016.

slowly dwindling, especially as old people increasingly came to be covered by old age and survivor's insurance.

But these remarkable results were not the product of some natural economic law. We had entered a period of full employment in the war and post-war periods, producing a shortage of labor. Special factors accentuated the shortage—the low birth rate of the great depression, the war demands for many able-bodied men, and the post-war concentration on further education through the G.I. Bill of Rights. These conditions helped create a vacuum which sucked disadvantaged groups into the labor force.

One important result of the operation of these forces was a change in the character of the labor force. The labor vacuum pulled into the labor force a large number of women, so that by 1957 almost 30 percent of all families in the United States had two wage earners. In addition, many wage earners had more than one job as moonlighting expanded. (Interestingly enough, families with both husband and wife in the paid labor force were concentrated among the upper income fifth of American families. Sixteen percent of those in the lowest income fifth had a husband and wife in the paid labor force in 1957 as compared to 41 percent of those in the upper income fifth.)

"Pockets of poverty" were, of course, present, and occasional public recognition was given to the plight of migrant laborers, tenant workers, old workers and other groups. But these groups were considered as special cases. Galbraith's term of "case poverty" seemed to cover them. By particularizing the poor, we avoided an overall summation of the groups in poverty, so that the scope was not comprehended in its totality.

By the late 1950's and early 1960's the suction power of the economy began to weaken. Our economy moved into a new industrial revolution, the cybernetic age. In this period, as the demand for labor increases, we can no longer depend on a corresponding reduction of unemployed and unemployable groups. This latest industrial revolution has created a labor demand aimed chiefly at the skilled and educated.

The theory that expanding aggregate production will funnel down to all income groups has collapsed as the gross national product has soared to an unprecedented half a trillion dollars. Production has continued to mount but so has unemployment. Six percent of the labor force are unemployed, with twice this rate of unemployment among the low-educated and unskilled and triple this rate for youth entering the labor force. Unemployment and poverty are not simple reciprocals of employment and production. The power of the unregulated economy to siphon off a large part of expanding production to the low-income groups has been reduced.

Our changing economy has to be related to the changing nature of poverty. Poverty is traditionally related to the cost of a fixed basket of goods and services that are required for survival. But as Galbraith has so aptly said, "people are poverty stricken when their income, even if adequate for survival, falls markedly behind that of the community . . . they are degraded, for in the literal sense, they live outside the grades or categories which the community regards as acceptable."

Poverty is thus not a fixed point. It is a moving escalator, reflecting the values of a society. Our conceptualization of poverty has been too narrowly limited to a dollars and cents standard. A more embracing standard is needed to include the distribution of nonmonetary resources, of education, recreation, medicine, old age protection, and similar services.

Moreover, we have tended to disregard the issue of inequality by giving too much importance to the fact that people were receiving more than they were getting before. Clearly, the shoring up of incomes does not mean that we are also automatically improving the relative position of low-income holders. For example, the average earnings of the non-white male increased from $1,800 in 1950 to over $3,000 in 1960. But these figures represent a slight drop in the percentage of Negro income, compared to the average white man's income, from 61 to 60 percent.

The recent tendency in American society has been to raise the absolute level while increasing inequality. The percentage of the total pie going to the bottom 20 percent has slightly declined in the post-World War II period. As Myrdal has observed, this trend results in widening the class chasms and stiffening the class structure.

We cannot presume that the tax structure operates to reduce inequalities and to redistribute income. The differences in the distribution of income before and after tax are amazingly slight. Tax evasion is partly to blame. The poor pay more of their income for taxes than families five times as rich since state and local taxes rely on regressive taxes such as the sales tax. The *Wall Street Journal* recently reported that "28% of family incomes under $2,000 a year is paid out in taxes." Increasingly, tax exemptions, fringe benefits, expense accounts, pension plans serve as hidden multipliers of economic advantage. Macauley estimates that a quarter of payroll costs in the United States are in the form of fringe benefits.

Today, little emphasis is placed on the direct redistribution of income as a means of reducing poverty and inequality. Education is increasingly seen as the important escape hatch and the Johnson "war on poverty" will likely emphasize education as the answer to poverty. A cult-like devotion to the magical aid of a high school diploma is developing. As educational achievement rather than family connections became more important in determining occupational possibilities, it was believed that inequalities and poverty could be reduced by expansion of educational attainments.

Education today does not seem to be effectively reducing the occupational and income inequalities in society, at least for youth coming from the lowest income families. The long-term neglect of schools in the low-income areas is only now slowly beginning to be rectified. Despite the additional investments in low-income schools, the relative per capita expenditures in better-off areas of the United States is still much greater. A recent Pennsylvania study by Rein and Hare reveals that in poor counties welfare expenditures are high and educational outlays low. In better-off counties the pattern is reversed. Suburban per capita expenditures for white middle class children usually far outdistance those spent for low-income white and Negro children living in center cities. Thus, present investments in low-income areas may serve only to increase the absolute level without strengthening the relative educational position of the poor.

The educational level needed for jobs which provide decent income and security is constantly moving upward. As low-income youth increase their absolute level of educational achievement, the educational achievements of the rest of the population also continue to rise. The best that can be hoped for is that low-income youth will maintain the same relative position. Maintaining the same relative position may in time represent a decline in opportunity as the overall volume of jobs declines in relation to a growing labor force and as educational credentials for jobs increase. The use of an absolute standard such as high school graduation as a national goal can be deceptive, because the meaning of this standard changes over time. Increasingly, high school graduation will be inadequate to gain a secure foothold in the American occupational structure.

An underlying assumption is that if we bring people up to a certain level in education, there will continue to be jobs for them. Despite expanded production, there simply may not be enough jobs to cover the rapidly growing labor force. Expanding educational achievement which leads to no work can be disillusioning for a young person. An educated, discontented, and deprived population is the kind of incendiary substance from which revolutions are formed. We have to re-think poverty and inequality in a cybernetic, affluent society.

The following principles are crucial in developing a successful strategy for reducing poverty and inequality today. Clearly, these suggestions do not represent detailed programs but broad organizing principles based on the reconceptualization of poverty.

Present programs are acting as though poverty is a short-run problem aimed at raising family income to some absolute standard. When the changing character of poverty is recognized, these short-term, remedial programs appear limited. It is necessary to institutionalize these programs rather than defining them as a temporary injection of limited funds to solve a short-term problem. *The present form of ad hoc tinkering with minor demonstration programs will not meet the long-range requirements.* It is unlikely that if we rely on fragmented remedial programs we can educate people as fast as industry's educational level is moving up. What is needed is a broad-scale, permanent program. For example, a program designed to provide a guaranteed college education for all low-income youths, much like the G.I. Bill's provision of a guaranteed college education for veterans, should be given thoughtful attention. The distribution of educational opportunity should be extended not only to selected groups such as those who have served their country in war, but to all individuals by virtue of citizenship in American society.

In place of short-term programs we need a broad redistributive program aimed at reallocating income and services. One step would be providing higher benefit levels for social insurance and public assistance that would directly and immediately aid many of the poor.

As we have suggested, poverty must be conceptualized to include the quantity and quality of services. Consequently, redistributing housing, educational, medical, recreational and other services would be important. And these services should be quality services.

The broadened concept of poverty antiquates the rigid *ideology of the minimum* in public welfare services which permeated nineteenth century economic liberalism. It was feared that the expansion of public provision would kill incentive to participate in the main economy. In a similar fashion our present emphasis on short-term programs is continually guided by the fear that a comprehensive approach to poverty would reduce incentives and destroy freedom. Consequently, in retraining programs, for example, we stop at retraining and neglect the important tasks of getting job and worker together. In economically distressed areas we do not provide subsidies to families to enable them to move, to locate a place to live and to secure a definite job. Implicit in these apprehensions is the assumption that unemployment in an affluent society is a result of personal inadequacy. Our present formulation of strategies of change continues to be chained to a nineteenth century ideology, of minimum help to the "laggards," rather than to a twentieth century notion of *adequate help* to the victims of society who frequently need pervasive aid to manage in the changing society.

Existing service-dispensing institutions have failed to alter the relative position of the disadvantaged. Many social institutions have ignored or dealt inadequately with the poor. Therefore, it will not be sufficient to simply provide these *institutions of failure* with more funds—to continue doing what they have always done in the past. *It is necessary to change social institutions so that they are more effectively responsive to the needs of the poor.* Changes in the programs of educational and welfare institutions and in the styles of professional intervention are needed.

Professionals must turn more to a concept of service, with less emphasis in the guild function of their professions. Hamlin at the Harvard School of Public Health recently recommended that voluntary agencies be made accountable to a public review board. In a similar fashion we think that it is important that independent sources of accountability be developed which would encourage and pressure welfare and educational institutions to be more responsive to the needs of low-income families. More services are not enough; they have to be changed and improved.

The operation of our economic system needs priority consideration. The growth of poverty and inequality may well be interpreted as free enterprise on trial. Present programs have avoided a confrontation on this issue. The favored action programs today are those directed at the machinery for inducting individuals into the labor force or retreading those who are already in the work market but unable to hold a job or compete for a new one. Free enterprise and the operation of our economy remain a privileged sanctuary in American society. It is acceptable to criticize voluntary agency programs, schools, and public welfare, but criticism of the economy is conspicuously absent. Long-range economic planning is neglected; public attention is concentrated on short-range issues designed to promote private consumption. As Galbraith has proposed, more attention needs to be paid to collective consumption. We need to reverse the equation of public squalor and private affluence. To do this we need to modify our traditional suspicion about increasing public budgets and we should be ready to make a very substantial investment in public expenditures for schools, hospitals, welfare services, roads and other forms which would expand collective consumption.

It is important to extend monetary and fiscal policy to include not only a broad investment in the public sector but also a greater investment in specialized industries. In an economy committed to promoting labor-saving industries by devices such as generous depletion allowances, a parallel investment needs to be made in the expansion of labor-intensive industries. Many low-skilled individuals—and there will continue to be many—will not be employable in the industries of the future. In this context, the expansion of the role of the sub-professional, as pointed out by Marcia Freedman in the January, 1964 issue of *American Child*, warrants special consideration as a device for expanding job opportunities. Labor shortages among the helping profession are acute.

Finally, we need to consider changes in social values. This calls for a two-pronged program aimed both at the present and the future. As far as the present is concerned, we must develop a broader view that permits us to see welfare programs not only as devices for creaming off those who are most able to participate in the economy but also for those who are not economically mobile. The true test of the humanity of a society is what it does with people who cannot participate directly or effectively in the economy. As for the society of the future, in which there may be a greatly lessened need for traditional work assignments, we must find new, socially respectable ways of getting financial support for families. Today, only people who make an economic contribution are assumed to have any value. The concept of work needs to be re-examined and new standards for the definition of social utility developed. We need new standards by which to measure *the moral equivalent of an economic contribution.*

Poverty cannot be studied and changed without studying and changing society.

FURTHER READINGS

Goode, William J. *World Revolution and Family Patterns.* New York: The Free Press, 1963.

Hoselitz, Bert F. and Moore, Wilbert E., eds. *Industrialization and Society.* Paris: UNESCO-MOUTON, 1963.

Hughes, Everett C. *French Canada in Transition.* Chicago: University of Chicago Press, 1943.

Lipset, S. M. and Bendix, Reinhard. *Social Mobility in Industrial Society.* Berkeley and Los Angeles: University of California Press, 1959. Paper, 1962.

Moore, Wilbert. *The Impact of Industry.* Englewood Cliffs, New Jersey: Prentice-Hall, Inc. Paper, 1965.

12

MASS SOCIETY AND
MASS CULTURE

Introduction

A PHENOMENON which is integrally tied to urbanization, bureaucratization and industrialization is the emergence of mass society. From the writings of Alexis de Tocqueville during the early part of the nineteenth century to the sociological commentators of the present, including Bernard Rosenberg, for example, this phenomenon and its concomitants has been a source of serious concern. Fear of the "tyranny of the majority" and the possibility of an artistic Gresham's Law—in which low quality art would lead to the rejection of high quality art—has led intellectuals and social scientists into a series of seemingly endless debates.

Harold Wilensky attempts to throw some empirical light on a number of issues basic to the ongoing debates surrounding these phenomena. He clarifies the assumptions made and places the issues into the context of the contemporary American societal structure. In suggesting the theoretical impact of his findings he holds that, "To be socially integrated in America is to accept propaganda, advertising, and speedy obsolescence in consumption." This suggestion might be profitably reviewed in the context of our Epilogue, Chapter 13.

Joseph Bensman and Israel Gerver contribute to our understanding of both mass society and "the withdrawal of artists from concern with social meaning during recent decades." They analyze both *pure art* as an art form and the changing role of the artist. In a thoughtful and penetrating analysis the writers suggest why the consumer of mass art is often confused by efforts of mass producers to manipulate his mind.

The movie has been an important mass medium in most societies throughout the world. Used both as a source of propaganda and entertainment, films produced in Hollywood reach all corners of the world. Herbert Gans reviews the changes in content of Hollywood movies during a selected period of time. A recent emergence, he notes, is the *problem-film*, "which deals explicitly with social, sexual and political problems and their solutions." Tracing the sources of these changes to the audiences for whom movies are made Gans suggests that film producers take the diverse backgrounds of their audiences into account in order to provide a better implementation of aesthetic values. Thus Gans holds, along with Mack and McElrath in Chapter 9, that there are important population differentials which should be encouraged.

∽ ᴗ∽

Mass Society and Mass Culture: Interdependence or Independence?

HAROLD L. WILENSKY

Several major questions about the social impact of affluence have come to dominate intellectual discussion concerning the shape of modern society. Some of them involve the nature, extent, and impact of mass culture and mass leisure. Everyone agrees that abundance everywhere brings a rise in mass communications, through radio, television, and press; the development of mass education and the concomitant spread of literacy; and, finally, mass entertainment on a grand scale. I propose to deal with these trends in the context of ideas about the "mass society." I will (1) analyze the interplay of high culture and mass culture, with special attention to the structural roots of cultural standardization and heterogeneity in rich countries; (2) present data on the quality of media exposure in a variety of occupational groups and strata in the Detroit metropolitan area—so that we may both gauge the extent of cultural uniformity and locate the sources of resistance

From *American Sociological Review*, Vol. 29, April, 1964, pp. 173-196. Reprinted by permission of the publisher and author. A paper presented at the 58th Annual Meeting of the American Sociological Association, Los Angeles, August 27, 1963. It is part of "Work, Careers, and Leisure Styles: A Study of Sources of Social Integration," a program of research made possible by the generous support of the National Institute of Mental Health (M-2209, 1958-63), the Department of Sociology of the University of Michigan, and the Center for Advanced Study in the Behavioral Sciences. The aim of the larger study is to discover those aspects of work and leisure which bind individuals and groups to community and society and those which foster alienation and estrangement. This paper is an elaboration and test of ideas in my "Social Structure, Popular Culture, and Mass Behavior," *Studies in Public Communication*, 3 (Summer, 1961), pp. 15-22; the material, used by permission of The Free Press of Glencoe, is based on a forthcoming book. I am grateful to Guy E. Swanson and David Gold for critical readings and to John C. Scott, Michael T. Aiken, and David Reynolds for research assistance.

to mass culture. My general aim is to fill in gaps in theories of the mass society and to arrive at a more valid vision of modern society.

THEORIES OF MASS SOCIETY AND THE FUNCTIONS
OF THE MASS MEDIA

Traditional theorists of "urbanism" or of the "mass society" tend to be pessimistic in ideology and macroscopic in sociology; their empirical critics tend to be optimistic—some would say fatuous—in ideology and microscopic in sociology. Both seek to interpret the impact of industrialism and urbanism on social structure and culture. Together they have given us most of the imagery with which we construct our picture of the affluent society.

From Tocqueville to Mannheim [1] the traditional theorists have been concerned with one or both of two problems: (1) the debilitation of culture-bearing elites (and of the core values they sustain) brought on by their diminishing insulation from popular pressures; (2) the rise of the masses, who, for various reasons, are increasingly susceptible to demagogues and extremist movements.[2] These scholars are said to believe that the mobility, heterogeneity, and centralization of modern society destroy or weaken the ties that bind men to the common life, rendering the mass manipulatable, leaving mass organizations and the mass media in control. Although they vary in their depiction of the generating forces, they tend to accent either the atrophy of primary and informal relations or the atrophy of self-governing secondary groups and associations.[3]

---

[1] Alexis de Tocqueville, *Democracy in America,* New York: Alfred A. Knopf, 1948, 2 vols.; Karl Mannheim, *Man and Society in an Age of Reconstruction,* London: Routledge & Kegan Paul, 1940.

[2] Cf. William Kornhauser's treatment of "accessible elites" and "available masses" in *The Politics of Mass Society,* New York: The Free Press, 1959.

[3] Cooley, Mayo, and their students emphasize the functions of primary groups in the maintenance of social order, and cite reasons for their declining functions and authority. Since the primary group is the training ground for good citizenship, its decline, they felt, would produce mass men who would produce a "mass society," "anomie," or "social disorganization." Charles H. Cooley, *Social Organization,* New York: Charles Scribner's Sons, 1927; Elton Mayo, *The Human Problems of an Industrial Civilization,* Cambridge: Harvard University Press, 1933, esp. pp. 122 ff. and *The Social Problems of an Industrial Civilization,* Cambridge: Harvard University Press, 1945, Chs. 2 and 5. Tocqueville, among other 19th-century observers, and Lederer, Neumann, and DeGré, among modern students of totalitarianism, tend to emphasize the functions of secondary associations in the maintenance of social order or democratic political systems, or both. Alienation from work, politics, and community, and a related susceptibility to mass movements, they argue, are mainly due to the weakness of independent organizations lying between the nuclear family and the state. Tocqueville, *op. cit.;* Emil Lederer, *State of the Masses,* New York: W. W. Norton, 1940; Franz L. Neumann, *Behemoth,* New York: Oxford University Press, 1942; and Gerard DeGré, "Freedom and Social Structure," *American Sociological Review,* 11 (October, 1946), pp. 529-536. Cf. Robert A. Nisbet, *The Quest for Community,* New York: Oxford University Press, 1953. Émile Durkheim was aware of the possible links of both primary and secondary groups to the level of social integration. He tended to stress the atrophy of primary group life as a source of

Now the empirically-minded critics—a later generation studying a more industrialized society—have countered with these propositions: Primary groups survive, even flourish. Urban-industrial populations have not stopped participating in voluntary associations, which in America and perhaps in other pluralist systems, continue to multiply. Moreover, in every industrial society, whether pluralist or totalitarian, there are potent limits to the powers of the mass media, the big organizations, and the centralized state.[4]

I count myself as one of the critics,[5] but I am restive about the way the debate has progressed.[6] The parties talk past one another and ideological blinders obstruct the vision far more than in other areas of sociological investigation. Nowhere is this more true than in the sketchy treatment of mass culture in theories of the mass society and in the almost ritualistic recital of the "two-step flow" slogan by the students of media ineffectiveness.

The main theme of the theorists is this: the *mass society* develops a *mass culture*, in which cultural and political values and beliefs tend to be *homogeneous* and *fluid*. In the middle and at the bottom—in the atomized mass—people think and feel alike; but thoughts and feelings, not being firmly anchored anywhere, are susceptible to fads and fashions. At the top, poorly-organized elites, themselves mass-oriented, become political and managerial manipulators, responding to short-run pressures; they fail to

---

anomie and expressed the hope that larger secondary associations (especially the occupational group or workplace) could emerge as new bonds of solidarity, new sources of civic virtue. *The Division of Labor in Society*, trans. by George Simpson, New York: The Free Press, 1947, pp. 1-31. (In later writings, Durkheim increasingly emphasized the second point.)

[4] In evidence, the critics say, look at the following studies: Fritz J. Roethlisberger and William J. Dickson, *Management and the Worker*, Cambridge: Harvard University Press, 1939; Paul F. Lazarsfeld, Bernard Berelson, and Hazel Gaudet, *The People's Choice*, New York: Columbia University Press, 1948; Morris Janowitz, *The Community Press in an Urban Setting*, New York: The Free Press, 1952; Scott Greer, "Urbanism Reconsidered: A Comparative Study of Local Areas in a Metropolis," *American Sociological Review*, 21 (February, 1956), pp. 19-25; Marvin B. Sussman, "The Help Pattern in the Middle Class Family," *American Sociological Review*, 18 (February, 1953), pp. 22-28; J. Smith, W. H. Form, and G. P. Stone, "Local Intimacy in a Middle-Sized City," *American Journal of Sociology*, 60 (November, 1954), pp. 276-284; Charles R. Wright and Herbert H. Hyman, "Voluntary Association Memberships of American Adults: Evidence from National Sample Surveys," *American Sociological Review*, 23 (June 1958), pp. 284-294; Daniel Miller and Guy E. Swanson, *The Changing American Parent*, New York: John Wiley and Sons, 1958; E. Katz and Paul F. Lazarsfeld, *Personal Influence*, New York: The Free Press, 1955; Michael Young and Peter Willmott, *Family and Kinship in East London*, New York: The Free Press, 1957; Joseph T. Klapper, *The Effects of Mass Communication*, New York: The Free Press, 1960; etc.

[5] See Harold L. Wilensky and Charles N. Lebeaux, *Industrial Society and Social Welfare*, New York: Russell Sage Foundation, 1958, Ch. 5.

[6] For an assessment of the evidence on the vitality of social participation see Harold L. Wilensky, "Life Cycle, Work Situation, and Participation in Formal Associations," in R. W. Kleemeier (ed.), *Aging and Leisure*, New York: Oxford University Press, 1961 and "Social Structure . . . ," *op. cit.*; for an empirical study of the integrative potential of various types of social relations see Harold L. Wilensky, "Orderly Careers and Social Participation," *American Sociological Review*, 26 (August, 1961), pp. 521-539.

maintain standards and thereby encourage the spread of populism in politics, mass tastes in culture—in short, a "sovereignty of the unqualified." [7]

The empirically-minded critics of such theories are impressed by the diversity of modern life. Concerning the leveling and fluidity of culture, they point to an extraordinary variety of cultural products, assert that it is easier to prove that mass tastes have been upgraded than that such tastes have been vulgarized, and protest that high culture has not declined but merely become more widely available. Concerning the role of the mass media in politics and culture, the critics cite considerable diversity of media content as well as persistence in habits of exposure. And where diversity of *content* falls short, they argue, there is everywhere enormous diversity in *response*. While the optimists are well aware of the limits of their studies, they seem always to come to the same punch line: the burden of evidence indicates that the media are not omnipotent; they are absorbed into local cultures via the two-step flow from media to local group to person; and this absorption involves a self-selection of exposure corresponding to previous attitude.[8]

It is a pity that these students of the media who know mass communications best are not more ideologically sensitive and not more concerned with general characterizations of society; equally unfortunate is it that the theorists, at home in the world of ideologies and utopias, are not more sophisticated in the handling of data. For systematic observation and theoretical problems must be brought together if we are to understand the interplay of social structure, high culture, and mass culture.

Mass Culture and High Culture. For my purposes here the most useful definition that distinguishes high culture from mass culture is one that emphasizes the social context of production. "High culture" will refer to two characteristics of the product: (1) it is created by or under the supervision of a cultural elite operating within some aesthetic, literary, or scientific tradition (these elite are the top men in the sphere of education, aesthetics, and entertainment who carry the core values and standards of that sphere and serve as models for those working in it); (2) critical standards independent of the consumer of the product are systematically applied to it. The quality of thought or expression of the cultural object and the social milieu in which it is produced define high culture. This definition has the advantage of leaving open questions about the organization and recruitment of cultural elites, the social controls to which they are subject (e.g., pressures from patron, market, or mass), the conditions under which a high-quality product—a Shakespearian play, a Mozart symphony—can become

---

[7] Cf. Philip Selznick, "Institutional Vulnerability in Mass Society," *American Journal of Sociology*, 56 (January, 1951), pp. 320-331; Bernard Rosenberg and David Manning White (eds.), *Mass Culture*, New York: The Free Press, 1957; and Kornhauser, *op. cit.*

[8] See e.g., Klapper, *op. cit.*; and Raymond A. and Alice H. Bauer, "America, 'Mass Society and Mass Media," *Journal of Social Issues*, 16 (1960), pp. 3-56.

popular, the ways in which the product is or is not absorbed into the culture of the consumer.

"Mass culture" will refer to cultural *products manufactured solely for a mass market*. Associated characteristics, not intrinsic to the definition, are *standardization* of product and *mass behavior* in its use. Mass culture tends to be standardized because it aims to please the average taste of an undifferentiated audience. Common tastes shape mass culture; critical standards sustained by autonomous producing groups shape high culture. Another frequent but not inevitable correlate of mass culture is a high rate of mass behavior—a uniform and direct response to remote symbols.[9] It is expressed in strong attachment to and dependence on distant public objects and concerns—e.g., acts, thoughts, and feelings regarding the nation (hyperpatriotism and xenophobia), class (Marxian class consciousness), race (racism). The definition leaves open questions about the relation of mass culture to high culture; the conditions under which a product of mass culture can meet the standards of high culture; the degree to which mass culture is fluid or, like folk culture, stable (characterized by little original creation in each generation); whether traditions of expression and performance develop in it; the extent to which the impact of the mass media is mediated by audience standards and the extent to which those very standards are themselves anchored in the media.

In short, these concepts permit sociological analysis of cultural products in the social contexts in which they are created and used. They have the disadvantage of being difficult (but not impossible) to apply in empirical research.

Theoretical Problem and Assumptions. Our problem is the relation of the main structural trends associated with abundance to the form and content of high culture and mass culture. The main research question is, "which groupings of modern populations acquire a 'mass' character and which do not—with what net effect on culture, high and low?" More precisely, will the heterogeneity of culture rooted mainly in the division of labor give way to the homogeneity of culture rooted mainly in the centralized state, mass education, the mass media, and mass entertainment?

Five assumptions about modern society have guided my approach to this question: (1) social differentiation persists, even increases; (2) cultural uniformity also grows; (3) in rich countries there is more independent varia-

---

[9] Following Blumer and Wirth, the "mass" is a collectivity which is big, heterogeneous (dispersed geographically and cross-cutting many groups and sub-cultures), and socially-unstructured (comprised of individuals who do not share norms and values relevant to the situation—individuals who are unattached for a time, not in role, and can therefore behave in a uniform, undifferentiated way). Herbert Blumer, "Elementary Collective Behavior," in Alfred McClung Lee (ed.), *New Outline of the Principles of Sociology*, New York: Barnes & Noble, 1946, pp. 185 ff.; and Louis Wirth, "Urbanism as a Way of Life," *American Journal of Sociology*, 44 (July, 1938), pp. 1-24. On the public, see also Robert E. Park, *Masse und Publikum: Eine Methodologische und Soziologische Untersuchung.* Inaugural-Dissertation der Hohenphilosophischen Fakultaet der Ruprecht-Karls-Universitaet zu Heidelberg, Bern: Lack & Grunau, 1904.

tion of social structure and culture than in poor ones, although some of this incongruity is due to imprecise measures of structure; (4) developments in the aesthetic-recreational sphere as well as the political sphere may remain isolated from those in the economy and locality for some time, so that in the short run mass behavior in one sphere may not become mass behavior in another; but (5) over several generations, and as rich countries grow richer, there is a strain toward consistency between structure and culture and between behavior in one institutional sphere and that in a second.

1. *Social differentiation persists, even increases.* It is rooted first in specialization by job and occupation and by the corporate and occupational communities that develop from work. It is rooted second in society-wide age-grading systems and in individual stages of the life cycle. (As sources of alienation from work and community, for instance, age and life cycle stages, which are fixed in both biological and social nature, are invariably more important than family income, which tends toward equalization.) Finally, differentiation is rooted in religious institutions, which everywhere mesh with kinship and friendship and often form a basis for wider but separate networks of affiliation. (The labor-leisure study shows that religion is a far stronger anchor for close friendships than occupation or workplace—as measured, for instance, by the religion, occupation, and place of employment of one's three best friends.) Of course, racial and ethnic groups do assimilate, but only slowly. If they serve as a basis for variants of religious communities, as among Catholics of diverse origin, or Jews, or for protest movements, as among Negroes, such groups maintain a tenacious hold, which is often reinforced by residential segregation. The ties of locality doubtless diminish, despite the evidence of occasional communities in the metropolis (again ethnic, racial, or class "neighborhoods" or at least "blocks").

There is, in short, no evidence that the bonds of economy, age, religion, and the nuclear family (with family and church often meshed with extended kin) are weakening in the rich countries, although the quality of those relationships may be changing and their influence in particular social contexts is still problematic. In much of the discussion of "mass" society or "totalitarian" society, the persistence and stability of such ties are underestimated. The masses have nowhere in any developed country been kept "atomized," "available," "unattached," "in motion." [10] Many writers, shocked

---

[10] A major theme in Kornhauser, *op. cit.*, a creative synthesis of literature on sources of extremism, is that totalitarian control depends on the institutionalization of "high availability" of the mass (p. 62). Totalitarian regimes deliberately atomize the mass (via forced migration, purges, terror), but since mass behavior is unpredictable, they need to "keep the masses in a state of constant activity controlled by the elite" (p. 123) and so, these regimes take steps to remain with their subjects "one gigantic movement" (p. 62). Three questions about this argument may be raised. First, the implication that Bolshevik power, as a key case, depends on "massification" and the latter makes the regime vulnerable, runs counter to the apparent stability of Soviet society. Second, if totalitarian nations had to keep the masses in a constant state of mobilization, we would

by the barbarity of the Stalinist and Nazi regimes, have generalized a vocabulary appropriate to brief historical episodes or, in the case of the Nazis, selected populations, and have thereby missed the main trend. The limits of terror have been encountered by every totalitarian elite committed to economic progress. Even the most monolithic industrial societies are forced to supplement coercion with persuasion and manipulation, and to attend to problems of morale and motivation. This is especially true when they confront skilled workers at every level, including cultural elites, and is most evident when persons in these categories are in short supply. The argument is both familiar and accurate: some tasks cannot be mastered without the development of more-or-less autonomous groups—crafts, professions, scientific disciplines, and other private enclaves. Such groups cultivate technique and celebrate it, motivate disciplined work, provide stable careers and professional conviviality. The arts and sciences that flourish in the Soviet Union are not merely those which are politically safe; they are the ones which prior to the rise of Bolshevism were characterized by a high degree of skill and organization and either an aristocratic tradition (music, the ballet) or a tradition of intellectual achievement (mathematics, linguistics).[11] In short, the necessity of mobilizing social support for the performance of complex tasks sets practical limits on the baiting of intellectuals and professionals.

While the "professionalization" of occupations is often no more than a struggle for the rewards of exclusive jurisdiction, and while there are many

---

expect them to become increasingly terror-ridden. Although the variable use of terror thus far does not provide sufficient evidence on long-run trends, much totalitarian terror has seemed to give way to other means of control. Finally, the treatment of mass "availability" is tautological. Availability is indicated by (1) a high rate of mass behavior and (2) lack of attachment to independent groups. Here the hypothetical causes of mass behavior are confused with the idea of mass behavior itself (cf. 40-41, 61-62). I have dealt with this in my study by maintaining a distinction between mass behavior as particular acts in time and space (e.g., responding to a gasoline ad or a demogogue without reference to group norms) and persistent structures that presumably give rise to it (e.g., a pattern of impoverished social relations).

[11] Within the general framework of a policy of strenuous intervention (even in strictly philosophical matters) the Soviet regime has alternated application and relaxation of controls over intellectual life. J. M. Bochenski in A. Inkeles and K. Geiger (eds.), Soviet Society, Boston: Houghton Mifflin, 1961, pp. 454 ff. Despite these ups and downs, Soviet commitment to modernization has forced some liberalization. In the short run (e.g., during the period of maximum Stalinist terror) the regime can do pretty much what it likes with particular disciplines: it can wipe out genetics by persecuting Mendelian deviationists; it can proscribe quantum mechanics as inconsistent with dialectical materialism. But over the long pull, some disciplines stand up better than others. For instance, some disciplines once purged now flourish in relative freedom (linguistics, poetics); others do not (genetics, history, literary history and criticism, economics). To demonstrate such variable resistance, however, we would need data on the degree of vulnerability to the purge in each case (number put to death, imprisoned, removed from any office, removed from top office only, merely forced to recant, etc.) and on the persistence of each group beyond the purge (men and resources devoted to the discipline, quality of output, success of efforts to maintain autonomy). To demonstrate further that resistance to state penetration is a function of the pre-existing organization and tradition of the discipline as well as the indispensability of its contribution to Soviet power would require the same systematic comparisons.

organizational and political threats to the autonomy of professional groups, the number of occupations that are given some freedom to organize their work seems to be increasing in every rich country. And while the freezes and thaws in the intellectual climate make it difficult to assess the persistence of cultural elites under political attack, here, too, autonomy based on social differentiation persists. Groups that could be expected to carry high culture maintain considerable social insulation, which stems from their unique training and jobs (and related differences in religion and family background). The separate worlds of work multiply.

2. *Nevertheless, cultural uniformity grows.* Even without the obliteration of social differences, modern society tends toward cultural standardization—a widespread sharing of beliefs, values, and tastes, cross-cutting groups and categories. The forces at work are well known: popular education and mass literacy; high rates of social and residential mobility; the emergence of national markets and a national politics, both making use of nationwide media of mass communication and entertainment. Of course rich countries vary in the level of these modern developments and none has yet experienced their full impact. Even in the richest of them all, the United States, a really mass education system has existed for less than two generations,[12] hardly time for its cultural influence to be felt. Nevertheless, it seems likely that on its production side, modern society displays increasing diversity of structure; on its consumption and leisure side, increasing standardization of culture.

3. *Structure and culture change at varying rates in all societies, but their independent variation is greatest at the highest levels of modernization.* The relevance here is that "mass culture" (and its correlates, standardization and fluidity of tastes in consumption and media content) can vary independently from "mass structure" (in which the mass lack firm ties to the social order and are easily mobilized into mass movements). This follows from my first two assumptions—the simultaneous growth of structural differentiation and cultural uniformity. In fact, the closest meshing of mass society and mass culture may appear neither in modern pluralist countries nor in modern totalitarian countries but instead in the new nations of Africa and Asia, where demagogic politicians, on radio, on television, in the village square, inveigh against imperialists and colonialists, manipulating a population torn loose from traditional tribal ties. As Shils suggests, "the availability of the media of mass communication is an invitation to their demagogic use —even more pronouncedly so where the populace is illiterate and scattered in many not easily accessible villages, and where there is the belief that

[12] Richard H. Bolt in a National Science Foundation study has analyzed numbers of baccalaureate and first professional degrees expressed as a percentage of the college-graduating-age cohort (median about 22 years). The ratio increased slowly from about 1.3 per cent in 1870 to about 2 per cent in 1910, and then increased roughly logistically to nearly 20 per cent by 1960. A similar acceleration of high school graduates had already markedly set in by 1900 and by 1960 high school graduates exceeded 70 per cent of the relevant age cohort. Unpublished manuscript, 1963.

the members of this populace must be 'mobilized' for the progress of the country." [13] Where intellectual elites have achieved only embryonic development, the prominence of modern communications also means that all culture, as it moves away from traditional patterns, becomes mass culture.

The characteristics of mass society and mass culture exist in some degree in every country undergoing rapid social change, but they are most compatible in the emerging nations, however they may blend with traditional ways of life. Because the level of economic and political development conditions the effect of "mass" structures on mass culture and high culture, we cannot assume any straight-line trend from simple, poor, and non-massified, to complex, rich, and massified.

4. Not only are structure and culture divergent in modern society as it has thus far developed, but *there is considerable independence among the separate institutional spheres.* Behavior in the aesthetic-recreational sphere as well as in the political sphere may for some time remain isolated from that in the economy and the locality. In my study I assumed the independent variation of patterns of work, social participation, exposure and response to mass culture, and vulnerability to mass politics; I took as problematic the conditions under which their influence is reciprocal. My data show that a modern population can display fluid politics or high susceptibility to media manipulation, propaganda, and advertising, and yet simultaneously evidence stable patterns of social relations at work and in the community. And for some men the gap left by impoverished social relations is filled by vicarious participation in television programs, vicarious involvement with media heroes, a symbolic sharing in the national non-political life which acts to constrain both apathy and mass politics. The data also demonstrate, however, that much behavior spills over from one sphere to another, and therefore are consistent with my fifth assumption.

5. *There is in the long run a strain toward consistency (1) among values and beliefs in diverse institutional spheres;* [14] *(2) among behavior patterns in diverse spheres; (3) between culture and social structure.*

The congruence of values in spheres as diverse as kinship, politics, and aesthetics—e.g., "idealistic" and "authoritarian" political values and child-rearing philosophies as reflected in literature—is well illustrated in a careful, sophisticated content analysis of the 45 most popular new plays in Germany and the United States in 1927.[15] In 44 per cent of the 45 German plays and only 4 per cent of the 45 American plays, "*idealism*" was a basic theme: a central character, standing above the masses, pursues high principle and is compelled to sacrifice conventional morality (as is the case of the

---

[13] Edward A. Shils, "Demagogues and Cadres in the Political Development of the New States," in Lucien W. Pye (ed.), *Communications and Political Development*, Princeton, N.J.: Princeton University Press, 1963, p. 67.

[14] William Graham Sumner, *Folkways*, Boston: Ginn, 1906, pp. 5-6.

[15] Donald V. McGranahan and Ivor Wayne, "German and American Traits Reflected in Popular Drama," *Human Relations*, 1 (1948), pp. 429-455.

patriot who, for the sake of his country, murders his beloved). The level of action was 51 per cent *ideological* in Germany, 96 per cent *personal* in America: the American hero must struggle against immoral or anti-social tendencies in himself or in others which block the achievement of personal happiness; the German hero, pursuing an ideal goal, must struggle against the normal practices of society itself. Personal ambitions and satisfactions, expressed within the bounds of conventional morality, are positively sanctioned in the American plays; such strivings are often portrayed as the root obstacle in the German plays, the "materialism" and "Philistinism" against which the idealist must fight. Literature and art are not mirror images of society, but in the rare case where the data are most solid and comparative, the congruence is striking.

Concerning consistency of behavior in the diverse spheres of modern life, a nation probably cannot forever have both high rates of mass behavior in consumption and low rates in politics (Britain) or rate low on mass consumption and high on mass politics (France). I assume that mass behavior in politics, consumption, and media exposure are correlated—that voting for Ike's personality is like responding to undiscussed gasoline ads, and the two can reinforce one another. Data reported elsewhere support this notion.[16]

Similarly, with respect to the congruence of structure and culture, I assume that a modern nation cannot forever have both an elite educational system and continued growth in mass culture (as in France, where the paid circulation of the *Reader's Digest* now exceeds a million, which, in proportion to population, is almost a third of its penetration in the United States), or high rates of mobility and stable, insulated leisure styles (class sub-cultures in Britain, ethnic sub-cultures in America). And the formulation sometimes advanced by students of American culture [17] that we have made progress by moving on from a concern with "politics" to a concern with "culture"

[16] Wilensky, "Social Structure . . ." *op. cit.* p. 21. Tabulations based on 678 interviews with a cross-section of white males in the middle mass (upper-working class and lower middle class) of the Detroit area, aged 21–55, show that our indicators of susceptibility in advertising and politics are indeed correlated. We assumed that candidate switchers—Democrats who went for Ike, the (less numerous) Republicans for "Soapy" Williams—were responding to personality appeals in recent campaigns. Then we asked those who own cars and notice gas ads, if, when they hear claims made in these ads, they "ever try a tankful or so to see how true the ads are." We also asked everyone how often he had bought something because he saw it advertised and then found he'd been stuck. Among those who never completed high school (whatever their income), and among young high-school grads with low family incomes (in this sample that means $5,000–8,000), it is the loyal party men who try a tankful; but among the vanguard populations—higher-education, higher-income men—it is the candidate switcher or ticket-splitter who takes a flier, especially among middle-aged, upper-income, high school grads and young college men (whatever their income). Incidentally, these same college-educated Eisenhower Democrats report that they get stuck in the product market quite often. The link between mass behavior in consumption and politics is most visible among men of the future.

[17] Winston White, *Beyond Conformity*, New York: The Free Press, 1961, and the early writings of David Riesman.

and "conformity," obscures the most interesting challenge—to discover the complex connections between them. Mr. Minow's travail suggests that cultural homogeneity is rooted in the political structure as well as the market place.[18]

Thus, we may assume that the influence of mass education, the media, and the centralized state will in the long run overcome the influence of variations in work, religion, age, and locality as sources of cultural values and leisure styles and we can expect mass culture in both Europe and America to penetrate structures now more or less insulated from it.

Educational institutions are strategic in linking structure and culture and the diverse institutional spheres. The education system is locality bound, but brings wider worlds to view; its curricula are highly differentiated, reflecting the specialized occupations for which it trains youngsters, but it is the central transmitter of core values and beliefs. Universities and colleges are the main source of what high culture there is, and to some extent they inoculate against mass culture; at the same time mass education uses the media, incorporates them into its content and technique and helps train the next generation in a style of leisure permeated by the great din of the media.[19]

Clearly, to understand the impact of abundance on culture and the limits and possibilities of public policy in overcoming cultural uniformity, we need to contrast the cultural life of countries whose governments differ in policy regarding education and the media of mass communication.[20]

[18] If there is more independent variation of politics and culture in the United States than in other rich countries, it may stem from our greater gap between intellectuals and the government, the split that Tocqueville noted between intelligence and action. In several parts of Europe, notably Britain and Scandinavia, the media to some extent feel compelled to reflect the work of the intellectuals—the statesman, the educator, the serious artist. In the United States, the media reflect more the work of the businessman as advertiser, the artist as entertainer, the politician as demagogue; they are typically managed and staffed by anti-intellectual intellectuals. Cf. Reuel Denney, *The Astonished Muse*, Chicago: The University of Chicago Press, 1957, p. 216; and Richard Chase, *The Democratic Vista*, Garden City: Doubleday & Co., 1958, *passim*.

[19] The reciprocal influence of the mass media and mass education has received little serious attention. A few of the obvious possibilities are: (1) Extensive exposure in the home accustoms the child to visual and oral communication of the simplest sort; teachers and curriculum planners respond by using the media to make education more entertaining, using the child's television experience (e.g., current events) as the basis for class discussion—generally displacing time otherwise devoted to a more systematic treatment of history or geography. (2) The average college receives students unaccustomed to disciplined reading and adapts assignments and techniques accordingly. (3) In school and college alike, manners, morals, and speech are more subtly influenced—with self-display becoming a new ideal, and publicity-consciousness a new set of mind. The "show and tell" sessions of our elementary schools, like the audience participation and panel shows of television, combine both. Whether the post-Sputnik spurt in "hard" subjects (a product of Cold War competition) together with the oversupply of youngsters (a product of the changing age distribution, which increases competition for college entrance) will offset the penetration of mass culture into the schools is unknown. As all these forces converge, the cultural tastes of the average college professor, like those of the school teacher, will weigh in the outcome.

[20] For some lines of inquiry, see Pye, *op. cit.*

SOCIAL STRUCTURE, HIGH CULTURE, AND MASS CULTURE:
AN EMPIRICAL APPROACH

Let us apply the larger debate about modern society to the mass media
and mass entertainment in America. We must first grasp the fact that the
mass media are the core of American leisure and that television has become
the core of media exposure. The sheer arithmetic is striking. Nine in ten
American homes average five to six hours daily with the TV set on. And it is
not just turned on; it is generally being watched. Eight in ten Americans
spend at least four hours a day viewing television, listening to the radio, or
both.[21] Additional time goes to reading newspapers and magazines.

The trend is up. An increasing fraction of the daily routine is devoted
to the products of the mass media. Mainly due to the rise of television, the
media together and on the average now take up almost as much time as
work; substantial minorities log more hours a year in TV viewing alone than
in working.

Both cause and consequence of this trend is the development of an enormous machinery of promotion. Today, our outlays for advertising are almost
equal to our current expenditures on public schools (elementary and secondary)—about 11 billion annually.[22] Additional billions go to PR and the
like. The more abundance, the more activity to increase the desire for it.

So far we are on safe ground. The size of this frenzied promotion effort
and the astonishing amount of exposure are well known. The *impact* on the
quality of American culture, however, is difficult to judge.

In tackling the problem I have tried to be specific: in approaching the
standardization of culture I have looked for media exposure and response
cross-cutting social classes, educational levels, age grades, and religious and
nativity categories. In handling the *heterogeneity* of culture I have searched
for variations in media exposure and response with special attention to structural facts obscured by these traditional categories of sociological analysis—
e.g., the quality variations within broad levels of education; the variations
in tasks, work schedules, occupational groups, workplaces, and job patterns
within broad occupational strata. The picture that emerges is more complicated than the assertions and counter-assertions of theorists and critics, but
it is also a more realistic reflection of modern life.

I will first present findings bearing on the structural roots of cultural
heterogeneity, and then findings that suggest the perhaps more powerful
roots of cultural uniformity. I will draw from data on the quality of media
exposure among 1,354 men ranging from highly-educated professors, lawyers,

[21] G. A. Steiner, *The People Look at Television*, New York: Alfred A. Knopf, 1963,
pp. 4, 112; and citations in footnote 30 below.
[22] Fritz Machlup, *The Production and Distribution of Knowledge in the United
States*, Princeton, N.J.: Princeton University Press, 1962, p. 104.

and engineers and executives matched for age and income, through a cross-section of the lower middle and upper working classes (the "middle mass") of the Detroit area, and down through 186 men unemployed and on relief.[23] We listed all their favorite TV shows, periodicals and newspapers read regularly, and all books they could name which they had read in the last two months. We then classified each program, each magazine, and each book in three "brow" levels—high quality, trash, or neither.

In coding for quality we were tolerant. The aim was to classify according to some fixed aesthetic standard, applicable to the medium, the more-or-less best performances and the clearly worst. Thus, the bias was that of Gilbert Seldes' *Seven Lively Arts*—sympathetic to the media. The product does not have to be aggressively educative to get by as highbrow, but if it is drama, the contrast is "Playhouse 90" vs. the most stereotypical detective, western, and adventure shows; if it is a paperback mystery, the contrast is Agatha Christie or Chandler vs. Spillane.

On *television programs* our staff made an effort to keep in touch with critical opinion and pooled judgments.

On *books, periodicals,* and *newspapers,* we compiled an initial classification and checked with experts. For the book code, for instance, two English professors reputed to have opposing views about the modern novel independently agreed on 97 per cent of the 200-odd high-quality titles. (That this code, like the others, is tolerant is suggested by the reaction of a literary critic who judged that perhaps half of the highbrow books would better be labeled "middling" or "upper middle;" clearly the list would not withstand the scrutiny of a Dwight MacDonald. But by that token it has the advantage of not understating the fallout from the "cultural explosion" as it appears in these samples—which, as it turned out, was scanty.)

In general these codes do *not* reflect a snobbish understatement of qual-

---

[23] The analysis is based on detailed interviews with probability samples or universes of six professional groups (100 solo lawyers; 107 firm lawyers in the 19 Detroit firms with ten or more partners and associates; 31 professors at "Church University;" 68 professors at "Urban University;" 91 engineers at "Unico" and 93 at "Diversico"—generally research and development specialists, supervisors, or executives); a probability sample of the middle mass (N=678); and, as a sharp contrast, two samples of underdogs, 81 Negro and 105 white, who were severely deprived. The interviews took place in the first half of 1960. Only males who were in the labor force, 55 years old or younger, and currently or previously married were interviewed. All the professionals had college degrees. The special selection criteria are described in Harold L. Wilensky, "The Uneven Distribution of Leisure: The Impact of Economic Growth on 'Free Time,'" *Social Problems*, IX (Summer, 1961), p. 38; "Orderly Careers . . . ," *op. cit.*, pp. 529-530; and "The Moonlighter: A Product of Relative Deprivation," *Industrial Relations*, 3 (October, 1963), pp. 106-108. It is important to note that the leading colleges and universities are well represented in the backgrounds of men in the professional samples. Three-quarters of the firm lawyers, for instance, are graduates of one of five elite "national" law schools—Chicago, Columbia, Harvard, Michigan, and Yale. Like the professors—full-time faculty in the humanities and physical sciences (including mathematics) in two arts and sciences colleges—these lawyers may be assumed to have had as much opportunity to acquire discriminating tastes as their counterparts in other cities.

ity exposure, and there is less disagreement at the extremes than one would expect.[24]

To establish the coherence, independence, and economy of my measures, I combined all samples and carried out two factor analyses—one of the content, social context, and psychological functions of exposure; the other, of media uses as part of leisure style. A resulting factor from each analysis will be used as a dependent variable below.

1. *"Much exposure to poor TV"* is a strong factor (12 per cent of the variance) in the media analysis. It is defined by: (1) high number of hours per week of television viewing; (2) many westerns as "favorite TV programs —the ones you almost always watch;" and (3) many detective and adventure programs as favorites. These defining items not only go together in the media experience of our 1,354 men but they are independent of such other factors as "privatized TV-viewing," "vicarious participation via television," and a variety of uses of print. The men who score high here are neither ardent sports fans nor devotees of panel, quiz, giveaway, audience participation, and general entertainment shows. But so far as one can become involved with the western-detective-adventure triumvirate, these men are: when they watch, they watch with others; when they are away from home they are likely to discuss television often with friends or relatives.

2. *"Low leisure competence"* (or *"compulsive absorption of much poor TV as a time filler"*) is a strong factor (22 per cent of the variance) in the analysis of leisure style, which included data from all areas—social participation, consumption, politics, as well as media exposure and response. It is defined by (1) much exposure to poor TV (above); (2) absorption of media, especially television, into groups beyond the nuclear family; (3) compulsive TV-viewing (when watching he often feels he'd rather do something else, but he just can't tear himself away); and (4) much restless, aimless, aggressive leisure (he "blows his top" often, does a great deal of aimless Sunday driving, says he would not watch TV more if the day were 26 hours long, but meanwhile names the late show or the late-late show as TV favorites).

Other correlates of this factor are: *deviance* (the man who is low in leisure competence is likely to be a McCarthyite, a cross-class identifier, have a deviant perception of his standard of living—i.e., he is a blue-collar worker who thinks he is better off than office workers or a white-collar worker who thinks he is worse off than blue-collar workers—and he hangs on to his cars longer than most people); *leisure malaise* (often feels he has time on his hands, doesn't know what to do with himself); subjectively *weak attach-*

---

[24] Two independent studies, using impressionistic judgments to rank magazines, arrived at results so similar to one another (a rank order correlation coefficient of .93 for 49 magazines) that one is tempted to defend a ranking of the entire range, not merely the validity of three categories. Babette Kass, "Overlapping Magazine Reading: A New Method of Determining the Cultural Level of Magazines," in Paul L. Lazarsfeld and Frank N. Stanton (eds.), *Communications Research: 1948–1949*, New York: Harper & Row, 1949, p. 133, Table 1.

ments to secondary associations and fluid friendships; and, as I shall show below, a *short work week.*[25]

The most precise summary phrase I can think of to describe the psychology of this leisure style is, "coping with restless malaise by an unsatisfying retreat to violent, escapist television." Students of the media who stress the absorption of television into the warm bosom of family and peer group should ponder what is being absorbed most effectively by whom with what effect.

Other, simpler measures of media behavior will be self-evident as I use them. I now turn to the sources of variation in the quality of exposure.

Structural Roots of Cultural Heterogeneity. The paradox of structural differentiation and cultural homogeneity is in part a spurious product of our weak concepts and measures of the attributes of social organization. If we pinpoint the groups and events that grip men in the daily round, some of the cultural phenomena which at first blush appear standardized turn out to be somewhat differentiated.

This can be seen in an analysis of the sources and correlates of (1) the number of media areas (television, newspapers, magazines, books) in which our respondents were exposed to any high-brow material and (2) their score on "much exposure to poor TV." In each case, 17 variables were related to these two media exposure variables. (See Table 1.) To determine the relative effect of each variable and to locate the incidence of high- and low-brow exposure within each class of each variable, I used a regression technique called "multiple classification analysis" which permits the use of non-continuous variables like religion and does not assume linearity in their effect (SEE APPENDIX ON METHOD).

Only 85 of these men were exposed to any high-brow material in three or four areas; 157 score in two areas, 305 in one; 807 men reported no quality exposure in any area. At the other extreme 138 men reported very high exposure to poor TV—25 and 30, even 35 hours of westerns, detectives, and adventure programs a week; 524 have medium scores; 692 avoid large doses of this type of program.

Although the main story is the general scarcity of quality exposure, which I will explore in detail later, Table 1 tells us something important: with sensitive measures of social position we can go far in explaining what cultural variation we do uncover. *The 17 variables explain over 46 per cent of the total variance in the number of areas in which quality exposure is reported and 25 per cent of the variance in exposure to poor TV.*

[25] These are items whose loadings on the Low Leisure Competence factor rank high, but which are either too weak or appear on two or more factors; they are sufficiently associated with the defining items to be taken as subsidiary meanings of the factor, but they may measure other phenomena as well. The results of this leisure style analysis are reported more fully in Harold L. Wilensky, *Work, Leisure, and Freedom,* New York: The Free Press, forthcoming. Correlation matrices were factor analyzed by the method of principal axes. Factors were rotated according to Kaiser's varimax criterion. In interpretation, loadings below 25 per cent of the average communality of the factors were ignored.

Table 1

RANK ORDER OF 17 SOURCES AND CORRELATES OF QUALITY
OF MEDIA EXPOSURE AND ADJUSTED MEANS FOR SUB-
CLASSES IN A MULTIPLE CLASSIFICATION ANALYSIS **

| | | Quality of Media Exposure | | | |
| | | No. Areas High-Brow | | Much Exposure to Poor TV | |
	N	Adjust. Mean	Rank as Predictor	Adjust. Mean	Rank as Predictor
I. PRE-ADULT SOCIALIZATION					
A. *Generation American, Religion, and Status of Religious Preference*					
Protestant					
Above average status of religious preference and four grandparents born in U.S.	98	.752		49.046	
Above average status of religious preference and three or fewer grandparents born in U.S.	133	.807		49.454	
Average or below average status of religious preference and four grandparents born in U.S.	144	.719		48.779	
Average or below average status of religious preference and three or fewer grandparents born in U.S.	217	.702		49.239	
Catholic					
Average or below average status of religious preference and four grandparents born in U.S.	70	.895		49.608	
Average or below average status of religious preference and three or fewer grandparents born in U.S.	351	.700		49.990	3
Jewish	77	.922		48.337	
No Preference	66	.943	2	49.774	
B. *Early Farm Isolation (number of years lived on farm, nature and number of activities while in school, and teen-age club memberships)* *					
Non-farm activist (40–49)	693	.772	17	49.752	4
Mixed farm-non-farm, isolation-non-isolation (50–59)	373	.751		49.093	
Much farm isolation (60–79)	90	.710		48.105	

Table 1—Continued

		Quality of Media Exposure			
		No. Areas High-Brow		Much Exposure to Poor TV	
	N	Adjust. Mean	Rank as Predictor	Adjust. Mean	Rank as Predictor
C. *Level and Quality of Formal Education (degree of exposure to liberal arts)*					
Less than high school graduate	235	.278		53.004	1
High school graduate	255	.303		52.391	
Some college (1–3 years)	124	.409		50.745	
Baccalaureate degree, low quality	173	.722		48.344	
Baccalaureate degree, high quality	63	1.040		46.865	
Graduate or professional degree, low quality	152	1.502		44.805	
Graduate or professional degree, high quality	154	1.729	1	44.707	
II. WORK CONTEXT, SCHEDULE, AND ATTACHMENT					
A. *Size of Workplace*					
Less than 49 employed	249	.655		48.475	
50–499 employed	194	.748		49.558	
500 or more employed	543	.940	3	49.306	
Self-employed	170	.337		50.950	2
B. *Work Schedule*					
Has orthodox work schedule	1039	.767	15	49.547	7
Has deviant work schedule	117	.696		48.206	
C. *Long Hours: Chooses Work Over Leisure (many hours per week and weekends, and has control over work schedule)* *					
Short work week (30–49)	575	.660		49.626	8
Medium work week (50–59)	446	.812		49.464	
Long work week (60–69)	135	1.013	4	48.320	
D. *Work Alienation*					
None	979	.755		49.362	
Some	126	.728		49.401	
Much	51	.928	10	50.377	13
III. AGE, ASPIRATIONS, MOBILITY, AND CAREER					
A. *Age of Respondent*					
21–29	121	.609		50.196	6
30–39	478	.818	6	49.710	
40–55	557	.744		48.981	
B. *Worklife Mobility Pattern*					
Up	385	.726		48.967	10
Stable	420	.776		49.672	
Fluctuating	335	.780	14	49.650	
Down	16	.727		48.238	

Table 1—Continued

		Quality of Media Exposure			
		No. Areas High-Brow		Much Exposure to Poor TV	
	N	Adjust. Mean	Rank as Predictor	Adjust. Mean	Rank as Predictor
C. Intergenerational Climbing of Couple (Respondent's father's occupational stratum → respondent's; respondent's father-in-law's occupation → respondent's; and educational level of respondent compared with father's) *					
Much status loss of couple (20–39)	99	.695		50.131	12
Little or no status loss of couple (40–49)	407	.753		49.327	
Some status gain of couple (50–59)	484	.800	9	49.347	
Much status gain of couple (60–69)	166	.700		49.375	
D. Occupational Aspirations (past, present, and for the next generation) *					
Low aspirations (30–39)	52	.670		48.659	
Medium-low aspirations (40–49)	398	.737		49.450	
Medium-high aspirations (50–59)	505	.778		49.466	16
High aspirations (60–69)	201	.784	13	49.390	
IV. PARTICIPATION, COMMUNITY ATTACHMENT, AND MISCELLANEOUS LEISURE CORRELATES					
A. Primary Range (index of range of values, interests, and status levels represented by relatives, neighbors, friends from workplace or in same line of work, and other friends) *					
Low primary range (00–04)	158	.706		49.006	
Medium primary range (05–12)	764	.738		49.500	15
High primary range (13–19)	234	.867	8	49.395	
B. Effective Mediating Attachments (much time and wide range of contacts in formal assns.; numerous assns. clearly attached to; and high political affect and strong mediation of campaigns) *					
Weak mediating attachments (30–39)	183	.766		49.391	
Medium-weak mediating attachments (40–49)	251	.778	12	48.966	
Medium-strong mediating attachments (50–59)	492	.775		49.443	

Table 1—Continued

		Quality of Media Exposure			
		No. Areas High-Brow		Much Exposure to Poor TV	
	N	Adjust. Mean	Rank as Predictor	Adjust. Mean	Rank as Predictor
Strong mediating attachments (60–79)	230	.702		49.844	11
C. *Community Attachment, Good Citizen Style (voted in recent elections; voted for school taxes; gives high percentage of family income to churches and charity; feels neighborhood is "real home" and reasons show local attachment)* *					
Weak local citizen (30–39)	61	.820	7	49.310	
Somewhat weak citizen (40–49)	354	.792		49.370	
Somewhat strong citizen (50–59)	676	.760		49.478	17
Strong local citizen (60–69)	65	.531		49.030	
D. *Leisure Malaise: Time on Hands*					
Never have time on hands	610	.793	11	49.009	
Not very often	461	.720		49.743	
Fairly or very often	85	.741		50.500	5
E. *Leisure Style as a Status Criterion: Taste (mentions manners and speech, books, music and art, and refinement of taste in defining class differences)* *					
Few references to taste (40–49)	376	.692		49.411	
Some references to taste (50–59)	649	.754		49.520	14
Many references to taste (60–69)	131	.985	5	48.871	
F. *Leisure Style as a Status Criterion: External Symbols (mentions houses, amount of money, clubs and organizations, and clothing in defining class differences)* *					
Few references to external symbols (40–49)	637	.748		49.080	
Some references to external symbols (50–59)	425	.765		49.848	9
Many references to external symbols (60–69)	94	.817	16	49.678	
Total N	1156				

* Items are combined in a factor score; the cutting points for scores are in parentheses.

** For explanation see "Appendix on Method." For details on measures which are not self-explanatory, see text. For participation measures (e.g. of the range of values, interests, and status levels represented by the respondent's social relations) see "Orderly Careers . . . ," *op. cit.*

Both the measures and samples of the larger study were designed to permit projections of social and cultural trends in the affluent society based on comparisons of vanguard and rearguard groups at the same stage of the life cycle and the same social level. Does modernization increase the level of education? Then compare college graduates of growing mass institutions with those of elite colleges, which produce a declining percentage of the educated. Does economic development bring rising levels of mass aspiration? Then compare the aspiring with the less aspiring. Does it bring the dominance of large, complex organizations? Then compare the self-employed with men in workplaces of various sizes and structures. Does it make for an uneven distribution of leisure? Then compare the long-hours men with the short. Does modernization change the social composition of elites? Then compare established Protestant elites with rising Catholic populations.

My findings underscore the importance of education and the persistence of older bases of differentiation—descent (religion and nativity), age and work situation. When we really peg the meaning of these as indicators of social position and discover their variable effects, however, we cannot help but be struck with the difficulty of predicting their future functions for the maintenance or decline of cultural diversity.

The three top predictors of quality of exposure in both "number of areas of high-brow exposure" and in amount of poor TV are: (1) an index of level and quality of formal education which I interpret as degree of exposure to the liberal arts—by far the single most important variable in both cases; (2) an index of "generation American, religion, and status of religious preference;" (3) work context (size of workplace and self-employment status). The more education, and within educational levels, the higher the quality, the higher the level of taste. Among religious-nativity categories Jews, those with no preference, and established Catholics (four grandparents born in the U.S.) stand out in taste while the most ardent consumers of low-brow TV are Catholics of more recent American vintage (three or fewer grandparents born in the U.S.); however, two of these same high-brow categories —established Catholics and men with no preference—also produce more than their share of enthusiasts for the western-detective-adventure shows. Jews and established high-status Protestants tend to avoid big doses of poor TV. As for work context, the good-taste categories are salaried men employed in big organizations; the poor-taste categories are self-employed or are employed in medium-sized workplaces. Long hours, a factor measuring choice of work over leisure, ranks fourth as a predictor of high-brow media exposure; short hours ranks eighth as a predictor of low-brow television exposure. Men 21–29 years old (all in the middle mass) stand out in low-brow exposure; men 30–39 stand out in high-brow exposure.

What can we make of such findings? We began with the macroscopic assumption that the division of labor, religious institutions, and age-grading systems persist as powerful sources of cultural differentiation and that mass education is a source of standardization. Now that we have pinpointed the effect of these variables, slicing things a bit finer, the picture is not so simple. Take one of our favorite sociological clues to social structure: education. Will rising education levels bring an upgrading of taste, or will mass education mean an efflorescence of *kitsch?* In answering such questions, the distinctions I have made are crucial.

Table 1 (variable I-C) reports the mean scores (for each of seven categories of education) for number of media areas in which the respondent reports any high-brow exposure and for much exposure to poor television. To take account of the increasing diversity of higher education,[26] the colleges and universities from which degree holders had graduated were divided into two quality levels. For professors, the top 20 graduate schools in the 1957 Keniston rating [27] were coded high quality, the rest, low. For lawyers and engineers, faculty in a position to reflect professional consensus were given the complete lists and asked to rank leading schools, second-line schools, and others. The ten leading and second-line law schools, and 17 leading and second-line engineering schools, were counted as high quality; the rest were coded low.[28] The aim, again, was to capture as much of the variation in exposure to the liberal arts as possible and to explore the cultural impact of the rise of mass education.

The main findings are these:

1. For the number of media areas in which high-brow exposure is reported, *amount* of education makes little difference from grade zero through "some college;" thereafter, both quality of education and sheer level count heavily. The biggest jump in mean scores is between baccalaureate level and graduate level (.462), but the difference between men with high- and men with low-quality undergraduate education (.318) is greater than the differences between less than high school vs. high school (an infinitesimal .025), high school vs. some college (.106) or even some college and low-quality baccalaureate degree (.313).

Ultimately the mere rise in the average education level will do little for the cultivation of taste in reading and in the broadcast media; what counts is the number who complete college, and especially the number fortunate enough to go through a few favored colleges.

2. For the avoidance of big slugs of poor TV, sheer level of education counts slightly more than quality, although the differences are tiny until we come to college populations. Here the three largest differences are be-

[26] The most perceptive treatment is David Riesman, *Constraint and Variety in American Education,* Garden City, New York: Doubleday & Co., 1958.

[27] Hayward Keniston, *Graduate Study and Research in the Arts and Sciences at the University of Pennsylvania,* Philadelphia: University of Pennsylvania Press, 1959, p. 119.

[28] Respondents are coded according to the highest degree attained. The category, "baccalaureate degree, low quality," includes 121 engineers plus the 53 men of the middle mass who have a degree; the 63 men with a high-quality baccalaureate are all engineers. I assumed that the best graduate and professional schools draw from the best liberal arts colleges.

tween "some college" and the low-quality baccalaureate (2.401), high-quality baccalaureate and low-quality graduate school (2.060), and low-quality and high-quality baccalaureate (1.479).

In sum: when we conceptualize "education" even at this crude level of "exposure to the liberal arts" and devise measures to match, we can gauge the cultural impact of abundance with more precision. These data suggest that the rising average level of education will protect against enervating amounts of the very shoddiest media content but it will not cause large populations to break the mediocrity barrier. As for the graduates of quality institutions, they will decline as a percentage of the educated and, as I shall show below, their exposure to quality print has declined and perhaps will continue to decline as a fraction of their leisure routine.

A final demonstration of the ambiguous effects of education and of the structural roots of cultural heterogeneity is in Table 2, which shows the impact of the organization of work and the level and quality of education on "leisure competence." In modern economies, group propensity and opportunity to work vary greatly even among occupational groups at the same social level; Table 2 ranges my samples in columns according to the proportion of the group or stratum usually working 44 hours or less a week. You will recall that the measure of "low leisure competence" is a factor score tapping a style best described as the compulsive absorption of much poor TV as a time filler.

The table shows first that a simple structural fact—group schedules of work—is a powerful source of diversity in leisure style. "Low" leisure competence ranges from 17 per cent in long hours groups to 65 per cent in short hours groups. The underdogs are similar to short-hours engineers and blue-collar workers: 61 per cent score low competence. Within various work contexts, how does the education of the individual affect his leisure competence? Exposure to the liberal arts has a heavy effect, which increases with shorter hours. For instance, among the short hours groups, a high-quality bachelor's degree brings the low competence rate down to 25 per cent; a low-quality bachelor's degree yields 45 per cent incompetence; some college or less yields a whopping 73 per cent. The 343 men comprising that 73 per cent are the largest group and have the lowest rate of competence in the table. Among men not accustomed to the wider universe made available by demanding work, it takes a long, expensive education to avoid an impoverished life. For students of American culture who look forward to the leisure-oriented society, in which we retreat from work to the more diversified joys of ever-shorter hours, the moral is that those who have most leisure have least resources for its creative use.

Structural Roots of Cultural Homogeneity. So far I have asked, "who in all these samples is exposed to high culture and who avoids the very worst of mass culture?" I have not dealt with the *extent* of high-brow exposure, the effects of diverse *types of media,* and above all, the *interaction between high culture and mass culture.* How much do men who could be

Table 2

SHORT-HOURS GROUPS AND MEN ON RELIEF ARE PRONE TO COMPULSIVE ABSORPTION OF MUCH POOR TELEVISION AS A TIME FILLER; GROUPS ON LONG WORK WEEKS DISPLAY HIGHER LEISURE COMPETENCE. QUALITY AND LEVEL OF EDUCATION INCREASE LEISURE COMPETENCE MOST AMONG SHORT-HOURS GROUPS

GROUP PROPENSITY AND OPPORTUNITY TO WORK: *	Long-Hours Groups			Medium-Hours Groups				Short-Hours Groups				Unemployed Underdogs on Relief			Sample Total
LEVEL OF EDUCATION:	Professional or graduate degree			BA or more		Some College or Less		BA or more		Some College or Less					
QUALITY OF EDUCATION:	High %	Low %	Total %	High %	Low %	Total %	Total %	High %	Low %	Total %	Total %	Negro %	White %	Total %	Total %
LEISURE COMPETENCE **															
High	89	78	83	64	55	33	42	75	55	27	34	33	43	39	47
Low	11	22	17	36	45	67	57	25	45	73	65	67	57	61	52
Total	100	100	100	100	100	100	99	100	100	100	99	100	100	100	99
N	(141)	(134)	(275)	(44)	(127)	(271)	(442)	(32)	(64)	(343)	(439)	(81)	(105)	(186)	(1342)

* Long-hours groups are "Urban U." professors and all lawyers, solo or firm; only 17 to 22 per cent work 44 or fewer hours per week. Medium-hours groups are "Church U." professors, Unico engineers, and white-collar men of the middle mass, any age; 32 to 38 per cent have short work weeks. Short-hours groups are Diversico engineers, blue-collar men of the middle mass, any age; 52 to 59 per cent have short work weeks. Men on relief provide extreme contrast.

** A factor score: 47 men scoring 20–30 on "Low Leisure Competence" and 599 scoring 40–49 were combined to form the high competence category; 89 men scoring 60–79 and 619 men scoring 50–59 comprise the low competence category. Twelve unemployed in the middle mass are excluded from this table. For details on measures, see text.

519

expected to have cultivated tastes expose themselves to high culture? To what extent are intellectuals insulated from mass culture? Which media of communication have most and least impact on the standards of cultural elites and educated laymen?

Not everything that is wrong with our intellectuals, as Shils reminds us, can be attributed to the media or to mass culture; high culture has always been precarious.[29] But what *is* new, unique to our time, is a thorough interpenetration of cultural levels; the good, the mediocre, and the trashy are becoming fused in one massive middle mush.

Structural trends in the organization of intellectual life are at the root of the problem; among *intellectuals* and their educated publics we see: large numbers, spatial scattering, intense professional specialization, and a loss of a sense of autonomy and intellectual community (America, with more college graduates than any other nation in the world, does not have a first-rate intellectual weekly like the *Observer* in Britain). For both *intellectuals and the general population*, as I have suggested earlier, the cultural atmosphere is permeated by the mass media.

These are all in some measure requisites or consequences of abundance. Hundreds of thousands, eventually millions, of specialized experts and intellectuals are indispensable in a complex society. And the spread of higher education to the average man is both a manpower requirement of modern economies and a great achievement in equality.

The problem is not that the taste of the masses has been debased, but rather that the creators and maintainers of high culture in the humanities, the arts, the sciences, have an increasingly difficult time doing their proper work. Intellectuals are increasingly tempted to play to mass audiences and expose themselves to mass culture, and this has the effect of reducing their versatility of taste and opinion, their subtlety of expression and feeling.

There is little doubt from my data as well as others' that educated strata—even products of graduate and professional schools—are becoming full participants in mass culture; they spend a reduced fraction of time in exposure to quality print and film. This trend extends to the professors, writers, artists, scientists—the keepers of high culture themselves—and the chief culprit, again, is TV.[30]

[29] Edward A. Shils, "Mass Society and Its Culture," *Daedalus*, 89 (Spring, 1960), pp. 288-31.

[30] Any assertion about long-term trends is inferential; we lack good base-line data. My position rests on three considerations. First, there is scattered evidence that the broadcast media in competition with print generally win out—in attraction, number of hours, perhaps persuasiveness, too. Reading, especially of books and magazines, declines. T. E. Coffin, "Television's Impact on Society," *The American Psychologist*, 10 (October, 1955), p. 633; L. Bogart, *The Age of Television* (2nd ed.), New York: Frederick Ungar, 1958, pp. 133 ff.; James N. Mosel, "Communications Patterns and Political Socialization in Transitional Thailand," in Pye, *op. cit.*, pp. 184-228; and Klapper, *op. cit.*, pp. 107 ff. Second, among the educated, total exposure to broadcast media has recently increased. Before television, radio listening among set owners averaged 4.9 hours daily; evening listening averaged 2.6 hours for all, 2.4 hours for

You will remember that media researchers emphasize the limited power of mass communications by invoking the idea that the audience sorts itself out according to predisposition. By that formula, we should find the highly-educated listening to Gerry Mulligan, watching Channel 9, and reading the *Partisan Review* (or at least *Harper's*); and the less educated should be listening to Elvis Presley, watching "Gunsmoke," and reading *True Detective*. The evidence is that the educated display, on balance, a mild tendency toward more discriminating tastes.

Studies consistently demonstrate that college graduates compared to the less educated have somewhat less exposure to the broadcast media, which are more uniform in their content, and somewhat more to print, which is more diversified. They are a bit more choosey in the regular programs they watch on television; they definitely read more quality magazines and newspapers; and they listen to more serious music.[31] Table 3, emphasizing the efforts of educational and occupational groups to be selective in their use of newspapers, periodicals, and television, confirms this picture. For instance, over two-fifths of the professors, a third of the lawyers, and a tenth of the engineers compared to one in a hundred of the middle mass and none of the underdogs read a quality newspaper. And in reading the newspaper, the professional groups are somewhat more cosmopolitan and serious; they include world and national news as sections important to them more often than do the middle mass or underdogs. Similar differences appear for qual-

---

college graduates. Program preferences did not vary much by education. P. F. Lazarsfeld, *The People Look at Radio,* Chapel Hill, N.C.: The University of North Carolina Press, 1946, pp. 97-98, 136. Today, even excluding highbrow FM, radio listening has not declined to zero. (The typical radio family that acquired a television set cut radio listening from four or five hours to about two hours a day. Bogart, *op. cit.,* p. 114.) Meanwhile, television viewing for the average product of a graduate or professional school rose from zero to three hours daily. Steiner, *op. cit.,* p. 75. If we assume no major increase in the work week of the educated, and no change in life style that can remotely touch television in sheer hours, their exposure to undifferentiated broadcast media has risen as a portion of the daily round while their exposure to serious print has declined. And the small differences in amount and quality of television exposure reported in the text indicate that the educated are not especially discriminating. Finally, the argument about the effect of intellectuals' participation in mass culture on the standards of performance and appreciation proceeds through example and counter example without the benefit of much systematic evidence. "Raymond Aron's thought," says Edward Shils, "does not deteriorate because he occasionally writes in the *New York Times Magazine.*" *Op. cit.,* p. 306. Unfortunately, we cannot know what the quality of Aron's thought would have been if as a young man he had been watching "situation comedies" instead of reading books. As a master of ambiguous polemic, Shils presents the best defense of the view that mass culture has little effect on high culture; but in listing the structural forces that threaten high culture, he gives inadequate weight to them and no weight at all to the major problem we confront here—central tendencies in the life styles of educated strata.

[31] Cf. Paul F. Lazarsfeld, *Radio and the Printed Page,* New York: Duell, Sloan, and Pearce, 1940; B. Berelson and M. Janowitz, *Reader in Public Opinion and Communication,* New York: The Free Press, 1953, Part 7; L. Bogart, "Newspapers in the Age of Television," *Daedalus* (Winter, 1963), pp. 116-127, and other essays in that issue; and the citations in footnote 30 above.

Table 3
EFFORTS TO BE DISCRIMINATING IN MEDIA EXPOSURE, BY

		Lawyers			Professors		
N		Solo (100)	Firm (107)	Total (207)	Church (31)	Urban (68)	Total (99)
DAILY NEWSPAPER *							
Reads at least one quality paper		22	50	36	26	50	42
Does not read a quality paper		78	50	64	74	50	58
RATING OF "SERIOUS" CONTENT IN NEWSPAPERS							
Mentions world news as important		55	67	61	81	87	85
Mentions national news as important		66	84	75	68	85	80
Mentions local news as important		56	42	49	29	22	31
Mentions political news as important		40	29	34	61	62	62
NO. OF QUALITY MAGAZINES READ REGULARLY **							
Three or more		5	13	9	67	64	64
One or two		31	34	33	25	13	17
None		64	52	58	3	1	2
Missing data		0	0	0	3	22	16
CULTURAL, "EDUCATIONAL," SELECTED "SPECIAL" TV SHOWS							
No favorite		72	58	65	42	51	49
One favorite		10	22	16	16	16	16
Two or more		18	21	19	42	32	35
INDISCRIMINATE TV-VIEWING (LETS WHATEVER COMES ON THE CHANNEL STAY, FROM ONE SHOW TO ANOTHER)							
Never		55	64	60	74	60	65
Seldom		23	21	22	19	10	13
Occasionally, often, or almost always		17	11	14	6	7	7
Missing data incl. "no TV" and "never watches"		5	4	4	0	22	15
CLEAR THEME OF CULTURAL CRITICISM APPEARS IN THE INTERVIEW							
Clear cultural criticism		38	50	44	74	76	76
No clear cultural criticism		62	50	56	26	24	24

* *New York Times, Herald Tribune, Washington Post, Christian Science Monitor, Manchester Guardian, St. Louis Post-Dispatch, Wall Street Journal.*

OCCUPATIONAL GROUP AND STRATUM, IN PERCENTAGES

Engineers			Middle Mass Age 21–29		Age 30–55			Underdogs		
Diversico (93)	Unico (91)	Total (184)	WC (69)	BC (54)	WC (251)	BC (304)	Total (678)	Negro (81)	White (105)	Total (186)
10	12	11	0	0	2	1	1	0	0	0
90	88	89	100	100	98	99	99	100	100	100
76	65	71	41	48	41	36	39	41	31	35
76	65	71	52	33	43	36	40	28	33	31
51	58	54	57	35	50	45	47	37	25	30
23	24	23	10	9	24	18	19	4	6	5
8	2	6	0	0	1	0	0	0	0	0
51	60	56	7	0	5	1	3	0	0	0
39	37	38	93	100	94	99	96	100	100	100
2	0	1	0	0	0	0	0	0	0	0
66	70	68	83	83	75	83	80	96	91	94
18	19	18	7	7	10	12	11	4	5	4
16	11	14	10	9	15	5	9	0	4	2
28	29	28	28	41	37	29	33	15	19	17
41	35	38	35	33	36	33	34	36	30	32
12	23	17	17	9	11	15	13	16	19	18
2	2	2	4	6	4	3	3	4	12	9
32	32	32	9	7	21	8	13	0	5	3
68	68	68	91	93	79	92	87	100	95	97

** Includes 41 non-professional periodicals, plus major law reviews, professional journals of engineering societies, and, for professors, all learned and professional journals.

ity magazines read regularly. But the differences in exposure to print among my samples, as well as those in other studies based on broader samples, are not great. Table 3 deliberately reports measures yielding the largest differences in media exposure one can get. Even here, if we pinpoint the groups and take interest in political news as a clue to wider perspectives, the most privileged, well-educated firm lawyers have only a 10 per cent edge over the middle mass; and engineers are about the same as lower white-collar workers. In his interest in world news, the solo lawyer has only a 7 per cent edge over the younger blue-collar worker. The differences in the proportion of diverse groups who rank local news as important to them in their daily reading are similarly small.[32]

Even more uniform from group to group are media habits tapped by more subtle measures of involvement with mass culture not shown in Table 3 —being a loyal rooter for sports teams, rating comics as an important daily experience, becoming deeply involved with media heroes. And when we come to television, at least in America, the constraint of structural differentiation seems doomed; uniformity of behavior and taste is the main story. Nowhere else has a "class" audience been so swiftly transformed into a "mass" audience.

A recent nationwide survey of TV-viewers, sponsored by CBS reports that those with more than four years of college average about 3 hours a day of viewing compared to the 4.3 hours of those with only grammar school education.[33] Admitted prime-time viewing is unrelated to education. When the CBS survey asked them to name their favorite programs (those watched regularly), over half of those at the top of the educational range named light entertainment shows, the overwhelming preference of everyone else. Comedy, variety, and action (i.e., western, adventure, crime, police, private eye)—these were only slightly less common favorites among the college educated than among the less privileged.

Unfortunately, the actual record of viewing—in diaries, for instance— reveals even fewer differences.[34] Education has a lot more to do with how people *feel* about TV than what they *do* with it. College graduates criticize

[32] If you are inclined to use the British as a case on the other side, you will receive little support from Mark Abrams' careful study of the media habits of the socio-cultural elite of Great Britain. "The Mass Media and Social Class in Great Britain," paper presented at the Fourth World Congress of Sociology, Stresa, Italy, September, 1958. The upper 1 per cent in education and occupational status (from a random sample of 13,620 adults, aged 25 and over) reported media habits so similar to those of the mass public, that one is reluctant to use the label "cultural elite." More of them read the *Daily Express* and *Daily Mail* than the *Times* or *Guardian;* their movie habits —both in frequency of attendance and choice of films—are hardly differentiated from those of the rest of the population. The only real gap between mass tastes and elite tastes is the preference of the latter for no TV or BBC programs over commercial programs. A qualification is in order: while prestige dailies lag in circulation, good Sunday papers—the *Observer,* the *Times,* the *Telegraph*—show a marked increase. Further, the recent return to BBC of large television audiences once lost to commercial competition tells us that a speedy decline in mass tastes is not inevitable, although it does not challenge the proposition that the interpenetration of brow levels threatens high culture.

[33] Steiner, *op. cit.,* p. 75.

[34] *Ibid.,* p. 161.

TV programming, but they choose to watch extensively, and in doing so, find themselves in Mr. Minow's wasteland, unable, because of the limited high-brow fare available, to exert much more selectivity than the general population. They clearly display more signs of guilt and uneasiness at this state of affairs, but apparently it's not so punishing that it makes them flick the dial to "off."

Perhaps the most telling data demonstrating the interpenetration of brow levels, not merely in television viewing but also in reading, come from my samples in the Detroit area. Most of those who read at least one high-brow magazine, also read middle- or low-brow magazines. Only 3 per cent of all these men read only high-brow magazines. How about books? *Among college-educated professionals, only one in four claimed to have read a high-brow book in two months.* Only about three in five of the professors and lawyers, the most highly educated, entirely avoid low-brow TV favorites. The typical professor crosses one or two levels of TV exposure. The engineers and executives, middle mass, and the underdogs on relief are quite similar in their TV-viewing habits. Television, again, appears to be a powerful force for cultural standardization, since these groups include men making more than $100,000 and others who have been unemployed for years. The department chief at GM, his foremen, and the unemployed autoworker on relief are bound together in the common culture of Huntley-Brinkley, "Restless Gun," and Mr. Clean.

If we consider magazines, books, newspapers, and TV together, what portion of these groups are exposed to any quality product in more than two areas? The answer: a minority of each group. Forty-three per cent of the professors score high on at least one item in each of three or four areas, 13 per cent of the lawyers, 5 per cent of the engineers and executives, 1 per cent of the middle mass, none of the underdogs.

The fact that the professors did so well in this generally dismal picture encouraged me to carry out a special analysis of deviant cases—those who use print and television for enlightenment and stimulation, and seek the quality product for entertainment.

Portrait of the Media Purist. Who are the media purists—men who insulate themselves fully from mass culture? We could not find one case in 1,354 who was not in some area exposed to middle- or low-brow material. By relaxing the definition, however, we located 19 men who make rather heroic efforts to cultivate the best in the media. They either (1) report some high-brow exposure in all four media areas (magazines, books, newspapers, TV) *and* are exclusively high-brow in one or more reading areas; or (2) have no TV set or never watch TV, have some high-brow exposure in the three reading areas, and are exclusively high-brow in one reading area.

The characteristics of the 19 men suggest that one must be a very odd fellow in America to avoid mass culture. All but two were educated in high-quality liberal arts colleges and graduate schools or were educated abroad —a very rare pattern. In occupation, 16 were professors (13 of high rank, especially in the humanities, mathematics, and physics); three were prosperous corporation lawyers. As a group, the media purists have inherited higher occupational status than their colleagues (their parents tend to be established professionals and executives)—which suggests that it may take rather close family supervision over more than a generation to inculcate a taste for high culture. In religion they are more often Jewish or have no preference or are inactive Protestants. Several are intermarried or in other ways have experienced cultural discontinuity. In origin, training, and position, then, this group is at once high status and marginal.

What constitutes the style of life of media purists? In consumption, they are almost ascetic; among the professors, their relatively high incomes are spent only minimally for luxury possessions, homes, cars, vacations, or charity. They are apartment-dwellers more often than home owners. They tend to be ambitious, independent-minded, like to "go-it-alone." Their media exposure is not only more high-brow; it is more extensive.

Although these media purists stand outside American society ideologically, they are well-integrated socially and politically. As one would expect, they are to a man highly critical of the media. They are also generally estranged from the major power centers in the United States—except for the federal courts, which they feel are doing an excellent job. In participation patterns, however, they belong to more organizations and are attached to more than their colleagues. The professors among them are almost all active, liberal Democrats; the lawyers are conventional, moderate Republicans.

In short, it takes such an unusual set of experiences in family, school, and career to produce a media purist that they are practically non-existent.

IMPLICATIONS FOR SOCIOLOGICAL THEORY

In applying the larger debate about the shape of modern society to the mass media and mass entertainment in America, I have brought systematic survey data to bear on the problem of the interplay of social structure, mass culture, and high culture. I have tried to resolve the paradox of a simultaneous growth of structural differentiation and cultural uniformity by re-examining the structural roots of media exposure and response. These data point up the need for a merger of the main characterizations of modern society—"mass," "industrial," and "urban." Specifically, three lessons can be learned.

1. The sketchy treatment of mass culture in theories of the mass society and the very limited idea of the two-step flow of mass communications, which accents the healthy absorption of the media into local cultures, demand more sophisticated treatment of the social structures in which the media are received. My data suggest that we need to slice up social structure in ways that capture both the persistence of older divisions (age, religion, occupation) and the emergence of newer ones (the quality and content of

education) and to do it more precisely than usual. To say "white collar" or "working class" is to obscure most of what is central to the experience of the person and the structure of society. To say "professional, technical, and kindred" captures more of social life but not much more. "Lawyer" and "engineer" moves us closer to social reality, for these men develop quite different styles of life, rooted in diverse professional schools, tasks, work schedules, and organizational contexts. To say "independent practitioner" is to say even more, and finally, to particularize the matter with "solo lawyer" vs. "firm lawyer" is to take account of the sharp contrasts in recruitment base (social origins, religion, quality of professional training), career pattern and rewards which divide the two.

In general, data both here and in other studies suggest that as predictors of life style variables—especially cultural tastes and ideology—sex, age, and social-economic stratum are far weaker than religion, type of education, work and career—variables that represent positions in established groups. The implication is clear: return to the study of group life.

2. Television, the most "massified" of the mass media, the one with the largest and most heterogeneous audience, has become central to the leisure routine of majorities at every level. The usual differences in media exposure and response among age, sex, and class categories—easy to exaggerate in any case—have virtually disappeared in the case of television. Even here, however, where we pinpoint social groups—an occupation supported by an occupational community, a religion buttressed by a religious community—some differences do remain. And among the printed media, where most competition prevails, the chance of such groups to stylize their uses of mass communications remains strong.

3. The paradox of the simultaneous growth of structural differentiation and cultural uniformity is thus partly a matter of our weak concepts and measures of social structure and our consequent failure to spot group-linked variations in life style. But it may also reflect the state of an affluent society in transition. In order to pin down the cultural impact of continued economic growth, we require data not now in hand. For countries at similar levels of economic development, having diverse cultural traditions and systems of education and communications, we need data on levels of mass taste, organization and self-conceptions of cultural elites, distance between educated and less educated in exposure to mass culture and high culture. Until we have such systematic comparisons, I will assume that structure and culture are congruent and massified in rapidly developing new nations and that they become increasingly *in*congruent at levels of development thus far achieved. Finally, as rich countries grow richer, homogenizing structures in politics, education, and mass communications combine with an already high level of cultural uniformity to reduce the hold of differentiating structures of age, religion, work, and locality, and bring about greater consistency of structure and culture—a new combination of "mass" society and "industrial" society, mass culture and high culture.

4. Many leads in my data point to the need for synthesis not only of

ideas about industrial society and mass society but also of ideas about pluralism and totalitarianism. I can here merely indicate the direction of these findings. Briefly, what takes place in the economy and the locality—work, consumption, and participation in formal associations—forms coherent styles of life, one of which I have come to label "Happy Good Citizen-Consumer." The style includes these pluralist-industrial traits: strong attachment to the community (supporting increased school taxes, contributing generously to churches and charity, thinking of the neighborhood as one's "real home," voting in elections); consumer enthusiasm (planning to buy or to replace many luxury possessions); optimism about national crises; a strong belief that distributive justice prevails (feeling that jobs are distributed fairly). It also involves long hours at gratifying work, little or no leisure malaise; wide-ranging, stable secondary ties and, to some extent, wide-ranging, stable primary ties—the very model of a modern pluralist citizen. But this benign pattern of work, consumption, and participation is independent of participation in and feelings about mass culture. And both happy good citizenry and the uses of the mass media are more or less independent of approaches to national politics—or at least go together in ways not anticipated in received theory. Thus, the good citizen-consumers tend to be unusually prone to personality voting (party-switching, ticket-splitting), dependent on the media for opinions on issues, susceptible to advertising and to mass behavior generally (e.g., they score high on a measure of susceptibility to manipulation by the media in politics and consumption). Men who have confidence in the major institutions of American society distrust "TV and radio networks"; men who trust the media distrust other institutions. Finally, men whose social relations are stable tend to have fluid party loyalties. *To be socially integrated in America is to accept propaganda, advertising, and speedy obsolescence in consumption.* The fact is that those who fit the image of pluralist man in the pluralist society also fit the image of mass man in the mass society. Any accurate picture of the shape of modern society must accommodate these ambiguities.

APPENDIX ON METHODS

To determine the relative effect of each variable and to locate the incidence of high- and low-brow exposure within each class of each variable, I used a technique of multivariate analysis ("multiple classification analysis") which is a simple extension of multiple correlation to situations in which the explanatory factors may be either membership in subclasses like religion or continuous variables divided into classes. The computer program was developed by Vernon Lippitt and the General Electric Company. The rationale is described in Daniel Suits, "Use of Dummy Variables in Regression Equations," *Journal of the American Statistical Association,* 52 (December, 1957), pp. 548-551, and J. N. Morgan *et al., Income and Welfare in the United States,* New York: McGraw-Hill, 1962, Appendix E. The main advantage is that no assumptions are made about the linearity of the effect. The main restriction is the assumption that the effects of various factors are independent or additive; interaction among the independent variables is ignored.

I dealt with this limitation by:

1. Eliminating variables with the most obvious overlap. Occupational group was eliminated because it is highly correlated with level and quality of formal education.

2. Running three- and four-variable cross tabulations where interaction effects might be likely. For instance, one such table shows that weak community attachment (IV-C), which ranks only seventh as a predictor of number of areas of high-brow exposure in Table 1, is strongly associated with high-brow exposure among men with graduate or professional degrees, especially those from elite schools; community attachment has little effect in other educational strata. Scoring low on "good citizen" strengthens the already strong relation between a good education and high-brow exposure; alienation from the local community goes with cultivation of the better products of print and television, and both are rooted in long exposure to the liberal arts.

3. As a further way to avoid reliance on the beta weights in the regression analysis I gave primary attention to the mean of each pattern of media exposure for each subclass of each variable. The several classes of one variable may together rank low as a predictor (II-D ranks 10th on "number of areas high brow") but one subclass based on a small N (51 cases of "much" work alienation) may be very deviant (much high-brow exposure, and, if we look at "Poor TV," much low-brow exposure, too).

Table 1 reports (1) the subclass means adjusted simultaneously for the effects of all the other variables and the intercorrelations among them; and (2) the rank order of the beta coefficients for 17 variables thought to be sources or correlates of media exposure. The categories, grand means, multiple correlation coefficients, variance explained, and "adjusted variance" for the two dependent variables follow:

NUMBER OF MEDIA AREAS IN WHICH RESPONDENT REPORTS ANY HIGH-BROW EXPOSURE	MUCH EXPOSURE TO POOR TV (HIGH NUMBER OF HOURS OF VIEWING; FAVORITES INCLUDE MANY WESTERN, DETECTIVE, AND ADVENTURE SHOWS)
Index Number	*Factor Score*
0. None	40–49. Least poor TV
1. One media area	50–59.
2. Two	60–69.
3. Three	70–72. Most poor TV
4. Four	
$x = .760$	$x = 49.411$
$R = .698$	$R = .530$
$R^2 = .487$	$R^2 = .281$
$R_a = .682$	$R_a = .500$
$R_a^2 = .465$	$R_a^2 = .250$
$p < .001$	$p < .001$

Because my hypotheses here included work milieu and feelings about work, the underdogs and 12 unemployed men of the middle mass were eliminated, leaving 1,156 men for this regression analysis.

Subclass means above the grand mean represent more than the average number of areas of high-brow exposure (.760) or more than the average exposure to poor TV (49.411) for these 1,156 men; subclass means below that are below average. The importance of a variable can be judged both by its rank order and by the size of differences between subclass means and their deviations from the grand mean.

The interpretation can be illustrated by considering variable IV-D, "leisure malaise." The three classes of malaise rank fifth as a predictor of low-brow media exposure. The adjusted means tell us that, holding constant all other classes of all other variables, there remains a moderate difference of 1.491 between (1) the above-average amount of poor TV (50.500) of the men who "fairly often" or "very often" feel they have "time on their hands" when they're not at work and "just don't know what to do" with themselves, and (2) the below-average amount of poor TV (49.009) of men who report they "never" have time on their hands. This variable is a weak predictor of high-brow exposure, however; the men without malaise have only a slight edge in high-brow exposure.

Why is the difference of 1.491 in exposure to poor TV among malaise categories "moderate?" The difference is moderate compared to the difference, say, between the bottom and top classes of education (I-C), the leading predictor. There the subclass "less than high school" scores a very high average of poor TV (53.004) and the subclass "graduate or professional degree, high quality" scores a very low average (44.707)—a difference of 8.297. The discussion of education in the text is based on differences in subclass means in Table 1; the cross-tabulation in Table 2, which uses a different measure of work context and another qualitative measure of television exposure, is consistent with the results of the regression analysis. For instance, the differences in adjusted means of the hours groups, variable II-C in Table 1, are larger between long and medium than between medium and short—the same pattern presented by percentage differences among hours groups in Table 2.

The present study represents an intensive search for cultural differences among subclasses; these differences, typically small, should not obscure the generally high absolute level of mass exposure in every subclass.

Art and the Mass Society

JOSEPH BENSMAN and ISRAEL GERVER

THE WITHDRAWAL OF ARTISTS from concern with social meaning during recent decades stems from two general sources: the *internal* rationalization of art, as found in technical and esthetic systems; and the *external* orientation of art, as indicated in the changing social position of the artist. In this paper both will be treated in detail.

The internal rationalization of art as an esthetic system refers to art as *pure art,* art as a form. As a medium apart from other media, art develops rules, logics and an internal economy of its own. The development of all modern art in the last two centuries is the history of explication, expansion, and development of "inner logics" both for the field and for schools of art. Over a long period of time the esthetic premises of the arts have become more rationalized, self-conscious and self-consistent. Consequently artistic fulfillment consists of expressing and exhausting the possibilities inherent in a set of esthetic assumptions.

Among and within schools there are rivalries between the partisans of divergent esthetic assumptions and techniques. Such factions do not remain static. When the limits of the traditional philosophy are reached, new assumptions are posited and new techniques and modes of creativity are permitted.

The consequences of this process are:

a) The major problems of art become primarily technical, and the artist becomes primarily concerned with problems of techniques. (4) As a consequence, the artist is constrained to focus his attention on methodological problems. The meaning of social experience becomes secondary and in some cases is almost excluded from the scope of art.

b) As the rationalization of each artistic medium develops, its techniques, methods, conventions, rules, language, and logic become more elaborate and precise. The position of artist then requires a thorough, intensive, and prolonged professional training, indoctrination, and practice. At the same time the appreciation of the artistic product increasingly requires a knowledge of those highly sophisticated criteria upon which the work is based. Since a knowledge of such criteria can only be based upon specialized and intensive training, art becomes more and more inaccessible and incomprehensible to those who have not acquired the esthetic standards of appreciation. The work of art is alienated from the taste of the lay public, and artistic interpreters (critics, educators, publicists, managers,

From *Social Problems,* Vol. VI, Summer, 1958, pp. 4-10. Reprinted by permission of the publisher and authors.

dealers) become important in determining the channels by which works of art are exposed to and accepted by an untrained public.

c) The development of self-conscious schools of art is not monolithic. The artistic and esthetic foundations of a school are the results of usage, acceptance by producers of commonly agreed upon esthetic propositions. Even though artists belong to numerous and competing schools, art is still peculiarly a means of personal expression. Specific artists of any one school will emphasize different tenets of a school. Given this situation, the general public is confronted with an overwhelming plentitude of artistic traditions which are presented side by side.

II

The relationship of artistic product to the social position of the artist has been studied and documented in the last century. One major type of analysis has been in the Marxist tradition. It has emphasized the relationship of the artist to the means of production, to the class structure, and to markets. In general, the major thesis of Marxist analysis is that artistic production "reflects" the system of economic and industrial production. The Marxist argument stresses the problems of the market for works of art. Taste is defined as a reflection of changes in the composition and character of the supporting strata for artists, the purchasers of artistic production who compose the market.

Marxists attempt to demonstrate a parallel between the class position of the artist and themes, symbols, avoidances and biases in his artistic production. This leads generally to a circumvention of esthetic considerations. Moreover, over-emphasis on external criteria of artistic productions results less in generalizations about art, and more in generalizations about society. These limitations do not completely invalidate external analysis, so long as it is not used as a simple-minded approach. The same stricture applies to internal analysis.

In modern times there have been many shifts in the relationship of art to society. The Renaissance entailed greater secularization. This occurred along with the rise of new classes with secular tastes, new financial resources for art purchases. The major change in the market relations of the Renaissance artist was primarily from religious to secular patronage.

While the artist had lower social status, the relationship of the artist to his consumer was a close one. The artist participated in and knew the life of his patrons. There was common universe of taste between artist and consumer generated by shared social existence and the special character of the patrons.

The rise of a large middle class in the eighteenth and nineteenth centuries resulted in mass market for art. For example, portraiture was transformed into a middle class art, but more significant than the class nature of such art is its mass character. With mass audiences whose only obligation was the purchase of a ticket, or a book, rather than employment of the artist, art reached monumental proportions. The full symphony orchestra became the characteristic expression of music and it performed for large audiences in architecturally appropriate halls.

Nineteenth century artists captured large audiences by adopting mass themes which expressed national, political, and social aspirations.

Within mass audiences, scientific technology increased the scope within which the artist operated, and the artist was increasingly removed from his audience. Indeed today the musician may make a reputation on phonograph records before he makes a live *début*. Major concert performers such as Artur Rubinstein and Joseph Szigetti were introduced to the musical audience in this country via the phonograph recording. In the past decade the long playing record has accelerated this procedure of promoting performers and composers (both dead and alive) by records rather than by risking expensive live performances. Similarly in painting, the reproduction of pictures has led to a mass audience, but the painter's relationship to the audience has been depersonalized.

The very impersonality of the market place removed the artist from the art consumer. As art consumption adjusted to the purchase price of tickets, books, etc., the type and character of artistic consumers was further differentiated, making it more difficult for the artist to absorb and share the clients' world. Since appreciation of art is associated with the price of a ticket, the intellectual requirements for art consumption are reduced.

The newer art consumers of differentiated background with feebler critical criteria have replaced the stable patron groups of previous eras; correspondingly, the canons of art have become less stable. The artist, not confronting a particular patron, can chose his public from a plurality of possible consumers. He is not bound to fulfill the artistic demands of a specific consumer, nor does he necessarily face a public whose standards are either firm or highly developed.

When the artist appeals to a mass audience, he encounters certain economic gatekeepers: the impresarios, promoters, critics, etc. whose often erroneous stereotypes of the public may become demands upon the artist.

In modern society, where artists have engaged in social commentary, they have more often than not rejected dominant social values. Serious art has generally been hostile or indifferent to industrialism and the middle class way of life. This rejection has not necessarily been programmatic, utopian, or revolutionary, but rather critical of the philistinism and shoddiness of materialistic society.

Serious arts may reject the world by avoiding it—in portraying a world in which formal esthetic concerns are dominant (impressionism, cubism, symbolism, abstract art, etc.)—or reject the world by portraying its most unseemly side (neo-gothicism, surrealism, naturalism, etc.). The very term "naturalism" has less frequently meant portrayal of the world as it is and more frequently refers to the ugliness of the world—the world as unnatural.

Since the artist is not directly concerned with a mass audience, the absence of direct pressures based on personal contacts with a patron frees the artist from all external demands and forces him to develop his own perspectives. The internal standards most directly relevant to the artist *qua* artist are those of technique.

From this there emerges another set of consequences. Art is essentially *exploratory*. Each product is an extension of the past and a feat of *virtuosity*. Mere reproduction of past work is avoided. *Novelty* in virtuosity becomes an end in itself. Freedom from the patron and the particular public, the production for an impersonal market, tends to isolate the producer from the consumer socially and economically. The artist's life patterns are separated from the rest of society, and esthetic concerns intensify this separation.

It is perhaps ironical that the development of the mass middle class audience enables the artist to reject middle class standards in asserting his independence. At times, such assertions of independence surpass the esthetic reasons for independence, for example the phenomena of bohemianism, in which the "artistic attitude" transcends artistic production. As art becomes increasingly concerned with its own dynamics, the freedom of art to pursue artistic ends places serious art at tension with the society.

III

The serious arts, as described above, exhibit two major interrelated tendencies. Serious, self-conscious artists become primarily concerned with the creation, development, expansion, exploration, and criticism of their central techniques and methods. As a result of this attitude, the artists either avoid the world in artistic self-preoccupation, or they reject the world because it ignores and rejects their central core of values. Thus, the artist forsakes the attempt at intellectual leadership where his art would be an instrument to define or influence the society.

This pattern is not true of the mass arts. In the mass arts, the concern with techniques is almost as great as in the serious arts, but the mass arts attempt to express themes and messages characteristic of either everyday life or more precisely what its consumers need or want to believe about everyday life. The mass arts may communicate inaccurately with major distortions but they do communicate!

Since the mass arts involve the use of vast and expensive communication networks, the mass arts are based on heavy capital outlays and fixed expenses. Even when unit costs are low, they can only be profitable when they have a high sales volume. This is especially true of the *"free"* mass arts, radio, TV, and to a large extent the press; for in these sponsored arts, circulation, surveys of readership, and Nielsen ratings are a substitute for sales volume.

Given this apparatus, the mass artists can only be viewed as technicians who are elements of vast and intricate administrative organizations geared to satisfying existing demands. They are assisted by market researchers, whether formally defined as such or not, by promoters, publicity men, agents, financial and other analysts, impresarios, critics, and agency representatives. The content of the artist's work is supplied to him by others, and he must execute the design within the limits of mass formulae. The genius in this field is the artist who is his own market researcher, that is, one who can predict when the largest market will be available for a given technical feat, be it the tough detective of Hammett *et al.* or the plastic models of religious figures which decorate automobile windshields as mass contemporary iconography.

While the mass artist is as involved in problems of techniques as is the serious artist, there are differences. As noted earlier, the technical preoccupations of serious artists result from attempts to solve technical and esthetic problems.

The mass artist can rarely define his own problems, because they are predefined for him by the keepers of the public taste. The solutions are necessarily simple, since they cannot go beyond public knowledge. This also holds for the means of presentation. The mass artist cannot go radically beyond established techniques, because this would violate the canons of established tastes. Instead he must rely on the serious arts to establish and develop new techniques. When these become acceptable to sufficiently large audiences, they can be adopted by the mass artists.

The economics of the mass market determine the content of art and its form. Under the compulsion of the mass approach, the businessman of the arts must attempt to find stereotypes of publics which will support merchandisable products. This is not an easy task. It has been assumed by many analysts of mass mentality that mass means lack of differentiation, and that mass society consists of a vast number of undifferentiated people. This idea reflects an inaccurate derivation of the character of the audience from the standardized products that they consume. Actually, the mass society is a conglomeration of different groups—classes, occupations, perspectives, traditions, geographic, and cultural backgrounds.

The mass arts have to find "meaningful" themes which evoke the experiences of these diverse groups. The cultural level of the mass arts is irrelevant. What is important is an audience large enough to justify a competitive return on an investment. In a society which has a sizeable population, there may be big enough "middle" and even "high brow" audiences to justify the costs of the relatively less expensive mass arts, such as the symphony and opera. When the specialized publics are sufficiently large, it is possible to make money with specialized mass productions addressed to different groups.

As the anticipated potential audiences increase in size, a number of limitations and restrictions are placed on producers. These have been analyzed elsewhere and will only be restated here.

a) The larger the anticipated audience, the greater is the care that the *thematic treatment should not alienate any interest group of the potential audience*. This means that controversial subjects must be ignored, unless the resolution of the conflict is neutral. Such themes should be stated so that no pressure group is likely to attack the work and thereby influence large numbers of potential consumers to boycott the product.

b) Concurrently, characters must be created so that diverse groups can identify them. These symbols of identification are stereotyped abstractions. "Realism" consists of adding external details to the "abstraction" rather than developing the themes and figures from their internal necessity; for example, the use of folk song flavor in movie background music in order to present a convincing rural background.

c) The mass media are constantly vulnerable to intimidation by legal censors and the would-be censors of pressure groups. The controllers of the mass arts must continually estimate and respond to the weights and influences of conflicting pressure and interest groups. The final product is almost always a compromise, an adjustment to these different estimates. It is this form of audience calculus, rather than the internal dynamics of the art form, the creative theme, or the internal logic of the characters and events portrayed, which largely determines the mass product.

d) Since the mass arts are the creation of semi-permanent institutions and associations, the merits of any particular *art product* are viewed by its owners as less important than the maintenance of the institution. Thus, good will, good public relations, respectability, a favorable public esteem are necessary. Artistic producers are always viewed both as technicians and as upholders of public, private, and political morality. Failure to measure up to these may result in catastrophe, even when no technical failure is present.

e) Because of the above factors, the mass arts are conservative. They rarely risk capital in presentations which are beyond the ascertained taste, experience, knowledge and illusions of the audience. This is true of political as well as artistic areas. When large numbers of the members of society go in a new political direction, it becomes feasible for the mass media to move in that direction. The dynamics of such changes lie outside of the sphere of the arts; but, because of this tendency to conform, the mass arts can be used as a device for estimating the underlying state of public opinion. (6) While the principle governing the mass arts is one of conformity to established norms, when marked changes occur, the prescient mass artist (if he guesses correctly) can give public expression to a trend.

The rise of science fiction especially during the post-World War II years provides an example. The number of pulp magazines more than quadrupled and the market spread to the slick magazines which started to publish science fiction. With the public faced with the power of science in the form of atomic bombs, guided missiles, rocketry, space satellites, etc., the mass market for literature involving futuristic possibilities of science was inevitable. Along with the popularity of science fiction there has also developed a distaste for dealing with the harsher potentialities of science for this world.

IV

We have until now emphasized the limitations of the mass arts. They cannot come to grips with reality in such a way as to alienate large segments of their calculated audience. Since in a complex society almost all "problems" are controversial (except where a predetermined solution is prevalent and respectable), the mass arts manifestly avoid these conflicts.

However, the avoidance of all problems *per se* would result in the economic collapse of art as an industry. The initial economic assumptions of the mass arts include their ability to stimulate interest. They must provide some points of relevance to the consumer. The mass arts, while they explicitly avoid the manifest problems of social experience, actually disguise it and mirror the psychological life of their intended audience.

Thus, the mass arts provide scope for identification. The identification symbol may either provide for wish fulfillment or for the release of aggressions and hostilities which the consumer cannot express. Hence, on the one hand, the identifying symbols tend to be wealthy, glamorous, exciting, and to have sexual access to desirable partners, at the same time the protagonists are threatened by outside forces, cannot control their environment, and give expression to types of brutal, violent, and anti-social behavior which are not possible in the ordinary life of the consumer. The mass art production is similar to the world of dreams and phantasy as described by psychoanalysis. All of the elements of reality are present in disguised form. Psychologically the mass arts are different from individual projections in that in modern society the projective mechanisms are alienated from their users. Modern man does not even manufacture his own illusions. Instead they are manufactured for him by an elite corps of scientific mass producers which provides him with comfortable illusions. The primary act of mass art consumers is the act of identification, and modern scientific mass psychological techniques makes such identification easy.

Whether this tendency is desirable or not is beyond the scope of this essay. One can argue that such mass illusion and deception makes it difficult for the consumer to come to grips with reality and hence understand his social world and deal intelligently with his problems.

It is also possible to argue that the mass arts tend to permit the gradual release and displacement of tensions which might otherwise be intolerable;

that direct facing of reality where individuals do not possess the ability or the power to deal with it might lead to radical reconstructions of the society in directions which are not necessarily desirable.

These speculations aside, the dominant fact remains that the world presented by the mass arts to the consumer is a world which manifestly does not exist. The symbolic apparatus of modern society does not adequately describe or clarify his way of life. In the public relations sphere, the consumer's experiences are interpreted in order to permit his manipulation. In the world of serious art his experiences are avoided. In the mass arts his experiences are transvalued so that the consumer can repond in terms of controlled processes of reaction which lead only to relatively crude and synthetic emotions. Thus in all spheres of symbolic communication, the consumer has to try to penetrate a confusion which is impenetrable, and at best he can only occasionally glimpse the underlying reality behind the arts either in their serious or mass forms.

ᕦᕤ   ᕤᕦ

The Rise of the Problem-Film: An Analysis of Changes in Hollywood Films and the American Audience

HERBERT J. GANS

I

SOCIOLOGISTS HAVE PAID ALMOST NO ATTENTION to the movies in recent years, but some significant changes have been taking place in the content of Hollywood films in the past decade. This paper is an impressionistic and highly speculative attempt to describe these changes, to trace the causes within the film industry and in the audience and, finally, to apply these conclusions to the role of movies in American society and to the making of better films.

Until the 1950's, the movies were undoubtedly the major staple in the American entertainment diet, and the major tellers of the fantasies and myths of American society. It is nearly impossible to generalize about the many thousands of films that came out of Hollywood and the many myths these told and retold, but in these films, and especially the *formula-films,*

From *Social Problems,* 9, 1964, pp. 327-336. Reprinted by permission of the publisher and author.

four myths were of major importance. One was the myth of *moral heroism,* portrayed most often in Westerns and mysteries, which described the efforts of a moral individual to achieve social justice and personal satisfaction in a lawless setting. A second myth, that of *youthfulness,* suggested that young people had only to overcome the evil or misguided opposition of an older generation in order to achieve social and individual rewards. The third myth, of the *priority of romance,* proposed that the most important individual reward for social usefulness was an encounter with, and the courtship of an attractive, loving woman, and the fourth myth, the *justification of social mobility,* showed that ordinary persons could strive for wealth without being corrupted by it.

The stars who played these myths to their happy ending were heroic but often shy males who used their virile power to set things right, and glamorous females who appeared to be bad, that is, purely erotic, but turned out to be good, that is, loving.

Movies about the old fantasies and myths are still being made, but over the past decade there has also appeared what might be called the *problem-film,* which deals explicitly with social, sexual and political problems and their solution. The typical problem-film shows how an individual or group is beset by the problem, weaves a plot around the causes and consequences of the problem, describes the moral or ethical issues—and dilemmas—raised both by the problem and by possible solutions, and finally ends with the hero taking appropriate action, usually including a morally difficult choice, which solves the problem, at least for him and his loved ones. Although a few films of this type appear all through Hollywood's history, the contemporary emphasis on the problem-film probably began with the shortlived race relations cycle of the late 1940's, and developed in earnest after the political demise of Joseph McCarthy. In the past few years, Hollywood has made films dealing with—to mention just a few topics— adolescent sexual precocity and juvenile delinquency (*Splendor on the Grass, Sin of Susan Slade, West Side Story, The Young Savages*); familial conflict (*Dark at the Top of the Stairs*); deviate sexuality among adults (for example in the films of Tennessee Williams' plays); McCarthyism and the dilemma of how to deal with ex-Communist liberals (*Manchurian Candidate, Advise and Consent*); foreign aid and the American government's dilemma in supporting right-wing or left-wing extremist governments among the new nations (*Ugly American*); and even atomic war (*On the Beach*).

At the same time, the old myths are being questioned in the *formula-films.* Justice is no longer so easily attainable, for right and wrong are harder to determine. Even young people are shown to have problems, a happy courtship does not guarantee a good marriage, and social mobility is not without its complications.

Similar changes are taking place in the characters of the films, and in the stars who play them. Heroes and heroines are frequently shown to be troubled people, and villains are not evil but sick. The depictions of the private lives of the stars—or the public versions thereof—which once featured an incongruous mixture of carefree romance and normal home-life, now emphasize the fact that they are fragile human beings with emotional problems galore. When Rita Hayworth made *Gilda,* no one wondered whether this love goddess—or the heroine she played—might be beset by personal difficulties, but today more attention is being paid to the difficulties than to the glamor of such contemporary love goddesses as Elizabeth Taylor and the late Marilyn Monroe.

The scope and significance of this change must not be exaggerated, however, and it is especially important to note that the explanation and resolution of the social problems depicted draw extensively on traditional formulas. Psychological explanations have replaced moral ones, but the possibility that delinquency, corruption and even mental illness reside in the social system is not considered, and the resolution of the problem is still left to a hero assisted by the everpresent *deus ex machina.* For example, in *The Young Savages,* delinquency is finally explained as a result of mental retardation and psychopathology; after an initial concern with poverty; in *Advise and Consent,* politicians are described as men who need worry only about their conscience and the consequences of youthful sexual mistakes. The real explanations of Congressional voting behavior: the role of the party organization, the pressure group and the need to placate the voters back home, are ignored, and the dilemma of what to do about the liberal who has lied about his past Communist ties is sidestepped—as in the novel —by a conveniently placed Senatorial suicide and the death of the President. In *The Ugly American,* the problem of reconciling left-wing and right-wing extremist leaders is eliminated by the killing of the former, and the civil war is ended when Marlon Brando strides heroically into the fray.

Thus, the problem is usually shown to result from the deviant acts of a troublemaker or sick person, and both problem and troublemaker are usually removed by a hero who still resembles the Western outlaw or the private eye. That some problems cannot be solved so easily, or that the solutions may require social and political reform is not often suggested. Moreover, few popular films concern themselves with such ordinary but widespread American problems as poverty, segregation, or the emotional and social conflicts of everyday living.

II

How can the change in content be explained? One necessary although not sufficient cause is the emergence of television and its takeover of the old fantasy themes. The formula B picture of the past is now an hourly segment in a television series, although in the last couple of years, the concern with social problems has infiltrated the small screen as well, for example in *The Defenders,* and *East Side, West Side.* A second explanation, heard most often in the film industry itself, is the change in the movie-

makers. At one time, the movies were made by poorly educated entrepreneurs who received their training in the garment industry; today, they
are made by college-educated and relatively urbane men who not only
want to turn out a profitable product but would also like to be considered
occasionally as artists or intellectuals. But this explanation is not sufficient
either. College-educated writers and directors have been the mainstay of
the film industry for well over a generation, but they have come to power
in Hollywood just in the past few years, *and only because the audience has
changed.*

The pre-World War II audience was, or could be conceived as, a mass
audience because so many of its members went to the movies regardless
of what was playing. Today, the audience is not only much smaller, but
more people choose what films they will go to see. As a result, the audience must be viewed as a set of diverse publics with different interests and
tastes that are expressed in the choices they make. These choices can be
shown to reflect *subcultures of taste,* each of which supports specific types
of films, magazines, books, music, and art, for every subculture has somewhat different concepts of beauty, levels of taste, and values concerning
leisure and consumer behavior. In what follows, I shall describe four such
subcultures, and I shall use the "brow-level" terms originally formulated
by Van Wyck Brooks, although I shall use them as descriptive rather than
judgmental categories.*

Perhaps the major elements in the old audience were the poorly educated adults and adolescents, working class in socio-economic level, and
rural or immigrant in origin, whose taste subculture may be described—
and non-pejoratively so—as low brow. The four myths I mentioned earlier
correspond quite closely to their own aspirations to achieve a romantically,
materially and morally satisfying life; and they reflected their own methods
for achieving this life: good intentions, hard work, and the elimination of
bad luck and evil persons who stood in their way. The *formula-films* which
this audience came to see had to justify the belief that a tough but honest
individual could by his own efforts and virtues achieve success in an in-

---

* Part of the discussion following the presentation of my paper argued the opposite:
that Hollywood had made problem-films in the past but was not doing so now, because of
McCarthyism and the still continuing blacklisting of left-wing movie-makers. Although
the blacklist has undoubtedly inhibited Hollywood in dealing with political topics, it
seems to me few films dealing explicitly with social or political problems and issues were
made in the past; even in the 1930's, only a handful of films dealt explicitly with the Depression. Moreover, most of the blacklisted industry members made the same kind of
entertainment and *formula-films* as their colleagues. The movies have always offered passing commentary on various social issues, some of it inserted deliberately, and much of it
the implicit or covert commentary on the society that is intrinsic to all art and entertainment, but the problem-film I describe is a recent phenomenon. Perhaps it is not as out-
spoken as such occasional past films as *The Grapes of Wrath,* but I suspect that this is less
a consequence of the blacklist than of the fact that the audience for such problem-films
is now becoming sizeable enough to make them commercially feasible. The discussion of
the effects of the blacklist is reported in Murray Schumach, "Sociologists Join Attack on
Films," *New York Times,* August 30, 1963.

creasingly bureaucratized American society. In fact, the myths stated several values and realities in working class life, especially in the action-film, with its insistence on a rigid black-and-white morality, the resort to violence, the manly but woman-shy hero, and the heroine whose good-bad ambivalence reflected the working class girl's conflict between being sexually responsive in order to be popular, and remaining virginal until marriage.

Today, no single subculture is dominant in the total audience, although numerically the most important is perhaps the lower-middle brow one, found largely among the high school educated lower middle class population. Since the nuclear family plays a more significant role in its life than among working class people, this subculture is concerned almost as much with marital stability as with romance. It values respectability, abhors eccentricity—which may help to explain the disappearance of slapstick in American comedy—and rejects conflict. It is more cognizant of the difficulties of daily life, and less prone to reliance on luck or fate.

This is not to say that lower-middle brow culture or the people who share it are ready to confront reality in the films. While this population is responsive to the problem-film, it prefers to watch the problems of other subcultures—for example, those of the delinquent or the idle rich—and then only those problems which can be resolved through existing institutions and the application of traditional moral judgments.*

Two other American subcultures, the upper-middle brow and the high brow ones, used to find their entertainment in the legitimate theater, and have only recently begun to attend movies. Although the disappearance of the touring companies has encouraged some of them to see the film versions of Broadway plays, they tend to choose foreign films. These deal more frankly with social problems, and they delve more deeply into characters. In recent years, the artistically most important European films, those made and seen by highbrows, have emphasized the search for identity and the inability to love, two themes which especially concern the serious artist, and an audience which would like to think of itself as artistic. It would be only a slight oversimplification to say that European film-makers have shifted from social problems to love just when Hollywood has begun to go in the other direction.

In addition, the adolescent audience, while always large, has grown in absolute numbers and as a percentage of the total audience, partly because of post war population changes, partly because of the development of separate youth subcultures, and partly because television programs cater mainly to adults and children. The problems of being an adolescent in America:

---

* The unwillingness to see films about one's own problems may be shared by all subcultures, for films that touch the basic concerns of better educated groups have generally not done well at the American art theater box office. Films about American problems are more successful in Europe, just as films about European problems are very popular in this country.

how to achieve adulthood, how to cope with the social and emotional contradictions of teenage status, and how to deal with sexual urges are considered in many films, and are acted out by the youngsters who have suddenly
become Hollywood's biggest stars. These themes are stressed even more
explicitly in today's popular music, which is written almost exclusively for
adolescents, and they are also apparent in the fan magazine treatment of
the romantic or marital troubles of the younger stars.

Hollywood has attempted to cope with the reduction, change and increasing diversity of the audience in a number of ways. One method—which
harks back to earlier days—is to make large budget spectaculars that try to
appeal to every public, with care being taken to provide enough action and
spectacle—not to mention violence—for the low brow group, a "serious"
story line for the middle brows, an array of stars that will attract teenagers
as well as adults, and two romances, one between an older couple, the other
between a younger one.

Another approach has been to film more Broadway plays and best-sell-
ing novels and to rely less on original screenplays. The fiction has already
been tested for its appeal to a mass audience, and the plays have been pre-
sold sufficiently through Broadway publicity to awaken the curiosity of
those interested in, but not yet quite ready to attend the legitimate theater.
The film versions of both are simplified and slightly bowdlerized, the ending is altered to be happy, or morally uplifting, and the stars are selected to
attract the lower-middle brow audience. For example, the film version of
William Gibson's play *Two for the See-Saw* featured Shirley MacLaine and
Robert Mitchum, who have usually played lower middle class and even
working class characters and are less "ethnic" and cosmopolitan—and also
more easily identified as heroine and villain—than Anne Bancroft and Henry
Fonda, who starred in the play.

Hollywood's treatment of social and political problems stems in part
from the use of plays and novels, but the creation of the problem-film is as
much a result of the availability of a sufficiently educated and tolerant audience as it is a transfer of content from other mass media. The same is true
of Hollywood's increasingly explicit treatment of sexual relationships, which
also began on Broadway and in the novel, but has been given considerable
impetus because it enables Hollywood to offer an attraction not yet possible
on the TV screen with which it is in constant and desperate competition.

But in some ways the most significant adjustment to the change in the
audience has been the breakup of the studio, that monolithic dictatorship in
which a single head directed the making of films—by a quasi-mass production schedule—for a single or mass audience. The rise of independent film
companies has enabled individual film-makers to make their own films
which reflect at least in part their personal ideas and tastes. The diversity in
film-makers and the films they make responds to the greater diversity that
now exists in the total audience.

III

I have argued that changes in film content can be traced to changes in the audience, and that the content changes are therefore ultimately to be seen as responses to transformations in American society. This raises an important and little studied question: how is the change in the audience translated into content change, especially if, as I have argued, film-makers are now able to express their personal ideas, and in light of the fact that Hollywood does not conduct market research, and thus gets little direct feedback from the audience?

For one thing, the movie-makers do operate in a market context, and must return a profit to their investors. Thus, they can be conceived as catering to, and campaigning for, the wishes of the audience, much like other businessmen or, perhaps more aptly, like politicians. There is, however, a considerable difference between the role of the audience in movie-making, and that of the voters in political campaigning. Politicians compete against each other in an election in which only one can win, and each candidate must therefore tailor the subject matter and the public image of his own person carefully to the expectations of the voters. Film-makers do not "run" against each quite so directly, and while a financially unsuccessful film may hurt their careers, a failure does not eliminate them from the competition. Thus, they need not be quite as conscious of the characteristics and the expectations of their constituents. They rely on general industry experience based on box office receipts (even if the meaning of these is at best ambiguous), their own intuitive judgments about what the audience will like and, above all, how well the individual scenes and the film as a whole "play", a criterion by which the movie-maker estimates how well these come across, perhaps to an imaginary audience member. Before the movie is released, there may be some changes (sometimes called artistic compromises) to enhance the likelihood of financial success.

Moreover, every creative decision made in the film, from the choice of a subject, the selection of stars, the emphases in the plot, the resolution of the dramatic tension, to the method of advertising the finished product has implications for who will come to see the film, and who will like what he sees. Thus, when the movie-maker makes a decision that accords with his own esthetic standards, he is also making a decision that will appeal to like-minded audience members, and repel others. Since films are a group product, the making of films can be analyzed to show how the final product is the result of a partial compromise between different people whose own tastes resemble those of different segments of the total audience. If the film-makers are successful, if their own choices are in agreement with a sufficient number of people to allow the film to show a profit, they are encouraged to make other films; if the film "dies" at the box-office, the film-maker who is responsible must change his approach until he is able to communicate to a large enough audience, or at least to persuade investors that he can do so.

The crucial point here is that today the successful movie-makers must share the tastes and preferences of at least part of their total audience; unlike the men who made the B pictures of the past, and now make the formula television series that appeal primarily to low brow tastes, the cultural gap between themselves and their audience is much reduced. As a result, the audience is "represented" at the camera, because the movie-maker is himself like the audience. To put it another way, while the politicians use *direct feedback* through public opinion polls and voter surveys, the movie-makers keep in touch with the audience through *indirect feedback* created by the sharing of tastes. Moreover, different movie-makers appeal to, and thus represent, different subcultures in the audience. John Huston or Billy Wilder make different films than Ross Hunter or Sam Goldwyn, and these differences reflect not only their own approaches to film-making, but at the same time the preferences of different audience publics. In this way, the diversity of the audience is mirrored in the diversity of the movie-makers.

Is this description of the movie-making process and the indirect feedback tie to the audience accurate? We do not know, for there are no studies of how film-makers choose the films they make, the way they make them, and the extent to which they have some picture of the eventual audience in mind as they work on the film. Moreover, almost nothing is known about how the audience reacts to the films it sees. Box office receipts tell the film-makers only how people felt about the film before they saw it, but not how they reacted to the film they paid for, except insofar as their word-of-mouth advertising is reflected in subsequent box office receipts. These are a poor source of feedback, however, for radically different conclusions about audience reactions can be reached from the same box-office figures, and it is impossible to tell which aspects of the film were liked or disliked.

Thus, no one knows how well the indirect feedback works, how well the movie-makers communicate with and satisfy the audience. There is no information about how the audience reacts to the new type of film content: whether people find it interesting, whether they would accept franker discussions and more adequate explanations of the problems filmed, or whether they would just as soon see the old fantasies. Since no one has asked the audience such questions, there are endless debates about audience reactions, with the critics claiming that Hollywood underestimates audience sophistication, and the movie-makers retorting that they do not. Nor is there any explicit concern with the diversity of the audience, for the critics do not think in terms of the ticket buyers, and the movie-maker who offers pronouncements on the subject in *Variety* usually projects his own tastes on the audience, and ascribes to the entire audience preferences that are actually held by only a part of it.

IV

My description of the changes in American films and of the movie-making process has so far been purely empirical, as befits a sociological paper. But implicit in what I have said there are value judgments. By making these explicit, I would like to show what implications the descriptive model has for the evaluation of films, and the making of better ones.

When I noted that the audience could be divided into several taste subcultures, I suggested also that each subculture has a somewhat different concept of what is good or beautiful: a film that is thought good by the lower-middle brow group may be judged bad by high brows, and vice versa. Implied in my description of these groups was the belief that each subculture is entitled to its own judgment. Elsewhere, I have argued that the esthetic pluralism resulting from the diversity of subcultures is justified because variations in esthetic judgments are ultimately the result of differences in socio-economic background and especially in education. While I would agree that the cultures of the "higher" brow levels are, on the basis of an absolute standard, more insightful, more satisfying and thus more desirable, they also assume a kind of sophistication that requires a liberal arts education of superior quality. Most high brows have had such an education and, without it, they would not hold and practice the esthetic standards they do. Unless and until other people can obtain—and accept—this education, one cannot expect them to share the requisite standards, and one must therefore respect their own standards, which reflect the desire for beauty and goodness as much as do high brow ones. One can only ask—but one can ask—that people pursue their own standards of what is good and beautiful, and that they live up to these standards in their esthetic choices. I distinguish here between what people think is good—esthetic standards—and what they want—esthetic choices—for they often want and choose things which they do not consider to be good. This is as true of the high brow, for example, when he reads detective stories, as it is of the low brow.

The existence of esthetic pluralism means that there can be no easy agreement as to what is a good movie or, for that matter, a bad one—although there may be some movies that somehow meet the standards of all subcultures, and there is probably some consensus among subcultures about what makes a bad movie bad.

How can the film industry deal with esthetic pluralism? Two conditions are necessary; that they try to make the kinds of movies they consider good, and that enough diversity exists among movie-makers to assure that all subcultures are supplied with what they consider to be good movies. The subcultures now served most poorly by Hollywood are the upper-middle and the high brow ones, partly because their needs are often met by foreign films, and the low brow one. This group, being unable to respond to the more sophisticated films made for the middle brow audiences has little choice among movies, and is therefore frequently victimized by shoddy or cliché-ridden "quickies". A more conscientious attempt to understand low brow standards, and to make films that meet this standard is badly needed.

The attainment of subcultural diversity also requires the development of film criticism that voices the esthetic standards of groups other than the upper-middle and highbrow cultures. At present, criticism is written for these cultures alone, and the rest of the population is served only by film reviewers. The critics pay most attention to foreign films and, in recent years, some have also rediscovered the Hollywood films of the 1930-1945 period. The detachment created by hindsight allows the critics to see social and cultural commentary in the old films that was not visible when these were first made, and as a result the critics have made high culture artists out of many popular directors and stars of the past, among them Humphrey Bogart and the Marx Brothers.

Now it is easy to ascribe these preoccupations to the perversity of the critics—as the film industry so often does—but a much better explanation can be found in the fact that they write for, and represent, a group which has always been more interested in European than American culture, and which has traditionally taken over aspects of older folk and popular cultures after these were dropped by the folk. The critics' interest in old Hollywood films is thus part of the high brow interest in old folk art. Demanding that these critics pay more attention to current Hollywood films is both unfair and useless; what is needed is the recruitment of additional critics who have sympathy with, and understanding for, the esthetic standards of other groups in the population, and who can write the kind of criticism that will be read by these groups.

Another important requirement for subcultural diversity is the development of audience research. If movie-makers knew more about their audiences—not statistical studies of audience characteristics that quantify the already known, but narrative analyses (including ultimately quantifiable ones) of how the various publics react to specific films, what they see in them, and how they understand and judge what they see—it would remove some of the uncertainty under which the film industry operates. If such knowledge were added to the intuitive ability of the movie-maker to appeal to an audience, it might allow him to get closer to the audience, to make movies that touch it more than they now do. In addition, greater knowledge about the audience might enable the movie-maker to be less fearful about what the audience will or will not accept, or what pressure groups representing only a small number of dissident ticket-buyers might do to hurt the films at the box-office. Research is by itself no magic cure for the ailments of the film industry, of course. Care would also have to be taken that it does not stifle the creativity of the movie-maker or cause him to respond mechanically to the data showing what people have chosen in the past. This danger is small, however, if only because people wish to be entertained—and therefore surprised. As a result, they do not have any overt wants that they can state in advance, and data on their past wants and choices are never directly applicable to the future.

Finally, the proliferation of the problem-film is likely to make Hollywood a more important source of social commentary on the issues of the day than ever before. I think this is a desirable change. The Hollywood films of the past generally made only veiled or covert references to social problems, and only the critics and the highly educated audience, trained to read between the lines, could perceive them. In the problem-film, this commentary has become explicit, and is thus available to many more people in the audience.

Hollywood films may therefore assume a more significant role in American society even as their function as a model for consumer and social behavior continues to decrease. The same people who read only the headlines in the daily newspaper or watch the five minute news telecast will spend two hours or more seeing films dealing with delinquency or Congressional politics. Thus, movies provide information for the citizenship role even as they entertain. Of course, they may at the same time offer distorted descriptions of and facile solutions to the social problems with which they deal; the ending that allows the audience to leave the theater happily can also mislead it.

Some distortion of information is probably unavoidable because it is unconscious and derives from the film-maker's participation in the predominant frame of reference of American culture. But distortion may also be conscious, and this must either be avoided or, better still, identified by an explicit statement of the film's and the film-maker's values. I am not arguing that the movies should become documentaries, however, for their fictional and dramatic form gives them a better opportunity of attracting those people now least amenable to accepting information and ideas from the news media and educational institutions.

Effects studies have shown that the movies can do relatively little to change fundamental ideas, but the magic of the medium is such that it can encourage audiences to think, and to question their preconceptions as they sit in the darkness of the theater, temporarily isolated from society. For this reason alone, the rise of the problem-film, even with all its present deficiencies, is a desirable development.

FURTHER READINGS

Kornhauser, William. *The Politics of Mass Society.* New York: The Free Press, 1956.

Rosenberg, Bernard, Gerver, Israel, and Howton, William, eds. *Mass Society in Crisis.* New York: Macmillan, 1964.

———, and White, David Manning, eds. *Mass Culture.* New York: The Free Press, 1957. Paper, 1965.

White, Winston. *Beyond Conformity.* New York: The Free Press, 1962.

13

EPILOGUE

IN CONCLUDING THIS VOLUME we reprint a modified version of an earlier paper written by the Editor which covers a variety of issues dealt with in the several chapters of this book. Although this paper is not sufficient to integrate all the ideas dealt with earlier it does attempt to provide an overview of the kinds of dynamic processes which are characteristic of American society and, perhaps, other highly urbanized-bureaucratized-industrialized societies. Our focus is on two concepts, alienation and anomie, which have been the subject of numerous papers and books not only in sociology but in the humanities as well.

Our goal throughout this book has been to stimulate thought about the basic fabric out of which American society is woven. Both its emergent social structure and its values have played upon one another to bring about what is probably the most complex social system the world has ever known. Thus its very complexity compels a kind of insight into its fundamental processes, something never really required of the participant in simpler societies.

Sociology, if it does not offer prescriptions, can certainly direct us to important questions, alternative solutions and probable consequences. These readings and our comments about them should make it clear that the sociologist of today and yesterday has a great deal to offer to the explication of social issues.

Alienation, Anomie and the American Dream

EPHRAIM HAROLD MIZRUCHI

Two CONCEPTS which have become increasingly important in the sociological literature are alienation and anomie. While the concept alienation has most often been associated with the work of Karl Marx, particularly his earlier writings, anomie was introduced to sociology by Emile Durkheim. In recent years sociologists have operationalized these concepts in order to utilize them in empirical research. Melvin Seeman and his students have developed measures of alienation which have been applied in a variety of research tasks and Leo Srole's anomia scale has also been fruitful in empirical analysis.

The present paper is more speculative and descriptive than the kinds of papers which characterize analytical reports which attempt to place a specific set of findings into a particular stream of thought. Our interest here is to suggest that these concepts can enhance our understanding of major processes occurring in contemporary American life. Thus our statements should be interpreted as hypotheses rather than conclusive generalizations.

Marx's concept of alienation was most clearly formulated in his *Economic and Philosophic Manuscripts of 1844*. Unlike Hegel and Feuerbach whom he derided for their metaphysical philosophies, Marx approached alienation within a specific institutional context, the economy.

Marx held that four types of alienation emerged directly from the work situation: (1) alienation from the *process* of work; (2) alienation from the *products* of work; (3) alienation of the worker from *himself;* and (4) the alienation of the worker from *others.*

Marx's concern, at this stage of his career, was with the impact of the Industrial Revolution on man. Like the existentialist philosophers who were his contemporaries, such as Kirkegaard, he was concerned with the complexities of achieving a meaningful, productive experience for the person in modern society. It was to man's *subjective* reaction to an *objective* societal condition that Marx's early efforts were directed.

Durkheim was also deeply concerned with the outcomes of the Industrial Revolution. From his perspective the disruptive processes created strains in man's relationships with others and his aspirations for himself. Noting that suicide rates increase both in times of poverty and prosperity Durkheim introduced the notion of *anomie* to the sociologists of the twen-

Adapted from "Alienation and Anomie: Theoretical and Empirical Perspectives," *The New Sociology: Essays in Honor of C. Wright Mills,* edited by Irving Louis Horowitz, New York: Oxford University Press, 1964; Galaxy Books, 1965, pp. 253-267. *Cf.* also, Ephraim H. Mizruchi, *Success and Opportunity: A Study of Anomie,* New York: The Free Press, 1964.

tieth century. Primarily interested in the effects of anomie during times of economic prosperity it was that aspect which had reference to the striving for unattainable goals which he stressed. Under conditions of relative stability social mobility is somewhat limited and man strives for limited but genuine goals. Under stable conditions, however, these limits are removed.

> The limits are unknown between the possible and the impossible, what is just and what is unjust, legitimate claims and hopes and those which are immoderate. Consequently there is no restraint upon aspirations . . . With increased prosperity desires increase.

Thus, unlike Marx's concept of alienation, which referred to man's feeling of estrangement from work and its products, self and others, Durkheim's concept was directed to a condition of the social system in which the rules of the group no longer provide limits to man's impulses.

During the past two decades Robert K. Merton's rendering of anomie has had a decided effect on contemporary sociology. Stressing Durkheim's suggestion that the *deregulation of goals* is not the only condition of anomie Merton focuses on the *deregulation of means*. To Merton, concerned primarily with the causal nexus surrounding deviant behavior, anomie is a result of the disjunction between socially mandated goals and the structurally available means for the attainment of these goals. More specifically, the great emphasis placed on "success" in American society and the lack of corresponding emphasis placed on legitimate means for its attainment leads to a "demoralization" of the means.

Furthermore, since there is unequal access to the remaining legitimate channels for the attainment of success goals there will be unequal utilization of illegitimate means. In short, the less access to legitimate channels the greater the deviant behavior in the form of crime, delinquency and the like. Thus Merton's theory has been widely used to explain what are presumably higher crime and delinquency rates in the relatively lower classes as compared with higher classes.

What is interesting in this context, among other things, is that although Merton presumably takes his cue from Durkheim, for whom the greatest impact of social change affects the *more* affluent classes, his theory suggests that the *less* affluent classes suffer most from these processes. Thus it is in those classes in which Marx identified the process of alienation that Merton expects the greatest effects of anomie.

In order to throw light on the Merton hypothesis the writer undertook an elaborate research project in a small city in upper New York state. By the use of interviews with 618 respondents in 1958 and 227 in 1960 it was possible to gain some insight into aspects of anomie as formulated by both Durkheim and Merton. Among the extensive findings, was that although there was a generally greater tendency for lower class respondents to obtain high scores on Srole's anomia scale, when multivariate analysis was utilized it was those in the relatively higher classes who were significantly more frustrated when they felt that their opportunities were circumscribed than were those in the lower classes. The same relationship held for employment status. Thus it was not the *lower* classes who felt the greatest impact of limited opportunity to attain success goals, it was the *middle* classes.

A close examination of the nature of the values associated with success, held by the various classes, adds some clarity to these observations. By and large the middle classes seek more nebulous and more difficult to attain goals associated with worthy *achievements* while the lower classes focus on *rewards*. In short, our data suggest that the middle classes suffer most from what we have termed the "Myth of Infinite Elevation," the notion that there is no end to one's expectations.

In this altogether too brief summary of some of our empirical data it is the nature of the differential definitions of success and its consequences which appear to be most meaningful in terms of the classical tradition. For the nature of work is integrally bound up with the kinds of goals to which the lower classes aspire and the peculiar condition of the middle classes *seems to encourage unrealistic aspirations.*

CONTEMPORARY AMERICAN SOCIETY

The analysis which we have presented here suggests that contemporary American society is suffering from the combined effects of both alienation and anomie. Let us look at these processes in several contexts.

WORK AND VALUES

The concern with *rewards* for performance rather than *worthy accomplishment* on the job, or *success* as contrasted with *achievement,* on the part of our numerically largest segment of the population makes it clear that work is not seen as an end in itself, a condition predicted by Marx. The emphasis on *rewards* as contrasted with achievement strongly suggests alienation from work in the relatively lower classes.

Marx, it will be recalled, held that work in industrial societies tended to give rise to two types of alienation in the occupational sphere. Alienation from the process of work itself represents one type. The second was alienation from the products of one's work. There is mounting evidence derived from a great deal of sociological research which supports Marx's speculative hypotheses. One excellent example of alienation from the process of work itself is reflected in an interesting study by industrial sociologist Donald F. Roy.

While observing in a factory Roy held a piece-work job on the assembly-line. Roy's observations suggest that mental self-manipulation appears to be characteristic of the assembly-line work process . . . "making out on piece-work could be a stimulating game only as long as the job represented a real challenge to the operator, only as long as the element of uncertainty was present in the activity's outcome." In short, work typically involved no challenge.

The many studies of work-group control of rate of output on the assembly line including, for example, the Roethlisberger and Dickson study, suggests that much of the activity which characterizes factory work is inherently alienative since work satisfaction seemingly is not an inherent outcome of the work process in these contexts.

In addition to the *process* of work itself there is little opportunity for today's factory worker to enjoy personal attachment to those objects which he has created, if only in part. The assembly-line method has homogenized the products of the worker's efforts to conform to the needs of a standardized industrial system. Parts made in Toledo, Ohio, must meet precise measures in order to fit other units which are assembled in a Detroit automobile plant.

One of our informants in the community in which the foregoing study was done took the researcher on a tour of the factory in which he has worked for almost two decades. Currently a parts inspector, this man has worked on the line from the beginning of his career. In describing the work and in showing the writer the parts which were made in the plant he seemed to be taking personal pride in the items produced and in the way things were done. But the very handling of the parts, the throwing and dropping and casualness with which they were treated, suggested that there is little opportunity for identification with the material results of one's efforts in this type of work.

In an essay, "The Myth of the Happy Worker," Harvey Swados also addresses himself to the attitudes which workers have toward their work and its products.

> The worker's attitude toward his work is generally compounded of hatred, shame and resignation. . . . They know that there is a difference between working with your back and working with your behind. (I do not make the distinction between hand-work and brain-work, since we are all learning that white-collar work is becoming less and less brain-work.) They know that they work harder than the middle-class for less money. . . . Nor is it simply . . . status-hunger that makes a man hate work that is mindless, endless, stupefying, sweaty, filthy, noisy, exhausting, insecure in its prospects, and practically without hope of advancement.
>
> The plain truth is that factory work is degrading. It is degrading to any man who ever dreams of doing something worthwhile with his life; and it is about time we faced the fact.
>
> *The more a man is exposed to middle-class values, the more sophisticated he becomes and the more production-line work is degrading to him.* [Italics ours.]

Swados' observations, made during his periodic employment as a factory worker, provide us with more than a description of alienation from the process of work. In the italicized statement it appears that both alienation and anomie are intertwined as factors in the relationship between aspirations associated with the larger society—presumably middle-class consumption values—and the work situation. This is consistent with our position that the two processes are bound up with each other. Furthermore there is the suggestion that one's self-esteem is bound up with work which alludes to alienation from self and others.

Swados also offers some instructive comments with respect to alienation from the product, in this case, the automobile.

> On the one hand it is admired and desired as a symbol of freedom, almost a substitute for freedom, not because the worker participated in making it, but because our whole culture is dedicated to the proposition that the automobile is both necessary and beautiful. On the other hand it is hated and despised—so much that if your new car smells bad it may be due to a banana peel crammed down its gullet and sealed up thereafter, so much so that if your dealer can't locate the rattle in your new car you might ask him to open the welds on one of those tail fins and vacuum out the nuts and bolts thrown in by workers sabotaging their own product.

We could well ask, given these circumstances in the working-class occupational sphere, would we expect to find an interest in excellence on the job or achievement values? We could hardly expect this kind of orientation to work. As we noted earlier emphasis on *rewards* is more characteristic of the working class respondents in our sample. *Achievement goals* must be attained in other types of occupations, primarily those associated with the relatively higher classes.

Similarly, emphasis on excellence is more likely to be associated with occupations reflecting emphasis on worthy accomplishments than those which stress rewards. Excellence, as a mode of performing, tends to be integrally bound up with occupations which reflect achievement rather than success values.

But what of the middle-class white collar employee? Is his work challenging and gratifying? While we have suggested earlier that there is a greater tendency to view getting ahead in achievement terms in the relatively higher classes this does not necessarily imply that the vast majority of workers in these classes are actually engaged in more meaningful work than those in the lower classes.

Swados has mentioned that "white collar work is becoming less and less brain-work." Standardization and automation are making robots of the middle-class worker as well. Even in teaching, educational television threatens to make more of an automaton of our teachers than the bureaucratic organization of formal education has already accomplished. In the white collar spheres as in industry personal gratification as a result of work as an end in itself and also as a result of the products of one's efforts is a feeling enjoyed by the few rather than the many.

This process was already in evidence during the Lynds' second study of Middletown during the middle 1930's.

It is important to note the strains which current cultural demands for dominance and aggression create in the individual personality. The pursuit of 'success,' particularly in the business world where the males of the culture struggle, involves the acceptance of a heavy burden of disciplines and constraints. Most people, as a result, spend most of their time doing things in which they are not particularly interested, at a tempo which is not their own but dictated by the system. As Lawrence K. Frank has pointed out, to be 'businesslike' means in our present culture to be 'impersonal.' This is but one of the false faces that the culture forces man to wear. Everywhere one is confronted by the demand that one be 'on time,' act 'like a man,' hide one's emotions, talk and appear 'successful,' be 'energetic,' 'sure of oneself,' and so on indefinitely through the stereotypes of being 'regular.' Along with this channeling of individual bent and temperament that the 'success pattern' imposes upon many businessmen must be noted in the case of the workingman the major constraints of inactivity due to recurrent unemployment and to being 'bottom dog' in a culture which habitually stresses and glorifies the traits and possessions of its 'top dogs.'

Galbraith too, has suggested that even achievement may no longer be a worthy goal among higher level employees in this quotation from *The Affluent Society*.

The rise of the public relations industry, which draws its clientele overwhelmingly from among business executives, shows that business achievement is no longer of itself a source of acclaim. At a minimum the achievement must be advertised. But the first task of the public relations man, on taking over a business client, is to 're-engineer' his image to include something besides the production of goods. His subject must be a statesman, a patron of education, or a civic force. Increasingly some artistic or intellectual facet must be found. A businessman who reads *Business Week* is lost to fame. One who reads Proust is marked for greatness.

What we are suggesting here is that: first, the conception of success values may be a reflection of the nature of the work process: second, the material level of living which a group aspires to or has attained and: third, changes are occurring in all spheres of work.

As work becomes more instrumentalized, and current tendencies seem to be in this direction, gratification as a result of the work process will diminish. Indications are that the Protestant Ethic with its emphasis upon work as an end in itself is on the decline as a normative system. If this is indeed occurring then one of the most important sources for meaningful activity and direction in American society is threatened with extinction.

The problem must next be confronted in functional terms. Since one of the important requirements in a social system is a system of *motivation* which will encourage group participants to perform those jobs necessary for the maintenance of organized group life, American society itself may be threatened by the process of increasing instrumentalization.

The problem of motivation leads us to a speculative hypothesis. We

suggested above that the middle classes are provided with an already existing avenue for attaining alternate achievement goals. The alternative to
which we are referring is formal social participation which affords recognition for the active member of the organized group. It is in the nature of
social processes that norms, for example, may emerge as a result of activities which are associated with processes having little to do with the
objectives of these acts. We would hypothesize that while in the lower
classes criminal norms have, in the least, been reinforced as a result of
aspirational strains, in the middle classes a set of counter norms has emerged
which has a tendency to limit the emphasis upon achievement goals in the
occupational sphere. As William H. Whyte, Jr., has shown there is a growing
tendency for the suburban middle classes to place greater emphasis upon
security than on hard work, a major pattern in the quest to attain occupational goals, and an almost intense pattern of participation in formal associations. If there has been a diminishing emphasis upon individualism, as
both Whyte and David Reisman have held, then this, in part at least, may be
viewed against the background of both general affluence and the emergence
of a set of norms which have resulted from reactions to the strains associated with circumscribed opportunities and intense competition in the
occupational sphere. Whyte has suggested that aspirations have indeed
changed although his explanation for the change is at variance with our
own. In his words,

> The young men speak of 'the plateau.' If they were to find this haven they
> would prove that the Social Ethic is personally fulfilling. For the goal of the
> plateau is in complete consonance with it; one's ambition is not a personal
> thing that craves achievement for achievement's sake or an ego that demands
> self-expression. It is an ambition directed outward to the satisfaction of mak-
> ing others happy. Competitive struggle loses its meaning; in the harmonious
> organization one has most of the material rewards necessary for the good life,
> and none of the gnawing pains of the old kind of striving.

In short, there is a more limited effort to forge ahead in the occupational sphere since achievement goals can be attained with much less hazard
in other spheres of American life and the minimum material rewards are
accumulated, at least for this segment of the population, without a great
deal of competitive effort.

Although this hypothesis is highly speculative it is consistent with our
explanation for lower class anomie as compared with middle class anomie
above.

We held earlier that certain processes, e.g., education, must be pursued
as ends in themselves in order to provide optimum performance on the part
of the individual. More important, however, we noted that institutional
processes are characterized by end-valuation rather than means-valuation.
Society cannot afford to have certain processes come about as a result of
chance factors alone. Thus certain patterns come to be perceived as worthy

of one's efforts. Of these patterns some become mandatory and are incorporated into the institutional system.

If work comes to mean little more than a means to a livelihood then it might well be that the functional prerequisites may not be fulfilled in a manner which will, in the very least, maintain the American social system. In short, if the will to work is threatened the social system is likewise threatened.

PROSPERITY, POVERTY AND ANOMIE

And what of man the person? What will be the sources of personal gratification for him?

The constant proliferation of new hobbies and do-it-yourself programs suggests that these could become the primary source of gratification for man in this society. Many of us are already deluged with the problem of excessive leisure time and the mass culture lamentors have been quick to point out that the leisurely are being misled. Emphasis appears to be directed to the novel and superficial rather than to *haute couture*.

Indeed, Durkheim was not unaware of similar processes accompanying anomie during periods of excessive prosperity. As he pointed out in *Suicide*, "A thirst arises for novelties, unfamiliar pleasures, nameless sensations, all of which lose their savor once known."

Leisure time activities *as they are currently constituted,* it would seem, are not likely to emerge as meaningful alternatives to work.

Although it is hazardous to generalize too broadly there seem to be few situations in American life in which unrealistic expectations do not constitute a problem. Daniel Boorstin has suggested this in somewhat dramatic terms in a recent book, *The Image*. Characterizing Americans in terms similar to Kluckhohn's in *Mirror for Man*, Boorstin describes us as engaged in efforts to "fill our void."

> We [Americans] expect too much of the world. Our expectations are extravagant in the precise dictionary sense of the word—'going beyond the limits of reason or moderation.' They are excessive.
>
> When we pick up our newspaper at breakfast, we expect—we even demand —that it bring us momentous events since the night before. We turn on the car radio as we drive to work and expect 'news' to have occurred since the morning newspaper went to press. Returning in the evening, we expect our house not only to shelter us, to keep us warm in winter and cool in summer, but to relax us, to dignify us, to encompass us with soft music and interesting hobbies, to be a playground, a theatre and a bar. We expect our two week vacation to be romantic, exotic, cheap and effortless. We expect a faraway atmosphere if we go to a nearby place; and we expect everything to be relaxing, sanitary, and Americanized if we go to a faraway place. We expect new heroes every season, a literary masterpiece every month, a dramatic spectacular every week, a rare sensation every night. We expect everybody to

feel free to disagree, yet we expect everybody to be loyal, not to rock the boat or take the Fifth Amendment. We expect everybody to believe deeply in his religion, yet not to think less of others for not believing. We expect our nation to be strong and great and vast and varied and prepared for every challenge; yet we expect our 'national purpose' to be clear and simple, something that gives direction to the lives of nearly two hundred million people and yet can be bought in a paperback at the corner drugstore for a dollar. . . .

We expect anything and everything. We expect the contradicting and the impossible. We expect compact cars which are spacious; luxurious cars which are economical. We expect to be rich and charitable, powerful and merciful, active and reflective, kind and competitive. We expect to be inspired by mediocre appeals for 'excellence,' to be made literate by illiterate appeals for literacy. We expect to eat and stay thin, to be constantly on the move and ever more neighborly, to go to a 'church of our choice' and yet feel its guiding power over us, to revere God and to be God. . . .

Never have people been more the masters of their environment. Yet never has a people felt more deceived and disappointed. For never has a people expected so much more than the world could offer.

The problems associated with the marked tendency towards instrumentalization of work seem to be symptoms of more fundamental conditions in which the very social fabric, i.e., the normative system is threatened with annihilation. Indeed, this is the import of the pleas being made by Erich Fromm, Hannah Arendt and Erich Kahler, to name only a few.

But some writers do not see this in what is simply a foreboding aspect. William Kornhauser in his *The Politics of Mass Society*, concludes his interesting study with the suggestion that the process of mass society carries with itself not only the possibility of social alienation but "enhanced opportunities for the creation of new forms of association . . . Modern industry destroys the conditions for a new society of small enterprises, but it also provides the condition of abundance which frees people to seek new ways of life."

"Abundance" is, however, a major source of difficulty for contemporary American society. If there is any one factor which Durkheim stressed which can be isolated as a major source of malintegration it is abundance.

It is doubtful whether Durkheim could have envisaged a society in which middle class families could reasonably expect to own two automobiles, as many television sets and untold numbers of radios. Nor is it likely that he could have imagined how extravagant expectations could become.

Boorstin's comments could apply only to a society of abundance and prosperity and this is, indeed, the *type* of condition with which Durkheim was most concerned.

Thus our more general observations, following Durkheim's lead, suggest that contemporary American society is in a paradoxical situation. Having achieved a very high—but by no means complete—level of *material* prosperity it is in danger of attaining also a condition of social and cultural *poverty.*

In a suggestive study entitled, *Troublemakers: Youth in an Affluent Society,* T. R. Fyvel makes some observations which are interesting when juxtaposed to Kornhauser's statement.

> . . . the rise of delinquency has to be seen as one among many similar symptoms of the growing social unbalance in the affluent society. Looking at the development in Britain of the last ten years, one can distinguish something which seems like a built-in conflict in this society—a conflict between, on one side, a growing sense of widening opportunities, of expansion, and opposed to it, an alarming drive towards purposelessness.

> . . . the affluent society holds out tremendous possibilities of a freer life for the ordinary man. [But there is also] undeniable evidence that a fairly large section of British youth felt frustrated, angry, bored and adrift without firm moral guidance.

Fyvel points out that this condition characterized not only the youth in British society but adults as well and, similarly, not only the British but American, Russian and other European societies suffered from the same condition.

A very recent report by the Council of Europe has provided similar data. Twelve member countries were requested to report on juvenile delinquency and all noted increases in non-utilitarian acts of theft and violence. Most note-worthy is that these phenomena appear much less often in the under-developed areas.

Fyvel's conclusions and the observations cited in the above report are compatible with our own. *Increased* opportunities can, if not recognized and anticipated, have undesirable consequences. And it is to the study of these factors that sociological research must now turn. Too many of the problems of deviant behavior and social pathology have been cast in the mold of poverty conditions. The time is ripe for studies of the concomitants of prosperity.

We Americans have always assumed that unfettered social mobility is necessarily a desirable condition for all. During times of prosperity mobility not only becomes more attainable but also forces itself upon the multitude. Few see the high cost which is paid in the form of striving toward unrealizable goals and the consequences in personal demoralization and despair. Increased opportunity for success has its counterpart in increased opportunity for failure. If a social system is to maintain itself it must provide a balance between societal needs, personal aspirations and the possibility of attainment. American society has not solved this problem and, indeed, it has not even seemed willing to entertain the possibility that such a problem does exist.

The fundamental question then becomes one of assessing the American Dream. Should it be tempered with cautionary folk wisdom or should we ignore the heavy toll which its pursuit extracts? What would be the consequences for American society of a system of motivation directed by the oft-heard injunction attributed to Confucius, "He who makes his bed close to the ground does not have far to fall"?

On the other hand there is little chance that the ideology can persist in the face of the realities of life. Ultimately some economic setback will occur, some limitations will be felt. What will be the consequences? Will America wait and watch and speculate or will a new set of goals emerge?

FURTHER READINGS

Bell, Daniel. *The End of Ideology.* New York: The Free Press, 1960.

Josephson, Eric and Josephson, Mary, eds. *Man Alone: Alienation in Modern Society.* New York: Dell Publishing Co., Inc., 1962.

Mizruchi, Ephraim H. *Success and Opportunity: A Study of Anomie.* New York: The Free Press, 1964.

Sykes, Gerald, ed. *Alienation: The Cultural Climate of Modern Man.* 2 vols. New York: George Braziller, 1964.

AUTHOR INDEX

SUBJECT INDEX